THE
CONSUMER'S GUIDE
TO PSYCHOTHERAPY

Jack Engler, Ph.D., and Daniel Goleman, Ph.D.

With a Chapter on Psychiatric Medication by
Eliot Gelwan, M.D.

A FIRESIDE BOOK
Published by Simon & Schuster
New York   London   Toronto   Sydney   Tokyo   Singapore

SIMON & SCHUSTER/FIRESIDE

Simon & Schuster Building
Rockefeller Center
1230 Avenue of the Americas
New York, New York 10020

SIMON & SCHUSTER, FIRESIDE, and colophon are
registered trademarks of Simon & Schuster Inc.

Designed by Irving Perkins and Assoc.
Manufactured in the United States of America

10 9 8 7 6 5 4 3 2 1
10 9 8 7 6 5 4 3 2 1 PBK

Library of Congress Cataloging-in-Publication Data

Engler, Jack.
The consumer's guide to psychotherapy / Jack Engler and Daniel Goleman.
p.   cm.
"A Fireside book."
1. Psychotherapy—Popular works. I. Goleman, Daniel. II. Title.
RC480.515.E54 1992

616.89′14—dc20

92-8425
CIP

ISBN 0-671-76826-3
ISBN 0-671-77851-X (pbk)

The information in this book is intended to make the reader a better informed consumer of psychotherapy services and more knowledgeable about choices available to them. Where it offers guidelines for decision-making, these are meant as guidelines only; they are not intended to replace diagnosis and treatment recommendations by competent professionals, nor to provide personal psychological, psychiatric, or other professional advice. For such advice, the reader must seek the service of a qualified therapist or physician.
The authors and publisher cannot be held responsible for the reader's use or misuse of the information contained in this book.
While the examples of different problems for therapy in this book are based on real people and their experiences, the authors have created composite characters and altered any characteristics that might identify individual clients.

To Our Families

CONTENTS

∎

INTRODUCTION

∎

Our goal in writing this book is to help you make informed choices as a client in psychotherapy. As with any other major decision in life, which therapist and what kind of therapy you should seek are not choices to be made lightly. When it works well, therapy can do more than relieve your emotional distress. It can have a powerful, even transformative, effect on your life. But when therapy does not go well, it can add to your problems. It can drag on and on, never quite ending, yet never quite helping. It can postpone your getting more effective help or discourage you from seeking further therapy when you might need it. This guide will help you minimize the risks that therapy can entail and help you avoid common pitfalls.

This book is organized into two parts. Part I, What You Should Know About Therapy, offers guidelines for knowledgeable decision-making about the major arrangements for therapy: how to decide whether or not you need therapy; how the therapy process works; how to find a therapist; what to expect when you begin; how to make therapy work and how to tell if it is working; ethics in therapy; and how to tell when it is time to end. Part II, The Therapy Guide, is designed to help you select the approach or approaches likely to be most effective for you and your specific problem. Difficulties such as a troubled marriage, a painfully shy child, or a severe depression each respond best to different kinds of therapy. Both kinds of information are crucial if you are to be an informed consumer and get the help you want.

The recommendations made here rest on three very different but complementary sources of data. We have incorporated the expertise represented by each. The first is the National Survey of Psychotherapists, a three-year study that led directly to the idea for this guide. The second is current scientific studies on the outcomes of therapy, which we reviewed specifically for the guide. The third is a panel of therapists with expertise in different fields whom we asked to review our recommendations.

One of the reasons a guide like this is particularly needed at this time is that the options available in therapy are greater than ever. It is no wonder the consumer is often confused. It was not so long ago that most therapists tended to take a relatively uniform approach to almost all problems—usually some sort of insight-oriented therapy. Back in the 1960s the distinctions between the different problems from which people suffer weren't so clear or so well understood. There was also a much smaller range of therapies to choose from. Most therapy was still individual. Group, family, and couples formats were still in their infancy or unknown. The preferred approach for most therapists, even those beginning to practice group and family therapy, was still based on psychodynamic principles, with the newer behavior therapies just beginning to make some inroads. Psychiatric medications were just beginning to be introduced, with many of the medications now considered standard practice still to come. Just how to combine medication and psychotherapy was poorly understood, and many therapists questioned the desirability of doing so. So much has changed, and a goal of this guide is to explain all the possibilities now available.

This guide has also emerged now in response to a recent innovation in decision-making about therapy called "differential therapeutics." This method, developed by clinical researchers and therapists at Cornell-Westchester Medical Center (Allen Frances, M.D.; John Clarkin, Ph.D.; and Samuel Perry, M.D. *Differential Therapeutics in Psychiatry*. New York: Brunner/Mazel, 1984; and Samuel Perry, M.D.; Allen Frances, M.D.; and John Clarkin, Ph.D. *A DSM-III Casebook of Differential Therapeutics: A Clinical Guide to Treatment Selection*. New York: Brunner/Mazel, 1985), allows a new level of flexibility and precision in matching a given person's presenting problem to an overall plan for treatment that best suits his or her individual situation. It recognizes, for instance, that all depressions are not alike: a twenty-year-old college student who has suicidal thoughts after a breakup with a girlfriend would be approached differently from a middle-aged, divorced mother of three who has suffered bouts of depression for years.

In other words, therapy can't be targeted just to the problem or issue. It needs to take the *person* into account: how *you* experience the problem; the ways you have been trying to handle it; and the key people in your life whose direct involvement in therapy might help.

Differential therapeutics provides a framework for thinking about what kind of therapy would be most appropriate for you, for your problems, in your circumstances. That framework focuses on the elements all therapies have in common, no matter how different they might seem on the surface:

- *Who will participate:* should you meet with a therapist individually? with your partner or spouse? with your entire family? or with a group of others who share the same problem?
- *Where you will meet:* will you meet in the therapist's office or clinic? or should you meet in some other setting?
- *How frequently you will meet:* should you meet the usual once a week? or more frequently? less frequently?

- *How long sessions will last:* Should you meet for the standard fifty-minute hour? or would that be too long? not long enough?
- *How long therapy can be expected to take:* should it be brief, six to twelve sessions? will it need to be long-term: months, possibly several years? or would it be better to leave it open-ended?
- And perhaps most important, *the kind of therapy that is best suited to your complaints:* psychodynamic, behavioral, cognitive, family systems, or supportive, or some combination of these approaches?

All these decisions, of course, should be made in consultation with a psychotherapist. But this framework can help you enter into that discussion with a clear sense of what to look for and ask about.

This guide also recognizes that the therapy is not always the right choice, or may even be counterproductive. Where appropriate, we have tried to suggest guidelines for recognizing when some alternative such as a self-help or support group would be appropriate and a better use of your time, money, and effort.

The National Survey of Psychotherapists

One completely unique source for our recommendations in Part II is the National Survey of Psychotherapists. This randomized survey solicited the clinical opinions of close to one thousand therapists from across the nation in the three major mental health professions: psychiatrists, clinical psychologists, and clinical social workers. (Details of the survey are in Appendix V.)

The psychotherapists were surveyed about the forty most common reasons people come to therapy, ranging from marital conflicts and adjustment problems of children, to depression and phobias. Our recommendations for psychotherapy draw on these responses.

Each psychotherapist was asked to respond only to questions about problems he or she was experienced in treating. The survey results thus reflect what most therapists recommend: what type of therapy tends to work best for which problem.

Despite the fact that the therapists expressing these opinons represent a diverse range of outlooks, from psychoanalysis to biological psychiatry, a distinct consensus emerged on the best range of approaches for the most common psychological problems. Where very recent research has shown the utility of a particular approach, we have tried to take that into account, too.

To be sure, for the majority of problems there is not usually an exclusive answer—this approach and no others. Instead, reflecting the state of the field, sometimes two or occasionally three approaches were recommended, sometimes in combination, sometimes in sequence, especially for more complex problems. But that narrows the choice considerably. It tells you what to look for and what to avoid. And it gives you a solid basis for making decisions about the two main features of therapy: the most effective approach to treating the problem, and the most appropriate format.

PART I

WHAT YOU SHOULD KNOW ABOUT THERAPY

◼

CHAPTER ONE

WHEN TO CONSIDER THERAPY

WHAT IS PSYCHOTHERAPY

The term *psychotherapy* is the general name for a variety of psychological interventions designed to help people resolve emotional, behavioral, or interpersonal problems of various kinds and improve the quality of their lives.

No single definition of psychotherapy is accepted by all of the many schools of therapy or by every therapist. Some therapists view it as a form of treatment akin to medicine, though psychological rather than biological; others see it as a form of social learning. Some see it as a way of resolving internal conflicts stemming from early life experiences; others see it as simply changing present patterns of thought, feeling, and behavior. Still others view it as a way of altering dysfunctional interactions in couples, marital, or family systems.

Almost all therapists agree, however, on two things. One, psychotherapy involves *a personal relationship of a special kind* between client and therapist, and it depends on this for its effectiveness. Two, its concern in the broadest sense is *personality and behavior change*—helping individuals, couples, groups, or families see, think, feel, or act differently. Where therapists and therapies differ is on what needs to be changed and how to change it. A person seeking help from a therapist wants change. They may not think *they* need to change. They may feel it is someone else or their situation that need changing. But whatever they see as the source of their discontent, they want to feel or act or manage better than they are, and a therapist agrees to help them achieve this goal.

In his classic comparative study of psychotherapies, *Persuasion and Healing,* psychiatrist Jerome Frank, M.D., pointed out four traits all varieties of therapy, ancient and modern, share. One is the *unique kind of relationship* therapy depends on: an alliance between a therapist and a client that is exclusively for the client's benefit. A second is the setting for therapy: *a safe place* in which what goes on is kept in confidence, entirely separate from the rest of your activities and relationships. A third is the *different perspective a therapist offers*—a different way of seeing and doing things than you are accustomed to that helps you to make sense of what feels bewildering and confusing. Finally, therapy entails *a set of procedures or techniques,* specific ways of working that flow from the therapist's viewpoint.

Therapy can be used in a variety of ways. First and foremost, it can be a vehicle or catalyst for change and growth. This is undoubtedly its most common use. But it can also be used as a source of support, helping you manage day-to-day difficulties when you feel temporarily overwhelmed and unable to manage on your own. It can also offer acute care or crisis intervention in a time of psychological emergency.

However it is used, psychotherapy is most powerful when it helps you to move from being a passive sufferer to an active agent on your own behalf, to take greater charge over what happens inside you, around you, or between you and others; and to find new and more appropriate ways to live and function—individually, in a couple, or in a family. It is most effective when it addresses the ways you are limiting yourself, or failing to develop and exercise your competence, self-mastery, and sense of self-worth. This often means helping you face the ways you may have had a hand in your own difficulties and distress; or in oppressive situations, finding ways where you can still take action on your own behalf to change the situation or change yourself, instead of remaining caught in the unproductive cycle of failure, blame, and guilt.

We take on ourselves and impose on others two kinds of suffering: suffering that leads to more suffering, and suffering that leads to the end of suffering. The first is destructive and avoidable—largely self-imposed and within our ability to do something about. The other kind of suffering is constructive and unavoidable—confronting and changing the ways we create suffering for ourselves and others can itself be a painful process.

While the immediate aim of therapy is to relieve discomfort and distress, most therapies have a longer-range goal: to modify or change the patterns of thinking, feeling, and acting that are producing the distress; and to learn new, more effective and satisfying ways of living.

THE BASIC ASSUMPTIONS UNDERLYING THERAPY

The first of the three major assumptions common to all therapies is that *something in us or in our behavior is constricting our freedom to be ourselves and live productively.* That "something" may be:

- A habitual pattern of behavior or coping that is no longer serving us well: drinking too much, for example; attention to detail that has become rigid, anxious, and obsessive; a take-charge style that has become overbearing and authoritarian.
- An inner conflict: over sexuality, a punitive conscience, ideals you are having trouble living up to.
- A block in psychological development: in the ability to experience, express, or manage emotions without losing control; to sustain intimate relationships; to feel competent and capable in work or love; to leave home or live independently.
- A trauma or stressful event: losing your home or job, the death of a loved one, physical or sexual abuse, violence.
- One of the many problems in day-to-day living that has become particularly distressing or intractable: conflict with an employer, difficulty managing work or school.
- A marital or family problem: constant arguing or fighting, a child who seems beyond your control.
- A major mental illness or psychiatric disorder: depression, manic-depression, panic attacks, a phobia, psychosis.

Therapy assumes that at least some part of the problem is *potentially under your control*—that you could take steps to do something about it but that for some reason you aren't. If what is distressing you isn't at least partially within your ability to affect or change, then therapy won't help.

People often come to therapy feeling just the opposite: discouraged or quite hopeless—stuck, stalemated, victimized, oppressed, either by their own problems and behavior or by circumstance—and helpless to do much about it. If this is the way you are feeling as you contemplate therapy, you should know you aren't alone. When they start therapy, a great many people feel uncertain that anything, including therapy, will really help.

What people often discover once they begin therapy, however, is that they have more resources for changing their situation than they thought. Even in cases of overwhelming trauma or victimization such as incest, physical abuse, rape, or violence, or in emotional disorders such as manic-depression that have a biological base, they find a shattered sense of self and self-esteem can be restored; that it's possible to rebuild trust in relationships and in oneself, and to again feel in control.

The purpose of therapy is to help you discover that you *do* have choices and options in ways to be.

This hopeful outlook toward the possibility of change is based on psychotherapy's assumption that *our feelings, thoughts, beliefs, attitudes, images of ourself, and behavior are to a large extent the product of our life experience.* All of these are learned—and what has been learned can be unlearned, or modified by new learning. Where learning isn't possible—in some genetically or biochemically based conditions, for instance—therapy has little to offer. Where the problems are primarily due to environmental factors such as poverty, discrimination, or political oppression, or where people are coming to therapy because they have to, not because they want to—referred by a court or school system, or bowing to family pressure—therapy is usually ineffective or irrelevant. At best, it's swimming against the current.

The third major assumption is that, *within limits, you have the capacity to grow, to know yourself better, and make choices that will further your development.* Therapy also assumes that your development doesn't have to be at the expense of someone else's, or be motivated by trying to meet their needs and expectations. Perhaps most important, psychotherapy assumes you can take more responsibility for yourself and the choices you make.

Some approaches directly explore the ways we limit ourselves, undermine our capacities to love and work, or fail to find purpose and direction in life. In these therapies, much of the work may simply be exposing your resistances and obstacles to growth: the role you may be playing in creating your own dilemmas without being aware of it, or in other ways holding yourself back. By uncovering resistances to growth and change, these approaches can help you extricate yourself from self-limiting attitudes and patterns of behavior and allow new capacities to emerge.

Other approaches concentrate instead on directly learning new modes of behavior. These therapies work by first pinpointing self-defeating habits—for example, the automatic thought, "I must do everything perfectly"—and then learning new, more positive ways of reacting in the same situation.

All therapies involve some degree of both identifying and unlearning old patterns, and learning new, more satisfying and productive ones.

Even when you can't do much about the circumstances of your life, your attitude toward your situation will have a lot to do with how they affect you. Your reactions are much more under your control than you imagine, even in coping with oppressive or distressing life events such as a life-threatening illness or incapacitating injury. If you can't change what is happening to you, therapy can at least help you take some control over your inner response to it.

The Goal of Therapy

The basic goal of therapy, therefore, is to assist you in taking more active and effective charge of your life. It isn't to advise, direct, or tell you what to do, though advice and direction may play an occasional role. A therapist may also suggest or recommend from time to time. But whatever the specific issue, the larger and fundamental goal is to support and promote your ability to think, feel, and act for yourself, never to preempt this capacity. The only time a therapist should—and must—substitute his or her insight and judgment for yours is in crisis situations where your own capacity is so impaired by trauma, illness, psychosis, or some other condition that you or someone else is in danger of imminent harm.

The central issue in therapy is competence: the experience of functioning effectively and appropriately. The therapist's goal is to help you develop this capacity, enlarge its scope, and learn to trust it in yourself. Change by itself isn't the issue. We are all ambivalent about change. We want things to be "different," but that doesn't mean we want to change or are prepared for change. Instead, change grows out of the experience of competence. In therapy, you are validated. You see that who you are and what you think, feel, and do matters to someone. You are treated as a human being capable of acting on your own behalf. In addition, you learn that what you do makes a difference and that you can change things for the better. This may be experienced first in the therapeutic relationship, but gradually your changed behavior affects your life outside. You see yourself respond differently and see that others respond differently to you. All of this reinforces the experience of competence, of feeling more in charge, more capable of effective living.

THE THERAPY RELATIONSHIP

The heart of psychotherapy, what makes it special, is the therapeutic relationship. This relationship is probably unlike any other in your experience. It is a curious combination of emotional intensity and detachment, of intimate involvement and objective distance, that allows you to share and confront your personal problems, your vulnerabilities, your darkest fantasies and deepest fears, with another person who is trained to help you without judging you, and whose exclusive concern is your needs and interests.

Though it need not be, the therapy relationship is often highly charged because it carries the burden of your expectations, disappointments, and fears from the relationships that have mattered to you most in the past. It may activate the very issues, feelings, and patterns of behavior that trouble you most. This may be crucial in helping you understand and master them, but it can also leave you occasionally feeling vulnerable and raw.

What makes this all possible is trust. You and a therapist will form a working bond, a therapeutic alliance, which will be based on a sense of mutual rapport, understanding, confidentiality, and commitment to working on your issues together. The relationship will also depend on your sense that this is someone who has your best interests at heart and will make them his or her sole concern. They will put their own personal needs and concerns aside to focus exclusively on yours.

You may not feel this trust all at once; as in any relationship, it takes time to develop. But you should have some sense from the very beginning that this person is trustworthy. Even if you have good reason *not* to trust relationships—if they have been bitterly disappointing in the past, for instance—some sense that this is a person you could *come* to trust has to be present. An important part of the process is to learn to trust both your therapist and the relationship.

HOW THERAPY WORKS

Every therapy entails a set of techniques, informed by a point of view, that aims to enlarge your freedom and ability to guide your life. Whatever the approach, the process has to be compatible with the basic goal of helping you to be more yourself and to function more effectively.

This means a therapist doesn't "do" something to you. Psychotherapy is often described as "treatment." The traditional terminology of *patient, doctor, diagnosis,* even *therapist*—borrowed from medicine by the first generations of therapists, who often were physicians—suggests the image of an active "doctor" healing a passive "patient." This image unfortunately survives in certain schools of therapy and in the minds of many clients at a time when it is gradually disappearing from medicine itself. Medicine has certainly had an excessive influence on the practice of psychotherapy. Seeing therapy through the eyes of medicine distorts it, as Freud was the first to point out. But the image survives largely because of the unexpressed wish most clients have in starting therapy that their therapist will "do something" to them to "cure" them of their problems. When we are in distress, it is hard to believe in our own resources. We are frightened. We are confused. We are hurting. So we tend to look to someone else—some expert, someone who seems to know the answers—to tell us what to do, do it for us, or make the bad feelings go away. Or we may feel so bereft or disheartened that we just want to be "given" to without anything being asked of us. Also, accepting responsibility for our own behavior and looking at the part we may be playing in our own distress can be painful. Remaining helpless is safer and easier.

While it is easy then—and powerful forces will push you in this direction—to look to your therapist as someone who will cure what ails you, psychotherapy has only a superficial resemblance to this outmoded medical model. Therapy is a *collaborative* process between you and your therapist that is based on your active participation. You must work together or therapy doesn't work at all.

The fundamental principle is that therapy is designed, not to change you, but to help you change yourself. This defines your and your therapist's respective roles.

The Therapist's Role

The therapist's role is not that of a doctor but of a consultant who acts as an agent and catalyst for whatever changes you, your spouse, or your family want to make. Depending on their training and theoretical orientation, therapists approach this task in different ways: by providing insight into inner emotional conflicts (psychodynamic therapy); by helping to correct distorting cognitions and beliefs (cognitive therapy); by helping to change behavioral sequences (behavior therapy) or to restructure the pattern of family or group interactions (a systemic or group approach).

But like any enterprise concerned with promoting someone else's development—parenting and teaching are other examples—a therapist can only help you "do" something. He or she can't "give" you anything, or do anything "to" you, that will directly cure, fix, or change you. Therapists won't be able to solve your problems, for instance. Solutions that may have worked for them or other clients probably won't address what is unique about your situation. What they can do is help you find a solution that works in the context of your life.

Whatever they think should happen, their main job is to help you examine what is troubling you and help you figure out what you can do about it or how you can do it differently. They can ask questions; help you examine your behavior, its meaning, its payoffs and punishments; probe your motives, goals, and aspirations with you; guide you in your efforts to understand how you may get in your own way, avoid or ignore possibilities for growth, or engage in self-limiting or painful patterns of behavior. They can help identify fears, inhibitions, or anxieties that might be holding you back. They can also help you regain control in your life, your marriage, or your family. They can offer support in managing problems of everyday living when these threaten to become overwhelming. But they cannot change you and should not try.

They should also not do things for you that you can do for yourself. This only reinforces fears of helplessness or inadequacy and confirms doubts about your competence. Any process that requires you, overtly or covertly, to surrender responsibility for yourself to the therapist is harmful and destructive and not genuine therapy.

The Client's, Couple's, or Family's Role

What you do is every bit as important—in many ways *more* important—than what your therapist does. In the long run, the outcome will depend even more on you than on your therapist.

Therapy catalyzes change in different ways because therapists follow different formats or approaches. Nevertheless, the catalyst for change always grows out of a joint examination of the area you want help with. This may also involve looking at other areas you didn't anticipate.

Whatever the problem and the therapist's approach to it, the effectiveness of therapy depends on your joining them in actively examining the issues, then being willing to try doing things differently.

THE STRUCTURE OF THERAPY

Effective therapy needs a good framework, one that you and your therapist can agree on and that will organize what you are doing. Every therapy comprises the same six structural elements. These are combined in different ways depending on the nature and severity of the problem, your therapist's theoretical orientation and expertise, and what will work best for you. Every therapy requires decisions about each.

These six basic elements are:

1. *The Approach:* what the client and therapist actually do together to address the issue or problem. The major orientations to therapy are psychodynamic, cognitive, behavioral, systemic, and supportive. Each has many variants. Chapter 2 provides a description of each.
2. *The Setting:* where you will meet. Most therapy is done in the therapist's private office or in a clinic. But it can also go on at a hospital, a day treatment program, or any number of other social service agencies or organizations.
3. *The Format:* individual, couple, family, or group, according to who directly participates. The traditional form of psychotherapy was a single client meeting individually with a single therapist. This is probably still the most common. But for marital problems, the couple is seen together. For most family problems, the therapist works with the family as a whole. Therapy can also be done in a group format, with a single therapist leading a group of six to eight clients.
4. *The Length of Sessions:* the current standard session for individual and couple therapy is fifty minutes, though some therapists see clients for forty-five minutes, others for one hour. Group and family sessions typically last ninety minutes because of the greater number of people involved.
5. *The Frequency:* how often you will meet. The usual arrangement is once a week, but that too varies, depending on need and on the type of therapy. At one extreme, psychoanalysis usually requires four or five sessions a week. Family therapy sessions may not need to be scheduled more than every other week or once a month. At the other extreme, supportive therapy for long-term psychiatric conditions may only require infrequent check-ins. Meetings are often scheduled more frequently during a crisis or hospitalization. You may need an immediate meeting during an emergency.
6. *The Duration:* how long therapy will last. There is no standard length of time that therapy should take. Ideally this will depend on the problems or issues you are addressing, the goals you set, and how slowly or quickly you progress

toward them. This in turn will depend on how ready and able you are to confront them. Other factors may also play a role: your finances may be limited or your health insurance may limit coverage to a set dollar amount or number of sessions per year (see Chapter 7, "Paying for Therapy"). *Brief, focal,* or *time-limited* approaches to therapy in which the number of sessions are specified in advance—anywhere from six sessions to six months—are also becoming more common for certain types of problems (see Chapter 6, "Contracting for Therapy"). By contrast, *open-ended* therapy can continue indefinitely. As a general rule of thumb in current practice, short-term psychotherapy is anything lasting several sessions to several months. Any therapy lasting up to a year or longer would be considered long-term.

IS THERAPY REALLY EFFECTIVE?

Perhaps the most important question about therapy is: does it work? This hasn't been an easy one to answer scientifically. A British researcher, Hans J. Eysenck, first challenged the effectiveness of therapy in 1952 with the claim that two-thirds of the people with a neurotic disorder improved over a two-year period whether they received psychotherapy or not. For the next twenty-five to thirty years, researchers heatedly debated just how effective therapy was, and whether it was in fact effective at all. Some studies showed psychotherapy worked, others found little or no effect, still others that it could have negative effects.

The resulting ambiguity from these evaluative studies actually troubled therapists much more than it did clients. Despite the controversy, millions of people continued to seek help from therapists. Most seemed to feel they improved, but doubts persisted because of the lack of clear, firm, unambiguous evidence. The effects of therapy proved hard to measure and harder still to predict. The causes of any measurable effects proved even more difficult to identify.

Why Research Findings Have Been Contradictory

In retrospect, it is not so difficult to see why the initial research findings were often contradictory. Different schools of psychotherapy have emphasized different goals: the reduction of symptoms, greater insight, the achievement or elimination of a specific behavior, a change in the pattern of social interactions, greater happiness and productivity. Effects of therapy also continue to accrue after therapy ends.

Effectiveness can only be measured relative to a particular goal, and the goals varied considerably.

Different studies also employed different methods of measuring effectiveness: ratings from therapists, client self-ratings, evaluations from significant others, various psychological tests. Outcomes were also measured at different points in the process:

from several weeks to several months into therapy, at the end of therapy, and from several weeks to several years after termination.

Much of the research was also done by therapists themselves, raising the possibility of bias in attempting to either defend psychotherapy or demonstrate the effectiveness of one approach over another.

The Two Major Claims Against Therapy

The debate was fueled in the 1960s by Hans Eysenck's original claim that psychotherapy was no more effective than "spontaneous remission": the success rates of therapy are no better than simply doing nothing and letting natural improvements take their course. In other words, psychotherapy doesn't make a difference.

The second argument granted positive results, but attributed them to a "placebo effect" resulting from clients' expectations that they would improve, not from anything inherent in the process itself. Clients in formal psychotherapy will improve, for example, but not significantly more than people "treated" by untrained "therapists" who are believed to be legitimate. In other words, people get better because they expect to.

Current Research Findings

For several decades it was difficult to refute these claims scientifically because of major methodological flaws in evaluative research. And because there is truth in both claims. People's situations do improve without therapy; and expectation certainly does play a role. Then in the 1980s a new generation of research based on more sophisticated methodology and statistical analysis began to settle some of these questions. An important innovation in evaluating outcomes was the introduction of a statistical technique called meta-analysis, which allowed the outcomes of many single studies to be examined conjointly, as if they were the result of one large study. Meta-analysis can tease out a powerful, overall effect from many studies that a single study may miss. The more recent generation of outcome studies has been encouraging and tends to confirm what therapists and clients have believed and felt about therapy all along.

Researchers also began to take into account the wide range of therapists, problems, clients, and approaches to psychotherapy. They stopped asking simply if psychotherapy "works" and began asking a much more useful question: which approaches work best, for which problems, under what conditions, for which clients? That question has informed our thinking here, and is the question you yourself should ask in thinking about therapy.

After a further decade and more of research, the most important overall conclusion is this: for the wide range of moderate problems that most people bring to therapy, whatever the approach, given a reasonably skillful therapist, most people can expect to make appreciable gains. The effects produced by the broad range of formats and approaches are not only statistically significant but therapeutically meaningful. Moreover, more sophisticated replication studies have shown that the gains people make are greater than if they had not gone into therapy—refuting the spontaneous remission argument. They are also greater than a simple "placebo" or "expectation" effect.

At the same time, research has also shown that not everyone who goes into therapy will be helped, or helped as much as others. Not everyone benefits to a satisfactory degree. Some will actually be harmed (more on this below). Nevertheless, whether the targets of therapy are narrowly defined and specific (symptoms of anxiety, depressed mood, an eating disorder, insomnia, a marital problem) or more global in nature (social or work adjustment, greater self-insight), the improvements therapy brings for most clients appear to be substantial.

Also, while some problems may recur, such as relapses in addictive disorders, benefits from therapy tend to last. Considerable evidence suggests that even brief interventions can produce enduring effects. Research shows that gains tend to be strongest when the therapy aims at enduring changes instead of just short-term relief. Gains are also more likely to endure if you experience the improvements as the result of your own efforts and continue to make an effort to maintain them. Lasting gains are also more likely if therapy includes helping you anticipate future life crises and challenges and how to handle them.

One of the more surprising findings is that differences in outcome for different techniques are not as great as might be expected. For most of the moderate difficulties people bring to therapy, little difference in effectiveness is apparent among the various therapy approaches and formats. If the therapist is skillful and well trained, either a behavioral or psychodynamic approach, for example, can apparently facilitate substantial improvement.

For certain specific problems, however, the approach does make a difference. Behavioral and cognitive approaches, for instance, have been shown to be more effective in treating such difficult problems as phobias, compulsions, sexual dysfunction, and eating disorders, and in treating severe disturbances such as childhood aggression and psychotic behavior.

In making the recommendations for treatment in the Therapy Guide, we have taken such research into account.

THE INGREDIENTS OF EFFECTIVE THERAPY

Not surprisingly, therapists themselves tend to attribute positive outcomes to their own particular approach and to emphasize their differences in technique. However, research is showing more and more clearly that certain interpersonal, social, and emotional factors are prominent ingredients of *all* types of therapy, and that these so-called "common factors" play a central role—perhaps the major role—in making any kind of therapy effective.

The most important of these are *factors associated with the therapy relationship* itself. Not surprisingly, people are helped by a therapeutic relationship that is trustworthy, warm, accepting, stable, and informed by good judgment and understanding. But these relationship factors turn out to be crucial even in approaches that emphasize the importance of specific techniques and downplay the client-therapist relationship. The effect of technical interventions is usually less than the influence of the relationship itself. This means that how well you and your therapist work together—your ability to establish and maintain a solid working relationship with each other—is the single most important determinant of a satisfactory outcome.

Other ingredients of successful therapy are *factors associated with the therapist*. Effective therapists seem to have certain personal qualities in common, whatever type of therapy they practice. The most important qualities turn up repeatedly in studies:

• warm but not possessive
• trustworthy and genuine
• able to enter into your experience and make you feel understood
• nonjudgmental and accepting of you as a person
• genuine and true to who they are; not performing or acting a role

Note that none of these is unique to a particular school or approach.

The therapist's conviction in the efficacy of his or her approach is also crucial. They should believe in what they are doing and be able to convey this to their clients. This belief should be realistic, based on reliable evidence and past experience rather than wishful thinking or a party line. It should be clear to you that your therapist confidently expects that he or she can help you. On the other hand, be wary of any therapist who overpromises or overpromotes him or herself or their approach, or offers any kind of a guarantee. Dogmatic insistence betrays doubt.

The therapist's competence is still another crucial ingredient. Most therapists aren't simply "good" or "bad" in an absolute sense. Rather they vary in the range of issues they work well with, doing better with certain kinds of problems than with others. Studies have shown, for instance, that even therapists who have generally poor results actually do well with some cases. No therapist is experienced or skilled enough to treat the entire range of problems equally. A successful outcome is more likely if the therapist is adept in handling the type of problem that brings you to therapy.

The outcome of therapy doesn't depend entirely on the therapist. It is becoming increasingly clear that *the client makes the greatest difference* in how effective therapy is. Certain client characteristics have been shown to be especially linked to good outcomes:

- *The amount of confidence and conviction you bring.* Perhaps the most important attitude you can bring to therapy is the belief that you can change, and that with help your life can improve. This doesn't come from blind faith or wishful thinking, but from past experiences that make you believe you are capable of change.

   Believing in therapy itself is also important. This shouldn't be a naive faith, but a level of confidence warranted by whatever information about therapy you have gathered that is relevant to your situation.

   Few people entering therapy have an unshakable conviction that they can change or that therapy can help them. Doubts are natural, a part of the process. Even so, therapy can still be effective if you begin with a sense that it holds promise. Even that may wax and wane, but if you manage to hold on to some sense of hope and expectation of help, therapy can work. By the same token, if you are convinced it can't work for you, or come to believe it can't, it probably won't.

- *Being actively involved.* Your sense of being actively involved is another crucial factor in making therapy more effective. Therapy has a better chance of making a real difference if the issues come alive for you, and you actively struggle with them.

- *Feeling as well as thinking.* A repeated research finding is that some degree of emotional arousal is essential for successful therapy. Obviously you don't want to be overwhelmed with emotion. But if you don't experience some strong feelings, strong at least for you, if the whole process is a dry, detached, intellectual discussion of what's upsetting you, not much is likely to change. What has upset you *should* be upsetting. If therapy is to be successful, in some way you will eventually need to reexperience the distress, fears, and confusion that led you to seek help. The crucial difference between therapy and your usual experience is that therapy offers a safe, trustworthy relationship in which you can confront the feelings with someone who can help you learn to handle them.

- *Your motivation, commitment, and follow-through.* The more honest you are about yourself, the more willing to confront what is troubling you, and the more motivated you are to follow through with decisions, exercises, and contractual agreements for therapy, such as keeping appointments, the more successful therapy will be.

- *Your comfort with the approach.* Therapy has a better chance of working if the therapist's approach makes sense to you and suits your preferred way of working.

It should also be suitable for your specific problem—a matter explicitly addressed in the Therapy Guide.

Circumstances Can Limit Therapy's Effectiveness

Despite all this, some circumstances beyond your control might limit how effective therapy can be for you. These include:

- little or no support or understanding from your spouse or family
- an unstable living or working environment while you are in therapy (unless this is the problem you are working on)
- crises that constantly preoccupy you, or interfere with keeping appointments or carrying out assignments
- a long interruption in therapy due to illness, accident, injury, absence, or an unplanned termination
- the absence of any clear precipitating event you can tie your problems to
- personality traits that make it difficult to establish a good working relationship with a therapist
- severe interference with your thought processes, and your ability to think coherently and realistically
- a prior experience of therapy that did not work out well or was directly harmful

Therapy *can* be effective in spite of these circumstances. But they may affect how much you can put in or get out, and it's well to be realistic about this. The wider context in which you do therapy can facilitate or hamper it.

So, is therapy effective? In broadest terms, yes. Most therapies do offer demonstrable help, especially for the wide range of moderate problems that most people confront. The gains are greater than relying on the natural course of things to improve, and what you gain from therapy you tend to keep if you make the effort.

The much more relevant question, however, is what therapist and which approach is likely to be *most* effective for you and your problems. The following sections and chapters in Part I are designed to provide guidelines for making informed decisions about each of these issues.

In the final analysis, how successful therapy is will depend primarily on you. You may need a therapist to help mobilize your resources and catalyze change. But change itself will be your responsibility. It will only come about as the result of your actions and choices. In this sense psychotherapy is more like education than medicine—more a process of learning than healing. It is not so much the teacher who teaches, but the student who learns.

THERAPY IS NOT FOR EVERYONE

People go into therapy for many reasons: a failing marriage; a feeling of lethargy and hopelessness; a teenage son who continually gets into trouble or a teenage daughter who is starving herself; a loss of interest in sex; a frustrating trail of failed romantic relationships; a drug habit; suicidal impulses; a fear of crowds . . . the reasons go on and on.

But therapy is not for everyone, nor for every problem. Emotional struggles are a normal part of life. While therapy might help with some of the distress of being out of work, or the breakup of a relationship, it is not a solution. If you can't find work, for example, or have run out of benefits, you need help finding a job, not therapy—unless your feelings of incompetence and inadequacy have convinced you that looking will be fruitless.

Therapy also doesn't change social injustices. If you are suffering because of ethnic or racial bias, or because you are gay or lesbian, or if you are a woman whose boss feels free to make suggestive remarks, the remedy is not therapy. The solution may be a complaint to a company ombudsman, a letter from your lawyer, or a civil rights lawsuit.

The inner turmoil you may feel can warrant considering psychotherapy as well, but the external situation causing your distress can only be changed by direct action. Therapy sometimes becomes a substitute for action, an excuse for putting up with a situation you should tackle head-on.

Deviance or distress by themselves aren't necessarily problems for therapy. If you find yourself the target of antagonism and resentment because you are a Buddhist, a radical environmentalist, gay or lesbian, or you've resigned from the firm to take up something else you've always wanted to do, what you are doing may be socially deviant but not something that indicates an emotional disorder—despite what others may say. "Deviant" behavior can be a sign of emotional problems, but also a sign of health. Taking a vow of celibacy to be a priest may be socially deviant in some quarters, but it isn't pathological. Being homeless, starving, or broke is certainly distressing, but not a problem for therapy.

Some struggles are actually signs of inner strength and social responsibility. Someone who chains herself to a tree to keep a virgin forest from being logged may be called "crazy" by some—but others will thank her. Putting yourself on the line in a life-promoting crusade may antagonize some people, but it can betoken a high level of moral maturity.

Some People Don't Benefit from Therapy

While it is now clear that psychotherapy is effective and can bring about significant and enduring changes, it is also clear that it doesn't help everyone. For a few, it can even have negative effects. This is important to consider given the amount of time, energy, and money therapy usually entails.

Since therapists tend not to report their failures, it is hard to say exactly how often therapy doesn't help. However, studies have found that about 10 percent of clients in therapy get worse instead of better. In the majority of cases, the harm isn't caused by therapy, but by the therapist. In the wrong therapy you may see little or no improvement; but even with the right approach, a bad or exploitative therapist will cause harm. This guide will help you avoid therapists who make clients worse.

Aside from bad therapists, other reasons why you are less likely to be helped, or may even end up feeling worse, are if:

- You have been in therapy a number of times without experiencing any benefit.
- You have been in several therapies and dropped out hurt and bitter with your therapist each time, or ended feeling caught up in an intense, drawn-out struggle that was never resolved.
- You tried several times, but you just can't establish a working relationship with a therapist. For some people, all relationships are so fraught with mistrust that they hold back from intimacy and keep contacts superficial. Such people often find it difficult if not impossible to relate well to a therapist, and therapy depends on a good working relationship.
- You are going into therapy for some ulterior reason that has nothing to do with the real goals of therapy. If you are involved in a lawsuit, for instance, in a child custody proceeding, or in a compensation claim, you might be entering therapy to prove you are getting help or are emotionally distressed, but it won't be therapeutic.
- You are going into therapy only because it is mandated by some third party. A court, for example, is mandating it as a condition of probation, or the Department of Social Services is requiring it as a condition of child custody. A good therapist probably won't see you under these conditions unless he or she thinks you are also personally motivated.

    Some offenders can benefit from therapy if they are genuinely distressed by their actions and are motivated to change. But for the great majority of those with long histories of antisocial acts, probation with mandated therapy instead of jail is useless. It is either a way for the state to keep the prison population down, or for the offender to stay out of jail.

    On the other hand, in cases where a family probate court orders mandatory counseling as a condition for custody, or a civil court mandates marriage counseling prior to granting a divorce, therapy often turns out to be useful.
- Your motive is not to examine your emotional life and behavior, but only to please someone else: a spouse, a parent, or a school system requiring it, for instance. This often happens in a marriage when one spouse insists the other

has some "problem" that must be "fixed" to save the marriage. What both partners may really need is marital therapy together.

- You are turning to therapy primarily for someone to lean on and take responsibility, or you have become a "career patient," content to remain in therapy because you have become dependent on your therapist.
- You are convinced your distress is the fault of others, bad luck, or circumstance. If this is genuinely the case, then the obvious strategy should be activist rather than therapeutic: do what you can to change the oppressive circumstances.
- The situation does not lend itself to therapy. In a marriage strained beyond repair, for example, it is simply too late to bring the spouses together. Certain severe psychiatric disorders sometimes follow a downhill course, especially in the early years. Some—but certainly not all—schizophrenic conditions are hard to arrest no matter what is tried. Advanced alcoholism and substance abuse are notoriously hard to interrupt.

The Time May Not Be Right

Timing is a critical but often overlooked factor in effective therapy. Even if your problem is appropriate for therapy, good reasons may exist to postpone or defer it until a more favorable time.

A vital consideration is your *readiness for therapy*. Rarely is anyone completely ready to confront difficult and painful issues, no matter how desperately he or she wants relief. But for therapy to work, the desire to do something has to be greater than the tendency to procrastinate, or to rely on "something happening" to take care of the problem.

Many people considering therapy have the confusing experience of knowing quite clearly that they need help, even genuinely wanting it—but still finding themselves not doing anything about it. They're unable to make that phone call; they never get around to asking for a referral.

This is only confusing if you don't understand the inevitable role of *ambivalence*. Almost everyone who seeks therapy has some reservations about it. The issue is the *degree* of ambivalence. If you want help but just can't get started, this may be a sign that you aren't ready yet or that some major obstacle has yet to be overcome.

Others may not realize they aren't ready until they actually start therapy. Once the initial relief of talking to someone about their distress is over and they begin confronting themselves and the need for change, they realize they don't feel prepared for the demands of therapy, or that this isn't what they wanted after all—at least, not just now.

Not feeling ready for therapy can simply be a normal response to a difficult and challenging self-examination. You should expect to feel this way to some degree. Everyone does. Normally, if you genuinely want help, these feelings won't deter you for long or prevent you from making good use of therapy once you begin.

Not *feeling* ready doesn't necessarily mean you aren't. It may simply signal ambivalence about getting help. "I don't know if I'm ready for this" is a common feeling at difficult moments in therapy when some demanding change is required. It is always confusing and frustrating when it surfaces. It can be mild or profound, and even temporarily immobilizing. But usually you can get past such moments with assistance from your therapist.

However, the feeling that you aren't ready may also be accurate. This may not be the time, whatever your wishes, no matter what your therapist says. Such feelings should be respected as valid, not treated as a "resistance" to be "worked through." When it isn't the right time, it's important you recognize this and not take your feeling as a sign of weakness or lack of resolve.

Certain situations signal that it is *not* the time for therapy:

- *Limited financial resources.* Therapy can be expensive. If it would place too great a demand on your finances, this is not the time to begin. At times the distress is so great you may feel almost any expense if justified, but most often this isn't the case and other personal or family matters have to take precedence. Be sure to inform yourself first about some of the ways to make therapy affordable at a reduced fee (see Chapter 7, "Paying for Therapy").
- *Time constraints.* It may simply not be possible to fit therapy into your present schedule. This may be true, for example, if the therapist you want to see has no openings at a time you can make, or if you would have to commute too great a distance for sessions. You may have started a new job that demands extra time, or you may have a new baby in the house and are needed at home. Once these pressures ease, scheduling therapy may be more realistic.
- *Marital and family considerations.* Sometimes going into individual therapy will only exacerbate a marital conflict or threaten a relationship you want to maintain. If your partner is unwilling to go into couples therapy with you, it may be better to wait until your partner changes his or her mind. Similarly, if it's a family problem that needs family therapy, but some members of the family refuse to attend, it may make matters worse to exclude them from the sessions. Or, at the present time, your partner, spouse, or family may not be able to stand the extra strain therapy would entail. Confronting issues between you might genuinely lead to a breakup that neither of you wants. These kinds of questions are best explored in a consultation first to see if you really couldn't handle them in therapy (see Chapter 4, "Consulting a Therapist").
- *Other pressing obligations.* This may be a time to keep your attention focused on work, family relationships, or some other important activity rather than on self-exploration. This may be particularly true if you have been in therapy before and find you tend to do better in therapy than in managing day-to-day living, or tend to retreat to therapy when active involvement becomes too difficult.
- *Emotional exhaustion.* This may be a time when you don't have the inner

strength, energy, perseverance, capacity for work, or the emotional availability for a close relationship that therapy requires. You may feel too fragile, emotionally exhausted, or physically ill. In these cases, a supportive therapy might help, but any other approach may be more than you could tolerate at the moment. Again, a consultation could help you clarify this.

- *Lack of motivation.* You may want help, but simply aren't motivated enough. Insufficient motivation is different from ambivalent motivation: it means you just aren't moved enough by your difficulties to take significant action. If this is so, then deferring therapy is usually a wiser course.

ALTERNATIVES TO THERAPY

Therapy is by no means the only way to get help for emotional problems or other issues many of us commonly face. Long before there were therapists, there were ministers and rabbis, wise men and women, caring friends and family. Though there are a wide range of alternatives to therapy, not all may be offered in your community. To find them, try the telephone book, directory assistance, your local community mental health center, or the municipal or state department of social services.

The many alternatives to therapy include:

- *Crisis intervention services.* If you have an emergency, crisis intervention services may be able to provide immediate help. These are available under such different names as Crisis Services, Community Mental Health, various Hot Lines and Help Lines, Emergency Call Line, Information and Referral, Suicide Prevention, and others. Ask directory assistance if you can't find one of these names in the white or yellow pages. Most larger cities will have a medical emergency line, a poison control center, a rape crisis line, a suicide prevention number, a drug crisis line, an alcohol information referral service, and lines for child abusers, senior citizens, runaways, cancer victims, heart patients, divorced people, single parents, and others. Typically, the hot lines are manned by volunteers rather than professionals, but they have usually received training and supervision and are well-informed about what courses of action you might take. Their job is to help you get through the immediate crisis, then help you find ongoing counseling if you need it.

- *Self-help and support groups.* These are peer groups of individuals who meet regularly to help each other handle a similar problem or life experience, usually without a therapist or any other professional involved. There is great power in being able to share your difficulties with others who know from firsthand experience what you are going through. They cannot only offer you practical advice, understanding, and acceptance, but also stand as examples of others who have successfully gone through the same struggle.

The first and most famous of self-help groups is Alcoholics Anonymous. Its "twelve-step" program is the model for many others. Self-help groups are now available for a surprisingly broad spectrum of problems and issues, from survivors of incest to overeating and anorexia, to gambling, to people with manic-depression, parents without partners. One of the most active is the National Alliance for the Mentally Ill, a national advocacy and support organization with regional chapters throughout the country for families with a member who suffers from a major mental illness.

If you decide to try a peer self-help or support group, don't be surprised if you encounter the same kind of backsliding, resistance, lack of concentration, drive, and follow-through that are common in psychotherapy. Just because it's self-help doesn't mean you won't have to deal with ambivalence and resistance to change.

Consult the general listing of self-help groups in Appendices I and II for addresses and phone numbers of their national headquarters. The headquarters can tell you if there is a chapter in your area. Or you can check your local telephone directory.

• *Skill training.* What is troubling you may not actually be an emotional problem but the lack of some specific skill in living: how to make a marriage work, raise children, succeed in a job or at school, handle stress, manage the family finances, meet people socially, or one of the many other skills modern living requires. If so, skill training in that particular area and developing a sense of mastery and competence through practicing that skill might be more helpful than therapy. Many kinds of skill training are now available, and at a reasonable cost.

Continuing-education programs, community colleges, junior colleges and universities, community mental health centers, health maintenance organizations, and various training institutes now offer a wide variety of educational programs for all kinds of problems: assertiveness training, parent effectiveness training, stress management and relaxation training, divorce and bereavement groups, and many others. These programs are typically advertised through local newspapers, class catalogues, clinic waiting rooms, and community bulletin boards. Instructors are usually competent and the focus will be very specific. In addition to low cost, you may feel more comfortable for now being a student rather than a client or patient.

• *Help from friends.* Friendships are wonderful sources of support in hard times, and sharing problems with friends can often deepen the relationships. If you have a friend you feel particular respect for and whom you especially trust, see if talking things over with him or her first will help you clarify the problem and find some solutions. Simply confiding in someone can sometimes bring all the relief that you need.

• *National agencies for special problems.* These focus on such specific problems as aging, alcoholism and drug abuse, child abuse, and other family problems.

They can often direct you to a local program. See Appendix I for a listing.
- *Legal aid.* If your difficulties include the need for legal advice you cannot afford to pay for privately—in determining your rights as a tenant, for instance, or your eligibility for social services or disability, or the laws regarding custody or inheritance—you may be able to get free legal counsel through your local legal aid society or bar association.
- *Counseling and planning services.* Often run by charitable organizations affiliated with local churches or by state and municipal departments of social services, there are counseling centers in most cities for vocational guidance, family planning, and financial advice.

Combining Self-Help Methods with Therapy

You can definitely pursue self-help methods and therapy at the same time. There need be no conflict; one should complement the other. If you are already in a self-help group, for instance, you might consider therapy if areas where you are psychologically vulnerable are becoming too stressed: if discouragement is in danger of turning into hopelessness and depression, for example; or tension threatens to become overwhelming anxiety and panic. If you're already in therapy, self-help methods can be useful if you need additional support between sessions, have to deal with difficult external circumstances unrelated to therapy, or need help with the practical as well as the psychological aspects of a problem.

In general, a therapist should support any efforts you make at self-help. With certain problems, many therapists will actually encourage you to become involved in a self-help group as an adjunct to therapy. In treating addictive behavior, most therapists will even require regular participation in a peer self-help group such as Alcoholics Anonymous or Narcotics Anonymous since psychotherapy alone is seldom sufficient to maintain sobriety. Self-help groups offer a different kind of mutual moral, emotional, and practical support than therapy offers. Your involvement in one enriches and broadens your experience in the other.

In the Therapy Guide, these groups are included among recommendations for treating specific problems where appropriate.

However, even though therapists generally support self-help approaches, they aren't likely to suggest you try these avenues first. If you can afford to be patient and think one of these self-help approaches may help, it might be a good idea to try that first. You can always consult a therapist later.

WHERE THERAPY CAN HELP

Psychotherapy offers help in three broad areas of living: personal growth, problems in everyday living, and emotional and behavioral disorders.

Personal Growth

You don't have to be desperate or in the throes of great distress to consider therapy. You may be experiencing a "higher dissatisfaction": perhaps you find you aren't as creative now as you used to be or would like to be, or as playful or as curious and open. You may have reached a point at which you have grown dissatisfied and want more out of life, or a new sense of direction and purpose. You may feel you're entering middle age, for instance, and you've begun to question the meaning of your life and how you've lived it. You want to reflect on how aging is changing your priorities. Or you may want to seek a more spiritual dimension. You may simply want to fulfill your psychological potential—to grow through self-exploration. Or you may simply want to understand yourself better.

Therapy is not the only way to pursue these questions, but it can be a very effective way, particularly therapies that take an exploratory, open-ended approach.

Problems in Everyday Living

Conversely, you may be experiencing dissatisfaction or distress over something very specific in your life. You may be struggling with one of the many "problems in living" that are part of everyday life. These are not full-fledged emotional disorders such as depression. They are normal emotional reactions to the many stressful situations that can arise in the course of living. But they can occasionally become overwhelming or tax your patience, ingenuity, or ability to cope.

A wide range of these unavoidable passages, events, and difficulties in life can make you miserable enough or stressed enough to consider getting help. Common ones include:

- trouble in a relationship
- conflict with parents
- doing poorly in school
- marital problems
- a parent-child conflict, or feelings of inadequacy as a parent
- a child who is having behavior or adjustment problems
- the death of a family member or friend that has left you deeply saddened and grieving
- a separation or divorce: yours, your parents, your child's, a sibling's, or a friend's
- losing a job, or the stress of long unemployment
- serious illness or disability
- envy of friends' successes in love or work, or disappointment that you have not been more successful
- struggling with long-simmering feelings of anger and bitterness over early rejection or neglect

- major life transitions: leaving home, getting married, having a baby, starting work, changing jobs, getting established in a career, entering middle age, losing parents, growing old
- confusion and uncertainty over what course your life should take

Problems in everyday living are the traditional arena of therapy. These are the most common problems people bring and the problems for which therapy is most reliably effective. The list above is only partial. You will find more detailed descriptions of the most prevalent "problems in everyday living" as well as recommendations for therapy in Chapter 15 of the Therapy Guide.

Emotional and Behavioral Disorders

These are *not* the unavoidable problems and difficulties of everyday life. Disordered functioning is different in both kind and degree: more serious, usually much more taxing and disruptive. Emotional and behavioral disorders are typified by mental or behavioral disturbances that appear as symptoms: feeling so hopeless, for example, that you can't get out of bed; being unable to stop after you've had your first drink; binge eating; inexplicable panic attacks; an irrational fear of leaving the house or being around people; repetitive nightmares and flashbacks reliving a traumatic event; the conviction that people are plotting against you.

Symptoms are recognizably abnormal ways of thinking, feeling, or acting, often associated with physical complaints as well. Unlike problems in living, symptoms are not everyday occurrences. Everybody confronts the difficulties of everyday living; not everyone experiences symptoms.

- *Disturbances in thinking* include marked difficulties in paying attention or concentrating; noticeably impaired judgment or memory; repetitive morbid thoughts; obsessions; irrational fears; thoughts that race out of control; irrational beliefs that one is absolutely convinced are true; hallucinations—hearing voices or seeing or smelling things that aren't there; serious thoughts of suicide.
- *Disturbances in feeling* include extreme moods such as chronic anxiety; sudden unexplained panic; unremitting depression; prolonged loss of motivation, energy, pleasure, or interest; elation and boundless energy. Also included here are pronounced mood swings: episodes of feeling very "high" alternating over days, weeks, months, or years with episodes of feeling extremely "low."
- *Disturbances in behavior* include compulsions; addictions; sexual problems; abnormal eating behavior such as self-starvation or binge eating; self-mutilation, such as cutting or burning oneself; planning or attempting suicide.
- *Disturbances in physical functioning* that can combine with other symptoms to indicate an emotional disorder include extreme weight loss or weight gain;

insomnia; and physical complaints that don't seem to be caused by an identifiable medical problem.

Taken in isolation, many of these disturbances in normal functioning are relatively common. We probably all experience some of them at different times. Insomnia is a good example. By itself, an individual symptom rarely constitutes an emotional disorder or indicates the presence of one. An isolated or transient symptom such as anxiety may be nothing more than a temporary reaction to stress. Only when individual symptoms *fall into a larger pattern* of emotional or behavioral disturbance and either *cause you distress or significantly impair* your personal, social, or work life might they signify a disorder.

In current psychiatry, each disorder is defined by a particular cluster of symptoms. Many symptoms show up in several different disorders—anxiety and insomnia, for instance, can be symptomatic of a major depression, a phobia, an obsessive-compulsive disorder, alcohol withdrawal, or posttraumatic stress. But the overall pattern of symptoms for each disorder is distinct.

Some disorders are more clearly defined than others. There is still controversy over the exact boundaries of some disorders that look similar. There is also debate over whether disorders should be defined by symptoms alone, or whether a true disorder should be marked by a particular prehistory, natural course, and genetic or biological vulnerability as well. Each successive revision of the standard *Diagnostic and Statistical Manual of Mental Disorders* brings some changes. But for the most part, research and clinical experience is gradually clarifying which symptom patterns mark the first type of emotional and behavioral disturbance, the so-called *"symptom disorders"*: depression, agoraphobia, alcohol abuse, hypochondriasis, sexual impotence and frigidity, posttraumatic stress syndrome, schizophrenia, manic-depression, and the like. The Therapy Guide provides a full description of the symptoms that characterize each of the main disorders.

Each emotional and behavioral disorder usually requires a different approach to therapy. Many of the innovations in technique, in fact, grew out of attempts to treat this range of problems. Usually more than one type of intervention is necessary as well. Individual therapy in particular is often not enough by itself. Frequently therapy is combined with medication to treat particularly troublesome or disabling symptoms. Hospitalization may also be necessary if symptoms become acute or disabling. The recommendations for treating these disorders in the Therapy Guide take this often complex picture into account. The Guide provides information about particular therapeutic approaches, medication, and other interventions that may be necessary as well.

In addition to the symptom disorders, contemporary psychiatry describes a second type of disturbance referred to as a *"personality disorder."* The personality disorders were much more difficult to identify as a distinct type of disturbance than the symptom disorders. Research into them is still evolving, and the boundaries between some of the different types is still being debated. What characterizes all of them, however, is that the disturbance shows up not so much in individual symptoms as in personality traits that are painfully disruptive and cause significant distress and disability. It is typical of this kind of disturbance, however, that the sufferers tend either to exaggerate their own sense of badness and guilt, holding themselves responsible for rejection and neglect; or they don't think they have a problem at all—rather, someone else is to blame, life has been unfair, or they are victims of unfair treatment. Unfortunately, in many cases they are partially right and all three are true. Many individuals who later develop disturbances in personality functioning were physically or sexually abused as children, or they grew up in severely dysfunctional families. Much of their own dysfunctional behavior is learned, either by modeling or out of attempts to protect themselves.

In the context of a personality disorder then, *disturbance* is not an altogether accurate term. These disorders involve blocks or gaps or twists in psychological development as much as disturbances in current functioning. For reasons that are still not well understood and probably involve many different factors, important psychological capacities have been arrested or developed imperfectly.

These individuals typically have difficulty tolerating even minimal frustration or rejection without exploding in anger or recoiling in hurt. Bearing and controlling strong feelings is difficult. Small sparks of irritation, for instance, can flare up suddenly and without warning into brushfires of anger or rage that feel overwhelming. Their mood tends to be chronically dysphoric and slightly depressed. They can fall into inner feelings of futility and emptiness when they don't feel much like a "real" person, or don't know who they really are. Relationships tend to be all-or-nothing: they either warily hold themselves aloof or abandon themselves to the other. The degree of closeness and distance never feels quite right. They long for closeness and intimacy but feel frightened by it, yet tend to fall apart when people they depend on let them down. If they do get close, they tend to submerge themselves in the other person—submissively, dependently, adoringly—and demand or expect that person to be exclusively there for them. Self-esteem is typically fragile and tends to fall apart with criticism, rejection, or neglect. They often feel and act quite entitled on the surface, while underneath they feel bad, guilty, unlovable, and undeserving. Outside and inside don't match.

In addressing the problems faced by individuals with a personality disorder, therapy can be useful as *crisis intervention,* to help them through one of the recurring crises they are prone to; as *focal, problem-oriented, short-term therapy,* to help them deal with one of the many ongoing problems they tend to encounter, especially in relationships and with addictive or self-destructive behavior; and as *long-term, reconstructive therapy,* to repair the underlying developmental deficits themselves. The Therapy Guide describes the different personality disorders that have been identified to date and the recommended approaches to their treatment. Since individuals with personality disorders are often prone to symptom-based disorders as well—alcohol and substance abuse, depression, and anxiety states are particularly common—the emotional and behavioral disorders section may need to be consulted as well.

Many terms are loosely used for both symptom-based and personality disorders. You have undoubtedly heard the terms *insanity* and *nervous breakdown*. These terms have no specific meaning in psychiatry. Mental health professionals do talk about "mental illness," usually to refer to the more severe disorders that have a strong biological or genetic base: schizophrenia, major depression, and manic-depression. But most emotional and behavioral disorders are not illnesses in a medical sense. The current revision of the *Diagnostic and Statistical Manual of Mental Disorders, DSM-III-R,* uses the general term *disorder* for all emotional and behavioral problems that are associated with a particular pattern of observable symptoms. The Therapy Guide follows this convention.

Special Cases

Psychotherapy can also offer help in two special cases related to medical problems.

When Psychological Factors Are Affecting a Physical Condition

Many medical conditions can be worsened—or improved—by psychological factors. A wave of recent research suggests that psychological and social factors clearly affect people's susceptibility to disease, as well as the course of illness and speed of recovery. Of course, disease is a complicated process, and such factors are only two among a wide range of interacting elements. It is not that psychology overrides biology, but that it can profoundly affect it.

The best-known emotional factor in disease is stress; its role in speeding the onset of illness or worsening of symptoms is well established in conditions ranging from rheumatoid arthritis to migraine headaches. In recent years, researchers have found that negative emotions in general—hostility and anger, anxiety and pessimism, depression and hopelessness—are themselves risk factors for disease of all kinds.

Illnesses aggravated by stress and other negative states include heart, respiratory, skin, and gastrointestinal diseases, and obesity and chronic pain. With such conditions, psychotherapy can be a useful addition to essential medical care (see p. 61 on behavioral medicine).

When Medical Problems Have Psychological Complications

A wide range of medical problems are complicated by the psychological reactions they provoke. One of the more common is severe depression or a brief psychotic reaction following open-heart surgery: it happens in more than a third of the cases. Such psychological complications call for therapy, and often for psychiatric medications as well.

A psychiatric specialty called liaison consultation has developed in recent years to deal with such mixed situations. It offers psychiatric expertise to attending physicians in cases where psychiatric complications arise.

Note: A Medical Condition Can Sometimes Present as a Psychological Problem

What looks like a psychological problem may not be: some medical disorders can cause psychological symptoms. When the medical problem is cured, the psychological symptom vanishes.

For this reason, if you are experiencing pronounced psychological symptoms of any kind, the first step before or as you begin therapy should be a comprehensive physical exam. A good therapist will recommend you have one before assuming your distress is purely psychological and treatable by therapy. He or she is not "reducing" your distress to biology, but recognizing that mind and body affect one another intimately. It is all too easy in our psychologically minded culture to assume that something that looks like an emotional disorder is one. You also need to be cautious about "interpreting" or "psychologizing" physical symptoms, or a physical state that feels like a medical illness. Many people, including many professionals, certainly do deny emotional factors, and you may see yourself as having a more "enlightened" attitude. But to act as if everything is psychology and that "cure" is simply mind over matter is equally unenlightened, as well as potentially dangerous. If emotional problems actually stem from a medical condition, therapy can be worse than ineffective: it may actually delay getting the appropriate medical treatment, as well as costing fruitless time, expense, and suffering.

Consult the Therapy Guide for a description of the conditions where this is likely to be the case.

WHAT KIND OF PERSON BENEFITS FROM THERAPY?

There was once a rule of thumb—a stereotype actually—that those who got the most out of therapy were "YAVIS," as therapists dubbed them: young, attractive, verbal, intelligent, and successful. That elitist view implies that those who make the best candidates for therapy are those who need it the least.

There may have been some truth to the maxim in early days of psychoanalysis when five-days-a-week analysis was something only a cultured elite with time and money could afford or would be attracted to. But today, with so many different kinds of therapies and so many systems for the delivery of services, formats and approaches are available to suit nearly every need.

Another common stereotype, still very current, is that you need to be "psychologically minded" to benefit from therapy, be a person who looks at behavior in terms of motives and unconscious motivation. This bias also derives historically from an exclusively psychodynamic approach. Psychological-mindedness in the traditional sense is not a prerequisite for most forms of contemporary therapy, which don't require any particular "psychological" sophistication. The introspective method that looks for unconscious motivation is only one approach to therapy today. You may also have heard you will have to "free associate" in therapy. You won't, unless you are doing psychoanalysis. Even there, free association is a skill that has to be learned, not a precondition. So you shouldn't hold back because you don't think you are psychologically minded enough, or because you mistrust "psychological" explanations—so do many therapists! The persistence of these stereotypes says more about the degree to which the idea of unconscious motivation has become part of popular culture than it does about contemporary therapy.

You also don't need to be exceptionally articulate. Verbal facility can just as easily be used to hide feelings as to express them. And putting things into words is only one way to express yourself. Some therapies today don't depend primarily on verbalization. The newer "expressive therapies" employ music, art, movement, dance, and drama as the main mode of expression (see p. 51).

Outcome studies have generally shown little correlation between a good outcome and the other attributes once thought to be prerequisites for therapy: social class, age, gender, or intelligence. In regard to gender, the majority of clients in therapy are women. Men tend to be more wary of it, perhaps being less at ease than women in disclosing their feelings. Whether this is true or not, despite the initial resistance some men may have to therapy, the evidence suggests that therapy works as well for men as for women. And in regard to intelligence, no clearcut minimum requirement for a good outcome in therapy has ever been established. Certain types of therapy may require a certain kind of intelligence—psychoanalysis, for example—but it is not a concern in most other approaches, such as behavior therapy.

A different kind of factor that both clients and therapists often assume is linked to outcome is the person's degree of disturbance or distress. It might seem that the more disturbed and distressed someone is, the less he or she would be able to benefit from therapy. The one disturbance that interferes most with a good outcome is confused, disorganized thinking. But this is often independent of emotional distress. Even if you are greatly distressed, you can benefit from therapy, as long as your distress isn't so great that it interferes with forming a bond with your therapist or following through with the treatment plan. Even in that case, if you are willing to consider it, distress can often be reduced by medication to the point where you can engage with good effect.

So, therapy is no longer the preserve of a cultural, social, or economic elite, nor are the attributes associated with these elites necessary to benefit from it. You do not need to be psychologically sophisticated. A wide range of approaches available today don't depend on psychological "insight." What will matter most are *wanting the help therapy has to offer and making the effort it requires; and—the most important factor—your ability to form a good working relationship with your therapist.*

WHEN TO CONSIDER THERAPY

What you want help with may be appropriate for therapy. You may be one of the many people who could benefit from it. But *when* should you seriously consider it? There are three considerations in deciding when to seek therapy:

1. Your level of distress: is it intense enough that you want to do something about it?
2. Your ability to handle your problems on your own: are you managing, or do you feel the need for more support?
3. How much your distress is affecting your personal life, your family, or your work: are your problems getting in the way of your ability to function? Are you, your family, or your work suffering significantly?

If an honest answer to any one of these questions is yes, it is probably time to consider therapy. If the answer is yes to all three, you need help *now*. At the very least, you should get a consultation as soon as possible (see Chapter 4).

Your Level of Distress

When does a problem become a "problem"? When does something turn from being an inconvenience, an irritant, a problem you can live with, and become something you need to do something about? Some people manage to live with symptoms of severe disturbance for years—delusions, hallucinations, periodic episodes of mania or depression, self-starvation or binging and purging, chronic tension and anxiety, impotence and frigidity, agoraphobia, polysubstance abuse, alcoholic blackouts and DT's—without seeking or even wanting help. Others go on living with abusive, alcoholic, or unfaithful spouses, persist in marriages marked by chronic fighting and arguing, bear with a hyperactive child, or tolerate behavior from their children that is clearly harmful and out of control. Still others blame circumstances, fate, or a malevolent providence for their problems.

In all but the most serious cases, or when your safety is at stake, what matters most is your own subjective level of distress. A problem becomes a "problem" when you think it is, or when it hurts enough. This will depend on two things: *what you're used to*—is this more than the usual struggle?—and *what you expect*—do you expect something very different from yourself?

As with physical pain, emotional pain is a sign that something is amiss. It is a signal to get help. Being aware that you feel anxious or distressed is actually a good sign. The more you are aware that things aren't as they should be, the more likely you are to do something about it.

Others may see your situation differently. Count on it, in fact. Families will typically try to reassure you that it isn't that bad—they don't want to see you suffer, and they are inclined to take it personally if you do. Friends will be divided: half will agree you have a problem; half will try to minimize it or talk you out of it.

Pain is a signal you can read better than anyone else. Your own feelings about how things are going, how well you are managing, how dissatisfied and unhappy you feel, and whether you need help are the best and truest gauge. By and large, if you think something is wrong, something probably is.

If you aren't sure, ask for a consultation from a therapist and get a professional opinion. While family, friends, and colleagues may minimize your troubles, a good therapist will listen carefully, see what is troubling you, and help you sort things out. No therapist expects you to have a cut-and-dried idea of just exactly what the trouble is. Part of the therapist's job is to help you get a handle on what is going on.

Whether You Can Manage on Your Own

We all know what it feels like to be depressed, irritable, anxious, or distraught from time to time. People have different degrees of tolerance for these feelings. Your situation may be stressful, but you may be handling it adequately with your normal supports and without significant disruption of your daily life. It's when you notice these feelings repeatedly getting the better of you, or when they become extreme, that it's time to consider getting help. We all get overwhelmed from time to time. It's when you find yourself feeling overwhelmed most of the time, or too much of the time, that it's probably time for help.

Not everyone who might need or who could benefit from therapy necessarily feels overwhelmed emotionally, however. Not everybody experiences anxiety and distress directly. Pay attention to other signs as well. You may be experiencing emotional distress physically, in your body, in the form of tension or physical complaints, or in behavior that is unusual or uncharacteristic of you. Unfortunately, a good many of us can tolerate more anxiety and distress than is good for us before we recognize and acknowledge a need for help.

How Much Your Life Is Being Affected

For many people the most reliable yardstick of the need for therapy is how well they are handling their affairs: their intimate relations, their family life, their job. Although subjectively you may feel "fine," how you are actually handling things may indicate that not all is going well. For a child, who may not have the words for feelings, or can't confront a painful home situation directly, the first signs of trouble are often bad conduct at school, a sharp drop in academic performance, or sudden belligerence at home.

OBSTACLES TO GETTING STARTED

Common Doubts and Reservations

Doubts and reservations are inevitable when people think about entering therapy. Some doubts are fed by ideas we hear from friends or in the media; others grow out of reasonable concerns. The most common include:

- I'll discover something about myself I'd rather not know about.
- I'll have to reveal painful things about myself.
- If I talk about things, it will only make them worse.
- If I need help, it means I'm weak.
- I won't be up to it. It will be too difficult.
- Nobody can help me.
- Therapy just adjusts people to the status quo.
- I have to do it by myself.
- Therapy will mean surrendering my independence.
- You only need therapy if you're sick or crazy.
- I won't be able to talk about my personal life with someone I don't know.
- I'll become too dependent on my therapist.
- It's too much time and money. It will break me.
- I'm afraid I'll find out I'm really disturbed.
- I'll lose my spontaneity and creativity.
- If I go into therapy, I'm admitting that all my/our problems are my fault.
- It will ruin my relationship with my family: I'll end up blaming my parents for everything. My parents/spouse will wonder if I'm talking about them.
- Once I start therapy I'll never be able to get out.
- I don't want to be labeled with a diagnosis.
- Therapy will make me dull and boring.
- I just want help with a particular problem; I don't want to dredge up my whole life.
- What will others think of me if they hear I'm in therapy?
- Being in therapy might be held against me in the future.
- Therapy doesn't really work anyway.

What makes these worries and doubts difficult to judge objectively is the ambivalence you probably have about entering therapy to begin with. Any or all of these can offer you a "good excuse" not to try it.

If you're uncertain which concerns are well-founded and which may really be excuses, a consultation with a therapist may be in order to help you sort this out.

Inner Blocks

Apart from common doubts and reservations, people considering therapy are often held back by personal resistance to seeking help for these kinds of problems. We tend to react to emotional difficulty quite differently from physical illness, in part because those around us tend to view them differently. Our culture legitimates physical illness and actively supports getting help for it; but it still reacts to psychological problems with alarm and moral judgment, even discrimination.

It is hard not to share these attitudes, which can make it difficult for you to recognize your emotional distress as a valid reason to seek help. A number of these attitudes can become inner blocks to seeking help:

- *The need to appear in control during an illness or crisis.* This is compounded by our particular cultural value system, which emphasizes self-control, self-discipline, strength of will. To seek help is to acknowledge a loss of control.
- *The need to maintain the illusion of self-sufficiency.* This, too, is a mix of personal and cultural pressures to support the myth that we can do it by the force of our own guts and self-determination. If we just try hard enough, we can pull ourselves together without anyone else's help.
- *The general fear of illness and disability.* Illness and disability leave us feeling weak, vulnerable, unable to defend ourselves. Instinctively we seek protective isolation and try to hide the revealing signs or symptoms of distress.
- *The specific fear of being stigmatized or labeled.* You may be afraid or ashamed of being called "sick," "crazy," "emotionally disturbed," "mental," "a head case." We don't know how our parents, spouses, or family members will react. A label is most hurtful when it's applied by someone at home.

The result of such inner blocks is that just at the moment when you are hurting the most and need to reach out, you are prone to doing just the opposite: withdrawing, isolating yourself, denying your need for help, understanding, and support.

Social Pressures

Specific social pressures can undermine your motivation to seek therapy. Sometimes the very people who may have urged you to go into therapy become its strongest opponents when it begins to conflict with their own needs. Initial support, even enthusiasm and advocacy, can turn into open or covert opposition. A last child at home who has struggled in therapy over the guilt she feels about moving out suddenly hears her mother say, "You have everything you need here . . . why leave?" An unhappy wife begins to encounter resistance from her husband when she proposes going to work now that their last child is preschool age. Friends may tell you that having been in therapy will be held against you in your career. The prevailing attitudes about therapy at your church or temple, or at your school, may also act as a deterrent. It is always hard to persist in the face of contrary opinions from people who carry weight with you and whose respect you want to keep.

Why Not Just Use a Friend?

People often ask themselves, do I really need a therapist? Can't a good friend do what a therapist can do? The answer is no.

There are limits to the kind of help a friend can provide, limits that make talking with a friend very different from working with a therapist. With a friend, you are more likely to hold back some of your darker feelings or emotional secrets. After all, this is someone you spend time with and see socially. *Complete* self-disclosure may leave you feeling awkward or vulnerable in the future.

Friends may also talk to someone else about your conversation. Even if they promise to respect your confidence, it may be difficult for them not to confide in another friend, a spouse, or a lover. Friends may feel anxious or burdened by what you've entrusted them with and may not want to carry it alone. A therapist is ethically and legally bound to respect confidentiality.

A friendship also involves a mutual give-and-take. Friends will rightfully expect you to be there as much for them as they are for you. They may experience it as unfair and one-sided if your conversations tend to focus on your problems and your feelings, and not theirs. Therapists, on the other hand, will expect this. Their sole commitment is to be there exclusively for you and your concerns.

Friends are also not trained to listen and respond as a therapist does. Therapists will hear issues or key aspects of the problem a friend may miss. They will bring a trained and experienced perspective to bear on human problems that a friend without that training can't. They will also be less hesitant to tell you what they hear than a friend will. A friend will find it hard not to be influenced by your friendship and what they think you want to hear. Your friendship will inevitably color their perceptions of you, what they tell you, and how they say it.

Finally, a therapist has been trained in methods for addressing specific emotional, interpersonal, behavioral, and family problems. They can bring a level of specialized professional skill and experience to bear that a friend simply can't.

This is not to say don't talk to a trusted and respected friend. Therapy doesn't substitute for friendship. Just don't expect a friend to do what a therapist can.

GETTING STARTED ANYWAY: POTENTIAL REWARDS AND SATISFACTIONS

With all these obstacles, little wonder that many people find it hard to get started in therapy, and that so many wait until they are feeling desperate before seeking help. Or that when they do start therapy, they have many doubts, fears, prejudices, and outside pressures to overcome. But if you wait until you have hit bottom to start, you put yourself at a disadvantage. You will feel under pressure to go with the first therapist you find instead of giving yourself time to find someone who is a good match for you and your needs. If you wait too long you won't have the same emotional resources and energy for the work. And the longer you delay, the more entrenched your problems and patterns are likely to become and the more difficult to change.

Whatever your reasons for considering therapy, if you are serious about wanting help, the best time to start is now. With the right therapist, you may start to feel some relief fairly soon. About half of all therapy clients say they feel better within the first six to eight sessions, even if it's largely from the feeling of no longer having to struggle alone. Even if you don't experience immediate relief, therapy can help you face what is troubling you with greater confidence. If it doesn't eliminate your problems, it can help you deal with them more effectively. It won't make you a new person, but it can help you to love and work better, improve relationships, ease recurrent anxieties, clarify your thinking, learn new ways of handling feelings, break unproductive or vicious circles, take more charge of your life and behavior, and thereby increase your sense of being a competent and worthy person. As you change, you may find that others around you seem to change for the better, too!

STEPS TO FINDING THE RIGHT THERAPY

Step One: Acknowledge That You Need Help

That can sometimes be difficult. Chapter 1 has reviewed those difficulties, and the kind of help you can expect from therapy.

Step Two: Identify the Issue or Problem

If you aren't sure—and it is sometimes difficult to pinpoint exactly—consult the Therapy Guide. The Guide describes in detail the major problems and issues therapy can help with, and the preferred therapy approach for each. The main therapy approaches are described in Chapter 2. You can use the Guide to help organize in your mind what you want to talk over with a therapist.

Step Three: Get Referrals to Several Therapists

Try to get the names of at least three therapists who offer the kind of therapy that you think you are looking for—the Therapy Guide should have given you a place to start. Chapter 3 will tell you how to find appropriate and reliable referrals.

Step Four: Ask for a Consultation

A consultation is an opportunity to interview a prospective therapist, not a commitment to go into therapy. It gives you a chance to see what a therapist is like and sense if you could work well together before you commit to therapy. Chapter 4 describes how to get a consultation, and how to use it to get an idea of the therapist's compatibility and competence.

Step Five: Weigh Your Options and Make a Decision

Ideally, you should consult with several therapists before deciding which one is most suitable. Chapter 5 explores the considerations that should go into a decision.

Step Six: Contract for Therapy

Once you've decided on a therapist, you and the therapist should then agree on your specific goals for therapy and exactly how you will work together toward them. Chapter 6 details what should go into the therapy agreement. Chapter 7 discusses how therapy is paid for: the range of fees therapists charge, how a particular fee is negotiated, billing, insurance coverage, and third-party payment.

CHAPTER TWO

■

APPROACHES TO PSYCHOTHERAPY

Next to choosing a therapist, the most important decision is deciding on an approach: how you and your therapist will actually work on your problems. With so many alternative methods and therapies available today, the choice of approach can be confusing. Therapists themselves often disagree on how problems should be approached in therapy and which technique is more effective.

The following overview describes the basic differences in orientations so that you will be able to talk with a therapist in an informed way about the options you have.

The categories we are using are: *psychodynamic, behavioral, cognitive, family systems,* and *supportive.* Each defines a distinct theoretical and technical approach to therapy. As you begin looking for a therapist, you will find most therapists tend to ally themselves with one of these approaches, even if they describe themselves as "eclectic." A therapist's approach is what defines him or her within the profession and constitutes his or her professional identity. A therapist may specialize in one well-defined method—cognitive therapy, psychoanalysis, biofeedback, or structural family therapy—but his or her thinking and practice will be informed and guided by one of these broad-based orientations.

Research shows these approaches can make a difference in treatment. One will clearly be the "approach of choice" in certain cases. For instance, an extroverted young woman who is otherwise doing well but has an irrational fear of driving would be better served first by a behavioral approach directed at her phobia, rather than a psychodynamic exploration of the meaning of her symptom and insight into

50

the unconscious conflicts that might cause it. In other circumstances, a particular approach will clearly be counterproductive: trying to explore the meaning of delusions and hallucinations with a young man undergoing an acute schizophrenic psychosis will only make him more psychotic. In the National Survey of Psychotherapists, practicing therapists themselves often clearly recommend one approach over another for most problems.

The differences between these approaches are real and important, but not absolute. They are more a matter of focus and emphasis—of adopting a particular perspective on human problems and their causes, and on the remedy for them. These approaches also aren't mutually exclusive, despite the dogmatic stance many schools and therapists take. They can be used in combination, either simultaneously or sequentially, to treat more complex problems. For instance, once behavioral techniques have resolved agoraphobic symptoms, and the person is able to leave the house and resume normal activities, a psychodynamic exploration of his or her underlying fears of separation may be necessary to prevent a recurrence of the phobia. A psychodynamic exploration of personal conflicts in individual therapy can be undertaken at the same time as a systems approach in couples therapy to resolve problems in a marriage.

These categories don't capture every nuance of every approach. Some therapies also don't fit comfortably within one of these five categories. The "expressive therapies," for instance—art, music, dance, and movement therapy, along with psychodrama—are here considered modalities that can be employed within any of the main approaches. The "supportive" approach also isn't a "school" like the others that embodies a specific view of human functioning and an independent body of techniques. Supportive elements are in every therapy. But it does constitute a separate approach when support, rather than emotional or behavioral change, is the main objective—supporting someone through an acute psychotic episode, for instance, or helping someone with a chronic condition manage the problems of everyday living.

There is no one "best" approach to therapy, or even to every problem. But one of these approaches may be better for you and what you are seeking help for. For most of the normal individual problems in living, the particular approach the therapist takes is less important. Nevertheless, one may feel more comfortable and intuitively right for you. Listen to the therapists you consult, but follow your own instincts and judgment, too.

THE PSYCHODYNAMIC APPROACH

The psychodynamic approach derives from the principles and methods of psychoanalysis, the first of the "psychodynamic" therapies.

The distinctive feature of this approach is its emphasis on the *subjective meaning* of experience; and the use of the therapeutic relationship itself to explore, illuminate, and transform your subjective world—the way you experience yourself and others.

Prior to Sigmund Freud, psychiatry assumed that the irrational ideas characteristic of mental disturbance were the result of an "infliction," much as fever was viewed as the result of infection. Freud reversed this assumption: it is irrational ideas that often produce the disturbance—and the symptoms. Moreover, these ideas can be linked with memories, impulses, desires, and fantasies that the mind keeps out of awareness in the "unconscious" through the mechanism of "repression." The notion of a dark, unconscious side of the mind itself was not new. It is as old as Plato in the West and the Vedas in the East. What was new was Freud's discovery that whatever was unconsciously repressed did not remain buried but continued to actively affect behavior—the meaning of "dynamic" in *psychodynamic;* and that the mind had to work to keep unwanted, forbidden wishes and fears from awareness and expression. This discovery became the foundation of the method that later became psychoanalysis. It remains the basis of the psychodynamic approach.

Most contemporary schools of psychoanalysis no longer follow Freud's notion that all unconscious conflict is rooted in the frustration of sexual and aggressive drives. *Object relations theory,* for instance, emphasizes the way the infant and growing child forms internal images of his or her primary relationships, and the way these internal representations become the basis of mental organization and all subsequent experience. *Self-psychology* sees the structure and development of the sense of "self" as the central organizer of psychological experience, emphasizing the role of others' empathic attunement in building a cohesive and coherent sense of selfhood.

But the concept of unconscious motivation and conflict at the root of emotional problems remains basic to the psychodynamic approach. These unresolved conflicts—fear of an angry and critical father, excessive dependence on an overinvolved mother, feelings of rivalry and jealousy toward a sibling, having to put one's own needs as a child aside to care for a dysfunctional parent, or perform for parents who viewed their children as narcissistic extensions of themselves—are seen as lingering on in ways that sabotage our ability to learn, to love, and to work. Because these ideas and feelings remain so painful, so threatening, or so at variance with our normal sense of ourselves, we continually try to clamp a lid on them—"repress" them beyond the reach of conscious memory and recall. This repression then distorts our perceptions of ourselves and significant others—we have to "not see" certain things about ourselves or them. But though we may be unaware of them, these desires, fears, fantasies, memories, and internal images of ourselves and others do not go away; repression is never totally successful. They continue to express themselves in disguised form and demand our attention in dreams, symbols, slips of the tongue, jokes, memory lapses, art, or relationship patterns.

If the conflict is strong enough, it may show up as psychiatric symptoms or other signs of emotional distress. The psychodynamic approach assumes that these unconscious dynamic beliefs, motives, and conflicts have to be gradually teased out into the open where they can be faced and dealt with. A large part of this approach is working with the psychological defenses that you employ to avoid seeing or knowing the unacceptable things you want, fear, or are projecting onto others.

The goal is to understand and resolve these internal emotional conflicts that originate in our earliest relationships and repeat themselves in our adult experience.

Unlike other approaches, which tend to be much more directive in devising a plan of action for each session, you are free to bring up whatever you want to talk about in this approach. This may be a situation at work, an argument with your spouse, a dream you had the night before, some decision you need to make. The therapist will take the problem you bring in at face value and help you work on it; but she will be particularly interested in helping you look more closely for links to underlying patterns of ideas, expectations, anxieties, desires, and frustrations that you may be struggling with. This offers you the chance to identify and grapple with what are sometimes impossible desires, irrational fears, or ancient angers. The therapist helps you confront these buried areas of experience by listening intently, with a nonjudgmental attitude, and reflecting back what you are saying in ways that help you expand your awareness of your inner life.

A psychodynamic approach assumes your most basic conflicts will inevitably come into play in the therapeutic relationship. How you act with—and react to—your therapist becomes one of the most important, if not *the* most important, sources of information about you. For this reason, the relationship with the therapist plays a central role, even more so than in other approaches. This relationship is designed to offer a new arena in which the conflicted feelings and thoughts can emerge and be dealt with. By watching your relationship with your therapist unfold, you see yourself repeating the patterns that continue to cause you distress. But with the therapist's help, you catch yourself in the act, seeing how these patterns are affecting you here and now. The fact that they become present and real in the relationship is what gives this approach its emotional immediacy and power to effect change.

The stereotyped view of the psychodynamic therapist as a silent, impassive, anonymous blank screen for projection has become outdated. Most therapists using this approach engage their clients actively. The central idea remains the same, however: while engaging you in a genuine emotional and personal relationship, a vital part of the therapist's job is to help you see how you are investing him or her with attributes and expectations that derive from relationships with significant others in your past that have shaped and limited your experience in critical ways. Together you will clarify the conflicting wishes, needs, fears, hopes, and fantasies that you are "transferring" to the therapist as a way of understanding the patterns—particularly the unresolved conflicts—that continue to shape your life. This "transference" itself becomes a microcosm of your psychological experience. As you both examine it, the patterns that dominate your life can be clarified and new ways of thinking, feeling, and acting tried. At the same time, therapists will try to be aware of their own reactions to you—their own spontaneous feelings about you, their "countertransference"—both to avoid reading their own issues into yours, and to use their own reactions as a guide to understanding how you are experiencing the relationship and what they themselves are contributing to it.

Therapists following this approach will tend to share only a limited amount of personal information about themselves. Your concerns should be the exclusive focus in any case, and what you think and feel about them is much more important than biographical information "about" them. They will also acknowledge and accept your desire for love, reassurance, and approval; but they will try to help you understand the underlying needs that may be making these desires so problematic, threatening, or intense. Short of an emergency or an action that would clearly be harmful, they will try not to take sides in your struggle with yourself. The purpose of this—which you may find frustrating at first—is to allow as many of your conflicting ideas and feelings to come to view as possible.

As these emerge, the therapist's role is to help you understand and come to terms with them. As you do, the tendency to repeatedly reenact these old angers, resentments, conflicts, and fears will diminish as they are mastered; and the irrational guilt or shame associated with them will gradually dissipate. Finally, you will be more free to choose for yourself how to live without being driven by unmastered conflicts and anxieties.

TYPES OF PSYCHODYNAMIC THERAPY

Psychoanalysis

Psychoanalysis is the original and probably still the best known of the psychodynamic therapies. What distinguishes psychoanalysis from the other psychodynamic approaches is its method, and to a lesser extent, its goal.

The central method of psychoanalysis is free association, the attempt to express everything that comes to mind without selection, reservation, or censorship, whatever your feelings about it—whether you think it unimportant, embarrassing, or unacceptable: all your thoughts, feelings, desires, fears, sensations, and memories as you become aware of them. Obviously, this is not an ability you start with; it is learned in the course of analysis. What you and your analyst observe and talk about will include not just what you say, but *all* expressions and communications between you, nonverbal as well as verbal.

The task of free association inevitably encounters opposition, manifested through a block in the flow of speech or in some kind of avoidance or evasion—changing the subject, remaining silent, withholding relevant information. The analyst will assume this is due to some interference, or *resistance,* of which you are not consciously aware. This then becomes a signpost to unconscious conflict.

Central to this method of uncovering is the management of the transference. In regular, once-a-week psychodynamic *psychotherapy,* the emphasis is more on the present than the past. The primary focus is on real-life problems and current dynamic patterns. There is less attempt to systematically reconstruct the past; it is brought in only as it directly bears on the problem at hand. The therapist will use your spontaneous transference attitudes and reactions to them to throw light on the problems you are working on, but won't encourage a systematic and full-blown transference. *Psychoanalysis,* on the other hand, makes the transference absolutely central to treatment. The process is designed to encourage the reenactment of all important underlying issues and conflicts in the transference; and it is in the transference that they are primarily explored and dealt with. Current problems and dynamic patterns, while taken seriously and worked on, tend to become starting points for a more systematic exploration of their roots in primary relationships.

The unique treatment arrangements associated with psychoanalysis are all designed to facilitate free association and transference. You would probably be asked to lie on a couch. This creates an element of mild sensory deprivation that narrows your focus to your inner thoughts, feelings, and fantasies and stimulates the free flow of ideas. Lying down is also a posture associated with reverie, imagery, and dreaming rather than logical thought. The analyst will probably sit behind and above you. This further promotes free association by removing the person you are talking to from your line of view; in addition, it tends to symbolically re-create the early parent-child situation, thereby facilitating transference reactions.

Another distinctive feature of psychoanalysis is meeting four to five times a week, again to facilitate a strong transference and an ongoing flow of associations.

Psychoanalysis doesn't aim specifically at relieving individual symptoms, though symptoms usually remit if the analysis is successful. The ultimate goal is to modify the structure of personality or deeply ingrained traits by gradually integrating previously repressed material into conscious awareness, so that it no longer has to be defended against by constricting and distorting your experience in self-limiting and painful ways.

The process tends to unfold slowly. It takes time to feel comfortable with free association, for the transference to become established, and to learn how to work in such an unusual way. Uncovering and understanding unconscious material also needs to be balanced with your ability to absorb and integrate often painful and difficult insights without being retraumatized by the experience. Thus analysis takes longer than any other therapy: typically the time frame is left open-ended, but three years is probably the minimum, and it can take as long as five to seven years, occasionally even longer, all told a considerable commitment of time, effort, and money.

Developmental Psychodynamic Psychotherapy

This form of psychodynamic therapy needs special mention because it is still not widely known. It is designed to treat problems that are more severe than the psychodynamic approach was originally intended for, particularly the personality dis-orders and other forms of severe disturbance such as schizophrenia. This approach is based on the idea that certain critical psychological functions have become arrested or derailed in severe forms of psychological disturbance; and that basic psychological structures have never been adequately developed. The arrests are seen primarily in the areas of emotion, body image, the sense of self, and the capacity for relationship. Therapy involves using the real, here-and-now relationship with the therapist—not the projected transference relationship—to repair basic functions or develop them for the first time, such as the capacity to experience emotion or tolerate anger or ambivalence without becoming overwhelmed or having to dissociate. It avoids the usual uncovering techniques of the psychodynamic approach such as free association and transference interpretation. These would only stir up thoughts, feelings, and memories that the individual doesn't have the internal capacity to handle. The idea is to build structure and adequate defenses, not uncover conflicts.

Brief or "Time-Limited" Dynamic Psychotherapy

The increasing reluctance of third-party payers to support long-term psychotherapy has made this time-limted approach a much more popular alternative. And it has also proven effective for a wide range of problems and disorders. The principles and methods are much the same as in longer psychodynamic therapy, but therapy is limited in advance to twelve to twenty visits. The goal is to resolve a specific problem or set of related problems quickly. The better-known types of brief dynamic psychotherapy are associated with their founders and institutions: brief psycho-therapy (Malan–Tavistock); time-limited psychotherapy (Mann–Boston University); short-term dynamic psychotherapy (Davanloo–McGill University); and others.

Short-term interpersonal psychotherapy is a specific type of short-term therapy originally designed by Myrna Weissman and Gerald Klerman to treat depression. This approach views interpersonal relations as both a cause of depression and as a method of cure. As in most short-term therapies, the therapist is very active. He or she will readily offer you direct advice and help in making decisions. In controlled studies, interpersonal psychotherapy has been as effective as antidepressants in treat-ing some types of depression.

Other Exploratory Therapies

Some schools of therapy have their distant roots in psychoanalysis and are explor-atory in nature but have changed so much they bear little resemblance to the usual psychodynamic approach.

Jungian analysis, developed by Freud's former student, Carl Jung, was the first. Jungian analysis makes greater use of the mythic and archetypal dimension in dreams and fantasy than is usually the case in psychodynamic therapies. These are used to plumb the "collective unconscious," a transpersonal level of meaning and identity that is expressed through cross-cultural "archetypes" often found in myth. A Jungian analyst will place relatively little importance on the childhood conflicts that are important in other psychodynamic approaches. Instead, he or she will try to help you find the meaning of psychological problems in deeper archetypes, such as the Great Mother. Rather than free associating to your dreams, for instance, you and the therapist work together to detect the archetypical meanings your dream symbolizes. Like Freudian analysis, Jungian analysis is less oriented toward curing specific symptoms. Its aim is more to help you find a sense of personal meaning and mission in life.

Gestalt therapy, developed by Fritz Perls and based on the principles of Gestalt psychology, focuses on emotion and feeling, and bringing the body into the realm of therapy. This approach sees repressed conflicts as inflicting a cost on the entire organism, and the work of therapy as increasing awareness of what the organism needs at the moment. Excursions into the past are irrelevant; the focus is on the here and now, as much on nonverbal clues to hidden feelings as on what is said. One technique, for example, dramatizes the client's feelings by having him sit in different chairs to play the various "parts" of himself—a guilty conscience, a resentful but submissive child, and so on. By making these splits blatantly obvious, the therapist helps the client bring them into harmony in an integrated whole.

Transactional analysis focuses on the typical kind of "scripts" that govern your interpersonal interactions. Though it is done in an individual format, it typically involves participation in a therapy group. How you interact with other group members becomes the basis for examining your habitual psychological stance toward yourself and others. As in gestalt therapy, the focus is on the here and now. Therapy is typically brief, usually for a fixed number of sessions. The goal is for your "adult" self to find a balance between the reckless and self-centered "child" in you and the punitive, judgmental "parent."

Existential psychotherapy springs from the philosophical outlook of European existentialism. It emphasizes a different kind of basic conflict at the root of human problems: not a conflict with repressed drives or with internalized significant adults; but the conflict that flows from the individual's confrontation with the "givens" of existence—certain ultimate concerns that are an inescapable part of living: death, freedom, isolation, and meaninglessness. The focus of therapy is on cultivating a direct, authentic confrontation with these intrinsic factors of life, the relationship with the therapist serving as a microcosm. The therapist attempts to be open and responsive, sharing his or her own sense of life as well as trying to understand yours. Like other dynamic therapies it is exploratory, but there is no theory of old psychic wounds skewing the present. Rather the focus is on embracing the fundamental anxieties of life and being open to your reactions to them. If a chaotic and tragic world leaves you anxious, then you learn to face this directly rather than turning away.

Client-centered therapy, developed by Carl Rogers, has been especially influential among educators and counselors. It, too, is exploratory in nature, but not in the direction of uncovering unconscious dynamics. Rogers, a leader of the humanistic movement in psychology, held that there is a basic drive in everyone toward health or "self-actualization": living up to one's full psychological potential. What holds us back is our perceptions of ourselves. If we are riddled with self-doubt, we hold ourselves back from emotional health. The goal in client-centered therapy is to help you come to a more positive view of yourself. The assumption is that at base you have the resources you need to explore your emotional needs; and that with warmth, support, and "unconditional positive regard" from your therapist, the inherent drive toward self-actualization will help you find your own way.

Somatic therapies, or body therapies, include Reichian therapy, bioenergetics, Rolfing, and numerous newer schools such as "Hakomi therapy." These therapies are also exploratory, but proceed from a different starting point. Their premise is that emotional traumas and issues leave their imprint on the body in the form of muscle-tension patterns. The therapist works actively with and through your body to try to unblock muscular tension or "body armor." Through releasing the patterns of your body tension, the feelings, thoughts, and memories associated with the original emotional trauma and "held" in that particular tension pattern will emerge.

THE BEHAVIORAL APPROACH

The distinctive feature of this approach is its emphasis on *modifying specific, observable behaviors*, using the principles of learning theory to alter what are viewed as self-defeating habits.

The main assumption is that emotional problems, like all behavior, are learned responses to the environment. Unfortunately they are maladaptive responses; but again like any other behavior they can be modified or unlearned. If they are rewarded or reinforced, they will persist. If they are not rewarded, not reinforced, or punished, they will desist. The behavior therapist then is not interested in increasing awareness of unconscious motivation or conflicts, or gaining insight into the childhood roots of your problems. He simply seeks to change observable behavior.

Unlike the psychodynamic approach, behavioral techniques did not evolve from one principal school of thought alone. They emerged instead from many experimentally based studies of the way behavior is learned—and unlearned—through *stimulus-response* and *operant* conditioning. In the first case, a particular behavior becomes associated with a specific stimulus that precedes it; in the second, a particular behavior is reinforced by the consequences that follow it. The result has been a wealth of scientifically based, systematic methods of changing or controlling specific maladaptive behaviors. This approach is most effective when it is directed to circumscribed target symptoms such as anxiety and phobias, or in dealing with specific problem behaviors: alcohol and substance abuse, eating disorders, sexual dysfunctions, smoking, stuttering, obsessive thoughts, compulsions, marital conflict, and many childhood problems such as separation anxiety, school phobia or refusal, bedwetting, conduct disorders, attention deficit, even autism. It is also effective in controlling exaggerated psychophysiological responses.

Behavior therapy is much more directive than psychodynamic and other exploratory approaches. Treatment begins with a detailed "behavioral analysis" of the specific events leading up to and following a particular unwanted behavior. You and your therapist will first delineate the problem or symptom in terms of specific, objective, measurable behaviors. When you come to a behavior therapist with a child who continually disobeys you, for instance, or with headaches from chronic tension, you will be asked to observe that behavior as closely as possible for a period of time—even keeping a written record, if need be, of how many times it actually occurs. This provides you and your therapist with an objective "baseline" from which to measure change and improvement.

Next, you and your therapist will try to analyze what is either triggering or reinforcing the behavior. For instance, you may find that your child becomes unruly when you are inattentive so as to get your full attention; or that when you get impatient, you snap at your child, which then triggers rudeness. Or you may find that your headaches occur whenever you have too many deadlines too close together.

You and your therapist will then design a treatment plan that will change the behavior. You will be asked to carry out a specific sequence of steps that will condition a more adaptive response, either by modifying the triggering stimulus or the factors that are reinforcing or rewarding the behavior. You may try, for instance, to spend certain times with your child when you give him your full attention; or you may systematically ignore him when he is bad and praise him when he is good. For headaches, you might learn to use a relaxation technique whenever you feel muscle tension building in your neck and shoulders.

Expect "homework" assignments in this approach. Therapy sessions themselves are devoted to analyzing behavior, devising steps for modifying it, and reviewing the effectiveness of the plan as you carry it out. The most important work is done between sessions when you implement the program, not during sessions as in other approaches.

The goal of behavior therapy is to extinguish the behavior—that is, let it die out by stopping whatever was reinforcing it—or to replace it with a more desirable response.

Methods of Behavior Therapy

The behavior draws on a wide range of techniques, many of them borrowed from education and child rearing. One of the oldest, although no longer the most common technique used, is *systematic desensitization,* developed by Joseph Wolpe, one of the first behavior therapists. The method is particularly useful for treating phobias. In this procedure one learned response, anxiety, is replaced with an incompatible one, relaxation.

This involves first mastering a simple relaxation technique, such as deep muscle relaxation. You and your therapist will then construct a hierarchy of situations that are progressively more anxiety-provoking. A hierarchy of ten to twelve scenarios in order of increasing anxiety is standard. If you are afraid of dogs, for instance, seeing a picture of a dog might be at the low end, and approaching a large German shepherd might be at the high end. You work up through the desensitization hierarchy gradually, mastering the ability to remain relaxed at each level before proceeding to the next. This may be done exclusively in the imagination, or the desensitization procedure may begin with imagined scenes and proceed to actual ones. At each level you learn to remain calm and in control.

Another behavioral method for treating anxiety and phobias is *flooding.* This approach assumes that escaping from an anxiety-provoking experience actually reinforces your anxiety through conditioning. The premise is that by not allowing you to escape, the conditioned avoidance behavior can be prevented and the phobic response eliminated. In this procedure, the therapist encourages you to imagine or actually put yourself in the situation you fear. Unlike systematic desensitization, no relaxation exercises are used; instead, the anxiety gradually subsides as you experience that nothing terrible actually happens. Someone afraid of heights, for instance, might ride a glass elevator on the outside of a hotel. Your therapist typically accompanies you in these situations to support your effort and help you realize that you have survived without the dreaded result coming to pass.

A variant of flooding is *implosion,* in which the imagined or real event is made worse than it actually is in order to desensitize the habitual anxious response. Both these techniques involve some psychological discomfort and work best with specific phobias. *Graded exposure* is also similar to flooding in that no relaxation training is involved. The phobic object or situation is approached through a series of small, graded steps, usually in a real-life context.

In two related methods, *assertiveness training* and *social skills training,* you learn to be more effective socially by analyzing your patterns of interaction and trying out new skills. Both types of training teach specific ways of responding appropriately in social situations, expressing your opinions and your needs in acceptable ways, and achieving your goals. A variety of techniques are used, including desensitization, role modeling, positive reinforcement, and experimentation and rehearsal.

Modeling, in which you learn a new behavior by observation alone, and *behavioral rehearsal,* in which you practice new behaviors and act out real-life problems under the therapist's supervision or direction, are two further behavioral techniques. As irrational fears can be learned by watching a model become unnecessarily frightened, they can be unlearned by observing another model—the therapist—confront the same object or situation without fear. The technique has been effective with phobic children who are placed with other children of their own age and sex who will approach what they are afraid of. Rehearsal is particularly helpful in managing more complex behavioral problems such as job interviews and shyness.

Operant conditioning techniques are used when a person's environment can be restructured to discourage unwanted behaviors and reward better ones. If a behavioral response is followed by a rewarding event—praise, food, some desired object or activity—it tends to be reinforced and to occur more frequently. This principle is often used in therapy for children. A child can be discouraged from unwanted habits by teaching parents how not to respond to them, or how to respond differently, or how to use a system of structured time-outs when their child is seriously misbehaving.

Other Behavioral Approaches

There are a range of behavioral approaches other than behavior therapy per se. They all focus on changing a target behavior through a sequence of steps directed and guided by the therapist.

Hypnosis or **hypnotherapy** is becoming an increasingly respected and widely used method. The therapist induces a "trance" state, a light, relaxed reverie that facilitates visual imagery, heightens sensory awareness, and accesses memory. In the beginning the therapist will use explicit induction techniques. As you become adept at entering a trance, these techniques can become quite minimal or free-form. Activating a posthypnotic suggestion may be sufficient to immediately induce trance.

Once the trance state is induced, the therapist will guide the imagery in the direction you have agreed on to accomplish a wide variety of therapeutic ends. Your assent is essential: you cannot be hypnotized into doing anything that is morally offensive to you or conflicts with your value system. Hypnotic visualizations can be effective in treating symptoms of anxiety, phobias, somatic conversion reactions, dissociative states, and obsessive-compulsive behavior. Posthypnotic suggestions given in trance to stop smoking will automatically take effect later when you are tempted to smoke. More recently, hypnosis is being used in conjunction with individual therapy to help repair the psychological deficits in severe emotional disorders: imagery and heightened sensory awareness can be used to build better self-boundaries, develop a more realistic body image, and develop a better capacity to experience and tolerate feelings.

Hypnosis is also beginning to play a major role in the treatment of posttraumatic stress once symptoms have stabilized: first to help create a climate of safety, then to help in gradually uncovering and working through different aspects of the traumatic experience. In an exploratory therapy, hypnosis can be used to access repressed memories or visualize alternative perspectives and new directions.

Behavioral medicine applies the techniques of behavior therapy to alleviate medically related problems: obesity, smoking, insomnia, anxiety, chronic pain, stress.

Assuming a mind-body connection and our ability to regulate our behavior given adequate feedback, it uses behavioral techniques to amplify feedback and promote conscious self-regulation.

One of the best-known methods is *biofeedback,* the use of a device that detects subtle changes in the body, such as the tension level of a muscle. Biofeedback allows you to use these subtle cues to learn to become deeply relaxed—a general antidote to anxiety. Other techniques used in behavioral medicine to teach relaxation include deep muscle relaxation, hypnosis, meditation, yoga, and autogenic training. Any emotional problem that is fueled by anxiety or stress can be relieved to some degree by these methods, occasionally instead of medication, or in instances where medication is not advisable or has not been effective.

Sex therapy is the term used for a range of methods, some adapted from psychodynamic and family therapy approaches, though most sex therapy is behavioral. For example, sexual unresponsiveness is treated by step-by-step relearning of the steps in the normal sexual resonse cycle. This takes place in the privacy of your home, with sessions devoted to reviewing the effectiveness of each step and planning the next one. See "Sexual Problems" (p. 511) in Chapter 17 where this approach is discussed in detail.

THE COGNITIVE APPROACH

The distinguishing feature of the cognitive approach is its emphasis on the *role of thoughts in influencing behavior.*

The cognitive approach has elements of both behavioral and psychodynamic therapies. Like psychodynamic approaches, it seeks to uncover underlying causes of emotional problems. But as in behavior therapies, it looks for the causes in learned behavior. The therapist is *directive,* helping you replace maladaptive responses with adaptive ones. The major difference from the behavioral approach is that the focus is not on explicit, observable behaviors, but on your thoughts and your patterns of thinking—your "cognitions"—especially the things you habitually repeat to yourself in the ongoing inner dialogue.

The cognitive approach reintroduced mental content into behavior therapy. It is based on the idea that our normal responses are mediated by cognitive processes that enable us to perceive reality accurately, or distort it. Its developer, psychiatrist Aaron Beck, labeled those persistent cognitive patterns through which we interpret our experience "schemas." Emotional problems are attributed to cognitive errors that produce negative schemas—distorted and self-defeating thoughts that tend to persist despite any and all evidence to the contrary. In therapy, these distorted ways of thinking are replaced with more realistic ones, and the conflicts they led to are resolved. By changing your thoughts, your feelings and behavior change as well.

In practice, cognitive therapy is often combined with behavior therapy. Indeed, many therapists identify their approach as "cognitive-behavioral." But the two approaches have their separate applications. Cognitive therapy has been shown in comparison studies to be especially effective for depression, for instance.

In the National Survey of Psychotherapists we included the cognitive and behavioral approaches as separate categories, allowing therapists to make different recommendations about each. One approach or the other was often highly recommended for many problems, and sometimes both equally.

If you go to a cognitive therapist, expect the therapist to take a firm hand in directing your observations of your distorted thoughts, to help you specify exactly what it is you are seeking to change, and to design a program for you to follow. Cognitive therapy is self-education, and the therapist is something of a tutor.

Your therapist will begin by explaining the role of distorted thinking in emotional problems and provide an explicit rationale for the treatment. Expect to have a more or less explicit agenda for each session and to be given "homework" to do between sessions.

One of the main techniques in cognitive therapy is examining "automatic thoughts," ideas that repeatedly spring to mind in certain key situations. For example, every time a friend fails to call you back when you leave a message, you might think, "She doesn't like me because I'm just not the kind of person people go for."

The next step is to put that thought to the test. Your therapist may help you find ways to actually tell whether the thought is true. For instance, he might encourage you to try an experiment. The next time your friend fails to call, instead of automatically feeling hurt, call her and ask why she didn't call. You are likely to find that she was just too busy and it had nothing to do with you or how likable you are.

As you and your therapist track your automatic thoughts, you are likely to see they fall into more general patterns or schemas. These are the implicit assumptions you make that are maladaptive and guide your life in self-defeating ways. One such schema would be, "If someone doesn't like me, it means I'm unlovable." Just as you test the validity of automatic thoughts, you can test the validity of schemas. Your therapist, for instance, may ask you to defend your assumptions, proposing any number of objections. If you had the unlovable schema, your therapist might ask you to recount the people in your life who actually do love you. Or you might be assigned to ask people who like you the reasons why. In this way, you challenge the self-defeating schemas with information and perspectives that contradict them.

Other cognitive therapy techniques are borrowed from behavior therapy, but adapted to identify and test the validity of your cognitive assumptions and learn new cognitive responses. One prominent technique is cognitive rehearsal, in which you envision a situation that gives you difficulty, then imagine the various steps in confronting and mastering it, breaking the problem down into small, manageable steps, and finally rehearsing each step mentally.

Other Cognitive Approaches

Rational-emotive therapy, developed by psychologist Albert Ellis, is based on the premise that emotions are a form of evaluative thought. Positive emotions result from experiences labeled "good" and negative emotions from experiences labeled "bad." Emotional problems are the result of the constant repetition of illogical thoughts, often reinforced by the harmful evaluations and irrational beliefs of family and society. Emotions are controlled by bringing rationality to thought; they are changed by reevaluating or relabeling situations.

Rational-emotive therapists will energetically confront and challenge your erroneous and self-defeating beliefs. They will help you identify the "self-talk" or things you tell yourself that lead to emotional disturbance. A common irrational idea is, "I must be competent at everything I do," or, "Everyone must like me." Such beliefs lead to feelings of inadequacy. The therapist will try to show you how these beliefs operate and teach you to dispute them—talk back to your own thoughts.

Reality therapy was developed in the 1950s by William Glasser. As the name implies, this approach tries to strengthen a practical understanding of reality and encourage concrete thinking and planning that will lead to a better and more satisfying adjustment. It emphasizes a down-to-earth focus on problems in the present. It is based on the assumption that a strong sense of personal identity and self-worth can come only from "doing": if you can develop a degree of responsibility and initiative, a feeling of personal success and effectiveness will result.

The therapist therefore begins by focusing not on how you are feeling, but what you are doing—your behavior—especially any attempts you are making to become more successful from your own point of view. If these are not working, or if you aren't able to make definite plans of this kind and commit yourself to them, the next step will be to encourage you to make a concrete plan. This is based on small steps that you can master without becoming overwhelmed. You next enter a contract promising to carry out these steps. If you are lonely, you will contract to go places where you might meet people. And you will report on exactly what you have done to fulfill the contract. Your therapist accepts no excuses, but also offers no punishment. Remaining in the situation that brought you to therapy is incentive enough.

THE FAMILY SYSTEMS APPROACH

This approach focuses on *the couple, marital, or family system, rather than on the individual.* The basic assumption is that couples, marriages, and families are organic units that have a life, personality, and dynamics of their own. Every marriage and family has its own culture: its own implicit and explicit rules, its own way of assigning and appraising roles, its own value system, its own set of loyalties and obligations.

And its own characteristic problems and ways of trying to solve them. Each member's actions are shaped by that culture. What any one person says, feels, or thinks affects all the others in some way and is affected by them. The influence of each person's individual personality and problems isn't denied, but the focus is on the relationships within the marital or family system as a whole.

Partners, spouses, and family members often find it hard to acknowledge that the problem may lie in the couple or the family itself—some way they are not communicating or functioning well together. Instead, one of the spouses or family members is often seen as the one who has the problem—or *is* the problem. In this view, however, if one member begins to have problems, it probably means there is a problem in the marriage or the family.

To take one example: according to the family systems approach developed by Murray Bowen, a family will resort to one or more of four basic "solutions" if there is increasing tension between the parents: family members will distance from each other; they will fight with each other; one of the parents or a child will deflect attention away from the marital problem by developing problems of their own; or the parents will band together over some shared concern—usually one of the children who has suddenly started misbehaving or doing poorly at school. Everyone will then join in worrying about the family member who has the problem. When the marital conflict becomes too stressful, the family will tend to overuse these "solutions" and they will lead to just the kinds of problems families usually seek help for: marital conflict, a dysfunctional spouse, or problems with one of the children.

Different schools of family therapy have different views of what constitutes a family "system" and what the most important forces in it are. All agree, however, that each member's behavior has to be seen in the context of the culture of that particular family.

The aim in this approach, then, is not to change individuals but to change dysfunctional patterns of communication and interaction within the couple, marital, or family system.

Typically, everyone involved meets with the therapist in this approach, at least for the initial evaluation. In couples therapy, this means both partners; in family therapy, parents and children. Members of the extended family may be invited in, too. Depending on his or her approach, the therapist may continue to meet with all of you together or with a particular subset of the family—the parents or the children alone, the parents and the "problem" child—or they may meet with different members at different times. Occasionally they may even suggest meeting in your home.

As a rule, a family therapist will be much more of a participant-observer than an individual therapist, often joining in with your family as you interact with each other, almost like a member of the family. The family therapist will also be directive: asking questions, making observations, facilitating interactions, dramatizing family patterns, assigning homework. In clinics and family therapy institutes, sessions may

be co-led by a male and a female therapist. Other therapists may observe through a one-way window and phone in suggestions from time to time. Expect to be active yourself with this approach. Family therapists usually like to get everyone involved.

The Main Orientations to Couples and Family Therapy

Therapists can look at couples and families from a number of different perspectives. Which is most effective in a given case is still a matter for research. But one may feel more congenial to you, or more intuitively appealing.

The Historical Perspective

Here your therapist will primarily focus on *the story of your relationship, your marriage, or your family.* How did you get to where you are? What are the traditions, roles, expectations, legacies in your family? He or she will assume that your relationship or your family has been shaped by past forces and events which have had long-range consequences you may not be aware of. The therapist will be particularly interested in helping you understand the way the problem is a reaction to unresolved issues in the previous generation that are still affecting your family life in the present: how a history of alcoholism, for instance, that required a child to learn early how to take care of a dysfunctional parent predisposed them to play an unsatisfying caretaker role in later relationships; or how the early and unexpected death of a father later on in life left a daughter excessively bound to her mother even after marriage. The goal of therapy will be to disentangle you—or each family member— from these predicaments.

Family therapists who take this past-as-present perspective tend to look to different kinds of past events and issues as crucial:

Contextual family therapists (following Boszormenyi-Nagy) will emphasize each family member's need for justice in the family: whether each of you feel you have received your due and have given others what was due them. Therapy will focus on discovering ways in which original loyalties and unresolved obligations to your family of origin, particularly parents and grandparents, are keeping you stuck in patterns that limit your capabilities as a spouse or parent. If you feel you didn't "repay" your parents for what they did for you, for instance, you may be attempting to balance the books by overpaying your own children. Forgiveness is the key here to halting the hurting and blaming that adds to the "family ledger" of injustices and debts.

The therapist will usually work with your entire family, often extended family members as well, to identify and resolve these "unpaid emotional debts" that are bequeathed across generations.

A related approach (following Norman Paul) will stress the impact of unresolved losses on your family. The goal will be to help the family complete the unresolved mourning process in a symbolic but real way.

Psychodynamically oriented family therapists will be more likely to focus on the role of projection in the family: the way some family members may be projecting onto others their own unfulfilled needs, fears, wishes, and ambitions; and how they are then unwittingly pressured to comply with these projections and take them on as their own. How a child, for instance, is tacitly expected to entertain a depressed mother or live out the disappointed ambition of a frustrated father. Or how you may have chosen a spouse to be the emotionally and sexually expressive partner in the relationship, or the objective, rational, and "grounded" one. Therapy will aim at minimizing this family projection process, which typically extends across two, three, or even more generations.

Family systems therapists (following Murray Bowen), on the other hand, are more likely to look at the difficulties previous family members encountered in separating from their family of origin as the explanation for current family conflicts. The focus will be on the cut-offs and triangles in the family that are preventing members from becoming their own person. Someone from the previous generation has been cut out of the family network, or someone from the next generation has been drawn into the conflict: a father and favorite daughter against the mother; a mother and her mother against the husband; a mother and father in effect keeping a problem child at home in order not to have to face each other, or the child developing problems that draw attention away from the problems in the marriage.

Therapy is designed to identify these patterns and to help family members individuate. The therapist will "coach" you on how to go back to your family of origin and search out clues from surviving members of your extended family, especially from older generations, about the patterns of triangles and cut-offs in the family, and how to interact with other family members in a less emotionally reactive way.

To facilitate change, the therapist taking a historical perspective will rely primarily on understanding as the main method of change, helping you see the way these unresolved issues continue to shape family patterns and affect family life, and the way your current patterns of interacting with each other are perpetuating the problem and frustrating one another's needs. To throw light on family history, the therapist may use diaries, photo albums, interviews with relatives, or reenactments of past events to complement or correct memory. To help you learn about current patterns of interaction, he or she might show you a videotape of your behavior during a session or use family sculpting, artwork, or role playing to increase your awareness of your own and other's experience of life inside the family.

The Interactional Perspective

In these approaches your therapist will primarily focus on the *current behavior patterns of the family,* especially those that are repetitive and frustrating, such as confusing patterns of communication. Family therapists taking this approach are typically not interested in history; their object is to clarify and change behavior that is apparent to everyone in the here and now. They will be particularly interested in sequences of behavior—what you are actually doing with each other; or in the family structure—the overt or covert roles and rules in your marriage or family that govern these sequences.

A therapist taking a *structural approach* will focus on the underlying organization of the family, particularly the boundaries between the parent and child subsystems: how well the lines of responsibility have been thought out, and how clearly and consistently authority has been defined. They will view problems—a daughter with an eating disorder, a teenage son in trouble with the law—as signs that boundaries are either too blurred and members too enmeshed, or too rigid and members too disengaged.

Therapy will aim at defining these structural boundaries within your family more clearly, strengthening parents' legitimate authority and protecting their privacy, giving tasks and privileges to the children in accordance with their gender and age as determined by your family's culture, and building a firm boundary around the nuclear family from outside intrusions—from grandparents or in-laws, for example. If a mother and daughter are acting like siblings, for instance, the therapist will try to find ways to strengthen the primary relationship between the spouses, while preserving the mother-daughter bond.

A therapist taking a *strategic approach*, on the other hand, will focus on the problem, not the family itself. He or she will take your specific complaint at face value and work on solving it with minimal emphasis on learning your family's history, or even on exploring the larger structure of your family. He or she will assume that the problem is part of a self-reinforcing cycle or sequence of behaviors that is perpetuating the problem. A husband complains of his wife's unfounded jealousy, for instance, neither of them realizing that her jealous questioning only reinforces his withdrawal, while his reticence and withdrawal only stimulate her questioning, ad infinitum. The goal in this approach will be to interrupt or block these kinds of vicious circles.

The therapist won't consider it essential to have all the family members present in this approach. He or she may prefer to see individuals or family subgroups separately, relying on a small change in an important relationship within the family to have a domino effect on the family as a whole.

Therapy ends when the presenting problem is resolved. A strategic therapist won't go on to tackle other dysfunctional behaviors in the family if they aren't experienced or presented as a problem.

Like strategic therapists, a *behavioral family therapist* will focus on behavioral sequences in family interactions and how they are maintained, looking at them in terms of the same principles of conditioning and reinforcement that underlie all behavior therapy. To facilitate change, the therapist in this approach will employ active interventions. He or she will elicit reactions, or direct one or more members of the family to undertake certain activities, either during the session or between sessions. The goal will be to directly change the interaction patterns within the family. These techniques may increase the family's understanding of itself, but they don't depend on insight. Most directives will be straightforward and overt—an instruction in how to improve the content of communication, for example. Others may be indirect and involve tasks that may seem odd or counterproductive to the family, but which are designed to lead indirectly to beneficial changes in the family's behavior or structure. This kind of family therapy is shorter, often ten sessions or less, because it won't be concerned with your family's history or the larger context of the problem in the family culture.

THE SUPPORTIVE APPROACH

The supportive approach is defined primarily by the therapist's intention and attitude.

The distinctive feature of this approach is that *the goal is support rather than change*. The assumption is that at times it is enough just to help someone get through an emotional crisis or handle day-to-day demands the best way possible. Sometimes it is too ambitious to aim for change. In this approach, the focus is on supporting your strengths and areas of competence, and helping you deal with anything that excessively taxes or threatens to overwhelm them.

All psychotherapies have supportive elements, but a primarily supportive therapy is the approach of choice in three situations:

- When you are having such a difficult time functioning that you are in danger of being overwhelmed. In this situation, the goal is to prevent a decline into total helplessness or dysfunction.
- In a psychiatric emergency, when you have temporarily lost your ability to cope—during an acute depression, for instance, an acute posttraumatic stress reaction, or a psychotic episode. The goal is to help you safely through the crisis, then help you return to your normal functioning as quickly as possible.
- In cases of long-term psychiatric disability where a therapist's support can be helpful in maintaining hope, preventing relapses, and managing the stresses and demands of everyday living. In this situation the therapist's role is to be a source of information, sound judgment, even advocacy. The therapist willl help you face and handle whatever is stressing you: your living situation, your finances, the ongoing discouragement of being disabled. If you feel incapable of handling things, the therapist will work with you to bolster your confidence. If you are having difficulties with your landlord, your family, or an agency, the therapist will help you solve the problem. The therapist is also someone with whom you can share your interests and accomplishments, someone who will appreciate what they mean to you.

Supportive therapy can be brief—a time-limited intervention during a crisis—or it can continue for years. During periods of crisis, you may meet with your therapist in short sessions several times a week. As the crisis subsides, you may meet less frequently. In long-term supportive therapy, you may see your therapist weekly, monthly, perhaps eventually only once every few months just to check in, report how things are going, and stay in touch. But the support therapist will always try to be available when needed.

CHAPTER THREE

■

FINDING A THERAPIST

Once you decide you want therapy, you face the task of finding a therapist. For a variety of reasons this is considerably harder than finding a good contractor or accountant or lawyer. One is that simply asking people to recommend a therapist tells them that you feel you need one—and you may not want to reveal that to just anyone. Nor should you. It's a personal matter and you don't want to leave yourself any more vulnerable than you may already feel.

On the other hand, feelings of embarrassment, shame, or reticence often lead too many people to simply end up with the first therapist they find, rather than with someone who has the best chance of helping them. Or you may feel afraid to "shop around" because you feel intimidated or uncertain about what to look for.

You should go about finding the right therapist in the same way you would go about tracking down a good lawyer or a good doctor. You should not take the first recommendation you get; you should do some homework first.

In looking for a therapist, keep in mind that you are contracting for a professional service. As a client, you have a right to be satisfied with that service. In fact, you will *need* to be satisfied if therapy is to be effective. You also have a right to ask questions about the service you are contracting for. As with any service, you have every right to comparison shop—to look around, ask questions, be selective—until you find someone you think can genuinely help you. Remind yourself you have a lot at stake: an important aspect of your life and your well-being is on the line.

This will also be a very personal and intimate kind of service. The relationship you will have with your therapist may be among the most intimate you will ever have with anyone. You will be entrusting them with some of your greatest vulnerabilities and fears. The more particular you are in your choice, the better chance you have of getting the help you want.

Just exactly what you should be looking for in a therapist is not always self-evident. The two most important things to look for are *compatibility* and *competence*. If your motivation and readiness for therapy are the most important factors in determining the outcome of therapy, the next most important are your therapist's skill and the personal chemistry between the two of you.

Ideally, of course, you want a therapist who has the right knowledge, skills, training, experience, and personal qualities. You can't take them for granted just because someone describes or advertises himself as a therapist. Unfortunately, degrees after the name and diplomas on the wall don't necessarily tell you whether a potential therapist meets these basic requirements. You are going to have to find out for yourself; this chapter can help you do that.

Compatability and competence are not so easy to assess in the case of therapy as in other human services. You should know, however, that some general guidelines, which this chapter will provide, will enable you to make an initial judgment with some degree of confidence. This chapter will also alert you to some less obvious things to look for that might not register consciously in your initial contacts, but that can profoundly influence how therapy is likely to go.

In looking for a therapist you should use the Therapy Guide in Part II to find out what kinds of approaches are most recommended for the particular problem or issue you are seeking help for. Once you know that, you can narrow your search by looking for a therapist who is expert in one of these approaches. The guidelines in this chapter will then help you decide among those therapists you consult.

STEP ONE: KNOW WHAT TO LOOK FOR

Therapists have a wide range of backgrounds, perspectives, and skills. They vary greatly in the approach to therapy they tend to practice and specialize in. Their fees also vary, as does the length of time they expect therapy to take. Being aware of the major ways in which therapists differ will help you to zero in on just what may be right for you:

- *Profession.* Therapists include all licensed mental health professionals: psychiatrists, psychologists, social workers, and psychiatric nurses, and in some states, marriage and family counselors. Also, many disciplines are not professionally licensed or certified, but their members also practice psychotherapy, such as pastoral counselors.

- *Format.* Therapists tend to specialize in individual, couples, family, or group therapy. Whatever their speciality, however, most therapists, with the exception of some family therapists, offer individual psychotherapy.
- *Approach.* Most therapists tend to practice within a particular theoretical orientation: psychodynamic, behavioral, cognitive, systemic, or supportive (see Chapter 2 for descriptions). Other approaches are mentioned and briefly described in the Therapy Guide in Part II.

One approach doesn't have to exclude another and sometimes a combination of approaches will actually offer the most effective help. Therapists are becoming increasingly aware of the need to adapt therapy to fit the problem. However, any given therapist will not be equally competent in every approach and may not be competent at all in some you are seeking.

- *Setting.* Therapists practice in a variety of settings. These include private-office practice, outpatient clinics or group practices, public agencies, community mental health centers, health maintenance organizations, hospitals, medical schools, and church-related pastoral counseling centers. The setting can affect the fee, and to a lesser extent, the kind of attention you get.

PSYCHOTHERAPY LICENSING

Strange as it may seem for such an exacting discipline with such potential to influence people's lives for good or ill, psychotherapy is not a licensed profession. Therapy is an "unregulated field." No regulatory body at any governmental level oversees certification and maintenance of professional standards for the practice of psychotherapy *as such,* though standards exist for psychiatry and the other professions most psychotherapists belong to. Legally, anyone can call him or herself a "psychotherapist."

The absence of an independent profession of psychotherapy has had several unfortunate consequences. One is the lack of universally accepted clinical or legal standards for practicing psychotherapy. Even professional training in one of the allied professions does not by itself qualify a professional to be a psychotherapist. Psychiatrists, psychologists, social workers, or nurses may be qualified to practice their profession but still not have received the specific training and supervision needed to practice therapy.

The absence of licensing and regulation of therapy as a separate profession means that many people can—and do—practice therapy without adequate training as therapists, even among licensed professionals. It is important that you, as a consumer, be well-informed in making choices about something as important as therapy. The old adage applies here as elsewhere: "Let the buyer beware."

While there may be other reasons for starting with a licensed professional, by itself this isn't a guarantee that he or she has received adequate training as a therapist.

This is perhaps most true in psychiatry. A psychiatric residency following medical school may focus on biological psychiatry—pharmacotherapy, neurology, or related areas, and on inpatient care and management—and may include little or no training in conducting psychotherapy.

Nevertheless, for a therapist to be licensed as a member of a regulated profession has two important implications for you as a consumer. It means they have received a certain level of professional training and supervision in a major mental health discipline, which includes several thousand hours of supervised work in the field, some of which will probably have been in psychotherapy. They have demonstrated an acceptable level of professional competence and have passed a national certifying examination in their discipline.

Second, it means they are legally bound to specific standards of professional and ethical practice in their field, including continuing education, and are legally accountable to a state licensing board for maintaining these standards in their practice, *including their practice of psychotherapy*. It also means they are subject to annual review and recertification by the licensing board. Both professional training and licensing offer important protection to the consumer, though they still are not a guarantee of competence in therapy.

DIFFERENCES BETWEEN THE PROFESSIONS

Psychiatrists. A psychiatrist is a physician. Like other physicians, they have completed four years of medical school, leading to an M.D. degree, and one year of a medical internship. Since psychiatry is a branch of medicine, a psychiatrist must have a general medical license to practice psychiatry.

In addition, he or she must have completed a three-year residency training program in psychiatry following their medical internship to be licensed in their state as a psychiatrist. In the past, these residencies were often limited to hospital settings and medical treatment of patients with major mental illnesses or acute conditions—schizophrenia, major depression, manic-depression, brief reactive psychoses, alcohol and substance abuse. The focus was on pharmacological or neurological intervention and case management, with little or no training in psychotherapy. In recent years, residencies have generally included at least some training in psychotherapy. In some, residents carry a psychotherapy caseload all three years, with the second year of residence devoted almost exclusively to outpatient psychotherapy with a wide range of clients.

About one in three psychiatrists are "board certified." Board certification is an additional credential awarded by the American Board of Psychiatry and Neurology following a nationwide oral and written examination after completion of residency training. Since the board examination focuses primarily on psychiatric diagnosis and psychopharmacology, board certification by itself does not certify competence in psychotherapy.

Unless their residency has included specific training in psychotherapy, psychiatrists who want training as a therapist, or training in one of the specialized modalities or approaches to therapy, will attend one of many postgraduate institutes in psychotherapy. The best known are psychoanalytic institutes, which train psychiatrists in psychoanalysis. But every major kind of therapy has its own training institutes— for group or family therapy, for Jungian, gestalt, behavioral, or cognitive therapy, among many others. If you want to know what kind of therapy a psychiatrist is most proficient in, asking what training institutes he or she has attended is one way to find out.

That question will tell you more useful information about a psychiatrist's qualifications as a therapist than finding out if a psychiatrist is board certified, or a member of the American Psychiatric Association, the main professional group for psychiatrists. Neither association membership nor board certification has anything to do with proficiency as a therapist. But having been trained at an institute does, as does membership in psychotherapy or psychoanalytic associations.

Psychologists. Psychologists are academically rather than medically trained and so come to the field by a very different route. As a licensed profession, the professional title of *psychologist* is controlled by state law. Only those meeting state certification or licensing requirements can advertise themselves as psychologists. This typically requires a Ph.D. in the subspeciality of clinical or counseling psychology or a related area, a one-year full-time internship in a mental health facility, a specific number of hours of supervised pre- and postdoctoral clinical work, and a national licensing examination. Some psychologists were certified or licensed under a "grandfather" clause if they had been in practice before the new licensing laws went into effect.

Licensing laws are also changing. The general trend is to make state licensing laws more stringent, requiring a Ph.D. in clinical or counseling psychology only, for instance, or requiring higher cutoff scores in the national licensing exam.

A relatively new degree, the Psy.D., now also qualifies for licensing in many states. This course of graduate study is oriented more toward professional practice and less toward research than the more traditional Ph.D. programs. It is offered by an increasing number of universities and freestanding graduate schools of professional psychology.

Not all psychologists, however, are trained in psychotherapy. Many subdisciplines within the field—developmental, social, organizational, and physiological psychology to name a few—are purely teaching and research specialities and have nothing to do with clinical work. Others, such as educational or counseling psychology, do incorporate clinical skills and practicum training in their curricula, but not necessarily training in psychotherapy.

Legally, once psychologists are licensed, they are free to work in any area of the field—another anomaly in professional licensing laws—but the American Psychological Association's code of ethics requires its members to work only in their area of training and competence.

A licensed psychologist with a degree in a speciality other than clinical psychology can ethically practice psychotherapy, but only if he or she has gone back or gone on for clinical training. As with psychiatrists, many psychologists who do therapy have had to get additional postgraduate training at an institute or some other training program.

The American board of examiners in professional psychology awards a more advanced certification to clinical psychologists who pass speciality examinations they are eligible to take after five years of postdoctoral experience. Most clinical psychologists choose not to apply for the diplomate status, even when they are eligible, probably because it is not necessary in their practice. However, it is an important additional qualification for you as a consumer to be aware of.

An additional resource is the *National Register of Health Service Providers in Psychology*. This was first published in 1975 and lists all psychologists who are licensed or certified in their state, have a Ph.D. in psychology, and two years of supervised experience in providing mental health services. These standards are minimal and don't testify directly to competence or experience in psychotherapy. But the listing is one way to assure yourself that a psychologist you may be considering is licensed and has some experience in delivering professional services. Membership in the American Psychological Association by itself does not imply any expertise in psychotherapy.

Social workers. Most states either license or certify social workers as they do psychiatrists, psychologists, and nurses. Social work training typically comprises a two-year graduate program leading to a master's in social work (MSW) that includes several field placements. These may be in any one of the wide range of human services that social workers provide, from rehabilitation and welfare work to child advocacy and hospital discharge planning. The traditional social work curriculum was oriented to casework, though some graduate programs now offer a concentration in clinical social work that requires field placement in mental health settings and may include training in psychotherapy, though not necessarily. Most social workers have a master's degree, though some have a doctorate (a DSW).

There are several levels of certification. Most states now certify or license social workers as an independent profession. State certification (CSW) or licensing as a clinical social worker (LICSW) requires two years of supervised postmaster's experience followed by a qualifying statewide examination. Already established social workers were "grandfathered in" and automatically awarded certification when these licensing laws went into effect. The profession itself, through the academy of certified social workers within its national association, awards a further level of certification (ACSW) following additional supervised postgraduate experience and examination.

The National Association of Social Workers has recently introduced a diplomate certification as the most advanced credential in social work. Like the diplomate in psychology, this is awarded on the basis of five years of supervised clinical experience plus a national written and oral examination. Also like the diplomate in psychology, it is not a necessary requirement and most social workers will probably not apply for it. Nevertheless, it is a further level of certification that you as a consumer should be aware of.

The National Association of Social Workers publishes a *Register of Clinical Social Workers,* which lists ACSW members who have two years of postmaster's experience in clinical social work practice.

As in the case of psychiatry and psychology, state certification or licensing does not testify to competence or even training in psychotherapy. That needs to be inquired into separately. If it has not been part of their MSW training, social workers may have attended a training institute or program in individual, group, or—increasingly common these days for social workers interested in clinical practice—family therapy.

Membership in the National Association of Social Workers says nothing about psychotherapy skills, though it may indicate a certain level of professional responsibility. Membership or affiliation with a therapy institute or association is more significant.

Psychiatric nurses. All states license or register nurses with a degree in nursing who have passed a state examination. There is no speciality licensing or certification for psychiatric nursing. The title refers only to the speciality area in which the nurse chooses to work. Traditionally, "psychiatric nurse" simply referred to a nurse who worked on a hospital psychiatric unit. More recently, it has come to refer to any mental health nursing, including seeing clients in outpatient clinics. Some schools now offer graduate training in psychiatric nursing, and some state nursing associations award a certificate in psychiatric nursing to nurses meeting a certain level of training and experience. However, the title itself does not indicate any training or competence in psychotherapy. Like other mental health professionals, nurses need to have had specialized training in addition to their professional qualifications to be competent to practice psychotherapy.

Marriage and family therapists. These are now licensed in more than two dozen states. Their training is generally a two-year master's program mainly oriented toward the therapy of couples and families, followed by two or three years of clinical supervision, after which they take a state licensing exam. As their title suggests, their speciality is problems that arise in couples or among families. Typically, they receive extensive training and supervision in this therapy, but many also get training in individual therapy and practice that, too.

OTHER KINDS OF THERAPISTS

In addition to licensed professionals from the major mental health disciplines, you will encounter people using many other titles in the field as well. Some of these people represent disciplines outside the mental health professions. Others represent a particular form of expertise and may designate themselves as that kind of therapist and also be licensed in one of the major professions.

The great majority of psychoanalysts, for instance, are psychiatrists by profession. Social workers trained in working with families often call themselves family therapists, but you will find psychiatrists, psychologists, and psychiatric nurses calling themselves that as well. Of course, you need not be professionally trained to call or advertise yourself as a family therapist—and many only have some training in doing family therapy. Remember, formal training isn't legally required to call yourself a "psychotherapist."

You need some idea of what the more commonly encountered titles are, what they mean, and what kind of assurance they offer you, keeping in mind that professional licensing or certification is an entirely different matter. Some of the most common:

- *Psychotherapist* is a generic term, simply referring to anyone who offers any kind of psychotherapy. A vague term, it tells you next to nothing about the person's background, training, or special expertise.
- *Psychoanalyst* refers to someone who practices psychoanalysis, the therapeutic technique developed by Freud. (Followers of Jung usually call themselves "Jungian analysts" by way of contrast.) Today there are numerous variations on that technique, but all psychoanalysts follow a psychodynamic approach (see p. 51). A psychoanalyst should have gone through training and supervision in analytic techniques at a training institute, but the term can legally be used by anyone.
- *Family therapist,* another term that can be used by anyone, refers to someone who typically works with entire families (usually, but not always, in a group). A family therapist should have been trained at one of the many institutes that specialize in this approach.
- *Pastoral counselor* is used by clergy who offer psychological counseling. Programs for training pastoral counselors are usually connected with a divinity school. Sometimes a clergy member will get additional training in psychotherapy at a training institute. But the term *pastoral counselor* can be used by anyone.
- *Biofeedback therapist* refers to a technician who will help you learn to relax through the use of biofeedback equipment. The only proficiency such a person need have is in using the equipment. There are training programs for using

biofeedback as part of behavioral medicine, but no degree programs in the field. Anyone can use the term.

- *Hypnotherapist* is the term for people who use hypnosis to treat such things as smoking and obesity. Training in and clinical use of hypnosis is not regulated. Reputable hypnosis training programs require that their students have degrees in a profession such as psychology. But anyone can call himself a "hypnotherapist."

- *Stress reduction* or *relaxation therapist* simply means that the person teaches a relaxation method. No particular training qualifies someone for this, and anyone can use the term.

- *Child psychotherapist* means that the therapist specializes in treating the problems of children. Special training programs exist for such therapists, but use of the term is no guarantee that a given therapist has received such training.

- *School psychologist* is a speciality within psychology that requires training in such topics as education and child development. The term *psychologist* is controlled by state laws; to use it a psychologist must be licensed or certified. Most school psychologists work with children who have such problems as learning disabilities or emotional difficulties, and they are hired by school districts.

- *Vocational* or *career counselor* is just that: someone who specializes in helping people make good career choices. They do not offer psychotherapy. The term *counselor* does not mean therapist and is not regulated by law; anyone can use it. There are, however, graduate training programs in various kinds of counseling, including rehabilitation counseling for people who have had incapacitating physical disabilities.

Sex therapists: a special case. This is one speciality in which discrimination in picking a therapist is called for. Competent treatment for sexual disorders demands extensive training, even if a therapist already is, say, a clinical social worker or psychiatrist. Institutes for training sex therapists require that their students already have at least a master's degree credential, such as an MSW.

Even so, the title *sex therapist* is unregulated, and some therapists have claimed expertise without having been properly trained. Simply being a mental health professional is not sufficient qualification for treating sexual problems. Although some sex therapists may have acquired sufficient expertise on the job, it is a safer bet if a sex therapist has been trained by a reputable institute specializing in sexual disorders.

Sexual problems are especially delicate because a failure in therapy can jeopardize a marriage. If you or your spouse have a bad experience with one sex therapist, it is all the harder to overcome the sense of defeat and to try again with another therapist.

Paraprofessionals. Increasing numbers of paraprofessionals are working with clients at psychiatric hospitals, mental health centers, drug and alcohol treatment facilities, or other public agencies. Most have college degrees, though not necessarily in a mental-health-related discipline; some have only a high school education. In most of these settings, paraprofessionals receive on-the-job training and are usually closely supervised by professional staff who have a stake in making sure the services provided are safe and reasonably competent. Paraprofessionals, ideally, can consult a supervisor when they need to, and they will be insured through the agency's group insurance policy for malpractice. But what you will get is more in the nature of counseling—don't expect psychotherapy. If a paraprofessional goes off independently and opens a therapy practice, there is no guarantee of supervision or quality of services.

THERAPISTS OUTSIDE THE LICENSED PROFESSIONS

Therapy is more than a set of methods: it is an interpersonal art, and the person your therapist is matters immensely. No therapy training program or state license guarantees human qualities such as rapport and empathy. These essential abilities cannot be certified by some exam or degree. Even so, human warmth and rapport, by themselves, are not enough. For therapy to work, a therapist must also be competent.

There definitely are gifted therapists outside the licensed professions, but caution is called for. They often offer their services under one of the unregulated terms listed above, such as *psychotherapist* or *counselor*. Many have had some specialized training in some aspect of therapy, but that's not guaranteed. An increasing number of therapists have been practicing without training or accreditation of any sort. Obviously, being in therapy with a person who does not have recognized credentials, and who may lack essential skills, involves risk. If you consult such a therapist, he or she may be incompetent. One thing you do know is that an unlicensed therapist has probably not had the many hours of supervised training that are required for state licensing.

Because no law regulates "psychotherapy" per se, anyone can offer it. Some practice without credentials for ideological reasons, believing that the therapy establishment is self-serving, adheres to faulty premises, or is a tool of social repression. A group of "radical" therapists, for example, sees a major source of clients' problems as rooted in social oppression and inequities, and they attack conventional psychotherapy as simply trying to make clients conform to social norms. In their view, therapy should be a process of education that includes raising the awareness of the client to the sources of social oppression and their role in the client's problems. For radical therapists, the mainstream institutions of psychotherapy—including state licensing—are anathema, even though many have received training in graduate programs and postgraduate institutes themselves.

Along with such principled nonlicensed therapists are some less scrupulous therapists just out to make a buck. This is the group to be most wary of. Such therapists are more likely, for instance, to make promises of a cure—something no reputable therapist would do.

Apart from these, some therapists are unlicensed in a given state not because they lack expertise and training, but because they have not completed all the requirements. Some have not yet finished their training and intend to do so. Some have moved to a state where their professional qualifications are not recognized (e.g., marriage and family counselors, a credential regulated in less than half the states). Some will fulfill the requirements and become licensed, others will not. Most therapists in this group see clients under the supervision of a licensed therapist, especially if they are on their way to becoming licensed.

Be cautious of therapists not licensed by your state because, should they do something unethical or incompetent in therapy, you have far less protection or recourse than if they were licensed.

RECOMMENDED: LOOK FOR A LICENSED PROFESSIONAL

By choosing a therapist with a license and credentials, you get several important protections. Your therapist will be accountable to a professional licensing board for maintaining standards and for continuing recertification. Most professionals are now required to take continuing education courses in their discipline each year to stay current. Your therapist will practice under the jurisdiction of specific regulatory bodies, with the ethical standards of his or her profession enforced by an ethics committee and a state licensing board. Should a breach in ethical standards come to a lawsuit for damages, only professionals are covered by malpractice insurance. Finally, if you have health insurance that covers psychotherapy, usually only a licensed professional will be included.

Does the Particular Profession Matter?

Just for psychotherapy, usually not. Much of the confusion and controversy between the major mental health professions centers around the question of who is qualified to do what. The truth is that all the modes of therapy—individual, group, marital, and family—are practiced by some members of all the professions. So are all the various approaches to therapy. No professional has special or exclusive expertise in any one area of therapy anymore. Where once family therapy was largely the domain of social workers, for instance, an increasing number of psychologists and psychiatrists are now trained and specialize in it, too. So you shouldn't choose a therapist solely on the basis of his or her profession.

The one possible exception is when medication is likely to be recommended in addition to therapy. In a number of the psychiatric disorders described in the Therapy

Guide in Part II, medication can have a significant effect in reducing symptoms. Since only a psychiatrist can prescribe psychiatric medications, you might want to consult a psychiatrist first for these conditions. You should know, though, that when medication is recommended, it doesn't have to be the therapist who actually prescribes it.

It is becoming increasingly common for nonpsychiatrists to be the main therapist even for someone who may be severely disturbed, and to have a psychiatrist, psychopharmacologist, or other physician supervise the medication. Many psychiatrists actually prefer to keep therapy and medication separate and will refer their therapy clients to another psychiatrist for medication. This is routinely the case in psychoanalysis, for instance, but is also common in many other therapies.

A second possible exception to the rule that a therapist's profession is not the main factor in choosing is when you or the person you are seeking help for is functioning so poorly that hospitalization may be necessary. If it's becoming impossible for the person to carry on daily activities, or there is a risk of self-harm or harm to others, a psychiatrist can often arrange a hospitalization more easily than other professionals, though even this is less true than it used to be, especially in metropolitan areas.

Most psychologists, clinical social workers, and psychiatric nurses are trained to recognize the range of problems clients can present. When necessary, they will usually know how to refer to other specialists, including to psychiatrists for medication, while still remaining the primary therapist. They will also know how to arrange for a hospitalization when necessary. For the most part then, the specific profession of your therapist shouldn't be a major consideration.

Psychological testing is occasionally recommended during an evaluation prior to therapy (less often during the actual course of therapy) to clarify some important aspect of a client's behavior or potential that may not be evident. Therapists in the other disciplines will refer to a psychologist in these cases. Psychologists assess a wide range of issues that may be important to identify in therapy: intellectual and cognitive functioning, neuropsychological functioning, personality traits, suicidality, homicidality, psychosis, learning disabilities, school achievement levels, and vocational aptitude. To date, this kind of testing and assessment remains mainly the domain of psychologists.

STEP TWO: ASK FOR REFFERALS

You can get names of potential therapists from many sources, including your family doctor, clergy, other therapists or mental health professionals, local professional organizations for psychiatry, psychology, social work, and nursing, community mental health centers, or psychotherapy institutes. But some sources of referrals are much better than others. *The guiding principle is this: how you find, learn about, make contact with, and what you come to know about your therapist becomes part of your therapy. To some degree it will influence not just the kind of working relationship you establish but the outcome of your therapy as well.*

Remember our discussion in Chapter 1 of the unavoidable ambivalence of every client who enters therapy. To some extent we want help and genuinely want to change; at the same time we may be afraid of change and so try to avoid it by finding a therapist who will unwittingly repeat the old patterns with us under another guise. The process of selecting a therapist is so important precisely because we are sensitive to these nuances in any contact with a potential therapist, whether we are immediately aware of it or not. Will this be a therapist who can provide a reasonably safe and secure frame for therapy that ensures privacy, confidentiality, objectivity, and an exclusive focus on you and your concerns? Or is this someone who will unwittingly accommodate your fears and anxieties about change, or bend the framework that successful therapy typically requires? No referral guarantees an excellent therapist, but some routes to therapy offer a better chance of getting the help you want.

RECOMMENDED REFERRAL SOURCES

For a Therapist in Private Practice

1. *Mental health professionals, especially other psychotherapists.* If you are trying to find the name of a competent therapist in private practice, one of the best sources is other therapists or mental health professionals. You should be aware, though, that many therapists refer through their own network to other therapists who often share their approach. That may not be the approach that suits your problem (the Therapy Guide offers some guidelines for deciding which approach that might be). Your problem may call for a family therapist, for instance. If you consult a psychoanalyst or a behavior therapist, you may not get the name of a family therapist. Therapists based in hospitals, clinics, or other facilities that provide many different kinds of services and employ professionals from all the disciplines tend to have a wider network and so may be more likely to refer to a broader range of therapists.

2. *The national professional associations, or their state or local chapters.* Another excellent source is the state or local chapters of the national professional organizations (see Appendix IV for a full list). The main ones:

- for psychiatrists, the American Psychiatric Association
- for psychologists, the American Psychological Association
- for clinical social workers, the National Association of Social Workers
- for psychiatric nurses, the American Nurses Association

- for marriage and family therapists, the American Association of Marriage and Family Therapy

If you call the local chapter, they will usually give you three names of members as referrals. To find the local branch, check your local phone directory, or in the nearest large city. They may also provide more specific information about the therapists' services, fees, or years of practice, if you ask. Appendix IV lists the phone numbers of the national headquarters, which can provide the name and number of the local chapter if you have difficulty finding them.

Some of the major associations also publish national directories of members, which you can consult to find names in your area. Psychiatrists are listed in the *American Psychiatric Association Directory,* and in the *Directory of Medical Specialists* if they are board certified. Psychologists are listed in the *American Psychological Association Directory,* and in the *National Registry of Health Service Providers in Psychology.* You will find social workers in the *Membership Directory of the National Association of Social Workers,* or in its *Register of Clinical Social Workers.*

These directories are available in most public or college libraries. They can also be obtained through the national headquarters of each association (see Appendix IV). Turn to the geographical listings to find out the professionals in your area, then check the individual listings, which provide background information on each professional, such as training and year of licensing or certification, and will tell you how many years they have been practicing.

3. A leading figure in the field. An excellent route to referrals is a leading figure in the field, such as the director of a psychiatry department at a teaching hospital or the head of a training institute. They are likely to know many therapists, and to have a sense of who among them would be good resources for you.

4. Friends or relatives. Friends or relatives can be a good source of referrals if their connection with a therapist they recommend is professional—they know them or know their reputation through professional contacts, *not* if they know them socially or have been in therapy with them. If you go into therapy with a therapist who has personal or social ties to people you know, it complicates and can sometimes jeopardize the therapy (see Chapter 11, "Professional Ethics," for more on this).

5. Self-help groups. Self-help groups such as Alcoholics Anonymous can often be helpful in recommending therapists who have a good record of helping people with a given problem.

For a Therapist in a Clinic Setting

Still another route to therapy is through a clinic. Many kinds of clinics offer psychotherapy along with other services: some are for profit, some are not; some focus on specific problems, such as alcoholism or family problems; some treat the gamut of emotional problems. Some clinics are freestanding, but most are affiliated with hospitals, medical centers, health maintenance organizations, universities, psychotherapy training institutes, community mental health centers, or agencies in the public or private sector.

One advantage of clinics is that their fees are usually lower than those of therapists in private practice. Most will work on a sliding fee scale that can accommodate your income. They can also offer you a wider range of services than any one therapist can. Additionally, they can give you an evaluation to determine just which kind of therapy would offer the best chance of help.

Clinics also have several potential drawbacks. They often have a waiting period of several days to several weeks before someone is available to see you, though any clinic should respond to an emergency. You probably won't be able to choose your therapist, who will usually be assigned by the clinic.

Clinics are also increasingly limiting the number of therapy sessions they will provide. This is especially true in health maintenance organizations, where the emphasis is on providing cost-effective crisis intervention rather than traditional psychotherapy. Also in many clinics, especially those affiliated with a teaching institution, the therapist you are assigned will probably be someone in training. This doesn't necessarily mean you won't get good therapy, however. The trainee will usually have had some prior experience and will be getting close supervision from an experienced therapist.

Clinic settings include:

1. *Mental health clinics*. You will find these in community mental health centers or local hospitals. These are usually staffed by professionals from all the mental health disciplines. Among these will be therapists at all levels of experience. Some therapy may also be done by trainees. These clinics will offer a full range of psychotherapy services, usually with a sliding fee scale, including assessment and evaluation, crisis intervention, and psychopharmacology. If they are publicly funded, they may have restrictions on whom they can see.

You can locate them through your local department of public health or mental health, or in the yellow pages, usually under "mental health services." You can also phone any local hospital and ask whether they have an outpatient mental health clinic.

2. *Social service or family service agencies*. These agencies are primarily staffed by professional social workers, with some psychiatrists and psychologists on staff as consultants. Some of the services may be provided by trainees. These kinds of agencies usually have specific eligibility criteria for services, as well as some restrictions on the length and kinds of services they can offer. They usually employ a sliding fee scale. Their focus is more likely to be on case management, advocacy, consultation, and counseling than on therapy, but this can often be exactly what individuals and families need.

They can be located through your local department of social service, or through the yellow pages.

3. *Medical school and university training clinics.* These are usually affiliated with a medical school or university-affiliated teaching hospital, or a university graduate department, all of whom often run clinics to train their students while providing relatively low-cost therapy to the community. They usually offer a fairly full spectrum of psychotherapy services, often with a sliding fee scale. Psychotherapy will be offered by trainees.

Unlike at most postgraduate psychotherapy training institutes (see below), these will be students who are still completing their professional training: psychiatry residents, psychology interns, social work interns, or graduate-level nurses training in psychiatric nursing. However, all trainees will be receiving supervision from a teaching therapist. You will have the benefit of up-to-date methods, as well as of the supervisor's experience and expertise. But the length of time therapists in training will be able to see you is limited (usually to the academic year). This is still much longer than most clinics can offer, and the fee may be more affordable.

4. *Psychotherapy training institutes.* These train and supervise therapists learning a particular modality or approach to therapy—family or group therapy, for instance; or a psychoanalytic, behavioral, or cognitive approach. You will find one or more of these institutes in most large metropolitan areas. You will get a lower fee, but you will also get a therapist in training. Unlike other settings, however, this doesn't necessarily mean someone who is unseasoned. A trainee at this kind of institute is often an experienced therapist who has returned for advanced training to expand his or her repertoire of skills or to learn a new method or technique. Again, you can be sure their work will be closely supervised, and you will have the benefit of the supervisor's experience as well.

5. *University or school mental health services.* These are normally available only to the academic community, but they can be an important first line of help. They employ professional staff primarily, often with some services provided by graduate-level trainees. Fees are typically low and often covered by student or faculty health insurance. Like health maintenance organizations, they are oriented toward providing emergency crisis intervention or evaluation and referral only.

To Be Used with Caution

1. *A therapist you have heard a lot about personally.* You should be cautious about a referral to any therapist whose personal life is known to you or you are likely to continue to hear about through mutual contacts or associations—even though you may have no personal contact with them.

2. *A therapist you are required to see.* Another questionable referral is one where you have little or no choice. Employee assistance programs at work sometimes require

therapy as a condition of continued employment. Judges and other officers of the court occasionally order a referral to therapy as a condition of probation, parole, or child custody. You may have no choice but to accept the referral in these situations. Mandated institutional referrals can sometimes be effective if the goals of therapy are carefully defined and limited, and you have some choice over the individual therapist you will see. Therapy under these conditions nevertheless begins under a cloud, already compromised by doubts about confidentiality and in whose interests it is really being conducted. If you have an option, you may not necessarily want to follow through on such mandated referrals, but seek a therapist of your own choosing.

3. Referrals from professionals who are not in the mental health field. These include physicians and family doctors, attorneys, clergy, school and vocational counselors, and others in the helping professions. While professionals in the mental health field are generally good sources for referrals, other professionals generally are not. Your lawyer, for instance, has no particular expertise in recognizing an able therapist, nor a professional network that could reliably inform him who is competent. The same is true of clergy, vocational and school counselors, though school guidance counselors may know of good child therapists.

Even physicians are not necessarily reliable sources for therapy referrals. The problem is that many physicians, understandably, have a medical bias. In fact, many try to treat emotional problems themselves—more psychiatric drugs are actually prescribed by family physicians than by psychiatrists! If they do refer to a therapist, they are likely to give the names of psychiatrists—but as we have seen, psychiatrists as such are not more qualified as therapists than other licensed professionals, and they tend to be the most expensive.

4. Arbitrary listings. Taking a name from a telephone directory or similar listing, for instance, or going to a therapist because you happen to pass by their office are potluck choices. You are entrusting your mental and emotional well-being to an entirely unknown figure. This is usually careless and unthinking and seldom leads to good therapy. Therapists listed in the telephone directory or yellow pages or in other public advertisements are not screened for their qualifications. Most qualified professionals do not advertise in such listings.

Avoid at All Costs

1. Any therapist with whom you have had more than minimal personal or social contact. Once therapists have been a friend, colleague, or social acquaintance, they cannot be a therapist for you. Especially in a psychodynamic approach, you are likely to experience therapy with them as confusing or even incestuous. It goes without saying that you should never enter therapy with a family member or relative, no matter how distantly related.

2. Referrals from friends and relatives who have a social, personal, or professional relationship with the therapist. For the very same reasons that apply to therapy with a therapist you yourself have a prior social or personal relationship with.

3. Referrals from former clients. Normally one of the most reliable sources of information about a professional service is satisfied consumers. However, just the opposite tends to be true in therapy. Recommendations from current or former clients are compromised by their emotional involvement. It is not that they don't know the therapist, but that their sense of the therapist is from their own perspective, which will not be yours. They are also too close to have an objective view. They rightfully *need* to believe in their therapist and *need* to believe that their therapy has worked for them. It may have, but how do you know? You *do* know they will be biased in the therapist's favor if they recommend them. Such referrals are often made out of a need to have their own experience in therapy confirmed by someone else, or out of the desire to share their therapist and have someone else involved with them.

Just as important, though more subtle, recommendations from current or former clients are also compromising. You can feel put under obligation by their recommendation and praise. It can exert a subtle pressure to ignore contrary, especially negative, impressions. It can establish a covert standard for comparison: making you doubt yourself and feel it must be your problem if it doesn't go well; inviting fantasies of doing even better than your predecessor if it goes well. Either can interfere with the natural course of your therapy.

On the other hand, you need not shy away from a therapist who has been recommended by other sources and who also happens to be recommended by a former client. The alternate source, if it is reliable, is an object corroboration of the former client's enthusiasm.

4. Public-source referrals. Seeing therapists on TV, hearing them on the radio, reading about them in the newspaper, or reading their articles and books are not reliable sources of referrals. The initial encounter is unavoidably a rich source of fantasy about them because of the aura media lend, but it tells you nothing about whether they are actually competent as therapists. Some therapists become newsworthy because of an innovative method, research they have done, or special expertise in an area they are being asked to consult on, but this does not necessarily give you much, if any, information about their skills as a therapist. Even if they are not self-promoting, becoming newsworthy or being publicized for whatever reason is no guarantee of actual competence. You would be putting your well-being in the hands of someone you don't have a reliable reference for.

5. Psychotherapy referral services. Steer clear of so-called psychotherapy "referral services," which are to be found in many cities. Many are simply ways for a single therapist, a training institute, or a group of therapists to recruit more patients. A "referral" can be more like recruitment as a client.

WHAT TO SAY IN ASKING FOR A REFERRAL

In asking someone for a referral, you may wonder how much to reveal. You only have to say enough to give the person or clinic a general idea of what you are looking for and why. You need not go into detail about yourself or your problems, and you should not give out any information that you consider private. People sometimes feel pressured to say more than is necessary in order to be sure they will get a response. If you can't get a response to your request for help without revealing more than you feel comfortable with, this isn't the person or clinic to be asking for a referral.

It's important to protect your confidentiality from the beginning. You will feel much safer and more trusting of therapy later if the process doesn't start with a self-disclosure you didn't want to make. This can leave you feeling already undefended, out of control, or at a disadvantage—feelings you may already have and don't need more of.

All you need to specify in asking for a referral are the following:

1. *In general terms, say what you are considering therapy for.* The Therapy Guide in Part II is available to help you formulate a more precise idea of the kind of problem that may be troubling you.

2. *Mention the kind of therapy you are interested in:* individual, couple, marital, family, or group therapy. If you are uncertain, the Therapy Guide provides guidelines on this. Therapists tend to specialize in different approaches. A final decision on which may be most appropriate will be made after your initial consultation (see Chapter 4). But it's good to begin with a tentative idea of what you're looking for.

3. *Ask about the kind of approach the therapist practices or specializes in:* psychodynamic, behavioral, cognitive, family systems, etc. (see Chapter 2). Again, the final decision about this will be made after a consultation, but you can use the Therapy Guide to get some idea of the kinds of approaches generally recommended for your problem. If you want help for a marital problem, for instance, you want to be sure you aren't referred to a therapist who specializes in individual behavioral therapy.

4. *Ask for a licensed professional.* As we discussed earlier in this chapter, a licensed professional offers you several important protections. Which profession is less important.

5. *In general terms, describe the kind of person you think you would work best with, and any personal preferences.* What kind of person would you feel most compatible with? You may want to refer to Chapter 5 to help you assess this. It is perfectly appropriate, for instance, to say you prefer a male or female therapist, an older therapist or someone your own age. A number of characteristics may be important to you. Feel free to mention them.

6. *Give a general idea of what you think you can afford to pay.* Insurance coverage may be a factor in determining this (see Chapter 7, "Paying for Therapy").

7. *Indicate whether you want a therapist in private practice or would be willing to*

consider a staff therapist in a clinic. What you can afford to pay may have a bearing on this.

8. *Indicate where you would be able to go for therapy.* You will want someone close enough to work or home so you can keep appointments on a regular basis.

Anything more than this is more information than someone making a referral needs.

Ask for several names; three is the usual number. Of special interest are therapists recommended by different sources. By reputation, at least, they are standouts.

RETURNING TO A FORMER THERAPIST

If you were in therapy before, should you go back to the same therapist? There is no absolute rule of thumb here. There is certainly no personal or professional obligation. Assess your preferences and needs, then make the same kind of informed decision you would make about a new therapist. Because it's harder to be objective with a former therapist, however, you should have some guidelines for making this decision.

One consideration, of course, is what you saw the therapist for then, and what troubles you now. If the problems have little to do with each other, and if your new problem is not within your old therapist's range of competence, then you need a new therapist. For instance, if you were in couples therapy for a failing marriage some years ago, and now you need help for depression or an anxiety disorder, a couples therapist may not be the best choice.

If your current difficulty *is* within your old therapist's competence to treat, you should not feel obligated to return. But here are some reasons to consider it if your experience was *positive*:

- To save time. If your current problem is urgent, your former therapist knows you already and so may be able to hone in on the difficulty and help out more quickly than a new therapist.
- If the problem is time-limited and you only need short-term help, someone who knows you is in a better position to provide effective help immediately.
- The same old issues are bothering you again. Your former therapist knows them already and understands your history, habits, and emotional patterns. This puts her or him in a better position to help you do further work on them.

Even if your experience with your former therapist was *mixed,* you should consider returning if:

- Changing therapists in the past hasn't helped. You're still no further along in resolving your problems.

- You feel there are lingering issues between you and your former therapist that you can work on and clear up—feelings of anger, mistrust, or disappointment, for instance. If you're thinking of doing this, though, be aware that you risk simply raising the issues without resolving them, since they weren't resolved with that therapist the first time around. You might seek a consultation (see Chapter 4 on how to conduct a consultation) with another therapist first, to evaluate whether this is a realistic goal.
- You find that the same difficulties you experienced with your former therapist, such as inexplicable anger or repeated feelings of being hurt, keep cropping up with other people in your life—people at work, your spouse, your family or friends. Then it might be worth going back to your original therapist to explore those issues more deeply. It might improve the rest of your relationships if you get to the heart of the difficulty this time.

People are sometimes held back from returning to a former therapist for the *wrong* reasons:

- Feeling that needing therapy again means they've failed.
- Being upset that the old problems have returned.
- Fearing that their therapist will be disappointed in them because they're having problems again.
- Dreading going back into the same painful issues again.
- Feeling resentment toward the therapist because their problems weren't cleared up the first time.

While such feelings may give you pause about a return, they are quite common and do not necessarily mean you should not return to your original therapist. They may simply indicate your reluctance to delve more deeply into whatever may be troubling you.

On the other hand, good reasons *not* to return to a former therapist are:

- Your previous experience was negative and unhelpful.
- You had deep reservations about whether you and your therapist were genuinely compatible. You had such basic differences in beliefs or values, for example, that these differences got in the way of understanding each other. Or your personalities and styles of interaction were ill-suited to each other. If you are unsure how to assess compatibility, Chapter 5 provides some helpful guidelines.
- You and your therapist have since established some social or professional association outside therapy or have otherwise had ongoing contact, or your therapist has since established a personal or professional relationship with a family member or relative.
- Another member of your family has since gone into therapy with your therapist.

- Your therapist behaved or acted unethically, or you have serious reservations about his or her professional conduct (see Chapter 11, "Professional Ethics").
- You have serious doubts about your therapist's competence.
- Your therapist's approach seems stale or irrelevant now, and you think another approach might be more suitable or useful.

STEP THREE: CHECK CREDENTIALS

Once you have a therapist's name, you can check on his or her credentials and training in several ways before you actually call for an appointment. One is to call the state licensing board if the therapist is a licensed professional: a psychiatrist, psychologist, psychiatric nurse, or in those states that license them, a clinical social worker or a marriage and family counselor. You can check with the county medical society for a psychiatrist. You can also check with state professional associations. These organizations are all charged with safeguarding the standards and reputation of the profession. They will tell you if the therapist holds a valid license or is a member in good standing of their professional association.

A second way to check credentials is to call the therapists you are considering. Say you are considering therapy, having been referred to them, and want to ask about their professional qualifications before making an appointment. Many therapists may be surprised at such a call—clients rarely ask about these things—but none should hesitate to answer your questions if they are at all interested in seeing you. You can ask their degree, where they have received their professional training, whether they are licensed or certified, their professional affiliations, and if they have any specialized training. Respectful questions should get a straightforward response.

Expect to be a bit nervous making these calls; most people are at this stage. But if you ask these preliminary questions by phone, it can help you narrow down your list to the two or three most promising candidates. In part you can eliminate therapists who refuse to answer or will only provide this information if you make an appointment—an expensive way to get public information you are entitled to. Also, even this brief phone contact will provide you with some initial sense of what it is like to interact with this person, and if you could work with him or her. First impressions count. Don't dismiss them.

What Credentials to Look For

The important credentials are somewhat different for each profession. Remember, too, that the best credentials are not a warranty of skill. They simply mean you can be a bit more confident in the therapist's background, and you have the added protections licensing and certification afford.

If you are referred to any *psychiatrists,* ask if:

- They have completed a residency in psychiatry, which included training in psychotherapy.
- They are board certified in your state.
- They are a full member of the American Psychiatric Association. Membership in the American Medical Association says nothing about their competence as a psychiatrist.
- They have any postgraduate training at a psychotherapy institute, and whether they are a graduate of the institute.
- They have membership in a psychotherapy or psychoanalytic society. This is a plus, but not necessary.

If you are referred to any *psychologists,* ask if:

- They have a doctorate in psychology or a related field: a Ph.D., Ed.D., or Psy.D.
- They are licensed or certified in your state.
- They have full membership in the American Psychological Association.
- They are registered in the national Register of Health Service Providers.

A psychologist may have additional credentials. These are a plus, but not necessary:

- Training in or graduation from a psychotherapy training institute.
- Diplomate status in clinical psychology.
- Membership in a psychotherapy or psychoanalytic society.

If you have been referred to any *clinical social workers,* ask if:

- They have a master's degree in social work (MSW) with a clinical concentration.
- They are licensed (LICSW) or certified (CSW) in your state (if your state licenses or certifies social workers).
- They have full membership in the National Association of Social Workers.
- They have evidence of clinical training, or specialized work in psychotherapy.

A clinical social worker may have additional credentials that are desirable, but not necessary:

- Membership in the Academy of Certified Social Workers (ACSW).
- Training in or graduation from a psychotherapy or psychoanalytic training institute.

- Diplomate status from the National Association of Social Workers.
- Membership in a psychotherapy or psychoanalytic society.

If you have been referred to any *psychiatric nurses,* ask if:

- They have an R.N. license in your state.
- They have a master's degree in psychiatric nursing from an accredited university.
- They are certified as a psychiatric nurse by the state nursing association, if this kind of certification is available in your state.
- They have evidence of specialized training in psychotherapy.

Psychiatric nurses may have additional qualifications that are desirable but not necessary:

- Training in or graduation from a psychotherapy or psychoanalytic training program.
- Membership in a psychotherapy or psychoanalytic society.

If you have been referred to any *marriage and family therapists,* ask if:

- They have a master's degree in marriage and family counseling.
- They are licensed or certified in your state.
- They are full members of the American Association of Marriage and Family Therapy.

Marriage and family counselors may have additional qualifications that are desirable but not necessary:

- Training in or graduation from a psychotherapy training institute.
- Membership in the American Academy of Marriage and Family Therapists.

If you have been referred to a *sex therapist,* ask if:

- They are licensed or certified in one of the professions in your state. No good sex therapy training institute will admit someone who does not already have established credentials in one of the other helping professions. You should then inquire about the credentials listed for that profession above, especially their standing in their professional organization.
- They have graduated from a recognized sex therapy training institute.
- They are members of the American Association of Sex Educators and Therapists.

If you have been referred to a *therapist outside the licensed professions*. Our recommendation is that you start with a licensed professional. Make this request clear to whomever you ask for referrals. However, should you be referred to a therapist who is not licensed and there is some compelling reason to consider them, you should ask:

- What skills and competencies does that person have that could be helpful?
- What kind of training have they had in therapy? How much of that was supervised training? Have they trained in or graduated from a psychotherapy training program?
- How much experience have they had?

Then consider whether their capabilities and skills outweigh the potential risks of their not being licensed. This is of importance should anything unprofessional or unethical occur; you will have no recourse to a professional association or state licensing board. Your only recourse will be a lawsuit for damages.

STEP FOUR: CONTACT THE THERAPIST

The best way to contact a therapist is by phone. When you introduce yourself, don't feel you have to tell your whole story or every detail of what is troubling you—just give the therapist a general idea. Keep it brief and to the point. The consultation (described in the next chapter) is the place to go into more detail. All you need say at this point is:

- who you are
- that you are considering therapy
- that you were given the therapist's name by X as a possible referral
- that you are seeking help with this problem or issue
- is he or she accepting new clients?
- would he or she be interested in discussing therapy with you?

If so, this is the time to ask about several other things you want to know before going ahead and scheduling a consultation:

If You Are Calling a Therapist in Private Practice

- How soon can the therapist see you, and will it be on a regular basis?
  Sometimes a therapist can see you for a consultation, but you won't learn until you are already in their office that their schedule is actually full. They might be able to see you in several weeks or several months, but you may want to see someone sooner than that.
- What hours are available?
  Therapists may have openings in their practice, but not at times you can make, or that fit easily into your schedule. You want to find this out before, not after, you are in their office.
- What is the fee?
  This is an appropriate question and the therapist should answer it. If you can't afford to continue at the fee he or she charges, there is no point in starting. It is acceptable to ask if a reduced fee is a possibility. Some therapists will say they prefer to discuss their fee after reviewing your financial circumstances with you in person. This is acceptable, but then feel free to ask them if their fee is negotiable and what their range of fees is.
- If you have medical insurance, will your particular policy cover their services?
  They should be able to tell you whether their services are covered by most major carriers, and what health plans they are providers for. For others, you or they may need to inquire. If you are uncertain, arrange that either you or they will inquire before scheduling an appointment.
- Do they charge for an initial consultation?
  Some therapists now advertise "free consultation" to attract more clients into their practice or because they, too, may be "shopping around." But most therapists bill for an initial consultation. This is a billable professional service when it is used to offer a professional assessment of your problems and needs in therapy, and you should expect to pay for it. This makes the process a little more expensive for you if you consult more than one therapist. But the cost is well worth it. On the other hand, a first meeting should not be considered a billable professional service if the therapist uses it primarily to provide the kind of basic information that should be available to you without cost by phone beforehand: their qualifications, orientation and specialities, fees, and availability.
- Do they do the particular kind of therapy you are considering?
  One of the most important questions to ask potential therapists in the first phone call is if they offer the type of therapy and approach you are considering. Many therapists are competent in more than one modality and approach, but none are skilled in all. Beware of someone who tells you that he or she does "whatever works." It may be a sign of overpromising results, poor training, or

a shoot-from-the-hip eclecticism that isn't well grounded in any substantial body of theory or practice. Therapists may be reluctant to peg themselves as adherents of a specific school, but every therapist needs an overall theoretical approach as a guide. They should be able to tell you what approaches they employ.

- What are their qualifications?

   If you don't know, or haven't been told by the person who referred you to them, this is the time to ask. Some therapists may be surprised to be asked about this in the first phone call, but you need this background information to help you decide whether to go ahead and schedule a consultation. It isn't an unprofessional question, and you should get a straightforward answer to it.

When you call for an appointment, you should *speak to the therapist directly.* You may be tempted to get a family member or friend, or the person who referred you, to do it for you. You may be anxious or afraid you won't know what to say. It may feel a bit intimidating and overwhelming. But to ask someone else to do what you can do for yourself is not the way to start when the goal is to help you help yourself. Therapists who let someone else pinch-hit for you are colluding with your fears and effectively treating you as incapable of acting for yourself. It suggests a childish, helpless role for you in therapy. You may also be wary of a therapist who has a secretary or receptionist respond to your initial inquiry. It could signify someone who doesn't respect clients enough to respond personally; at worst, it suggests someone who needs to maintain distance and control.

Other therapists will take your call, but avoid answering any questions on the phone. Therapists shouldn't answer questions that don't bear on the services they provide, or any questions that require them to know something about you, such as what the therapist thinks about your situation, whether he or she thinks therapy would help, or how long it might take. These kinds of questions are best deferred until a consultation.

On the other hand, therapists should be ready to answer the questions outlined above about their services. If they won't answer these questions, or put you off by telling you they'll discuss them when you see them—for a fee, of course—this is probably someone who feels you have no right to the information or are entitled to it only if you pay.

If You Are Calling a Clinic

If you are calling for an appointment at a clinic, your questions will be somewhat different. You may not know who will be assigned from the staff until you make your appointment. At that time you will want to ask the same questions about the therapist's qualifications and competencies as you would of a therapist in private practice. Questions about scheduling, fees, and insurance or third-party coverage will normally be answered by clinic receptionists or by an intake coordinator.

But in your first call to the clinic you will also want to ask:

- Do they see people who live in your area?

  Many public clinics are restricted to a particular geographic zone or "catchment area" that they serve. This is almost always true of public clinics and agencies such as community mental health centers.
- Are they restricted from seeing clients above a certain income?

  Some public clinics and agencies can only see people with no health insurance whose incomes are low. Others will see any area resident, but their fee will range from full to free, depending on income.
- How soon can you be seen?

  Is there a waiting period or a waiting list? Some clinics are walk-in and you can be seen immediately. Most will require you to schedule the initial appointment in advance. This may be with the therapist you will see; it may be with a staff member who will then assign a therapist on the basis of an evaluation.
- What kinds of therapists are available?

  What professions are represented on the staff? What level of training do they generally have? Are you likely to be assigned someone in training, or a staff therapist? If it is someone in training, what kind of supervision will your therapist be getting? Will you be able to request a particular kind of therapist, or will you simply have to take whoever is assigned? What is the procedure for requesting another therapist if the assigned therapist doesn't work out?

Unlike with a therapist in private practice, in a clinic or institutional setting you usually can't expect to talk with a staff therapist directly when you first call for an appointment. Nevertheless, you are sill entitled to the same information. Try to get it from whoever handles your call. Otherwise, get it from the therapist who is assigned to you for the first meeting.

FIRST IMPRESSIONS COUNT: ASSESSING THE FIRST CONTACT

You don't get a second chance to get a first impression. If this initial phone call is your first contact with the therapist, use it to form an initial sense of compatibility. First impressions count a great deal. Your intuition is a source of crucial information about a therapist. Even by the end of that brief contact, you will know a lot about the therapist, though you may not realize it.

Here are guidelines on what to look for in the initial contact:

How and Where the First Contact Is Made

Favorable

- the first contact is by phone
- the therapist answers your call personally
- the therapist has an answering machine service, and returns your call within one day, or two days, or has a good reason for the delay
- if you are calling a clinic, the phone call is routinely taken by a receptionist, or by another staff member who is designated to respond to inquiries

Questionable

- you called and left a message, but the therapist doesn't return your call for several days or longer
- you are only able to talk with the secretary or receptionist (unless you are calling a clinic)

Unacceptable: Don't Consider

- the therapist answers the phone and talks to you about an appointment while another client is in the room
- the therapist doesn't return your call for a week or more (unless they have been away or out sick)
- the therapist doesn't return your call or acknowledges having forgotten when you try them again
- the therapist has a secretary or receptionist call you back to make an appointment, without talking with you first
- the therapist has his or her spouse call you back
- the therapist is willing to discuss your situation and make an appointment at a social gathering or chance encounter in the community

Who Makes the First Contact

Favorable

- the therapist expects you to make the first contact yourself or insists on your calling directly
- the therapist readily accepts a call from someone else when there wasn't any other choice: on behalf of a child who is too young to call; an adult who is

physically or mentally incapacitated; or someone who is in an acute state and needs immediate attention but is refusing help: e.g., someone suicidal, homicidal, experiencing a toxic drug reaction, or so psychotic or paranoid that he or she is out of touch

Questionable-Unacceptable

- the therapist allows the person who referred you to make an appointment for you, or someone else you asked to do it for you

What Happens in the First Contact

Favorable

- the therapist conveys warmth and concern, but is also tactful, professional, and to the point
- the therapist asks how you got his or her name (this is important because some prior connection between the therapist and the person referring you might rule out his or her being your therapist)
- the therapist is willing to answer questions about services, credentials, and availability
- the therapist is willing to see you for a consultation first, rather than suggesting or implying that the first appointment is for therapy
- the therapist is able to offer you an appointment within a week or two, or immediately if it is an emergency

Questionable

- the therapist discusses in detail your problems or history over the phone
- you have a sense that the conversation is continuing after you have the information you need
- the therapist doesn't seem to respond to your sense of urgency
- the therapist can't schedule a consultation for several weeks
- the therapist offers explanations or recommendations on the basis of the phone call

Unacceptable: Don't Consider

- therapists who avoid or refuse to answer legitimate questions about their services, credentials, or availability, or say they will discuss them when you make an appointment (for which you will be charged)

- therapists who tell you personal information about themselves beyond their professional qualifications and services
- a psychiatrist who agrees to a request for medication or gives advice about medication before a full consultation
- therapists who agree to see you for a consultation when they know they won't have time to see you in therapy, unless they make this clear ahead of time and you still want their professional opinion
- a therapist who continues to explore your problems, makes irrelevant conversation, asks unnecessary questions, or extends the phone call after you've covered everything you need to

How the Therapist Handled an Emergency

If your first contact with a therapist is because you are in urgent distress, the response will be especially telling. Crises call for special responses. Examples: acute stress or trauma; violence or assault; severe depression; suicidal or homicidal feelings; acute psychotic reactions; extreme symptoms of any kind; acute interpersonal crises such as a death in the family or abuse or abandonment by a spouse; getting a diagnosis of a potentially terminal medical illness.

Favorable

- the therapist offers to see you that day, or at most, the next day
- if a therapist can't see you, he or she helps you find another therapist who can
- if you are in imminent danger, he or she refers you to a hospital emergency room or urgent-care clinic and helps make the necessary arrangements
- the therapist makes himself or herself available to you by phone for any necessary follow-up, or if your situation worsens while you are waiting for your first appointment

Unacceptable

- the therapist either ignores or misses obvious signs of crisis or extreme distress
- the therapist offers an appointment several days from the time you call
- the therapist recognizes the emergency, but doesn't offer his or her professional assistance in getting help

Step Five: Ask for a Consultation

If you are satisfied with this initial phone contact, the next step is to make an appointment to meet the therapist in person. In asking for an appointment, you are not asking to start therapy. You are asking for a consultation to discuss your situation in more detail, and to get the therapist's professional assessment and recommendations. Ask explicitly for a "consultation." Some therapists may offer a "first appointment" or talk about this meeting as a "first session" or "our first meeting." That implies there will be others. It suggests that in making this appointment you will already be starting therapy. Reserve that decision for yourself, after you have met with and gained an impression of the therapist. So be sure to clarify that what you are asking for is a consultation to talk *about* doing therapy.

Feel free to schedule consultations with more than one therapist. You might do well to talk with several of the therapists you obtained referrals to before making up your mind. This is a bit more costly, but well worth the additional expense if you can afford it. You will have some basis for comparison, you will see how different therapists bring out different sides of you, you will have an opportunity to ask further questions and get different perspectives on your situation. It will feel more like your own choice and will help you commit more seriously to the therapist you eventually choose.

A therapist should respect this. If the therapist you contact balks at the idea of consultation, or seems put off or defensive by the thought of your consulting someone else, he or she is not the therapist you want. Most good therapists will encourage you to speak with several others before making up your mind: They will certainly not discourage you.

CHAPTER FOUR

■

CONSULTING A
THERAPIST

THE PURPOSE OF A CONSULTATION

At this point you should have an idea about the kinds of help that are available, obtained several reliable referrals, checked their credentials, contacted the therapists or clinics by phone, and scheduled an appointment to meet at least one of the therapists in person for a consultation.

Why a consultation first? Why not begin therapy as soon as you have a good referral to a therapist who has agreed to see you? The consultation is actually the most crucial step of all. It is where you and the therapist will make a decision about therapy, where you will get the most important information you need about the therapist's competence and suitability, and where the therapist will determine whether he or she can be of help to you. Most important, it's the place where both of you will be assessing what it would be like to work together—whether you can establish the kind of working relationship that will make therapy successful.

Since a consultation is a *mutual interview,* the main focus should be on sharing information. You want to know about the therapist and the kind of therapy he or she does. The therapist wants to know about you and what you are looking for. You should describe your situation as well as you can. The therapist should tell you how he or she works, what kind of therapy is recommended and why. You should feel free to ask questions. This is also the time to fill in any gaps you have in basic information such as the therapist's credentials, services, approach to therapy, availability, and fees.

A consultation gives you and the therapist a chance to size each other up. Much of what goes on will be between the lines: your impressions of each other; your sense of compatibility and rapport; your sense of whether you seem able to communicate and understand each other; whether you agree or disagree on important matters.

If you think some personal characteristic of the therapist could affect your working together—such things as gender, age, race, religion, sexual orientation, personal values or beliefs—this is also the time to discuss that. Despite many therapists' denials, a therapist's basic values *do* influence how he or she approaches you. But you may not find it easy to get the information you want: some therapists will claim personally held values don't enter their work; others feel it is harmful to therapy to provide any personal information about themselves. If a therapist declines to answer questions about values, or about any personal or demographic characteristic that you sincerely think might impact on your working together, then you have to decide whether you will be comfortable working with that therapist.

The idea of interviewing a therapist may seem intimidating. If you're distressed, feeling pressured by your problems, uncertain of yourself, and all you want is relief, just the thought of it may seem beyond you. But it sounds harder than it actually is, particularly if you keep in mind that you are not interviewing "your" therapist yet, only talking to someone you don't know about contracting for his or her services. It is a chance to talk about therapy without making any commitment beyond this consultation. It also safeguards and supports your right to make *your* choice.

AVOIDING THE IMPULSE TO LEAP INTO THERAPY

If you can resist the natural temptation to leap into therapy with the first person who sees you, you have a much better chance of getting a good therapy. This may be hard to do if you're in emotional pain. But if you simply take the first opportunity that presents itself, you run a greater risk down the road of feeling trapped in unhelpful therapy, no better off than when you started. Worse still, you run the danger of ending up disillusioned with the whole process. Consulting with someone first will minimize these risks.

PREVENTING THE THERAPIST FROM LEAPING INTO THERAPY

No matter how clear you make it that you are just looking at this point, some therapists will take it for granted that you are there to start therapy. You are *not* starting therapy. Signs that the therapist is treating the consultation as a first therapy session include:

- Interrupting your account of your situation to pursue a single issue.
- Trying to get a detailed case history immediately. This is premature. A therapist's first job is to listen to you describe in your own words why you are there and what you are looking for.
- Not giving you the chance to ask further questions about the therapist's credentials, experience, orientation, or the type of therapy they do.
- Offering psychological interpretations in the first meeting.
- Giving you instructions or therapy "homework."
- Talking as if you will be working together rather than talking about it conditionally ("when we" instead of "if we").

If a therapist seems to be assuming that you will be working together, remind them that you are still deciding what to do. You are considering working with him or her, but first you want to explore all possibilities.

HOW LONG SHOULD A CONSULTATION TAKE?

A single meeting may be enough to obtain the information you need to form a definite impression—especially if your first impression tells you right away that this isn't someone you want to work with. On the other hand, you may need more than one meeting to feel comfortable in making a decision. Consulting two or even three times with a therapist before making up your mind is a good practice if you're uncertain after the first meeting.

An alternative approach is to consult each therapist once. Then ask for a follow-up consultation with the one you rated most highly in terms of the criteria suggested later in this chapter. This will give you the chance to check out your first impression and to explore areas you may still have questions about after the first meeting.

If you are going to a clinic, HMO, or agency instead of a therapist in private practice, they will typically require one or more "intake interviews" or evaluation sessions with someone who will then assign you to a therapist. The intake interview functions much like a consultation, except that you will not have a chance to assess your potential therapist. Only after you have been assigned and begin meeting with the therapist will you have a chance to assess their compatibility and competence (see p. 108). If you have a strong negative reaction, you should request another therapist. If your reservations are well-founded and your request is reasonable, most clinics and agencies will try to honor it.

SHOULD YOU PAY FOR A CONSULTATION?

Therapists vary on charging for a consultation. Some will charge only if you decide to begin therapy with them. Others will charge even if you don't, since they have still rendered you a professional service. This is fair if the consultation is used to assess your problems and discuss ways of approaching them. They should probably not charge if they use the appointment primarily to provide information they could have provided on the phone regarding their qualifications, orientation, fees, and availability.

You should always ask in advance if there will be a charge for the consultation. Don't be lured just because a therapist offers free consultation. You may be fortunate enough to have been referred to a therapist who takes the view that the consultation is part of finding the right therapy and should be offered gratis. But some therapists use the lure of a free consultation to attract clients into their practice.

HOW TO CONDUCT A CONSULTATION WITH A PRIVATE THERAPIST

Opening the Interview

The therapist should attend to arrangements and get things started. You are not on your home ground, after all. You may be upset, you are certainly anxious, especially if you've never been in a therapist's office before, and no matter how well you've prepared for this, it's natural to feel unsure of yourself.

Typically a therapist will begin by coming into the waiting room, introducing himself to you, and inviting you into his office. If it isn't immediately clear where you should sit, he should indicate this and invite you to sit down. Once you are seated, he will usually begin by asking a general question like, "How can I help you?" or "What brings you here today?" or "Tell me a little about why you've come." A question like this invites you to present yourself and what you are seeking in the way that is most comfortable for you.

Some therapists may simply wait for you to begin. Whether they begin with a general question or comment or wait for you to begin, you should start by saying that you are considering therapy and that your purpose in being there is to explore the possibility of working together. You need to clarify at the start that you are not there to begin therapy but to see if there is a basis for the two of you working together.

As you begin talking about yourself, an important part of the therapist's job is to help you feel more at ease. You should get the impression that this is a warm, empathic, respectful person who is capable of helping you. If you don't feel these qualities in this first meeting, this is probably not the therapist for you.

The therapist, not you, must make the consultation a "success." If you try too hard—to create a favorable impression, to make the therapist like you and want to work with you, to click—that can get in the way or registering your own impressions of the therapist and how you are interacting. Whether you feel a positive chemistry or are put off or have grave doubts, you have learned what you are there to find out.

What to Go Over in the Interview

Assuming that you have already asked about the therapist's credentials, orientation, availability, and fees when you first called, you should cover certain important areas in the consultation. You won't be able to cover them in depth, but you should come away with some understanding of each. If you don't and you still want to consider this therapist, then consider extending the consultation and ask for another appointment before making a final decision. The sequence in which these areas are covered is less important than making sure you cover them all.

Why you are there and what you want from therapy. Once you are comfortably seated, whether the therapist invites you to begin or simply waits for you to begin, you should start by describing why you are considering therapy and what you want to get from it. You should do this in your own words rather than searching for technical terms. Be as simple and direct as you can. As you talk about yourself, the therapist may occasionally ask questions to clarify the nature of your problem, how you experience it, and how and when it started.

A therapist may prefer a standardized initial interview, going through a more or less set sequence of questions designed to elicit information the therapist thinks he needs. In most cases, it is better if the therapist lets you describe what you want help for in your own way, then asks for any additional information late in the interview. If the therapist does follow a set protocol, some of what is asked about will be irrelevant to what you want help with. You don't have to provide all the information such a protocol asks for—only what you think is relevant to why you are there. Feel free to question any queries from the therapist you don't think are relevant.

If you have been in therapy before. At some point, usually near the beginning, let the therapist know if you've been in therapy before (see Chapter 13, "Starting Again").

The therapist (or intake evaluator at a clinic) will be interested in the following: when it took place; your reasons for going into it; what kind of therapy it was; how long it lasted; how you experienced the relationship with the therapist; whether or not you felt it helped; and why it ended when it did.

Be sure to mention if you encountered any problems in therapy, or with the process. You should also mention any experiences of unprofessional or unethical behavior by a previous therapist. This is often very hard to talk about, particularly in meeting another therapist for the first time. If you don't mention it, however, and it doesn't get talked about, the chances are great that this previous experience with therapy may compromise and even undermine future therapy. The therapist needs to be aware of it, even if the two of you agree to defer talking more about it until later.

What the therapist thinks about your problems and goals for therapy. After talking about the nature of your problems and hopes for therapy, you now want to know the therapist's reactions to what you have said. If the therapist doesn't offer any reactions, however tentative, ask for specifics: how serious does the therapist think it is? Does he or she see things the way you do? Does the therapist think other issues are involved? What should the goals for therapy be? Can therapy help? Is what you want realistic?

The therapist's ideas may be different from yours about any or all of this. It isn't uncommon to leave a consultation with different ideas about what your goals should be—that's often a sign of a successful consultation.

How the therapist would work with you. You will want to learn the basics of how the therapists would handle your case. What *kind* of therapy do they recommend? As the Therapy Guide explains, some problems are best treated in, say, family therapy or couples therapy. Do they recommend combining individual therapy with, say, couples or family therapy?

What therapeutic *approach* would they take? If you have used the Therapy Guide to familiarize yourself with recommended approaches, are their recommendations similar or different? If they are different, consider discussing that with them, realizing of course that each case is unique. The therapists may see something in your case that doesn't fit the general pattern, or they may have had success with another kind of approach.

Another set of questions concerns the *course* of therapy. Can they give you an idea of about how long they think it might take to accomplish what you want? How frequently would they suggest meeting? For how long each session? What problems would they anticipate might come up?

Finally, can they themselves offer you the kind of therapy you and they think you need? Have they successfully dealt with this problem before? Is their approach or expertise suitable for it? Most important, what do they think about the match? Do they think you could work well together?

Other recommendations the therapist might make. In addition to recommendations about therapy, the therapist might suggest you proceed by:

1. Obtaining records or other kinds of information. The therapist may want additional information beyond what you have provided in the interview.

If you have been in therapy before, the therapist may want to contact the therapist who worked with you. They might also want to contact a psychiatrist who has prescribed medication for you, a hospital where you were admitted, or a physician who treated you for physical problems that affected your emotional well-being. They may particularly want to consult with anyone treating you at the moment if they think it bears on your problems or could affect therapy—a physician who is prescribing medication with psychological effects, for instance, or is treating you for a medical condition that could be affecting you emotionally. If the therapist is considering recommending you be evaluated for medication, he or she may want to consult with a psychiatrist or physician who prescribed medication for you before.

If you are already under a physician's or psychiatrist's care for medication, or anyone else is treating you, they may want to confirm that and discuss how the two of them will work together. Less frequently, a therapist may want to talk with someone closely involved with your current situation: a physician, a lawyer, a child care worker, an employer, a clergy member, a probation officer, or a family member or spouse.

Occasionally the therapist will want written records of previous treatment, but usually they will phone. *All such contacts require verbal or written permission from you.* Usually you will be asked to sign a "release of information" form. See page 258 in Chapter 11, "Professional Ethics," on what should be in this form to safeguard your right to confidentiality. Verbal permission is probably enough to get started, particularly in an emergency, but it's good practice to follow it up with a signed release.

Agencies and clinics routinely ask for this kind of written permission at intake; private therapists less so. In either case, you should never consider this a "routine" request. It concerns how much and what kind of information will be shared about you. You should always discuss these requests carefully, and it should be clear to you why the therapist wants this information. Typically, the purpose is either to help the therapist better understand your situation, make more effective recommendations, or coordinate therapy with other forms of care. All these are good reasons. But it does mean widening the circle of confidentiality, and there should be clear need related to your current problems and request for therapy. You should also know how the therapist or the clinic keeps this kind of information confidential, especially any written records.

If the therapist or clinic requests additional information and you agree, this may mean extending the consultation to allow time to obtain it. In this case, you will probably need to meet at least one more time.

2. Psychological testing. Occasionally, a therapist will recommend psychological testing to aid in an evaluation. *Testing* is actually a misnomer. These are not tests you pass or fail, but a battery of instruments designed to provide information about different areas of functioning as well as problem areas that you may be unaware of. They are especially valuable in providing information about underlying personality structure and patterns of thinking that may be difficult for a therapist to evaluate on the basis of an interview alone. Occasionally, these evaluations aid in diagnosing a psychiatric disorder.

Three types of instruments are used. *Cognitive tests* provide standardized measures of intellectual functioning. The most widely used are the Wechsler Intelligence Scales: the WAIS-R (Wechsler Adult Intelligence Scale–Revised) for adults, and the WISC-R (Wechsler Intelligence Scale for Children–Revised) for children aged six to seventeen. These yield the standard IQ scores familiar from school. But their purpose is different in a therapeutic context. The various subscales and the relationships between them can provide important information about relative strengths and weaknesses in intellectual abilities; and about specific areas of functioning that may be related to your difficulties.

Self-report tests typically ask you to check off items that you think apply to you. Like cognitive tests, these are also based on various standardized scales. Unlike cognitive tests, they are usually designed to measure various personality traits, preferences, aptitudes, or symptoms. The best known and probably still the most widely used is the Minnesota Multi-Phasic Personality Inventory (MMPI), recently reissued in a revised version.

Projective personality tests are probably the tests most associated in the public mind with psychological testing. These include the famous Rorschach inkblot test and the Thematic Apperception Test (TAT). These two present you with relatively unstructured stimuli—an ink blot in the first case, an ambiguous picture in the second—that you are asked to make sense of by saying what you see. Projective tests are based on the idea that the way you respond to and make sense of an unstructured stimulus provides information about the way you see yourself and others, the way you tend to pattern your thinking and feeling, and the meanings specific behaviors may have for you.

Clients are sometimes asked to participate in psychological testing for research purposes—before and after therapy, for instance, to study the effectiveness of a particular approach. You should not feel obligated to participate. More importantly, it should never be made a condition of receiving therapy. This kind of research is valid and important, but it runs a significant risk of compromising the therapy. Consciously or unconsciously, it can lead you or the therapist to "steer" the therapy in certain ways. It can also lead to "measuring" the therapy against criteria that may have nothing to do with you or your goals in therapy.

If the therapist recommends psychological testing, ask why and be sure you understand the reasons for it. The recommendation should have some direct bearing on your case. The testing itself is usually done in a separate session by a psychologist to whom the therapist will refer you, and you will be charged. You should *not* be charged for any testing you agree to do for purely research purposes.

You have a right to know the results of any psychological testing, and you should always ask ahead of time that the testing psychologist go over the results with you afterward. Do not agree to testing if the results won't be made available to you. Going over results with the person taking the test is a routine practice. Any good tester should be glad to honor your request.

3. *A medication evaluation.* The therapist may recommend you be evaluated for medication in addition to therapy. Most problems in everyday living that people bring to therapy won't require medication, but major emotional disorders may necessitate combined treatment. If the therapist you are consulting is not a psychiatrist and thinks you may be suffering from an emotional disorder treatable with medication, he or she should refer you for a medication evaluation. This should be to a psychiatrist who is familiar with psychiatric drugs, not to a regular physician. Any physician can prescribe them, but nonpsychiatrists won't be as knowledgeable about psychiatric medications. The best workups for medication are done by psychopharmacologists—psychiatrists who specialize in psychiatric medications. Don't be surprised if the therapist who refers you to such a specialist is also a psychiatrist. Many psychiatrists eventually specialize in psychotherapy and may not feel as current or competent in psychopharmacology. Other psychiatrists prefer to keep therapy separate from medication in principle. This is a common and acceptable practice.

Since medication is a major intervention in its own right, and every medication entails the risk of some side effects, you may want to get a second opinion if medication is recommended. In some cases, a clear case can be made for it. In other cases, it is a matter of clinical judgment. A second opinion can be useful if a consultant has recommended medication and you have strong feelings in principle against taking medication.

If medication will be prescribed by someone other than your therapist, you should give both written permission to confer. Any other arrangement doesn't make sense and runs risks. But the prescribing psychiatrist does not need to know details of your therapy. It is your therapist who needs to know what is happening with your medication.

4. *A complementary therapy.* Therapists will occasionally suggest doing another type of therapy along with individual therapy. Most commonly group therapy or family therapy is recommended in addition to individual therapy. Or several different approaches to your problem might be recommended, either concurrently or in sequence. Either kind of recommendation is acceptable practice, but it will entail additional expense. It will also require careful discussion and planning so the goals of the different procedures mesh. Be sure you understand why an adjunctive modality or approach is recommended, and in what ways it may be helpful.

5. *Extending the consultation.* The therapist may feel that more than a single interview is needed: to clarify what is troubling you, to arrive at a mutually agreed on set of goals, to decide on the right approach, or perhaps to determine whether he or she is the right therapist for you. Therapists and clinics will rarely suggest extending a consultation unless they think it necessary. They like to get started with

therapy as soon as possible. Another consultation won't produce any more income than beginning therapy. So take this recommendation seriously. Beginning therapy is an important step that shouldn't be rushed.

The potential risks of going into therapy. Another matter, which therapists rarely bring up, is if they foresee any risks. As we pointed out, therapy can sometimes harm as well as help. It can have unanticipated consequences, or can affect others close to you in ways they may not immediately welcome. (see Chapter 1, p. 29). Inquire about any risks the therapist might anticipate if you make the changes you want.

The therapist's contractual arrangements. Finally, what would the ground rules of therapy with this therapist include? How often would you meet, how long would each session be, what is the fee, when and how will you be expected to pay, and how will missed appointments be handled? (See Chapter 6, "Contracting for Therapy.")

Concluding the consultation. If at the end of the consultation session, you or your therapist aren't really sure whether you want to go ahead or what the best way to proceed is, the consultation can be extended over another session or two.

HOW TO CONDUCT A CONSULTATION AT A CLINIC OR AGENCY

A consultation at a clinic or agency usually follows a slightly different procedure, though its purpose from your point of view should be the same, and it should cover the same ground. An "intake" or "screening" interview is usually not set up primarily as a way for you and a therapist to mutually explore needs and expectations. Its main purpose is to get the information from you that the clinic needs to see if you are eligible for their services, to make a preliminary diagnosis, which they are legally required to do before starting treatment, and to recommend a treatment plan. This information is also used to assign a therapist and to acquaint him or her with your situation before he or she meets you. Your purpose, on the other hand, should still be to get all the information you need to make an informed decision about therapy and a therapist.

The person who conducts the intake interview may not be the therapist who will eventually see you for therapy. But the intake interviewer often has discretion in assigning a therapist, and in recommending the kind of approach to take, so make your preferences clear.

These interviews often follow a set format if you are coming for the first time. In addition to asking about your present problem, the intake interviewer will probably ask for other background information, some of which may not seem directly related to why you are there. This might include psychiatric history or history of previous emotional problems, medical or work history, educational background, developmental milestones, and social history. This interview can be one-way, the therapist getting information from you, and can be both intimidating and impersonal. But you needn't just follow along, passively answering all the questions and hoping for the best. If you don't want to discuss some issues, say so. If you don't see the relevance of certain questions, ask. If you have ideas about what kind of treatment you are seeking, let the therapist know what they are and why.

While most clinics will take your preferences into account in assigning a therapist, they may be limited by such factors as what therapists have openings at the times you can come in and the kinds of therapists on the staff. There is less freedom to make compatibility and match a primary consideration. Nevertheless, from your point of view, the consultation continues into the first session with the therapist you've been assigned to. While the therapist may assume therapy has begun, you should take the view that this is a tentative arrangement. You still have a chance to assess the therapist's competence and your mutual compatibility. If you have serious reservations about either, discuss them with the therapist frankly.

If you're still not satisfied, request a change of therapist. Ask for a follow-up consultation with the person who did the intake interview and express your dissatisfaction. A poor match is sometimes worse than no therapy at all—it is worth making waves about. Most clinics and agencies will try to honor a reasonable request. After all, therapists don't enjoy working with people they're poorly matched with either. If you still can't get satisfaction, you might consider going elsewhere.

In clinic or agency settings, there may also be a waiting period before your first meeting with the assigned therapist. Feel free to ask how long this is likely to be, and if it is too long or your need is urgent, be sure to let the intake interviewer know this. If they can't do anything about it, you may want to consider trying somewhere else.

IF YOU ARE CONSIDERING OR ARE REFERRED TO GROUP THERAPY

If you are considering group therapy, you won't just be working with an individual therapist but with other members of the group as well. You will want information about the group as well as about the therapist.

Before joining a group, it is customary to meet with the group therapist alone for one or more sessions to prepare for starting the group. You should treat these sessions as you would an interview with an individual therapist—as a consultation. This is your chance to get detailed information about the group in advance. The therapist will usually take the initiative in providing this information and give you an opportunity to ask any questions you might have. The therapist will not expect you to know much about how group therapy works if you haven't been in a group before.

You will want to discuss:

- What is the purpose of the group?
- How many people are in it?
- What is the composition of the group? What is the age range? How many men? How many women? Any other characteristics that may be important to you.
- What kind of problems or issues do people bring to the group?
- How does the group handle these?
- What kind of things go on in the group? How do people interact with each other?
- What is the therapist's role?
- What will be expected of me as a group member?
- What about confidentiality? How can I be sure what I say in the group will stay in the group?
- What are the group's ground rules?
- What makes group therapy different from individual therapy? How will talking about my problems in a group help me more than talking about them with an individual therapist?
- (If the group isn't just starting) How long has the group been running?
- How often do people enter and leave the group? How stable is it?
- If I don't like the group, can I leave it?

In addition to assessing your fit with the group, these preparation sessions allow you to gather impressions of the group therapist as well, and whether you feel compatible. You will want to go over the same ground as you would in a consultation with an individual therapist. The same criteria for evaluating the consultation will apply (see later in this chapter), as will the same guidelines for assessing their compatibility and competence (see the next chapter).

IF YOU ARE CONSIDERING OR ARE REFERRED TO COUPLES OR FAMILY THERAPY

It isn't practical or necessary for each member of the family to interview a family therapist separately. Such meetings won't tell you what they are like to work with when they are meeting with the couple or the family. The reactions that count are not yours alone but those of everyone who is going to be in the therapy.

It is common in couples or family therapy to consider the first session or two a consultation to the couple or the family. Just as in individual therapy, you should specifically request a consultation first, without any commitment to doing therapy. The therapist should readily agree to this. During the consultation, be alert to the signals mentioned previously that suggest the therapist is assuming you are already embarking on therapy. Everyone who will be participating in the therapy should also understand and be in agreement that this first session is just a consultation.

In the consultation itself, you will want to cover much the same general ground as in any other kind of therapy, though the focus of course will be on issues in the couple's relationship, or in the family. The same general criteria apply for assessing the consultation, as do the same basic guidelines for evaluating the compatibility and competence of the therapist. This, however, involves several additional guidelines since more than one of you will be making the final decision (see p. 131).

"THIRD-PARTY" EVALUATIONS

A "third-party evaluation" is different from a consultation. People are sometimes sent to a therapist by some "third party" for an evaluation of their mental or emotional state. Like a consultation, it involves one or at most several meetings only. Unlike a consultation for therapy, however, the purpose is to provide information about you to someone else. Usually that someone else—the "third party"—is an insurance company or other health plan that is paying for your therapy and wants to substantiate its necessity or efficacy, or that is trying to evaluate a disability claim.

But a psychiatric or psychosocial evaluation is often requested in several other instances. Some psychiatric evaluations are court ordered. Competence to stand trial is sometimes the issue or sentencing or fitness as a parent in a custody determination. Another instance is to evaluate fitness or aptitude for certain kinds of employment, such as positions requiring a security clearance. Applicants for the ministry and some religious orders where emotional maturity and stability is considered crucial now often go through routine psychological evaluations, too!

Usually the third party will pick the therapist or the clinic to do the evaluation. But if you are seeking an evaluation for your own purpose—perhaps to support a custody case or a disability claim—you will need to make that explicit when you first contact the therapist so the therapist will not automatically assume you are coming for a consultation for therapy. Also, not all therapists or clinics do third-party evaluations and you want to be certain the one you have contacted does.

When you first contact the therapist or clinic by phone, explain that you want an evaluation, what it is for, and whether it is at your initiative or at the request of a third party. If they don't do such evaluations themselves, ask them to refer you to someone who does.

A CHECKLIST FOR THE CONSULTATION

By the end of a consultation, whether it takes one interview or several, you should have a lot of information and a lot of impressions. Both will be important in making a decision. The following checklist concerns the *basic information* you should expect to get from a consultation. Ask yourself:

About Therapy

- Are you clearer about your problems and goals for therapy?
- Do you have a sense of what the therapist thinks about them? Do you agree on the problem areas and expectations for therapy?
- Do you understand how the therapist would work on these areas with you: the type of therapy he would do, and the approach he would take? Do you feel comfortable with this? Is it compatible with the kind of person you are and how you tend to approach things?
- Do you understand how therapy would proceed: who would be included; how often you would meet; where and when you would meet; what you would be expected to do or not do; how long therapy would probably take?
- Can you afford the fee? Or would the therapist be willing to negotiate a reduced fee?
- Did you discuss potential risks?
- Do you understand any other recommendations: medication, for instance, or a medication evaluation, another type of therapy; psychological testing? Are you in agreement?

About the Therapists

- Have you checked their qualifications, if not beforehand then in the course of the consultation? Credentials, training, experience, institutional and professional affiliations? If they are still in training, what kind of supervision will they be getting?
- Do they have the personal qualities and background you are looking for in a therapist?

Assessing the Consultation

Your *impressions* of the therapists—what kind of people they seemed to be, how they conducted the consultations, and how they interacted with you—are just as important as what kind of therapy they would do, and more important than their credentials and qualifications. Above all, how did they handle the framework of this first interview?

Favorable—The Therapist:

- treated you with courtesy and respect throughout.
- made it easy for you to talk about why you were there, listened well, and seemed to understand what you were talking about.
- brought in little or nothing of her own personal life or personal opinions, but kept the consultation focused on you. When she asked questions or commented, it was to clarify things you said and help you understand your situation better.
- answered your questions about professional qualifications straightforwardly.
- apart from shaking hands when you came in and when you left, had no physical contact.
- after listening and exploring your reasons for therapy, told you briefly and to the point what kind of therapy he would recommend and whether he thought he could provide it.
- outlined what the ground rules of therapy with him would be.

Questionable—The Therapist:

- seemed angry.
- didn't seem very involved with you or your problems, or to care very much; or seemed preoccupied, daydreaming, or just not paying good attention.
- talked as much or more than you did.
- expressed a lot of personal opinions, made comments of a personal nature, or told you personal things about himself.
- frequently interrupted you or made you lose your train of thought by too much questioning or commenting.
- was mildly flirtatious.
- made nonsexual physical contact: patted your hand if you were anxious, gave you a reassuring pat on the shoulder as you were leaving.
- didn't say explicitly whether he or she could help you, didn't talk about the kind of therapy he or she would do, or didn't describe what the ground rules of therapy would be.
- asked you to lie down on a couch for the consultation.
- agreed to include in the consultation someone you had brought along unannounced, unless it was an emergency.

Unacceptable—The Therapist:

- was condescending, tactless, or disrespectful.
- talked a lot more than you did, constantly interrupted you to ask questions, offer comments, or talk about himself or his own ideas.
- was verbally or physically abusive to you.

- made you feel manipulated.
- did not respect your physical boundaries: hugging you, touching you when talking with you, even nonsexually.
- was seductive.
- suggested meeting socially outside the office or clinic.
- was clearly unprofessional in approach: overly personal, revealing private things about herself.
- gave you the feeling you were there to meet his needs for an audience, an admirer, or someone to make him feel good about himself.
- gave a lot of unsolicited advice and instructions about what you should do when you hadn't contracted for therapy yet.

ENDING THE CONSULTATION: YOUR OPTIONS

At the end of the consultation, you have several options:

- *If your impressions are clearly negative,* and you know this isn't the therapy or therapist for you, you should thank the therapist for the consultation and say in a simple and straightforward manner that you won't be making another appointment. A brief word of explanation is a courtesy if it feels appropriate and you want to, but it isn't required.
- *If your impressions are mixed and you aren't sure,* let the therapist know you still feel uncertain. Be frank about this. If you feel quite uncertain, say you will phone back if you decide you want to pursue it. A little time and distance afterward, or a consultation with another therapist in the meantime, may make things clearer. Or if you feel another meeting might resolve some of your doubts, ask to schedule another consultation appointment before leaving the office.
- *If your impressions are basically positive but you don't feel ready to make a decision,* tell the therapist you feel positive but need more time. You might feel there are still important things you want to discuss with her or other possibilities you want to explore. In that case, make another appointment. Or you might just want to interview someone else to have a basis for comparison—always a sound idea. In that case, say you will phone them back when you decide.
- *If your impressions are clearly positive,* you still have several options. You can decide to start therapy. The next step then would be to contract for it (see Chapter 6) and set up an appointment schedule. If this is the first therapist you have consulted, however, a better course is to interview at least one other therapist you have been referred to, for all the reasons mentioned earlier. This is particularly true if you have never been in therapy before. As positive as your impressions of this first therapist may be, you still have no basis for comparison. There is no one "right" therapist. Many different kinds of therapists can be

"right" for you, and you may be surprised how different therapists can pull out different sides of you. Your choice of therapist should be an *informed* choice, not simply an immediate response to a favorable impression.

DEFERRING A DECISION UNTIL AFTER THE CONSULTATION

Some therapists may tell you that you have to make an on-the-spot decision about therapy with them if you want to be sure of getting an available hour. Or they may cite some other reason why they "need to know now." Don't respond to this. If the therapist has only limited time available and can't hold it open for you beyond a certain point, then he or she should inform you of this matter-of-factly. If you feel pressured in any way to make a decision when you still have doubts, or you still want to consult other possible therapists, this in itself betrays a lack of sensitivity to your legitimate concerns and should make you wary of this particular therapist.

A final decision is best made outside the consulting room, when the consultation is over. Then, you are not under the influence of the therapist's presence or your own sense of urgency. You can think about what you have learned, marshal your impressions, and make an informed choice. The following chapter provides guidelines for evaluating the information and impressions you have gathered from these initial interviews.

CHAPTER FIVE

◼

DECIDING WHICH THERAPIST TO SEE

The time has come to make a decision. Ideally, by now you will have contacted and interviewed several therapists you were referred to. If you can choose your therapist and aren't limited to someone your clinic or health plan will assign, you now need a way to sift through the information and evaluate what you have learned. Even if you will be seeing an assigned therapist, you still need to decide whether this is someone you can work with.

This assessment is best done at home, away from the immediate pressures of the consulting room and the therapist's presence. You may have discussed therapy with family or friends. That may have helped. But their different ideas about what would be best for you may also have been confusing.

Whatever advice you've gotten, *the choice needs to be yours* if you are going to commit yourself and take responsibility for this challenging and often demanding process. Since therapy also depends on your being able to establish a special relationship, only you can judge whether a therapist is someone you can work with.

If the choice of a therapist isn't clear to you at this point, the following guidelines should help. If the choice does seem clear, these guidelines may still help you confirm that decision.

The most important guidelines concern a therapist's *compatibility* and *competence*. Another concerns the *appropriateness* of your relationship: how your therapist understands your situation, and whether his or her approach is suited to your issues.

ASSESSING COMPATIBILITY: THREE DIMENSIONS

Compatibility is the most important judgment you will make, because research has shown it is the single most powerful factor in determining the outcome of therapy. Are you and your prospective therapist well matched for doing this kind of work together? You may seem perfectly well matched in other ways—for friendship, for romance, for a business partnership, for discipleship—but still be poorly matched for therapy.

The most important dimension of compatibility is the *personal chemistry* between you and your therapist. A good match also depends on certain *personal characteristics* of the therapist that will enable you to work together in a climate of mutual trust and respect. Some are characteristics all good therapists need; others are more specific to your own personal style and preferences. Compatibility can also involve *similarities* in background, interests, and values.

Personal chemistry is a subjective judgment: you feel it or you don't. Personal characteristics of the therapist that are important in therapy, however, have a more objective basis. Research has definitely shown that specific qualities in therapists are associated with effective therapy. Similarity of background is sometimes important, sometimes not. It is more likely to matter, for example, if you are a member of a minority with special concerns about relations with other groups.

In assessing compatibility you have to trust your own instincts. First impressions count. Use them. In fact, your initial observations and immediate reactions to the therapist are particularly important because you have encountered him or her fresh, before the inevitable filtering that later goes on after you have started working together.

The Chemistry Between You

Chemistry is a vague term, more a matter of feeling than thought, but it points to the most important aspect of a therapist's suitability to your needs: how comfortable you feel with him or her as a person.

At times therapy won't feel so comfortable. Then it will be the relationship, the bond between you, that will see you through. No matter how skilled or experienced your therapist might be, he or she needs to be the kind of person *you* can work with in this intimate way, someone with whom you can establish a relationship that will survive the difficult moments—even be enriched by them.

What you need most is someone you can work with closely in an *atmosphere of mutual trust*. This means a person you can talk with easily, with whom you feel you can be yourself, someone whom you feel comfortable not just approaching, but also questioning or even disagreeing with. It should be someone who not only understands you and your problems, but makes you feel understood.

Your therapist must also be able to tell you things in a way that you can accept, even when it is something you don't want to hear. What your therapist says to you should have meaning for you and feel pretty much on target—at least most of the time. Finally, you should enjoy and respect your therapist as a person and feel enjoyed and respected in return.

A compatibility checklist. After the first meeting or two, ask yourself these questions to gauge how comfortable you would be with a prospective therapist:

- How comfortable did you feel in talking about yourself?
- How easy did he or she make it for you to explain why you were there and what you wanted from therapy?
- Did you find yourself holding back and screening your thoughts and feelings, or did you feel free to express yourself?
- Did the therapist welcome your questions or discourage them?
- Did you feel he or she was attuned to you and understood what you were talking about—that you were on the same wavelength?
- Did the therapist talk in a way you could understand (for example, not using unfamiliar technical terms) and that was meaningful to you?
- Did you get a sense the therapist was genuinely engaged, interested in you, in what you had to say and in what you were feeling?
- Did he or she make you feel that what you had to say was important?
- Is this someone you could come to trust and have confidence in?
- Did you feel responded to as a person, not just as a client?
- Did you feel a genuine concern?
- Did you like him or her? Did the feeling seem to be mutual?

Personal Qualities of the Therapist

Because the essence of therapy is a relationship, the human qualities of a therapist are especially crucial. Research has consistently shown a therapist's personal qualities, attitudes, expectations, beliefs, and values matter more than technique, approach, or theoretical orientation in making therapy work. The therapist's personal qualities are a prime ingredient in the chemistry between you; the better that chemistry, the brighter the outlook for therapy.

The qualities in a therapist that have been found to make the process more effective, no matter what approach is used, are:

- courtesy and respect, so you feel valued and treated with regard.
- warmth, a genuine and active care and concern for your welfare, but in a supportive manner, without being intrusive, possessive, or overly involved.
- interest in knowing you and learning who you are.

- empathy, the ability to understand your feelings and what it is like to be you.
- engagement, a willingness to engage with you as a real person, not as someone filling a role or fitting some theory.
- understanding, so that you feel not just heard, but listened to.
- trustworthiness, instilling confidence that he or she will be ethical and responsible, serve your interests, and not take advantage of you or of anything you disclose.
- sensitivity to your feelings and to how confused, vulnerable, and embarrassed you can sometimes feel.
- insight, sensing things about you that you are not aware of and that you would probably not discover on your own.
- accepting and affirming your individuality and your need to live your life in your own way, and conveying a positive regard for you as you are.
- nonjudgmental of you or your problems, attitudes, feelings, choices, and values; but not afraid to challenge you when you aren't being true to yourself.
- unafraid of your stronger feelings, your fears and anxieties, your often mixed reactions toward therapy, or of your resistance to change, and ready to face these feelings.
- credibility, a confidence in the therapeutic process, in his or her own professional judgment, skill, and experience, and in your ability to change for the better and make your own choices.
- personal maturity, characterized by genuineness, self-acceptance, and a sense of ease.
- some touch of human wisdom, the sense of an understanding that goes beyond mere technique and theory.

On the other hand, certain qualities in therapists have been shown to be clearly *unhelpful,* no mater what the therapist's orientation. Be cautious if you experienced your prospective therapist as:

- disrespectful
- aloof, remote, or cold
- indifferent
- excessively sympathetic or solicitous
- possessive
- passive
- evasive
- angry or argumentative
- critical or judgmental
- insensitive
- patronizing or condescending

The one quality clients are most likely to complain about and find unhelpful in a therapist is remoteness or coldness. The stereotype of the aloof psychoanalyst is an unfortunate and destructive parody of the original ideal of someone who would remain accepting and nonjudgmental—who would take an evenhanded stance that family and friends typically cannot. A detached attitude has no place in therapy, including psychoanalysis as it is actually practiced. On the other hand, it is also destructive to have a therapist who is overly sympathetic and solicitous, so eager to make you feel better or quick to sympathize that he or she fails to help you confront your fears.

Other Danger Signs to Watch For

It is particularly important to recognize therapists who may exploit clients to meet their own needs. The therapy relationship is particularly vulnerable to this, and you want to avoid any therapists who bring destructive personal needs into their work with you. These problems do not usually emerge until after therapy has started, but some signs in the very first interview can alert you to the danger.

This kind of therapist typically:

- comes on too strong, so you feel overwhelmed.
- uses jargon or "psychobabble" that confuses you or seems empty.
- talks a lot more than he or she listens.
- tries to impress you with his or her brilliance or reputation.
- offers too quick or clever interpretations.
- takes over the session, so you have little or no chance to talk.
- seems too eager to please.
- is consistently overly sympathetic or solicitous, to the point that you feel uncomfortable.
- tries to impress you with a casual, personal style of talk, manner, dress, or behavior, or with being up-to-date, fashionable, or successful.
- tries to impress you with being professionally avant-garde in approach.
- makes you feel like just another client in some assembly line.
- makes you feel worse about yourself as a person.
- seems to hide behind the therapist's role rather than engaging you as a person.
- displays signs of excessive anxiety, poor self-control, or other personal problems: e.g., a strained or pressured way of talking, forced friendliness, nervous tics, chain-smoking, or other awkward mannerisms that make you feel uncomfortable.
- shows signs of personal immaturity.

All of these traits signal therapists who probably need you more than you need them.

Your Own Preferences

Don't neglect these. Compatibility isn't some general, objective trait: it's compatibility with *you*. Good therapists tend to have the personal qualities listed above, but every therapist also has his or her own interpersonal style. This may or may not be compatible with how you think you would work best.

There is no point in trying to work with a therapist who, even though skilled and a good person, seems a poor match for you. Precisely what kind of person you would feel most comfortable with is largely a matter of taste. Apart from the positive and negative guidelines above, a gray zone exists where your personal preferences matter most.

Would you work best with someone who:

- is more active or more quiet?
- will talk a lot or will mostly listen?
- is more parental or seems more like a contemporary or peer?
- is more definitive or authoritative in responding to you or more inclined to question and explore with you?
- tends to be more affirming and accepting or who will be tougher and more challenging?
- is more formal or businesslike or more relaxed and informal?
- tends toward the serious side or the lighter side?
- is younger or older?
- is male or female?

Similar Background or Outlook

Your therapist's background doesn't have to be the same as yours, or even all that similar, for therapy to be effective. As a rule, similarity in experience is less important than your therapist's ability to appreciate the meaning those experiences have had for you. Your therapist needn't have lived through events like those in your life to understand their importance and impact. A therapist who can empathetically enter into your experience can help.

Nevertheless, in some instances you may feel you want a therapist with *shared experience*. If you are going into marital therapy, for example, it's reasonable to want a therapist who is married or at least has been. If you are struggling to parent a child, you may feel more confident with a therapist who knows what it is like to raise children.

Having a therapist who shares a *basic cultural and value orientation* with you is more important as a rule than similarity of background. Though many therapists will deny it, maintaining they are impartial, all therapists bring two sets of values into therapy that invariably influence their work.

The first set are fundamental therapeutic values that guide all good therapy as a process of growth and change. Despite some heated opinions to the contrary, therapy is not a value-free science. It rests upon certain basic values, whether these are consciously espoused or not. These typically include a belief in people's responsibility for their actions and lives, that people's freedom and individuality should be respected, and that therapy can help people lead a life more to their liking.

In addition, therapists' personal values—like anyone else's—are shaped by their cultural, ethnic, religious, and social backgrounds. You want a therapist who is clear, open, and unembarrassed about his or her commitments. A perfectly neutral, impersonal, culture-free therapist doesn't exist. Such a therapist probably couldn't help you much anyway, because therapy involves a relationship with a real person, not a technician or machine.

If you and your therapist share similar values, the two of you usually have a better chance of working well together. Someone who has a somewhat similar outlook will be more likely to understand what you mean and feel, not just what you say; what you are striving toward as a person, not just what you want to get relief from; which therapy approaches will feel more natural to you, and which may be technically right but insensitive.

If your basic values are different, you have a judgment to make about how great, for example, differences in age, gender, culture, or sexual orientation feel—to take the four that tend to be of most concern to clients—and how relevant they are to why you are in therapy. The more substantial and relevant such differences feel, the more demands this will inevitably place on your therapist to be alert to how his or her own values and biases may be affecting therapy.

If you sense a great gap between you and your therapist in outlook, ask yourself: does this therapist seem to be sensitive to these issues and equal to the extra demands? Even if this therapist seems up to the task and rates high in other ways, do you still feel strongly that you need someone with a similar background?

Keep in mind that similarities in background or orientation, as important as they might be to you, are still no substitute for competence, or for the other personal qualities in a therapist that make for effective therapy. For example, if you belong to a minority group and prefer someone from your group for a therapist, make sure that whomever you are considering is also a good therapist. You might be better off in the long run choosing a therapist who is highly skilled, even if not a member of your own group.

Still, substantial cultural or value differences with your therapist can place greater demands on you. Most therapists are part of the social and economic mainstream. This is particularly true of licensed professions, such as psychiatry and psychology. If society doesn't consider you or your reference group part of the mainstream—if you belong to an ethnic minority, or are gay or lesbian, for instance, or a social activist or feminist—you are only too aware of bias and stereotyped perceptions.

But you may not realize the extent to which these can permeate therapy as much as any other profession. Despite their training, therapists are not immune from the biases and misperceptions of the society as a whole.

You don't necessarily have to have someone of exactly the same background or orientation as you, but you do need a therapist who won't approach you or your issues with the same biases you confront outside therapy. At the least, you want a therapist who will be open to exploring them with you, and honest in acknowledging when they may be present.

It isn't always easy to get this kind of information. Many therapists don't like to be asked about their values. Some will claim personally held values don't come into their work—a naive position. Others feel it is asking for personal information about them that will compromise the therapeutic process. It *is* personal, but it also is information you are entitled to ask about because it directly bears on your prospects for successful therapy.

Of course your best source for this information is not the therapist's words, but the attitudes he or she conveys. At a minimum, if the therapist has declined to answer any questions about basic values, or any significant attitude or characteristic that you sincerely think bears on your working together, you ought to reconsider.

Women. In general, the sex of a therapist probably has less to do with the course and outcome of therapy than does the therapist's attitudes toward gender issues. That said, many women are dealing with issues that are more comfortably raised with a woman therapist: the complexities of a woman's role; balancing marriage, career, and children; the burdens of choices that may seem "unwomanly" in the eyes of society at large; dealing with sexism.

Therapists, like anyone else, are vulnerable to subtle expectations and stereotypes about women that can bias therapy. Even so, therapists should be more aware than most of such biases. And although a woman therapist is more likely to be understanding of the struggles of a woman in contemporary life, a therapist's gender is no guarantee of a feminist outlook.

In short, whether you are considering a male or female therapist, you would do well to screen his or her attitudes on some key issues that may be signs of a bias you want to avoid. Such issues include abortion rights, whether a mother of toddlers should stay home rather than work, being a single parent. If any such women's issue is likely to come up in the course of your therapy, you would do well to get a reading from your therapist on it from the outset. You are looking for therapy, not for an argument.

If feminist issues are of great importance to you, you might consider seeking a feminist therapist. While feminist therapists vary in the school of therapy they use, they agree that therapy should include a raised awareness of the forces of sexism and the need for change. They tend to agree, too, that the therapist-client relationship should be an equal one, and that therapy should help women see how sexist social attitudes have shaped their problems. If you see a feminist therapist, be sure that she is also experienced in working with the particular problem that brings you to therapy.

Minorities. America is, more than ever, a melting pot. But in the more recent waves of immigration there is a greater trend than before for ethnic groups to preserve what is distinctive about them rather than to try to blend 100 percent with the American mass. At the same time, Native Americans, Hispanics, and blacks have a greater sense of pride in the uniqueness of their identity.

Beyond that, many minorities have tended to be poorly served by the mental health community, either because they were among the poor, or because language or other ethnic norms got in the way. And of course, some therapists have the same biases that can make daily life a hardship for members of many minorities.

For all these reasons, many minority members feel more comfortable with therapists who belong to their own group. If you can't find such a therapist who is also experienced in treating your problem or issues, then you should explore a prospective therapist's attitudes toward your group. While no therapist is likely to admit bias, you can often sense from how he or she talks about the issue whether you will be comfortable in working together. Be especially sensitive to how understanding and respectful the therapist seems.

You can also look for a therapist who, even though not a member of your group, has had many clients who are. This person will not only be more familiar with the special circumstances of those in your group but also is likely to be someone whom others from your group have felt comfortable with. If you have any concerns along these lines, bring them up immediately.

Gays and lesbians. Like those in many minority groups, gays and lesbians face a high level of hostility and bias in society at large. Indeed, a few therapists still harbor an outdated attitude that saw homosexuality itself as a psychological disorder. The current view, of course, is that a person's sexual orientation is only an issue if that person is upset about it.

There are therapists, both gay and straight, who specialize in treating gays and lesbians. They are particularly attuned to the issues homosexuals must deal with: coming out, keeping antigay hostility from becoming self-hatred, the complications of intimate relationships, dealing with unsupportive families, handling bias.

For lesbians who view their sexual stance as a political statement, a woman therapist is highly preferable; a feminist therapist is most appropriate. But for many lesbians and most gays the sex of the therapist is less important than his or her sensitivity and understanding of the issues that surround homosexuality.

If you are going into therapy because of issues that relate directly to homosexuality, then you should seek a therapist who specializes in the area. But if you are seeking therapy mainly for some other problem, then you should look for someone who is experienced in treating that problem, then screen him or her for attitudes toward gays or lesbians.

Older people. Many psychological issues come to the fore in life's later years. These include dealing with retirement and chronic illness, with the death of loved ones, and with a loss of income. For those who take many medications, the side effects or interactions can sometimes create psychiatric problems such as depression, apathy, or anxiety.

Even so, older people are often reluctant to seek help from a therapist. Many have the attitude that, at their age, it is too late to change or that they should be able to handle their problems on their own. But many emotional problems and issues, such as depression or adjusting to the death of a spouse, that would otherwise diminish the quality of your life can be dealt with readily in therapy.

In recent years the expertise and numbers of therapists specializing in the psychological problems of old age have surged. If you can, find such a "gerontologic" therapist.

In general, whether or not you go into therapy with a gerontologic specialist, you may find yourself more comfortable with a therapist who is older rather than younger. And if you are not with a specialist in gerontology, then you should try to find someone who has at least some experience in treating older people. Finally, be wary of any therapist who seems to be an "ageist," showing signs of bias or condescension toward the elderly.

Spiritual orientation. For people who have deeply felt religious beliefs, a therapist's attitude toward spirituality can be important. For example, Albert Ellis, founder of rational-emotive therapy, has been dismissive of religious belief as irrational thinking; some psychoanalytic thinkers, including Freud himself, have also viewed religious belief as more neurotic than healthy. If your religious outlook is relevant to the issues that you will address in therapy, then you should at the minimum be sure your therapist does not hold a bias against them.

For the deeply religious, seeing a therapist who holds the same set of beliefs can be helpful. There are, for instance, therapists who are explicitly Christian in their approach to therapy. The same is true for Orthodox Jews. "Transpersonal therapists" specialize in helping people of all beliefs deal with general spiritual issues in therapy.

A reminder. No matter what personal qualities the therapist you are considering has, and no matter how similar your backgrounds or orientations, the final and only judge of the match is you. If you don't feel good about a therapist, if you have real doubts about being comfortable enough to work together fruitfully, then this is probably not the therapist for you.

Remember, this is not a minor matter: studies show the match between client and therapist is the single most important factor in determining the success of therapy. Your relationship is the foundation for the therapist's approach to work. It is the medium in and through which therapy operates. If you and your therapist don't have good chemistry, there will be no positive reaction!

ASSESSING COMPATIBILITY IN GROUP THERAPY

Group therapy requires two assessments: how comfortable you feel with the therapist, and how comfortable you feel with the group. Your first impressions of the therapist will come when you meet to prepare for joining the group. But you should consider this provisional. Meeting with your therapist alone will be different from meeting in the group. Your therapist may seem different to you when you aren't the only other person in the room.

One quality to look for in a group therapist is the ability to make each member of the group feel important and respected as an individual who has something to contribute. So it is best to defer a final judgment until you have seen how the therapist actually treats you and other members in the group itself.

At the same time, though successful group therapy requires a particular set of technical skills from the therapist, it depends just as much on compatibility and a good match with the therapist as does individual therapy. So you will want to consider the same factors: personal chemistry, the therapist's qualities and characteristics, your own preferences, and how important a shared background and values are to you.

You also won't be able to tell how comfortable you feel in the group just from the therapist's description of it. So your final judgment will have to wait until you start actively participating.

Most groups allow a trial period so both you and the others in the group can see how things go. The trial period gives you a chance to see if this is the right group for your issues, and if you feel comfortable and fit in. The group will be interested in who you are and whether your being a member feels like a good match for the group.

Sometimes the therapist and the group may want a commitment from you before you actually join. If so, contract with the group and commit to a specific number of sessions—perhaps three or four—before making a final decision. If the group won't agree to this, reconsider joining.

ASSESSING COMPATIBILITY IN COUPLES OR FAMILY THERAPY

How can you judge compatibility if you are going into therapy as a couple or as an entire family? Couples or family therapy does present a different challenge. Each person will invariably have his or her preferences, and in all likelihood, you may not be able to find a therapist with whom everyone will feel equally comfortable. However, this isn't necessary to get started. As discussed in the previous chapter, it is common in couples or family therapy to consider the first meeting with the therapist a consultation, much as in individual therapy. If anyone has an extreme negative reaction to the therapist rather than to the idea of being in therapy, you should consider another therapist.

On the other hand, if you all more or less agree despite individual reservations, you can proceed by contracting for a limited number of sessions to start—six is common, but fewer is also acceptable. At the end of this time you pause and review how therapy has gone, with the option to recontract for another specified number of sessions if you all agree. This procedure builds in an ongoing assessment as part of the therapy and allows all the participants to feel they are not locked into a process with someone they may have initial reservations about.

ONE FINAL CAVEAT: AMBIVALENCE AGAIN

Remember, everyone has some ambivalence about going into therapy. For one, it means confronting difficult, often painful, things about yourself, and the need to depend on someone else for help. It also involves a perfectly normal ambivalence toward change—any kind of change that really matters and requires you to do things differently.

This ambivalence can color your assessment, taking the form of a negative impression of *any* therapist you consult. A convenient way to avoid confronting yourself and your problems is to convince yourself that no therapist is right for you. Or this ambivalence can take the form of being drawn to a therapist who will covertly collude with the side of you that doesn't want to face yourself. Such a therapist will help you create the illusion of change without the substance.

This kind of collusion is more a problem in a psychodynamic therapy than in more directive approaches such as behavior therapy. If you are seeking psychodynamic therapy, be wary if you find yourself immediately attracted to a therapist who seems charismatic, powerful, and seemingly all-knowing; or someone who seems to be "the" person you have been desperately seeking; or someone in whose presence you feel a warm glow that makes other relationships pale and other activities seem less important. These may be signs that you are being drawn to a therapist who will not help you confront the darker sides of yourself.

The angry, fearful, vulnerable, traumatized side of you probably sees such a therapist as someone who will do therapy for you or make it unnecessary. The bond with this seemingly very good and wonderful person is enough to make you feel differently about yourself, without having to look more closely or make any fundamental changes in your behavior. This kind of bond is often marked by a sense of immediate and overwhelming relief, along with grandiose expectations, extreme dependency on the therapist, and the idealized view that your therapist is "perfect."

ASSESSING COMPETENCE: WHAT TO CONSIDER

Even though the overall quality of the therapeutic relationship is the single most important predictor of a good outcome, therapy with the most trustworthy, understanding, and supportive therapist can *still* be undone by a lack of skill.

Assessing a therapist's competence is not easy. You are the best and only judge of their compatibility. But how can you judge a therapist's competence if you're not a professional yourself?

Of course, we form such opinions all the time—we have to. When we seek out a pediatrician for our child, for instance, or a lawyer or contractor, we try to make an informed choice, based in part on how competent we think they are. Criteria exist for making a similar judgment in choosing a therapist.

Your initial assessment of a therapist's competence will be provisional, of course. While you can get a fairly accurate impression of a therapist's personal qualities in one or two interviews, competence only fully reveals itself as the therapy progresses. Nevertheless, you need to be assured of at least some reliable level of competence at the start, provisional though your judgment must be.

In assessing your therapist's competence, look for:

The Therapist's Credentials

What are your therapist's education, professional degrees, and training? Check whether your therapist is licensed or certified by the state, and whether he or she has any advanced professional certification or special training in the specific therapy approach you will be using.

Credentials don't guarantee competence, but they are one place to start. We recommended as a rule that you start with licensed professionals because of the additional professional and legal safeguards licensing affords you (see Chapter 3, p. 74). You can also be certain of a certified level of professional training.

Refer back to Chapter 3, Step Three, page 92, for guidelines on assessing credentials.

Refer back to Chapter 3, Step One, page 72, if you are still uncertain what licensed professions are and what different credentials mean.

Chapter 3, page 80, also provides guidelines on what to look for in evaluating nonlicensed therapists.

Your Referral Sources

How did you learn of this therapist? Who recommended her to you?

A reliable referral source is the only real outside reassurance you have of competence. Referral sources vary widely in reliability, some trustworthy, others questionable, still others almost certainly unreliable. Weigh this reliability strongly in your assessment of a therapist's competence.

Refer back to Chapter 3, page 83, for guidelines on rating your referral sources.

The Therapist's Professional Affiliations

Is your therapist a member in good standing of the relevant national professional associations or their state chapters? Is he or she associated with a psychotherapy training institute, or a member of a psychotherapy society? Is your therapist on the staff or faculty of a medical school, a hospital, a mental health department, a clinic or agency?

Like credentials, professional affiliations do not testify directly to competence as a therapist. But they do provide some assurance against incompetence.

Refer back to Chapter 3, page 74, for information about professional affiliations.

The Therapist's Area of Specialization

Does this therapist have expertise or much experience in working with the problems or issues you are bringing to therapy? Is this an area in which he or she specializes? Is this therapist's approach appropriate to the problem?

You can ask your referral source, as well as asking your therapist directly. You can also ask if the therapist has had any specialized training in the area you need help with, or whether he or she is affiliated with an institute or clinic that specializes in treating this problem.

This factor is a little harder to assess than others, but you should weight it strongly.

In thinking about the appropriateness of the approach recommended, refer to Part II, the Therapy Guide, which offers information on the preferred approaches to most of the problems people bring to therapy.

How the Therapist Handled Your First Contact

Consider how your therapist (or the clinic or agency) handled your first contact. Whether by phone or in person, this was your first direct experience of your therapist's manner of interaction. How competently therapists handle this first contact already reveals a lot about the kind of therapist they would be, and the way they would conduct therapy. Weight this factor strongly.

Refer back to Chapter 3, page 98, for guidelines in assessing this first contact.

How the Therapist Handled the Consultation

As the first extended contact with the therapist, the consultation probably helps most in assessing compatibility. But it also enables you to make a number of judgments about competence. Weight this factor strongly.

Refer back to Chapter 4, page 116, for guidelines on assessing how the therapist handled the consultation.

MAKING A DECISION

By now you have all the information about your therapist you can reasonably expect to get at the outset. The rest will have to wait until after therapy has begun. Therapy itself is a process of ongoing learning, about yourself and your therapist. Implicitly or explicitly, you will continue to assess how things are going and whether therapy seems to be working or not (see Chapter 10, "Evaluating Therapy"). But now you need to make a decision. Though subject to review as therapy proceeds, this decision should be made with a firm sense of committing yourself to a person and a course of action.

What to Compare

In evaluating the information you have obtained, these are *the most important factors* to weigh. To evaluate a single therapist, check the "1" column if your answer is positive, the "2" if you are neutral or unsure, and the "3" if the answer is negative. To compare several therapists, rank each one first, second, or third for each factor in the following checklist.

THERAPIST _____

1   2   3

[ ] [ ] [ ]   *Referral Sources:* How reliable are the sources through which you were referred?

[ ]   [ ]   [ ]   *Personal Chemistry:* How good is the match?

[ ]   [ ]   [ ]   *Personal Qualities of the Therapist:* Does he or she have the qualities of a good therapist?

[ ]   [ ]   [ ]   *Shared Background or Values:* If this is important to you, is there a match?

[ ]   [ ]   [ ]   *Professional Competence and Skill:* Do they have solid credentials, training, and experience? Are they licensed or certified? How did they handle the first contact and the consultation?

[ ]   [ ]   [ ]   *Suitability of Format and Approach:* Is this right for your problems or issues?

[ ]   [ ]   [ ]   *Special Expertise:* Do you need help for a specialized problem? If so, does this therapist have special expertise in it?

[ ]   [ ]   [ ]   *Availability:* Can the therapist see you now, or will you have to wait longer than you want or can afford to?

[ ]   [ ]   [ ]   *Contractual Arrangements:* Can you afford the fee? Will therapy be covered by your insurance? When and how will you be expected to pay?

Ranking prospective therapists relative to each other on these grounds gives you a rough objective measure. But you can't make a final decision about a therapist simply by comparing their scores.

Therapy involves a working relationship with another person and so raises inevitable issues of trust, respect, compatibility, and confidence. You can't stand back from it and make a decision purely on "rational" or "objective" grounds. You have to be involved in the decision in a personal way; the decision demands an element of "feel" or intuition.

Think of it not so much as a decision as a *choice*. You are choosing someone to work with in a very personal way. Choice always involves a subjective, nonrational weighing of preferences. You can't arrive at such a choice simply by weighing pros and cons. If you have gathered the necessary information and considered it carefully, then rely on your inner feel and judgment to tip the balance. The only essential element of your choice is that it be yours.

IF YOU STILL HAVE SOME DOUBTS

Don't ever let yourself be pressured into starting with a therapist you have doubts about. If you are just not sure but feel good enough to start, an option is to defer a final decision until after three to six sessions. But you should make it clear to your therapist that this is what you are doing. Chapter 9 provides guidelines for making therapy work that may be particularly useful in giving yourself and the therapist the best chance. Chapter 10 provides additional guidelines for telling whether therapy is actually working once it is under way. "Your Working Relationship with Your Therapist" on page 230 is particularly useful for assessing your reactions to the therapist after several sessions, and whether this is likely to be a good match for you.

IF NONE OF YOUR OPTIONS SEEM RIGHT

If You Have Reservations About an Assigned Therapist

You may have been assigned the therapist you will be working with. This is likely if you went to a clinic or agency, belong to an HMO, or were restricted to specific providers by the terms of your insurance policy (see Chapter 3, p. 85). Even though whoever saw you for the initial intake interview (see Chapter 4, p. 112) may have tried to take your needs and preferences into account, you may find you have serious reservations after meeting with your assigned therapist.

If your reaction was mostly negative, or you have serious doubts about the therapist or the match, you should let the therapist know you think you would work better with someone else. Clinics and agencies don't like to reassign therapists as a rule, but most will usually try to accommodate you if they feel you are making a well-considered request.

The assigned therapist will probably want to discuss your reasons with you, however, before supporting a reassignment. This can be awkward, but you will find it easier if you stress the issue of compatibility rather than the therapist's competence.

Some clinics ask that you try one or two additional sessions before they are willing to switch you. Unless your reaction was decisively negative, you should probably go ahead with a few more sessions. The first meeting with an assigned therapist can often be skewed by feelings about being assigned to someone you haven't chosen, or even seen before. Your second impression may be different.

Some clinics have an unstated policy against transferring clients to another therapist. You still have the right to press your request for another therapist, perhaps with the head of the clinic. If you protest enough, you may get a change. If not, you can try to work out your problems with the therapist directly.

This usually isn't worth a protracted struggle, however, unless you have no choice. You are there to get help for yourself, not to struggle with someone who wasn't your choice in the first place. Discussing reservations and issues is one thing; trying to work through unambiguously negative feelings is another. It probably isn't wise to try. Therapy requires a net balance of positive feelings over negative ones, and you don't have that. In that case, it's best to look elsewhere if you can.

If None of the Therapists Seem Right

This does happen. Even if your referrals have been from reliable sources (see Chapter 3, p. 83), it is possible that you just won't match up well with any of the therapists you've consulted. They may be good therapists, but still not right for you. In that case, you have no alternative but to get more referrals and try again.

On the other hand, if no therapist ever seems quite right, the problem may not be with the therapists. Constant dissatisfaction or difficulty connecting suggests other influences may be at work. Your past experience of helping relationships may have been problematic, leaving a residue of wariness and mistrust, or perhaps a need for perfection, that is sabotaging the chemistry with each therapist.

Another possibility is that you are actually much more ambivalent about going into therapy than you are aware of. You may be finding reasons to dislike each therapist as a way of protecting yourself from facing your own ambivalent feelings. If ambivalence seems to be keeping you from getting off to a good start, review the reservations commonly stirred up when someone thinks about entering therapy: the conscious doubts and fears; the inner blocks to getting help; and inhibiting social and cultural factors (see Chapter 1, p. 46).

If you think any of these may be at work, a good option is to schedule another appointment with the therapist you had the fewest reservations about and discuss whatever you think may be holding you back. An alternative is to schedule a consultation with a new therapist, but this time discuss your reservations directly. In either case, you may find that exploring your reservations will help you to overcome them. If your conclusion is still that your hesitations are well-founded, then the next step is to go back and get additional referrals.

If You Have Little or No Choice

Clinics or agencies where a therapist is assigned to you are not the only situations in which your choices may be limited. Few therapists may live in your area, or few with the particular expertise you are seeking. Your financial resources may be limited. Your need for help may be so urgent that you don't have the time or energy to interview several therapists.

If the match is less than ideal, but you feel your only choice at this point is to continue, you can still take several steps. First and foremost, be straightforward in acknowledging your reservations with the therapist and try to discuss them. No therapist enjoys an unhappy, ineffective therapy, and any competent therapist will try to address your concerns. Second, keep the therapy brief and time-limited. Contract for a specific number of sessions or time, and decide later if you want to continue. Third, keep therapy focused on your immediate problems. Finally, if your situation changes or becomes less urgent, take the opportunity to find a therapist who is a better match.

REMEMBER, EVALUATION IS ONGOING

Once you make a decision about your therapist and start, evaluation of your therapy and your therapist doesn't stop. As you will see, you can—and need to—monitor how well you and your therapist are doing as you go along. You are not trapped by a therapist you chose. At the same time, you need to make a definite commitment to therapy and to your therapist at the start or you will get little from it.

CHAPTER SIX

■

CONTRACTING FOR THERAPY

Once you have decided on a therapist, the next step is to work out an explicit set of agreements in three major areas: the *goals* you will be working toward, the *methods* you will use, and the *contractual arrangements* for therapy. These should be discussed and agreed on *before* you start therapy, as the last thing you do in the consultation, or the first thing you do in your initial therapy session.

Discussing the terms of therapy before you become emotionally invested gives you a much better chance of coming to an agreement. Once therapy is under way and the therapist becomes "your" therapist, it becomes harder to negotiate basic terms. Discussing these terms before you start will also give you an idea of how well you and your therapist will be able to work out more substantive issues later on in therapy.

YOU ARE CONTRACTING FOR A PROFESSIONAL SERVICE

It may seem odd to have to be so formal about such a personal relationship. A lot of people rush into therapy—and a lot of therapists allow them to—just because the personal chemistry feels right. They assume everything else will then work out. Not so.

To this point we have stressed the personal side of therapy and the importance of a good match. But therapy is a professional relationship as well. As in other professional relationships, both parties will have certain *expectations* of each other, as well as certain *obligations*. In fact, no other relationship is such a strong blend of the personal and the professional. Most of our relationships tend to be one or the other, and we tend to think of them as mutually exclusive.

There is a great deal of pressure to focus only on the personal in therapy. We need this other person. We want a therapist to think well of us. We want to like them. Often the personal qualities, the way a therapist engages with us and makes us feel about ourselves, mean most to us, especially in confronting our vulnerabilities and perceived failures. Precisely because therapy *is not* impersonal, it can touch, move, mobilize, and change us.

But this is just the rub. Calling attention to the professional side of the relationship is often experienced as distasteful, painful, or personally embarrassing. Dealing with the business details seems to detract from the personal qualities of the relationship, as if a therapist cannot provide both a professional service and genuinely care about you at the same time. This feeling tends to resurface at critical junctures later on in therapy, often during times of difficulty or disappointment; or when your therapist seems unempathic; or when you may be feeling particularly vulnerable; or when issues of trust emerge.

Another reason why we often want to minimize or overlook the professional side of therapy is that we want this setting to be a protected and privileged place where the messy and overwhelming details of life—things like money and schedules and ground rules and contractual obligations—can be left at the door.

Still another source of reluctance to deal with the business side of the relationship may be a fear of committing ourselves to explicit goals or a course of action. Suppose we fail or don't measure up? If we don't make explicit commitments, we can avoid being held accountable. Paradoxically, we come to therapy to deal with what isn't working, but we somehow expect it to be the one place where ordinary rules and necessities don't apply.

Sometimes an opposite impulse is at work. We may try to avoid the personal side of the therapeutic relationship precisely by overfocusing on contractual details.

In any case, contracting for therapy involves recognizing that this will be a professional as well as a personal relationship, and that these don't have to be mutually exclusive, even though it might feel that way at the beginning. Contracting for therapy is an opportunity to begin bringing these disparate parts of our life together at the very start.

THE NEED FOR EXPLICIT AGREEMENTS

Why spell out these agreements? Because in a very real sense, you are contracting with your therapist for therapy. Your agreements may or may not take the form of a written contract (see p. 158), but the model of a contract in which you make your mutual expectations and obligations explicit is what you should have in mind.

Agreeing to an explicit plan on how you will proceed together stimulates confidence, sets goals against which to measure whether therapy is actually working, and ensures that both of you will be pulling in the same direction. An explicit set of understandings also protects the alliance between you as therapy proceeds. If you clarify how you are going to work together and toward what goals, there is less chance of the therapy ending in stalemate, misunderstanding, or disagreement.

An agreement also makes you mutually accountable to each other. It establishes the fact that a successful outcome will depend on both of you. This will help to balance the other inequalities you are bound to feel in the relationship as you start. It gives you a more active and responsible role from the outset by acknowledging that the goals and conditions of therapy have to be defined by both of you.

And if you need to change these goals or conditions later, this will also be easier. The principle has been established that this is a joint effort, and you will already have had the experience of working together to arrive at a mutually acceptable agreement.

In short, you shouldn't consider yourself "in therapy," or let the therapist talk as though therapy has begun, until you have worked out agreements in the following areas.

AGREEING ON GOALS

Clarifying your goals was one of the jobs of the consultation. Your therapist's ability to help you clarify what you wanted from therapy was presumably one of the reasons for your choice. Now you want to agree explicitly on what you will be trying to accomplish. This can be easy when you know exactly what it is that you want. But exactly what you want from therapy may not be all that obvious to you, and it may take the two of you some time to figure it out.

You may have your ideas about what you need while the therapist has others. You may have a specific, concrete goal in mind: for instance, you may simply want to stop being too shy to date. But you may find your therapist encouraging you toward a more encompassing goal, such as exploring your problems with intimacy and your tendency to avoid close relationships of all kinds.

Conversely, you may have broad and ambitious goals—changing parts of your character you don't like, or leading a more fulfilling life—and find your therapist encouraging you to focus on changing specific behaviors instead.

While the goals of therapy vary greatly from person to person, the most helpful goals have four characteristics:

- They are *clear,* framed in easy-to-understand terms: "I want to be able to talk with my spouse about what's upsetting me without blowing up every time." "I want this misery and hell of depression to end." "I want my kids to mind me." "I want to be able to ask my employer for a raise."
- They are *specific.* Enough so that you and your therapist can tell whether or not you are reaching them. "I want to stop avoiding a place where I was mugged and being frightened whenever I see someone who resembles my attacker." "I want to be able to talk in front of a group of people at work without my heart racing, my palms sweating, and my mind going blank." "I want to begin by not having a drink for one day/one week/one month" instead of "I want to recover from my attack" or "I want to stop drinking."
- They are *mutually understood* by you and your therapist. Don't settle for a formulation by your therapist that you don't really understand. Put it in your own words and make sure your therapist agrees.
- They are *realizable.* Your goals should be realistic: something you can reach in this kind of therapy, with this therapist. At the outset your therapist has an obligation to let you know if your goals seem unrealistic—either too broad and encompassing, or too restrictive and limited.

Once your goals are set, your therapist's professional responsibility is to work toward them. If your therapist disagrees with your goals at the beginning, and if you still can't agree after he or she explains why, then you don't have a contract for therapy and should not proceed further.

Goals can also change in the course of therapy. Some may prove unrealistic. Others may prove irrelevant to the problem or not what you really want. New ones may emerge. Since the basis of working together is mutual agreement on what you are working toward, either of you is free to raise the question of goals and suggest a fresh look. But whenever that occurs, modifying old goals or agreeing on new ones should still be done by explicit and mutual agreement between you. This is part of your ongoing contract with each other.

AGREEING ON METHODS

During the consultation, you and your therapist should already have talked about the methods he or she would use. *Methods* here means the basic framework of the therapy you will be doing:

- whether the format will be individual, group, couples, or family therapy
- what approach the therapist will take
- where you will meet
- how often you will meet

- how long each session will last
- how long therapy can be expected to take, or how many sessions you will agree to meet for

And if your therapist has made a recommendation for medication, psychological testing, or a complementary type of therapy or support group, now is the time to agree about how it will be done.

These *basic elements of every therapy* are discussed in detail at the beginning of the Therapy Guide in Part II (p. 310), and you should review them there. Specific recommendations for each kind of problem are included in the Guide itself. However, some of the issues to consider when contracting are:

Format. Is your therapist recommending individual, group, couples, or family therapy? Are the reasons for this choice clear to you? Do you agree? Or do you have reservations—either about the appropriateness of the format, or about your comfort with it? If the recommendation is couples or family therapy, will you be able to convince the other person or family members to come? If you decline a recommendation for group, couples, or family therapy, would the therapist agree to see you individually? Would this still accomplish your goals? If you will be doing individual therapy, will the therapist nevertheless want to include your spouse, or perhaps other family members, from time to time? How do you feel about that? Will the therapist want you to do another type of therapy in addition, either now or later?

Approach. The therapeutic approach or method you will be following is perhaps the single most important area to agree on explicitly. Your therapist probably won't be able to identify each individual technique or procedure he or she might use in advance, nor is this necessary. But you should have a fairly good idea of the overall approach your therapist intends to take, and what will be expected of you.

Is the therapist proposing a psychodynamic approach, where you focus on internal conflicts and the influence of past experiences? Or an approach based on identifying and modifying specific habits or patterns of thinking? Or on the ways you and other family members interact? Will it include the introduction of dramatic techniques or body work, or various methods of creative self-expression such as music, movement, or art?

Each of these approaches will mean a very different kind of experience in therapy. For more details on the differences between the main approaches, refer back to Chapter 2.

Setting. Where will you meet? Usually this will be the therapist's office, but it may not be, particularly if you are going to an agency or clinic, or if you will be doing group or family therapy. In any case, is this setting acceptable to you and reasonably convenient? Is there an alternative if it isn't?

Frequency. How frequently will you meet? This can vary greatly, depending on the format, the approach you are following, your goals in therapy, how distressed you are, and the pace you are comfortable with. The main point is that whatever frequency you agree to, you should understand the rationale for it, it should be appropriate to your goals, and it should be a pace that you can manage. See Chapter 14, p. 327, for guidelines.

If your therapist proposes some arrangement that departs from standard practice, do you understand the rationale for it? Do you agree with it? What will be the arrangement for an emergency? Will the therapist be available to meet with you outside the regularly scheduled time? If not, will they at least be available by phone?

If your therapist proposes meeting less frequently because of financial considerations, you should ask: will he or she really be able to help you as well if you have to meet less often? If that frequency is less often than the therapist thinks your problem warrants, then why is he or she willing to meet on that schedule? Will the therapist want to increase the frequency if you can afford it later?

Length of sessions. How long will you meet for each time? Normally the length is set in the beginning and remains the same throughout therapy. The standard is fifty minutes for individual and couples therapy; seventy-five to ninety minutes for group and family therapy (see Chapter 14, p. 328, for these guidelines). If the therapist suggests leaving sessions open-ended, insist on agreeing on a fixed length of time.

An emergency or crisis is another matter. You may need to meet for shorter but more frequent sessions. What will the arrangement be in this situation?

Duration. Your therapist won't be able to tell you exactly how long therapy will take because this depends on so many factors. Nevertheless, it is important to discuss duration, even though it can't be specified precisely. The important consideration is what you hope to accomplish. Therapists should be able to give you a general idea based on their past experience using their approach with people like yourself with similar issues. So instead of asking, "How long will therapy take?" ask, "How long do you think it will probably take for me to accomplish the goals I've set?" That expectation will help orient you for the work to come.

It is also a good practice to agree at the outset that you will periodically *pause and review* the therapy and possibly renegotiate the terms of your agreement. Taking an objective and critical look at how things are going and how you and your therapist are doing together gets harder the longer you work together. Contracting beforehand for a specific number of sessions, or for periodic reviews in the course of therapy, takes the burden off the two of you. Evaluating the therapy from time to time becomes a matter of course rather than a sign of dissatisfaction or a potential source of conflict. It also builds in a light at the end of the tunnel should you need it. See Chapter 14, page 328, for guidelines.

Additional Considerations

Medication. Is medication being considered? Even if it is not, you should have an explicit understanding with your therapist about medication regarding:

- Your therapist's stance toward medication: will he or she recommend you consider medication if it might be helpful? Some therapists will not recommend it under any circumstances, or very, very rarely, because they are opposed to using medication in combination with therapy. Under what conditions would your therapist be likely to suggest you consider it? If you request an evaluation for medication, will your therapist support it? If your therapist is generally opposed to medication, would he or she continue seeing you if you are on medication? Will it color your therapist's attitude toward you, or the approach taken?
- Your attitude toward medication: will you agree to be evaluated for medication if your therapist recommends it? Are you opposed to taking medication for any reason? If the outcome of an evaluation is a recommendation for medication, will you take it?
- The arrangements for getting an evaluation: does your therapist regularly work with a psychiatrist or psychopharmacologist you would see? Would your therapist agree to your seeing someone else?
- The arrangements for taking medication if it is recommended: what medication(s) will you be taking, and on what schedule? *Be sure you understand what you are agreeing to.* Your agreement to take medication should be based on an understanding of potential drawbacks as well as advantages. People's responses to a medication are highly individual. You can't predict in advance which medication, if any, will help you. You should know what the typical side effects are, and what to notify the medication doctor about if you start to experience any. (See Chapter 18, "If You Need Medication," for specifics of your medication.)

If you will be taking medication but it will be prescribed by someone other than your therapist, what will the arrangements be for coordinating care with the prescribing physician? How will your therapist and the prescribing physician share information? This will require your explicit consent, and you should give it to both of them. It is hard to imagine a situation in which it would be in your best interest to prevent them from keeping each other informed about your care. At the same time, the prescribing physician does not need to know the personal details of your therapy—only information, usually about current symptoms and mental status, that bears directly on the use and effectiveness of the medication.

Finally, do not agree to take any medication unless you understand completely what it will do for you, what to expect from it, and how and when you will know if it is working.

A physical examination. Does your therapist want you to see a physician for a medical checkup before beginning therapy? Some therapists suggest this routinely. It doesn't necessarily mean they think anything is wrong. They probably just want to be sure your difficulties are not related to any medical condition. If you are coming to therapy for help with a problem such as severe depression where specific symptoms are prominent, your therapist may recommend tests to eliminate a physical or neurological basis for your symptoms. Take these recommendations seriously, but also understand the reason for them before simply agreeing.

Psychological testing. Is your therapist recommending psychological testing? Again, before agreeing to this, you should understand the reason for the testing, and how this will aid in your therapy. Are the tests to clarify a diagnosis? Is the purpose to determine if there are underlying learning disabilities or problems in intellectual functioning? Is it to gain a better grasp of underlying personality dynamics and emotional patterns? Is it to gain a better idea of your vocational skills and aptitudes? You should discuss any concerns you have about being tested in these areas.

You should also agree in advance how you will be informed of the results, who will go over them with you, who they will be shared with, where the test materials will be kept, and how they will be kept confidential.

CONTRACTUAL ARRANGEMENTS: FEES, BILLING, AND PAYMENT

Money is a most uncomfortable topic for therapists and clients alike. Some therapists who don't like to talk about it act as if they couldn't possibly accept payment for helping someone in distress. Clients are often hesitant to bring up money with someone they are asking for help and can't afford to offend.

The best foundation for a therapeutic relationship is trust, and nothing builds trust faster than paying attention to the underpinnings of the relationship. One of these is what you will be paying and how you will be paying it. Your relationship with your therapist will be based in part on this financial understanding. So if your therapist doesn't bring up money, be sure you do. A clear agreement about the financial side of therapy can prevent or minimize misunderstandings later.

The fee. Ideally, you and your therapist have already discussed the fee during your consultation. If you haven't, you need to know in order to decide if it is reasonable and you can afford it. The fee is normally the figure the therapist charges per session. How affordable that fee is for you, however, may also be related to how often your therapist is proposing you meet. Can you assume a regular schedule for purposes of estimating how much therapy will cost? Raise the question to be sure.

Occasionally a therapist may suggest meeting less frequently if you can't afford the regular fee. As a general rule, how frequently you meet should be a therapeutic decision, not a financial one. There is no point in meeting every other week, say, instead of weekly, if that doesn't permit the degree of intensity or follow-through you need. You can make therapy affordable at the cost of not getting much out of it.

Some problems and issues lend themselves to less frequent meetings. If your therapist has recommended a particular frequency, then is willing to adjust this when he or she learns you can't afford it, at the very least you want to know why your therapist is willing to compromise the original recommendation. Don't be afraid to ask, and don't settle for a vague answer.

A therapist may also propose meeting on a particular schedule now, but with the option of meeting more frequently later if you can afford it. Again, ask why your therapist is willing to see you less frequently if he or she really thinks you need to be seen more often.

Sliding fee scales and reduced fees. Therapists will sometimes negotiate a reduced fee for clients who cannot afford their regular fee. This varies from therapist to therapist, but is always worth asking about if you think you have a legitimate case for requesting a reduced fee (see Chapter 7, "Paying for Therapy").

Many clinics also take your ability to pay into account, usually by adjusting fees according to different income levels.

Advertised discount fees and "bargains" are very different from reduced fees based on eligibility requirements, ability to pay, and a standardized sliding-fee scale. Any therapist who advertises these should be considered suspect.

Missed appointments. In addition to paying for a therapist's competence, you are also paying to reserve a specific time for you each week in his or her schedule. If you can't make the appointment, what will happen?

Therapists and clinics have different policies about this. Many therapists insist you are responsible for the time regardless, since you have leased the time whether you use it or not. Since extra clients aren't lined up for the same time—unlike many doctors' or dentists' offices, for instance—missing an appointment means that you are asking your therapist to take a loss. This policy is also meant to encourage you to take the appointment—and therapy—seriously as an ongoing commitment.

Other therapists and clinics will allow you to cancel a session without payment if you have a legitimate reason and notify them sufficiently in advance. Some therapists will bill for all or part of a missed session, even with advanced notice, unless they are able to fill that particular hour—perhaps with a consultation or a rescheduled meeting with another client.

The important issues to resolve are:

- Will you be billed for all missed sessions?
- Will you be billed for unavoidable absences due to sickness, accident, or other emergencies?
- Will you be billed for absences that are your choice, such as vacations?
- If you will be billed for all missed sessions, will your therapist offer makeup sessions or agree to reschedule a session you can't make?
- If you will be allowed to cancel sessions under certain conditions, how much advanced notice will your therapist want?

In general, private therapists are less rigid now than in the past about automatically charging for missed appointments. Expect clinics to have less flexibility, however, since they have to adhere more closely to standard policies and since the budget of a clinic depends upon consistent reimbursement.

A legitimate case can be made for charging for missed appointments. However, if the therapist doesn't offer to schedule makeup sessions, and doesn't consider why you needed to cancel, you may want to check his or her overall attitude and approach for signs of rigidity or insensitivity to your individual needs.

Billing and payment schedule. When does your therapist want to be paid—at the end of each session? Weekly? Monthly? Quarterly?

The most common arrangement in private practice is for clients to be billed at the end of each month, and for the bill to be paid before the end of the next month. Many private therapists and most clinics, however, will request payment at the time of each session: clinics before the session, and private therapists at the end of the hour. For clinics and therapists, this is simply easier in most cases and ensures they will get paid. Experience shows that people typically pay doctors and therapists last, after all their other bills have been paid, and sometimes not at all. Many therapists also feel that clients benefit more if they are paying for therapy as they are engaged in it.

Therapy is a significant expense, even at a reduced fee, and there are good reasons not to run up a big bill. A large debt between you and your therapist can burden the relationship and create feelings in both of you that will probably tinge your work together.

For you, getting behind in paying the bill can turn therapy into one more problem you don't need—instead of a way of getting help for the problems you brought to it. Feelings about an accumulating bill also tend to escalate: you may start by feeling somewhat guilty, then resentful that therapy is just adding to your feelings of being burdened or inadequate. Next, you find yourself missing appointments. As the bill grows still larger, you may begin to question whether therapy is really worth it, and finally, whether you're really obligated to pay the bill at all since you've gotten so little out of it. Since therapy is often difficult and the results can be slow in coming, getting into debt can undermine the commitment it takes to stick with it and make it work.

For a therapist, not getting paid produces the same feelings you would expect in anyone else: frustration, mistrust, resentment, and finally anger—much of which many therapists will try to conceal since they aren't supposed to get angry at their clients. A growing debt threatens therapy from the therapist's end as well. At some point a therapist will have to decide whether to continue to see you without hope of getting paid or whether to stop. Therapists often side with their clients' difficulties and overlook the business and professional side of their work. Too many will simply continue to see their clients—but with covert resentment and diminished commitment that will eventually result in unproductive therapy.

If you are entering a longer-term or open-ended therapy, you can also probably expect the cost of services to rise slightly each year as in other professions (see p. 164). You should ask at the outset if this is your therapist's practice. Ask how long the current fee will be in effect and how much it is likely to increase over time.

Third-party payment. If you both have health insurance or a similar form of coverage, you and your therapist will need to arrange for third-party payment. If your therapist is already a designated provider for your insurance company or health plan, should he or she bill them directly, or bill you and you then apply for reimbursement? What percentage of the fee will be covered—most plans don't reimburse 100 percent— or up to what total dollar amount per calendar year? How will you be billed for the remainder? Who fills out the insurance forms? Do you each fill out part? Who will send them in?

If your therapist isn't already a provider, is he or she eligible to become one? If so, will your therapist agree to apply for provider status so you can use your insurance?

If your therapist is not eligible to become a provider for your particular plan (usually this is because either your therapist is not a licensed professional, or the plan restricts you to approved therapists), can you afford to see him or her anyway?

Who gets the bill. If you are being billed privately, you may not want the bill sent to your home or your office. If your insurance company is reimbursing the therapist directly, you should know who will know that you are seeing a therapist and what kind of information will be included on the form you or the therapist fills out. These arrangements affect confidentiality and can have a lot to do with how secure you will feel in therapy (see Chapter 7, "Paying for Therapy").

THE APPOINTMENT SCHEDULE

Lateness, absence, and rescheduling. Life is often unpredictable. Your car doesn't start, the baby-sitter is late, or there's an emergency at work. The issue here is not money but time. If you are unavoidably late, will your appointment still end at the usual time? Most often the answer is yes because your therapist has someone scheduled after you. But if not, will your therapist agree to extend the session?

What are acceptable reasons for being late? What not?

If you have to miss a session, will your therapist try to reschedule it? Under what conditions would he or she agree to reschedule? How much advanced notice will he require?

Vacations. You need explicit understandings on your therapist's policy toward clients' vacations. Will your therapist expect you to discuss the timing of these before you make your plans, or will he or she simply expect to be notified sufficiently in advance? Will you be charged for appointments missed while on vacation?

You also need to ask about your therapist's usual vacation arrangements so you can plan accordingly. When does he or she usually take vacation time? This may or may not fit well with your schedule, particularly if this is to be a short-term or time-limited therapy and your therapist is likely to be gone in the middle of it. If you are entering a longer-term or open-ended therapy, how many weeks vacation does your therapist usually take a year, and how long is he or she usually away at any one time? This may be longer than you want to go without regular meetings.

Will you be able to reach your therapist during vacations in an emergency? Or will another therapist "cover" while your therapist is gone? Will this be someone you can meet with, or someone available only by phone?

CONFIDENTIALITY

Therapists are ethically bound to keep everything that takes place in therapy confidential (see Chapter 11, "Professional Ethics"). Nonlicensed therapists are not bound by state licensing laws and the codes of ethics that bind members of the national professional associations, but they would generally consider themselves equally bound to keep what you tell them in confidence. In only a few, very specific situations—mostly where your own or someone else's safety is at stake—is confidentiality superseded by a law requiring therapists to report information. The therapist should inform you at the start about these occasions. If your therapist does not, you should ask about them so you both have the same understanding.

Apart from these specific and relatively rare situations, *a therapist should not provide any information about you, written or verbal, under any circumstances, to anyone without your informed and written consent.* Nevertheless, violations do occur, and confidentiality can't simply be taken for granted. It is best to spell out explicit guarantees as part of your agreement, including:

- Does your therapist agree to get your signed consent to release any information about you to anyone? (See page 258 for what should go into a release-of-information form.) Will your therapist also agree to show you what is sent before it goes out? Most therapists will not send anything without your authorization, but many may not want to show you what they are sending.

  Rationalizations for this abound. They may say you won't understand the material properly. It is their job to help you understand it. They may say they are afraid it will be "harmful" to you to see it, or that you aren't "ready" to handle it. That not only reflects arrogance and condescension on their part, but should be a cause for alarm on yours.
- Will your therapist be presenting work with you to a supervisor? If you know your therapist is in training, you can take this for granted. However, even experienced therapists seek supervision and consultation on their cases from time to time. This sound and time-honored practice should work to your benefit. But you have a right to know with whom your therapist will be discussing your therapy, and how your confidentiality will be protected.
- Therapists sometimes present aspects of work with clients at case conferences or professional meetings, or in journal articles or books. This is good professional practice, advances the field, and is a way of getting feedback. If your therapist wants to present some of your work together, will he or she discuss this with you ahead of time and go ahead only with your permission? How will they protect your anonymity? It is up to you to decide whether any material about you should be presented, and what details should be left out to protect your identity.
- At hospitals, clinics, and training institutes, clients are sometimes asked to allow consultants to interview them in a case conference or seminar where other staff members and trainees can hear the case. Those attending will usually be invited to ask you brief questions as well, and of course they will be able to observe your reactions.

  These conferences serve important teaching and training functions, and your therapist does get the benefit of expert opinion. However, you are under no obligation to participate, and you should never allow yourself to be pressured into taking part. You may want to ask your therapist if he or she foresees your ever being asked to participate in such a conference. Will your therapist respect your feelings if you decline? If you agree, how would you prepare for it together, and how would you handle any repercussions in the therapy afterward?
- Does the therapist ever tape-record sessions? Taping requires your informed and written consent. Taping sessions without your knowledge should never be tolerated and is a gross violation of your right to privacy and confidentiality.

- Will your therapist be taking notes during or after sessions? This is a fairly common practice for recording therapy. Notes are also used to review therapy sessions with a supervisor. In either case, the therapist must inform you and obtain your consent.
- Who has access to your file? This is a particularly important question if you are going to an agency or clinic, but it should be clarified with a private therapist as well.

THE THERAPIST'S AVAILABILITY

Clinics vs. private practice. If you are seeing a therapist in private practice, the odds are good that you can count on he or she being available to you for therapy for as long as you need, barring some unforeseen disruption in his or her personal or professional life. In clinics, community mental health centers, and training institutes, however, some therapists may stay for only one or two years until they have met training or licensing requirements, or until they move on into other positions or into private practice. If you are seeing a staff therapist, or a therapist in training, you may want to ask how long he or she intends to remain at the clinic.

In short-term therapy, this is usually not an issue, unless it is a clinic or an HMO where you will be returning periodically for care and would like to return to someone who knows you. If the therapist will be leaving, he or she may be able to take you into his or her private practice, though usually at a higher fee. However, therapists are often contractually bound not to take clients with them if they leave.

Outside professional commitments. Therapists often teach, consult, write, lecture, do hospital work, sit on committees of their professional organizations, or hold other professional positions. They may occasionally have to interrupt their regularly scheduled appointments because of these commitments. If this isn't acceptable to you, this is the time to ask how often they expect to have to cancel sessions for this reason. If it is acceptable, the therapist should still keep these interruptions to a minimum. If your therapist has to cancel, will he or she try to reschedule the appointment?

Emergencies. A therapist has a professional responsibility to be available to you in emergencies. Most therapists will take this for granted, so much so that it should be a red flag if your therapist says his or her policy is to be available only during regularly scheduled meeting times.

But what constitutes a crisis or emergency may not always be clear. What may feel like a crisis to you may not seem as urgent to your therapist. Conversely, what you may tend to downplay or minimize your therapist may feel should be taken quite seriously. You should agree on what kinds of situations will be considered crises or emergencies by both of you. And you should agree on whether your therapist will be available in person or just by phone.

If you should be unable to reach your therapist, what is your next line of help? This may be a person on call at a clinic or the emergency room of a nearby hospital. If your therapist is out of town, can you contact him or her somehow, or will you be given the name of a colleague?

Phone calls. A sometimes sensitive and touchy issue is the matter of phone calls between sessions. Standing arrangements can vary widely. Some therapists feel that phone calls should be limited to saying you will be late or need to cancel, feeling that the phone is not an appropriate way to work out problems. In a crisis, others will use the phone as an extension of therapy or in place of a meeting if it can't wait. Still others might build in scheduled phone contacts between sessions as part of the therapy itself, depending on the approach, the format, and the issues you are working on—or schedule phone sessions.

The important thing is to have a clear agreement about phone contact in advance: will your therapist take phone calls from you between sessions? If so, under what circumstances? When can you call—anytime, or only during certain hours? At what number? Are you likely to get your therapist, an answering machine, or an answering service? How often does your therapist check for calls, and how long might it be before you can expect a call back? Suppose something comes up that you feel can't wait until the next session?

Extra sessions. Will your therapist schedule extra sessions if you request them? If so, under what circumstances? Because of the importance of keeping to a secure and predictable frame for therapy, therapists will only rarely schedule an extra session simply at your request. But circumstances may warrant one.

Third-party evaluations. Clients sometimes want or expect a number of additional services from therapists that go beyond meeting for therapy, such as third-party evaluations. Some therapists will respond to these requests; many won't. It is important to know from the beginning what your therapist will and won't do for you outside therapy.

If it is relevant, you might ask if your therapist will do an evaluation of you for a third party if you request it. For instance, clients sometimes ask therapists to substantiate a disability or insurance claim; to determine parental fitness in a child custody case; to support certification for a license; or to provide expert testimony in a lawsuit or legal case.

Clinics, insurance companies, and health plans also vary: this is sometimes a covered benefit, sometimes not, in which case you will have to pay for it yourself and may have to go to someone else to get it.

Intercessions on your behalf. Clients also occasionally ask therapists to intercede on their behalf with family, friends, or employers. Most therapists will be reluctant to do this. They will want to protect the boundaries of the therapy and not become entangled in the problems you are coming to therapy to sort out. For example, they won't see it as their role to try to persuade your spouse to come to therapy, to convince another family member to get help, or to ask your employer to modify your workload or excuse an absence.

Their appropriate professional role is to help you help yourself with these kinds of problems. An exception is supportive therapy with severely disadvantaged or disabled clients who may need someone to advocate actively for them.

Arranging a hospitalization. Clients occasionally ask their therapists to arrange a hospitalization for a family member or friend they think needs help. No therapist will—or should—assist in hospitalizing someone on your say-so, or anyone they haven't seen and evaluated personally. Even if the person agreed to be evaluated, many therapists will not want to do this themselves in order to safeguard the boundaries of your therapeutic relationship. What they should agree to do is advise you how best to get help and refer you to someone who can provide it if the person consents to an evaluation.

The one exception to this is a life-threatening situation. If they are authorized by their state to hospitalize people against their will when their safety or the safety of others is clearly at stake, they may agree to arrange an involuntary hospitalization without seeing the person, but usually only if they are requested to do so by a colleague whose professional judgment they trust and who has personally evaluated the person. Otherwise, they should at least advise you how to get immediate help.

Only psychiatrists are empowered in all states to authorize involuntary hospitalizations directly. A number of states now grant state-licensed psychologists this authority also. But involuntary commitment is a legal procedure carefully regulated by state statute. No therapist, not even a psychiatrist, has the power simply to call up and have someone committed (see Chapter 11, "Professional Ethics," p. 269). In an emergency, your therapist will probably recommend bringing the person to the nearest medical or psychiatric hospital emergency room as the quickest and safest way to get help.

ARRANGEMENTS FOR ENDING THERAPY

It may sound strange, but you and your therapist should agree on how and why you will end therapy even as you start it. On your side, you should have the right to end therapy if you feel that it isn't working after a fair trial. Your obligation in this case is to inform your therapist in advance and to discuss the reasons for your dissatisfaction.

Does the therapist have the same right? This is more complicated because the therapist's obligation to you is different. In cases where the therapist feels (1) that you aren't engaged or working in therapy, or (2) that therapy has reached an impasse that the two of you haven't been able to resolve, your therapist has an obligation to bring this up and discuss it with you. In these two situations, however, if you still want to continue, your therapist is obliged to give you a reasonable length of time to engage in therapy or to work through the impasse together.

In other situations the therapist is professionally and ethically obligated to terminate therapy whatever your wishes. This is the case whenever a therapist genuinely feels that (1) the problems you are presenting can't or won't be resolved through therapy and some other method is more appropriate; (2) he or she isn't the right therapist for you; (3) the format or the approach is wrong, and your therapist is not competent in the format or approach you need; or (4) your therapist feels he or she has given you all the help he or she can at this time.

What happens if you don't agree? How will the two of you agree to handle this situation? You have the right to ask him or her to continue for a while longer to test their judgment. But you also may not want to continue working with someone who has lost confidence in the effectiveness of what you are doing together.

Of course therapists also have the professional right to terminate your agreement if you aren't living up to your contractual obligations: if you are regularly missing appointments without reasonable cause or notice or are not paying your bills on time or at all. They also have an ethical obligation not to allow you to run up a large debt you can't afford. Rather than terminating, they may suggest suspending work together until you catch up.

Therapists should never use a threat of termination as a way of pressuring you to agree with them or to some new arrangement. A good therapist will not threaten you in this way in any case, but an agreement about duration will provide added reassurance and protection. If it should still happen, terminate the relationship yourself.

A coercive therapy is positively harmful, and worse than no therapy at all.

ADDITIONAL GROUND RULES FOR GROUP, COUPLES, AND FAMILY THERAPY

The therapy agreement in couples, group, and family therapy becomes a bit more complicated, taking into account the needs of everyone participating.

Confidentiality in multiperson therapy. Confidentiality is harder to enforce and protect in couples, group, and family therapy. Information shared with many people is not protected in the same way it is in a client-therapist relationship. Usually this isn't a problem, but it's important to have an explicit agreement among all the participants that whatever is said and done in therapy remains confidential.

In couples and family therapy, this ground rule should be discussed and agreed to by everyone at the very start.

In group therapy, you should discuss it with the therapist before joining the group and review it with the group upon joining. Each time a new member joins, the entire group should explicitly recontract with each other for confidentiality along with the group's other ground rules.

Beginning and leaving group therapy. Many group therapists will typically want you to meet with them for several sessions individually in advance of your joining the group. In these sessions you will talk about any prior experience you may have had of groups, any anxieties you may have about participating in a group, the way the group operates and what to expect, and its ground rules.

Because others will be involved as well, and because each member of the group will depend on every other member, the ground rules about entering and leaving the group are different from individual therapy. You may be required to attend a certain number of sessions as a trial period at the start before acceptance as a permanent member of the group. You may also have to give longer notice when you intend to leave so others will have the chance to discuss your leaving and say good-bye.

Socializing outside group therapy sessions. An important ground rule in group psychotherapy is that members not socialize outside group sessions. If you are in a group, you naturally feel closer to some members than to others and are inevitably pulled to strike up friendships or get together with people who are sharing a deeply personal and intense experience with you.

But social contacts outside the group, however well-intentioned, always have divisive consequences. They lead to pairs, cliques, or coalitions invariably undermining the group process, either by doing the work of the group outside sessions, or using the process toward their own ends during sessions. They also lead to private communications and secrets being kept from the therapist and other group members.

Sexual involvement between group members is *always* damaging and harmful, both to the individuals and the group. A group can stir up intense feelings between members, including sexual attraction or romantic feelings. Because of this, the group needs to remain a safe, protected place where these feelings can be approached and worked through without the members being afraid they will be acted on. One of the benefits of group therapy is learning that you and others can have a wide range of feelings that can be discussed without threatening anyone. Even feelings of sexual attraction can be talked about if it is clear that not acting on these feelings is a ground rule of the group.

Acting on them, on the other hand, is invariably experienced by those within the group as a form of incest. Often the two members will experience it this way as well. It is the same kind of boundary violation as sexual intimacy in individual psychotherapy (see Chapter 11, p. 248).

Some group therapists take the position that social contacts are permissible as long as any issues they bring up are talked over in the group. Others believe, usually somewhat naively, that what the support group members can get from each other outweighs the potential complications. You should be wary of any therapist or psychotherapy group that does not have a ground rule against socializing outside the group, particularly in a psychodynamic therapy.

Self-help groups, on the other hand, because they have a different purpose, often encourage social contacts outside regularly scheduled meetings. Your meeting people and forming new relationships with others who have shared similar experiences is part of their explicit intent.

NEGOTIATING CHANGES IN THE AGREEMENT

Both your goals and methods can change in the course of therapy, particularly in long-term therapy. Your original goals may prove too broad or ambitious, or conversely, you may discover that you are capable of more than you thought you were. A change in goals can also lead to a change in approach.

Your initial arrangements for therapy may also need to be renegotiated, for example, if your income substantially decreases. You may incur additional medical or college or family expenses and no longer be able to afford the fee. You may change jobs and not be able to meet at the same time or as regularly as before. Your therapist may take on other work or a new position and not be as available as before.

Having a mutual agreement at the start of therapy does not mean you are stuck with it if circumstances change. You can always amend your agreements. Having a clear set of agreements to start with helps make clear exactly what may need to be renegotiated. Your experience negotiating the original set of agreements with your therapist will make it that much easier to negotiate any subsequent changes.

RENEWING THE CONTRACT

A standard practice in family therapy, contract reviewing, has been slow to take root in individual therapy. However, it is just as applicable there, especially in long-term or open-ended therapy.

Instead of simply entering into an open-ended agreement for therapy with a therapist—assuming your benefits aren't limited by the terms of your insurance coverage—work together for a specific amount of time to start with. You can discuss what that length of time should be in view of your goals. At the end of that time, the two of you will agree to review the course of the therapy to date.

Building in review ahead of time removes the suggestion of criticism from either side. It will make it easier to take a more objective look at how things have been going. Are your goals still the same and are you making progress toward them? Do the format and approach still seem right? What has proven helpful and what not? Are there any problems with any of the contractual agreements?

This will also be a chance for your therapist to share his or her perspective with you. Some therapists, often more traditionally trained psychodynamic therapists, may be reluctant to give you their opinion about how they think things are going, psychoanalysts in particular. Don't expect an analyst to say too much, but even they have a professional obligation to review your progress with you if you ask them to.

Therapists are occasionally reluctant to agree to a periodic review because they don't feel comfortable having their work subject to critical scrutiny and may be anxious about what you might say. Therapy is different from other professions in that the person can't be so easily separated from the work. Because therapy depends on a personal relationship and requires the therapist to use him- or herself in a direct way, reviewing the therapy means reviewing the relationship and the therapist.

Nevertheless, you wouldn't agree to contract with a professional in another line of work who wasn't willing to have his or her work examined. Therapy is no different, even though it is more personal. All licensed therapists have had their work looked at in detail by supervisors during their training. Many still present it for supervision and consultation. The profession requires this, and therapists should be willing and able to review their work with the person who has contracted for their services.

Part of an agreement for a periodic review is an option to recontract or renew the agreement for another specified period of time. The final arbiter of how things are going is you. If you are getting what you want out of therapy and want to continue, then the conclusion of the review is a renewal of your agreements together until the next periodic review.

DO YOU NEED A WRITTEN CONTRACT?

Most contracts between clients and therapists are oral agreements. Lately, however, the idea of a formal written contract has been gaining some support, particularly from consumer advocacy groups. Most therapists, particularly psychiatrists, tend to resist the idea of a formal written contract, probably because it runs counter to the traditional hierarchical relationship between doctor and patient that puts the power and authority in the doctor's hands.

Some therapists view formal contracts as placing arbitrary limits on the therapy. Though they may not admit it, many also object because they are afraid it will make them more vulnerable to malpractice suits—a misreading of the purpose. A more valid and perhaps understandable objection is the feeling that written contracts are somewhat unnatural when mutual trust is the basis of the therapeutic relationship.

The main issue is not whether the contract is formal or informal, verbal or written. The point is that the obligations and expectations you both have of each other should be *explicit* and *mutually agreed* to.

IN SUMMARY

The main points you and your therapist should review and agree on before you begin include:

- clear, specific, and explicit goals for therapy and ways to reassess those goals as you go on
- the format you will use
- the approach you will take
- where, when, and how often you will meet
- the length of each session
- how long you can expect therapy to take
- arrangements for periodically reviewing how therapy is going
- whether medication will be recommended, and arrangements for coordinating medication with psychotherapy
- fees and how they will be paid
- policy on canceled sessions or missed appointments
- ground rules for contacting your therapist outside sessions if necessary, especially in emergencies

CHAPTER SEVEN

PAYING FOR THERAPY

THINKING AND TALKING ABOUT MONEY

Unless your income is high, money will probably be a factor in your choice of a therapist. Because you have to consider not only the therapist's basic fee, but also how long therapy might take, financial considerations may also affect where you go for therapy, and indirectly, what kind of therapy you do. Private psychotherapy can be expensive. Even a reduced fee or a lower fee at an agency or clinic can add up to a significant expense over time. With insurance, you will still probably have to pay a portion of the cost. Because psychotherapy represents a significant investment, you should consider its cost and your own financial resources carefully.

Yet thinking about money in connection with psychotherapy tends to be difficult. Money can be one of the more uncomfortable topics to broach with a therapist. For many people, it is even more difficult to talk about than sex. Before getting into the nuts and bolts of how therapy fees are set, what you can expect to pay, and how costs are covered in different settings, it is worth looking at what makes money so difficult to talk about, and some of the emotional issues you may have to deal with along the way.

Just thinking about money is fraught with symbolic meaning. You may equate spending it on someone else with how much you care about them, for instance. Having money can also affect whether you feel in control of your life or dependent on someone else. If you are like most people, your ability to earn and manage money probably has a lot to do with how you feel about yourself as an adult: how competent, how independent, how grown up.

Powerful inner taboos exist against *talking* too openly about personal finances.

Fellow employees, for instance, rarely talk about their salaries. It is considered bad form to talk about your net worth at a social gathering. These internal inhibitions usually derive from certain deep-seated fears. We often feel that we will lose what we've gained, or have it taken away from us, if we let others know what we have. Hiding the details of our financial worth insures its safekeeping.

Another kind of internal prohibition stems from wanting to be respected for our financial accomplishments, but at the same time feeling afraid these will expose us to envy or disapproval, or to being seen as ambitious, greedy, or not generous enough with what we have.

Feelings about holding on to money, spending it, or losing it are often intimately related to worries about whether we have what we need, whether we are as capable as we need to be, and whether the world around us is a safe or threatening place. They are also related to concerns about whether we are loved, feel good about ourselves, and have the ability to take care of ourselves.

Such fears may be realistic, irrational, or superstitious, but they are usually operating in the background as you try to deal with money in therapy.

Beyond these general meanings of money, additional, unique pressures are at work in therapy that make talking about money even more difficult. Bringing up money in the context of the deeply personal issues that are discussed in therapy can feel inappropriate. It can reinforce feelings of being vulnerable, dependent, or unable to solve problems on your own. You may feel embarrassed to have to pay someone to help you with problems other people seem to be managing by themselves. It can also feel dangerous to bring up something that will risk alienating the very person you need help from and want to like you.

From their side, therapists are not only subject to the same internal fears and inhibitions as everyone else, they are also subject to unique pressures from the therapeutic situation. Many see themselves, for instance, as healers whose main concern is their clients' well-being. This can make them feel conflicted over charging anything more than a minimal fee for their services, or even charging anything at all: how can they make a living from someone else's emotional suffering?

Feelings about money can continue to be sticky and troublesome long after a fee is agreed upon. If, for instance, your therapist agreed to a reduced fee because you couldn't afford the regular fee, you can feel embarrassed. It can also reinforce any feelings you may have of being incompetent, or raise doubts in your mind about how committed your therapist will be to working with someone who isn't paying the full fee. You might find yourself feeling guilty about spending any extra money on yourself or concealing personal spending from your therapist.

If therapists feel guilty about their fee, or about having to charge for their services at all, they typically try to compensate in any of several ways: by working extra hard, being too available or too accommodating, not confronting you when you need to be, giving in to your wishes and demands, or allowing the boundaries of therapy to become blurred. And if your resentment lingers, you may accept all this as just compensation for the inequalities and indignities you experience in the relationship: someone is benefiting from your suffering by accepting a fee.

No therapy is free—emotionally or financially. This frustrates one of our deepest fantasies about getting perfect and unconditional care. These fantasies often crystallize around the issue of money, making it one of the most difficult things to talk about. Nevertheless, you will need to do it. If you avoid it, it can be the source of endless resentments and entanglements. On the other hand, it can be the occasion to begin working through some of the important issues related to getting and accepting help—which usually turn out to be related to the problems you are bringing to therapy in the first place.

HOW THERAPY FEES ARE SET

The Standard Fee

Most therapists and clinics have a standard fee per session. This is typically based on the so-called psychotherapy "hour," which may last anywhere from forty-five to sixty minutes, depending on the therapist. Fifty minutes is now the general norm for individual sessions. The fee for a shorter or longer session is usually prorated on that basis.

Factors affecting the fee. The fee per session also varies according to the *format* of the therapy. In general, the standard fee for family therapy is slightly higher than for individual therapy. In part, this is because more people are involved and the demands on the therapist are different. Also, family sessions typically last longer—usually an hour and a quarter or an hour and a half, depending on the therapist. The standard fee for group therapy is often half that of individual therapy, or even less, because of the number of people participating, even though, like family therapy, group sessions are typically longer.

The *professional discipline* of the therapist also affects the fee. This is particularly true in individual therapy, though these differences are slowly narrowing. Rightly or wrongly, a definite hierarchy exists among the professions when it comes to fees. In general, expect psychiatrists to charge the most, followed by psychologists, clinical social workers, and psychiatric nurses. Marriage and family therapists' fees tend to be the next lowest per hour, though the couples and family format lends itself to a higher absolute fee per session. As a discipline, pastoral counselors tend to charge the least, in part because of the church settings in which they work. The fees of nonprofessional therapists, who are not state licensed or certified, vary widely.

There is no inherent reason why the discipline of the therapist should make such a difference in the therapy fee. There are some differences in training (see Chapter 3, p. 74), but the major differences have to do with what distinguishes each profession, not with training as a therapist. Psychiatrists, for instance, who generally charge most, often receive less training and supervision in psychotherapy than those in other disciplines. Therapy may only be a subordinate part of a residency curriculum that emphasizes symptom-based diagnosis, neurology, biochemistry, and psychopharmacological treatment. Psychologists as a rule receive the most formal training and supervision in psychotherapy, if they have graduated from a doctoral program in clinical psychology that included a one-year internship. But their fees are traditionally lower than psychiatrists'. And some insurance plans will reimburse outpatient psychotherapy only if it is done by a psychiatrist.

All of this makes little sense. It reflects the relative social status and political power of the different professions in our society more than it does their relative competence as psychotherapists. In some cases, it also reflects the salary hierarchies among the professions in institutional settings. If the mental health clinic or agency is based on the medical model, the highest salaries will go to physicians, even though the medical model has little application to the discipline of psychotherapy. Just as a therapist's profession is no guarantee of competence as a therapist, neither is a therapist's fee.

Another variable affecting the fee, as in any profession, is the *experience and expertise* of the therapist. If you see a staff therapist in a clinic or agency, this usually won't be a factor. You or your insurance company will be charged a set fee, no matter whom you see. If you see a therapist in private practice, however, the more experienced, the more likely the fee will be higher. A therapist with expertise in some speciality may also charge higher fees, regardless of his or her discipline. Conversely, if you see a therapist in training at a psychotherapy institute (see Chapter 3, p. 86), you will usually be offered a reduced fee.

The *setting* in which you see a therapist is one of the major determinants of how much you will pay. In general, a private therapist's fee will be significantly higher than the fee a clinic or agency will charge for one of their staff therapists.

Where you live will also affect fees. Fees tend to be slightly higher in the South, the East, and West than in the Midwest. In a 1991 survey of psychologists, social workers, and marriage and family counselors, for example, median fees were $75 in the Midwest, and about $5 higher everywhere else. Fees tend to be highest in large cities and suburbs, close to the median in smaller cities and small towns, and lowest in rural areas. Indeed, therapy fees vary fairly directly with the cost of living in a given area.

Regardless of format, profession, experience, expertise, or region, individual therapists vary much more than you might think in what they charge, from well under $50 to well over $100 per session. It definitely pays to shop around. In most parts of the country, the situation is increasingly competitive for therapists, and like other professionals, they have to adjust their fees accordingly.

A final word of caution. Inexperienced therapists getting started may try to give the impression they are well established by charging a midrange fee, while a highly seasoned but less ambitious therapist may charge the same. A therapist charging a top fee may be either well established with an outstanding reputation or simply an ambitious entrepreneur. Don't choose a therapist who charges a high fee just for snob appeal: unless that therapist has a special expertise that is relevant to your problem, there is no reason to pay more.

Sliding Fee Scales and Reduced Fees

While most therapists and clinics have a standard fee, some do make exceptions based on your ability to pay. Some work according to what is called a sliding scale: they will negotiate a reduced rate according to your income and family size. This is a common practice at many public sector clinics and community mental health centers. When therapists tell you what their standard fee is, it is always worth asking, if you think you may qualify, if they use a sliding scale or ever see anyone for a reduced fee. Within limits, fees are sometimes negotiable as well. If you like a therapist but feel the fee is too high, don't be afraid to ask if he or she will see you for less.

If your financial circumstances change. If your financial picture changes—say, you lose your job or your insurance coverage—you may no longer be able to afford the fee you agreed on. Most therapists will be sensitive to your situation. Many will adjust their fee downward if you run into legitimate and serious financial difficulties.

In some of the helping professions, therapists have an ethical obligation to do some *pro bono* or free work. Your therapist may accept you on this basis until your finances improve. However, it may be unreasonable to expect your therapist to continue seeing you indefinitely at a much lower fee, though you should always ask. Unfortunately, changed financial circumstances do sometimes mean that therapy will have to end, at least for the present.

Conversely, your income may substantially increase during therapy. Can therapists raise their fees if it does? No. Raising their fees beyond their usual range because you can afford it is not considered professional or ethical. How much you earn does not determine the value of therapists' services.

If your therapist is no longer happy with the fee you set just because you are now worth more, that is not your problem. But if it affects his or her work with you, discuss it and maybe even reevaluate continuing. A therapist can raise the fee only if he or she has been seeing you at a reduced fee based on your previous inability to pay, but in any case not beyond their regular fee. You do have an ethical obligation to inform your therapist if you can now afford the regular fee.

Periodic Fee Increases

In short-term or time-limited psychotherapy, whatever the format, the fee usually won't change while you are in therapy. In longer-term or open-ended therapy of a year or more, your therapist may announce an annual increase in his or her fee. Therapists disagree about this. The more traditional view is that once a fee is agreed to, that remains the fee throughout, no matter how long therapy lasts, because it is part of the secure framework of therapy that should not be changed.

The more common view today, though, is that rising expenses are a fact of life, and therapists, like other professionals, must raise their fees year after year. Overhead rises yearly. Malpractice insurance continues to rise dramatically. For the last several years, the median rise in therapists' fees has been between five and ten dollars every two years.

Setting Fees for Adolescents

Setting fees for adolescents can be complicated since most are not in a position to pay for their own therapy. Should the fee be based on the assumption that the parents or the parents' insurance will be paying the bill, or should the adolescent be responsible for at least part of the cost of therapy? This issue inevitably involves other important questions about the therapy itself. If the parents pay the adolescent's fee in whole or in part, should they be involved in their child's therapy? If so, how? Directly, or by being kept informed of its progress?

Parents will often expect to be directly involved, or to be told details of each session. Adolescents need confidentiality in therapy as much as adults. At the same time, this has to be balanced against the parents' need and right to be kept informed at least in a general way about their child's course of treatment.

Money has just as many possible meanings for adolescents going into therapy as it does for adults. Adolescents may see their parents as cold and uncaring and want to burden them with a high psychotherapy fee as a way to get even. They may want to find out how much their parents care, or whether their parents see how miserable they are, by seeing if they will pay for professional help. They may feel their parents are smothering and too ready to rush in to get them anything they want, as if therapy were another expensive present.

In practice, most therapists and clinics will set a fee based on the parents' ability to pay. However, most therapists think it a good idea for adolescents to have some financial stake in their therapy, however minimal, and for them to pay at least a portion of the fee if at all possible. This should be something they can afford but that still catches their attention. Having adolescents contribute may provoke initial resentment, but in the long run it tends to support their independence, increase their commitment, foster a greater sense of responsibility, and in general help to make it "their" therapy.

It is also best for them to pay their portion directly to the therapist rather than simply to reimburse their parents. This asks more of the therapist. Not every therapist feels comfortable relying on adolescents for payment. But their portion will usually be small and the principle is vital, even with very ill or disturbed adolescents. It also asks more of the parents. It is always easier simply to pay yourself than to fight your teenage children over paying their share. But once decided, neither you nor the therapist should yield on this principle easily.

MEDIAN FEES

From our own National Survey of Psychotherapists and from other surveys, the following table presents the *median fees* charged for therapy nationally by profession. Half of all therapists will charge more than this; half will charge less.

Psychiatrists	$100
Psychologists	$85
Social workers	$70
Marriage and family counselors	$75
Other counselors	$65

How much you actually pay can differ from these median fees significantly. For comparison, 15 percent of psychologists charged $90 or over, and 5 percent charged $55 or under. But for social workers, only 1 percent charged $90 or more, and 22 percent had fees $55 or under. So, although fees clearly differ between the professions as a whole, the fee for any particular therapist can vary virtually across the entire range.

These data are as of 1991. Since the mid-1980s, therapy fees have been increasing at a rate of $5 to $10 every two years. Assuming more or less the same rate of change, you can calculate what you may expect to pay currently.

The median fee for *group therapy,* based on an hour and a half session, was $40 nationally in 1991.

ARE THERE OTHER WAYS OF REDUCING COSTS?

Can you reduce the cost of therapy by going for *shorter* or *less frequent visits?* Generally this is not a good idea if you want therapy to be most effective. Decisions about frequency and length of sessions should be made on a therapeutic basis, not to save money. You may reduce costs but at the price of not getting what you need. If you truly have no other option, discuss this with your therapist, but with very careful attention to whether it will meet your needs (see Chapter 6, p. 146).

Bartering services in return for therapy has recently been touted as a "creative" or "innovative" approach. You provide some service—e.g., accounting, if you are an accountant—to your therapist in lieu of cash. While this kind of arrangement may seem to make perfectly good sense, it is unfortunately open to serious abuse and skews the therapy since it constitutes what is called a "dual" relationship. For that reason, all professional codes of conduct rule out barter as unethical (see Chapter 11, "Professional Ethics," for a detailed discussion), though some therapists will accept the arrangement.

Psychotherapy Fees Are Tax Deductible

One bright note is that the cost of psychotherapy is tax deductible as a medical expense, even though it is not truly a "medical" service. Whatever portion of the fee you are paying out of pocket can be taken as an itemized deduction, if you qualify for medical deductions.

HOW THERAPY IS PAID FOR

Self-Pay

Until fairly recently, if you were in therapy, you paid for it yourself like any other professional service, sometimes helped by parents or family. That changed with the gradual application of the medical model to psychotherapy and its inclusion in health insurance policies and public health programs as a covered "mental health" benefit.

Currently about one in three people in therapy pay for their therapy entirely out of pocket. Even with insurance or some other form of "third-party" payment, you will still either have to bear some of the cost of psychotherapy yourself, or else limit the number of sessions. The only exception to this are individuals whose low incomes qualify them for "free care" in public sector settings.

Third-Party Payment

"Third party" means, literally, that some third person, other than you or your therapist, is a party to your treatment, usually because they are paying for it in whole or part. They are a party to it in more direct ways as well. Precisely because they are footing the bill, they have a right to know certain things about it and about you that you should be aware of—an important issue discussed below.

In general, you can be covered for mental health services, including psychotherapy, by:

1. private or group health insurance
2. a health maintenance organization (HMO) or a related form of managed health care
3. public-sector services

Are you covered for psychotherapy? The major types of health insurance coverage today, including HMOs and managed health care, include both inpatient and outpatient mental health benefits. Inpatient benefits are typically more extensive since the primary intent is to cover the more severe emergency and acute-care situations that require hospitalization. Some policies insure only for psychotherapy that takes place in a hospital. Most, however, will pay part of your clinic and office visits as well.

If you are thinking about starting therapy and have some form of insurance, check your policy to see if it includes psychotherapy. If it doesn't, you might be covered through the policy of a spouse, or a parent if you are a dependent minor.

If you have no insurance and think you might qualify for free care or a reduced fee at a community mental health center or clinic, call and ask what the eligibility requirements are.

Restrictions on psychotherapy benefits. One of the ironies of mental health care in our society today is that free psychotherapy is available only to the very affluent and the very poor. Only an "executive" insurance policy or free care in a public-sector clinic will cover the entire cost of therapy. Normal third-party payment is limited in one of three ways: by the total dollar amount of coverage per year; by the number of visits per year; or by the type of therapist you can choose from. Each type of coverage has a different type of restriction.

Third-party reimbursement requires a psychiatric diagnosis. Applying the medical model to psychotherapy has certain adverse consequences, and this is one of them. Strictly speaking, health insurance is for health problems, and benefits are therefore restricted to recognized medical and psychiatric conditions.

If you want to be covered, and most people do, you and your therapist must be prepared to call your problem an illness or a disorder. If it isn't, it can't be covered. This means you are assigned a psychiatric diagnosis on the claim form (see Chapter 11, p. 259, where this issue is discussed).

This should concern you for several reasons. Therapeutically, the issues for which you may quite rightly be considering therapy may not be psychiatric illnesses as defined by either of the two standard diagnostic systems that insurance companies, HMOs, and publicly financed clinics use: *DSM-III-R* and *ICD-9* (see Chapter 11, p. 259).

You may want to understand a repeated difficulty in intimate relationships, for instance, a conflict with a spouse or child, a death in the family, or problems at school or work. These problems in living are not psychiatric disorders such as depression, anorexia, or panic attacks. But if you want to use your insurance to cover therapy, your therapist will have to assign a psychiatric diagnosis to you. If your therapist is willing, he or she will assign a "diagnosis of convenience" to qualify you for benefits—a formal diagnosis that can be justified as having some bearing on your complaint. Since therapists are aware of the costs of therapy to their clients, they may even suggest this, in fact, once they learn you have insurance. But they also tend to downplay its implications. And you may understandably be eager to agree with this "technical procedure" because anything that will defray the cost of therapy is welcome.

While this has become a common practice that the insurance companies themselves are quite aware of, it is not as innocent an arrangement as it sounds. It is actually illegal as well as professionally unethical for your therapist to do this, even though most will because they know therapy is expensive and most budgets are tight. For the most part insurance companies themselves have implicitly gone along with the fiction. But you and your therapist are in an untenable position if the insurance company should challenge the diagnosis and review the therapy.

Additionally, even though you know it is a fiction of sorts, it can subtly affect the way you think and talk about yourself in therapy, especially if there is a grain of truth in it. Are you really "sicker" or "crazier" than you think? It can subtly influence you to start acting more like a "patient" than a "client." It can raise doubts about how your therapist "really" sees you—does he or she think you may actually have a psychiatric disorder?

Most important of all, it can raise doubts about your therapist's integrity and approach, and the quality of care you are likely to get. You want a therapist whose honesty and professional integrity you can rely on. To begin therapy in part on a deception, even though it is to your financial benefit, contradicts the basic premise therapy rests on—honesty.

Accepting a psychiatric diagnosis just to access a health care benefit, which is usually limited anyway, could affect you in other ways. Because it establishes a "pre-existing condition," it might lessen your insurability later on, say for life insurance or even for subsequent health insurance if you should need or want to change carriers. It also puts you in a bind if you are asked, in a job interview for instance, "Have you ever sought treatment for an emotional or nervous disorder?"

All of this in part is another unfortunate consequence of applying a medical model to psychotherapy and trying to make it fit a medical model of diagnosis and treatment. No one wins. The present system functions only because all involved—the insurance company, the therapist, and the client—feel they get something from it and are willing to look the other way at its contradictions and the untenable positions it forces all the participants into. If you decide to go ahead with a diagnosis of convenience when no clear psychiatric disorder is involved, at least do this with full acknowledgment and discussion of what you are doing, and anticipate any likely consequences with your therapist—and your insurance company.

INDIVIDUAL AND GROUP HEALTH INSURANCE

Until the introduction of HMOs and managed health care, individual or group health insurance policies were the standard form of third-party coverage for medical expenses. Originally these covered medical illnesses only. In time, the medical benefit was extended by many carriers to cover "mental health" as well, though this is still not true of every policy. Health insurance is still the major form of coverage.

How you get it. Most people obtain health insurance through their employer or business as part of their benefits package. An employer may pay anywhere from 50 to 100 percent of the premium, with the balance being deducted from the employee's salary. Health insurance can also be purchased privately, though this is usually much more expensive than the group policies offered through a business or employer. The best-known carrier of this type of insurance is probably Blue Cross/Blue Shield.

The psychotherapy benefit. If you have this type of health insurance and want to use it for therapy, you need to check two things: (1) Does your policy cover outpatient psychotherapy? Some only cover inpatient services. (2) If you are covered for outpatient therapy, how much are you covered for? The total amount covered will usually be limited in one of two ways:

- *By total dollar amount per year*. Most insurance policies that allow you to choose your own therapist typically offer a certain total dollar amount of coverage per year, irrespective of the therapist's fee. This can vary from a few hundred dollars to a few thousand, with $500 per year probably representative. You pay everything above this. Some policies pay the first $500. Others pay a percentage of each fee per session, usually 50 to 80 percent, with you paying the rest, until the total amount "covered" for the year is reached.
  Though $500 may sound like a lot, at today's fees it does not cover many sessions. If you are considering open-ended or long-term therapy, you should count on being able to afford most of the annual cost yourself with this type of policy. Check your policy to see what the total dollar amount actually is.
- *By a percentage of the fee per session*. This percentage is usually 50 to 80 percent, though only up to a certain amount per session according to a standard scale of fees set by the insurance company. If your therapist's fee is higher than that allowed by the policy, they will still pay the stated percentage of the maximum allowable fee, but you will be responsible for any cost above that. Even so, this is obviously a more advantageous type of coverage, but as you might expect, it is also less common. This type of policy often carries a several hundred dollar deductible as well.

Treatment for Alcohol and Substance Abuse. Even though alcohol and substance abuse are psychiatric disorders, they are sometimes treated differently from other mental health problems in some insurance policies and health plans. They may have an altogether different benefit structure. You should check your policy or health plan to see if they are included in the general mental health benefit or covered separately and, if separately, what the benefit is.

Providers. The main advantage to individual or group health insurance is that it allows you to choose your own therapist. However, you will have to choose someone the insurance company approves and certifies as a "provider" of the service. For most companies, this will usually be a therapist who is state licensed or state certified in any one of the major mental health professions. In practice, this is not a burden-some restriction; it gives you a wide range of choice. Moreover, a licensed therapist offers you a number of important advantages and protections anyway (see Chapter 3, p. 72).

Some insurance carriers, on the other hand, may restrict your choice *by profession*. They might cover outpatient psychotherapy only if it is provided by a psychiatrist, or only psychiatrists and psychologists. Or they may cover nonmedical licensed therapists only if you are referred to them by a physician. This means you have to see a physician or psychiatrist first, and they must be willing to refer you to someone other than a psychiatrist. Many states have now passed "freedom of choice" legislation that requires insurance companies to reimburse policyholders for psychotherapy provided by nonphysicians, though these therapists must usually still be licensed mental health professionals.

If your therapist is not an approved provider. Most therapists don't apply to become providers for a particular insurance company until a client with that insurance requests it. Feel free to ask if your therapist would be willing to apply for provider status. If some additional qualification is necessary, you should inform your therapist of it.

If your therapist is licensed and your company covers that profession, he or she may be eligible. Getting provider status with some companies, however, is no longer as automatic or easy as it used to be. An increasing number of provider panels are being restricted. Some are even closed. Most therapists will respond to your request, but you can't enter therapy assuming a particular therapist will be automatically credentialed as a provider if he or she isn't already.

If you are dependent on insurance and your therapist isn't a provider and isn't eligible to become one, you can ask your employer if they offer another type of insurance that would cover your therapist's services. Failing that, you will probably have to find a therapist who is a provider or is eligible to become one.

Reimbursement procedures. Usually your therapist submits a claim directly to your insurance company on a standard reimbursement claim form he or she will fill out. On occasion, you will pay your therapist the full fee, then apply to your insurance company to be reimbursed.

Not all therapists accept insurance. The great majority will, but some still oppose it because of the detrimental effects they believe third-party involvement has on therapy (see p. 168). Others have experienced delays in payment, disputed claims, and red tape with insurance companies. It's best not to assume the therapist you are considering accepts insurance—ask.

HEALTH MAINTENANCE ORGANIZATIONS AND OTHER FORMS OF MANAGED HEALTH CARE

HMOs are increasingly offered as an option to employees through their business or employer. The business or firm contracts with an HMO to provide comprehensive medical and mental health services to all employees who sign up. As with traditional health insurance, the employer pays anywhere from 50 to 100 percent of the monthly premium, with the balance deducted from the employee's pay. The premiums support medical centers run by the HMO, each with a permanent professional staff.

All HMOs offer comprehensive inpatient and outpatient services. If they don't run their own hospital, they contract with local hospitals to serve their patients. Most HMOs have their own mental health department or department of psychiatry with a salaried staff of psychiatrists, psychologists, social workers, and psychiatric nurses.

Other managed health care plans, "preferred provider organizations" or PPOs, rely on a pool of therapists who have been signed up to work for the health plan. The health plan will automatically pay for your therapy—up to a predetermined limit—if you see one of these therapists. But if you go outside the pool of preferred providers, ordinarily your therapy costs will not be covered.

Access to therapy in HMOs is likely to involve one step not necessary with other insurers: you may have to get prior approval first, either from your primary care physician or from a mental health professional who screens therapy referrals. They will then refer you to a specific therapist. Review your coverage booklet carefully for your plan's procedures, or inquire from their customer service department.

The psychotherapy benefit. Instead of providing a specific dollar amount of coverage each year or a specific percentage of each session fee, HMOs typically offer a specific number of mental health visits per person—or per family member if you have the family plan—each calendar year. This usually varies from ten to twenty, with one "visit" based on the standard psychotherapy "hour" of fifty minutes. This figure includes all visits, not just therapy. If you are seen for a consultation or evaluation, for crisis intervention, or for a medication check, or if you are seeing someone for group, couples, or family therapy in addition to individual therapy—all count toward the total number of visits.

However, some types of visits don't need to be full hours—medication checks, for instance. And since the number of visits is based on the standard fifty-minute hour, HMO therapists will sometimes see clients for shorter sessions so they can be seen more often or will see clients at greater intervals so they can be seen over a longer period of time. This helps someone who needs to be seen regularly for a serious condition or suffers from a recurrent condition that will flare up from time to time. But for someone seeking regular psychotherapy, reducing the length and frequency of meetings can be a disadvantage.

Accountability and cost effectiveness are emphasized in HMOs. This doesn't mean inferior therapy, but rather that the emphasis is on brief treatment and quick return to normal functioning. The HMO model works best for short-term or brief focal therapy where the goals are specific and time limited. It also works well for crisis intervention and emergencies.

But the limitation on visits is significant in treating problems that require more sustained therapy, especially chronic or recurrent conditions. Precisely because of this, however, insurance commissions in some states have begun requiring HMOs to lift this restriction and continue to provide services, particularly in cases of severely disturbed clients or major mental illness. Whether these restrictions on visits will be lifted for all subscribers is still unclear. What is clear is that HMOs are not the place to look for long-term therapy, especially psychodynamic psychotherapy.

Some HMOs will allow you to continue in therapy after you have exhausted the benefit for another specific number of visits for half fee, and then for full fee beyond that if you are willing and able to pay. Some also take "fee-for-service" clients, who are not subscribers and not covered by the HMO but are willing to pay full fee, as they would to any private therapist. In either case, however, you can't count on your therapist continuing to be available. HMOs are contractually obligated to give first priority to clients covered under the plan who haven't exhausted their benefits. Most HMO therapists just aren't available for extended therapy. Trying to do longer-term therapy when you can't count on the availability of your therapist is a prescription for frustration and disappointment.

Therapists. An HMO requires you to see one of their professional staff, which will usually include therapists from all the major mental health professions. If the available staff cannot treat a particular problem, or it requires outside expertise, the HMO will usually pay for outside treatment.

This usually gives clients a fairly wide and representative range of choice. The mental health staff also work closely with the HMO medical personnel, making it easy to coordinate medical and mental health care.

Your choice of a therapist in an HMO can occasionally be limited by availability and scheduling. You will usually be assigned a therapist at first, rather than getting to choose from the entire staff. But you can indicate your preferences regarding age, gender, and so on, and the HMO will try to take these into account. You should treat the first meeting or two as a consultation (see Chapter 4, p. 106). If it doesn't work out or seems to be a bad match, an HMO has the advantage of having other staff available, and you are free to request another therapist (see Chapter 4, p. 113). However, you are out of luck if none of the therapists at the HMO feel compatible to you.

THERAPY IN THE PUBLIC SECTOR AND OTHER FORMS OF FINANCIAL ASSISTANCE

Many mental health services and programs are federally, state, or municipally funded, each targeted to special levels and types of need. These provide psychotherapy to individuals and families who meet certain eligibility requirements and could not otherwise afford it. They range from community mental health centers with their own staffs to financial aid programs, such as Medicaid and Medicare, that reimburse other providers.

The one common eligibility requirement for most of these public-sector programs is that you have a low income and lack insurance. In addition, a number of programs target specific groups or populations in need who cannot afford private services or health insurance, such as children, the elderly, veterans, students, the mentally ill, or the disabled. Most public-sector services are also "catchment area"–based: you must be a resident of the particular area that clinic or program serves to be eligible for its services. That may be a town or city, a county, a regional area comprising several municipalities or counties, or the entire state. Most federally funded programs are administered locally through municipal, county, or state offices.

The standard of therapy in many of these programs is comparable to private care, particularly those associated with teaching hospitals or training programs. It does not automatically mean second-rate or second-class care by any means. It is not well known, but for individuals with severe, chronic, or recurring conditions, public-sector mental health often offers a much greater and more diversified spectrum of services than private insurance or even HMOs will offer. Clients can be seen more or less frequently as they need to be, for as long as they need to be.

Community mental health centers. These centers, supported in part by government funds, are open to anyone. Fees are set solely on the basis of your ability to pay. If an intake interview establishes your need, they must offer you services. In most cases, this will be some kind of therapy on a sliding fee scale. If your income falls below an established minimum, the fee will be waived altogether.

The state department of mental health. In addition to community mental health centers, states operate a spectrum of other mental health programs and facilities designed for low-income people. Services are generally on a sliding fee scale, from full fee to free care. To find out about your eligibility, consult your local state department of mental health office listed in the phone directory with other state government listings.

Medicaid. This federal-state financial aid program allows people with low income to get medical and mental health services at no cost from any qualified provider, based on a determination of needs. Each state administers its own program and sets its own eligibility requirements. In some you have to be virtually impoverished and unable to work; in others the requirements are less stringent. Your local welfare office—unfortunately, often a frustrating place—is the place to find out about eligibility.

Medicaid does pay for psychotherapy and allows you to choose your own therapist as long as he or she is enrolled as a qualified Medicaid provider. In most states this means they are state licensed or certified in their profession. However, therapists are reimbursed at below their usual fees and are understandably prohibited from charging the client for the balance. For that reason many therapists will not accept Medicaid clients.

Beware of two unethical procedures some therapists use to increase their fees. One is asking clients to sign forms for fictitious appointments. Another is seeing you for a short session but billing Medicaid for an entire hour. Both are illegal.

Medicaid will support longer-term psychotherapy if it is justified. However, many state programs now require "prior approval" for a specific number of sessions before authorizing reimbursement. As each series of approved sessions nears its end, another prior-approval authorization must be submitted.

Medicare. Medicare is the parallel federal government health services program for people over sixty-five who are receiving social security disability benefits. Like Medicaid, Medicare includes mental health services, among them psychotherapy, based on a determination of need. Also like Medicaid, it allows you to choose your own therapist as long as he or she is a qualified provider. In most states this means a therapist must be state licensed or certified. Medicare then pays a portion of the cost. However, also like Medicaid, Medicare tends to reimburse below therapists' usual fees and prohibits them from charging the client the difference. Consequently, not all therapists are willing to accept Medicare. If you are planning to use Medicare, ask if they accept it and are already enrolled as a provider.

Apply for Medicare at your local social security office.

Social security disability benefits. Depending on your income, you may be eligible for social security disability benefits if you have been unable to work for a year or more due to physical or emotional illness. These benefits include income support and Medicare coverage. Medicare coverage will pay for psychotherapy. SSDI benefits also continue for six to nine months after you start work again to assist in rehabilitation. Application is through your local social security office.

State rehabilitation commissions. This program is much less well known than those above. Each state has federal funds, administered by a state rehabilitation commission, earmarked to help people with physical or psychological problems, particularly those that interfere with their ability to work or attend school. You apply for an evaluation of needs to see if you meet their eligibility criteria. If you do, you can go to any licensed therapist. However, the type of therapy rehabilitation commissions reimburse for is usually brief and aimed at getting you on your feet within a few months. Since their reimbursement is usually below the regular fee of many providers, the therapist must be willing to accept a lower fee.

Veterans Administration. Veterans with a service-related illness or disability qualify for health care from the Veterans Administration. If resources are available, the VA offers services to veterans who can't afford private care, even if their disability is not service connected. However, the VA will now apply for reimbursement for treating non-service-related conditions if the veteran has private health insurance. All veterans with honorable discharges are eligible. Like all other VA services, therapy is free but must be for the purpose of treating a specific mental health disorder or condition.

Health insurance for dependents of federal government uniformed service personnel (CHAMPUS). This plan covers dependents of uniformed service personnel. The client pays 20 to 25 percent of outpatient mental health costs, along with a deductible. Most therapists will accept this coverage since it usually pays full fee.

College counseling centers. Most colleges offer students psychological counseling through the college health services. If the school has a graduate program in psychology or counseling, it may also operate an outpatient psychotherapy or counseling center. Such therapy is often high quality, and the therapists are highly experienced in working with the stresses students are under. However, therapy will usually be short term and oriented toward evaluation and crisis intervention. If the problem requires more extended treatment, college health services will usually refer you to a good local clinic or community mental health center. They will also make referrals to private therapists if you request them.

CONFIDENTIALITY ISSUES IN THIRD-PARTY PAYMENT

Confidentiality cannot be complete. If you will be relying on any form of health insurance or community-based services to defray the costs of therapy, it will affect one of the most important underpinnings of therapy, its confidentiality.

Most clients assume that whatever they tell their therapist will be held in the strictest confidence, guaranteed by law. That is not entirely the case. Even if you are paying privately for an individual therapist, your confidentiality can be broken when the law deems your right to privacy is outweighed by a higher public good. Therapists are legally bound, for instance, to report instances of child abuse that come to their attention in therapy, in order to protect the child from further harm. Normally, however, in private therapy what you tell your therapist remains private. No one will even know you are in therapy or for what unless you yourself tell them.

This won't be true if a third party is paying. You will be required to provide the third party certain information about yourself in order for either you or your therapist to be reimbursed. This information will stay somewhere—probably in a medical or personnel file or record.

What kind of information will you be asked to disclose? First of all, a third-party payer will want to know enough about you to determine your eligibility for benefits. Typical registration and insurance forms ask a wide range of questions. You may be surprised at the amount of information they ask for. (See Chapter 11, p. 259, for the typical items of information asked for on a representative Blue Shield outpatient reimbursement form.) For instance, they ask what you are in therapy for, what kind of therapy you are getting, how long you have been in therapy, and whether you missed any work because of your problem.

Probably the single most important item required is *a formal psychiatric diagnosis*. Many clients object to being given a diagnosis, particularly if they are seeking therapy for a personal issue or couple or family conflict rather than a psychiatric disorder. But even if you are seeking help for a recognized psychiatric condition, or are willing to accept a psychiatric diagnosis because it qualifies you for benefits, be aware that the diagnosis will go into your health insurance records.

If your coverage is through work, you should be very concerned if it goes into your personnel file as well. Unlike medical diagnoses, psychiatric diagnoses can stigmatize you if they become public knowledge.

Therapists often try to protect clients by assigning a diagnosis that is less pejorative. Unfortunately, this is basically dishonest and a violation of the therapist's professional ethics. Again, therapist and client agreeing to a deception at the start undercuts the therapeutic relationship and can plant seeds of doubt about the therapist's integrity, no matter how well intentioned the action. And pragmatically, the more benign the label, the shorter the authorized benefits are likely to be. If you have a more serious problem that needs more extended care, you won't get it.

Utilization review. Additional information about your therapy itself may be required for "quality assurance" or "utilization review." Third-party payers are becoming increasingly concerned about cost effectiveness in light of the spiraling costs of health care. In utilization review, an insurer asks other therapists (or sometimes, people without training in therapy) to evaluate the worthiness of a payment claim for psychotherapy; in "managed care" the review is done by a case manager. The goal is to minimize costs for insurers by matching a patient's needs to the most effective, but lowest cost, form of therapy.

Utilization review committees are not interested in personal or intimate details of what you and your therapist talk about. But they will require general information about what you are working on, how you are working on it, and what kind of changes, if any, therapy is bringing about. They will want to know your overall psychological and emotional state.

You have to give your consent to have information about your therapy released to a utilization review committee. However, there is a strong chance you will be denied benefits if you don't. Similarly, if your therapist doesn't provide enough information, the review board is likely to hold up the claim until he or she does.

While many or even most utilization reviews are carried out by competent professionals, that is not always the case. There have been complaints from therapists that some among the hundreds of companies that manage mental health payments for corporations or insurers have hired inexperienced people to review therapy cases. For therapists, that can mean that someone who is not qualified is second-guessing their clinical expertise.

Some therapists complain that the reviews can be as often as every three days for hospitalization and every three to six sessions for psychotherapy. Since an adverse review of progress in therapy means that payment will be cut off, the reviews can introduce an extra element of anxiety into therapy. There have even been reports of reviewers who confronted clients with the demand that they justify the therapy they were receiving.

At its best, however, utilization review and managed care helps insure that the psychotherapy you receive is well-matched to your needs. At its worst, it can mean that your insurer denies coverage of your therapy without having to explain either to you or your therapist the grounds for the denial. At this writing several states are considering laws to regulate how psychotherapy is managed by insurers, and to make the guidelines explicit.

Potential effects of third-party involvement on therapy. You may know your third-party payer is bound to confidentiality as much as your therapist, but even so, the presence of third-party "observers" to your therapy can still cause you to hold back, leave vital things out, or to misrepresent yourself without really intending to. Some of that concern may be irrational; some of it may not be, particularly if you are not sure who is going to know what about you and whether any information provided to the third-party payer will be held in confidence. Concerns about confidentiality— your insurance provider's no less than your therapist's—always pose the danger of compromising the effectiveness of your therapy. If these concerns worry you, there are several things you can do.

The best thing to do is to discuss them candidly with your therapist at the start, and any time you have reason to be concerned thereafter. Be sure you understand your therapist's reporting responsibilities to the third-party payer: what kind of information he or she will be asked to provide about you, to whom it will go, and how it will be used. You should especially discuss the diagnosis your therapist will have to assign. Be sure you understand the rationale for it and agree with it. Confront any ethical issues involved in assigning a diagnosis of convenience squarely and honestly—together. Don't allow yourself to be talked into an arrangement you don't believe in or want to accept responsibility for. On the other hand, be wary of a therapist who agrees to a diagnosis of convenience too readily, or who is insensitive to the ethical issues involved.

Second, you can ask to see any claim forms before they are sent in.

Third, you can ask your insurance company, HMO, or whoever is paying for your therapy what their procedures for protecting your confidentiality are. You can also ask what use will be made of any information you or your therapist provide.

Finally, don't sign any "release of information" form, authorizing anyone to obtain or release information about you, until you are satisfied you know just what information will be sent to whom and for what purpose. Be sure the release of information form specifies the exact nature of the information you are releasing (see Chapter 11, p. 258, for this).

CHAPTER EIGHT

■

BEGINNING THERAPY

There is no one "right" way to begin therapy. Each person has a unique way of entering a new relationship or starting a new undertaking, based on patterns of experience and character developed over years. Being aware of your own style of beginning can help you anticipate and understand some of the difficulties in getting started. Are you the kind of person, for instance, who:

- is cautious and only reveals him- or herself slowly?
- needs to develop a considerable amount of trust before making a commitment?
- leaps right in without checking too much out first?
- wants to be liked or wants approval and therefore tries hard to make a good impression?
- wants to impress with his or her competence and togetherness?
- is quick to find fault?
- is quick to take offense?
- gets involved easily but also loses interest quickly?
- sees involvement as a commitment?
- is wary of getting trapped?
- is pretty adaptable?
- usually feels disappointed after a promising beginning?

These characteristics aren't mutually exclusive; you may recognize yourself in more than one. Recognizing these and acknowledging them with your therapist can help you feel more at ease.

TYPICAL REACTIONS TO STARTING THERAPY

However you tend to begin a relationship, you will probably have strong feelings at the start of therapy, a time when you are particularly sensitive and open to first impressions, are trying to figure out what is expected of you, and are getting comfortable with how therapy works. You are also feeling your way into a relationship with someone you don't know, but who is already important to you and may eventually have considerable influence on your life.

Reactions are typically complex, and not particularly consistent. One moment you may feel understood, at another misunderstood; you may feel accepted and supported for who you are, then the next minute feel challenged or criticized. It may be a relief to unburden yourself of things you haven't been able to talk about. Or trying to talk about things that make you feel embarrassed, anxious, guilty, or foolish can be difficult.

Though grateful that you've finally found someone who can help, you may still find it difficult to accept that you need "professional" help. You may resent feeling dependent on your therapist. You may not understand how you can possibly feel such conflicting emotions about being in therapy, about your therapist, or about yourself.

This contradictory mix of feelings is normal—all of it. An uncomplicated and constant set of feelings at the start of therapy is the exception, and it usually means the client either isn't really engaged or is determined to keep things superficial. Avoid making yourself feel something you think clients are "supposed" to feel when they start therapy—relief, gratitude, hopefulness, excitement, dedication—and notice what you actually *do* feel. Observing your reactions can lead to learning important things about yourself. Self-observation is one of the major capacities therapy cultivates and depends on.

Reactions to Starting Therapy

- I look forward to the next session.
- I dread going in.
- My therapist seems to like me and be interested in me.
- I'm afraid I'm boring. I don't feel like I have anything really interesting to say. I'm afraid my therapist won't be that interested in working with me.
- Maybe I'll be one of my therapist's "special" clients.
- I can't seem to make myself understood, or say what I really mean.
- It's a relief to finally be able to unburden myself.
- I feel uncomfortable in there, anxious and ill at ease.
- I don't like having to think about certain things, much less talk about them.
- I don't like the fact that I get so upset during sessions.

- I feel stimulated and challenged.
- I don't like feeling this vulnerable.
- My therapist seems to insist on doing things his or her way.
- This is more intense than I expected.
- I thought this would be more intense. I feel kind of bored and disinterested.
- This just seems to be a lot of talking. How's that going to change anything?
- I feel accepted and understood.
- I can't tell what my therapist is thinking.
- This seems to be a one-way street. I have to do all the talking and giving. I want to know more about him/her.
- My therapist seems to hold all the cards. I don't like feeling anyone has so much power over me.
- I think our couples therapist likes my spouse better than me.
- I'm embarrassed when we argue or fight in front of our therapist.
- I feel better already just starting.

THE MAIN TASK: ESTABLISHING A GOOD WORKING RELATIONSHIP

Therapy's effectiveness—no matter what approach is taken—depends to a great extent on establishing a good working relationship with your therapist. If you haven't been in therapy before—or in a good therapy—it's easy to be confused about exactly what the therapeutic relationship is. It resembles other good relationships in many ways, but in important ways it is *unique*. What makes it so special?

Your needs come first. Therapy is not based on a mutuality of obligations. Unlike other relationships where the personal needs and concerns of both people are equally important and get attended to in a mutual give-and-take, your needs and concerns *always* come first and are the exclusive focus of the relationship. Your therapist's personal needs are not of concern—or shouldn't be.

This creates a uniquely safe environment in which you are free to express yourself, to make your needs, problems, and feelings known without fear of criticism or rebuke, and without having to worry about taking care of your therapist's needs. If you don't need to worry about your therapist, you are free to experience your thoughts, feelings, and actions as they are. You are free to do something about them because *you* want to, not because someone else expects it.

The therapist is the expert. This relationship is with someone who has expertise with the kind of problem you are having. He or she has seen others struggle with similar problems and is trained to listen, understand, and intervene. You can reliably count on this person to know how to help you. Even though family, friends, and other nonprofessionals may be well-intentioned, they won't have the same skills, training, and resources.

The therapist has a special influence and power. There is no avoiding the unique power and status differential in the therapeutic relationship (see Chapter 1, p. 19). Each of you is equal in dignity and worth, and worthy of equal respect, but the therapist has special expertise in precisely the area where you feel vulnerable and in need of help. Consequently, therapists can exert an exceptional amount of influence, either deliberately or not.

The therapist is responsible for defining the rules of therapy and the limitations of what he or she will and won't do. But the therapist is also responsible for helping to right the initial imbalance: to help you eventually feel empowered both in therapy and in daily life, to the point where his or her direct influence recedes as you gain mastery over your difficulties, feel better able to manage on your own, and come to value yourself and your capabilities more.

The relationship has specific boundaries. You meet at regularly scheduled times, rather than whenever you want or feel the most need to. You meet in a specially designated place—usually an office or clinic—instead of wherever you feel like. You pay a fee. The therapist may or may not be available to you between sessions.

Other boundaries besides those on meeting concern the nature of the relationship itself. Your therapist's professional code of ethics dictates that he or she has no social or business involvement with you whatsoever, and certainly no romantic involvement. Your therapist's own personal concerns and problems are off-limits.

The therapist is also bound by confidentiality. With some important exceptions, such as data reported to your insurer (for details, see Chapter 7, p. 167, and Chapter 11, p. 259), anything you say or do in this relationship is privileged communication. Legally and ethically, your therapist may not reveal anything about you or your therapy to anyone else without your explicit written permission.

All of these boundaries have one purpose: to establish a relationship in which you can be confident that your concerns will be paramount and that you will not be taken advantage of. These secure boundaries allow you to express your thoughts and feelings or examine your behavior, without worrying about rejection, retaliation, or abandonment from your therapist, or about disappointing someone else. They make it possible to have a relationship that is personal and intimate but still professional.

A therapist is not a kind of friend. Therapists make poor friends for their clients, and even poorer substitutes for friends. They don't do—or shouldn't do—the kinds of things friends do: hang out with you, share problems, invite you out to dinner, loan you money, intercede for you with family or other friends, take trips with you. They're trained not to. So you need not try to win your therapist over by putting your best foot forward, as you might a friend, or by trying to make a good impression.

For therapy to work, your therapist needs to know you honestly, your strengths and weaknesses, the things you like about yourself and the things you don't. You wouldn't try to start a friendship by revealing your vulnerabilities and deficiencies, but these are just the reasons you come to therapy and the areas you want a therapist to help you change. The therapy relationship, unlike many friendships, thrives in a climate of complete honesty.

If a therapist needs to find friends among clients, or turn clients into friends, he or she may need help as much as you do. If you try to make a friend of your therapist, you stand an excellent chance of compromising your therapist's objectivity and neutralizing his or her ability to help you. Every therapist who has heard a client describe his previous therapist as a "good friend" can guess why this client is still looking for help.

Therapy is often compared to a parent-child relationship. This is somewhat misleading. Like the parent-child relationship, the therapeutic relationship tries to create a favorable environment for growth that supports independence in a context of care and respect for the other's individuality. But that's where the similarity ends. Parents have their own needs and agendas with their children as well; a parent's acceptance and love is rarely unconditional. At worst, parental acceptance may depend upon the child's being able to satisfy the parent's needs.

Good therapy, on the other hand, depends upon the therapist's being able to keep personal needs from intruding.

The therapist is not a teacher or a guru. A therapist doesn't impart a moral or spiritual teaching or recommend a particular path of life. Though certain contemporary schools of therapists claim to be "value free," therapists *do* represent certain values: commitment to inquiry and self-examination, alleviation of suffering and distress, safeguarding of personal choice, acceptance of responsibility for one's personal decisions and behavior, the importance and necessity of interdependent relationships in life.

But therapists do not teach these values as "truths." They do not tell you what you should believe or how you should live your life. The values embodied in the therapy are compatible with a wide range of lifestyles, careers, ethical and spiritual commitments, personal preferences and activities. Good therapists have the personal qualities and professional expertise to help you with certain kinds of problems, but they aren't authorities on living.

Your Therapist's Part in Establishing a Good Working Relationship

Your therapist's most important job at the outset is to create the only setting in which effective therapy can occur: a place where you feel safe enough to be yourself without fear of criticism, retaliation, or abandonment. In this safe setting, your therapist's next responsibility is to provide a relationship that will encourage you to express yourself freely and confront whatever it is that is causing you distress—the good, the bad, or the ugly.

How a therapist does this is less a science than an art. It requires skill and experience, but is not a matter of therapeutic "technique." Technique doesn't establish a therapeutic relationship. You will know the difference, because a relationship that rests on technique alone will feel superficial and hollow—"professional" in the worst sense. A therapist may have considerable training and expertise, but if he or she doesn't inspire openness and trust, if you don't feel understood and accepted for who you are, that training and expertise will be irrelevant.

Your therapist's part is to listen, to observe carefully, to try to understand, to call attention to what you may not see, and to help you discover what he or she learns. And as therapy continues, your therapist's role is to expose you to new perspectives and possibilities, and to lead you into new routes of self-awareness and action.

Your Part

You can do a lot to help establish a solid working partnership. The most important part is to *be as open as possible about yourself* and the issues you want help with your thoughts, your feelings, your behavior. Therapy is about you, and only you can provide the material—whether you are an individual or a member of a couple, a group, or a family. No matter how attuned, your therapist won't be able to read your mind. You must present as much information about yourself as possible that bears on the problem you want help with.

Psychotherapy used to be known as "the talking cure." Open-ended talking is not as important in all the formats and approaches used today as it continues to be in psychodynamic therapy, but no matter the approach, your therapist depends on your making your thoughts, feelings, needs, wishes, and reactions known. Talking not only conveys information, it helps in and of itself because it stimulates thinking, elicits feelings, and finally, reduces anxiety. It also furthers self-mastery. If you can put something into words, you know what it is, are less afraid of it, and feel more in control.

Talking openly with your therapist begins to lift you out of the isolation and withdrawal that accompanies unhappiness, hurt, or distress.

Guidelines in Talking About Yourself

Depending on approach, personality, and style, your therapist may be active and directive—asking you questions, offering comments or observations, even making recommendations—or be more nondirective, letting you take the lead. Your therapist's approach can make a large difference in determining what aspects of yourself you will talk about most, and just how you will talk about them.

Whatever the format or approach, you can follow these general guidelines in talking about yourself and letting yourself be known:

- *Talk about what seems most important to you.* By and large, you can assume that it is always appropriate to talk about those issues most meaningful and urgent for you. If there are several, don't worry about choosing the "right" one. Any one will be a good starting point.
- *The more specific and direct you can be, the better.* Talk about actual situations. Describe concretely how you felt, what you thought, how you acted. For example, "Last week I had to go for a job interview, and for days beforehand I had trouble sleeping and eating. When I walked in, I felt panicky, I had trouble breathing, my heart started racing, and I started sweating uncontrollably" is much better than "I get nervous when I meet people for the first time." Being specific brings your experience alive in the telling and makes it easier for your therapist to understand what is really going on.
- *Say things as you think or feel them.* Don't change their tone or recast them in polite or polished language that you think your therapist wants to hear. Instead of saying, for instance, "My husband doesn't like to help out around the house," tell the truth: "I feel like I could murder the SOB when he just sits there while I cook and clean!" Use your everyday language.
- *Speak from your own position when talking about experiences or events.* Don't focus on what others did, on their experience, or on their motives. Speak from the center of your own experience: "I think . . ." "It felt to me like . . ." Or "I feel guilty when my sister seems angry at me and my mother seems upset" instead of "My sister always blames me for the trouble she causes, but she's the one upsetting our mother."
- *Include your feelings and reactions to situations; don't just describe what happened.* Focus on what you thought, what you did, how it left you feeling. For example: "After my girlfriend and I had a fight I was feeling real down and hopeless, and I thought that having a drink would cheer me up, so I went to a bar and drank so much that the next morning I felt even more depressed than before, plus guilty and ashamed." Not: "Last Friday I went to Frank's Pub and had four bottles of Coors and three White Russians."
- *Be as open and candid as possible.* You may not be very open and honest to start, despite your best intentions. However open and spontaneous you may

have been once upon a time, or are in some relationships, these qualities aren't second nature; they often have to be learned, or relearned.

Clients hide all sorts of things from their therapists, usually by leaving them out. Despite paying therapists a rather substantial fee to get relief from whatever is haunting them, clients so routinely hold back their most intimate thoughts, anxieties, and past deeds that a lot of therapy never gets off the ground. Candor is the only way you will get genuine relief.

Some subjects almost all clients find hard to talk about. Money and sex are usually the hardest. As a general rule, anything you feel shame or guilt over will be difficult to bring up. What you find hardest to talk about may be a clue to where you most need help.

As you begin to talk about yourself, you may be worried about how your therapist will react. You won't expect your therapist to come right out and tell you that what you just said was pitiful or disgusting, but you may wonder what he or she secretly thinks. In the beginning, you will implicitly expect your therapist to react to your actions as you do, or as others have—usually with some kind of judgment.

Nothing begins to provide perspective on yourself faster than noticing that your therapist doesn't react the way you expected. And nothing will be more convincing or will build trust quicker than testing his or her responses to your candid communication.

- *If you feel stuck, draw a momentary blank, or suddenly don't know what to say, describe that experience to your therapist as well.* This experience is part of most therapy. "My mind has suddenly gone blank." "I've suddenly lost my train of thought." "I can't remember what I was just talking about." "I don't know what else to say." "This makes me feel very awkward and uncomfortable. I feel sort of stupid." This momentary loss for words usually signifies some inner block, a resistance to some topic or memory that was about to emerge. If you stay with it, the material will often emerge and you will see what was difficult or painful about it.

Especially in a psychodynamic approach, this kind of experience can push therapy to a new level. But if it's too uncomfortable and you feel you are floundering, ask for some guidance: "This feels terrible. I don't know where to go from here. I need help."

Keep in mind that people do not let themselves be known all at once. A therapist will understand that. Don't worry; go at your own pace. But also recognize when you're ready to take the next step.

Listen to What Your Therapist Has to Say

Listening is as important as talking and is often just as difficult when you're starting out. You're likely to be a bit anxious, on edge. You may be on guard against being told what to do or what to think. You're apt to be preoccupied with your problems and telling your story rather than with finding out what your therapist has to say. You may find yourself a little afraid of what your therapist might say: his or her comments might suggest your problems are bigger than you thought.

If what your therapist says makes you anxious, your reaction will be to tune it out. Watch for signs you may be doing this:

- not being able to grasp the gist of what your therapist is saying
- focusing on how your therapist says something rather than on what he or she is saying
- mentally correcting your therapist's grammar, phrasing, or ideas or mentally putting down your therapist for any mistakes
- dismissing what your therapist says because it wasn't entirely accurate or right on the mark
- finding yourself bored, critical, or irritated at how your therapist puts things

Any of these may be signs that what is being said is getting to you—but you are not getting it.

On the other hand, if your therapist adopts a style or tone that strikes you as critical, insensitive, or demeaning, the problem may well be with your therapist, not with what is being said. But if you have generally started well together, chances are that your difficulties in listening have more to do with you.

Ask questions if you don't understand. Part of listening well is asking questions. If you don't understand what is being said, don't be afraid of looking "stupid"—ask your therapist to clarify it.

Stay in Touch with What You Want from Your Therapist

Stay in touch with the goals you agreed to work toward together, and the methods your therapist employs to help you reach them. But week to week, what you want and need from the relationship itself often changes as therapy progresses. Some of what you want may be realistic, some may not. Therapy is an opportunity to learn what you actually can and can't expect in relationships and from life.

Let Your Therapist Know How You Think Things Are Going

You can help your therapist by offering feedback on how therapy is working. A therapist starts out with a tentative plan—a format and an approach—that he or she thinks will be most effective, but a therapist can't always be right. Your input will let your therapist know just how best to work with you and your needs.

You may worry about offending your therapist in providing this kind of feedback. You're just starting this relationship, and you don't want to appear tactless or critical. But if you have chosen reasonably well, you can trust your therapist to know the difference between criticism and helpful feedback. If you still feel awkward speaking about this frankly, discuss this concern directly: "I have a hard time giving you feedback—can you help me figure out the best way to do it?"

Stay Open to New Ways of Looking at Yourself

Even in this beginning phase of therapy, you may begin to view yourself and your problems in new ways. Your perspective on what brought you to therapy might change somewhat. You may begin to make connections between events or feelings that seemed totally unrelated until now. You may also begin to develop a clearer sense of how therapy might help you as you understand the process better and your role in it.

Don't be surprised by these initial shifts in perspective. It doesn't mean you were wrong before, or that you and your therapist have to start all over again. Especially in a psychodynamic therapy, this shift is very common; it's a good sign. Share these new perspectives with your therapist. Use them to further refine and develop your goals for therapy, and your sense of how you might use it.

PROGRESS IN THERAPY DOESN'T FOLLOW A STRAIGHT LINE

Most clients begin therapy with the expectation of steady, gradual improvement. Progress may be fast or slow, there may be bumps along the way, but they expect their understanding to grow, problems to be steadily resolved, and things to get progressively better. However, therapy doesn't proceed this way, and starting with a more realistic grasp of how the process actually unfolds may ease the inevitable moments of discouragement and self-doubt.

"Progress" in therapy *doesn't follow a straight line*. Emotional repair and growth, like any other kind of learning, is often two steps forward and one step back. Or one step forward and two steps back before you are ready to take another step forward again. Whatever therapy you do, the learning curve won't be linear.

You will be trying to make changes that you haven't been able to make on your own. Trying to do things differently will call up and bring into play forces in you or your environment that are opposed to change or afraid of it. So at times you'll approach, at times you'll avoid, and at times you'll do both at once!

The fact that change isn't steady is one of the difficult aspects of therapy. You want to be able to see constant improvement; instead, you experience ups and downs, plateaus, times when it seems nothing is happening. You want to be able to show something for your effort, but hard work doesn't always yield an immediate result. Finding out what is causing a problem doesn't automatically mean you will be able to do something about it: insight and change aren't the same thing.

Above all, you may find yourself disappointed if initial progress doesn't lead to the rapid changes you were encouraged to expect. Instead, you might find yourself having to face and rework the same things over and over. But each reworking adds a bit more understanding, makes a bit more difference in the way you act, loosens a bit more the grip of old patterns of thinking, feeling, and acting, and adds a bit more sure footing in new territory.

If you understand that changes in therapy are less likely to be dramatic and constant than gradual and intermittent, therapy will be much easier to bear with and benefit from. Growth in therapy comes much the way it does in living: in spurts, and often when you least expect it.

PHASES IN THERAPY

In addition to ups and downs, therapy has different phases. Whatever its format, approach, and duration, every therapy has a beginning, middle, and end. Each is a more or less distinctive phase with its own unique features and dynamics.

At the beginning, if you've chosen well, you will probably feel some sense of relief or gratitude at having found someone who takes your distress seriously, is willing to listen, is reasonably confident something can be done about it, and seems to know how to proceed. Significant changes for the better often occur in this first phase. Your motivation is high and your therapist is likely to provide immediate help with some of the difficulties you have been facing.

But often, as therapy goes on, people find their attitude changing as some problems linger and progress doesn't come as steadily, quickly, or easily as they'd like or first imagined it would. Nor does the therapist seem to have some magic that makes problems dissolve. If this happens with you, you'll begin to see that the work is hard, perhaps harder than you first thought. Your problems may appear more intractable and the task more complicated. You'll begin to realize that the job is large and will take a lot of work on your part.

During this *middle phase,* you will probably be pleased at times at the progress you are making, but you may often find yourself frustrated by the problems that remain, discouraged by the slow rate of change. You may feel stuck in all the same old patterns. You may also be dismayed to find new issues starting to surface that you hadn't been aware of before or were unable or unwilling to face. As you open up to them, you may temporarily feel overwhelmed and panicked about your ability ever to get on top of them. At times you may feel worse off than when you started and begin to doubt the wisdom of continuing or of having started therapy at all.

This dilemma occurs, often more than once, especially in longer therapy, and almost always in psychodynamic approaches. When it does, it is always a fork in the road. Typically you feel caught: you can't go on, but you can't turn back. Moreover, you don't want to go back. You don't like the way things were before, and your experience in therapy so far has usually shown you that they don't have to be that way. The question is whether you will change, because at these moments you feel confused, discouraged, and can't see a way forward.

The *final phase* of therapy begins as goals are eventually met, some problems resolve, others prove intractable for now or are left for the future by mutual consent, and the end approaches or a termination date is set. Whatever gains you've made are consolidated. Some of the original problems or symptoms typically resurface for a last look and a chance to reassure yourself that they are manageable. The course of therapy is reviewed, both accomplishments and regrets are acknowledged, and plans are made for any remaining work to be done.

This chapter and the remaining chapters in Part I are meant to help you understand how therapy proceeds. They offer guidelines for working your way through its ups and downs, for making it work, and for telling if it is actually working.

CHAPTER NINE

■

MAKING THERAPY WORK

What actually happens in therapy? What do you do? What does your therapist do? Once therapy is under way, a number of issues will arise that have to do with the *process* of therapy itself, such as how to begin and end sessions; learning to feel comfortable in the sessions; handling areas that may be particularly sensitive, such as understanding feelings that you and your therapist develop about each other; working with negative feelings that might emerge; and connecting therapy to events between sessions and outside therapy.

You will probably not have encountered many of these issues before because they only crop up in the context of therapy. Handling a long silence, for instance, almost never occurs in conversation with a friend because social convention usually keeps talk flowing. Understanding how to handle these issues will make therapy much more effective and rewarding.

At first you may be surprised to find yourself reacting more to the small things about therapy than to such large issues as your therapist's methods and procedures. You may feel some discomfort over practical arrangements: what you call each other; whether you shake hands; how you start and end a session; how you keep track of time. You may wonder whether there will be interruptions or whether you can smoke or ask your therapist personal questions. Your therapist may use technical terms or jargon you don't understand. These practical issues affect how safe the process will feel, and without a feeling of security, you won't take the personal risks that let something of consequence happen.

BEGINNING SESSIONS

In more open-ended psychodynamic therapies, you usually start each session by bringing up something you want to talk about. Often this will be some issue related to your reason for seeking help. But it can be anything on your mind: your anger when you talked to your mother last night; a dream; a feeling that your therapist was being critical of you last session; your apprehensions about taking a new job. Starting with whatever feels most immediate and pressing has a better chance of leading to real engagement with your key issues and getting you emotionally involved. It will also get your therapist involved! It doesn't have to be something dramatic, just something uppermost in your mind at the moment. Whatever your starting point, rely on your therapist and on the train of your thoughts and feelings to lead you into therapeutic issues.

In cognitive, behavioral, and systems approaches, or in brief therapy, the therapist will be more directive, often leading you by suggesting the topic for the day, working out a behavioral protocol with you, or reviewing how an exercise assigned in the last session went. Of course, in these approaches, too, you are free to bring up anything you feel is urgent.

In the first session or two, you may feel the burden of getting the session going and not being sure of what you should be talking about. Or you may easily find things to talk about but then suddenly find yourself running out of things to say and wondering where to go from there. Should you start talking about your childhood? Your dreams? Whatever comes to mind? Or should you sit back and wait for your therapist to ask questions? This experience is more common in psychodynamic therapy. But in all approaches, there is normally a transition period after the first few sessions during which the two of you will learn to work together and establish an ongoing rhythm.

If these initial feelings of awkwardness and uncertainty don't pass, or if it's still difficult to find anything to talk about, discuss it with your therapist. You might be able to figure out what makes it so difficult—perhaps unexpected resistance to facing the issues you are there to resolve. If the difficulties persist, it may signify problems in the therapeutic relationship itself or could mean you aren't ready to tackle these particular issues yet.

If you tend to be late or absent with any regularity, it may simply mean that you don't plan well. But it may also signify you find something difficult to talk about, or perhaps that you are dissatisfied with the therapy. Perhaps your relationship with the therapist is becoming too intense, or you are afraid of becoming too dependent. Lateness and missed appointments should be discussed as soon as they become habitual.

DURING SESSIONS

During sessions you can always:

- *Ask questions.* Question anything you are confused about or need your therapist to clarify.
- *Share your reactions* about what your therapist is doing, your sense of how therapy is going, or how you feel about it. Your therapist can't read your mind and depends on your feedback to keep therapy on course.
- *Stay informed* about the basic arrangements for therapy and your therapist's policies. If your therapist does something that departs from your basic agreement, or does something that bothers you and that you haven't agreed to, it is important to ask for an explanation.
- *Refuse any procedure* or intervention your therapist proposes if you don't feel comfortable with it, or don't think it is in your best interest. That is your legal right as a client. But make sure you understand the procedure and the rationale for it first so you can make an informed decision.

How to Address Each Other

The way you address each other should reflect the kind of relationship you have. A good rule of thumb is to begin by using the name your therapist used in introducing himself or herself to you. A growing number of therapists today will start off on a first-name basis and invite you to do the same. There is no objection to this if you feel comfortable with the familiarity. But many therapists still use their last name and professional title if they have one—"Dr." X, for instance, in the case of a psychiatrist or clinical psychologist.

You may actually feel more comfortable using your therapist's last name, or even avoiding using his or her name at all, until you feel more closeness and equality in the relationship. But to address your therapist by first name when your therapist did not introduce himself or herself that way—or hasn't addressed you by your first name—assumes a false familiarity and is patronizing.

After you've worked together for a while, many therapists will address clients by their first name. If this reflects a growing closeness in your relationship, it isn't disrespectful. If it doesn't, it represents a condescending familiarity that you may resent, especially if your therapist uses your first name while continuing to insist you address him or her by last name and title.

Some therapists will continue to call you by your last name no matter how long you have worked together. This is often a way of showing professional courtesy and respect. But it may also reflect a lack of warmth, excessive reserve, or rigid adherence to the professional role that inhibits a genuinely personal relationship. You will probably sense the difference.

The important point is that how you address each other should reflect the nature of your relationship, and this may change over time.

Couch or Chair?

Despite popular depictions of therapy that have the client lying on a couch with the therapist sitting behind, that arrangement is unique to psychoanalysis. Freud originally introduced the couch to facilitate free association, the heart of the psychoanalytic method. A reclining position and the removal of the analyst from sight promotes an unrestricted flow of ideas, images, and feelings from within. In almost all other types of therapy, sitting in a chair facing your therapist is the usual arrangement. This is the posture of active engagement. Sitting up promotes thinking, communication, problem-solving, interaction with the outer world. Lying down facilitates associations, fantasy, dreaming, and surrender to the emotions and impulses of the inner world.

The method should fit the goals: your posture should be appropriate to your therapy. In the great majority of cases, this will be sitting up facing your therapist. Even in psychoanalysis, the first few sessions are usually conducted face-to-face, while client and analyst are getting to know each other and discussing how they will work together—a reality-oriented, problem-solving task.

Some therapists who don't have psychoanalytic training like to have their clients use the couch, but you may want to be cautious. The couch is a potentially powerful technique, and a therapist needs to be trained and experienced in the use of it. Some inadequately trained therapists, however, use the couch because they want to feel they are doing "analysis," but they may not be skilled in handling the internal forces that the couch elicits. As a general rule, if your therapist suggests you lie on a couch during sessions but isn't trained in psychoanalysis, don't agree unless it is part of another approach he or she is skilled in, such as biofeedback or relaxation training. Even if your therapist has analytic training, if you don't feel comfortable using a couch, feel free to express your reluctance. You are not missing any "magic" by not lying on a couch, and you should not let yourself be talked or intimidated into using it.

Your Therapist's Interpersonal Style

Therapists vary in their personal style: some tend to be more formal, others quite informal. This is largely a matter of personality and preference, but the degree of formality also depends on what your therapist thinks will foster a sense of comfort and trust.

Neither style by itself is necessarily better. A more formal style can still be compatible with warmth and caring, and a therapist with an informal style can take you just as seriously and work with you just as professionally as one with a more "professional" manner. The main thing is that you should feel comfortable with your therapist's style, since this can influence your forming a solid working relationship. If you don't, say so. In general, whatever is natural for both of you is best.

Small Talk

Small talk is a natural part of any relationship, including therapy: movies, politics, vacations, even the weather. It is a way of getting to know each other and building rapport. It is also natural to be interested in each other. But too much small talk can shake you out of a mood you've brought to therapy and need to discuss. It can distract you from the business at hand. Small talk also tends to revolve around topics that interest your therapist more than they do you. To please your therapist, you may find yourself bringing up gossip, tips, or other "special" information you have access to that your therapist seems to be particularly interested in. Or your therapist may pursue these things longer than you'd like. If so, it's hard not to go along—it makes you feel like an interesting person.

But if small talk happens too frequently, or too often at your therapist's initiative, you will find yourself resenting your therapist for using your time for purposes that have nothing to do with your therapy. If you feel this is the case, call it to your therapist's attention.

Smoking

Given the health hazards of "passive" smoking—inhaling the smoke from someone else's cigarettes—there is no justification for any smoker to subject others to smoke. If both of you choose to smoke, so be it. But if only one of you is a smoker, the courteous thing to do is to ask permission to smoke, or simply to wait until the session is over. This should be agreed on at the start of therapy.

Note-taking, Recording, and Taping

Traditionally, therapists have made their notes on sessions immediately after their client leaves. But more and more therapists are taking notes during sessions. Audio- and videotaping have also become more common, especially in family therapy. Some therapists ask permission; others take it for granted. You have a right to know how these records will be used. Are they just for your therapist's use or will they be used with a supervisor? Such uses are generally in your best interest as long as confidentiality is protected. But they may also be used for research purposes, for articles and books, or for seminar and conference presentations. These uses benefit your therapist but don't directly benefit you. Whatever the situation, your consent cannot be taken for granted. Your therapist should explain their purpose and get your express permission. If the notes are for your therapist's own review, or because a clinic or agency requires that each session be documented, the note-taking shouldn't intrude. If you find it disturbs you or disrupts the flow of the session, ask your therapist to make notes afterward.

Interruptions

Ideally, sessions would never be interrupted, but it is sometimes unavoidable. Your therapist should, however, keep interruptions to a minimum. Interruptions undermine the feeling that therapy is a protected place where your needs come first. Phone calls are the most common interruption. Unless your therapist is "on call" for a hospital, clinic, or agency, or dealing with an ongoing emergency, he or she should arrange to have all calls held during sessions or diverted to an answering machine. Some therapists justify taking calls by saying they want to be available to clients in an emergency, including you. However, few emergencies can't wait until the end of your session. If your therapist does take a call, he or she should keep it as short as possible and call back after the session ends. After all, this is your time. If it is an extended essential call, your therapist should offer to make up the lost time, either by extending the session or scheduling an additional one.

If your therapist does take phone calls during sessions and you don't like it, let your therapist know and discuss it.

Asking Your Therapist Personal Questions

You may find yourself wanting to know more about your therapist—wondering if he or she is or has been married or has children or whether he or she thinks your decision to divorce is brave or selfish. Clients often feel somewhat embarrassed or guilty for having these thoughts. They vaguely sense that it might not be appropriate to inquire—it feels like stepping over a line they should respect. After all, their therapist is offering a professional service, not personal friendship. And yet this professional relationship is a personal one, too, and often an intimate one at that. It's natural to be interested in who this person is.

Your interest can have many meanings. You may simply be curious about someone who has become important to you. You may think it would help you to know how he or she handles life and its problems. You may think knowing something personal would help you feel closer. You may want to know if your therapist can possibly understand your experience and the kinds of things you are talking about.

Your interest in your therapist's personal life can serve less therapeutic purposes as well. Finding out something personal or private may provide a secret sense of control, "having something" on him or her that will make your therapist less intimidating, or expose feet of clay. At the very least, insistence on knowing biographical facts "about" your therapist beyond professional qualifications can distract you from actually engaging—or from the task of looking at yourself.

Whatever your motive, therapists respond in various ways. Some won't answer. Others may deflect the questions or redirect them to you in some way, or give partial, but reluctant, responses. Still others will answer simply and directly if they think a question is relevant or a way to illustrate a point. Some, unfortunately, are all too ready to talk about themselves.

By and large, your direct interactions will tell you a lot about your therapist as a person—usually all you need to know. A large part of what is reparative in therapy results from that person-to-person encounter and collaboration; it doesn't come from knowing facts about your therapist's life.

Avoiding Your Legitimate Questions

It is an altogether different matter when therapists avoid answering questions that *are* relevant to therapy. Some therapists take the narrow view that answering *any* question or expressing *any* opinion is detrimental to therapy because it unduly influences you. Also, the more neutral they remain, the more they feel clients are forced to reveal themselves and assume responsibility for their actions. This stance has a certain place in psychoanalysis, and occasionally in psychodynamic therapy, but is inappropriate in most forms of therapy, particularly when it is important to you to know how your therapist feels about an issue you are struggling with, such as whether to sue for child custody or send an elderly parent to a nursing home.

In these cases you are not asking a personal question about your therapist's beliefs; you want help in thinking through an important issue and sorting out your own feelings. Part of that process is taking other perspectives into account, seeing yourself as others may see you, and dealing with attitudes that may not coincide with your own. Of course, you should still explore your own attitudes first. And in psychodynamic therapy, you may find it helpful to explore the meaning your therapist's attitudes have for you and why they are important. But once you've done this, your therapist has no reason to hide his or her perspective behind a stance of supposed neutrality.

Your requests for clarification should be treated the same way. Questions such as "Why did you ask me that?" "Why am I so depressed?" "Why am I having these nightmares?" "What did you mean when you said I saw myself in my daughter?" are straightforward, relevant to therapy, and deserve an answer. To take a doctrinaire stance that any answer from the therapist allows the client to avoid necessary therapeutic work is inappropriate. Often a clarification can help move you to a deeper examination of the issue.

Professional Jargon

Like professionals in any field, therapists have their own jargon. For the most part, therapists should avoid using it in therapy and speak in everyday terms. A therapist who regularly spices the conversation with jargon is trying to impress you or himself. A substitute for genuine thought and understanding, jargon tends to be impersonal and implicitly condescending. Still, even good therapists lapse into it on occasion. Some terms have particularly rich associations for them and come naturally to mind in certain situations. But if your therapist uses any jargon you don't understand, be sure to ask what it means.

Touching

Touching of any kind between therapist and client that suggests personal intimacy, especially sexual intimacy, raises serious ethical questions. Sexual intimacy is never permissible in therapy. It is a gross violation of trust and a breach of every code of professional ethics. It is always the therapist's responsibility to see that sexual feelings do not lead to sexual involvement, even if it is the client who initiates it (see Chapter 11, p. 250).

On the other hand, some kinds of physical contact can be a natural part of interacting: a handshake, for instance, or an occasional pat on the back, or even a hug. And if you are in a "somatic" or body therapy, touch is part of therapy. Even here, however, touch must stay within professional bounds, with no hint of sexual intimacy or a sexual motive.

Exactly what constitutes nonerotic, socially acceptable physical contact has become more ambiguous today because of changing social mores. Men who know each other well may routinely greet each other or say good-bye with a hug, for example, something that would have raised eyebrows not that many years ago. The main principle is that physical contact will probably not be harmful if it is spontaneous, comfortable for the two of you, and a socially acceptable form of expression that is appropriate in a professional relationship.

Therapy is not like other relationships, not even other professional relationships. Because of the special pulls on both therapist and client, and the need to keep this relationship a safe place where you can reveal yourself without fear of being taken advantage of, the boundaries have to be drawn tighter. A hug from your therapist at a time of distress, for instance, might show caring and support. But you might also experience it as an invasion of your personal space, or as being sexually provocative.

As a general rule of thumb, whatever your therapist's intentions, if *you* experience the physical contact as inappropriate, then it is. Part of your therapist's job is to be sensitive to and respect your feelings and boundaries for physical contact. And the corollary is, whatever your wishes or behavior toward your therapist, it is still his or her responsibility to safeguard appropriate physical boundaries in the relationship.

Unprofessional Behavior

All therapists, of course, have personal reactions to their clients. They use these reactions as a guide in therapy to understand what clients are thinking, feeling, and struggling with. It is a maxim among therapists that in order to help a client, they have to be able to identify with something about that person. They also need to like their client—or at the very least, like things about him or her—to form a good partnership.

You wouldn't want a therapist who didn't react to you personally. It would be like working with a robot or a computer. You want a therapist who knows how to use his or her own reactions to engage with you and understand you better. But this is no easy task. Normally we act on our reactions more or less unthinkingly. We don't stop to appreciate the extent to which our background, preferences, needs, interests, and feelings may be entering into and coloring what we see and how we react. Unless we make a conscious effort to keep our own feelings separate and ask what they may be telling us about the situation, our reactions aren't always a reliable guide—they will reveal more about ourselves than about the person or situation we are confronting. Part of therapists' training is learning to guard against this natural tendency to take everything their clients say or do personally, and to sort out their clients' expectations and perceptions from their own. Once in practice, a therapist will use consultations or supervision with another therapist, even personal therapy, to manage his or her reactions.

Despite these safeguards, therapists *do* make mistakes. On occasion, they will do or say something stupid, misunderstand, get angry, interpret incorrectly, become defensive, even retaliate. These kinds of reactions are not necessarily the same as unethical behavior or conduct that violates the ethical standards of the profession. They are the occasional lapses in professionalism that inevitably accompany all professional work done by less than perfect craftsmen. Nonetheless, they can be painful, awkward, irritating, or disruptive.

Following are some of the insensitive or just plain incompetent things therapists sometimes do that may upset you:

- *Overreacting* to something you said or did. Clients tend to become particularly upset if their therapist gets angry at them. Occasional anger, if appropriate, can be therapeutic if it can be talked about. It can teach what you may do that makes someone else angry, how to deal with another person's anger and your own fear of it, and how anger doesn't mean the end of the relationship or of caring.
- *Showing bias or prejudice,* especially against your sex, race, age, sexual orientation, or socioeconomic class. This can be an insurmountable stumbling block if it can't be openly faced and overcome.
- *Remaining cold, distant, or aloof.* This may show up as disdain or as a lack of genuine interest in you. It may also manifest as an inability to engage with you or empathetically enter into your experience. A therapist has to be able to form a relationship with you to be of any help, and you have to feel your therapist is connected with you in a caring and understanding way.

• *Intruding their personal life,* problems, or interests into your therapy so that your therapist becomes a focus of attention or discussion. In effect, the therapist uses your session to deal with his or her needs.

Any of these need discussion. You have a right to be listened to, have your concerns taken into account, and be understood. Most therapists will hear you out and take your observations seriously. If you have a reasonably good working relationship, count on it to help the two of you work the issue through. It can help to see how your therapist handles his or her own mistakes or just plain off days. This is actually when therapists are at their best, and when some of the best work in therapy gets done.

On the other hand, if such lapses are habitual, it may be a sign of general incompetence or impairment. You may want to consult with another therapist to get advice on how to resolve the issue. Or you may want to consider seeing another therapist.

Gifts

Is it appropriate to give your therapist a gift on a special occasion? This depends in part on your therapist's policy about gifts. Some will accept them; many prefer not to. It also depends on what giving a gift means to you.

Some gifts are clear: something bought or homemade. Some are more symbolic: sharing a secret or a piece of gossip, giving an inside tip, referring another client. Certain times for giving a gift are obvious: a holiday, ending therapy. Some are more subtle: just before or after an absence such as a trip or a vacation; on your therapist's return from maternity or paternity leave; on an impulse of gratitude after a break-through in therapy.

Whether or not your therapist accepts the gift, he or she may want to explore your impulse to give it, particularly if he or she is taking a psychodynamic approach. True, sometimes a gift is just a gift. On the other hand, giving your therapist a gift is part of the therapeutic relationship and an important communication between you that can be explored like any other. It can add to what you are learning about yourself—you may be surprised to find other motives at work, for example, seeking your therapist's approval or feeling guilty for being angry at him or her. Or you may have a hard time expressing your appreciation in words or want to do something that will mark you as special and different in your therapist's mind. You may feel you need to give your therapist something extra for putting up with you. Or you may want to send him or her another client to take your place when you are thinking of leaving. Sometimes a gift is *not* just a gift!

This doesn't mean your impulse wasn't a generous one, only that it may have other meanings as well. Your therapist should always acknowledge your generosity and gratitude, even if he or she encourages you to explore some of your other motives as well.

A gift is never required. It is not even expected. Your therapist's only expectation is that you pay your fee.

ENDING SESSIONS

Ending sessions, like beginning them, can feel awkward for a while. In general, your therapist keeps track of the time and lets you know when the session is over. Therapists often do this by having a clock positioned somewhere they can conveniently glance at without disrupting their concentration or the flow of the session. Any glance at the clock, though, can provoke a range of reactions in you: "My therapist can't wait for the session to end—I must be boring" or "Thank God the session's almost over—I was just about to bring up something really disturbing, but I'll save it now until next week" or "I still haven't got to what I wanted to talk about, and now I feel hurried and pressured."

You may find yourself experiencing other kinds of reactions when your therapist tells you the time is up for the day: "I'm not prepared—I didn't get enough warning." "Thank God it's over!" "I feel cut off." "I feel like I'm being dismissed and I don't like it!" "How can it end now? I'm too upset to leave." "I want more time." "I feel abandoned." "Why can't I be the one who ends sessions?"

All of us struggle with endings because they are associated with loss. Attention to these feelings is important. If they seem particularly intense or persistent, explore them with your therapist.

You, too, can take some responsibility for tracking time in the session. Ideally the therapist's clock should be somewhere you can see it, too. If you find yourself ignoring the time, it may indicate some underlying issue or need: wanting to be unconditionally cared for; not wanting to accept full responsibility for yourself; expecting or hoping that therapy will work like a medicine that you take without active participation on your part; relying on your therapist to manage things for you; being afraid to take charge.

There is no single "right" way to end a session. Not all therapists handle endings well. Some give no warning and signal the end by looking pointedly at the clock or abruptly announcing that the session is over. Others give a five-minute warning. Many have a good sense of timing and manage the ending within the flow of the session. Some are casual about the time, sometimes letting you run over; others are exact. You and your therapist may need a little time before you arrive at a way of ending that feels comfortable to the two of you. If the way your therapist ends sessions continues to irritate you or throw you off, discuss it. Your therapist should be able to accommodate you on this issue.

BETWEEN SESSIONS AND OUTSIDE THERAPY

Talking About Your Therapy with Others

What transpires in therapy is not sacrosanct, but you may want to keep what goes on between you and your therapist in *individual* therapy largely between the two of you. In *group* therapy, a basic ground rule is that members not talk about what goes on in the group outside the group, in order to protect everyone's right to confidentiality. Members are even discouraged from talking with each other about the group between sessions to safeguard the integrity of the group as a whole. The situation is different in *couples* or *family* therapy. Since these formats involve someone else you are usually living with, and because they often involve joint homework exercises between sessions, talking about therapy is unavoidable—in fact, you may be encouraged to do so.

On the other hand, there is no reason not to talk to other people about the *issues* you are grappling with in therapy, whatever the format, if there are others in your life whose views you particularly value. For therapists to insist you not talk about these issues outside the office implies they think they are the only person who can help you, or that you can't or won't bring them up once you've talked them over with someone else. Anything that deepens your understanding, helps you to function better, furthers your growth, or enriches your life is consistent with the goals of therapy and should be encouraged.

In individual therapy, where only your own right to privacy is at stake, there is no reason not to talk about your therapy with others if you want to. There is a danger in making the therapeutic relationship off limits to the normal kind of discussion you might have about any important relationship with others you are close to.

At the same time, if you do talk with others about therapy, you should let your therapist know about it. Otherwise your other conversations may become a substitute for bringing up feelings about therapy in sessions or for dealing with your therapist directly. If you get ideas about therapy from others and don't bring them in for discussion, they can subtly undermine the trust and openness the therapeutic relationship depends on. If you talk to others, be careful you don't set them up as rival sources of authority, second-guessing your therapist.

If you're talking with everyone else but your therapist about your problems, you have to ask what is going on. It may be a sign of dissatisfaction with the therapy. You may feel blocked from talking about certain issues in your sessions because you think your therapist isn't interested or because you are feeling intimidated. You may be angry at your therapist for some reason and covertly retaliating. Or you may be avoiding these issues in the one setting where you would have to face them and do something about them.

Social Contact with Your Therapist

As you work together and get to know each other, you might find yourself wishing you could occasionally have some "normal" contact with your therapist outside sessions. This isn't a good idea. As long as you are working together, everything that happens between you happens within the context of a therapeutic relationship.

The psychotherapy relationship is not the same thing as a friendship, no matter how warm and friendly the feelings between you. Your therapist can't be a friend and a therapist at the same time. Many clients—and a surprising number of therapists—don't want to hear this. But the principle is so important it has been incorporated in professional codes of ethics, which prohibit therapists from entering into parallel or "dual" relationships with their clients (see Chapter 11, "Professional Ethics," for more details). These compromise therapy because they are a betrayal of trust, whether the client and therapist acknowledge it or not. If the rationale still seems questionable to you, it shouldn't be to your therapist.

The situation is different when you simply want to invite your therapist to an event that marks an important milestone for you, particularly if this is related to work you are doing in therapy: a graduation, a wedding, a baptism, a bar mitzvah, an exhibition or recital, an opening of a business. Some therapists will accept your invitation in support and appreciation of how important the event is for you, depending on their conception of their role as a therapist, their feelings about you, how important they think the event is to you, and how related to therapy they think it is. Some will decline, even if they might like to attend, feeling it is important to preserve the boundaries around therapy.

Clients don't always appreciate how uncomfortable and self-conscious they can feel having their therapist at an event with family, friends, or colleagues. You should never feel obligated to invite your therapist to such occasions, nor should you invite him or her only as a test of feelings about you. Your therapist may want to discuss your reasons for the invitation, as well as his or her reasons for accepting or declining.

If, after starting therapy together, you discover you work, travel, or socialize in the same circles as your therapist, you should also take this up. It can definitely complicate your therapy. Sometimes it's unavoidable, particularly in smaller cities, towns, or rural areas. If you foresee this happening ahead of time, you may want to find a therapist you are less likely to cross paths with outside sessions.

Running Into Your Therapist by Chance

This can and does happen on occasion—on the street, at a movie, in the supermarket, in the clinic itself if you happen to be in for another appointment. Don't be surprised if it feels awkward. A simple greeting or hello is fine. Your therapist won't expect any more than that. If you don't feel comfortable acknowledging your therapist in public at all, he or she should also understand that. In either case, you may want to review what the encounter felt like in your next session.

Making Major Decisions or Life Changes While in Therapy

Therapists used to discourage clients from making major changes in their lives while they were in therapy. The rationale was that issues and feelings stirred up in therapy would influence important decisions before they had been resolved. The concern is a valid one to a degree, and some therapists still follow that policy. In general, though, the practice belongs to a bygone era when the pace of life was much slower and therapy was the prerogative of a more leisured class. You can't—and shouldn't—put your life on hold while you are in therapy. You entered therapy to grow, to change, to be more productive, to do things differently; not to stop living.

Ideally, you should give yourself time to think through any major decision and allow your feelings about it to emerge and be acknowledged. If you face a major change while you are in therapy, your therapist can help you weigh the pros and cons, sort out your feelings, anticipate consequences, and forestall rushed decisions. Therapy is also a good place to deal with unexpected consequences afterward. On the other hand, you shouldn't force a decision prematurely just because you are in therapy and will have your therapist's support if it doesn't work out.

Books, Lectures, Courses, and Workshops on Therapy

Some therapists will not only discourage clients from talking about therapy, but from informing themselves about it through reading, lectures, workshops, or other means outside the therapy process itself. Their rationale is that whatever you learn elsewhere might confuse you or dilute therapy. This is a narrow and anxious view; it certainly doesn't express much confidence in you. As with any activity you are engaged in, therapy may stimulate your interest and curiosity and you may be inspired to learn more about it. The more you learn, the more possibilities you will see in therapy. It is also true that the more you expose yourself to new perspectives, the more questions and doubts you will have. But these should enrich your therapy, not impoverish it. Therapy relies on a spirit of investigation and self-examination, which should never be limited or cramped. Indeed, some therapists may assign or recommend books that complement the work done in sessions.

Referring Friends to Your Therapist

If therapy is going well and you are enthusiastic about your therapist, it may seem natural to refer friends who are looking for a therapist. A large number of people do actually find their way to a therapist through friends who have been clients. But oddly, as a client, you aren't the best source of a referral.

If it does not work out, you may be left feeling bad for your friend, your therapist, or both. If it doesn't, you will worry what your therapist thinks. You will also question your own judgment: did you misgauge the match that badly? Does it mean you really don't understand your therapist that well? Are there things about him or her you've missed? You will also wonder how it will affect your relationship with your friends: will they hold it against you? Think you don't really understand them? Be resentful that they failed where you are succeeding? Will they think you are more interested in finding another client for your therapist than finding the right therapist for them?

On the other hand, if it does work out, what will it mean for you both to be seeing the same therapist? You may want your therapist to prefer you to your friend. You may worry about privacy and confidentiality: will you feel free to talk? Will you be able to talk about this friendship if you need to? What might he or she be telling your therapist about you? These issues are particularly important when you are thinking about referring a member of your own family. Most therapists won't see two members of the same family in individual therapy for those very reasons.

A final reason to be cautious is that your motives for recommending your therapist may actually be quite mixed. You may want your friend to have a good experience in therapy, but you may also want to do something extra for your therapist, or something that will make you special in your therapist's eyes, earn his or her gratitude, or make you feel more equal in the relationship. You may like the feeling of having your therapist indebted to you. You may be angry and refer someone you know will be difficult.

None of these issues is insurmountable by itself. They are reasons to be cautious, not reasons never to consider referring a friend. The only person you should normally *never* refer is another member of your family, unless it is to do couples, marital, or family therapy together. Discuss any referral with your therapist if you are considering making one.

Many therapists won't accept referrals from their clients for these reasons. Their view is that working with people who know each other puts the boundaries of both the therapeutic relationship and the friendship at risk and can cause unnecessary complications. Some therapists will accept your referral, but only after exploring what it might mean to you. This approach builds in some safeguards, but still runs risks. Other therapists may actually encourage referrals, feeling that any issues that emerge are simply grist for the therapeutic mill. This position is unwise and naive at best, self-serving at worst, and puts your therapist's needs ahead of yours.

If your therapist declines a referral from you, make sure you understand why. Most will be glad to suggest the name of another therapist.

MAKING THERAPY WORK

Therapy Is Hard Work

Make no mistake. Any illusions about this can set you up for disappointment. Whatever your goals in therapy, all will require work. Your therapist can do many things—listen, support, encourage, observe, confront, offer insight, advise, even coach—but only you can change. And if changing were that easy, you—or your partner or spouse or family—would have done it already. You're in therapy because you're trying to change things that you haven't been able to change on your own. This won't happen by wishing or by waiting. Rely and depend on your therapist, but as a collaborator, not a crutch.

Common Feelings Clients Have During the Middle Phase of Therapy

Whatever the format or approach, and whether your therapy is brief or long-term, the learning curve is never smooth. You may commonly feel during therapy:

- *encouragement,* feeling off to a good start, that things are happening and you are making genuine progress.
- *discouragement,* feeling stuck or stalled, or feeling that no matter how hard you try, you can't do it, and you might as well give up.
- *excitement,* feeling stimulated by new insight into yourself, by changes you are making, or by the process of therapy itself.
- *boredom,* feeling that nothing much is happening, feeling uninvolved with therapy, wondering what else you could be trying or what other therapist you could be working with.
- *confidence,* feeling that therapy works, that your therapist knows what he is doing, that you can do it and everything will work out.
- *doubt,* about therapy, about your therapist's abilities, or about being capable enough to really benefit from this kind of process.
- *love,* for your therapist, for everyone who is struggling so valiantly with problems, for family and friends, even for yourself.
- *anger*—toward the very same people!—for not understanding, for making things so hard for you, for being so unsympathetic and unsupportive, for asking and expecting too much from you.
- *clarity,* getting a new and liberating perspective on yourself or your issues, suddenly seeing how things fit together or what you can do to make a difference, feeling a new sense of direction or purpose.
- *confusion,* feeling that you don't know where you are headed or why.
- *liberation,* feeling freer, feeling that you are finally getting out from under old problems that have oppressed you; that more choices are becoming available, and you don't have to go on in the same old unsatisfying way as before.

- *entrapment,* feeling trapped in old patterns that you can't seem to shake off and are even more painful now that you see them more clearly.

It's important not to deny any of these feelings. Growth and change don't come from avoiding what we wish we didn't have to feel, or from pretending we're feeling better than we are. They come from facing our situation squarely at each step, with someone who can and will face it with us and who will not lose faith.

Strengthening the Therapeutic Relationship

Since therapy is a professional relationship, you tend to take it for granted as you might the relationship with a lawyer, accountant, or your child's teacher. But because therapy is also a personal relationship, it requires continual effort to strengthen the bond between you and your therapist and keep it creative and vital. In fact, learning how to do this is usually a key to making the changes and growth you want.

The first thing you can do to strengthen that bond is continue developing the skills that were important in establishing it:

- letting you therapist know as much as possible about the problems or issues you want help with
- listening to what your therapist says
- learning to observe and listen to yourself
- asking questions
- keeping your goals in view
- letting your therapist know how you think things are going
- staying open to new ways of seeing things
- taking emotional risks that will let you change and grow

An additional task specific to the middle phase, particularly with a psychodynamic approach, is *learning to balance the growing closeness and intimacy you and your therapist develop with the equally important need to develop your own independence.* You've been working together for a while now, and you've come to see this person as someone you can trust and depend on. You may feel grateful for your therapist's understanding, help, and support, but at the same time, you may start to feel uncomfortable as you continue to reveal more about yourself. It can sometimes feel as if your therapist knows *too* much about you, has too much influence on your life—even that you are in danger of losing your own point of view. You may find you have difficulty disagreeing with your therapist, needing his or her approval or confirmation. Feeling wary, your reaction may be to back off.

This tension between wanting to be close and wanting to be separate is part of any healthy and vital relationship. The therapy relationship offers an excellent opportunity to experiment with new and more satisfying ways of experiencing *both* closeness and separateness, mutuality and individuality.

It is important to make your thoughts and feelings about the relationship part of the therapy. You will have thoughts and feelings about what your therapist says, does, or doesn't do. At different times you will find yourself feeling respected, hurt, pleased, annoyed, grateful, furious, cared for, criticized, or rejected. Some of your reactions will seem well-grounded and completely justified; others will feel irrational or embarrassing.

Why bring these feelings up? Are they really relevant? Won't it just complicate the relationship, alienate your therapist, and deflect attention away from what you're actually trying to accomplish? A lot of therapists would say yes. Some therapists—because of their theoretical orientation, preference, or temperament—just don't feel comfortable or skilled in focusing attention on their interaction with you.

The position taken here is that, whatever your therapist's approach, the interaction between you is as much a part of therapy as the issues you bring to sessions. How you experience that interaction and what you do with your feelings about it can't simply be put aside while you are "dealing with your problems."

Whatever affects the therapeutic alliance affects the outcome to therapy. At the very least, anything that you feel is interfering with your working relationship should be brought up for discussion. This is part of working out a meaningful relationship with your therapist as you would with anyone else.

Therapy offers a unique opportunity to focus on your experience of an an important relationship while you are living it, where you can express your thoughts, feelings, and anxieties about it openly without fear or repercussions or the pressure of having to worry about someone else's reactions. Therapy offers the invaluable experience of seeing how a vital relationship can repair itself after inevitable misunderstandings and disappointments.

Remembering What You Want to Talk About

Frequently, something comes up during the week that you make a point to bring to the next session, only to find you've forgotten it when you walk through the door. This can signal "resistance" when sufficient anxiety is associated with the thought to make it uncomfortable to remember or talk about. But preoccupation with daily needs can also make it difficult to attend to private, inner thoughts.

To remember these transient thoughts, carry a pad and pen and jot down a note of any idea or memory you don't want to lose. Or keep a diary when you start therapy. A diary has the advantage of allowing reflection, in addition to keeping a record, and can support the process of self-examination.

Don't worry too much about "forgetting" an important thought. If it is important to your therapy, you will either remember it in a later session, or the issues involved will come up in some other way.

Silences

Even talking therapy has its moments of silence. If you are uncomfortable with silence or you expect therapy to be continuous talk, silence can feel unnerving, but it has a definite place. You and your therapist may fall silent after a shared moment of insight or feeling. Silence may be necessary for reflection, to recall an idea or memory or to get in touch with a feeling. Silence can follow emotional release, as you sit quietly in the presence of your feelings. Silence may be the appropriate expression of sudden realization, surprise, or deeply felt gratitude.

Some silence is purposeful. If you have been talking on the surface of things, skirting an uncomfortable topic by distracting yourself with chatter, a silence can give you a chance to get at what is really on your mind. Your therapist may even ask you to be silent to help you focus. A reflective silence can help you get in touch with what's below the surface that may be really bothering you.

Silence can also indicate a block between you and your therapist. Discomfort, anger, and resentment toward a therapist often get expressed by withdrawal into silence, sometimes followed by a stubborn waiting for the therapist to break the silence or to comment on it. Your therapist's job is to sense what kind of silence it is; it is up to you to break a resentful silence by letting him or her know what the silence is about.

Therapists can also retreat behind silence. Clients sometimes experience therapists' silences as lack of concern or boredom. If they are otherwise attentive to you, you are probably reading your own fears or feelings into this. But if your therapist clearly is not paying attention or does not remember important things you've said to them, your negative sense of the silence is probably accurate.

If you are seeing a therapist in training or a relatively inexperienced therapist, the talk-to-silence ratio may be shifted strongly in one direction. You may find your therapist either talking too much, afraid that too much silence will reveal an inadequacy as a therapist, or talking too little, because he or she doesn't always know what to say or is imitating the stereotype of the silent analyst.

Asking Your Therapist for Advice

You may find yourself wanting to ask your therapist for advice—about taking or leaving a job, getting married or filing for divorce, whether to have another child, breaking off a relationship. Some therapists, like some friends, are all too ready with advice. Others will give it, but reluctantly. The problem is that therapists are not just friends. Their job is to help you in the decision-making process, but not to make decisions for you. If your therapist does, it undermines your ability to make them for yourself; it even conveys a covert message that you can't. What your therapist *can* do is help you reflect on what's at stake, clarify your options, uncover the blocks to your commiting yourself, and anticipate the consequences of whatever decision you do make. And he or she can also support you afterward in dealing with the results.

Some therapists rigidly refuse to give advice or make recommendations under any circumstances. This is irresponsible. At times a therapist must be prepared to advise, even at the risk of rupturing the relationship. This is always the case when clients' insight or judgment is so impaired by trauma, severe depression, psychosis, intoxication, panic, or some other internal state that their essential well-being, or someone else's, is at risk. Even short of these extreme situations, it would occasionally be irresponsible or unfeeling not to offer a point of view or recommend a course of action. For instance, you may be so anxious you can't see how to handle a situation that may affect whether or not you keep your job. A therapist can suggest several courses of action, leaving the actual decision up to you.

Even in the most directive therapies, a therapist's suggestions are meant to help you resolve a specific problem, not to tell you how to live your life. Life decisions are still in your hands, no matter how emphatic your therapist may be. The point of all therapy is to become more self-directing, not more dependent on a therapist.

Managing Anxiety

An old axiom among therapists is that a person who doesn't feel anxious about something is a poor candidate for therapy. Anxiety is both a signal of distress and a motive for change. If what you and your therapist are trying to accomplish doesn't make you feel anxious at some point in the therapy, it may mean you're not engaged enough to bring about real change. Examining yourself or your behavior, exposing the areas where you feel weak and vulnerable, trusting a stranger, taking risks in doing things differently, are anxiety provoking. Since there's no way around feeling uncomfortable from time to time, it's best to simply expect it.

Anxiety takes different forms, some physical, some emotional. Physical symptoms include sweating palms or forehead, rapid and shallow breathing, quickened heartbeat, and so on. Emotional symptoms are more diffuse but equally unmistakable: a state of inner tension, an inability to relax, a feeling that something bad is about to happen.

An important part of therapy is learning to know when you are feeling anxious and why: to call these feelings by their right names and to identify what is causing them. This converts what can be an amorphous feeling, threatening and hard to manage by its very vagueness, to a specific fear that is linked to a specific situation. Anything that may be making you anxious about therapy itself is particularly important to call by its right name. Learning how to do this in therapy will not only make therapy more effective, but will carry over outside therapy as well.

However, feeling anxious and feeling overwhelmed are not the same. Moderate, even intense, anxiety can be therapeutic; chronic anxiety or overwhelming states of panic mean something is seriously wrong. Your therapist won't see this degree of anxiety as therapeutic and certainly shouldn't encourage it since it makes doing therapy very difficult, if not impossible.

Resistance to Therapy

In therapy, resistance refers to the subtle and covert ways of blocking change. The paradox of therapy is that even though people come in wanting to change, they are ambivalent about changing. Change demands facing truths that are painful and altering the status quo—as unsatisfying as it might be. Resistance, then, supports the wish *not* to change and expresses the *fear* of changing.

In some types of therapy, little or no time is spent on dealing with resistance because it is largely irrelevant to the therapist's approach. But if resistance interferes with your ability to deal with your issues or gets in the way of your working alliance with your therapist, it has to be dealt with.

At some point, even if you got off to a good start, *therapy itself will evoke resistance* and bring all your characteristic ways of avoiding change into play. Three points in particular typically trigger resistance: when you are close to making a decision, on the verge of a discovery, or coming to a realization about something that is going to cause you distress or discomfort. Each means seeing yourself, your past, your family, or others around you more realistically. A part of you will correctly anticipate that this is likely to involve surrendering some long-cherished hope or illusion that has sustained you; experiencing some regret or sadness; and facing the need to do things differently, as well as your doubts about whether you can. Some part of you may feel it isn't a risk worth running.

Say you have gone into therapy because you feel others take advantage of you in relationships. It's confusing to you because you don't like it, you have tried to avoid it, and yet it keeps happening. The pattern of avoiding conflict may be self-defeating at present, but it may have been a reasonably effective solution to a painful dilemma in your childhood—coping with an alcoholic parent, for instance. You've relied on the pattern and giving it up would leave you feeling vulnerable. Think of resistance as the way you continue to protect yourself in therapy from experiencing the painful feelings this pattern was originally designed to help you avoid.

What makes resistance to therapy difficult to spot is that it mostly shows up in disguise. You have to consider the likelihood of resistance if you find yourself:

- regularly coming late to appointments
- repeatedly missing appointments altogether
- not calling to cancel when you have to miss an appointment
- "forgetting" appointments
- beginning to find fault with your therapist when things get rough
- suddenly starting to question your therapist's competence when you've always respected it before

- suddenly wondering, "What's the use?" or feeling abrupt impulses to quit
- suddenly doubting yourself and feeling hopeless
- talking too long about inconsequential topics such as the weather, recent events, a movie or book—anything other than the topic you need to work on
- changing the subject—e.g., talking about someone else's problems, rehashing old grievances, wanting the therapist to talk about him- or herself

Your therapist may point out the resistance or may simply call attention to your behavior. If you find yourself becoming defensive or irritated, that is a further sign that you are probably confronting some resistance that warrants exploration.

Identifying and understanding what is getting in the way of making the changes you want is a vital step in therapy. Working through this can start the process moving again in unexpected and beneficial ways. Since the same blocks are typically interfering with life outside therapy as well, working them through can lead to doing things differently outside therapy also.

When you are finally able to work through resistance in therapy, you usually discover one or more of the following:

- *Self-defeating beliefs.* These distorted, self-limiting assumptions we make color our outlook and influence our decisions and behavior. Typical beliefs of this kind are: if I'm good, everyone will love me; having problems must mean I'm a weak person—strong people don't feel anxious/uncertain/sad; I shouldn't be angry at my mother/father/spouse/children; I'm being selfish if I put my own needs first; I shouldn't burden others with my problems; if someone really gets to know me, they won't like me.
- *Self-defeating patterns.* These are the things we do that are self-destructive, but are rewarding or satisfying enough in some way that they are hard to give up: drinking or eating too much; getting our feelings off our chest without caring whom it hurts; not succeeding or doing poorly to defeat someone else's expectations of us; starting an affair to punish a partner for his or her neglect; getting attention for making trouble. Such behaviors undermine self-esteem, cause pain, and disrupt relationships.
- *Obsolete solutions.* We tend to hang on to what has worked in the past even when circumstances change. "The past" often means childhood and the coping strategies we developed as children and adolescents in our families of origin. If you were frightened as a child of rage from your parents, for instance, or were afraid of being abandoned or neglected, you may have learned to avoid conflict at all costs as a means of buying security or avoiding calling attention to yourself. In your later adult relationships, the price you pay is never bringing up your own needs or resentments out of fear it will provoke conflict or abandonment.

"What has worked in the past" doesn't necessarily refer only to patterns learned in childhood. Outmoded solutions can include the way you approached a first marriage, a first job, a first adjustment to adulthood. What may have worked well enough to get you through an earlier phase of life may not be as well suited to the present.

The truth is that all these self-limiting ways of thinking, feeling, and acting have also been successful in some way. Thus the *paradox of neurosis:* a learned response that does ease your anxiety, but exacts a cost at the same time. You put up with that cost because you feel relieved—until the next time, when you have to go through the anxiety-relieving maneuver again. Neurosis is a temporary solution, not a lasting resolution.

Often the path to change in therapy lies through *appreciating what we are giving up first*—not just intellectually acknowledging it, but feeling it in our bones. Recognizing how useful your old solutions were in the past will help you let go of them now that they are no longer needed.

Letting go of them is often accompanied by *grieving.* You may need to mourn the person you were, the sufferings you endured as well as the things you said and did that were hurtful to others. You may need to mourn your innocence, your ignorance, the ways in which you deluded yourself, did not stand up for yourself, or were abandoned or betrayed. Don't be surprised if you experience some sadness and some anger—even quite a lot—as you work through your resistance and begin to make the very changes you hoped for.

Although absences and lateness to therapy, sudden silences, and impulses to quit can often signify resistance, they may be reactions to inappropriate or harmful interventions by your therapist. They may be a symbolic protest against incompetent, unethical, or unskillful behavior (see Chapter 10, p. 232). You may occasionally have a good reason to "resist"! If you think this might be the case, bring it up with your therapist. Discussing it directly rather than expressing your feelings in symbolic behavior—where it may be misunderstood—will be much more productive and helpful (see the next chapter on Evaluating Therapy).

Acknowledging Gains

Therapists may have no trouble pointing out when a client is being resistant, but they often hesitate to point out gains: achieving a new level of understanding; mastering a new skill; unlocking feelings that weren't available to you before; saying things you never believed you could, such as saying no to an unreasonable demand. For some therapists, it's actually harder to share in your gains and appreciate them with you than it is to empathize with your discomfort.

What is at stake here is a principle vital to all growth and change. Accomplishments become more real when we see them reflected in someone else's eyes. In individual therapy, your therapist's recognition helps you know you aren't deluding yourself.

In group therapy, individual members recognize each other's gains. In couples, marital, and family therapy, gains need to be shared to be more effective, but it is often the therapist who needs to acknowledge and confirm these for the couple or the family.

When and how gains are acknowledged is also important. Your therapist's actions and feelings toward you will be more reassuring and reliable than his or her words. Superficial reassurance can actually block your progress by undermining your confidence that your therapist really does know how hard this is, and how afraid and doubtful you feel. Knowing that your therapist understands and is genuinely delighted with the progress you have made can help you consolidate your gains.

The Need for Social Supports

Growth and change in therapy requires the support of family and friends, and sometimes employers, colleagues, and neighbors, but they may not always know how to help you change. Overtly or covertly, they may even resist it. People close to you may be comfortable with the old you and feel threatened if you begin to think or act differently. They may depend on the very pattern you are trying to change—being the caretaker, for example, or the Rock of Gibraltar whom they can always count on to hold things together, or the one who brings zest into the relationship. Attending Al-Anon or Adult Children of Alcoholics may violate the unspoken agreement in the family not to call a parent an "alcoholic," for instance.

Resistance can also come from the community at large: many women who have used therapy to become more independent have had to fight a resisting family and society as they put their inner change into effect. Gays and lesbians may find it difficult to be members in good standing in their churches or synagogues and to feel good about being gay or lesbian at the same time. For these reasons many therapists will make the impact of the society a focus of therapy. Some will support social and political action as therapeutic; others will even encourage it as a means of personal empowerment and a way to change social conditions that affect your well-being. On the other hand, very traditional therapists may take the position that these wider sociocultural concerns lie outside the province of therapy.

Whatever your therapist's position, he or she should be willing to help you get more support for the changes you are trying to make and help you figure out ways of approaching others for it. For example, your therapist can help you find self-help groups that are designed to support you in the very change you are striving for. If you are trying to get off drugs or alcohol, fight a depression or other major mental illness, cope with an eating disorder or compulsion to gamble, survive trauma, rape, or incest, there is probably a group in your community that can help you. Belonging to such a group can be a huge help in putting the changes you seek in therapy into effect. Appendix I lists a wide range of such self-help groups.

Working with Dreams

Many clients assume that all therapists will want to hear about their dreams as part of therapy. Not necessarily, and in many cases, not at all. Working with dreams may not be relevant to your goals or a part of your therapist's theoretical orientation and approach.

Dreams are more likely to be part of the work in longer-term psychodynamic approaches where expanded self-understanding is either a goal in its own right or an important catalyst for change. Psychoanalysis always involves work with dreams. Other psychodynamic approaches usually involve some dream interpretation, though how much will vary with the therapist. Few therapists have specific training in dream interpretation unless they have been trained in a psychoanalytic institute, but a therapist may be interested in working with dreams that feel particularly significant to you. You should simply ask if your therapist considers them relevant.

If so, you may be worried about remembering them or afraid you won't have any to discuss. If you normally don't recall your dreams, you may believe you don't dream much. The issue is actually *retrieving* your dreams, not dreaming itself. Research shows that dreaming is part of the normal sleep cycle. We all dream, even if we don't remember.

To increase your dream recall, tell yourself you want to dream before you get into bed. You will be surprised how effective just having an explicit intention to dream can be. If it's important enough to you, tell yourself you want to wake up after an important dream in order to remember it. If you do wake up, review the dream and fix it in your mind before you let yourself drop off to sleep again. Or better yet, keep a notepad by your bed or use a tape recorder. You needn't remember the whole dream or all the details. Even dream fragments can lead to productive insights.

The premise of all approaches that consider dreams relevant to therapy is that dreams have psychological meaning; and that this meaning is often quite different from what we consciously think and feel in our normal waking state. According to this view, in the dream state we are open to moods, associations, and images of ourselves and others that are often screened out of everyday awareness. In therapy, dreams can reveal perspectives and feelings about issues that we may not otherwise be aware of. Freud termed dreaming "the royal road to the unconscious."

Interpreting dreams isn't an arcane or mysterious process. With some training and experience, it needn't be difficult either, though it may seem difficult because dream events are so different from ordinary waking-state experiences. It is still *you* thinking and feeling—just using another language and logic.

When you dream, you communicate in visual images as well as words. And the rules of normal perception and common sense don't apply. The significance of dreams can be figured out, but it is a matter of knowing how to interpret them.

The basis of interpretation will be your own *associations* to the various elements of the dream. This should be the first thing your therapist asks you for, before offering any interpretation. In relating a dream to your therapist, first report it as you would any other experience. As much as possible, try to recapture the mood of the dream and the feelings the various events or images stirred up in you. In reexperiencing the dream, you may begin to get an intuitive sense of what it is about.

The trigger for a dream is often something that happened the day before, or an event you are anticipating. Going over the dream again in light of recent or upcoming events may help to capture its meaning.

Exactly how your associations will be interpreted will depend to a large extent on the theoretical orientation of your therapist. Psychodynamic therapists are more likely to interpret the meaning of the dream in terms of emotionally charged issues and inner conflicts. Jungian therapists are more likely to look for archetypal themes that you are living out. Whatever framework of interpretation your therapist is using, any interpretation you arrive at should ideally be a collaboration. If your therapist's interpretation doesn't ring true, don't accept it. An interpretation must make emotional sense to you. It must not only sound right, but feel right.

Dreams can have meanings on different levels. In the different logic that governs dreaming, meanings aren't mutually exclusive. If you're working with a dream, don't stop as soon as you think you have an insight into it. Look for other levels of meaning as well.

Therapists who work with dreams will typically try to see if the dream also reveals something about how you may be experiencing the therapeutic relationship, particularly in the dreams you have the night before or the night after a session. Therapists occasionally overwork this approach. Not every dream you have will be about therapy. Again, the rule is that the interpretation must make sense to you.

Where to Focus: Past or Present?

Therapy typically starts and ends in the present. You enter therapy because of some current problem and ideally end when you have developed the capacity to deal with it. Along the way, it may or may not be important to reconstruct events of the past as they relate to the present. It usually won't be important in brief therapy or cognitive-behavioral therapy, where the goal is to address a specific behavior—a phobia, for instance. It also won't be important in many types of family therapy where the focus will be on here-and-now interactions between family members. It is usually more important in psychodynamic approaches where present problems and issues are thought to be related to earlier unresolved conflicts.

When it is important to reconstruct the past, it is not the events themselves that are important but rather the *meaning* they have for you or others in your family. Your past is important in therapy only insofar as it has shaped your feelings and attitudes, crystallized a certain set of beliefs about your life, and conditioned certain patterns of response. Understanding how this happened can help you understand your present reactions.

Establishing these links between past and present is often described as gaining "insight." Many clients in psychodynamic therapy erroneously believe it is insight that leads to change. They are inevitably disappointed and confused when it doesn't. What can lead to change in exploring the past is the *actual reconstruction of it with your therapist*. All memory is a reconstruction from the perspective of the present, never a simple retrieval of historical "facts" that have their own self-evident meaning. How you remember events, which ones you remember, and what significance you assign them depends in large part on how they fit into the larger, ongoing fabric of your life. What seemed important at one time may seem relatively trivial now, and seemingly insignificant events may loom large in retrospect as turning points. We are constantly rewriting our history, retelling our story. This actual reconstruction of our past, revision of the narrative of our life, *with someone else* can be therapeutic.

This retelling can confer a sense of coherence and meaning where there seemed to be none. It can convey a feeling of being in charge of your life rather than a passive victim of events. It can be the basis of forgiveness and compassion—toward yourself as well as others. It can help you let go of guilt, anger, or shame as events are seen from new perspectives. As a collaboration with your therapist, it can be a shared experience that helps to overcome isolation and self-doubt—the sense of being "different," "sick," or incapable of being understood. As a review of possibilities seized, lost, or denied, it can uncover the role of choice, decision, and will—as well as chance—and mitigate feelings of being fated, irredeemably stuck, or permanently scarred.

Sometimes, however, delving into the past in session after session is a way to avoid talking about problems in the present. At the other end of the spectrum are those who believe that the past is not all that relevant to the problems you want help with. And if you feel the ground has been gone over to the point of diminishing returns, you needn't continue just so your therapist can fill in the gaps.

Pacing Therapy Through Different Phases

It is understandable that you want to hurry therapy along, especially because it takes time, costs money, and occasionally hurts. And indeed you can help it along by doing the kinds of things that make therapy work better, such as cultivating a good working alliance with your therapist. But *making therapy work is different from making it go faster*. Making therapy work well doesn't speed up change; it makes change possible.

Each of us has our own pace of growth and change, depending in part on what we are dealing with and how supported we feel in confronting issues and making changes. A lot of it depends on your state of *readiness* at the time you enter therapy. Wanting therapy, having the intention and the will, does not mean the conditions for change are right.

Therapy also proceeds at different rates at different times. Sometimes there are rapid breakthroughs; other periods feel barren or fallow, nothing seems to be happening, the goals you want so badly seem beyond your reach, and old painful conflicts keep resurfacing. But actually a period where "nothing" seems to be happening may be a time of gathering strength or of slow integration of new gains. Remember, because therapy involves personal growth, it isn't like recovery from an illness. It is not a simple straight line of continual "improvement."

Homework and Exercises

Several major approaches routinely assign specific exercises for you to do during sessions or as "homework" between sessions. In a session, for instance, you may be asked to "role-play"—take on the persona of someone else in your life such as your boss, spouse, child, or parent—and enact an imagined scene with someone else playing you. Other key parts might be taken by others in your group if you are in group therapy, or other family members in family therapy, or by your therapist. Role-playing gives you a chance to see a situation from another perspective, or to get in closer touch with the feelings a relationship evokes in you. It can also give you the chance to rehearse an encounter you're nervous about. Such exercises are particularly usefulf for building social skills you may need to strengthen, such as assertiveness.

Behavior therapists often give homework assignments and almost always use special exercises. In behavior therapy, the exercises may involve imagining yourself in an anxiety-provoking situation while you try to stay relaxed. Or your therapist may work with you to create a list of the most to least anxiety-provoking situations concerning a phobia. Or you may be taught a method for deep relaxation. Some behavior therapists actually accompany their clients to a situation—such as a place where they have been attacked—that is anxiety-provoking.

In cognitive therapy, too, exercises and homework are standard. For example, you are certain to be asked to track your upsetting feelings during the day, and the situations and thoughts that triggered those feelings. You will also be taught to "talk back" to distorted ways of thinking about those situations and encouraged to keep a record of the instances in which you did so, and what happened to your feelings.

In a family therapy session, you may be asked to change places or roles with another family member. You may be asked to help construct a "map" of your family over generations, tracking influences from one generation to the next. Some family therapists are very directive, suggesting, for example, that the family try new living arrangements, such as having a grown child move out.

In all these instances, the exercises and homework are designed to help you achieve your therapy goals. But you should never feel coerced into trying them and should discuss any reluctance with your therapist. The final decision is always up to you.

FEELINGS BETWEEN YOU AND YOUR THERAPIST

Your feelings toward your therapist can be strong, though often they are more muted and in the background. But they are always present, even in short-term therapy. Therapists understand the nature and role of these feelings differently depending on their theoretical orientation and approach, but they all agree on their importance.

All schools agree, for instance, that positive feelings toward your therapist are a prerequisite for a good outcome. Without them, you won't feel safe enough to fully reveal yourself or your problems. This doesn't mean you won't have negative feelings as well. It means that *on balance positive feelings should prevail*. An overall positive, confident regard for your therapist will enable the relationship to survive the difficult times, as well as the times he or she disappoints you, does something insensitive, misunderstands, or has a bad day. At times negative feelings may come to the fore and you find it impossible to believe your therapist has your best interests at heart or even likes you. At times you may doubt your therapist's competence or compassion. But these times should be temporary and relatively brief. A therapy that gets stuck in protracted negative feelings toward the therapist usually turns out badly. Often it has to be terminated.

Your experience of the relationship can teach you a great deal about yourself. This is because therapy doesn't so much elicit new feelings and response patterns as *manifest* and *magnify* habitual ones. In addition, therapy is structured in such a way that you have an opportunity to experience as well as observe yourself simultaneously. To act and to be aware of your actions is the prime condition for learning anything about yourself and is one of the hallmarks of a healthy ego. Additionally, you have a chance to explore your feelings and reactions to your therapist firsthand, whereas your interactions with others can only be explored secondhand in therapy. Interactions between the two of you are right there in the room. They are the one thing you both have direct experience of. Their immediacy is tangible and convincing. Because of this, your reactions to your therapist have a special power to engage you emotionally and catalyze understanding and change.

Your Feelings Toward Your Therapist

Some feelings typically occur over the course of therapy because of common elements in the therapeutic relationship, whatever the approach. Initial perceptions, for instance, are often idealized. If you've made a good choice, early on you'll probably be quite impressed with your therapist's sensitivity and insight. You may see your therapist as more knowing or able than he or she actually is or could be. Your very need for someone you can depend on who knows more than you do encourages such perceptions. The exclusive focus on your needs also tends to elicit unrealistic fantasies of care and nurturance. Because therapists are always there for you and don't withdraw their acceptance, it is easy to feel you have found the perfect parent, lover, or friend.

These initial idealizations are typically tempered as therapy continues, usually as a result of the inevitable disappointments that occur, some large, most small. You begin to see—sometimes reluctantly, sometimes with a sense of relief—that your therapist is not a magician or perfect parent, and your view gradually becomes more balanced and realistic.

Several developments often complicate this pattern, however. Not all therapists will welcome your disillusionment. They may prefer your admiration and encourage your continued idealization of them. And you may find yourself wanting their admiration as well. You may not be feeling good about yourself, or your sense of being special is being called into question, and you can feel reassured just to think this exceptional person admires you. You may find yourself doing or saying things to make yourself special in his or her eyes or to encourage a more personal interest in you: arriving early for appointments, dressing to please your therapist, becoming interested in his or her interests. Becoming sexually interested in your therapist can be motivated by a similar wish: to be intimately connected with this special person.

Wanting to be admired by your therapist is a natural impulse and can even be therapeutic. But it can subtly distort the way you present yourself or begin to be a major motivation for therapy. At worst, wanting your therapist's admiration can become a goal in itself and a substitute for genuine change.

An idealized image of your therapist also condemns you to an inferior position. Therapy is not about substituting one form of dependency for another, no matter how thrilling or gratifying in the short run. The therapy relationship also can't take the place of missing or less ideal relationships in your life. Even your therapist's understanding of you, no matter how insightful, is finally not the point. What counts is how well your therapist can help you understand yourself and reach the goals you set for yourself.

You may also have unique reactions to your therapist based on your past relationships and what you have come to expect from them. If you think you are a dull person, you may be on the lookout for signs your therapist finds you dull. A yawn, a distracted look or gesture, a flat tone of voice, will immediately be taken as proof. If you are used to women finding you sexually attractive, you will expect a female therapist to, also. If your therapist seems to be reacting to you in some way that others tend to, there's a good chance you're seeing your own expectations rather than your therapist's actual feelings toward you. Learning to distinguish what you believe others think and feel about you—in this case your therapist—from their actual thoughts and feelings can be an important part of therapy. Psychodynamic therapists call this "working through the transference," but it is at play in every type of therapy to some degree. Since you will tend to relate to your therapist in the same way you relate to others, it's an opportunity to see how certain selective or unrealistic perceptions may be limiting you in all your relationships.

How intense your feelings are about your therapist will depend in part on the kind of person you are. If you are characteristically reserved, you will probably be reserved toward your therapist. Strength of feeling is relative and less important than clarity of feeling. It will also depend on the kind of person your therapist is, the type of therapy you are in, and which phase. Psychodynamic approaches that explicitly make your experience of the therapeutic relationship a part of therapy tend to encourage and elicit stronger feelings. How important therapy is to you will also affect the strength of your feelings toward your therapist.

So be wary of setting up some arbitrary standard against which you rate yourself. Others may describe an intense relationship with their therapist, while your own experience may be more quiet. Effective therapy does require emotional investment, but that doesn't mean the process has to be intensely emotional. *Intensity is different from involvement.* Some people can be involved without being intense; others can be intense without being involved.

There is no "right" way to feel about your therapist. The most important thing is to be open to experiencing your therapist as he or she actually is, not as you wish, and to learn how to tell the difference. All that counts is how meaningful your therapy is to you, not how it compares to anyone else's.

Your Therapist's Feelings Toward You

Your therapist, of course, does not experience all of this with detached impassivity. This is not always for lack of trying. It is now generally recognized, even in the psychoanalytic tradition, that a therapist can deny an emotional relationship with a client but not avoid one. Even detachment is a form of emotional relationship. Sitting behind a couch listening is a communication. Psychotherapy outcome research has repeatedly shown that effective psychotherapy depends on a therapeutic relationship that is warm, genuine, and empathic. Therapists *do* have feelings about their clients. And these feelings tend to run the same gamut as their clients' feelings about them. The difference is that the therapist's special skill and responsibility is to recognize these feelings for what they are and to use them constructively to help understand you. The inexperienced or immature therapist will deny the presence of these feelings, and the incompetent and potentially harmful therapist will put them ahead of the needs of clients.

Like clients, therapists tend to experience certain common reactions in doing therapy. They tend to like clients who like them. They tend to get anxious and defensive in the face of hostility. They may occasionally respond with anger themselves. They may try to win over, appease, or withdraw from clients they think don't like them. When their clients have problems similar to the ones they themselves are actively struggling with, they may understand them better, but they tend to be less effective.

Therapists also have their personal preferences. Personality is relatively consistent.

They don't become different people once they enter their offices. If a male therapist feels more comfortable with women, he will be more comfortable with women clients. If a therapist is nurturing by nature, he or she will tend to prefer clients who want to be nutured. A therapist with an authoritarian personal style will prefer submissive clients. And a therapist who is a recovering alcoholic may particularly value working with clients with drinking problems.

Of all the feelings therapists can experience toward clients, sexual feelings are potentially the most problematic. Therapists do occasionally find themselves sexually attracted to a client. Sexual attraction is a normal experience, for therapists no less than for anyone else. But sexual attraction by itself need not be a problem unless it turns into something more than a transient feeling or the therapist allows it to influence his or her behavior or professional judgment. Finding a client attractive is one thing; acting on those feelings, or permitting a client to act on them, is something else entirely. The therapist's professional obligation is to avoid any kind of intimacy or involvement. The consequences both inside and outside of therapy are always destructive. (Chapter 11, p. 248, discusses the entire issue of therapist-client sexual intimacy.)

CHAPTER TEN

■

EVALUATING THERAPY

Evaluating how your therapy is going isn't an option; it's a necessity. You shouldn't take for granted that therapy will go smoothly if you just ask a few questions from time to time. While it's easy to simply trust that everything is working out, it may not be. Like any other consumer you should be concerned about whether you're getting what you're paying for. Evaluating how things are going—what is working well, what isn't, what could be working better—also helps keep you aware and actively engaged on your own behalf.

Therapists know the importance of scrutinizing their work from their professional training and experience. But like most of us, most of them don't like to have doubts raised about their effectiveness. Since the personal relationship plays such a central role in therapy, therapists tend to take personally questions about the efficacy of therapy, or to interpret them too quickly as "resistance." Agreeing at the outset to build in *periodic reviews* of your work together can prevent this misunderstanding.

Periodic reviews help keep both of you from getting stuck, or unwittingly repeating in a subtle way the very patterns you came to therapy to change. They are also opportunities to reevaluate goals—to modify them or set new ones if necessary.

OVERCOMING RELUCTANCE AND INHIBITIONS

Don't be surprised if you experience some trepidation at the prospect of a review. Several common inhibitions often make it difficult:

Fear of what you may find out. "If I question how therapy is going, it may raise doubts in my therapist or confirm my own. That would undermine the help I'm finally getting. I can't afford to question what I'm doing."

Feeling dependent on your therapist. "Alienating my therapist would feel like biting the hand that feeds me. Sure, there are things I have questions about. Maybe it could be going better. But if I question what we're doing she'll see me as a 'problem client' and lose interest in working with me. Anyway, there's no alternative. I don't have anywhere else I can turn."

Wanting your therapist to like you. "I want him to like me. I *need* him to like me. I'm not feeling so likable or lovable right now, and I want to be able to count on his unconditional positive regard. I'm not going to expose myself to someone who doesn't like me."

Self-doubt. "What do I know? She's the expert. Trust is the basis of therapy, isn't it? She's seemed trustworthy up to now. With all her training and experience, she wouldn't do anything she thought was harmful to me. I'd feel awfully stupid bringing this up when there's probably a perfectly good explanation for it. I'm sure it will prove to be in my best interests in the long run."

Fear of disrupting therapy. "If I bring this up, it will really disrupt things. Things have been going pretty smoothly on the whole. I need to stay focused on what we're working on. I'm afraid we'll never get back on track if I bring this up now."

Needing to excuse or rationalize your therapist's mistakes. "My therapist's anger took me aback. Maybe she wanted to make me see how my own anger makes other people feel."

Confusion about closeness and intimacy. "I feel uncomfortable with all the questions my therapist seems to be asking about my sexuality, but I feel embarrassed to say anything about it."

The fact is that you are evaluating therapy and your therapist all the time. You may not express these reactions out loud, but everything that happens in therapy contributes to your sense of whether therapy is "working" or not.

Reliable vs. Unreliable Feedback

Because of the mixed feelings and motivations we bring to therapy—especially toward risking change and toward the need to depend on someone else for help—not all kinds of feedback are reliable in this ongoing evaluation. *Immediate feelings of relief are the most problematic.* Just seeing a therapist who seems to understand what has been confusing to you, or finally finding someone you feel you can depend on, can and should bring relief. But this immediate relief can be confused with the more lasting relief that comes from genuinely facing your issues and resolving them.

There are also counterfeit forms of relief. You may get an inexperienced or incompetent therapist to agree with you, for instance, that someone else is really to blame, or that it's the way you were treated or that you had no choice. That buys short-term relief at the cost of conveying a message that your life is out of your hands and you can do little to influence it.

The most reliable issues to focus on as you begin to evaluate your therapy are:

- *How well your therapist is maintaining a secure framework for therapy.* How safe does the therapeutic relationship feel? Do you trust your therapist to keep what you say confidential, have your best interests at heart, and not let his or her own needs or issues intrude?
- *Whether you feel seen, appreciated, and believed in.* Do you have the sense that your therapist truly understands you?
- *Your sense of increased competence and self-mastery.* Are you finding that you are functioning better at work, in close relationships, with other people in general?

No matter how disturbed you may be, a part of you—this is true even in psychotic states—senses whether things are going as they should. The most important source of this feedback will be the impressions you are continually forming of your therapist's comments, manner toward you, and overall approach.

Occasionally you will find yourself making an explicit judgment in the course of an hour: "I really don't like the way she puts things when we talk about my problems with my family." "He's expecting too much of me—I won't be able to do it." "I thought she wouldn't see that." Or you may leave a session and try to sum up how you felt about the hour just past: "This doesn't seem to be working." "That was really helpful." "I hate it, but he doesn't let me get away with my usual stuff."

These ongoing intuitive evaluations are also expressed in the way you talk about therapy with others, in the way you find yourself responding to your therapist, and in your feelings about being in therapy. If you and your therapist are in touch with this stream of ongoing commentary, it can be an important additional source of information for the two of you about how things are going.

WHEN TO REQUEST AN EVALUATION

In addition to the kind of spontaneous session-to-session feedback that should be part of therapy, time should be set aside for more formal *periodic review*. In this session, you and your therapist review how therapy is going, your progress toward your goals, and how long therapy is likely to take.

Some therapists have explicit reviews built into their particular format or approach. Behavioral and most cognitive therapies, for instance, proceed by setting specific goals and tracking progress toward them by observing and measuring the results of specific interventions. Reviewing the outcome of the preceding intervention is the basis for designing the next. Family therapists who make "homework assignments" will begin the next session by reviewing how you have carried out the assignment. Family therapists are also more likely to contract for a specific number of sessions at a time, ending with a review and an option to recontract for another set number of sessions.

In most other formats and approaches, you will need to build the idea of a periodic review into your initial therapy agreement. Otherwise, you will need to let your therapist know that you think a review would be helpful or that you want to discuss specific issues. It is best to mutually agree to and schedule reviews in advance instead of waiting until problems or a crisis develops. That ensures a less pressured and more dispassionate look, without the connotation of blame or the suggestion that something is wrong. Even in long-term therapy, you should review your progress at least once or twice a year. If you are already working with a therapist who doesn't routinely review and you haven't included periodic review in your initial agreement, then you have to bring it up.

In addition to scheduled periodic reviews, you can ask to review your therapy anytime you feel there is good reason to.

A reassessment can be useful in all phases of therapy. In the early phase, you might want a review because it is still a bit unclear to you whether therapy is going as it should. In the middle phase, it can be useful in pinpointing areas that may still need attention, identifying new areas that need work, clearing up misunderstandings, addressing any lingering grievances about something your therapist has said or done, getting feedback from your therapist, recommitting yourself to the work. Toward the end, a review is the place to assess if you have finished what you set out to do and if it is therefore time to end.

Special Circumstances

Special circumstances that call for a review now rather than later are when you:

- aren't working well together
- consistently feel your therapist doesn't understand you
- dread going to sessions
- find yourself thinking about quitting
- have serious questions about your therapist's competence
- feel uncomfortable about how your therapist is acting or have doubts about his or her professional behavior or ethics
- have been approached sexually by your therapist or feel your therapist is being seductive
- have become sexually involved with your therapist
- feel increasingly stuck or stalemated

- feel you are actually getting worse rather than better
- find yourself constantly upset about how things are going
- feel you are adrift or have lost your sense of direction and purpose
- feel bored and unchallenged, or that therapy has become routine and predictable
- have serious reservations about the approach your therapist is using, a procedure she wants to introduce, or a major departure she is suggesting from the approach you have agreed on
- want to change your goals
- have serious doubts that you've made any progress, despite substantial time and effort; you can't tell whether this is simply a plateau, a fallow period, or an impasse
- find your therapist's personal life, opinions, or concerns are taking over your sessions
- experience your therapist as insulting or belittling
- are "at risk" to hurt yourself or someone else. For instance, if one of the following situations arises in the course of therapy, doesn't respond to therapy, or gets worse during therapy:

  - threatening or violent thoughts or behavior
  - suicidal thoughts, plans, or behavior
  - physically or sexually abusing others, especially children; or entertaining fantasies of abuse or perverse sexual practices, again especially with children
  - becoming the victim of physical or sexual abuse yourself
  - repeatedly finding yourself in dangerous situations that expose you to harm
  - abuse of drugs or alcohol
  - not functioning well enough to take basic care of yourself or to work
  - hearing voices that tell you to hurt yourself or someone else
  - loss of control over your own thoughts
  - severe depression
  - overwhelming anxiety or panic attacks
  - severe phobic reactions that interfere with your daily life or work
  - states of disorientation, disorganization, or delirium

Normally these "at risk" situations call for an *immediate* consultation, and always if the symptoms emerge in the course of treatment. If the conditions or symptoms are ongoing and therapy hasn't made an appreciable difference after a reasonable length of time, something more *must* be done.

Not all therapists are trained or experienced enough to deal with such grave problems. Even if your therapist is skilled and competent in handling these problems, psychotherapy alone may not be enough, and you and your therapist may temporarily need the support and safety of an inpatient setting. The Therapy Guide in Part II provides information on the treatments these conditions normally require. This is not a substitute for a consultation, however. All these situations call for urgent reassessment.

Some of the options to consider with your therapist in "at risk" situations are:

- hospitalization until you have regained sufficient control or the crisis is over
- psychiatric medication to help control the symptoms or dangerous behavior
- if you are on medication, a psychopharmacological consultation to assess whether you are on the right type and dosage
- a change in the structure of your therapy: a different format or approach, more (or less) frequent sessions, longer (or shorter) sessions until the behavior or symptoms are under control
- an additional therapeutic modality: couples or family in addition to individual, for instance
- a supportive self-help group such as Alcoholics Anonymous or the various support groups for victims of physical or sexual abuse, eating disorders, chronic major mental illness, and many other problems (see Appendix I)
- another therapist who specializes in this particular problem if your therapist doesn't

WHAT TO REVIEW

Your Focus and Goals

Are your purposes for being in therapy and the goals you set still clear to you? Do the two of you still agree on them? Do you still understand them the same way? Are you still agreed on how to approach them? Or are you confused about where you are headed? Ask your therapist if he or she is still confident of reaching the goals you set or thinks they need to be changed.

You may simply need to see how far you've progressed toward your original goals. Or what seemed important when you started may seem less relevant now as other issues have emerged, and therefore your goals for therapy may need to be reassessed.

Your Progress: Are You Satisfied?

"Progress" is a slippery notion. How far you've come can be hard to judge since so many factors may be involved. It can be particularly hard to judge if you're having a difficult time right now, or if this is one of the fallow phases or plateaus. And yet you have to have some sense of whether you are accomplishing what you wanted to.

The following guidelines may help:

- First, be specific. Progress is relative to a specific goal. Evaluate your progress toward each of your goals separately, as it may differ.

- Don't just look at how you feel now. Look back over the entire course of your therapy to date. Allow for steps forward and steps back.
- If you are in cognitive or behavioral therapy, or most kinds of family therapy, progress will probably be easier to measure. The goal will be a particular behavior and steps toward it will be measured in discrete behavioral terms. In other approaches, the measure of progress may be more subjective: your own sense of satisfaction or dissatisfaction about how far you've come—or haven't. Therapists know that clients usually have the best sense of how things are going and they learn to trust it. So should you.

Your Working Relationship with Your Therapist

Compatibility should have been the most important consideration in choosing a therapist (see Chapter 5). How well you and your therapist are actually working together is the most important area to review since it plays the greatest role in determining satisfaction with therapy and its effectiveness.

Not only is it difficult to be candid about compatibility, but it's probably the most difficult aspect of therapy to assess. How do you evaluate a therapeutic relationship? What criteria should you bring to bear? Since reviewing the relationship means reflecting on what each of you is contributing individually and how you are doing together as a partnership, you should consider:

On Your Part

- Have you been forthright about the issues you want help with, or have you found yourself holding back important information—facts, feelings, thoughts, behavior—your therapist needs to know?
- Have you generally been receptive when your therapist suggested a new perspective or a different way of doing things, or have you often found yourself resistant?
- Have you been able to ask your therapist questions about things you didn't understand, or do you still feel hesitant?
- Have you been able to listen to what your therapist says, or do you often find your mind wandering or forgetting what you talked about?
- Have you been able to figure out what you want from your therapist and how to get it, or are you still uncertain?
- Have you been able to give your theapist feedback about therapy, or are you hesitant to let him or her know your reactions?

On Your Therapist's Part

- Do you still seem like a good match? Or have you discovered qualities in your therapist that put you off and interfere with therapy?
- Whatever your therapist's temperament and style, do they convey warmth, caring, genuine concern?
- Do you feel taken seriously and accepted as a person? Or do you feel criticized, judged, tolerated?
- Does your therapist believe in your ability to change and grow?
- Does your therapist see your strengths as well as your weaknesses?
- Do you feel your therapist has your concerns at heart? Or does he or she impose goals or a theoretical point of view on you?
- Does he or she respect your independence and your right to make your own decisions, and your basic beliefs and values?
- Is your therapist willing to challenge your behavior or your ideas? If so, does it feel helpful?
- Does your therapist respect your wishes not to engage in a particular technique or approach?
- Is he or she considerate and dependable, or have you found appointments changed abruptly, sessions ended early, or phone calls not returned?

As a Partnership

- Do you like each other?
- Are you on the same wavelength?
- Do you understand your problems in the same way?
- Do you agree on goals for therapy?
- Do you have good rapport?
- Do you respect each other's point of view?
- Do you feel he or she is helping you?
- Does this feel like a joint effort?
- Can you work out misunderstanding and disagreements?
- Can you see you will eventually accomplish what you came to therapy for?

You should feel free to bring up any questions a review of your relationship raises. If you can't, if your therapist is unwilling to confront any doubts, the relationship won't be therapeutic.

Negative Reactions to Your Therapist: Telling Incompatibility from Resistance

Do negative feelings about therapy mean that therapy isn't working? Not necessarily. They can actually be a sign that therapy *is* working, doing exactly what it should. But if it is, then why are you feeling antagonistic toward it? The answer is *ambivalence:* our tendency to have opposite feelings about one thing at the same time.

When therapy is working, you may be confronting aspects of your life you wish you didn't have to face, as well as doubts that you will ever be able to do anything about them. The more real the possibility of change becomes, the more frightening and daunting the prospect can seem. Entrenched habits, long-nurtured images of yourself and others, deeply held beliefs about how life works—or should work— may be restrictive, the source of considerable unhappiness, but they are familiar. The anxiety of the unknown can feel worse. To move ahead may also mean leaving something of yourself behind: some painful but cherished image of yourself; some childlike hope that you won't be disappointed; or a stubborn insistence on a parent's being the way you want him or her to be.

Like most people, you may get angry with therapy and your therapist when a breakthrough is at hand and try to block the therapy in some way to avoid having to understand or change. Since therapy without resistance is an illusion, if you don't experience resistance at times, you probably aren't coming up against anything that matters greatly to you.

In evaluating the therapeutic relationship, it's important to distinguish negative feelings that signal *resistance* from negative feelings that signal *incompatibility*. Negative feelings about your therapist that stem from resistance are often signs that therapy is going well, if the fear behind them can be talked about and understood. Negative feelings about your therapist that stem from incompatibility or from shortcomings in your therapist suggest therapy may not be going well.

Your Therapist's Professional Conduct

Unprofessional conduct is another source of strong negative feelings about therapy. Each of the major mental health professions spells out explicit professional standards for its members, and recognizing conduct that violates ethical and professional norms is fairly easy. Chapter 11, "Professional Ethics," describes the various kinds of ethical misconduct in detail.

Consider Your Therapist's Competence

This may seem presumptuous: how can you, as a client, judge your therapist's competence? The truth is, you are the *only* person in a position to judge his or her competence directly—*by its effects on you.* You are unlikely to be able to judge your therapist's technical competence. Only their supervisor or a senior colleague can do that. But you don't have to. Your gauge of competence is very different: the effects of what your therapist says and does on you.

Three Criteria for Assessing Competence

The same criteria apply that you use in forming impressions about therapy all the time:

- *Whether you feel a growing sense of self-mastery and competence,* particularly in the areas you are working on together.
- *Whether what your therapist says and does makes you feel seen, heard, understood, and respected, and whether it conveys belief in your ability to be more self-determining.* The essential point here is that you experience feeling supported both in your need for an empathic relationship on which you can depend, and in your strivings for independence and maturity.
- *Whether your therapist has maintained a secure framework for therapy.* Unless you feel safe, any gains you make in therapy will be superficial and small. For this reason, whatever the format or approach, how a therapist manages the framework of therapy is probably the central measure of his or her competence.

Review the Structure of Therapy

You should also review the basic elements of your therapy: the setting, the format, the approach, the length and frequency of sessions, and how long you expect therapy to take. Arrangements that made sense at the start may need to be changed.

Reviewing the format and approach to therapy is more important than reviewing any of the other elements. Any change should be considered carefully since it may involve changing therapists as well. If your therapist isn't skilled in the approach or format a review shows you may need, he or she should refer you to someone who is. Many will prefer to continue working with you by modifying their own approach. Discuss this issue thoroughly. Make sure they either have the training or background to do it or will get supervision from someone who does. Some speciality areas, such as sex therapy, should *only* by done by a therapist certified in that speciality.

If you are under unusual emotional distress, you may need to meet more often until the crisis passes. But it may also mean meeting less often if it becomes clear that meeting once a week for an hour, say, is actually more intimacy than you can bear, is too stimulating, or leaves you feeling overwhelmed. A review can be the time to make that adjustment.

Finally, a review is an opportunity to reassess how much longer you can expect therapy to take. This will depend to a great extent on how close to your goals you feel you are. Having a sense of time and timing is vital to keeping focused and on course.

On the other hand, if you are very unhappy with the way things are going, the problem probably *isn't* in the structural arrangements. It's more often in the way you and your therapist are working together—something just changing the structure won't correct. In fact, focusing on such changes may be a way of avoiding a more difficult discussion of your relationship.

Generally, if the initial consultation has been adequate and you have worked out a reasonable set of arrangements, it is usually best to keep to them unless a change is clearly indicated by a crisis, a major shift in goals, an obvious lack of progress, or any of the "at risk" situations described above.

GETTING A SECOND OPINION: CONSULTING ANOTHER THERAPIST IF NECESSARY

What a Therapy Consultation Is

Unlike the initial consultation to talk about going *into* therapy, a therapy consultation is a discussion with another therapist *about* therapy. If you've thoroughly talked things over with your therapist and you're still confused, remain dissatisfied, or continue to have serious doubts, consider a consultation before simply stopping.

Usually the consultant meets with you privately. Rarely would you and your therapist sit down with the consultant together. He or she may ask your permission to talk with your therapist separately as well; you are also free to request this. Normally it is a good idea, and most therapists will agree if your request is reasonable. They often seek help from colleagues and supervisors themselves.

Many clients don't realize they can request a second opinion, or that it doesn't require their therapist's consent. Like getting a second opinion for a medical problem, it's an opportunity to talk over doubts you have about your therapy with another professional. A consultant can provide an independent point of view, bring a fresh perspective to bear, and help you see if your doubts are well-founded. When there has been some major failing—an inability to work together, a wrong format or approach taken, an ethical lapse, or gross incompetence—the consultant can help you move on to another therapist or to deal with the emotional wounds from the therapy.

Whatever your reason for seeking a consultation, you are not obligated to consultants in any way. You don't have to implement their recommendations or give them an accounting. Most important, you are not asking to go into therapy with them, only for their help in sorting out your present therapy and what your options are. Nor should they try to exploit your dissatisfaction by encouraging you in any way to consider therapy with them.

When to Consider a Therapy Consultation

Consider a consultation when:

- You've talked with your therapist and you can't agree on what is wrong.
- You agree on what the problem is, but not on how to resolve it.
- Your therapist is engaging in unprofessional or unethical conduct (a consultation is a must, *even if* you and your therapist can talk about it).
- You find yourself unable to bring up problems in the relationship.
- You've developed a poor working relationship and you think it can be improved.

Discuss It with Your Therapist First

Therapists are more likely to be receptive to any recommendations consultants might make if you discuss the idea with them in advance. A consultant's recommendations may mean changing your original therapy agreement, and since that agreement was worked out together, you will have to renegotiate it together.

Many therapists welcome consultations when therapy has stalled or is otherwise not going well. You may be surprised to learn that they feel it's time for a change, too, or that another therapist may have something to offer you that they don't. Consultations are particularly common among family therapists, but they are used in all the other approaches as well.

Not all therapists will be open to a consultation. Temperament, professional pride, and circumstances will all play a role. Some will take it as an affront to their competence or as an accusation that they have failed you. Almost every therapist will be inclined to see it initially as a form of "resistance"—which is certainly possible. It's worth exploring this and considering what they have to say. Even if your therapist reacts defensively, take some time to talk it over. You can still pursue a consultation while you continue to talk.

What to Consider in Choosing a Consultant

If you decide to get a consultation, you can locate a consultant through the same kinds of referral sources recommended in Chapter 3 for finding a therapist. Give yourself time to find an appropriate consultant since you will get different feedback depending on whom you choose.

Should a consultant have the same approach to therapy as your therapist? If the trouble seems to be with your therapist's competence or compatibility, then seek a consultation from a therapist with a similar approach. He or she will be better able to evaluate your therapy than someone who isn't as well informed about the approach you've been taking. Going to someone with a different approach is likely to call into question the entire way you've been doing therapy, though it may be appropriate if you feel the approach is the problem.

If your concern is your therapist's professional conduct or ethics, then the state or local chapter of their professional association should be able to provide a consultation (consult Appendix IV).

What to Discuss with the Consultant

However well founded their concerns, clients often hold back in talking with a consultant out of a sense of loyalty or guilt. Or they are so upset and disillusioned that they paint a one-sided picture of incompetence and failure.

It's crucial that you be as straightforward as possible, even about things you find difficult to talk about. If the consultant doesn't understand why you really felt the need for the consultation, then the effort will be wasted. Try to be fair, but don't pull your punches. You are counting on the consultation to help you make a major decision about therapy. You could end up worse off and more confused if you try to follow recommendations based on inadequate information.

Be prepared to review at least the following:

- a brief introduction of yourself and your history
- why you went into therapy
- your goals in therapy
- a brief description of how therapy has gone
- your reasons for wanting a consultation

You'll want to ask the consultant about your concerns:

- how well founded are they?
- how serious?
- are they correctable?
- is it worth the time, effort, and cost?

You will also want to ask:

- are you benefiting from your current therapy?
- are you being harmed in any way?
- what could be improved?

Finally:

- what do they recommend?

Evaluating the Consultation

Weigh what the consultant has to say, but remember that his assessment is based on a limited knowledge of you, and unless he has consulted with your therapist, too, only on your description of your therapy. A good consultant will be able to tell much even from a single consultation, but you shouldn't look to him for "the" answer. You have to decide what to do with his recommendations.

How to Proceed: Considering Your Options and Making a Decision

Generally, a consultation has one of the following outcomes:

- It helps clear up some confusion between you and your therapist, and therapy can now continue.
- The consultation confirms specific problems, but also some solutions to these within your current format and approach. These can be incorporated without any major change in your therapy.
- It is reasonably clear that a different format or approach would be more suitable. If your present therapist can't provide it, you will need to terminate and look for a new therapist.
- It confirms irresolvable problems in the therapeutic relationship: the match is poor; negative feelings toward your therapist are too pervasive; you and your therapist are in a downward cycle of misunderstandings and mistrust; your therapist has engaged in unprofessional or unethical conduct. Therapy should be terminated.
- You are still uncertain and want to continue therapy while you decide what to do.
- It confirms that your therapy is on course and you can continue with a renewed sense of confidence.

Ideally, the next step is to bring the consultant's ideas and recommendations and your own thoughts about them back to your therapist before making any decision. If your therapist has agreed to the consultation, or better yet, participated in it, this should pose no problem. It is the rare therapist who will not be at least a little defensive in talking over some of the consultant's ideas. But he or she is a professional and you have a right to a professional response. You can probably expect to feel a bit defensive yourself. But most therapists will be as eager to straighten things out as you are.

If your therapist was opposed to a consultation, is not open to reviewing your therapy or renegotiating your agreement, or won't acknowledge problems in the relationship, this discussion will be a lot more difficult or perhaps impossible. In certain instances, a consultant may even recommend you end therapy without talking it over with your therapist first. In certain cases of ethical misconduct, for instance, there may be no basis for discussion. It may even be unwise to return. Action may be called for rather than talk. As a general rule, however, it's best to discuss in person your reasons for ending.

CHAPTER ELEVEN

∎

PROFESSIONAL ETHICS

The psychotherapeutic relationship can be abused. The nature of therapy requires you to open up to someone you don't really know and to reveal sides of yourself that you have probably been hesitant to reveal even to those you love and trust. Your therapist can use these revelations to hurt, coerce, or manipulate you rather than to serve your interests. Therapy elicits, if not actually encourages, a dependency on this person who will have unique influence in your life. Therapy is also an arena where the most basic needs and fears can come alive, and where you can feel a special vulnerability that you normally don't experience in any other relationship.

The psychotherapeutic relationship also requires therapists not only to put someone else's needs ahead of theirs but to put their own needs aside altogether. It requires therapists to act exclusively in the client's interests, while exposing them to the client's powerful hopes, fears, needs, fantasies, anger, envy, and criticism. It asks the therapist not to take all this too personally, but to see it as the client's struggle.

Above all this relationship asks the therapist not to react the way people normally do: not to react to criticism and anger with rebuke or retaliation; not to react to idealization by feeling or acting special; not to react to a request for help by trying to rescue; not to respond to wishes for affection by becoming a friend or lover; not to react to questionable behavior with judgment.

So both are vulnerable: the client to being taken advantage of; the therapist to taking advantage. But by far the greater vulnerability is the client's.

For these reasons, all the licensed professions have adopted a professional code of ethics. The American Psychological Association was the first to adopt such a code, in 1953, the Ethical Standards of Psychologists, which became the model for similar codes in the other mental health disciplines. The original standards have themselves undergone several revisions since that time. These codes govern how your therapist should and should not behave toward you. They are also meant to safeguard your rights as a client. Strictly speaking, they are binding only on members of the licensed professions.

Some therapists are not licensed, since therapy per se is an unregulated profession. But even unlicensed therapists would agree that therapy is governed by certain ethical principles, and most would agree with those stated in the ethical codes of the licensed professions. Of course, unlicensed or uncertified therapists aren't accountable to professional or state ethics committees and licensing boards. But they aren't protected by them either, nor are you if you see an unlicensed therapist.

The great majority of therapists conduct therapy ethically. The issues in this chapter arise infrequently for the most part—but they are of vital urgency when they do occur. This is not meant to make you distrustful of your therapist, but you should not be naive, either. Being an informed consumer is your best protection.

Whenever therapists violate the trust clients have to place in them, their misconduct not only takes advantage of the client, but inevitably undoes much of the work that has been accomplished in therapy.

It may be disconcerting to think that therapists can act unprofessionally, unethically, or even illegally, but some do:

- A woman who has been in therapy for three years is astounded to hear from a friend that her therapist has been telling stories about her—and joking about them—at a dinner party with other therapists and their spouses, including her friend.
- A businessman becomes so enthralled with his therapist that he invites the therapist to go into business with him as an "adviser." After several years, the therapist ends up owning a majority interest in the business.
- A man and his wife are each seen separately by a therapist. In the course of therapy they separate. The woman stops therapy and starts dating the therapist, and the husband, who is still in therapy, is outraged when he learns of this.
- An accountant is convinced by his therapist to give up part of his practice, take a cut in pay, and come to work in the therapist's clinic while he continues in therapy.

All these cases exemplify unethical conduct. In most of them the therapist's misconduct is clear. But in other cases you may be less certain where the profession draws the line. Is it unethical, for example, for a therapist to kiss clients, but acceptable to hug them? Is it unethical for a therapist to trade therapy for a service from a client instead of a fee? If a therapist socializes with a client outside sessions, is this simply an extension of the warm relationship that may have developed between them, or an ethical violation that compromises therapy?

VIOLATIONS OF ETHICAL PRINCIPLES: WHAT TO LOOK FOR

The central ethical principle that underlies all others is therapists' concern for the welfare of their client: therapists must honor the trust placed in them as professionals. Your therapist is obligated not to take advantage of you, either intentionally or unintentionally through negligence or ignorance, and to act only in your best interests.

A therapist violates this principle of concern for your welfare when he or she:

• *Makes suggestions that are blatantly immoral, illegal, or harmful.*

☐ Your therapist proposes that you submit insurance claims listing twice the number of sessions that have actually taken place, offering to split the extra money with you.

☐ Your therapist advocates using MDMA, a psychedelic drug, in sessions to help you "get beyond your blocks" when you believe taking nonprescription drugs is not only illegal but unethical in the context of therapy.

A therapist is bound to honor not only current legal standards but also your own moral standards and may not pressure you into anything that would violate them.

• *Acts with discrimination.* Therapy cannot be denied on the basis of race, religion, sex, sexual orientation, age, or national origin. But discrimination can be subtle and can take many forms, often masked by invoking psychiatric authority.

☐ A therapist tells a gay client that his sexual orientation has to be considered a "perversion" from a psychiatric point of view (as it once was, but no longer is) and that he needs treatment to "cure" him of homosexuality.

☐ A therapist tells a woman client that her place is in the home—she should be happy taking care of her children and give up her aspirations to go back to school and start a career.

Therapists do have a professional right to limit their practice to a specific category of client—children, adolescents, women, minorities, and families are common instances—when this is their area of primary competence or is a speciality. But this is clearly different from discriminatory or prejudicial denial of services.

• *Offers services outside his or her area of competence.* Therapists are ethically bound to limit their practice to the kinds of clients and problems that fall within their expertise.

☐ A therapist who many years ago had just one course in sex therapy and no supervised experience in actually doing sex therapy decides to try it with a woman who originally came complaining of depression, but later brought up her problem with reaching orgasm.

If a problem comes up in therapy that your therapist isn't experienced in treating, he or she can continue working with you, but should consult a therapist who is expert in working with that problem. Otherwise your therapist should refer you for concurrent treatment to someone else who specializes in it.

• *Offers services when incapacitated.* Therapists are ethically bound to stop practicing as long as any illness, life crisis, or personal problem is likely to make them ineffective or could lead to harm for their clients.

☐ A therapist who is a recovering alcoholic starts drinking again, telling himself that he is a "controlled" drinker. His clients begin to notice that his attention wanders, he sometimes nods off during sessions, and he often forgets what they have talked about earlier in the same session.

☐ Another therapist, who has a life-threatening cancer, continues to see her clients even as she grows weaker and weaker. While she is very devoted to her clients, she does not seem to realize that her powers are waning, that some of her clients are becoming frightened, and that their concern over her condition is taking over their therapy.

You may become aware that your therapist is under stress, or you may begin to notice subtle, but continued, lapses in functioning. If this should happen, you should call it to your therapist's attention. When therapists become aware that their functioning is compromised—or are made aware of it—they are obligated to get a professional consultation or treatment to decide whether they should suspend or limit their practice until the problem is dealt with.

• *Imposes his or her values on you.* One of the main ethical obligations of a therapist is to safeguard and promote his or her clients' freedom of choice and self-determination. Your therapist must respect your value system and your right to make choices for yourself.

☐ A therapist works in a community mental health center that is in danger of closing because of local and state budget cuts. She pressures her clients to advocate for pending legislation that would provide funding to keep the center open.

• *Avoids or denies responsibility.*

☐ A family in which the father physically abused his wife and two children was seeing a family therapist. During therapy, one of the children, a sixteen-year-old boy, said he was depressed and had considered killing himself with his father's hunting rifle. The therapist did not take the threat seriously.

- *Violates moral or legal standards of behavior in the community in which they practice.* A therapist has an obligation to be aware of the moral and legal standards of the community. Therapists must also be aware of the impact their personal as well as professional behavior might have on their clients or their profession if it deviates significantly from these standards. Under certain circumstances, a legal violation can in itself constitute ethical misconduct.

☐ A psychologist was accused of forcing a teenage girl to have sexual relations with him in his home. In the resulting legal action, the judge noted that his use of force with a minor demonstrated a potential threat to clients—even though the minor was not a client—and he was sentenced to three years probation. The state licensing board subsequently suspended his professional license as well on the grounds that his actions were not consistent with prevailing moral and legal standards and also compromised the profession itself.

☐ A therapist decided to offer a marathon weekend therapy group. During the marathon, one of the men in the group, who was also seeing the therapist in individual therapy, turned to a woman and told her that her fundamentalist beliefs were keeping her repressed and that she needed to feel free about her body and her feelings. To help her "loosen up" he put a hand on her breast. Proud of his client's "progress," the therapist did not interfere, though the woman fled in tears.

This particular principle is probably the least widely known—among therapists as well as clients—but it is as binding as any other, and for the same reason: the obligation therapists have to put their clients' welfare and concerns first, and to uphold public trust in the profession.

- *Enters into a dual relationship with you.* This form of ethical misconduct, which is probably the most damaging to clients, has come to the forefront of national concern. Because it is so important, it is discussed separately and in detail below under "Special Ethical Situations."

VIOLATIONS OF ETHICAL PROCEDURES: WHAT TO LOOK FOR

The second kind of ethical misconduct involves violations of *procedures*. A therapist must conduct therapy in a way that safeguards clients' rights to confidentiality, voluntary participation, adequate care, and ethical treatment.

A therapist violates these rights if he or she:

• *Doesn't maintain or protect confidentiality.* One of a therapist's main obligations is to keep anything a client says, does, or reveals to them in strictest confidence. A therapist can only disclose anything with the client's informed and written consent.

A therapist should not even acknowledge that you are in therapy with him or her to any third party who might ask, unless this is part of your agreement— e.g., if your name has to appear on an insurance claim. In most states, therapists cannot even share information on a child they are treating with a noncustodial parent unless they have the permission of the parent who has custody. Nor can they legally or ethically respond to a subpoena for records or testify about a client unless the court issues an order.

☐ A client is shocked to hear his therapist being interviewed on a radio show, talking about his own case. The therapist does not mention him by name, but tells enough about his profession, his family, and his problem that people who know him would be able to recognize him.

☐ A university graduate student is seeing a therapist at the university health center. One day she is at the back of a crowded elevator in a campus building and is dismayed to hear her therapist unwittingly ask a colleague for advice about a "difficult" client— herself—and discuss details of her private life.

• *In couples, group, or family therapy,* where other people are present, the ethical situation is a little different since other participants in the therapy aren't bound by a code of professional ethics. Confidentiality is still binding on the therapist, of course, and should always be an explicit ground rule of the group agreed to by everyone. The therapist must inform everyone of this beforehand, or when they join. However, if one of the participants violates confidentiality, you do not have the same legal recourse as if it had been your therapist. Communication isn't privileged in many states when more than one person is present.

☐ A woman in group therapy told a confidant outside the group what went on during therapy sessions. The confidant worked in the same office as another man in the group. The therapist leading the group had never discussed the need to keep what went on in therapy confidential within the group.

The only exceptions to confidentiality in most states are cases of child abuse, which must be reported to the relevant public agency when they come to a therapist's attention, and specific threats of harm to a third party that are made in therapy. A therapist is legally obligated to inform anyone of threats made against them if they are clearly in danger.

A therapist *can* discuss your case with colleagues without your consent for professional reasons—to get supervision on it, for instance, or to get a consultation on some aspect of the therapy. But then they can ethically discuss only information that is relevant, and the supervisor or consultant is then equally obligated to keep the discussion confidential.

- *Doesn't obtain your informed consent.* A therapist must inform you about *the nature and extent of the therapy* he or she proposes to do: what procedures he or she will follow, what will be expected of you, when and where you will meet, about how long to expect it to take, and what costs you might expect to incur. Not obtaining your informed consent to these arrangements before beginning therapy is ethical misconduct.

☐ A social worker who had been treating a couple for marital problems received a subpoena to testify about the mother's fitness to have custody of the children. The social worker testified in court, even though during the therapy she had never discussed that this might happen.

- Therapists sometimes want to—occasionally even need to—consult with other professionals or people who know you well, such as a former therapist, your primary physician, your spouse, your employer, your priest, minister, or rabbi. They must obtain your informed, written consent to do so. The only exception is a life-threatening situation where your safety or someone else's is at stake.
- *Three other situations* occasionally arise where your informed consent must be obtained in advance: (1) if your therapist wants to try an experimental procedure; (2) if your therapist wants to incorporate your therapy into research; (3) if your therapist wants to publish an account of your case.
- In addition, minors, patients committed to a hospital involuntarily, prisoners, psychotic and retarded individuals, all are considered to have diminished capacity to provide informed consent by virtue of their condition. When working with such clients, the therapist is obligated to uphold their best interests and avoid diminishing or violating their rights.
- *When a person isn't mentally competent to provide consent,* therapists are still obligated to try to make the nature of the therapy clear to the client, but must negotiate suitable arrangements for protecting confidentiality with the legal guardian.

☐ A fifteen-year-old autistic boy whose parents had cared for him at home was admitted to a psychiatric hospital. A staff psychologist designed and administered a program of adversive conditioning therapy without consulting the boy's parents.

- *Doesn't allow for voluntary participation in therapy.* This is usually not an issue in individual, couples, or group therapy, where you are usually participating because you want to. The one exception may be court-mandated therapy, but the party requiring treatment in that case is the court, not the therapist. This is more likely to be an issue in family therapy. The therapist may want to see all the members of the family, and not everyone may be willing. If the family therapist does require all family members to be present, he or she must inform the family of this in advance and must also let each family member know he or she can still choose not to participate.

□ A family therapist refused to see a family unless all members came to the sessions. One family had a teenage daughter who did not want to come. To get the daughter to come, her parents threatened to make her stay home nights for a year. Once at the session, the therapist did not tell her that she was free to leave.

• If one or more family members exercise their right not to participate, and the therapist's approach depends on having everyone present, the therapist is not ethically obligated to proceed.

• *Doesn't make appropriate use of other professional resources when these are called for.* Therapists are not just obligated to offer you their own expertise; they must make full use of all available resources that will serve your best interests (see discussion, p. 247).

□ A woman comes to therapy with a variety of physical complaints in addition to feeling anxious and depressed. In the course of therapy, she focuses mainly on these physical symptoms, which seem to shift from week to week, consistently complaining that nothing is helping and no one understands. The therapist tells her these are "mostly in your head," though he does agree that her distress is real. During several sessions she specifically complains of uterine pain and asks if she should consult a physician. Used to her complaints about what seem to be imaginary medical problems, the therapist turns her attention back to current stresses in her life and ignores the question about seeing a physician. The client consults one anyway, and an ultrasound reveals a large fibroid growth on her uterus that requires surgery.

• *Offers therapy to you when you are already in therapy with someone else.* A therapist occasionally learns from a client that he or she has started seeing another therapist at the same time. When this happens, it is usually because the clients feel discouraged with the pace of change or have doubts about the ability of the original therapist to help. But they are afraid to bring this up or are afraid to end the therapy because of what they imagine their therapist's response will be.

Clients always have the right to consult another therapist if they think their therapy is not going well, though it is a courtesy to inform their therapist in advance. Letting your therapist know you intend to consult another therapist and discussing why you feel the need can be the stimulus for working through blocks in the therapy. Another therapist can ethically agree to see a client who is in therapy with someone else for a consultation, though normally the second therapist would want the client to inform the original therapist about it.

However, a therapist cannot ethically offer therapy to a client who is already in therapy with someone else. If you consult a second therapist who then offers to see you, realize this therapist is acting unethically and may not hesitate to put his or her interests above yours.

The only time it is ethically and clinically sound practice for two therapists to be seeing the same client is when the client's problem calls for different but complementary *formats,* for instance, individual and group therapy for alcohol abuse; or different but complementary *approaches,* e.g., supportive psychotherapy along with desensitization therapy for treatment of severe agoraphobia. But in these situations, each therapist's role is clearly differentiated, there is ongoing consultation between the therapists, and the plan is worked out and agreed to by both therapists along with the client.

• *Doesn't act when he or she learns of another therapist's unethical behavior.* If one professional learns of another professional's ethical misconduct, most professional codes of ethics obligate them to bring it to their colleague's attention. As you can imagine, this is often a delicate matter and can put therapists in awkward situations. Nevertheless, ethical violations are so destructive of the clients the profession serves, of the integrity of the profession itself, and of the public's confidence that most professions make their members responsible for general oversight of professional activity.

The Ethical Standards of Psychologists, for instance, is very clear on this point. If the misconduct of a colleague is relatively minor in nature—that means it appears due to a lack of sensitivity, knowledge, or experience—other psychologists who become aware of it are obligated to try to resolve the issue by bringing the lapse to the attention of their offending colleague. If the misconduct can't be resolved informally, or if it is more serious, they are then obligated to bring it to the attention of the appropriate state or national committee on professional ethics and conduct.

Special Ethical Situations

DUAL RELATIONSHIPS

When a therapist becomes involved in a *dual relationship* with a client, not only is this gross ethical misconduct, it can be among the most destructive events that can occur in therapy. A dual relationship with your therapist means any link that you have apart from your therapy: social, sexual, financial. Any involvement your therapist has with you outside therapy taints what goes on in therapy. It impairs his or her professional judgment as well as your own, and makes it difficult for the therapist to be truly impartial or to act solely on the basis of your best interests. Dual relationships invite exploitation of the client by the therapist because you and your therapist are not on equal ground: you are open to your therapist's influence in a way your therapist is not open to yours. Your therapist knows such things as what you are afraid of, where you feel inadequate or vulnerable, where you can be hurt or influenced.

As a client, you have a need and distress that brought you to your therapist for help and that leads you to depend on him or her for guidance. Beyond that, a certain power accrues to a therapist because the role itself has taken on some mythic qualities in our society—the qualities that used to be accorded to traditional healers: a greater wisdom, compassion, power to heal. That idealized view is sustained by the need of clients to believe in their therapist's ability to understand and help them.

Sexual Intimacy

Sexual involvement between therapist and client may be the most frequent type of dual relationship. It is the most common complaint against therapists before state licensing boards, courts, and professional ethics committees. It is devastating to the client and to therapy itself. The time-tested principle is: *when sexual intimacy begins, therapy ends.* There are no exceptions.

Ways sexual intimacy develops. Client-therapist sexual contact can develop in many ways, and though it often does not reach the point of sexual intercourse, it can have damaging results regardless.

□ A woman whose problems stemmed from sexual abuse in childhood fell in love with her therapist. He said he felt the same about her; during therapy they would hug, and once they kissed. But he refused to have sex with her; hurt, she quit therapy.

□ A woman who had been attracted to her therapist learned that he was getting divorced. She asked him about it, and soon their therapy sessions were spent mostly talking about his problems, not hers. He asked her to dinner, and she accepted. They started dating, but never made love. After they broke up, she stopped seeing him as a therapist, but could never find another therapist whom she felt she could work with.

Sometimes the therapist uses emotional coercion or drugs to create an extreme dependence.

□ A therapist arranges to give an addicted client drugs in exchange for sex once a week. The client is so heavily addicted that she is terrified of losing her source of supply.

□ A charismatic woman therapist tells her clients that she knows exactly what is best for them. By a combination of intimidation, humiliation, and threats of ending treatment, she gradually develops what amounts to a cult of followers, all of whom center their lives around "therapy" with her. For many it takes the form of sexual favors.

A therapist may misrepresent patient-therapist sex as a "treatment" for sexual problems.

□ A woman comes to a therapist because she does not experience orgasm and is told that she should engage in "systematic desensitization" with him. During the sessions he has her disrobe and discuss her feelings of anxiety, while he comments on how well she is doing and how attractive she looks. The sessions progress to her masturbating in his presence, and finally to her having intercourse with him. For years afterward the woman failed to have orgasm, but she did not seek help because of a deep mistrust of therapists.

Sometimes a therapist may dismiss the significance of inappropriate sexual contact by saying things "just got out of hand."

□ A woman finds herself having sexual fantasies about her therapist and feeling sexually aroused in the quiet intimacy of his office. After months of agonizing, she finally tells him about her sexual feelings. When she does, he comes over, hugs her, and kisses her on the mouth. Upset, she consults another therapist, who agrees with her that this is misconduct. But when she confronts her therapist, he becomes angry and denies that anything was wrong. The woman is plagued by guilt, both over what happened with her therapist, and over having consulted a second therapist.

A therapist may excuse a sexual transgression because it did not occur during the therapy session itself.

□ A brash and successful businessman asks his therapist, a woman, to meet him at his office to help him through a crisis he is having at work. The therapist agrees. That "session" leads to more meetings outside therapy, often over dinner. Gradually, the therapist ends up spending the night with him.

A therapist can take advantage of a client's emotional needs.

□ A young woman whose parents have been distant and cold is told by her male therapist that she needs a "corrective emotional experience." The therapist begins by holding and soothing her, as she craved to be held and soothed by her parents. It ends with him seducing her. After that, she finds that she has trouble forming close relationships with men she is dating.

Sexual feelings in therapy. Clients—and many therapists—are often confused about the kind of sexual feelings that can come up in therapy. They mistakenly assume any kind of sexual feeling is inappropriate and tend to feel embarrassed or guilty. It is important here to understand the difference between *sexual attraction* and *sexual involvement* in therapy.

Finding someone sexually attractive is natural and spontaneous. It can occur in therapy just as anywhere else, but both clients and therapists can feel frightened or guilty because it feels "as if" they were already sexually involved, or about to be. If a therapist in training feels this way, the problem is often handled with good supervision. If an experienced therapist feels this way, it is probably a signal he or she is emotionally overinvolved and either needs to consult a fellow professional or to consider referring the client to someone else. Sexual attraction is in most cases manageable, but in all cases, the therapist is ethically obligated not to become sexually *involved*.

At certain points in therapy therapists and clients frequently experience more complex sexual fantasies and feelings about each other. These may surface simply because of the emotional intimacy that can develop in therapy, especially if it is longer term, but often they have to do with complex transference and countertransference reactions. Again, the burden is on the therapist to recognize the distortions in these feelings and fantasies on both sides, not to confuse them with reality, and above all not to act on them, but to use them to help clients understand themselves better.

In the course of therapy—especially with psychodynamic approaches—it may even be necessary to explore sexual feelings, fantasies, shame, and guilt, particularly if these turn out to be related to the issues that brought you to therapy. The therapist must not subtly exploit these themes in order to gratify his or her voyeurism, or to make the client sexually vulnerable.

The ethical issue: sexual involvement. The ethical issue in therapy is *not* the natural sexual feelings or fantasies, but *whether these are acted on* and become *sexual intimacy*.

Who actually makes the first move may matter in other ways, but not from the ethical standpoint. All the mental health professions are clear about this: whatever the client may have felt, thought, said, encouraged, or allowed, the ethical responsibility is the therapist's. The therapist's duty is to know better, to safeguard his or her client from exploitation, and to maintain therapy as a place where it is safe to have such feelings and to talk about them candidly without fear they will be acted on.

Sexual intimacy and gender. While most sexual misconduct occurs between male therapists and female clients, it also occurs where both therapist and client are female, both are male, and where the therapist is female and the client is male. And though rare, therapists have involved clients in group sex.

The absolute prohibition on sexual contact and sexual intimacy. This prohibition is now explicitly stated in the formal ethical codes of every major mental health profession. The prohibition is absolute: no matter what the client says or does or wants, no matter what the situation is, there are no exceptions; sexual misconduct between client and therapist is *always* the *therapist's responsibility*.

The courts have consistently upheld the principle that sexual intimacy between therapist and client constitutes ethical misconduct. They have affirmed the authority of state licensing and certification boards to suspend or revoke the licenses of therapists who violate the prohibition. In addition, several states have passed legislation making therapist-client sexual intimacy illegal. Expert testimony is no longer needed in these states to establish that sexual intimacy violates professional standards—that is understood to be so by the courts. Similar legislation is pending in many other states.

Three common misconceptions. Many clients—and too many therapists—still believe there is nothing wrong with sex between client and therapist if it occurs outside therapy. Whenever you are in therapy with a therapist, there is no "outside" to your relationship. He or she is as much your therapist between sessions as during sessions. That is why the consequences are every bit as negative as if the sexual contact occurred during the actual sessions. Thus *wherever and whenever* sexual intimacy occurs, it violates the ethical prohibition against dual relationships and constitutes misconduct.

A second misconception is that a sexual relationship is acceptable if it begins after therapy ends. While many years ago even some therapists believed this, that is no longer the case. This is a much easier situation to rationalize. Unlike involvement during therapy, you may not feel any apparent conflict or harm, at least initially.

Even so, the evidence suggests that later sexual contact can still be damaging to both client and therapist because of the special nature of the therapeutic relationship. Therapy may have ended, but this person will never stop having been your therapist. Many of the same potentials for abuse or exploitation as in the client-therapist relationship remain.

Previous gains in therapy can be undone by the therapist imposing his or her needs on the relationship, even after therapy has ended. A sexual relationship can also raise doubts about what you accomplished: did he or she really have your best interests in mind during therapy? It can also create new issues that you won't be in a position to work through with your therapist, who will no longer be disinterested, since he or she will have a personal stake now in how you look at things. In addition, having a sexual relationship with your therapist can make forging a good working relationship with another therapist difficult if you decide to go back into therapy again.

For all these reasons, some professional codes of ethics—the Ethical Standards of the American Psychological Association is one example—explicitly state that a sexual relationship is never allowable, *even if therapy has ended,* no matter how long afterward. No state has a regulation that defines a particular time when a therapy relationship ends for similar reasons.

A third common misconception is that sexual involvement is acceptable if the client initiates it. *Nothing a client does* justifies a therapist's becoming sexually involved, in the same way that nothing a child does justifies incest.

Other Kinds of Physical Contact

One school of thought holds that therapy should begin with a handshake in the first session and end with a handshake in the last session, with no other physical contact in between. At the other end of the spectrum are many of the expressive therapies—dance therapy, movement therapy, somatic therapies—which incorporate various kinds of physical contact as part of their therapeutic technique.

It is hard to set an absolute ethical guideline on physical contact. Indeed, surveys of therapists have shown they disagree. Clearly, not every kind of physical contact between therapist and client—a handshake or even a friendly hug, for instance—constitutes sexual intimacy. Changing social norms also complicate the picture. It's now quite common for men who know each other well to hug by way of greeting, for example.

Whether this kind of nonerotic physical contact is appropriate depends on the context. A reassuring pat on the back when a client is leaving a session, or even a brief hug between a therapist and client when the client is particularly upset and spontaneously initiates it, may be perfectly appropriate. The same hug in another emotional context may be erotic. In general, physical contact other than handshakes should not become a standard practice between you, since it may signal a breakdown in the frame that keeps therapy a safe and secure place.

The genders of the therapist and the client are also relevant. When a male therapist touches a female client, or a female therapist touches a male client, in any way other than a handshake, the contact usually has some erotic overtones, even if not intended. This includes little reassuring pats on the arm, or a comforting hug. Physical touches are also not a wise practice if you are gay or lesbian and working with a therapist of the same sex.

Appropriate physical contact also depends on what is natural for the therapist and the client. Some people are spontaneously demonstrative—they give and want hugs or pats for emotional reassurance. Others bristle or feel invaded by touch.

If there is a general guideline here, it is that any kind of physical contact that *you* experience as erotic indicates insensitivity on the therapist's part at the very least, and perhaps some degree of ethical misconduct. Even if he or she doesn't intend it to be sexual, your therapist must be sensitive to your boundaries and respect them at all times.

Consequences of Sexual Intimacy

Clients and therapists, and even society at large, can sometimes rationalize client-patient sexual intimacy and deny its destructive consequences. The overwhelming weight of both clinical experience and research, however, is that it clearly has harmful effects:

- *For your present therapy.* Not only don't you get the benefit of therapy for your original difficulties, but these are often made worse. In addition, new problems are created by the complications of a destructive sexual relationship.
- *For any future therapy or situations in which you may need help.* The most universal reaction to therapists' sexual involvement is the loss of trust in therapists altogether. Having been betrayed by one therapist makes it extremely difficult to fully trust another therapist in the future. It makes it particularly hard to get into therapy that can help deal with the very emotional wounds the sexual relationship creates.

  This mistrust can easily extend to the entire therapy profession: to the legal and ethical boards that regulate therapists, the schools that train them, the clinics where they work, and the institutions they are affiliated with. If a civil suit is pressed, it can extend to the courts as well where the civil process is often long and complicated, and can be humiliating and ultimately unsatisfying compared to the damage done.

  Clients often find it hard to talk to anyone at all about what happened, including their closest friends or family. For one, they may feel a deep shame, thinking they were somehow seductive and may be blamed for what happened. They may find themselves lying awake at night, filled with doubt, with no one to turn to.

  That typically happens with clients who, after a sexual contact with a therapist, begin to center their lives around the incident. This kind of obsession can come from a combination of preoccupied introspection about what happened with being cut off from anyone else because of mistrust. The result is an isolation that can have disastrous effects on marriage, friendships, children, and the ability to work.

- *For you personally.* The immediate emotional impact on clients is usually devastating. Any feelings of fulfillment or triumph are normally very short-lived. The typical effects include an inability to trust; feelings of emptiness and isolation; difficulty concentrating on other things; feelings of betrayal; loss of confidence in your own judgment; sharp swings in mood; a deep feeling of guilt and self-reproach; and a collapse of self-esteem.

  Sexualizing the therapy relationship can unleash an emotional storm: rage or suppressed anger; severe depression; confusion; nightmares or "flashbacks"; a preoccupation with the sexual encounter that can intrude suddenly and unpredictably on anything else you are trying to do; even homicidal and suicidal thoughts and impulses.

  Some of these feelings may surface immediately, others not until years later. These symptoms bear many of the marks of a posttraumatic stress reaction—it *is* traumatic. Sexual contact with their therapist is often experienced by clients as a form of incest or rape.

  Perhaps the most corrosive and debilitating effect is the undermining of confidence in your own judgment. Not only is it hard to trust therapists again but you begin to feel your own judgment is faulty and you can't trust yourself to make a wise choice of therapist.

  Clients may be left constantly questioning their motives as well, not knowing whether to put themselves blindly in the hands of an authority they can't trust or to refuse any kind of help when they need it and risk the anxiety, depression, and helplessness that comes with feeling alone. Sexual involvement leaves them with an excruciating dilemma.

  Another common effect on clients is a deep and often enduring confusion about sexuality, and sometimes, their own sexual identity. This is particularly true when the therapist justified the sexual contact with a mystifying mix of jargon, professional-sounding terms and arguments, and appeals to a "therapeutic" rationale. The clients who are most affected are those who originally came for help with a sexual problem, or with a history of sexual abuse.
- *For your significant others.* Sexual involvement can have tragic consequences for family, friends, and others close to you. Perhaps the worst is the breakup of a marriage, or even a family. When one spouse learns another is sexually involved with a therapist, it can lead to a bitter divorce that can take years to resolve, and through a ripple effect, may entangle friends and relatives, who are called on for financial help or moral support.

Early warning signs. Explicit sexual contact is not the measure of sexual misconduct. The spectrum of unethical behavior begins with early warning signs and ends with actual sexual involvement.

To help spot signs that your therapist is becoming inappropriately intimate with you, consider these questions (adapted from Kenneth Pope, Ph.D.):

- Does your therapist seem preoccupied with his or her own personal problems and discuss them with you?
- Does your therapist seem to get a vicarious pleasure in discussing your sex life and suggest that you try certain kinds of sexual activity?
- Does he or she seem to take undue interest in your sex life, initiating the topic or steering conversation there?
- Does your therapist interfere in your sex life? For example, has he or she told you not to have sex, or to stop a sexual relationship for "therapeutic" reasons, although the suggestion does not fit your experience of the relationship you are in?
- Does your therapist seem seductive to you, either in dress, manner, or the way he or she talks?
- Does he or she encourage you to act in a seductive fashion?
- Has your therapist suggested that you meet socially outside of sessions for drinks, dinner, or a date?
- Does it seem your therapist is scheduling your sessions at a particular time of the day or week that allows him or her to spend more time with you or allows for greater intimacy—at night, for instance, or at the end of the workday?
- Does your therapist discourage you from consulting a physician or other professionals when your situation seems to warrant it and you feel you should?
- Does your therapist seem to be sexually attracted to you or aroused in sessions on a regular basis?

If the answer is yes to any of these, a caution light should go on. At the very least, you should mention your concern to your therapist and discuss it to your satisfaction. If your therapist refuses or becomes angry or excessively defensive, you should tell your therapist that you would like to get a second opinion from another therapist. If your therapist tries to talk you out of this, refuses to cooperate, or becomes even angrier and more defensive, this will confirm that therapy was taking the wrong direction and that this is the wrong therapist for you.

Socializing Outside Therapy

Professional codes of ethics don't explicitly prohibit a therapist from socializing with a client outside sessions, but experience has shown that this, too, can have an adverse effect on therapy, particularly with the psychodynamic approach. Initially you may experience this as a sign of your therapist's interest. It may even give you the feeling of being more equal in the relationship.

But some part of you may experience this as a violation of the safe frame of therapy. It may eventually raise questions in your mind about trust and confidentiality. You may also find yourself wondering about your therapist's motives in working with you. All this inevitably compromises therapy.

You should protect your therapy by not involving your therapist in your life outside therapy, innocuous as it may seem. Any therapist who respects the boundaries of therapy won't, for instance, expect to get an invitation to a party or to a family function such as a baptism, bar mitzvah, wedding, or funeral.

In certain settings—small communities, for instance, or overlapping social or professional networks—it may be impossible to avoid all social contact. You may not know for sure whether your therapist will be at a particular social event. If so, the best course is to be friendly and as natural as possible—you don't have to avoid saying hello, for example—but not to engage your therapist in any extended way. You also don't have to acknowledge that this is your therapist: that fact is part of the privileged communication between you and is no one else's business. If you run into each other by chance, you don't have to go out of your way to be friendly, just courteous.

Therapy with Family or Friends

It is unethical for a therapist to offer therapy to immediate family members, relatives, or friends. This is a dual relationship with the greatest potential for conflicts of interest, as well as lack of privacy and confidentiality. You should never agree to therapy with someone you know as a friend, and certainly not with a relative. Such therapy is hopelessly compromised from the start. It can be either harmful in itself, or harmful to the family relationship or friendship.

That does not mean, of course, that you cannot go into therapy with someone you have met or know casually. In some cases, though it isn't preferable, it may be unavoidable. In many smaller towns, or in some social circles, therapists and clients may know each other in the natural order of things. But if the social relationship is close, if you are likely to see each other regularly, or you have many close friends in common, you should avoid going into therapy.

Business and Professional Associations Outside Therapy

Therapists are ethically bound not to offer therapy to employees or business associates. Conversely, they are obligated not to enter into any professional or business relationship with any client in therapy with them. Both situations create conflicts of interest, and once a therapist's self-interest enters the picture, it compromises his or her ability to care for you as a therapist.

Gray areas. The boundaries between therapist and client contain a number of gray areas where it is hard to apply an absolute rule, and where therapists themselves differ on what is ethical. One of these is becoming a friend—not a sexual partner— of a client after therapy ends. In one survey of psychologists, more than half said they had done so, though close to three-quarters thought it was not ethical. Likewise, four in ten had gone to a party given by a client, though close to six in ten thought it was a breach of ethics.

In these gray areas, you will have to consider the specifics of each case. For instance, a therapist might go to a party for a client if it is for some honor the client is being given. The therapist might see his or her presence there as an appropriate show of support.

CONFIDENTIALITY AND RECORDS

Your trust in your therapist is built, in part, on the sense that he or she will safeguard what you say in therapy. Unlike some other ethical issues, all therapists agree confidentiality is the foundation on which your being able to work together rests.

Apart from those very few instances excepted by law and detailed below, only you have the right to release information about yourself. It is not up to your therapist, or to any agency or clinic that he or she may work for. If your therapist violates that trust, you have grounds for an ethical complaint, and perhaps a lawsuit.

Today, however, the biggest threat to confidentiality in therapy is not from therapists but from those who pay for therapy: insurance companies, HMOs and other "managed health care" systems, and the like. A new factor is at play in preserving confidentiality today: the need of those who pay the bill to know what they are paying for and to have enough details to be sure it is a justifiable expense.

Requests to Release Information

When you first see a therapist or start at an agency or clinic, they may ask your permission to get records of any previous medical treatment or therapy, or to talk with someone else who is currently involved in treating you. Most of these requests are routine and should pose no problem. Their purpose is to help your current therapist understand the context in which you are looking for help, what kind of help you received in the past, or how to coordinate therapy with other care you may be getting.

Or your therapist may be asked to provide information about you or your therapy by some third party: another doctor who is treating you, the lawyer who is helping you prepare a case for court, a probation officer if therapy is court mandated, or someone else's lawyer.

The important thing to know is that *any release* of information about you to anyone *requires your informed, written consent*. Normally this involves your signing one of two forms: either a "release of information," which gives your therapist permission to release certain information about you to a third party who is requesting it; or a "request to release information," which grants some third party permission to release information to your therapist. Both are legal procedures, and the forms themselves are legal documents that safeguard your right to control who knows what goes on in therapy apart from your therapist.

You may have reasons for not wanting your current therapist to talk with a former therapist, for instance, or to see your previous records. This may or may not handicap your therapist, but it is your right. At the least, you should make your reasons known and discuss them. Consider the therapist's point of view, then make your own decision. In general, therapists will not—and cannot—refuse you services just on this basis, unless they have reason to believe there is undue risk to you in starting therapy without this information.

Administrative Forms

If your therapist is part of a mental health center, clinic, or hospital that receives federal, state, or municipal funding, you may also be asked to sign a release of information that allows statistical information about you—such as age, sex, marital status, income, and the like—to be forwarded to the funding source so these governmental bodies can make more informed decisions about allocating their mental health resources. Normally this doesn't pose a threat to confidentiality because of the regulations governing collection and distribution of this information. Nevertheless, your name, address, social security number, and anything else that identifies you personally should not be part of the form. If you have doubts about your confidence being kept, don't sign: you can't be denied services if you don't.

What Should Be Included in a "Release of Information" Form

If you choose to sign a release of information form, check to see if the document includes:

- today's date
- a place for your signature
- a place for the signature of a witness
- the *specific* information to be released
    This is the most important thing you want control over. It should be indicated explicitly. If you don't understand the meaning of some term, or the reason for including some item, ask.
- the specific person or agency to whom the information is to be sent
- a statement that you have the right to revoke your consent at any time
- a statement that you have the right to review any information that is sent out about you

- an expiration date on the release, or a statement that your authorization ends when you end therapy

Information Requested by Third-Party Payers

The other instance in which you or your therapist will be asked to forward certain information about you and your therapy is if you are using some type of medical insurance to pay for all or part of it (see Chapter 7, "Paying for Therapy"). Whoever pays will want to know some specifics before paying a claim. How much information they will want varies from carrier to carrier. To give one example, Blue Shield currently asks for:

- date of birth
- sex
- date you were first seen for this condition
- whether the condition is related to your employment
- whether you have suffered from the same condition previously and the dates
- whether you are able to work
- the dates of total or partial disability due to the condition
- the name and address of the facility where you received services
- a psychiatric diagnosis
- the dates of therapy sessions
- the type of therapy you received
  This refers to the format—individual, group, family, couples—the length of the sessions, and whether it was an initial evaluation, crisis intervention, or ongoing treatment. Note that it doesn't ask for the approach or technique used.

Insurance forms generally do not and *should not ask for any details of your therapy sessions* themselves, or any personal information you reveal in the course of them.

Probably the most sensitive piece of information is the psychiatric diagnosis almost all third-party payers require your therapist to assign before they will reimburse a claim. (The therapeutic and ethical issues this can raise and its potential impact on therapy are discussed in detail in Chapter 7, p. 167). You have a right to know what this formal diagnosis is. You should also know what it means. Since many psychiatric diagnoses aren't mutually exclusive, and more than one can often be assigned of greater or lesser severity, your therapist may be assigning more than one. Different diagnoses carry different implications for how you might be viewed if they became known. Be sure you discuss with your therapist all the issues involved in assigning a diagnosis before signing a reimbursement claim.

Confidentiality Issues in Third-Party Payment

What will be done with the information you or your therapist is required to provide? The limits of confidentiality are already extended. Who will see the information? And will they keep it confidential?

In some cases, insurance claims for therapy, like other medical claims, are handled through the personnel office where you work. That means that some fellow employees will know you are seeing a therapist and why—at least in terms of a diagnosis. Generally employees who handle such information are required to keep it confidential, but you can't take absolute confidentiality for granted. The same is true with employees at your insurance company, though at least they are remote from your personal, and usually your professional, life. However, at least a few insurance companies have been known to cancel or refuse to renew a policy on occasion for someone who has filed a claim for therapy services.

Employers are more likely than insurance companies to want to know more than they are entitled to, and to try inappropriately to find out from a therapist what is wrong. Confidential information obtained by employers can have adverse consequences. In rare instances, people have been refused promotions or even jobs on the grounds that they received psychiatric care. For that reason, you should beware of an employer who asks you to sign a release for "all medical information"—that includes your psychiatric as well as medical history. This is an abuse of your right to confidentiality.

On the other hand, progressive employers and employee assistance programs encourage their employees to seek mental health services for problems. Alcohol or substance abuse is a common example. Some even pay for initial consultations.

Because of the lingering possibility that someone connected with the payer may find out details of your therapy, you may want to consider paying for it yourself, if you can afford it. The sense that someone else is listening in, even from a distance, sometimes holds clients back from revealing their deepest secrets and painful emotional history to their therapists. This needn't be an insurmountable obstacle if you and your therapist remain alert to it throughout your work together.

Therapy That Is Being Supervised

In most clinics, therapists will regularly discuss their work with colleagues, either in supervision or in staff meetings. Therapists in training, even at an advanced-training institute, will be presenting each of their cases to a supervisor under whom they work. Therapists in private practice also routinely get consultations.

It is not considered a breach of confidentiality for your therapist to seek this kind of consultation. In fact, it's good professional practice and in your best interest, as long as you aren't identified by name. Your therapist is still obligated to protect your anonymity, and the consulting or supervising therapist is no less bound to keep anything discussed confidential as if they themselves were your therapist. But you should know if your therapy will be discussed, and with whom.

Case Conferences

Therapists at clinics affiliated with teaching hospitals or training institutes occasionally present their work with a client at a so-called teaching or case conference. If so, they should ask the client's permission and discuss it with him or her ahead of time. They may also want to invite the client to appear in person to be interviewed so attending staff members and trainees can see and observe the client for themselves. Sometimes only the consultant will ask questions; occasionally the client will be asked to take questions from others in the audience.

The clients may or may not get the benefit of learning what the consultant or the staff think about them and their problems. Whether you will be present or not, therapists should assure you that they will not use your name or any information that might identify you. As soon as they become aware of it, they should invite anyone who might know you to leave the conference. You are under no obligation to participate personally and shouldn't let yourself be pressured into it under any circumstances.

Observations of Therapy

In some therapy training institutes, sessions are conducted in a room with a one-way mirror, behind which therapists being trained observe the session. The therapists in training are obligated to keep whatever they see confidential. You may, however, find it inhibiting to feel "observed" and must give your consent first. Do not let your therapist pressure you into doing so.

Records

Private therapists as well as clinics are required by law to keep records of any treatment they provide. You might want to ask your therapist what will go into your record, where it will be kept, who might have access to it, and how confidentiality will be assured.

Notes, Tape Recordings, and Videotapes

In addition to formal record keeping, therapists sometimes want to tape-record, videotape, or take notes during sessions. These are usually used to discuss the progress of your therapy with a supervisor or consultant, or occasionally as the basis for lectures, articles, books, or seminars. In each case, they require your informed written consent. Taping or recording a session without your knowledge is a gross ethical violation. If you give your consent, this material must be kept in the same confidence as anything else you say or do in therapy.

Lectures, Books, and Articles

Your therapist might discuss your therapy in a report at a professional meeting or in a journal article or book. This is not considered a breach of confidentiality as long as the specifics are sufficiently disguised that no one will be able to recognize you. However, informing you is a courtesy your therapist should extend.

EXCEPTIONS TO CONFIDENTIALITY

Some states have adopted regulations that limit privileged communication and confidentiality. In those states the "public good" is considered to override the individual right to privacy in some situations. Courts have ruled that in these cases "the protective privilege ends where the public peril begins."

These exceptions to confidentiality include:

- *You make an explicit threat against someone or reveal an intention to harm or injure them.* Therapists are now obligated to protect that person—if identifiable by name or description—by warning the person, or someone else who can notify the person, of the threat. Most therapists will take additional steps, usually arranging to have the client committed to a hospital, or notifying the police.
- *You reveal child abuse or neglect.* Therapists are obligated in most states to report child physical or sexual abuse or neglect to child welfare authorities or the local police department.
- *You reveal neglect or abuse of the retarded or elderly.* In some states, this must also be reported.
- *There is a clear risk of suicide or self-harm.* If your therapist believes you are suicidal and/or at clear risk to hurt yourself in some way, they are obligated to seek an involuntary commitment to a hospital. They will base this decision on several factors: how serious your thoughts about suicide or self-harm are; whether the danger seems imminent; whether you have an active intent; whether you have a plan, the means, and an opportunity to carry it out; or whether you can contract not to hurt yourself while you and your therapist work on your problems.

If a therapist is not authorized by state law to commit a client to a hospital in these circumstances, the therapist is obligated to seek commitment from someone who is—a psychiatrist or a licensed psychologist in those states that authorize psychologists who are state-licensed or -certified.

Most therapists know that the great majority of people who attempt suicide have very mixed feelings about living and dying, and that most suicide attempts are desperate cries for help. Their assumption is that, given some time, the reasons for living will prevail, especially if help is made available.

Undoubtedly some therapists mistakenly think breaking confidentiality in this situation will "risk" rupturing the therapeutic relationship, and some won't interfere with a client's right to self-determination on principle. A therapist who would stand by and do nothing for whatever reason is not only acting unethically, but without compassion.

Clients who are aware of a therapist's ethical and legal obligation to take steps to prevent them from killing themselves sometimes don't want to reveal what they are thinking or feeling for this very reason. Thoughts of suicide as a solution to an overwhelming problem are not uncommon, especially in depression.

If you have felt this way, or feel this way now, you should not be afraid to talk about it with your therapist—your therapist needs to know just how bad you feel, and you may find comfort in revealing it. Your therapist will not break confidentiality about it unless you are in imminent danger, in which case your therapist should. If your therapist does not act to protect you, your trust that your therapist really does care for you and can help you will be undermined, and may actually increase the level of risk.

- *You disclose an intention to commit a crime.* Many states now require therapists to report to the police any client who reveals an intention to commit a felony.
- *You are ordered by the court to be examined by a psychiatrist or psychologist.* In this case, the therapist is required to report their findings back to the court.
- *The court orders therapy as a condition of probation.* The therapist is obligated to keep a probation officer informed if a client under court order is keeping appointments, but it is questionable whether the therapist is obligated to report the content of sessions. Usually courts or probation officers will not inquire into these details anyway.
- *Certain court proceedings.* A therapist may be asked to testify in a civil proceeding regarding whether a client should be involuntarily detained in a hospital; in a trial if a client uses the "insanity defense"; or in a hearing about a client's mental competency to stand trial. But these exceptions to confidentiality vary from state to state. Should you be involved in such a proceeding, the best course is to get a good attorney to advise you.

ETHICAL ISSUES IN FINANCIAL ARRANGEMENTS FOR THERAPY

Setting fees. A therapist should inform you what his or her standard fee is before beginning therapy, and if they employ a sliding scale for clients who can't afford it.

A therapist should *not* begin by asking how much you can afford to pay. Therapy fees should be based upon the value of the service provided, not upon the ability of the client to pay.

The acceptance of barter for payment. Bartering therapy for *services* in kind is considered unethical by most therapists because it involves the therapist and the client in a dual relationship. The ethics of bartering *goods* is less clear, especially if a fair market value of the goods is clearly established prior to beginning therapy. However, it is still generally considered an unwise practice. Barter can be a way to avoid paying legitimate taxes. It also borders on the exchange of gifts, which can sometimes have detrimental consequences.

Billing two insurance companies separately. Submitting claims for reimbursement to two separate insurance companies for the same sessions is outright fraud—whether you do it or your therapist does it. If you suspect your therapist is doing this, check by looking at the monthly or quarterly statements you will get from your insurance company, showing how much your therapist was paid, when, and for what.

Billing an insurance company for sessions that never took place. Again, check by looking at your insurance company statements.

Falsifying a fee to an insurance company. To check if your therapist is collecting more than the fee negotiated with you, look at your insurance company statements.

Assigning a "diagnosis of convenience" on an insurance claim to ensure reimbursement. Since most major insurance companies will only reimburse for a diagnosable condition, therapists will sometimes assign a formal psychiatric diagnosis when none is warranted so you can use your insurance. This is not only unethical but fraudulent. A more common practice is to assign a diagnosis that is related to the condition they are treating you for, perhaps has some features in common, but doesn't accurately or fully represent it.

Both practices are often engaged in by therapists who say they "don't believe" in diagnoses in therapy or "don't take them all that seriously." Some will justify it by maintaining they are protecting the client by assigning a "less serious" or less stigmatizing diagnosis. Given that it is hard to guarantee confidentiality outside therapy and that many psychiatric diagnoses do still stigmatize—even the knowledge that someone is seeing a therapist can sometimes be hurtful—it is hard not to be sympathetic to this reasoning. At the same time, it may represent a subtle collusion with you to minimize the seriousness of whatever may be troubling you.

Trading a reduced fee for cash payment. This is clearly unethical if it means the therapist reports less income than was actually earned. It involves you in your therapist's tax evasion and taints the therapy by making a personal interest of the therapist paramount.

ETHICS IN ADVERTISING AND PUBLIC STATEMENTS

While therapists may advertise their services, they must represent themselves and their services, as well as the institutions and organizations they are affiliated with, accurately. Certain practices are prohibited, including: testimonials from clients; statements that are likely to create unrealistic expectations of positive results; any statement suggesting that only this therapist can do the job or has unique, "one-of-a-kind" abilities; statements playing on clients' fears about what might happen if they don't get this kind of help; statements claiming one therapist's services are more effective than others'; and any direct solicitation of individual clients by mail, telemarketing, or the like.

If a therapist you are interested in engages in any of these unethical advertising practices, it should be a warning to you to stay away.

OFFERING A CONSULTATION

It is unethical for another therapist to try to convince you to leave your present therapist and come into therapy. This sometimes happens when therapy is not going well and you seek a second opinion (see Chapter 10). As a client, you are always free to request a consultation with another therapist. If you feel the second therapist may be more effective for you than your present therapist, you are free to discuss the possibility of terminating with your current therapist and continuing therapy with the second. However, the consulting therapist must not try to persuade you to make the switch.

RESEARCH WITH CLIENTS

Occasionally clients are asked by therapists to take part in a research project. Such participation is for the general good: it advances scientific understanding and in the long run will help improve the effectiveness of therapy. But it may mean letting information about you become part of a larger study.

You do not have to participate, and you should not until you have thoroughly discussed it with your therapist. Do not take part just to please your therapist. You may end up feeling "observed," which may inhibit what you will be willing to reveal. It may lead to feelings of being exploited or treated as a guinea pig.

On the other hand, being asked to participate may be flattering and appeal to your sense of self-importance. This, too, can lead to pressures to "live up to" expectations you think the researchers have of you and derail your therapy.

These pressures aren't insurmountable, but pose a risk that you and your therapist should take seriously.

These issues aside, no research should be done with clients unless it follows certain ethical norms, which your therapist should review with you in advance:

- *Informed consent.* You should know the general purpose of the research, the procedures that will be followed, and later the overall outcome if you are interested. Only after all your questions have been answered should you sign a form consenting to take part.
- *Voluntary participation.* It should be made clear to you that your participation is completely voluntary. It is unethical to force clients into participating. You are free to withdraw at any time without jeopardy to your therapy or your relationship with your therapist.
- *Protection from any physical or mental discomfort, harm, or risk.* You should be informed of any possible risks and have recourse to help from your therapist during—and even after—the research if it results in stress or harm. Your therapist is ethically obligated to look out for and correct any undesirable consequences.
- *Confidentiality.* If you do take part, no identifying information about you should become part of the research data. Instead of using your name, for instance, the researchers should give you a code number. If you have any concerns about confidentiality, exactly how it will be protected should be explained to you.
- *Treatment.* If you were a member of a control group—that is, an experimental group that did not actually receive a treatment that was tried with a comparison group—you should have the option of receiving the treatment later if it proved effective.

PARTICIPATION IN NEW OR EXPERIMENTAL TREATMENTS

A therapist has an ethical obligation to provide you with competent service, but new approaches to therapy are always emerging for which there aren't established standards yet. If your therapist wants to try an innovative method with you, he or she should let you know beforehand that it is still unproven and experimental. This does not mean that such methods should never be tried—just that they should be used only after you understand that they are innovative and have given your consent. Your therapist should also have specialized training or supervision in the method before attempting it with you. Ask before giving your consent.

REFERRALS TO OTHER PROFESSIONALS

Your therapist is obligated to use all the professional, technical, and administrative resources available that serve your best interests. It is unethical for a therapist *not* to refer you to another professional for a service you need.

For example, non-M.D. therapists must refer you to a physician if they suspect any medical problems. Similarly, if therapists suspect any neuropsychological problems such as a learning disability or memory impairment, they must refer you to a neuropsychologist for testing.

If your therapist is not a psychiatrist and your problem is one for which medication has clearly proven effective, he or she should discuss the role of medication in its treatment and how that might supplement psychotherapy, then refer you to a psychiatrist or other physician for a medication consultation. The Therapy Guide in Part II will tell you which conditions are now routinely treated with medication. You can also consult Chapter 18 on the use of medication in therapy.

YOUR SAFEGUARDS AGAINST ETHICAL MISCONDUCT

The two best safeguards against a therapist's misconduct are the therapist's training and adherence to a professional code of conduct and an informed consumer—you.

The therapeutic professions have established three kinds of external safeguards to protect the public. Unfortunately, because psychotherapy per se is an unlicensed profession, these are binding only on therapists who are members of a mental health profession that is licensed or certified in your state. You do not have the same protection—or recourse—in the case of therapists who are not members of one of these regulated professions.

1. **Professional codes of ethics.** Each of the major mental health professions has developed a code of ethical standards specifically related to its goals and clients. Therapists licensed by a particular profession are accountable to a state licensing board, as well as to the ethics committee of their profession. If you are interested, you can request a copy of your therapist's professional code of ethics from the national professional organization to which he or she belongs.

The ethical codes of the major therapy professions don't only establish minimal standards of behavior for avoiding censure or punishment. They also establish certain ideals to which therapists in the profession should aspire. The highest ideal is the promotion of human welfare and well-being. In the pursuit of this ideal, members are obliged to be responsible, competent, honest, respectful of their clients and colleagues, and aware of community, moral, and legal standards. These are more than lofty sentiments; each translates into specific obligations for practice in therapy.

For example, the mandate to be responsible means, among other things, that a therapist should not go on vacation without offering clients alternative coverage with another therapist or a way to contact him or her in an emergency. The ideal of competency means that a therapist should stick to areas and methods within his or her range of competence. For instance, if a therapist has only a cursory knowledge of sex therapy, he or she should not try to treat clients for sexual problems best treated by a sex therapist.

2. State licensing or certifying requirements. Professional codes of conduct establish ethical standards for practice; state licensing boards establish legal requirements and sanctions. Psychologists, social workers, or psychiatric nurses can belong to their national professional organizations without being licensed or certified in their states. A state license means that the professional has met legal qualifications required by that state for practice. Licenses must be renewed regularly. Many states have established continuing-education requirements as a condition for renewal, in an attempt to ensure that the professional keeps up with developments in the field.

A state license can be revoked or suspended if the state licensing board finds that a professional has violated the laws governing that profession. Complaints can be filed with your state licensing or certifying board directly. The boards can also initiate their own inquiries.

3. Legislative statutes. Beyond state licensing requirements, professionals are bound by laws that govern negligence, malpractice, and professional liability. These laws are the basis for civil suits, and for criminal suits in more serious cases. In some states, the boards and agencies that regulate the professions implement regulations, which are available to the general public on request.

CLIENT RIGHTS

In addition to the ethical norms and legal requirements that are binding on all professional therapists, you are also protected by certain rights as a client, whatever the circumstances under which you are in therapy. Like ethical norms, these safeguard therapy as a place where you will not be taken advantage of and can count on your needs being the focus of concern.

Constitutional and civil rights. You obviously retain your basic constitutional and civil rights, even in the event you have been involuntarily detained in a hospital for your own or others' safety. These include your right to religious freedom, to vote, to freedom of association, to self-determination and freedom of choice, to an attorney, and your right of communication and of control over your personal possessions. You can sue anyone who tries to deprive you of these rights, unless they were temporarily curtailed while you were at risk to hurt yourself or someone else or were unable to care for yourself. Even then, a legal procedure is required, and you retain all of your constitutional and most of your civil rights.

Rights of clients in treatment. In addition to basic constitutional and civil rights, numerous federal and state laws guarantee certain rights to people in need of or undergoing treatment. These include:

- The right to adequate care and treatment. Even if you are involuntarily detained in a hospital, you cannot simply be held there. You have a right to active treatment for your condition while you are detained.
- The right to be treated in the least restricted setting given your condition. If you can be adequately treated in your community or while living at home, you have a right to be treated there instead of, say, in a hospital or residential setting.
- The right to be treated with dignity and respect.
- The right to confidentiality and privacy.
- The right to informed consent. You have a legal right to know what your therapist intends to do as part of treatment: the kind of therapy, the steps it entails, how long it will take, what it will cost, what the alternatives might be, and any risks or side effects.

  Sometimes—perhaps often—therapists don't take the time to provide all the information you want or need, or they go over it in a perfunctory way that leaves you unsatisfied or mystified. You should feel free to ask questions until you understand. If you were too upset or confused when you began therapy to ask, or other questions arise, you can ask later. You should understand the explanations you are given—you are entitled to plain language, not technical terms or jargon.
- The right to refuse treatment. You always have the right to refuse treatment, including medication, and to end therapy at any time. But you should be cautious about acting too hastily, especially when things get difficult, as they often do. The greatest gains are often made through the most difficult stretches, and you may be jumping to conclusions based on a misunderstanding of what is going on. Before deciding to stop, talk over your reasons thoroughly with your therapist (see Chapter 12, "Ending Therapy").
- The right to due process. No state allows people who are emotionally disturbed to be detained or hospitalized against their will unless a strict legal procedure for "involuntary commitment" is followed.

  This means that, despite popular belief, your relatives cannot arbitrarily "railroad" you into a mental hospital with the help of a psychiatrist. Any psychiatrist who participated in such a scheme would be acting both unethically and illegally.

  A person also cannot be involuntarily detained in a hospital indefinitely, but only for a specified period of time—usually three to ten days. If the person is still at risk at the end of that time, the hospital must return to court to petition for another involuntary commitment, again for a predetermined length of time. The client has the right to appear at that hearing, as well as the right to legal representation.

Some lawyers specialize in mental health law. If you cannot afford a private attorney, you can obtain legal counsel through the court, or through your legal aid society or the Mental Health Law Project (see p. 647).

If a person has admitted himself to a hospital voluntarily and wants to leave before the hospital staff feels he is ready for discharge, he has the right to sign a "notice of intent to leave." This legal document mandates a waiting period of three to five days, depending on the state. At the end of that time, the hospital must go to court to obtain an involuntary commitment if they believe the client cannot provide for himself or is at risk to hurt himself or someone else. Again, the client has the right to counsel. If the hospital decides the client isn't at risk, or the court refuses to grant a commitment, the client is free to leave even against medical advice.

• The right to refuse medication. People cannot be medicated against their will unless there is a clear need to protect them or someone else from harm. In those rare instances where caregivers feel medication is necessary even when the person is not at risk of physical harm, they must initiate a legal process to obtain a "medication guardianship" from the court. In court, the person is entitled to a lawyer.

• The right to see official records of your treatment. Records are the legal property of the therapist, agency, or clinic, but you have a right to review them. Usually your therapist or another professional must be there to review them with you to clarify anything you do not understand.

IF YOUR THERAPIST ACTS UNETHICALLY

WHY CLIENTS DON'T SPEAK UP

It can be difficult to admit to yourself that your therapist has done something wrong. Should you ever find yourself in this unhappy situation, powerful internal forces may be at work to hold you back from speaking up, making you feel weak and humiliated. But knowing what these forces are can diminish their grip and help you to take action:

• *The difference in power.* You and your therapist aren't on an equal footing. You depend on your therapist; he or she is not dependent on you. Your therapist is an expert; you are not. You're vulnerable, but not your therapist—or so it feels. It is difficult to be objective about someone you need and depend on as much as you do a therapist, let alone voice your feelings. The fear of being criticized, rejected, or abandoned—even if you are right—can make you feel too intimidated to suggest that anything is wrong.

• *No one wants to be seen as a complainer.* Questioning your therapist's behavior or judgment can feel like whining. No one likes a complainer, least of all—you imagine—your therapist, who is supposed to know what's in your best interests and is trying to help you.

Whining is not the same thing as expressing dissatisfaction with professional services. It is always legitimate to speak up when you have grave doubts about something that has happened in therapy. A competent therapist will want to hear any such doubts or complaints. So will reputable clinics and agencies. They may not like what you have to say, but they will be concerned to maintain their reputation and professional standards.

• *You will have to admit you made a poor decision in the first place.* This is a hard admission because it tends to make you question your own judgment, not only about choosing this therapist but about choosing another therapist in the future. It can even lead you to doubt your judgment in relationships in general.

However, we all make mistakes. You probably made the best judgment you could based on the evidence you had. You don't know everything about a therapist all at once. Nor can you know how someone will act under all the infinite variety of situations that arise in therapy. You can't be faulted for assuming a professional therapist will treat you ethically, with respect and dignity.

• *A fear of suffering consequences.* It is natural to worry that your therapist might retaliate if you speak up: criticize you, ridicule your doubts, make you feel foolish, withdraw concern, become less involved, or stop the therapy. If you file a formal complaint, you may be afraid this will expose you to public ridicule or that the nature of your problem will become known.

Some therapists *will* retaliate, but if your therapist does, it will help you decide you should not be working with him or her.

A formal ethics complaint or civil suit will end therapy, but if your therapist has been acting unethically, it should. Some confidentiality will also be lost in initiating a formal complaint. In a civil or criminal suit, your therapist's records will become public information. But if you file a complaint with the state licensing board or the ethics committee of your therapist's professional organization, they won't. Licensing boards and ethics committees are legally and ethically bound to observe confidentiality in their hearings.

• *A feeling that it won't do any good.* Clients often feel daunted by the prospect of going up against a therapist. Not only does the therapist have training, experience, professional affiliations, and prestige on his or her side, but therapists are also in a position in the session to dismiss, counter, or explain away their behavior. At the worst, they can always blame the client. In ethical, civil, or criminal proceedings, too, you can feel up against a long, costly, complex process of uncertain outcome that a therapist may be better prepared to handle than you are.

Confronting your therapist individually may or may not change his or her attitude or behavior. Either way, you will learn something you need to know. If it does do some good, it may reestablish enough trust to continue. If it doesn't, it will suggest the only sensible course is to stop therapy.

The day is past when unethical therapists could rely on public indifference to protect them. These days, bringing therapist misconduct to the attention of regulatory agencies and professional organizations almost always results in an official inquiry. Oversight boards are no longer loathe to censure, suspend, or permanently revoke the licenses of professionals who violate ethical and legal standards. When this occurs, the name of the therapist, the principle or law violated, and the sanction invoked are published in professional journals to notify colleagues.

- *Ambivalence toward therapy in the first place.* Because of the ambivalence that people bring to therapy, they are often all too willing to accept compromised and even damaging forms of therapy as long as they don't have to see themselves too clearly. Paradoxically, working with a therapist whose behavior is questionable can even make us feel better in the short run, by letting us feel more comfortable with our own failings.

  This ambivalence is the most subtle of the forces working to keep clients from speaking up or taking action. The more damaging forms of ethical misconduct are not hard to recognize, but if you experience reluctance to acknowledge them or to act, don't be surprised. If you are in doubt, seek a consultation from another qualified therapist.

- *Ignorance of the channels that are available to you.* Unless they take active steps to inform themselves, clients don't usually know what recourses they have to report therapist misconduct. This is the easiest problem to deal with. The next section describes the various channels available and the procedures they entail.

HOW TO TAKE EFFECTIVE ACTION

If you feel you have a valid ethical complaint—not just some gripe or disappointment—you have several options. Consider them all carefully. *No one course of action is right for everyone.* Each has different consequences, both for you and for your therapist.

1. Talking It Over with Your Therapist

The first thing you can do, of course, is talk to your therapist. This is always a good place to start unless it is a major ethical offense, or the nature of the offense is such that talking it over would expose you to further abuse or humiliation.

If you do decide you want to talk it over first, realize that your therapist will hear whatever you might say as a criticism and may be defensive. It will help if you are as clear and specific as possible about what is bothering you and why. Avoid generalizations. Most minor complaints can be cleared up this way.

2. Requesting a Consultation or a Second Opinion

If you aren't satisfied after talking it over, or if you are in doubt about whether your therapist really has acted unethically, you can consult another therapist about what happened and how you feel about it. It's probably best to see another therapist who does the same type of therapy as yours.

Getting a consultation on therapy is a standard practice, though you should inform your therapist of your intention. You can consult with another therapist on your own, but you can also request your therapist to meet with the consultant after he or she has talked with you. You would not have to be present.

The second therapist should help you clarify your questions. If it turns out to be a misunderstanding, the consultant will probably refer you back to your therapist, but with suggestions for making therapy work better. If the consultant agrees that some ethical misconduct has occurred, he or she can advise you on your options and discuss how to proceed—either to work it out with your therapist, to find a new therapist, and/or to proceed with a formal complaint.

3. Filing a Formal Complaint

At this point you can either stop therapy without further action or consider going ahead with filing a formal complaint.

Before you embark on a formal complaint, you should know that route will require a sustained commitment and considerable courage on your part. The process can be lengthy, time-consuming, and stressful.

Whom can you file with? You have two options:

A. The Ethics Committee of a Professional Association

If your therapist belongs to a professional association, you can file a complaint with them. You can quickly learn if your therapist is a member by simply calling the association. For psychiatrists, you should file a complaint with the American Psychiatric Association; for clinical psychologists, the American Psychological Association; for most clinical social workers, the National Association of Social Workers; for marriage and family counselors, the American Association of Marriage and Family Therapy (see Appendix IV for the association addresses). Each has an ethics committee that handles complaints.

Sometimes a therapist will belong to more than one professional organization. It's always best to file a formal complaint with their national and state professional association because they will carry the most weight. But you may want to file with the therapist's other professional organizations, which include those representing a particular modality of therapy—individual, group, couples, and family—and those representing the various schools of therapy, such as psychoanalysis, behavior therapy, cognitive therapy, and the like.

All the professional associations have their national headquarters in Washington, D.C., but the complaint itself is filed with the state chapter. Get the address of the chapter in your state from the national headquarters. Ask the state association to send you information on their procedures for filing a complaint. Once you've gone through this carefully, you should call them back with any questions you might still have, such as:

- How long does it usually take for a complaint to be resolved?
- What evidence will the committee need?
- Can you appear before the committee? Do you have to?
- Will your therapist be required to appear in person? Can you be present if you want? If so, will you be able to ask questions?
- Will your therapist be shown whatever evidence you offer, and will you be able to rebut his or her response?
- Over the past several years, how many complaints similar to yours were filed? What percentage were found in favor of the complainant? What actions were taken against therapists who were found in violation?
- How will the committee announce its decision? Will you be notified in writing? What other announcement will the committee make? Will the committee notify its full membership, or the appropriate licensing board?

Some clients who have gone through the difficulty of filing a complaint have ended up feeling betrayed when they could not find out what decision was taken after months or even years of waiting.

You may still want to protect your privacy at this stage. The association will not need to know your name in order to answer any inquiries about procedures for filing. They will need it if you decide to actually file, since ethics committees generally will not investigate anonymous complaints.

A formal, signed complaint will probably need to include at least the following points:

- your name, address, and telephone number
- the name and address of the organization and/or therapist you are filing against
- the specific nature of your complaint: the behavior or practice you have been subjected to, and how you feel you have been harmed
- an account of any efforts you have already made to resolve the issue
- copies of any correspondence or documents pertaining to the matter
- any additional background information about yourself, your therapy, or the circumstances that you think will help in evaluating the complaint
- your signature

The typical ethics complaint procedure. Once your completed form is received, an investigatory subcommittee is usually appointed. They then contact you for further information, any substantiating documentation, and names of any witnesses. You are asked to waive confidentiality at this point, and a copy of your complaint is sent to your therapist. He or she must then reply within a specified time—often fourteen days—with documentation of his or her own, along with names of witnesses, if the complaint is being contested.

The subcommittee considers the evidence from all sides and makes a recommendation to the full ethics committee, which then reviews the case. A vote is taken. If a penalty is recommended, this is submitted to the board of directors of the organization for final disposition. Both you and your therapist are then notified. If your therapist appeals on procedural grounds, a formal hearing will be held to review the case a final time.

Keep copies of any documents and correspondence you submit, and copies of any correspondence from the association to you.

What professional organizations can and can't do. Knowing the possible outcomes of filing with a professional ethics committee can minimize potential disappointment, bitterness, and frustration from unrealistic expectations.

The three things professional organizations do *not* have the authority to do is revoke a therapist's license, stop him or her from practicing, or grant financial compensation. The professional organizations sometimes don't make this sufficiently clear on inquiry.

On the other hand, if the ethics committee finds that your therapist has violated ethical standards, it *can* take one or more of the following actions: (1) expel the therapist from the national and state associations and notify all its members of the expulsion; (2) suspend the therapist from the association for a period of time; (3) formally reprimand the therapist; (4) require the therapist to put his work under supervision; (5) require continuing-education courses and further training; (6) require the therapist to enter personal therapy.

These kinds of action don't benefit you directly or directly redress the wrong done to you; but they do powerfully validate your complaint in a public way. They do affect the therapist's ability to practice and earn a livelihood. And they do protect other present and future clients.

B. The State Licensing or Certification Board

A second option is to file a complaint with a state licensing or certification board. All states license psychiatrists and clinical psychologists. About half license clinical social workers. More than twenty license marriage and family counselors. To find out if your state has a licensing board for your therapist's profession, contact the state department of consumer affairs or department of health services, or a similar branch of your state government. They can tell you how to contact the right licensing board to file a complaint.

Remember also that not all therapists are professionally licensed or certified. Though licensing laws themselves are generally adequate, licensing boards have no jurisdiction over any therapist practicing without a license. An individual can also have his or her professional license suspended or revoked and still continue practicing under an unregulated title such as "counselor," "therapist," "analyst," or "teacher."

You can get information from your state licensing or certifying board in the same way as from professional organizations. After reviewing this, you may want to call them directly and ask the same questions as above. The filing procedures and the processing of formal complaints are also quite similar.

The typical licensing complaint procedure. Once the licensing board receives back their completed form, it is forwarded to a state investigating body, often in the attorney general's office, if the board finds the complaint warrants further action. This body undertakes a preliminary investigation, and if it finds grounds, recommends a formal inquiry to the board, which can accept or reject the recommendation. If accepted, the complaint is formally filed and the case becomes part of the public record, as is true of any legal proceeding.

A deputy attorney general is assigned to the case, who may propose a settlement to the board. If the board rejects this, the case will be heard before an administrative law judge, without a jury or members of the board present. The judge's decision is then forwarded to the licensing board, which decides what disciplinary action to take.

It is the licensing or certifying board that can suspend or revoke a therapist's license to practice as a professional. But they cannot prevent him or her from continuing to practice therapy, as long as he or she does not practice under his or her professional title.

Nevertheless, losing their license usually has severe consequences on therapists. It becomes a matter of public record, makes other professionals much less willing to refer new clients to them, and disqualifies them from reimbursement by insurance carriers, a major factor in the economics of a therapy practice. It usually leads to expulsion from their professional organizations as well.

In addition to revoking or suspending certification or licensing, boards have the authority to make continued practice conditional upon any number of factors, including working under supervision, prohibiting therapy with certain kinds of clients, mandating a lower caseload, or requiring further training.

In the best of all worlds, licensing boards would act swiftly and efficiently in order not to compound the injury. Unfortunately, this can be a stressful procedure for you as well as your therapist, and it is best to be well informed about this ahead of time. At some point after you file the complaint, for instance, state investigators will interview you. In some states these investigators have police training but no special sensitivity to the therapy situation. You may find yourself inadvertently questioned in a way that upsets or further traumatizes you.

Another drawback is the time it takes for most states to follow through on a complaint. You may not be contacted during the entire pretrial period, for instance. This can lead to considerable anxiety while you wait.

Clients who have been severely abused—sexual involvement is the prime example—often find it hard to get on with the rest of their life until there is a resolution. This may take months, even years. The long process can be so harmful that subsequent therapists have sometimes advised a more vulnerable client not to pursue it.

If you are uncertain of your case, consult an attorney who is familiar with malpractice law. If you are uncertain whether you want to make the commitment or have concerns about your case becoming part of the public record, consult another therapist. But you should at least consider this option and not abandon it lightly, particularly if you have been harmed or the ethical violation was serious. It may also protect other clients in the future.

4. Bringing a Civil Malpractice Suit

If you feel you have suffered serious harm from your therapist's unethical action, you can file a civil lawsuit for personal damages. A lawsuit will not affect your therapist's status in the profession or his or her license to practice. But unlike a formal complaint to an ethics committee or licensing board, a successful civil suit can result in an award of damages to you.

Bringing a civil suit depends on demonstrating *malpractice,* not ethical misconduct. Unethical conduct simply refers to something your therapist did that violates the ethical norms of professional practice. In law, malpractice refers to therapists' *negligence in executing the obligations they owe to a client.* Often, of course, such negligence takes the form of an ethical breach.

It is important to understand that only a *licensed professional* therapist can be sued for malpractice. Nonlicensed therapists will usually be held to the same standard of care by the court, but you can't count on it.

To prove negligence, you will need to demonstrate four things:

1. There was, indeed, a professional relationship between you and your therapist—fairly easy if you paid your bills.
2. What your therapist did fell below a generally accepted standard of care. It is not enough to show that your therapist was unable to help you; you need to show that what he or she did actually harmed you. It also isn't malpractice if your therapist didn't employ a level of skill, knowledge, or expertise beyond the ordinary. The law also doesn't prefer one form of therapy over another. The court will usually measure your therapist's professional behavior by the standards of the approach they are following, provided that is supported by at least a "respectable minority" of his or her profession.
3. You suffered real damage: lost a job, became unable to work, had your reputation ruined, suffered emotional distress, or had your marriage break up, for example, or been hurt in some way that a jury can understand.
4. This damage was the direct result of your therapist's conduct, procedures, or negligence. To demonstrate this connection, you may need an expert witness, usually another mental health professional, to testify on your behalf in court. This may sound straightforward, but it often isn't. Getting a competent professional to stand up in court and testify that a colleague was negligent, or that some specific action led to the condition for which you are seeking damages, is not always easy.

Attorneys who specialize in malpractice law will usually be able to help you locate one. Just be sure the attorney you retain also comes with good references! Questionable attorneys lead to questionable "expert" witnesses who lack credibility and may only make you feel further demeaned by the whole process.

The one growing exception to the need for an expert witness is sexual intimacy. Courts are increasingly recognizing this as negligence per se, though the fact that it has occurred still needs to be demonstrated.

You will have to waive confidentiality if you pursue damages. A civil suit will make details of your therapy—and your problems—public. Trials of therapists also tend to be covered by journalists, as well as special-interest groups intent on publicizing and advocating for particular causes. Consider carefully how this might affect you and your family, or your work.

Retaining an attorney. If you decide to sue for damages, shop around until you find an attorney who has both the right expertise and whom you feel you trust enough to work with. Get references. Ask how many similar cases they have tried, and how they turned out. And be sure the chemistry is right; you'll probably be working together for a long time.

Be clear about financial arrangements from the start. Ask if the attorney expects a flat fee, and what that fee will be, or if he or she will be paid a portion of the damages you receive if you win. Ask for a sense of the likelihood of winning your case: do you have a strong case, or is it a long shot?

No One Course of Action Is Right for Everyone

Because each of the ways you can take action has a very different outcome, you need to reflect on which is in your best interest. Of course, you can pusue any or all of these avenues.

Consider retaining an attorney even if you are filing a complaint with a professional ethics committee or a state licensing board. If you decide to file more than one complaint, for instance, or both a complaint and a civil suit, an attorney can advise you whether filing them together or sequentially, and in which order, may be more advantageous. How you file and where you file affects when your therapist learns there will be an investigation, and under what circumstances. For instance, if you have already begun a lawsuit, your therapist may be forewarned and on guard should you file a complaint with the licensing board.

Finally, the impact for a therapist of such a lawsuit or complaint can be devastating. Weigh your case and be sure it is justified before you take action. If you feel it is, even though filing a complaint or bringing a civil suit can be grueling, it can also be therapeutic in knowing that a wrong has been righted, and that you need not passively accept being a victim of someone else's unprofessional conduct. It can also be the means of preventing further harm to others. In all those ways, it can be an important, positive, and healing experience.

CHAPTER TWELVE

◼

ENDING THERAPY

When clients think of ending therapy, they tend to think of the moment they'll walk out of their therapist's door for the last time. Actually, the decision to end therapy, no matter how it comes about, is usually only the beginning of a process called *termination*.

This last stage of therapy has its own rhythm, its own moods, its own challenges and rewards, and above all makes its own special demands on client and therapist. Just as it took you some time to settle into therapy, to get to know your therapist and feel comfortable, you will need to take some time preparing to end such an important personal and professional relationship. It takes time to get used to the idea of not meeting anymore, time to prepare yourself emotionally for saying good-bye.

Why Termination Is the Most Important Phase

Termination is the most important phase of therapy. The work you and your therapist have done together now jells—or doesn't. The two of you will look back over your work and decide what has been accomplished and what remains to be done. It is a time of consolidating gains, as well as dealing with any lingering disappointment over goals you didn't quite reach. If the work has gone reasonably well, termination can be the richest and most emotionally satisfying phase to both of you. The hardest work is behind, and you can—and ought—to share in the confident feeling of a job well done. That shared satisfaction, if it is well founded, will do more than anything else to consolidate your gains.

Special work needs to be done in this phase that can't be done at any other time.

Apart from the issues you have been addressing in therapy, the decision to end raises issues around separation and loss. Endings are difficult because even in the best of cases they can involve disillusionment—the need to surrender our secret fantasies of fulfillment and perfect satisfaction, our dream of becoming someone completely different, our expectation that someone was going to change us. Termination requires us to face our limitations, however much we have accomplished, and to accept that what our therapist could do for us, however much, was still limited. On the deepest level, separations and endings involve a confrontation with our finiteness and mortality.

This doesn't mean that all therapies will emphasize these issues during the termination phase. That will depend in large part on what approach your therapist is following and on how short or long term your therapy has been. The more psychodynamic and long term your therapy, the more likely termination will explore these issues. However, in most therapy, termination will still be treated as a separate and vital phase.

Deciding to End

When you first came into therapy, you may have had a fantasy that therapy would "cure" your problem, whatever it was. Usually in therapy you learn to appreciate the limits of what therapy can do, and to develop a greater appreciation for your own limits. Ending therapy often brings you up against those original fantasies again as you realize there is no such thing as a perfect solution to your problems.

This is particularly true if you came to therapy not to overcome a specific symptom but because you wanted to work better, love better, improve your relationships, be less depressed and unhappy, grow as a person. If you wait until you have been "cured," or make your decision contingent upon finding the one right solution to your problems that will tie up all loose ends, you will either never leave therapy or will leave it frustrated and disillusioned.

You should end therapy when you have developed the ability to manage on your own what you needed help with and when you are confident you can tackle this next period of your life with your own resources. The idea is *not* that you have become entirely self-sufficient, but rather that you feel ready to handle your issues without the help of your therapist.

Resistance to Ending

Deciding to end therapy can bring specific resistances into play. No one willingly or easily leaves something that feels as intensely important and personal as therapy can, particularly coming as it did at a time when one needed help. It means leaving someone you have come to depend on, someone you have been personally involved with and have probably come to feel close to.

Much as you may recognize it is time to leave, thinking about it may bring up anxiety about how you will cope. Terminating tends to awaken echoes of past endings, such as finishing school, leaving home, the death of a loved one, or separation or divorce. At a deeper level still, the end of therapy may mobilize fundamental anxieties about your mortality—the dread of an ultimate ending. For all these reasons, leaving is probably the most difficult issue for human beings to face, the one we are most anxious about and manage least well.

This will be true for your therapist as well. Though therapists are trained to recognize and handle these feelings, they experience them just the same.

Therapy Is Vulnerable to Frame Breaks During Termination

The strong impulse to reduce the tension of ending makes improprieties in therapy more likely at this time. There is often a temptation, for instance, to begin easing or even erasing some of the boundaries that have ensured a safe and professional relationship. Your therapist may begin sharing personal things that he or she hasn't before. You may find yourself trying to turn the relationship into a friendship that will continue. If there has been sexual attraction, the basis may now be established for sexual involvement after therapy ends. You may find yourselves talking about ideas for some kind of professional or business collaboration afterward.

It is easy for both therapists and clients to rationalize these breaks in the frame. They can be seen as a way of equalizing the relationship; a way of ending therapy on a warmer and more intimate note; or a way of allowing the client to get to know the therapist better. Or client and therapist may tacitly agree that the work is over and boundaries aren't as important now. All sound deceptively plausible.

But the hidden agenda of such breaks is to defend against the deep experience of loss. These maneuvers may succeed temporarily. But they cheat you out of the chance to use the termination phase to come to grips with your fears about separation and loss, and to reduce their hold on you. These anxieties may be connected on a deep level with the very problems that brought you to therapy, or with a tentative and fearful stance toward life itself. So to the extent you bend or break the rules that safeguard therapy at the end, the work on your issues will remain incomplete as well. A major break in the frame at the end can even undo the previous work you have done.

Make Ending Therapy a Process

You and your therapist should make ending therapy a *process* rather than an isolated decision or action. This will give you an opportunity to clarify your reasons for wanting to end, to explore any resistance, to look back over your work together, and to say good-bye. Do this no matter what format or approach you have been following, or however short or long your therapy has been. Even if you have met for no more than three or four sessions, you can devote the last half hour, say, to the work of ending. You may be surprised what a difference it will make in your sense of accomplishment and in your feelings about the relationship.

YOU SHOULD DECIDE WHEN TO END

Ordinarily, the decision to end therapy is yours. Some clients would rather their therapist make this decision and wait until he or she suggests it. But it is best for you to recognize you are ready and raise the issue. There will be signs in yourself and in the therapy that only you can really judge, and it is important for you to take responsibility for this decision. This can help consolidate a sense of yourself as someone now ready to continue the journey on his or her own. Once you have taken the initiative, your therapist can help you clarify your thoughts about leaving.

In fact, unless you are in brief, focal, or time-limited therapy, most therapists will wait for you to bring up the idea of ending. They will see your raising the issue yourself as a sign you are really ready to end. In an open-ended therapy, many good reasons support this practice. It encourages and safeguards your initiative and capacity to be self-directing and supports your ability to judge your own progress. It encourages the independence that comes from stopping and affirms your own sense of accomplishing what it was you set out to do. If your therapist is the one to suggest stopping, he or she may be allowing personal or professional needs to take precedence over yours.

The Major Exception to This Rule

If your therapist is concerned that stopping would expose you or someone else to a *serious risk,* he or she will be obligated to recommend that you continue treatment. Such risks include:

- suicide or other self-destructive behavior
- homicide or assault
- inability to provide minimal care for yourself: food, shelter, clothing, hygiene
- psychosis
- symptoms of a severe ongoing psychiatric disorder

If you are in crisis, and your therapist hasn't already discussed it with you, he or she may even recommend a more intensive level of care than therapy alone: inpatient treatment in a hospital setting, for instance, or medication.

If you nevertheless refuse their recommendation and insist on stopping, your therapist will be legally required to take steps to arrange for an involuntary commitment to a hospital for your own or others' protection. There you would receive around-the-clock care until the danger is past. In addition, your therapist will probably urge you to continue therapy during the hospitalization, either with him or with someone else (see p. 269).

HOW TO RECOGNIZE WHEN IT IS TIME TO STOP

If therapy has gone reasonably well, the realization that you are ready to end will probably come gradually. If you came to therapy with specific, well-defined goals that are easy to measure, then it will be relatively easy to recognize when you have reached your goals, or when you have made as much progress toward them as you can at this time.

If your goals are more broadly defined, more concerned with self-understanding and self-esteem or long-standing patterns, look for some improvement in the areas you wanted help with. Your therapist and others can say they see improvement, but only you will know if you actually feel better or if things have really changed. The difficulties that brought you to therapy should seem less troublesome and should no longer interfere with your life in major ways. This doesn't mean they are necessarily resolved; it means you feel you are managing them better and with greater confidence. There should also be significant subjective relief from the emotional distress they were causing.

You should also notice certain other changes in yourself, as well as in the therapy relationship, that add up to the feeling that you are ready to leave and continue on your own.

The principle of diminishing returns may also set in: you will begin to feel that the time, effort, and cost of therapy is outweighing its benefits.

Changes to Look For

In Yourself

These are some of the things clients typically notice about themselves as they start feeling ready to end. Not all apply in every case, or all of the time. With that qualification, you are probably ready to think about ending when *for the most part* you are:

- happy about your progress
- more hopeful about the future
- more accepting of yourself
- more able to appreciate your good points
- less anxious or self-critical about the things you still don't like

- more confident in your ability to take care of yourself and handle everyday problems
- better able to avoid getting caught in old self-defeating habits of thought, feelings, or behavior
- enjoying smoother and more satisfying relationships with others in your life
- deriving more satisfaction from work
- feeling less overwhelmed
- more ready to accept responsibility for yourself without blaming others
- able to think and see things more clearly
- more aware of your feelings and what they are telling you
- more able to let go of past hurts and resentments
- more ready to engage with life, and to tolerate its inevitable anxieties, burdens, and disappointments

These changes don't constitute perfection or an ideal way of life. Don't expect them to. No matter how satisfying, they undoubtedly won't live up to your original fantasy of how you were going to feel or what a changed person you were going to be when you finished. But they are significant all the same. They can be the basis for a much more satisfying and productive engagement with life and with others.

You also won't notice a change in every one of these areas, and those changes you do notice you won't feel all of the time. But when you begin to notice some of them, and they feel more genuinely part of your general outlook than before, that is a good indication that the end may be approaching.

Two questions can help make these changes clearer. Ask yourself:

Do I feel satisfied with the changes I've made so far? Or do I feel there is still farther to go?

Do I feel this way most of the time?

In other words, do these changes feel reasonably stable and well integrated? You don't want to end therapy at the first sign of progress. Gains need time to be consolidated. A fairly definite yes to both questions is a reliable sign that you are ready to think about ending.

In the Therapy Relationship

As you gain more self-confidence and mastery over your problems, your attitudes toward your therapist are likely to change:

- you begin to see your therapist realistically rather than with awe
- you find it easier to accept his or her limitations without becoming angry about them or feeling betrayed
- you trust your judgment and ability to see things more clearly, independently of your therapist

- you can disagree without doubting or second-guessing yourself, or worrying unduly how your therapist will react
- it becomes easier to speak up and confront your therapist when you think he or she is wrong
- you are more active in sessions, relying less on your therapist to lead the way
- you can set more realistic limits and goals for yourself
- your sessions become lighter, more humorous, with more sharing of information and reflection on your experiences together
- you can think of leaving without becoming panicky or wondering what will become of you without your therapist
- you feel restless in anticipation of a session and wonder why you're bothering to go

Dreams, Stories, and Associations Can Signal Ending

If you know what to look for, you may also find the sense of ending signaled symbolically in dreams, stories you find yourself telling in sessions, or memories and other associations about endings, separations, and losses. They will have themes of leave-taking, of moving on, of growing by leaving something outmoded behind. The feelings will be those you would expect: grief, sadness, anxiety, regret, excitement, anticipation. The stimulus will be the realization that the work of therapy is more or less complete and that the time to end is at hand. Even if your therapist is following an approach that doesn't work with this kind of material, you may notice it on your own, both between and during sessions.

Thoughts and Feelings About Ending Suggesting Caution

Other thoughts and feelings about ending suggest not readiness but impulsive flight, resistance, or avoidance. Check for:

- Thoughts and feelings about stopping that simply appear out of the blue and don't fit with what is going on in therapy at the moment, particularly if you still don't understand the how and why of what is troubling you.
- Thoughts about stopping at a time you are feeling particularly resistant to therapy.
- Impulses to stop before you are confident that the changes or relief you feel are durable, or before you have given yourself sufficient time to test them.
- Themes and images in things you talk about that suggest premature flight, escape, or a need to cover up and hide, i.e., stopping defensively to avoid a genuine confrontation and resolution.

All these suggest unfinished work that thoughts about ending are defending against.

HOW TO TERMINATE

Discussing the Issue with Your Therapist

Talking about ending therapy can be uncomfortable for both client and therapist. Both of you may be tempted to avoid it. You may be reluctant to bring it up—afraid of your therapist's reaction. You may imagine that your therapist will feel angry or rejected.

If you put it off until you are 100 percent certain you are ready to leave, there will never be such a moment. Instead, a much better practice is to discuss the issue with your therapist *whenever the idea of ending comes up*. At this point you are not saying that you want to end. Rather, you are telling your therapist that the thought has occurred to you and you want to talk it over.

Your therapist's job at this point is to help you clarify your thoughts and feelings about ending. He will help you explore your reasons whether other motives may be at play in ending at this particular time. Given how mixed our motives and feelings often are about important decisions, this is a vital step in coming to a clear and confident decision.

If Your Therapist Has Reservations

Your therapist may have reservations and he or she should spell these out. Because therapists sometimes find it difficult to express their own reservations to a client directly, they may interpret your thinking about ending as resistance or avoidance. This is unprofessional as well as unfair to you. If you suspect this is happening, ask your therapist directly if he or she disagrees with you.

Even if your therapist's reservations are well founded, he or she should *not* try to persuade you to continue or force you into staying, any more than he or she should make any other decisions for you. Your therapist's responsibility is to clarify what is involved in your decisions, but to leave the decisions up to you.

It is particularly unprofessional for a therapist to try to change your mind by predicting a relapse if you leave. They should discuss anything they think may leave you vulnerable to a relapse, but never in the form of a prediction, and never to scare you or bend you to their point of view. If this happens, it raises a serious question whether the therapist is capable of handling the termination properly.

Even if your therapist thinks terminating would involve a serious risk of harm—unless your condition is so serious that it meets the legal criteria for involuntary commitment in your state—the most he or she should do is make recommendations for continued care.

If you still have the sense that it is time to end but your therapist disagrees, you are in an awkward position. You have to try somehow to win his or her support, leave without it, or stay in therapy primarily because your therapist feels you should.

Few clients are able to simply stick to their decision in this situation and walk away with confidence.

If you're uncertain how to proceed, you may want to consider asking for an outside consultation.

Setting a Date

If you are in open-ended therapy, once the decision is made, the next step is to set a date so that the remaining work can be done with a definite end in sight. This will define the termination phase of your therapy.

Your therapist should allow you to fix the date for the last session because you know best how much time you think you will need to finish and say good-bye. The amount of time you will need can vary considerably—a week, a month, several months. As a general rule, the longer you have worked together, the more time you should allow for ending. But many other considerations are also important, and no rule about the length of the termination phase is hard and fast.

If you are in time-limited therapy, or if the total number of sessions is limited by the terms of your insurance or health plan benefits, you will have known from the beginning when therapy will end. In this case, the task will be planning how to use your final session(s) meaningfully.

In either case, having a specific date for ending establishes a limit that you and your therapist will have to work within. That helps keep this phase of therapy focused and on track—a check on the natural tendency to procrastinate to avoid or minimize the intense feelings that can come up.

The Main Tasks of This Phase

1. Exploring Your Reactions to Ending

Since endings always stir up ambivalent and complex feelings, a common temptation is to try to avoid these feelings by suddenly deciding to extend your termination date. Or you may find yourself downplaying their impact. But in the end you won't be able to avoid these reactions, nor should you want to; they offer a special opportunity to do some important work. Allow yourself to explore your reactions, make an effort to notice them as they occur instead of screening them out, and bring them into your final sessions. The following may help focus this task.

Common reactions to ending:

- sadness over having to stop
- a sense of loss

- pride and satisfaction over how you've handled therapy and what you've accomplished
- guilt over abandoning your therapist
- fear of being rejected, e.g., thinking your therapist will be relieved to see you go and won't miss you
- anger or resentment over having to stop
- anxiety about being on your own
- excitement about being on your own
- delight at having the time and money back you were giving up to therapy
- relief at no longer having to go to sessions
- gratitude toward your therapist
- numbness, an inability to feel much at all about ending
- disappointment that you didn't get more out of it or accomplish all you'd hoped
- denial of the importance of leaving
- denial of the importance of therapy or the relationship
- reluctance to give up the secondary gains of therapy ("Don't expect too much of me. I'm in therapy.")

Reactions such as these come and go as you work through this final stage. There is no one way you "should" feel. Don't be surprised if you find yourself reacting one way one session, and quite a different way the next. Acknowledging and working through these shifts in feelings can leave you with a special resiliency in the face of change, as well as a deep sense of appreciation and gratitude for what you have been able to accomplish.

The meaning this ending will have for you will also depend on your personal experience with endings in the past. As we have said, leaving therapy is likely to evoke how you felt during important endings and losses in your life up until now. Or the connections may be more indirect. You may find that the feelings being stirred up have an oddly familiar feel about them that you can't identify right away. Exploring these personal meanings can be a vital part of the termination phase. How extensively you do this will depend in part on the approach your therapist is following, but some exploration of what endings *mean* to you is important and should be undertaken in most kinds of therapy.

Nearly all clients have doubts about leaving. Your ambivalence may express itself in different ways:

- I'm not sure I can make it on my own.
- My problems seem to be returning.
- So many new issues that I need to talk about are coming up since I've decided to leave.
- Since I've decided to stop, I've been developing new symptoms.

• I was looking foward to ending. Now I realize a part of me doesn't want to end.

Having doubts about leaving does not mean you shouldn't leave. Having doubts is *part* of leaving.

2. Reviewing Your Therapy

Whether it takes place in one wrap-up session in a brief therapy or over many sessions in a long-term therapy, one of the most meaningful tasks of the final phase is to reflect on what has gone on. This is vital in integrating and consolidating the work you have done.

Where possible, it's helpful to tie up loose ends, and where impossible, accepting that, too, is an important part of leaving.

For most people, the most important part of reviewing the therapy is reviewing their relationship with their therapist: how you began together, how your working relationship developed, where you worked well together and where you didn't, and especially, any crises in the relationship or times it may have seemed fruitless to go on. It's often helpful to look back together at specific things your therapist said or did or other events and your reactions to them. In retrospect, these moments often turn out to be turning points when something shifted between you. More difficult to talk about but useful if you can are the different perceptions you had of your therapist, changes in your feelings toward him or her, and the different ways you felt he or she reacted to you.

You might reflect, too, on what is most memorable about your work together, also any lingering resentments or regrets, and what you particularly appreciated. Finally, you can go over what you are likely to remember about your therapist and the experience of therapy, and how you feel about saying good-bye.

3. Acknowledging What You Accomplished and What You Didn't

In this final phase of therapy, it's important for you and your therapist to talk over explicitly what you accomplished and what you did not. Changes in ourselves become more real and convincing when we see them reflected in the eyes of someone else whose recognition matters. You don't want superficial reassurance or encouragement. You need frank acknowledgment and affirmation from your therapist. An honest assessment will help you consolidate your gains and see your therapy—and yourself—realistically.

4. Avoiding New Work

Deciding to end therapy can often trigger the resurfacing of old problems or the appearance of new ones. This is normal and related to the particular kind of anxiety associated with termination, but this isn't the time to begin work on new areas unless they are directly related to termination. Often the problems that suddenly flare up at the end of therapy and seem terribly urgent lose much of their urgency after you end and your anxiety subsides.

5. Allowing Yourself to Mourn

Foremost among all the mixed reactions to ending is mourning the losses involved. Sadness, even grief, can mark the end of a relationship that has been unique, important, and at its best, healing. But there are other, less obvious losses as well:

- *Your therapy.* You may feel relieved that therapy is ending or pleased that you no longer need it. You may be ending with a genuine sense of accomplishment and gratitude. And yet you may still find yourself anticipating the loss of a safe, understanding place where the focus was exclusively on you and your needs, where you could feel accepted and supported, where you could gradually discover a sense of greater mastery and confidence in yourself. The regular ritual of meeting with your therapist may have been a reassuring anchor in the tumult of daily life.
- *Your therapist.* You may particularly miss certain qualities in your therapist—warmth, a sense of humor, directness, honesty. Beyond that, someone who has been close to you, whom you have entrusted with aspects of yourself you don't generally let others see and who has lived through your personal struggles, is no longer going to be part of your life.
- *Aspects of yourself.* You may find yourself missing aspects of yourself left behind in therapy: personal traits, old patterns and habits, hopes and dreams that turned out to be unrealistic, or long-cherished views of yourself as someone better—or worse—than you turned out to be. Clients and even therapists often overlook the kind of grieving that needs to be done over aspects of yourself that were once essential. You may be glad or relieved they are gone. That may even have been your goal. But you may still be surprised to find yourself mourning the person you were.
- *Your expectations.* Change during therapy never turns out to be what we imagined it would be. Ending therapy is about confronting our illusions about therapy as a process of perfect and completely fulfilling growth and change. If you are like most clients, you may have dreamed of even grander accomplishments for yourself and expected even more from your therapist than you got. If you can face your disappointments in yourself and your therapist and accept that some of your expectations were unrealistic, you can begin to feel good about what you did accomplish and avoid bitterness.

This acceptance will help you anticipate and deal with difficult times in the future. You have learned that not all loose ends can be tied up neatly, nor all problems anticipated. With fewer illusions and less wishful thinking, you may be able to more clearly foresee areas where you may be vulnerable, problems that are likely to recur, or events that are likely to be difficult: your children leaving home, for instance, or the death of a parent. Anticipating future problem areas and vulnerabilities with your therapist is another important part of ending therapy.

Managing the Termination

Keeping to the Termination Date

Despite the pulls that will make you want to prolong therapy, keeping to the original date defines the boundaries you are working within and frames a backdrop against which issues specific to this phase will emerge and be seen clearly.

Short of a clear emergency or some other unavoidable change in circumstance, not keeping to the date you fixed is usually a sign of underlying anxiety and avoidance, and it can make the job of ending more difficult and less satisfying. It may even compromise the process. It raises questions about whether you are actually ready to end. If therapists go along with it, it raises the additional question of whether they are having trouble with terminating themselves. Keeping to the date you set is a good sign that you are indeed ready to end.

Some therapists may suggest gradually tapering off the sessions, to once every other week, to once a month or every few months. The rationale is usually that this will give you a taste of what ending therapy will be like and help you prepare for it.

Tapering off like this is most appropriate for long-term supportive therapy, especially in cases of serious and chronic disorders such as schizophrenia or severe depression. But as a general rule of thumb, it is usually better to keep the same frequency of sessions right up to the end, for the same reasons it is best to keep to a fixed date.

Shifting Your Roles

The client's role during this phase is sometimes described as learning "to become your own therapist." A catchy idea, but a misleading one. You can't be your own therapist. What you *can* do is become more active in sessions and take more initiative, as you will have to once therapy ends. You should gradually feel less dependent and more confident in your own insight and judgment. Your collaboration should begin to feel more like a genuine partnership.

Your therapist's role should shift correspondingly. He should allow himself to become less important by playing a less central role in sessions: allowing you to take more of the initiative, joining with you on a more equal footing, and supporting your capacity to do your own work. His job in this phase is no longer to help you resolve the issues that brought you to therapy, but to keep the termination on track, not letting anxiety about ending—yours or his—sidetrack or derail it.

Maneuvers to Avoid in Combating Termination Anxiety

If you or your therapist don't recognize termination anxiety or don't address it, you may try to minimize the discomfort of separation. This can lead to an unsatisfying ending to therapy and reinforce your experience of all important endings as unhappy.

Reflect on how you've dealt with past separations. If they have been difficult, there's a good chance you are dealing with this one in a similar way. You may be coping with ending by:

- *Ignoring or avoiding it.* It's possible to come up with many "reasons" not to say good-bye: it's really not *that* important; your therapist really won't care anyway; you'll spare yourself and him an awkward and painful moment; it's actually been a disappointing experience and you don't want to have to say that.
- *Finding something to argue or get angry over.* Getting mad at the end is much less devastating than feeling sad. Picking a fight keeps the relationship alive; sadness acknowledges that it is over.
- *Devaluing therapy or the relationship.* It's much easier to leave something—or someone—that was no good than to leave something—or someone—we really cared about and valued.
- *Putting it off and hanging on.* Staying longer than you need to or should because a little feels better than nothing.
- *Downplaying its importance.* "Ending isn't such a big deal. My therapist is making too much of it. I'll be fine."
- *Not having any feelings about it.* This is the most effective form of denial, and the surest sign that denial is at work!

The important thing is to recognize the anxiety around ending for what it is. Just identifying and acknowledging it will go a long way toward making it tolerable. For your therapist, your anxieties about ending will provide signposts in guiding your therapy to a good resolution.

The Last Session

The last session may be less eventful than you anticipated. Or it may move you more than you imagined it could. Exactly what is appropriate in saying good-bye depends on the relationship between you and your therapist, on your personal styles, and on social convention. Clients are most often uncertain about whether to give their therapist something to show their gratitude, and what kind of physical contact is appropriate.

You may feel you'd like to give your therapist a gift at the last session—something to remember you by or a way to say thank you. Giving a gift is seldom as simple an action as it appears (see Chapter 9, p. 201). The most important thing to know is that your therapist will not expect it. He or she will be satisfied with a warm good-bye. Many therapists would actually prefer you not give them anything; others will consider it inappropriate. In any case, a gift at the end of therapy is very much the exception rather than the rule. If after reading the section on giving gifts you still want to give your therapist something, the most appropriate gift would be something small and inexpensive. It is best given in a spirit of appreciation and remembrance, not so much as an expression of gratitude.

In our culture, good-byes are usually accompanied by some form of physical expression. For most, a handshake at the end will feel right and is the rule in most therapies. Intimate physical contact—even a hug—may feel inappropriate.

How you and your therapist say good-bye to each other should simply feel right to the two of you and reflect the relationship you've had. Be yourself. There is no need for anything special.

LESS DESIRABLE FORMS OF TERMINATION

Stopping Early

When Clients Stop Prematurely

Clients often stop therapy before they reach their goals or before they adequately resolve the issues they wanted help with. There are *legitimate reasons* for stopping early—times when you *should* stop whether you have accomplished your aims or not. Your therapy may not be helping. You may like your therapist, but feel that the therapy itself is unproductive. This feeling may be the result of unrealistic expectations or a misunderstanding of how therapy works, but if attempts to clarify this still leave you feeling you aren't being helped, there is no reason to continue.

Another good reason for stopping early is if your therapy is actually harmful or if your therapist is incompetent. Therapists are sometimes quick to call this "resistance" or "acting out"—and this is always possible—but you may simply find you're becoming worse instead of better the longer therapy continues, either because the therapist is mismanaging the therapy or violating one of the basic ground rules that ensure a safe framework (see Chapter 11, "Professional Ethics"). It may still make sense to continue if these problems can be adequately discussed and corrected. But if that isn't possible, then it's best to work toward a termination that will allow you to get help under less compromised circumstances.

Premature terminations are also triggered by much more problematic impulses, including:

- *Resistance:* anticipating that some particularly painful issue, pattern of behavior, memory, or feeling is about to be tackled, and quitting to avoid it (see Chapter 9, p. 212).
- *Overestimating initial gains:* leaving at the first sign of progress in the overly optimistic belief that you will be able to manage from here; or taking an initial improvement to mean the work of therapy is done.
- *Refusal to acknowledge your need for help:* leaving because you are afraid of becoming too dependent, or of admitting that you can't do it by yourself.
- *Fear of intimacy:* leaving when you feel yourself becoming too close to your therapist.
- *Disappointment or feeling rejection:* leaving because your therapist has said or done something hurtful.
- *A "flight into health":* leaving because you suddenly feel fine and your difficulties seem to have evaporated, when nothing has really changed.
- *Reenacting unresolved issues from past endings:* sometimes quitting is part of a larger pattern in life, such as abruptly ending a relationship when you are angry, hurt, or anxious.
- *Self-sabotage:* quitting may be yet another instance of a long-standing pattern of self-defeating habits, in this case sabotaging therapy just as it starts working.

A *sudden* and *abrupt* decision to end therapy should make you suspect your motives. Unless the reason was frank misconduct on your therapist's part, it may mean that one or more of these impulses is at play. Leaving prematurely usually does bring short-term relief from the anxiety of anticipation, but at the cost of not dealing with the underlying issues.

When Therapists Stop Prematurely

Therapists can also end therapy prematurely, and for equally good or bad reasons.

They may rightly feel they can't help you any longer. Their particular approach or style may no longer be what you need or a good match for your temperament. They may be at their wits end and out of ideas.

Unfortunately, it's almost impossible not to experience this as a rejection, even if a change is in your best interest. Allowing enough time to end is all the more important so some of these feelings can be acknowledged and addressed. Otherwise you may be disillusioned about further therapy, or your next therapy might be seriously compromised by anxieties about eventual rejection.

Alternatively, a therapist may also suggest taking a temporary break before resuming. They may sense that you could use time off to integrate what has been accomplished. But unless you understand and agree with the reasons for this, you run the same risk of feeling rejected.

Most damaging by far is when therapists suggest ending therapy for reasons that have little to do with their clients' needs. They may feel frustrated by a client's lack of responsiveness, or a slow pace of change. This may leave them feeling personally inadequate, professionally incompetent, or guilty about not being of more help. Stopping provides relief, although it is not necessarily in the client's best interest. In the worst case, they may even exaggerate any signs of progress to convince themselves and the client that therapy has been successful and the client is ready to end.

It sometimes happens that a therapist simply doesn't like a client and doesn't want to work with him or her anymore. Or worse, the therapist may have agreed to see someone only until a "better" client shows up—someone more interesting, compatible, or status enhancing. This is blatantly unethical.

Therapists will occasionally end for reasons completely unrelated to therapy: they want to write a book, they want more vacation time or time away from clinical practice, or they want to do research. If therapists stop therapy early purely out of their own interests, it can undermine any work you've done to that point. It can be harmful and is unethical. A therapist who does this is not likely to own up to it, so there will usually be some deception. Responsibility for ending may be put on the client to salve the therapist's guilt: you are "resisting" therapy; you are "not psychologically minded enough"; you aren't "motivated"; the therapy "isn't going anywhere"; or you just are "not a good candidate for therapy." Or they may *appear* to take responsibility: "I'm afraid I just can't help you anymore."

If this happens to you, try to see it as your therapist's problem, not yours. Get a consultation from another therapist if you are unsure. A consultation can help ease and put into perspective the hurt, angry, confused feelings you are likely to be left with.

Delayed Ending

When Clients Put Off Ending

Clients hang on to therapy for many reasons:

- *You may be anxious about making it on your own.* If new problems come up or old ones resurface, your therapist won't be there to help you. Therapists sometimes unwittingly reinforce this anxiety by expressing concern about your ending or raising questions about how you will handle certain problems.
- *Therapy has become a substitute for living.* The relationship with your therapist or group may be taking the place of unsatisfying relationships in the rest of your life instead of becoming a bridge to better relationships. Or your time in therapy

may feel more satisfying, comforting, intense, or real than anything else you do.

- *You've become "addicted" to therapy.* You need your weekly "fix" to face life. You need to remain dependent or your therapist needs to maintain control.
- *You may be reluctant to give up the side benefits of therapy.* Therapy can be a handy excuse to escape other responsibilities, e.g., "Don't expect too much of me—I'm in therapy." "I'll have to talk it over with my therapist first."
- *You may be afraid of offending your therapist or group.* You may be tempted to stay to avoid their real or imagined rejection or disapproval. Therapists and groups sometimes *do* feel guilty or inadequate. You may be trying to spare yourself or them painful feelings around leaving.
- *If you can just hang on long enough, you will be "cured."* You may have the idea that with enough therapy you will finally "get it together," problems won't bother you, you won't feel anxious or be afflicted by self-doubt, you'll feel good and won't have to worry. Leaving may be bringing you up against your limits and may mean giving up fantasies of wholeness or perfection.
- *It may be easier to hold yourself responsible than confront an oppressive situation.* You may be trying to avoid the fact that no amount of work on yourself will change racial, gender, or age discrimination, abusive or alcoholic parents, limited economic opportunities. Blaming yourself can also help mitigate a painful separation you are contemplating: leaving home, a marriage, or a job.
- *You may simply be avoiding separation itself,* and inevitable feelings of sadness and loss, especially if past separations have been difficult or painful.

When Therapists Put Off Ending

Sometimes therapists try to postpone or prolong ending. Their work may feel incomplete. Like any professionals, therapists want to finish what they've begun, especially when they see the potential for further growth. They have invested a lot of time, attention, and skill. Giving you up may also feel like losing a chance to further their own growth and professional development.

If they are in private practice, your fee may be an important part of their income. A private client in once-a-week therapy represents an income between $2,000 and $6,000 a year. If they don't have a waiting list and they're not sure about new referrals, your leaving may be a significant loss of income. Responsible therapists won't let that influence them, but unacknowledged financial anxieties can sometimes subtly bias decisions about when to end.

Your therapist may find you particularly rewarding to work with for some special reason—you may be charming, interesting, attractive, exceptionally bright, have a good sense of humor, or belong to a world or social niche beyond his or her usual network. You may have some special status or notoriety. Working with you may be a source of personal prestige or an entrée to other prominent and affluent clients.

But probably the single most common reason for prolonging ending is when the relationship has been so meaningful to both the client and the therapist that they feel a pull to continue it long after the original goals are met and anything much is left to do. If you find yourself in this situation, acknowledging openly what the relationship has meant to the two of you and the difficulty you are both having in letting go will make its loss easier to accept.

Ending Unexpectedly

When Clients Have to End Unexpectedly

You may lose your job or insurance coverage, move out of state, or become seriously ill or disabled and thus have to end therapy.

Be sure the event is genuinely a reason for stopping and you aren't seizing on it as a way out of continuing. Many times you can find a way. If you suffer a drop in income, for instance, you can ask your therapist if he or she will see you for a reduced fee. If you get sick, you can discuss a sick leave and a return to therapy when you are sufficiently recovered.

Even if stopping is genuinely beyond your control, exploring your reactions to a forced ending can be important and revealing. You may find that you're secretly relieved, for instance, or that you feel terribly guilty and ashamed. You may feel angry or cheated. Whatever your reactions, you will still probably experience having to end as a real loss. You will leave feeling very differently about having to end before you'd planned if you can bring your reactions into therapy and discuss them.

When Therapists Have to End Unexpectedly

Your therapist may have to end unexpectedly for similar reasons. However "understandable" the reasons, you will probably feel rejected, abandoned, or betrayed. These aren't completely irrational responses for which you should feel guilty. Whatever the reason, your therapist is allowing some other factor to take precedence over your relationship. When ending is unavoidable, your therapist should be prepared to tell you why he has to stop. He should also give you enough advance notice to express and explore your reactions. If you want continued help, your therapist also has an obligation to refer you to another therapist, or in the case of temporary illness or disability, provide coverage while he is out.

Even in unexpected terminations, the last sessions should still be used to review what you've accomplished to date and what remains to be done. Even if you don't feel like continuing immediately, you should still discuss your future options for completing any remaining work.

If therapy has been ended abruptly without any chance for discussion or good-bye, you should definitely consider seeking another therapist's help, at least temporarily, to deal with the feelings you are left with. This helps prevent the abruptness of the ending from undoing any gains you've made and casting a pall over the entire therapy experience.

When Neither of You Can End

Deciding to end is often difficult enough when you've accomplished the goals you had agreed on or come as close as you can reasonably expect. But deciding to end when therapy has dragged on for months or years without much progress is particularly difficult. When is enough enough? Even if you want to continue, should you?

Therapy Can Feel Interminable

Therapy can feel interminable, yet not be. In an overpromised age of five-second sound bites and weekend growth seminars, the prospect of a process that may take weeks, months, or even years is daunting if not suspect by contrast. The truth is that changing ingrained patterns of thinking, feeling, and acting takes time.

You cannot force the pace of your growth. When sudden change does occur in therapy, it is invariably because the groundwork was already laid and entering therapy triggered what was only waiting for a catalyst. Impatience with therapy sometimes results from misplaced expectations of quick change, fueled in part by a misunderstanding of how change comes about, in part by your own desire for immediate relief, and in part by current cultural myths of instant transformation.

Therapy Can Become Interminable

On the other hand, therapy can be interminable, dragging on endlessly for no reason other than that neither of you can end it. That kind of therapy has become "chronic" and is producing a "chronic" patient. Some clients know it is unproductive and yet continue anyway with no end in sight. Others don't even sense a problem and just keep coming to sessions week after week.

You can get stuck in a chronic therapy for a variety of reasons. You may have made therapy the central event in the week that sustains you, a life preserver you need to stay afloat, even when you're bored, angry, or frustrated with it.

It may have become vital to your self-esteem. If nothing else is working well or you can't feel good about much else you are doing, at least you are in therapy. The fact that your therapist has invested so much time and interest in you, or has found your problems so difficult, may give you the feeling of being different and special.

You may have been through a profound trauma or deprivation earlier in your life and may be finding it difficult to give up the feeling that you are owed—you have a right to the care and nurturance you never got, or that will make up for the pain. The therapy relationship can come to represent all you feel you've been denied, all you should have gotten. Giving it up means accepting the injury and the fact that nothing will ever fully compensate for what you suffered or missed.

Still others become locked in an endless battle with their therapist, defying their therapist to change them and defeating their attempts at every turn.

You aren't well served by continuing in an interminable therapy. Chronic therapy will wear out both you and your therapist. It will perpetuate the fantasy that life will somehow, someday, finally fulfill your dreams—or your demands, all you feel you have a right to—only to disappoint you in the end once again. It will undermine any incentive to try life on your own. It will inevitably sap your therapist's enthusiasm and energy for the work, no matter how much he tries to sustain it. You will sense him straining and running out of ideas. You will feel you are getting less and less—and you will be right. At some point therapy will end in stalemate. You won't be able to hold on, but neither of you will be able to let go: you because you'll feel your needs still haven't been met; your therapist because he will feel guilty over abandoning someone he doesn't know how to help any longer. Each of you will think it's the other's fault.

Despite your resentment and your fear of going it alone, this kind of therapy needs to end, whether you feel ready or not. When you do, you may actually be surprised to find you are more capable than you thought, and that you can build on what you have gotten from therapy. The option to go back into therapy is always there if you find you can't make it. But then you should try a different therapist with a different style, format, or approach.

CONTACT WITH YOUR THERAPIST AFTER THERAPY ENDS

Many clients are content to let their relationship with their therapist end with therapy, even if it was close and satisfying. Others would like to continue some kind of contact. The most common feeling is probably wanting to let your therapist know how things are working out, or to inform him of important events that you think he might be interested in hearing about. Most therapists won't expect this so you shouldn't feel any sense of obligation, but these are natural impulses.

Ordinarily you won't have direct contact with your therapist once therapy is over. Professional codes of conduct absolutely prohibit therapists from entering into romantic, sexual, or business relationships with their clients *even after* therapy ends. This is to protect clients from exploitation via the inequalities in the relationship and the unfair position of influence a therapist enjoys (see Chapter 11, "Professional Ethics"). Posttherapy relationships also raise the question how disinterested your therapist's motives really were, and who the therapy was really for—doubts that can undermine any gains and sow seeds of mistrust toward other helping relationships. For similar reasons the professions do not prohibit but do discourage turning the therapy relationship into a friendship once therapy ends.

However, if your therapy was successful and you enjoyed a good relationship, follow your impulse and let your therapist know what is happening in your life, particularly when some major event occurs. Most therapists won't initiate follow-up contact, but in addition to their personal interest, they have a stake in how you are doing, particularly in anything that therapy may have helped make possible—remarriage following a divorce, for instance, or a switch in jobs or career. Your continued progress reflects on their work and how helpful they have been.

A card or letter is probably the most appropriate form of contact. Be prepared if they don't respond. They may, but they won't want to intrude on your personal life. They may also have had many clients and may have decided it wouldn't be right to respond to some if they can't respond to all. Even if they don't answer, however, be assured that they will be interested to hear from you and will appreciate your making the effort and remembering them.

CHAPTER THIRTEEN

■

STARTING AGAIN

A course of therapy is not a once-and-for-all experience. As you may have found, it can help you make major changes—in yourself, in your marriage, or in your family—but it doesn't "cure" you or "fix" you forever. It may have made you more confident and resourceful in dealing with new challenges since therapy ended, but it won't have made your life problem-free or immunized you from disappointments, conflicts, or anxieties. You may find yourself wondering about returning to therapy, especially if it proved helpful in the past.

You *can* return to therapy whenever the need arises. Trends in mental health coverage, especially in HMOs and other managed health care systems, are encouraging this kind of repeated use. Newer benefits policies that limit therapy to ten to twenty sessions annually assume that therapy will be brief, problem focused, and repeated as the need arises over the years. But quite apart from the changing structure of health insurance, there are good reasons why therapy *cannot* be a once-and-for-all experience.

Each Phase of Your Life Has New Tasks to Be Mastered

At no point is psychological growth complete. The context of your first therapy was, inevitably, the phase of life you were in at the time, and the perspectives, tasks, and problems of that phase. But each phase of your life since then will have presented you with new developmental tasks to be mastered and a fresh psychological challenge. Depending on when your first therapy took place, this may have been leaving home, finding a personal and professional identity, marrying and becoming a parent, embarking on a career, entering midlife or old age. Even dying is a developmental

302

step with its own challenges that can be lived through as an affirmation or a defeat depending on how one responds.

Core Issues May Need to Be Worked Through Again

Even successful therapy won't have made you into someone else. It won't have altered the influences that shaped you, your basic ways of thinking, personality traits, or behavior patterns that make you recognizably "you." What may be harder to appreciate, however, is that therapy also won't have completely eradicated *core issues and conflicts*. These are defined by early, formative life experiences, and they tend to remain points of vulnerability over a lifetime. Therapy helps us to recognize them and be less influenced by them, but it seldom resolves these core issues once and for all. It's not uncommon to find old problems resurfacing in a different context or at a later stage of life—a child of alcoholic parents, for instance, taking care of a dysfunctional spouse; or a first child being vulnerable to jealousy and anger as an adult when she has to collaborate with a younger colleague who threatens to upstage her. When this occurs, it may become necessary to confront the old issues anew. This doesn't necessarily mean going back into therapy, but if you do go back, reworking these core issues will normally be easier since you will have worked on them before.

Living Involves Confronting Existential Issues and Ultimate Concerns

You also cannot avoid confronting certain existential "givens": death, freedom, aloneness, and the struggle to find meaning. These urgent experiences, which existential psychotherapists refer to as "boundary" situations, often encourage people to consider therapy again.

Your Previous Experience in Therapy Makes a Difference

If you're considering therapy again despite a *bad experience,* there is a good chance that what is drawing you back is, in part, unresolved problems from before: wanting to work out what still nags, wanting to succeed where you felt you failed.

Whatever your reasons, if you've been burned once, you'll understandably be wary of trying again. Since about 10 percent of people in therapy do have a negative experience, this situation is not uncommon. Fortunately, the second attempt at therapy is often more successful than the first. Clients who have been in therapy several times often report that a later therapy has been the most satisfying. They are more aware of shortcomings in potential therapists, know better what to look for, are more knowledgeable about how therapy works, and are better able to focus on getting what they need from it.

If you do decide to enter therapy again, let your new therapist know that your previous experience was an unhappy one and why. Go over it in some detail at the start and you will both be aware of what to look for and have a much better chance of avoiding a repeat performance.

If you find yourself thinking about therapy again after a *good experience,* you're probably being drawn back because you see it as resource for addressing new issues:

- Your circumstances may have changed: an illness, a death, a personal or family crisis, a new phase of life may be bringing up old issues in a new way.
- You find yourself coming up against unexpected problems that you feel you need help with.
- You haven't made as much progress as you thought you would or haven't adequately consolidated your gains.
- Your goals have changed. You want to work on something different or more ambitious than you did the first time.

OVERCOMING RESISTANCE TO STARTING AGAIN

It's not uncommon to find yourself struggling with some of the same inhibitions you experienced the first time. In addition, there can be *special resistances* to going back into therapy, even if your previous experience was a good one:

- Admitting that you need help again can feel like admitting you failed: "I ought to be able to work things out on my own by now. If I can't, there's something wrong with me." Unfortunately, family and friends can contribute to this feeling: "You're addicted to therapy." "You're just indulging yourself." "After all the money it cost you the first time, how can you think of doing it again if it didn't help?" You may find yourself tempted to prove them wrong by not going back.
- You may feel disillusioned about the process: "Shouldn't once be enough? Why should I have to go back?"
- You may feel discouraged just thinking about having to do it all over again: "Therapy did help me, but it was such hard work and took so much time, effort, and money. I don't know if I can go through all that again."

THE SAME THERAPIST OR A NEW ONE?

There is no hard-and-fast rule about whether it's better to return to your first therapist or start with a new one. Obviously it depends in large part on the kind of relationship you had. But it also depends on your reasons for going back into therapy.

If you are going back to do some *short-term work* on a particular problem for which your former therapist's approach is still suitable, seeing him or her is probably best, assuming you worked reasonably well together before. He or she knows you, will be familiar with your issues, will know how you like to work, and you won't have to spend a lot of time developing a working relationship. A former therapist is in a particularly advantageous position to help you with a brief consultation about a specific issue that doesn't warrant actually resuming therapy. Trying a consultation with him or her first may actually prevent your needing to go back into therapy.

If your *needs have changed* and your old therapist's format or approach isn't right for the issues you are facing now, or they aren't in his or her area of competence, then you should definitely go to the trouble of finding a new therapist.

If you are going back for long-term psychodynamic therapy, you might find yourself drawn to your old therapist for obvious reasons, again assuming you enjoyed a good productive relationship. If your previous therapy was short-term, this is probably the best place to start. If you've already been in a long-term therapy with him or her, however, you should ask yourself why you are considering someone who may not have much new to offer. Is it because you're afraid to try somebody new? If you find yourself thinking that no one else could possibly produce the same results, remember that therapy is a joint effort. Given another good match, you should be able to do just as well the second time, and having been through therapy once should make it easier to adapt.

If you were with your previous therapist a long time, definitely consider a different therapist if your goal is to push into unexplored areas or develop new sides of yourself. It can be worth the effort of getting a new referral. Even if they belong to the same school or take the same overall approach, they won't see things, or work with you, in quite the same way.

You should consider whether it might be some unresolved aspects of your old relationship that are pulling you back to a former therapist: a strong bond of affection and a desire to resume a relationship you miss; disappointment that he or she never really understood you and a hope that this time will be different; anger over slights or hurts and a wish to confront your therapist and demonstrate how well you've managed on your own.

In this case, you're really not returning to therapy but to your former therapist. Working out important leftover feelings from the old relationship may be a good reason for therapy, but it should probably be with a different therapist, who can help you with the feelings without rekindling all the things that provoked the feelings in the first place.

STARTING WITH A NEW THERAPIST

Once you have a referral, ask for a consultation first. Begin by describing briefly why you have decided to go back into therapy. Then describe your previous experience, especially why you have decided to see someone new. That will provide a background for this therapy and help define how you want it to be different. You should cover:

- what led you to seek therapy the first time
- the goals you set
- how you and your therapist worked together toward those goals: the type of therapy, the approach, how frequently you met, how long you met for, and any special techniques employed
- how long therapy lasted
- the reasons therapy ended
- what you feel you accomplished
- how you felt about yourself when therapy ended
- what was most helpful to you
- and especially, *what your relationship was like:* how you felt about it; what worked well between you and what didn't

In starting work, be alert for signs your new therapist may be competing with your old. If you sense pronounced competitiveness, especially any overt put-downs of your former therapist, you may need a different therapist.

Therapy the second time around should not be a rehash of old material; you should have a sense of breaking new ground. Since you will already know how to establish a relationship with a therapist and understand how this relationship works, in all likelihood you will be able to use your therapist in a more focused way to get what you need. You will know what works best for you and what to avoid. You will probably be less hesitant in bringing problems to your therapist's attention and talking them out.

PART II

---◼---

THE THERAPY GUIDE

■

CHAPTER FOURTEEN

USING THE THERAPY GUIDE

The Therapy Guide is designed to help you match the problems you are bringing to therapy with the most effective approaches to treatment.

The listings. The Therapy Guide lists the problems most frequently seen by therapists. These include common "problems in everyday living" as well as psychiatric disorders. The latter are based on the *Diagnostic and Statistical Manual of Mental Disorders III-R* (third edition, revised), published by the American Psychiatric Association. While not every therapist finds this manual's way of organizing and diagnosing mental health problems useful, it is the standard in the field, and the vast majority of therapists, clinics, agencies, and insurance companies use it to make and record diagnoses of specific mental health problems. (A new revision, scheduled for 1994, is expected to refine existing diagnoses rather than altering the list substantially.)

We have not included every disorder listed in *DSM-III-R*. Some are purely organic in nature, such as Alzheimer's disease, for which psychotherapy is not an appropriate treatment. Others, such as sleep disorders and stuttering, are best treated in specialized clinics, not in a psychotherapist's office. Still others have been omitted because they are simply too rare.

Using the Guide. The Guide follows a uniform format. Each entry begins with general information about the problem. Included here are such things as a brief history of the particular diagnosis, data on its most common course, as well as guidelines for when a given problem is not serious enough to require therapy.

This background section is followed by "Signs to Look For," a description of the main characteristics that will help you identify the problem. For the psychiatric disorders, the "Signs to Look For" lists the main symptoms professionals use to diagnose a given problem. *Do not try to diagnose yourself.* These listings are meant to provide background information to facilitate your discussions with your therapist. Until you talk to a qualified therapist, these diagnostic descriptions are, at best, working hypotheses to help you make a best guess about what kind of therapy to seek.

Next, there is often a vignette, based on one or more actual cases, illustrating how a particular problem actually mainfests itself in daily life. Finally, there is a section on the most appropriate form of therapy for that problem.

Therapy. Most sections on therapy open with a summary of the recommendations practicing therapists made in the National Survey of Psychotherapists (see Appendix V). This special feature of the Guide will look like this:

What Therapists Recommend

Approach. This lists the major approach or approaches most therapists recommend for this specific problem.

Medication. This tells you whether therapists commonly recommend medication in addition to psychotherapy for this problem.

Setting. This describes the *place* therapists recommend treatment take place. Usually this will be the therapist's office, but it may be a hospital, a day treatment program, or a residential setting in more serious cases.

Format. This is the recommendation for individual, couples, marital, family, or group therapy, or some combination of these.

Frequency. This indicates how often most therapists would expect sessions to be held.

Duration. This is approximately how long therapists think therapy should take, or whether it should be left open-ended.

A few problems were not included in the Survey. Discussions of therapy in these sections do not open with a summary in this format, but do still include specific recommendations.

The final section is "What You Should Know About Therapy," which gives a more detailed explanation of the recommendations. It also incorporates current thinking and research in the scientific and clinical literature.

Of course, no general recommendations will apply in every case. But knowing the consensus among therapists on these key points can help you discuss your own situation with prospective therapists and help you find your way to the most appropriate therapy.

General Guidelines

Apart from the specific recommendations for each problem, general guidelines govern the choice of approach, setting, format, frequency, duration, and medication. Keep the following considerations in mind as you consult the Therapy Guide.

APPROACH: WHAT KIND OF THERAPY?

As we found in the National Survey of Psychotherapists, one of the major approaches—or a certain combination of approaches—tends to be most highly recommended for a *specific* problem, but no single approach is best for *every* problem.

As we explained in Chapter 2, we have used the five most widely accepted major categories in making our recommendations. These are:

- The *psychodynamic* approach, which focuses on examining the psychological issues and conflicts that underlie emotional problems.
- The *behavorial* approach, which focuses on learned, observable behavior that can be modified through new learning.
- The *cognitive* approach, which focuses on distorted patterns of thinking that can be corrected.
- The *family system* approach, which focuses not on the individual, but on dysfunctional patterns of interaction within the couples, marital, or family system.
- The *supportive* approach, which focuses on providing day-to-day support rather than facilitating change.

Chapter 2 provides a detailed description of each of these approaches. What follows are some general guidelines suggesting who is most likely to benefit from each approach.

The Psychodynamic Approach

Who is most likely to benefit. Psychodynamic approaches demand that you have some ability to put your thoughts and feelings into words. You should feel reasonably comfortable in talking about yourself as well as your problems. You should have a genuine interest in understanding yourself better, and you will need to observe yourself and reflect on what you see. You will also observe your interactions with your therapist and your attitudes toward him or her, making your relationship with your therapist a part of therapy. You will confront feelings, needs, and fantasies that you have not been aware of; what you find out about yourself may sometimes be disturbing, and you will need to be able to handle anxiety.

The problems best suited for this approach. The psychodynamic approach is best suited for issues arising from long-standing internal conflicts rather than from social pressures. It is best suited for problems that interfere in your life to some degree, but not to the point that your behavior is out of control—as in psychosis, alcoholism, or substance abuse. The psychodynamic approach also works best if your goal is to make some fundamental changes in yourself rather than to address one specific behavior. A modified psychodynamic approach, "developmental psychodynamic therapy" (see p. 55), can also be used for personality disorders and between acute episodes in some forms of severe disturbance such as schizophrenia and manic-depression.

If your problems can't be significantly changed, a psychodynamic approach may only make things worse by making you more aware of them. Time may also be a factor: this approach typically progresses at a slow pace. It also isn't appropriate if what you need is immediate help for a specific symptom such as a phobia or a sexual dysfunction, or for emergency symptoms involving risk. Behavior that is clearly out of control such as impulse disorders, eating disorders, and addictions requires behavioral intervention, not psychodynamic exploration. Immediate problems resulting from sudden changes, such as losing your job, a death in the family, or separation and divorce, are generally not best handled by a psychodynamic approach, though they may bring up issues that could be fruitfully explored after the crisis passes.

The Behavorial Approach

Who is most likely to benefit. In behavior therapies the therapist is active and directive, collaborating with you in devising a treatment plan to carry out specific behavioral steps. You must be willing to take direction and responsibility for following that plan, without feeling undue resistance or resentment. You will also need to be motivated to carry out homework assignments between sessions and be willing to accept focused and limited goals.

For people with anxiety problems, most behavorial techniques require you to gradually expose yourself to the very situations you dread. In some methods, such as "flooding," this will mean doing so all at once. For obsessive-compulsives, it means trying to resist the anxiety-relieving compulsive ritual, even when the urge to perform it seems unbearable.

The problems best suited for this approach. The behavioral approach is best when what you want help for is clear, discrete, definable symptoms or behaviors. These include phobias, obsessions, and compulsions; psychosomatic symptoms; behavioral deficits such as faulty social skills, shyness, or lack of assertiveness; personality trait problems such as hostility, anxiety, or loneliness; facial and other tics; stuttering; tension and migraine headaches; and the major sexual dysfunctions.

The behavioral approach may also be used in combination with other approaches to help control or stop smoking, drinking, overeating, alcoholism, substance abuse, impulse disorders, eating disorders, and obesity, and many of the behavior problems and conduct disorders in children. It is usually the principal approach for eliminating a wide range of maladaptive habits such as hair pulling, scratching, nail biting, difficulty voiding, intractable hiccuping, sneezing or vomiting, head banging and other self-destructive behaviors in children, exhibitionism, and unwanted fetishism. It can also be used to reduce the symptoms of autism, mental retardation, and psychosis.

When this approach is not recommended. Behavior therapies are not used to gain a deeper understanding of the psychological roots of your problems. Behavior therapy is purposely limited in focus, and its techniques are most effective when the problem is specific. This isn't the best approach when the problem or issue isn't a discrete, definable behavior or symptom; or when you think the problem may be associated with internal psychological conflicts.

The Cognitive Approach

Who is most likely to benefit. If you are comfortable thinking things through logically, then cognitive therapy will be easy for you. On the other hand, if your heart rules your head, don't turn your back on cognitive therapy: it may be just what you need to bring some rationality to your emotional life.

The therapist in these approaches is very directive, advising you what you should try to do. It will help if you appreciate such an approach, rather than rebelling against it. You will also be given "homework" between sessions—things to try and report back on. Since the success of cognitive therapy depends in part on your carrying these out, your willingness is crucial.

The problems best suited for this approach. Cognitive approaches were originally developed for use with depression, where they proved highly successful in many cases. Over the years the range of applications has steadily expanded, particularly to anxiety problems such as phobias, panic attacks, and agoraphobia. In several studies, cognitive therapy has shown itself as effective as medication for the treatment of mild depression and anxiety.

But because distorted thinking is at play in so many emotional problems, cognitive approaches have relatively wide applications beyond depression and anxiety: obsessive-compulsive, psychosomatic, eating, and paranoid disorders, and even chronic pain problems. The approach can also help with the problems of everyday living—feeling bad about yourself, lacking confidence or direction, loneliness—any problem that stems from distorted beliefs about yourself, your world, or your future. A recent application of the cognitive approach is to marital problems.

When this approach is not recommended. A cognitive approach is probably not what you are looking for if you want to use therapy to gain a deeper understanding of yourself or the psychological roots of your problems. Even so, some cognitive therapists have begun to explore "core schemas," those mental and emotional habits formed early in life that continue to exert a powerful influence. The cognitive approach may also be difficult if you find you can't tolerate the direct confrontation with your self-deprecating attitudes or change ingrained habits of passivity.

The Family Systems Approach

Who is most likely to benefit. A family systems approach usually requires that both partners or spouses, or all members of the family, come to sessions and be willing to work. However, a systems approach can be taken even in individual therapy. And a reluctant or unwilling family member need not mean that the whole family is kept from therapy.

But if you are considering a family approach, the key family members need to participate for it to work. That does not mean that everyone needs to be getting along—if you were, you wouldn't need therapy.

Perhaps more important is that you be willing to have your marital and/or family relationships challenged. No one in the system will remain unaffected.

Unlike individual therapy, in which everything that goes on is kept confidential between you and the therapist, in a family approach everyone is involved and everything that happens in therapy is shared. Some of your family secrets may be given a wider airing than you may be comfortable with.

The problems best suited for this approach. A family systems approach is the right choice whenever a couple or family agree they have joint problems. But as we discussed in Chapter 2 (see p. 64) identifying the roots of the problem is not always so clear. Many "problems in everyday living" are actually symptomatic of problems in the marital or family system, problems at work or school, for instance, reflecting problems at home. Children's problems, such as chronic misconduct, a sudden drop in school performance, or school phobia, are notoriously tied to problems at home, often to parental conflict. This is why virtually every problem that brings a child to therapy can be treated with a family systems approach. All this may be difficult to sort out, but as a general rule, anytime a member of a family or a couple sees a problem as a "family issue," an initial couples, marital, or family evaluation is in order.

A family systems approach is frequently combined with other approaches to treat such individual problems as alcoholism, substance abuse, or major mental illness, which affect the entire family. Not only does the family itself need support, but involving them in treatment is essential to the family member's recovery.

The Supportive Approach

Who is most likely to benefit. This is the choice when the object of therapy is not to bring about change, but to provide a supportive therapeutic relationship until some crisis or emergency passes (see Chapter 2, p. 69).

The problems best suited to this approach. Supportive therapy is designed to help you through acute turmoil that undermines your ability to function, such as the loss of a job, the death of a loved one, a divorce, or a serious illness or disability.

An important component in long-term therapy for chronic mental illness, therapeutic support can help people manage the demands of day-to-day living and maintain themselves in their community. It is also the right approach when they require a professionally organized and supervised social network, and when they can't tolerate more active or direct interventions.

More typically, a supportive approach is taken during the acute phase of mental health problems that are highly disabling: drug and alcohol abuse, major depression, mania, psychotic reactions, schizophrenia. In these cases, stabilization and a return to normal functioning is the immediate goal.

Frequently, the supportive approach is combined with other approaches.

MEDICATION: WILL YOU NEED IT?

Medication is almost always prescribed for the symptoms of major mental disorders and other psychiatric conditions, not for problems in everyday living. There are exceptions. A trend in psychiatry today is to sometimes prescribe medication, for instance, in cases of mourning or mild depression, and not to restrict it to biologically based conditions. By and large however, if you are seeking help for one of the normal problems in living that most people bring to therapy, you need consult this section no further.

For the *psychiatric disorders,* the Therapy Guide tells whether medication is usually recommended for a problem, as well as which type. All of the main psychiatric drugs and their uses are described in detail in Chapter 18.

There is no longer any question that psychiatric medications can help many people during periods of emotional or mental suffering, and with many behavioral problems. If life has been a black, bottomless pit for months on end, antidepressant medications can help. Severe symptoms that confuse and terrify individuals and their families, and that might otherwise result in physical restraints, hospitalization, or homelessness, can be mitigated with antipsychotic medications. Antianxiety medications can enable people to function in their everyday lives without embarrassing and often crippling panic attacks. Unless therapy alone suffices, or there is some other specific reason not to, for a psychiatrist not to recommend a medication trial in these and other situations runs counter to standard practice.

Combining Psychotherapy and Medication

At one time, many therapists believed that taking medication would undermine therapy by making people less motivated to explore psychological issues. Conversely, many psychiatrists thought that medication was superior and should replace therapy. You may still encounter these attitudes, though experimental and clincial evidence now shows that medication and therapy can be combined quite well. Research suggests that each is more effective with different target symptoms, so that in many cases the combined effect is greater than either alone.

Medication may be recommended along with psychotherapy when:

- The problem you want a therapist's help with is accompanied by specific symptoms that have been shown to respond to medication: depression, manic-depressive mood swings, acute anxiety states and panic disorders, obsessive-compulsive disorders, and psychotic disorders.
- Disabling symtoms need to be alleviated first. This is particularly true of intractable anxiety states and panic disorders, acute depression or mania, and acute psychosis. You can't benefit as much from therapy—or engage in most forms of therapy at all—until your most disabling symptoms are brought under control.
- A life-threatening emergency occurs: your behavior is self-destructive or you are actively assaultive or homicidal.

Medication and psychotherapy can be combined in two different ways: either simultaneously or sequentially. Normally they are prescribed at the same time, but in the acute phase of some conditions, medication is started first and psychotherapy begins when the person's condition has stabilized.

Some physicians and psychiatrists may recommend medication alone in some circumstances. When they do, they should arrange to meet with you more or less regularly to monitor your use of medication and its effects. They should also make time to talk with you about how you are doing in a way you might talk to a therapist. But this will be briefer and less formal, and the psychiatrist may not be a trained therapist. You should always feel free to ask about psychotherapy when medication alone is prescribed. Ideally, medication should always be prescribed within the context of a therapeutic relationship.

The aim of medication, like therapy, is to eventually eliminate the need for it. This isn't always possible. Some disorders, at least as we understand them at present, can be lifelong conditions, either chronic or recurrent. Depression, manic-depression, alcoholism, drug dependence and other addictions, and schizophrenia are examples. As with diabetes, parkinsonism, or epilepsy, medication may be required periodically.

Referral for a Medication Evaluation

If your therapist is not a psychiatrist and thinks your symptoms would respond to medication, he or she should refer you to a psychiatrist or psychopharmocologist for a medication evaluation. Don't ever begin taking psychiatric medication before having a formal evaluation first. This should include a medical history and a physical examination, since all medications have potential side effects. If the psychiatrist says you don't need medication, he or she is probably right. If your therapist, family doctor, or some other caregiver says that, take it as a reasonably informed opinion but not an authoritative one. Some therapists hesitate to refer clients to a psychiatrist for medication because they're afraid of losing the client and the fee. You should always feel free to ask if your condition would respond to medication, and if so, to request a medication evaluation.

Who Makes the Decision About Medication?

You do! A psychiatrist can only recommend. You should always take a recommendation seriously and be sure you understand the reasons for it. But the choice is finally yours. The point is to *make an informed choice* if medication is or isn't recommended.

In only two instances can you be required to take medication. One is the relatively rare situation when a family member or caregiver petitions the court for a *medication guardianship* and the court determines that not taking medication represents a serious risk to your own safety or others, finding you legally incompetent to make an informed choice. The second is a medical emergency when you are in imminent danger of hurting yourself or someone else.

As you try to evaluate taking medication, be aware that your own beliefs about medicines will come into play. Some people find a chemical solution to emotional problems reassuring, preferring to see the problem as biological. But this attitude can keep you from investigating the psychological factors that may be at work and lead to an incomplete resolution.

Others find the idea of taking medication for an emotional problem repugnant or "unnatural." If you see medication as somehow "unhealthy," you may find it hard to evaluate the recommendation fairly or to keep taking medication as prescribed. Half of all prescriptions written are never brought to the pharmacy!

Side Effects

Messages in the brain are transmitted by way of chemicals called neurotransmitters. Psychiatric medications work by imitating nature's plan, but they are at best rough approximations of the brain's own chemical balances. They are not perfect: all have side effects. And the problems they are used to treat all involve complex brain processes. Altering the brain's balance in just one way, as such medications do, may or may not correct the problem for you.

For psychiatric drugs, side effects are particularly bothersome since they are often the result of a direct effect on brain function and thus show up as cognitive, emotional, or psychological disturbances. The side effects of each of the major psychiatric drugs are described in Chapter 18; many can be controlled.

THE SETTING: WHERE THERAPY SHOULD TAKE PLACE

Your Therapist's Office

The standard setting for therapy is your therapist's office. The main exceptions are psychiatric emergencies or crises requiring full or partial hospitalization.

Short-Term Hospitalization (several days to several weeks)

In a psychiatric emergency, the therapist's rule of thumb is to consider personal safety first—your own and others'. In certain high-risk situations, the appropriate setting for treatment is a hospital or other inpatient facility. These situations include:

- acute suicidal thoughts or wishes, or command hallucinations telling you to kill yourself
- assaultive or homicidal thoughts or threats
- self-mutilation or other intentional self-destructive acts such as burning or cutting oneself, or deliberately engaging in high-risk behavior that courts injury
- drug overdose or drug-abuse emergencies

- severe alcohol or drug withdrawal
- incapacitating anxiety or panic reactions
- incapacitating depression
- acute psychosis
- starvation, dehydration, or severe electrolyte imbalance from an eating disorder
- acute posttraumatic stress reactions
- inability to care for yourself

A hospital is the appropriate setting as well if:

- your judgment, ability to plan, or sense of reality is seriously disturbed
- you aren't responding to active outpatient intervention and your condition continues to worsen or rapidly deteriorates
- your therapist or physician sees a need for supervised observation and diagnostic tests, or a change of medication that needs close monitoring for potential reactions
- your family is overwhelmed by your condition or cannot continue to provide care at home

Day Hospital (sometimes called partial hospitalization)

A day hospital is a short-term treatment program that you attend during the day only. Like a hospital, and often on hospital grounds, it provides a structured setting with a full psychiatric and support staff to provide immediate and intensive intervention during an emergency. The ratio of staff to patients is high, and medical personnel are available as needed. The aim is to provide rapid evaluation, stabilize your condition, and get you back to your normal level of functioning as quickly as possible without the need for hospitalization.

For people whose emotional problems are severe and ongoing, day hospital programs are often a good alternative to full hospitalization during acute episodes or relapses.

Not all hospitals or community mental health centers have day hospital programs. When they do, they are often every bit as effective as inpatient hospitalization, sometimes more so.

Long-Term Day Treatment

Long-term day treatment is similar to the day hospital setting, but is designed to be ongoing: several weeks to several months to a year or more. Like a day hospital, it provides a structured setting with a daily program of therapeutic activities, usually from nine A.M. to three P.M. two to five days a week. Long-term day treatment programs are based on the idea of a "therapeutic community." Treatment takes place largely through many different kinds of group and community activities, typically in conjunction with once-a-week therapy.

This is often the setting of choice for people with long-term mental health disabilities who are currently unable to work and for whom interacting with others is difficult, but who can live in the community and work toward further training, eventual employment, and better relationships if they have the help of a daily structure and more intensive support than psychotherapy alone. Social and vocational skills are the major focus of treatment.

You must be reasonably motivated, with living arrangements and income stable enough so you can attend. Despite impairments in social skills, even a considerable degree of social withdrawal, you still need to be able to tolerate being around others and participating in groups.

Related though somewhat less structured settings are various types of drop-in centers based on a "social club" or "clubhouse" model. These are for people with long-term psychiatric disorders who may not be able to participate in an active treatment program, or who simply want the after-hours support and a place to meet other people.

One advantage of both types of programs is their morale strengthening and confidence building, essential for people who have been demoralized by years of disability, illness, or repeated hospitalization.

Long-Term Psychiatric Hospitalization

Once very common for severe and persistent major mental illness, this setting is rapidly becoming a thing of the past. It has not worked very well for most people. Long-term hospitalization, especially in large state mental hospitals, has often created as much or more psychological disability as it has cured. Also, it is prohibitively expensive, especially with so many more effective and less expensive alternatives. Most insurance carriers and managed health care systems provide only limited benefits, and utilization-review procedures have established relatively strict guidelines for its use. Recognition of the "least restrictive setting" principle long sought by clients' rights advocates has also reduced long-term hospitalization. Clients have a right to be treated in the least restrictive setting possible, ideally in the community where they live, and not be cut off from family and friends just because they suffer from a psychiatric disorder. The availability of modern psychiatric medications and better aftercare now allows most people, even with major mental disorders, to live in the community and continue treatment as outpatients.

Long-term hospitalization continues to be an option for those few whose psychiatric problems have not responded to treatment or respond exceptionally slowly. Even here, it is justified only if people are a danger to themselves or others, or if they cannot provide minimal self-care.

Supervised Living

This option has replaced long-term hospitalization for most people who need supervised care. It is designed for those with debilitating symptoms who, with regular supervision, support, and mental health services, can still live on their own in their community. Someone with residual schizophrenia, for instance, may continue to experience mild hallucinations even with medication and lack the sustained energy to hold a job, but still be able to live in a supervised apartment, group home, or halfway house on his or her own.

The key in these situations is case management: a social worker or mental health aide sees that the person keeps medical and therapy appointments, perhaps attends a day program, gets disability checks, pays his or her bills, and takes medications.

FORMAT: WHOM TO INCLUDE IN THERAPY

Individual therapy has been the traditional format since Freud's time, but though still dominant, it is by no means the only one. The four standard formats are individual, couples, family, and group, and the most appropriate depends on several factors. For each of the psychological problems in the Therapy Guide, there is a specific recommendation, based on the National Survey of Psychotherapists and current clinical thinking and research, but some general considerations also apply.

If you are seeking therapy for one of the many problems in everyday living, the single most important question you should ask youself is: Is this an "I" problem or a "we" problem? Clarifying that, perhaps with a therapist's assistance, will go a long way to determine the appropriate format.

Individual Therapy

This is the format we usually associate with therapy: you and your therapist meeting in the privacy of his or her office. Individual therapy is the appropriate format when the difficulty is an "I" problem, one that primarily derives from you or concerns you: internal conflicts, for instance, or deeply ingrained personal habits that are causing repetitive patterns of self-defeating behavior. If you are primarily seeking relief from a specific symptom or condition such as a phobia or panic state, or if the problem is so private or potentially embarrassing that it needs the privacy of individual therapy, this is the format of choice. Consider individual therapy first if your primary need is for individual support in managing a difficult transition: a divorce, the loss of a parent, retirement, or unemployment.

Individual therapy is also recommended when your emotional patterns are repeatedly sabotaging your personal relationships. The intensity and focus of the personal relationship with your therapist can be reparative in a way that would not occur in another format.

The special strength of individual therapy is its atmosphere of complete confidentiality. Time in the sessions is yours alone. A basic trust is inherent in the individual format that ultimately derives from your experience of parental relationships and other early caretakers. The individual format is a familiar one.

However, the price of confidentiality is that therapists only get to know you as you are in the therapy sessions, and as you choose to reveal yourself. They inevitably get a partial and biased view—yours! Even a thorough exploration of the transference in a psychodynamic approach won't capture the range of reactions and behavior you would show, for instance, in a family or group format.

Another drawback to the individual format is that other people in your life can't be drawn into therapy to help you change. For many problems, such as addictions, this is often crucial. In a couples, family, or group format, others can also observe and confront your behavior, and you might hear their feedback better than you would hear your therapist's. There is also less chance to influence your environment and others who are affecting you than there is in a couples or family format.

Individual therapy can also have the unintended effect of labeling you the "patient" in your relationship, marriage, or family, conveying the message that you are the cause of the problem, and any change depends on your changing.

Lastly, individual therapy is the format that is most likely to permit, or even encourage, an excessive dependency on the therapist and an unconscious delegation of responsibility to him or her, even when you are both aware of this potential problem.

Family Therapy

As explained in Chapter 2, the problem is not always "in" one person. An individual family member's problems can be symptomatic of a troubled family. If that's the case, one member's going into therapy will do little or nothing to change things. The solution is to work with the entire family as a single system.

Family therapy is the appropriate format when:

- Everyone in the family agrees this is a "family" problem.
- The problem involves patterns within the family system to which everyone is contributing in some way, though it may require a consultation with a family therapist to clarify this.
- There are major problems in the way family members perceive and communicate with each other: each tends to blame the other for their problems; members are superficially close but actually distant; or family relationships are characterized by shifting alliances, with members often feeling betrayed by someone they thought was on their side.

- An adolescent is acting out in some major way: through alcohol or substance abuse; delinquency; promiscuity.
- An adolescent is having difficulty leaving home and separating from the family.
- A child or adolescent rules the house or is continually defiant.
- When one member of the family starts to do better, another member starts to have problems or begins to do worse.
- Another form of therapy isn't working, e.g., someone in individual therapy uses it mainly to talk about family problems.
- More than one family member needs therapy, but there is only enough money for one therapy.

Like other formats, the family format has potential drawbacks. If the children aren't involved in parental conflict, including them may distract the parents from focusing on their marital difficulties; marital therapy is then the right format. Certain intimate marital issues, such as sexual difficulties, are also best kept between spouses.

Couples and Marital Therapy

Couples or marital therapy is the format of choice when the problem is between the two of you. It may not seem to be a shared problem; from your point of view the problem may seem to be all his—or all hers. Or one or both of you may be too ready to blame yourself and accept sole or primary responsibility when the real problem lies between you, in the relationship.

Couples or marital therapy is the appropriate format when:

- You both agree the problem is in the marrige or the relationship.
- The therapist you consult sees the difficulties as in the relationship, with each of you contributing.
- There are major problems in the way you perceive and communicate with each other: you each blame the other for all of your problems; you keep shifting back and forth in the way you feel about each other; superficial closeness masks the ways you are actually distant; you typically misunderstand each other's goals.
- One of you begins having problems or starts to do worse when the other starts to do better.
- You or your spouse/partner haven't benefited from individual therapy, or you find yourself using most of your individual sessions to talk about your marriage or relationship problems.
- Your spouse or partner won't accept therapy in any other format.
- More than one of you needs help, but financial considerations will only allow for one therapy.

For couples or marital therapy to have a realistic chance, it is best if you start it while there is still a commitment between you to make things work. Many couples consider therapy after it is too late: one has already decided on divorce, for instance.

Frequently, the partner who initiates couples or marital therapy has an agenda: to get the partner to a therapist who can tell him (her) just how wrong he (she) is. But couples and marital therapists do not take sides, or shouldn't. Their role is to bring some objectivity to a highly charged situation, to open up blocked lines of communication, to help a couple find the ways they may both be contributing to the problem and ways they can jointly resolve it, and to offer a safe, structured setting in which this can be done.

If you are trying to get your partner to agree to couples or marital therapy, keep trying. Don't threaten or shame. It will defeat the purpose. Just talk. Focus on how important your marriage or your relationship is to you, how much you want to work out your problems, and how committed you are to working them out together. Couples therapists generally go out of their way to make the partner who may have felt "forced" into therapy feel not just comfortable, but actually welcomed and supported. If your partner or spouse is trying to get you through the door, be assured you won't be blamed or ganged up against.

In couples and marital therapy, the therapist has the chance to actually observe how you interact with each other and to hear both points of view. You will both be less likely to blame the other; instead, you will feel supported and encouraged to share responsibility for your problems. Couples and marital therapy also tends to check excessive dependency and reliance on the therapist. Your partner's presence is a reminder that the real world is just outside the door and that therapy isn't a retreat from problems. Lastly, the format provides the opportunity for simultaneous change and growth in both of you, so that one of you doesn't get better at the other's expense or at the cost of unbalancing the relationship.

Couples and marital therapy also has potential disadvantages. The resistance of one partner can block the more motivated other from getting needed help. The fear of having to reveal embarrassing things you have done can also be a factor in every format other than individual. Even in an intimate relationship, some secrets are probably better kept to oneself. By making a more open exchange possible, a couples or marital format can sometimes backfire if the partners seize upon therapy as a justification for finally unloading stored-up hostility. A good therapist will usually be able to forestall or contain this, however. Lastly, if you tend to live through and for your partner and have difficulty asserting your independence, individual therapy in conjunction with couples therapy may be appropriate if you can afford it.

Group Therapy

While the standard format of therapy is one-to-one, most problems that can be dealt with individually can also be handled well in group therapy. And for certain problems group therapy is generally superior. The idea of talking about intimate feelings in a group may be intimidating at first, but most people who give groups a fair try are glad they did.

Groups vary in composition and size. Many therapy groups are *"mixed"* or "heterogeneous" in the sense that the members have each come because of different emotional or interpersonal problems. People in this type of group can vary greatly in age, background, personality, and strengths as well as problems. In spite of these differences, mutual acceptance and support develop in the group. You discover you are not alone and that your experience is not uniquely crazy. You gradually find yourself more able to talk about yourself and your issues, take risks with others, listen to what they have to say, accept their feedback, and provide feedback to them. You learn others can help you at the same time you discover you have something to offer them. The different interactions in the group afford you the opportunity to test the assumptions you typically make about yourself and how others see you, correct distortions, discover how others regard you, and learn new and more satisfying ways of interacting.

The approach to therapy can also vary. Most of the same approaches taken in individual therapy have also been applied to group therapy.

The optimal number of members in a mixed group is six to eight, but slightly smaller and larger groups can also work well. The group should probably not exceed ten nor be held with less than three. Membership is relatively stable. This is your group and you meet with them regularly, usually once a week for an hour and a half. Members leave when they have accomplished their goals, but the group is usually ongoing. More recently, various types of brief or time-limited psychotherapy groups have also been introduced.

More and more over the years, *"single-focus"* or "homogeneous" groups have emerged. In these groups everyone shares the same problem or ones closely related. The problem may be being a single parent or divorced, having been a victim of rape or child abuse, or being addicted to alcohol or drugs. Or the problem may be a psychiatric disorder: agoraphobia or some other anxiety disorder, bulimia or anorexia, a manic-depressive disorder or schizophrenia. Such groups are now standard features of psychiatric hospitals and mental health clinics. And they are the mainstay of the mushrooming self-help movement.

Unlike heterogeneous group therapy in which interactions between members are normally restricted to sessions and members are asked not to socialize outside therapy, homogeneous groups will often encourage their members to support each other between sessions in the problem area—maintaining sobriety, for instance.

One of the great advantages of single-focus groups is that everyone shares your problem. This means, for instance, that you need feel no shame or stigma about it; others will feel an instant empathy for what you are going through and are likely to be understanding and welcoming from the start. And by being with people who are a little further along in the process than yourself, you can learn an immense amount that is helpful, just as you can have the good feeling of helping a recent arrival with a struggle you've just gone through.

Homogeneous groups tend to vary more in size, depending on whether they are conducted primarily as a therapy or a support group, and whether the personal interactions between group members are viewed as important to the process. A support group can be larger than a typical therapy group. How frequently the group meets is also more variable. If the goal is primarily support, attendance may be on a drop-in basis rather than on a fixed schedule.

One of the most therapeutic aspects of group therapy is the positive models it provides. Even though others in the group will have come because in some sense they are troubled, each person will also have strengths—a kindness, a straightforwardness, an intuitive sense, an ability to put their feelings into words, a capacity for empathy—that you can admire and imitate.

As you come to trust the group and yourself in it, you will find yourself experimenting with new ways of being, taking risks about things that have held you back. And what you find yourself able to do for the first time in the group you will gradually start trying in the rest of your life.

Interpersonal problems are particularly well suited to treatment in group, including loneliness, shyness, social and work inhibitions; a tendency to be overly dependent and timid, or argumentative; problems with authority; lack of assertiveness; difficulty sharing or appreciating others' experience; a negative self-image or an opposite need for adulation. Group therapy can also be the format of choice when other formats haven't worked for you, or you've gotten as much help from them as you can. A group format may also work better if you have a tendency to become so involved with individual therapists that it interferes with therapy; or conversely, if you find you can't tolerate the intimacy of one-to-one therapy.

Self-Help Groups. The most common form of single-focus group is the self-help group, the prototype being Alcoholics Anonymous. Many of these groups are listed in Appenidx I. Because they are so valuable, we have included the relevant self-help group whenever one is available in our treatment recommendations for each problem in the Therapy Guide. A separate listing of local clearinghouses to help find self-help groups is in Appendix II.

One drawback of some self-help groups is that they actively discourage your seeking any other kind of help. Some are explicitly "antipsychiatry" or "anti—mental health" and reject in principle anything that a therapist might have to offer. Some individual AA groups, for instance, will actively discourage the use of psychiatric medication, even when a person may be showing signs of some other mental disorder such as depression—not uncommon in recovering alcoholics.

If this should happen to you, you need to confront the issue directly. Discuss it with your group. Discuss it with your therapist and prescribing physician. You may find support among some group members who have been in a similar situation. Your therapist and/or physician should take your dilemma seriously and help you find a solution. As a last resort, you will usually be able to find another group who will tolerate and even support your use of other therapy or medication.

Single-focus groups, especially self-help groups, have two other potential drawbacks. Because they will focus more or less exclusively on the specific problem that all members share, other important areas may be neglected. Secondly, they tend not to explore resistances. If you aren't highly motivated to begin with, you may not be made to feel as welcome, even though you might benefit, unless you give up your reservations or change your point of view.

FREQUENCY: HOW OFTEN SHOULD YOU MEET?

How often sessions should be scheduled to produce the best results has never been clearly established. Consequently frequency varies, depending on the format and approach. Once a week has become the standard for most individual and group therapy, but this is more because of convenience and convention than because it is an ideal. Psychoanalysis is usually four or even five times a week. Couples and family therapy is typically more spread out, every other week or monthly. Crises, on the other hand, can require meeting more frequently.

The frequency of sessions usually remains the same over the course of therapy, though in some approaches you may meet less often toward the end or during a follow-up period. Couples and family therapists will sometimes adjust meetings to the needs of the individual couple or family they are working with. A primarily supportive therapy can also vary in frequency from weekly sessions to monthly check-ins to twice-yearly visits.

Some therapists will work with you less than once a week if that is all you can afford given your income or insurance coverage. Spreading out meetings means the overall duration can be longer. Or they may suggest starting at once a week, then cutting back once therapy is well under way.

If your therapist recommends a particular schedule based on your problem but is willing to meet less frequently, you should ask why. Will he or she really be able to help you if you have to meet less often? If that's less often than the therapist thinks your problem warrants, why is he or she willing to do it? Will the therapist want to increase the frequency if you can afford it later? On the other hand, therapy will not automatically go faster if you meet more frequently. In fact, meeting more frequently can sometimes prolong the process. More frequent sessions can expand the focus, allow additional material to emerge, and change your relationship with your therapist in ways you can't anticipate. Increasing the frequency can facilitate greater intensity of feelings when this is appropriate to the goals and the approach you are pursuing. It can also help defensive clients who find it hard to become involved in once-a-week therapy to become more engaged and use therapy better.

But as a general rule, more is not necessarily better. Some people move faster and do better meeting once a week than two or three times a week. You can't force-feed change, or your own growth. It will have its own pace and rhythm.

LENGTH: HOW LONG SHOULD EACH SESSION BE?

This usually depends on the format you are using. In individual and couples therapy, the usual arrangement is to meet for forty-five or fifty minutes—the so-called "fifty-minute hour." Family and group therapy sessions typically last longer: an hour and a quarter to an hour and a half. The approach can also make a difference: a primarily supportive therapy can often be managed very well with shorter sessions. In some cases, length can also depend on you. For some people with certain kinds of personality disorders or psychotic illnesses, or for individuals who have minimized their social contacts, forty-five to fifty minutes is more closeness than they can bear. It's also too long for someone in an acute state of psychosis, paranoia, mania, or depression, though therapy for these conditions would probably be taking place in a hospital or other inpatient setting anyway.

As a general rule, however, the length of sessions will remain the same throughout the course of therapy.

DURATION: HOW LONG SHOULD THERAPY LAST?

Unless you are doing brief, focal, time-limited therapy, your therapist won't be able to specify exactly how long therapy will take. The Therapy Guide makes general recommendations for different problems, but these are averages only, because duration depends on so many factors apart from the specific issue you are addressing.

What you hope to accomplish best suggests how long therapy is likely to take. Your therapist should be able to give you a general idea based on his or her past experience with similar issues. Just expect therapists to be less definitive about this aspect of therapy than others, because it depends on how open you are to the process, how hard you work, your confidence in your therapist, and your belief in the effectiveness of therapy. The therapist's compatibility and competence will also play a major role. Some of this may not be clear at the outset.

Some psychotherapies are explicitly time limited. This is the case in so-called "brief," "focal," "short-term," or "time-limited" psychotherapy, where a fixed number of meetings is part of the format, and this is spelled out in the initial agreement. Therapy is implicitly time limited in health plans or managed health care systems where the psychotherapy benefit covers a fixed number of visits per year. Even in longer-term or open-ended therapy, however, it is a good practice to build in an agreement to periodically review the therapy at set intervals and possibly renegotiate the terms of your agreement.

Other Therapy Options and Their Usual Duration

A handful of alternative options have standard durations or ways of thinking about how long therapy should last. The shortest is *crisis intervention,* a brief, intense therapy usually lasting a few weeks or a month at most. But during that period sessions may be almost daily, particularly at first. This approach is most common after trauma or during a psychiatric emergency.

A far wider range of problems are treated in *brief therapy.* While some "brief" therapies last up to forty sessions, most last between eight and twenty once-a-week sessions. As many kinds of brief therapy exists as there are therapy approaches; their one common denominator is their shorter length. All approaches have their brief versions: you can get time-limited behavioral therapy, cognitive therapy, exploratory or psychodynamic therapy. This is becoming an increasingly common format, partly because third-party payers see it as more cost-effective, partly because it is effective in bringing about specific changes within a limited time.

One variation of brief therapy is *time-limited therapy.* Here therapy is not necessarily brief, but it is limited to a specific number of sessions with a predetermined date for ending.

CHAPTER FIFTEEN

◼

PROBLEMS IN EVERYDAY LIVING

Problems in everyday living are not mental disorders. They center around an issue that life presents, such as the building tension between spouses when a marriage falters, the difficulty of grieving for a loved one, or the specter of losing a job or failing in school. Unlike psychiatric disorders, they have no specific symptoms, no checklist of signs, but cause day-to-day distress.

These problems are identified by *the issue* they revolve around, not by their psychological impact on you. One partner in a failing marriage, for instance, may find herself overwhelmed by rage and hurt, while the other is overcome with sadness and anxiety. What the couple needs to focus on in therapy, though, is the core issue: their relationship.

Finding the right kind of therapy is less important than in treating such disorders as depression or phobias since most approaches are equally effective in handling problems in living. What matters more is the format and finding the right therapist. To maximize the likelihood that therapy will work for you if you seek help for a problem in living, review the steps outlined in Chapter 3, "Finding a Therapist."

MARITAL PROBLEMS

Spouses have marital difficulties as varied as the reasons for getting married in the first place. The desire for companionship, for emotional closeness, for sex and physical intimacy, for financial security, for children—all these can become sources of marital distress, just as they can draw a couple together.

Sex, emotional closeness, or money, for instance, can each raise issues of who has what say, whose needs get met, who feels burdened or cheated, whose resentment grows to anger or rage. The hurt silences, or the tears and raised voices of marital arguments, are likely to revolve around these issues or similar ones: how to raise the children, how to balance the demands of work and family, getting along with relatives.

Problems are more likely to flare during transitions: the first year of marriage, the birth of a child, an undesired pregnancy or abortion, or when a child enters school or leaves home. Even the most robust, harmonious marriage, and the most well-balanced spouses, can and do experience times of tension.

How do marital problems begin? How did ours begin? These are questions you are sure to ask—but probably should not. Because asking *how* it all began is sure to lead to a cycle of blaming.

Who started it is beside the point. The truth is that marital problems are a difficulty *in the relationship,* not in either or both of the partners. The problem is in the way you relate to each other and manage your relationship together.

If it is truly a marital problem, you are both, in different ways, contributing to it. And so you need to work it out together. What needs therapy is what goes on *between* husband and wife, not just what is happening to one or the other of you.

The signs of trouble are often not the obvious fights, threats, accusations, and weeping that typify a stormy union. Often they are more subtle: not being able to talk about an issue, each partner blaming the other for a litany of ills; an emotional abyss that is hidden in a false cordiality, a deadening routine, or a retreat into role-playing. Any of these can eat away at the core of caring and trust that nurtures a healthy marriage.

It may be hard for one or both of you to admit to a serious problem in your marriage. It's upsetting to think you may have "failed" as a wife or husband, and frightening to think of things not working out.

But having trouble in your marriage is not a sign that the two of you have "failed." Rather it's a signal that you could use help for a time to work on your marriage. Even if things seem to have gone too far, if you seem to have genuinely irreconcilable differences, counseling can help you begin talking to see if some hope for the marriage remains.

Sometimes there is no obvious crisis, but things have gone stale: you feel bored, have lost interest in your partner emotionally or sexually, or both. Or you may want to explore together how to make your marriage more alive, a source of greater challenge and growth. Marital therapy can help with that, too.

Often one partner is outspoken about what is wrong, while the other denies much is wrong except that the other "complains too much" or is "overly sensitive." Usually one partner is extremely reluctant to enter therapy, while the other is more willing.

Most approaches seem to work equally well for most marital problems. What matters more is that you *focus in therapy on the relationship.* The earlier in the progression of a problem a couple seeks help, the better are the chances that it can be worked out. For that reason the rule of thumb is: *If one partner feels there is something seriously wrong in a marriage, there usually is.*

But before you consider therapy make a good-faith effort to work out your problems together first if you haven't, perhaps with some advice from friends or family. The final responsibility for your marriage is yours; if you can work through problems together on your own, this will only strengthen it.

Remember, even if you are having problems, therapy may not always be necessary. It takes attention, caring, and effort to make even the best marriage work. Only after you've tried to handle things on your own without success should you turn to a marital therapist.

Signs to Look For

There is no one symptom that indicates a marriage is in trouble. A given person's reaction to marital distress can range from anger, sadness, or anxiety to emotional numbness—or some combination of all of these and more.

> ☐ Ed was an accountant, Sandra a schoolteacher. Ed's firm had many large corporations as key clients and he was often out of town.
>
> When Ed was in town, he would want to have sex almost every night; Sandra would be in the mood at most about once a week. To Ed, Sandra was "frigid" and "withholding"; to Sandra, Ed was "insensitive" and "sex crazy."
>
> Sandra said she couldn't have sex unless she felt close to Ed, and that his constant traveling made that almost impossible. She was bitter about the emotional distance between them. How could he expect her to pop right into bed when they never even talked? But Ed said he felt sex was a way of reconnecting with her. Ed felt he needed this contact after working so hard and resented Sandra for withholding herself from him.

> ☐ Steve made a good salary as an insurance salesman. But he liked his wife, Sandy, to handle their finances and pay the bills. Sandy was conscientious and did a good job of managing their money. Her main problem was Steve: with no knowledge of their finances, he spent as though they had unlimited funds and ignored her warnings that their finances were getting out of control.

Every month when the bills would come in, Sandy and Steve would have the same argument: she would accuse him of reckless spending, and he would complain that he "made plenty of money" and criticize her for being inept at managing their finances. Time after time he promised to sit down with her and work out a budget for his spending. But somehow he never managed to get around to it.

What Therapists Recommend

Approach. The great majority of therapists recommed a family/marital systems approach, which focuses on the dynamics between the couple. Almost as many recommended combining this with a psychodynamic or a cognitive approach, focusing on distorted patterns of thought. Most also stressed the need to provide ongoing support to the spouses.

Medication. Does not apply here.

Setting. The therapist's office.

Format. Therapists are virtually unanimous in recommending couples therapy for marital problems, since the main trouble is in the relationship, not in one partner or the other. Over half recommend individual therapy in conjunction with couples therapy. This may reflect the bias of therapists who specialize in individual therapy; couples and marriage therapists see this as unnecessary and likely to dilute the work between the couple, which all agree should be primary.

Frequency. Once a week is standard. Extra sessions may be needed during an especially turbulent time or when a major decision is pending.

Duration. Marital therapy is most often short-term, one to six months, or less often, up to a year. If a couple works well together and finds therapy particularly helpful, it can be left open-ended.

What You Should Know About Therapy

Finding a marital therapist. Marital therapy is a speciality practiced by a wide range of professionals, with an even wider range of orientations and approaches. Many therapists have master's-level training in marriage, family, and child counseling, while others are psychologists, social workers, or psychiatrists. As with all problems in living, your therapist's experience with the problem is more important than their discipline or theoretical orientation. One way to find a marital therapist is through the American Association of Marriage and Family Therapy (see Appendix IV).

The initial understanding. Couples commonly agree with a marital therapist to focus on specific issues, and to try therapy for a specific number of sessions. Six sessions should be enough to give you a sense of whether the therapy is helping; any fewer may not give it a fair chance. After six sessions you and your therapist should review the therapy to date and decide if you want to continue.

Getting started: what if one partner doesn't want to go? There is usually one partner—typically the wife—who is the emotional barometer of a marriage. That partner spots problems sooner and is more sensitive to the emotional ups and downs of the relationship. When that partner senses something is amiss, then it is generally time to get help.

But what if the other doesn't want to go?

This is almost always the situation in marital therapy, at least at first. But after trying it, the reluctant partner is often surprised to find therapy less burdensome and more helpful than he or she expected. Not infrequently the partner who was initially reluctant becomes the more enthusiastic of the two.

Still, the fact is you can't—or shouldn't—force your partner into therapy. If you do, you won't get what you want out of it. For therapy to work, both of you need to find a reason to be there, even if one of you is there to end the relationship and the other to save it. At least you're in the same room, talking with a therapist about it.

Instead of asking for a commitment to participate in marital therapy, you're probably better off asking a reluctant partner just to consider a consultation. This offers the two of you a chance you may not have had to talk in a safe setting about how each of you sees things and what your options may be. It also allows each of you to meet a potential therapist and get a sense of how you would feel continuing in therapy with him or her.

Individual therapy vs. couples therapy. The rule of thumb is that marital problems are best solved *when both partners are in therapy together,* not with one or both partners in individual therapy. If you are in individual therapy and find yourself spending most of your session talking about difficulties with your partner, this may be a sign that you might do better with couples therapy.

If your partner refuses to go into therapy with you, you might consider starting or continuing individual therapy for yourself in the meantime. It can help you through tough periods, offering you emotional support and the chance to clarify your needs and desires. If you take this approach, be sure to let your therapist know what you are doing: that your long-range goal is marital therapy, if and when your partner is willing.

An alternative is to suggest that each of you try individual therapy, with the eventual hope that you will go into therapy together.

If you are already in individual therapy, you can continue it while doing couples therapy. Indeed, many therapists recommend that marital therapy go hand in hand with individual therapy for each partner, though expense often prohibits this. Concurrent individual therapy is a good idea only if many of the problems in the marriage are due to psychological problems in one or both partners. These problems may be better handled in individual therapy, but the ways in which they interfere in your marriage are still best dealt with in marital therapy.

If finances force a choice between individual and marital therapy, talk over which to choose with both your therapist and your partner. The rule of thumb is that if the problems are mainly in you—deep-seated anxieties, say, that make you clinging and dependent—then you would probably do better in individual therapy. But if the trouble is mainly in the relationship—constant tension about feelings of emotional distance; resentments about too little or too much sex—then the choice is marital therapy.

If you start marital therapy after having been in individual therapy, it is generally better that you see a new therapist. If you both see your old therapist, your partner is likely to perceive the therapist as "yours," biased toward your point of view.

Family therapy. For some marital problems, family therapy may be the best cure. This is the case when the problems between husband and wife focus on other members of the family, such as troubled interactions with a child. Another is when a husband or wife is so closely enmeshed with a parent, or a parent is so intensely involved with your marriage, that it is having an ill effect. Addressing "the family problem" may force you to face your marital conflict. Or once it becomes clear that it is a marital, not a family, problem, the rest of the family can be excused and you and your spouse can continue in marital therapy.

If the problem is sex. Most often this involves conflicts *over* sex or disagreements about it. But if the problem is a specific sexual dysfunction, then you may need sex therapy, not marital therapy. Sex therapy is a speciality for treating such sexual dysfunctions as failure to achieve orgasm, premature ejaculation, and impotence (see p. 519 for descriptions of these and others). However, if sex is leading to marital conflict, and neither of you have a sexual problem per se, then marital therapy is the appropriate choice.

Dealing with your own reluctance. Even if you are the one who initiated the move into couples therapy, expect to feel some hesitation. It can feel like "exposing" your shortcomings in your marriage to someone else—and in front of your partner! That may seem like an open invitation for more fights or outright humiliation. You may think, "Why stir things up? Aren't they bad enough already?"

If your partner is the more emotionally expressive and more adept at reading the nuances of relationships, you may also feel a bit intimidated. Your partner, you may fear, will win over the therapist to his or her side, leaving you at a disadvantage, or with both of them ganging up on you. Or you may be afraid that your partner will gain the therapist's sympathy, making you look like the villian.

A good marital therapist will be sensitive to these feelings and put you at ease about them. If the therapist is not sensitive to them—either discounting them or not helping you handle them when you bring them up—then this is the wrong therapist for you. You must feel he or she is even-handed, "siding" with neither you nor your partner, and able to understand you both.

When one partner has had enough. Even if you have already decided you want a separation or divorce—or if your spouse has—marital therapy can still be useful as long as this is clear from the outset. For one, it allows a reconsideration of the decision with the help of someone who is impartial. You, or your spouse, can think it through to be sure it is really the best thing, and that all the consequences—such as the impact on the children—have been adequately considered.

Some couples can actually use marital therapy to facilitate a less destructive and painful divorce, though this is possible only in couples who still have some reservoir of affection and degree of a working relationship. At the very minimum, a couple will need the ability to talk together without its escalating into a fight.

If this is just not possible, then you might consider seeing a therapist on your own, to help you manage the emotional tumult of separation.

PARENT–CHILD CONFLICT

Conflicts between parents and children are inevitable, whether it's with a balky, fretful two-year-old or a defiant twelve-year-old. Most are handled in the normal course of family life. But when problems get out of hand, and the family reaches a stalemate, then some special attention from a therapist may help.

It is too easy to see it as your child's problem and to think that your child needs therapy. More often than not, the trouble is the relationship *between* you and your child. Needing to see a therapist for help with this relationship does not mean that either of you is "crazy" or has some mental disorder.

Some troubles are predictable. Every family has a life cycle, much like an individual. Crises and troubles are more predictable at points of change and growth, when new opportunities also create new demands, adjustments, and vulnerabilities: the birth of a child; a child's entering school or leaving home; adolescence.

Other events that can turn up the pressure between children and parents include: the family's moving; separation, divorce, or remarriage; someone's losing or changing a job; a death in the family. Any pressures that raise the overall tension level at home can try even the healthiest of families.

Of course, sometimes it is the child's behavior that creates the tension: getting bad grades, being rebellious or rude, hanging out with undesirable friends, refusing to do chores, and the like. But even so, your relationship may hold the key to the misbehavior.

Stepparents are especially vulnerable to these difficulties. Sometimes the children will resent the stepparent, blaming him or her for their parents' divorce, or the children will feel disloyal to the divorced parent if they become too close to the stepparent. Or perhaps the stepparent has a different parenting style—often stricter—and the children resent it.

Turbulence between parent and child is not isolated; it affects everyone in the family. Other children, for instance, can resent the "problem" child for getting so much attention.

The problem may be more subtle than a constant struggle between parent and child. One parent may be intensely jealous of the other's close relationship with a child, or one parent may be overly involved with a child, neglecting his or her spouse. A family can have severe distortions in how members see each other, so that each is always blaming and attacking the others. Family roles can be blurred so that a child "runs" the house rather than the parents. Or relationships may be continually stormy, with shifting alliances so that one moment two members are close, and the next they are enemies.

Raising a child takes a great deal of caring and sustained effort. Just because a problem seems particularly difficult does not automatically mean you need therapy. But it may be called for, however, if tensions between you and your child are constant, no matter what you try to ease them. Your teenage son, for instance, gets furious with you whenever you question his choice of friends, or your daughter storms into her room every time you object to her dating habits.

If such problems fester, they can destroy your ability to talk together without either skirting the most crucial topics or ending in a shouting match. Sometimes the result is a child or parent who refuses to speak to the other, a child's leaving home, or a parent's ordering a child out of the house.

If a parent-child conflict seems to widen and worsen as weeks and months go on, then it is becoming serious enough that a therapist's help is appropriate. By that time the initial spark of trouble will probably have spread so that everyone is on edge and practically everything that happens fans the flame. By then everyone involved is likely to have a different view of what the trouble is and who is to blame.

If you and your child seem headed for such an impasse, you might benefit from consulting a therapist together. But before you do, try to work out the problems on your own, perhaps with the help of friends or relatives, or a minister, priest, or rabbi. If you manage to solve the impasse on your own, your relationship with your child will be the stronger for it.

And remember, every family has its troubles from time to time. It does not mean you are a failure as a parent if you need some help from a therapist. A healthy family is not one that never has troubles, but one where family members learn to manage their ups and downs and know when to get help.

Signs to Look For

No specific set of signs signifies that a severe parent-child conflict is at hand. Such conflicts can take many different forms, from an icy coldness between parent and child to constant battles. The hallmark is simply that the troubles originate in the relationship between the two individuals and are not due to some larger disturbance in either one of them.

☐ Joey was never in trouble at home until his mother got divorced and remarried. From the time Joey's stepfather began to live with them, the two were at odds. Larry, the stepfather, thought his wife was too lenient with eleven-year-old Joey, "spoiling" him. Joey thought Larry was a "dictator." They argued almost daily: about mowing the lawn and other chores, about cleaning Joey's room, about Joey's being too noisy or listening to music that was too loud. Finally Joey announced that he was moving out, to live with his father in a distant city.

☐ Cindy and her mother had always been close. But that changed almost overnight when Cindy turned fourteen. Cindy was physically mature for her age—she could pass for twenty-one—and enjoyed the attention of older boys. Her new boyfriend, Eddie, was twenty-four and out of work. Rumor was that he dealt drugs. Whenever Cindy's mother tried to talk to Cindy to convince her not to see Eddie, Cindy would run to her room in angry tears and slam the door. When her mother grounded Cindy, she snuck out of school to meet Eddie. Her mother felt Cindy was out of control; Cindy said that her mother "just didn't understand."

What Therapists Recommend

Approach. Family systems is the strongest choice since it focuses on the patterns of relationship within the family. Psychodynamic therapy is another strong choice, especially for individual therapy that is in tandem with family therapy.

Medication. Not appropriate, unless it is needed for some other disorder the parent or child may have.

Setting. Office visits.

Format. Family therapy is the format of choice. But most therapists also recommend individual therapy for the child in addition, especially when the child is troubled apart from the parental conflict.

Frequency. Once a week. But in a period of crisis you may want to schedule more sessions.

Duration. No strong consensus. Some therapists see no need for more than six months of therapy, but about as many say to leave it open-ended.

What You Should Know About Therapy

The term *family therapy* does not imply any particular theoretical orientation: family therapists can have any of a large range of approaches (see p. 64). The one unifying characteristic of family therapists, though, is that they will see the family together (or in different combinations) rather than just treating a single member.

Getting started. If you are seeking professional help for an intractable conflict between parent and child, begin with an evaluation. If your child seems troubled in other spheres of his or her life as well—at school, with friends—consider getting a psychological evaluation for him or her, too. It may be that the tensions between you are signs of some wider psychological problem your child is having.

If you have decided to try family therapy, the prospective therapist will want to see everyone in the family together at a single meeting to see how you all interact and to get an idea of whether family therapy is feasible. Sometimes in addition to meeting with everyone together, the therapist will also meet individually with each family member, or with the children and the parents separately, to get a better picture of exactly what is going on.

How long therapy should last: brief therapy. Many family therapists negotiate a fixed number of sessions at the outset, with an option to decide at the end if therapy should continue. Often the number of sessions agreed on is six or so. That gives you enough time to see if therapy is making a difference—or even to clear up your problems.

While there is not strong consensus, brief therapy is the most highly recommended duration. *Brief* usually means up to twenty sessions, which takes less than six months. Most of the results of family therapy are accomplished by then, research suggests. Brief family therapy is particularly appropriate when there is a specific conflict to focus on.

One advantage of "time-limited" family therapy—for instance, saying you will come for just six sessions—is that the deadline can often catalyze a change. Everyone knows this is his or her chance to fix things and works harder at it.

Long-term family therapy—more than twenty sessions—is also recommended in certain circumstances. One is when your family is having several complex problems at once, none of which is easily pinpointed.

Individual therapy. Most therapists surveyed recommend individual therapy for the child, typically in addition to family therapy. The more the child is in distress apart from the parent-child conflict, the more he or she would benefit from individual treatment.

Individual therapy itself may be the better choice if the parent or child involved is so extremely disturbed he or she is unable to participate in family sessions. Paranoid delusions, extreme agitation or mania, intense hostility, or psychosis may make participation impossible.

If the parents are having a tough time in their relationship and are unable to work together to help the child, then therapy for the child alone is better. That is also the case if the child is adamant in refusing to join in family therapy.

Hospitalization. In extreme situations, a child may need to be hospitalized for a brief time if he or she is reckless, violent, or self-destructive. This can happen if the child is becoming psychotic, severely depressed or manic, is "acting out" and out of control, or is abusing drugs. If the family can no longer manage the child at home, hospitalization or a residential treatment center is an option. But even if your child is being treated in such a facility, family therapy is often part of the treatment program; the goal is to return your child to life at home.

However, some psychiatric hospitals specializing in treating adolescents have come under sharp criticism for "marketing" themselves too vigorously, getting parents to hospitalize their children unnecessarily. The hospitals benefit because insurers will cover their costs. Adolescent admissions to psychiatric hospitals has been one of the fastest growth areas in therapy.

If you are in doubt that your family can manage your child at home while treatment goes on, get an evaluation from a therapist who is not connected with a particular hospital.

When family therapy won't work. In some instances family therapy is impractical. One is when someone in the family has a "valid secret," someting that he or she insists on keeping from other family members (usually younger children): your daughter has a secret pregnancy and is getting an abortion; you and your spouse are struggling over the fact that you are having an affair.

Another is when the family is already so fractured that it is virtually impossible even to get them together to try to heal the rifts. Or it may be that one family member—usually the child you are having problems with—has already become so estranged that he or she will not come to therapy sessions, views therapy as too stigmatizing to participate, or is just not motivated enough.

FAMILY PROBLEMS

The problems that can trouble a family are as varied as those that can affect an individual. The family is a system, an organism of sorts, and like any other organism is susceptible to a wide range of afflictions in its internal relationships. One person in a family may seem to be the "identified" problem—the one who is most obviously troubled—but everyone else in the family may still be upset or just as affected, but in less obvious ways.

For instance, a teenage daughter who becomes pregnant out of wedlock creates a troubling reality everyone else in the family will have to adjust to, whether she decides to have the baby or an abortion. Her father may be enraged, her mother depressed; her sister may feel the need to protect her from her father, while her younger brother may be more upset by the mother's depression.

Families handle most of their inevitable problems on their own, but outside assistance may be needed if the problem is so distressing that it affects not only the tenor of family life (constant arguments, high tension), but spills over outside the family: the children are having trouble concentrating at school or are getting into fights, or the parents are so preoccupied that their work or marriage is suffering. If a serious family problem persists for more than a few months without any resolution, then you should consider seeing a therapist.

Signs to Look For

The hallmark of family problems is that they affect each person in the family and distort the communication and relationships between family members. Some of the more obvious and serious of these include:

- incest or physical abuse
- a death in the family or of a close family friend
- moving to a new house, neighborhood, or city
- problems with conception: unwanted pregnancies, a miscarriage, or abortion
- divorce and remarriage
- loss of a job by the main money earner or other threats to financial stability
- life-threatening or chronic illness or serious injury to a family member
- bankruptcy or foreclosure of your home mortgage
- trouble with the law by a family member

Other issues that crop up in families reflect *relationships between family members:* the way the family works—or doesn't—to nurture and protect its members. If one child seems to be favored over others, for instance, that can be a chronic source of family tension. Another is the inability of some members of the family to communicate with each other. The *behavior* of one of its members can become a problem for the whole family. A parent may begin drinking or become abusive. A child may suddenly do poorly at school, get into trouble with the law, get involved with drugs, or become promiscuous.

Sometimes the problems are between generations. Grandparents and in-laws can be sources of tension if, for instance, some members of the family perceive them as too intrusive or controlling. Sometimes the tension will be because the mother and *her* mother are at loggerheads, or the father and his in-laws can't get along. Or some family members, such as a grandparent or parent and a child, may "gang up" against another member, the mother or father, for instance. Or a son or daughter may not be fulfilling their parents' expectations of them or their parents' own unfulfilled ambitions.

What Therapists Recommend

Approach. Family problems are normally addressed by a family systems approach, which addresses the family as a whole (see Chapter 2, p. 64).

Medication. Not relevant.

Setting. The therapist's office.

Format. The therapist should meet with and evaluate the entire family at the start, or with as many members as are available and willing. The therapist can then decide with you whether to continue with family therapy; whether to meet with the parents separately, for couples or marital therapy; or whether to meet with parents, children, and the whole family at different times.

Frequency. Family therapy sessions often vary. They may be once a week or once every other week to start. The frequency can then be adjusted, depending on members' schedules and how much homework is assigned between sessions. Once a month is not uncommon. In general, family meetings are held less frequently than individual therapy sessions.

Duration. How long therapy may last also varies considerably, depending on the family, the issue, and the particular type of family therapy the therapist is doing (see Chapter 2, p. 64). Many family therapists prefer short, time-limited interventions lasting under a few months and often as short as six weeks. Many others suggest leaving the duration open-ended.

What You Should Know About Therapy

If you are considering family therapy, you should ask for a family evaluation first. Usually this requires one or two interviews with a family therapist with everyone in the family in attendance. The purpose is to assess how family members interact and to gather specific information needed to decide if family therapy is appropriate. Usually the entire family will be seen together. Sometimes the therapist will see the parents together and then the children together, or individual members separately.

In some instances family therapy may not be appropriate. Not all issues are best discussed in front of the family: an unwanted pregnancy, an extramarital affair. Sometimes family therapy is not in the best interests of one member, such as a young woman who has just managed to become independent and move out on her own. Dragging her back for therapy with the family might compromise her hard-won independence.

Crisis intervention. This form of family therapy is devoted exclusively to helping the family handle a crisis. It usually lasts a month or less, or until the immediate crisis passes. Meetings can take place daily, weekly, or as needed.

Crisis invervention is called for when an emergency situation is threatening the safety or stability of the family, or is threatneing to destroy relationships between its members: the suicide or attempted suicide of a member; the revelation of a devastating secret, such as incest; physical threats or violence by one member against another. It can also focus on mobilizing family resources to help prevent the collapse of a single member, or to help the family find its way back together in the wake of a tragedy, or to hold together following parental abandonment, death, or divorce.

Brief family therapy. Brief family therapy can take as few as six sessions or as many as twenty. It rarely takes more than six months and almost always focuses on a specific family problem. Brief therapy is best suited to a specific problem in a family. Its chances of success are greatest when family members are highly motivated to change and cooperate. Some family therapists set a specific limit at the outset on the number of sessions. This often catalyzes family members to become involved and to change while they have the chance. At the end of the "contract" period, you and your therapist can reevaluate to see if more sessions are needed.

Long-term family therapy. If you and your therapist decide to leave therapy open-ended, it can become long-term—generally six months or longer. Long-term therapy is more appropriate when your goals are not narrowly focused, but are more ambitious. This is true, for instance, if multiple problems in the family are so complex they don't lend themselves to a single focus.

You may also want to consider long-term therapy if you have already tried a short-term approach but the problems persist.

RELATIONSHIP PROBLEMS

Even the healthiest relationship is susceptible to periods of tension and estrangement. Quite apart from the special cases of marriage and family, any of the other significant relationships in your life can cause you enough strain that you may want to consider getting help.

Normal problems in getting along, working things out together, understanding each other, trying to mesh your different interests and ways of doing things, adjusting perhaps to each of you being at different stages in your life—these issues crop up in all kinds of relationships: between romantic partners, among coworkers, with neighbors, friends, or within a close-knit social group. More often than not, the tension passes and the relationship goes back to normal. But when it doesn't, you can feel more and more upset and discouraged about the relationship.

Another range of problems may have to do with your own style or pattern of relating to people. If you are by nature shy, you may feel chronically lonely, wanting an intimate relationship or wanting to feel closer to others but not knowing how to go about it. Or you may have trouble getting along with people—at work, with neighbors, or among friends—continually feeling at odds with others or that people are "ganging up" on you. Or your romantic relationships may always end up disastrously, with you feeling disappointed, taken advantage of, and intensely resentful. Or perhaps you have a history of run-ins with people in authority.

Signs to Look For

There is no specific checklist of symptoms that signal relationship problems. The kinds of problems and your reactions to any one of them can vary enormously.

What Therapists Recommend

Approach. If you are looking for help with a particular relationship, a systems approach, which looks at the patterns of interaction between you, is the preferred approach.

Psychodynamic, behavioral, and cognitive approaches are also used, usually in individual therapy if couples therapy isn't possible, or if the problems ultimately prove to be personal.

Medication. Not relevant.

Setting. Normally in the therapist's office.

Format. Couples therapy is the preferred format for working on problems in a current relationship. This assumes that both of you are available and willing. See Chapter 14, p. 323, for a more detailed discussion of couples therapy. Individual and group therapy can also be appropriate alternatives if couples therapy isn't possible, or if the problems are due to habitual relationship patterns or personal conflicts.

Frequency. Once-a-week sessions are standard.

Duration. If there is a specific issue, therapy can be short-term: six sessions or less on average. Otherwise expect therapy to last longer.

What You Should Know About Therapy

The best approach to therapy depends on whether the problem is primarily in the relationship or is your own personal problem. If you have a long history of a specific kind of relationship difficulty, such as unhappy romances, an exploratory approach in individual therapy is better suited to investigating the underlying personality traits and conflicts that may be causing your troubles. A psychodynamic therapy that focuses on the evolving relationship with the therapist will provide you a "laboratory" where you can see your relationship problems in microcosm and address them.

If your problem is shyness or a particular pattern of behavior, behavioral approaches have proven highly successful. Cognitive therapy has been effective in changing distorted patterns of thinking that may be affecting your relationships—for instance, the assumption that "I don't deserve any better anyway."

Consider also group therapy. The advantage of a group is that you can explore and learn ways of relating to people in a no-risk situation and get candid feedback on how you are doing. A group often seems like the last thing you would want if you're having problems with relationships, but while it may be hard at first, it will give you a chance to work directly with others on practical issues that individual therapy may not get to. Ask about the option of a group in your first consultation with a therapist.

Do you really need therapy? Just because you are having problems in your relationships, or with a particular person, doesn't automatically mean you need therapy. Such problems are part of life. Your first effort should always be to confront the difficulties head-on and try to work them out with the person or people involved.

Even if you don't—or can't—do this, remember that such problems often resolve themselves with time, maturity, or a change in circumstances unless they are linked to underlying character traits. If you can manage them on your own, or with the support of family or friends, this reinforces your sense of competency in relationships. Turning to therapy—particularly individual therapy—too quickly can be a way of avoiding having to face the problem or person directly.

Consider therapy only (1) if the problem continues over a fairly long period; (2) you can't make any headway with it on your own; and (3) you feel enough distress that it interferes with your daily life or goals.

PROBLEMS RELATED TO WORK OR SCHOOL

Problems Related to Work

With people and families working harder and longer to keep up financially, work has increasingly become a source of emotional stress. You may find yourself in a high-stress job or feel dissatisfied with some aspect of your work: demands being made of you that are unreasonable or conflicting, being held to poorly defined responsibilities, having too much—or too little—to do.

Many work-related problems reflect inner emotional conflicts. A fear of success, for instance, which shows up in a range of self-defeating acts, from getting crucial work done late to being unprepared for important work responsibilities—even though you are perfectly capable. Or the feeling that your success is somehow fraudulent, that you are an "impostor" and will eventually be found out.

Another work-related problem is doubt about career choices: what job to seek, what kind of training to get, whether to switch jobs or career.

A different kind of problem is conflict between work and family. You may feel dissatisfied, for instance, if you are a mother at home but want to be pursuing a career. On the other hand, many parents who have to work feel conflicted because they would rather be at home raising their children or feel they "should" be.

Transitions at work are often difficult. Changing jobs, being promoted or demoted, facing layoffs, getting a new boss, seeing other people advance ahead of you, having to leave an old department, friends, and a familiar routine, approaching retirement—all these transitions put great emotional pressure on you. And being fired is undoubtedly one of the most stressful, demoralizing experiences in work life.

Another source of some of the most trying work-related stress is the sale of your company, a merger, or a corporate takeover. If you work for a company that has been bought by another, you are bound to feel anxiety as your company is reorganized. You may feel anxious about job security or about fitting into the new structure. Even years later, you may feel an "outsider" or "orphan" because your company was the acquired one and the people at the top are now mainly from the other firm.

Signs to Look For

Most work problems are best worked out by negotiating a change at work. But therapy can help you with some work-related problems, including:

- a sense of being blocked, unable to perform the essential tasks of your job
- a feeling of stagnation or dissatisfaction with what you are doing
- a history of friction at work with your peers or employers
- intense or constant envy of others at work
- a string of self-inflicted failures in your work life
- the constant fear of failure
- excessive anxiety about your job performance, your job security, or new responsibilities
- strong self-doubt about having skills needed to do your job and fear of being exposed as an "impostor"
- procrastination to the point that your performance suffers
- perfectionism; not being able to finish a task until you feel it is absolutely perfect, and so working much harder or longer on it than is necessary
- workaholism; working so long that it crowds out the rest of your life

□ Ed loved his work. A jeweler, he crafted gold and silver into exquisite pieces. He had built his craft into a successful business, with his own shop as well as several in other cities that carried his work. Ed thought nothing of working ten or twelve hours a day, including Saturdays and most of Sunday.

But his wife, Rita, came to hate her husband's work. She was pleased that he was doing so well and that he enjoyed it. But she felt it consumed him to the point that he never had time for her or their two young children. She'd see him off in the morning and not see him again until she was in bed at night. She finally told him that unless he cut back on his schedule to make room for her and their family, she would consider a divorce.

□ Sam worked at a large corporate law firm, where he was considered one of the most promising among the forty or so lawyers aspiring to become partners. In law school, he had been editor of the law review and had been chosen to clerk for a state supreme court judge. He had been with the firm for fourteen years, and broad hints were made that if he stayed with the firm and kept it up, he'd be made a partner in a few years.

Despite his great success, Sam was terrified that he was a "fraud," that he did not really know what he was doing, and that one day he would make a terrible mistake that would expose him. No matter how much praise he got for work well done, he always discounted it as undeserved.

Problems Related to School

Problems at college, graduate, or professional school are likely to resemble those that can develop in the workplace: perfectionism; procrastination or failing to get work done; fear of failure; boredom; trouble getting along with classmates or teachers. Some are unique to the educational setting: undue anxiety about exams or other evaluations, writing papers, or speaking up in class. Other problems are due to a more general difficulty in defining goals or finding a direction. This can be reflected in chronic vacillation about what to major in, frequent changes in your course of study, what to do about further training, or, after graduation, feeling paralyzed with anxiety about what to do next in the "real" world.

The most common signs of trouble are failing grades and underachievement in general—simply not performing up to your ability. Doing poorly can then set in motion a chain reaction of feelings: anger, self-blame, a sinking sense of futility and helplessness, and finally just feeling overwhelmed.

Performance at this level of education is notoriously susceptible to outside pressures. Poor performance may have to do more with family troubles at home, the breakup of a relationship, worry over student loans and accumulating debt or the financial resources to continue, the need to work full-time while going to school. This may be the first time you have left home, or moved beyond the orbit of your family, and had to adjust to new people and settings and make new friends. Or you may be returning to school after working or raising a family, and finding it difficult to juggle school demands with the ongoing responsibilities you have now.

If the academic or school-related problem has been persistent, it may be a sign of some underlying emotional difficulty or ongoing problem outside school. These kinds of problems are often reflected in persistent boredom with school. If you suddenly begin having academic difficulties, it is more likely to be situational: a reaction to some current stressful event or situation.

Signs to Look For

The hallmark of school problems is that you have difficulty functioning in school up to your natural abilities. Some typical forms this can take include:

- performance anxiety or fear of failure
- indecision about what course to pursue
- self-blame for your performance
- perfectionism, so that work is done over and over before being turned in
- procrastination, putting off work until it is too late
- boredom with or apathy about schoolwork

What Therapists Recommend

Approach. Psychodynamic therapy is the most highly recommended approach. This helps you identify underlying anxieties and conflicts that may be interfering with your work or academic performance, or your adjustment to school or work in general. Sometimes a little additional support from a therapist is enough to get you through a temporary block or crisis. Cognitive therapy can also be effective in identifying and changing self-defeating, distorted ways of thinking about the demands of school or work and the demands you place on yourself.

Medication. Normally irrelevant to these kinds of problems, unless work- or school-related anxiety or depression becomes disabling.

Setting. Office visits.

Format. Most therapists recommend individual therapy, though many also recommend either a therapy or support group as well. Most school counseling centers and employment assistance programs (EAPs) in the workplace now offer both.

Frequency. Once a week is standard. During a crisis, however, such as a layoff at work and panic at losing your job, or temporary inability to perform at school, you may need to meet more frequently.

Duration. Most therapists estimate one to six months is sufficient if the focus is kept to the work- or school-related problem itself.

What You Should Know About Therapy

Some problems at work or school turn out to be related to underlying issues that reach beyond the immediate work or school problem: a distorted way of thinking about your ability to perform, for instance; or conflict with authority. You must be clear about your goal: do you want help primarily with the immediate work or school problem? If this does turn out to be related to broader issues, do you still want to keep the focus on the specific problem at hand? Most of the time that is possible. A focused therapy can be helpful without opening up broader issues. Or do you want to explore those broader issues? This will undoubtedly lead to a longer and more complex therapy. If you do consult a therapist, this is important to discuss at the outset and agree on.

Even if the problem is due to circumstances at work or school that therapy can't directly change, therapy can help in several other ways. It can give you support when you need it most. It can help you clarify the issue so you can make a better decision on how to proceed. And it can help you handle your emotional reactions to the situation. Therapy can also help you maintain a belief in your ability to do something about the situation—if not now, then eventually.

Alternatives to Therapy for Problems Related to Work

Not all complaints about work are best handled by therapy, however. Sometimes direct action is called for: asking for a meeting to talk the issue over; clarifying what is expected of you; negotiating changes in your job description, work situation, or contract. Therapy can actually be a substitute for taking the practical steps that might resolve the issue—a way of avoiding actually *doing* something. The most effective step may be to take the issue to your boss, union representative, or shop steward, or to use your company's grievance procedure or employee assistance program. If your grievance is widely shared by other employees, you may even have grounds for a collective action within the company.

If the problem is simply stress on a job you enjoy, then a stress-management course, or a behavioral program that teaches methods of stress reduction, might be more appropriate. Such a program would include techniques like relaxation skills, an exercise program, and time management.

If your problem is doubt about what career to pursue, or whether to change careers, a career counselor is probably more appropriate than a therapist. A career counselor will explore your interests, test you on aptitudes and abilities, and suggest what career choices might suit you best and how to pursue them.

Alternatives to Therapy for Problems Related to School

Like work problems, some problems with school are best handled directly: asking for a meeting to talk the problem over; clarifying what is expected of you; discussing poor performance or clashes in teaching and learning styles with your teacher directly. Therapy can substitute for actually *doing* something about the problem. If you have already discussed it with your instructor, the most effective next step might be to take the issue to the next level—the school guidance department, the chairperson of the department, the academic dean or the dean of students—or to use the grievance procedures available to students in most schools today. If the issue is unfair treatment, gender or racial bias, sexual harassment, or other forms of ethical misconduct, use of the grievance procedures might be the most important first step, particularly if your grievance is shared by other students. Filing a complaint with the relevant regulatory agency or legal action if warranted may be more empowering than therapy in these instances, though not necessarily a substitute for it if the experience has been traumatizing.

DIFFICULT LIFE TRANSITIONS

Problems can arise from such obviously disruptive life transitions as the birth of a child or a move, or simply from the psychological issues that reaching a certain point in life stirs up. For instance, many men and women during middle age start to count the number of years remaining to them rather than how many years they have lived. This new perspective leads them to question the meaning and purpose of their lives.

A marriage, retirement, getting a job with greater responsibility, becoming a parent—all these are positive changes, but stressful ones nevertheless. The stress comes from the countless adjustments and new burdens each of these transitions brings, however welcome.

First-time parents, for instance, are often shocked at the massive upheaval in their routine that having an infant brings. Few new mothers are prepared for the day or two—or sometimes the week or two—of postpartum blues that so often occurs in the wake of a moment that is so long looked forward to. The sleep lost to a crying baby, the need to be constantly vigilant, the added concerns that caring for a baby bring, add up to a burden that can sometimes temporarily outweigh the joy.

Retirement is another transition that can bring unexpected stress. People who have been active, engaged, and essential may find that having open days is not as pleasant as they had anticipated. Instead these open days may symbolize being irrelevant or may be so unstimulating that they create the restless stress of boredom.

Moving to a new city—even one you have long wanted to live in—can also bring on unexpected malaise. Uprooting yourself from friends, family, and familiar routine can mean you feel a pervasive sense of loss. And because it typically takes a year or more to make friends who are close enough to replace the old ones left behind, the first several months in a new place may leave you feeling lonely.

Some life problems are due to no discernible change at all. A career that you spent years trying to build may have plateaued, so that you feel unchallenged and uninterested in what you're doing. A marriage that has lasted for decades may seem sterile and unexciting. You may yearn for some vague, unarticulated change, or for a renewed sense of commitment and meaning.

Stress and strain. Life changes are more likely to overwhelm you when they are unexpected, when many of them come all at once, and when the strains they cause you are unremitting. Thus, having a baby who is cranky and keeps you awake much of the night, in tandem with moving to a new house, is far more likely to create problems than would either one of these alone.

Recent research on stress shows that even more important than the raw number of life changes is what they *mean* to you. A divorce you experience as a liberation and the start of a new life is much less onerous than one you feel means the loss of everything you've held dear.

Many changes that most people take in stride can be particularly upsetting to others. Among them are entering the army, starting college, moving to a foreign country, changing or losing jobs, or suffering a drop in income. If you are having an extreme reaction to such a situation, psychotherapy can help.

Signs to Look For

The hallmark of problems with a transition is that you feel distressed by some change you are going through (first-time parenthood, a move) or a phase of life you are in (such as middle age). Apart from that distress, you have no psychological disturbance.

□ Robin had been eagerly awaiting the day she would graduate from college, move to the city, and find a job in publishing, the career she had set her heart on. But now, six months after the move, she was anxious and depressed, not excited. The job she had found in publishing was as a secretary, not an editorial assistant. She hated it but had been turned down for twenty others. The roommates she had found to share her apartment with were sloppy, difficult, and ignored her complaints. She hadn't made a single friend she felt close to. If she could move back home to her parents without feeling she was an utter failure, she'd do it tomorrow.

□ Mario was a writer and enjoyed the fact that his work was completely portable. When his wife, Wendy, got the chance to transfer to a post abroad with her firm, they were both delighted. But the change was disappointing for Mario. He found it hard to adjust to life in New Delhi, a dusty, noisy, congested city. He felt out of place; everything was strange, from the food to the language. Wendy, who spent her days in a large office with other Westerners, didn't mind. But Mario found himself miserably lonely, afraid to go out on his own, unable to sleep at night, and suspicious of everyone he met.

What Therapists Recommend

Approach. Psychodynamic therapy, where you investigate the underlying emotional issues that make this situation so troubling, is the most highly recommended. But supportive therapy, in which the focus is on helping you adjust to and cope with the situation, is also highly recommended. These approaches are often combined. Also well recommended is cognitive therapy, which explores the beliefs you hold that may be distorting your reaction to the situation.

Medication. Normally there is no reason for medication since the issue is not symptoms but a life transition. A very few therapists thought there might be occasion to use medication, presumably for short-term management of anxiety or depression.

Setting. Office visits.

Format. This depends on the nature of the life transition. If the issue is a personal one, as in the first case above, individual therapy is recommended. If the transition involves your spouse or family, as in the second case, couples or family therapy is recommended. Some therapists also recommend group therapy, or a peer support group, with others who are going through or have gone through the same transition.

Frequency. Once-a-week sessions are the norm. If the transition is particularly overwhelming, you may want to meet more than once a week for a time. As the difficulty resolves, you may meet less frequently.

Duration. Short-term therapy is usually enough—several weeks or more. If the problem itself is long-term or ongoing, therapy may need to be open-ended.

What You Should Know About Therapy

Just about any therapeutic approach can help, but be sure you find a therapist with whom you feel rapport and who seems to understand you (see Chapter 3, "Finding a Therapist").

If your problem has occurred before in roughly similar circumstances and seems to be part of some deeper pattern in your personality, you may benefit from therapy that explores lifelong character traits. For example, if you find that you become morbidly depressed after you move, and that pattern extends back into your childhood, then a deeper emotional issue may be at play. The psychodynamic therapies are particularly well suited for this.

On the other hand, most problems triggered by a change in your life situation are short-lived and can be addressed through short-term therapy. Psychodynamic approaches, unless they are explicitly time limited, are often open-ended and can last longer than necessary. No matter what kind of therapy you are beginning, be clear with your therapist at the outset what your goals are and determine how long he or she expects therapy to last.

Do you really need therapy? You may not. Though many life transitions are difficult, most people manage them without needing therapy. For one thing, the difficulties of a transition tend to fade with time no matter what you do. For another, the support and advice of family and friends is often enough. Peer self-help and support groups are often available, such as groups for new mothers or parents, community groups to welcome new neighbors, men's and women's groups for people at midlife, retirement groups, and many others.

However, if you are having more difficulties or feel more stressed than other people going through similar changes, or if your distress continues longer than it seems to in others, or the support of family and friends hasn't been enough, then therapy is a good resource.

BEREAVEMENT

One of the most painful moments in life is losing a loved one or having someone close to you suffer a life-threatening illness or injury. The loss, or anticipated loss, does more than disrupt life—it changes for a time how you experience yourself and the world. It can challenge the very meaning of life.

The mix of grief and other emotions that the death of a loved one brings can be evoked by other kinds of losses. A loved one's becoming incapacitated or senile, a separation or divorce, emigrating to a strange culture, moving away from your familiar social network or family, loss of a job—all these can trigger feelings of bereavement.

Anticipated losses, too, can lead to such feelings. These might include a family member's or a friend's becoming terminally ill, or one's parents or grandparents clearly getting old and beginning to fail. Or having one's first or last child leave home.

Then there are losses of what never was or never can be: a broken engagement, a career cut short by an injury, or learning you cannot have children.

In many of these cases you may not recognize that what you are feeling is bereavement because it isn't what you expect. But mourning is a healthy way of coming to terms with any meaningful loss.

But mourning is often precarious and can go awry in many ways. Any meaningful loss can undermine your sense of security and well-being. For a time, the world no longer seems so benign. How you grieve is crucial to how you will find your way in life afterward.

Normal grieving. Bereavement involves far more than simple grief. Indeed, sometimes you may feel no grief at all. Bereavement seems to involve *phases*—a period of intense anguish, for instance, may be followed by days or weeks of feeling numb or feeling very little.

That fluctuation of grief with numbness gives you a chance to adjust your feelings at a pace you can handle. You can expect grieving to continue in phases for as long as it lasts.

The first reaction is often one of shock or denial. You minimize or deny what has happened. To escape its emotional impact you may lose yourself in distractions or through compulsive activity at home or work.

Even so, the reality of the loss can hit you when you are most vulnerable: as you drift off to sleep, make love, or when you are deeply touched by something, such as a song or a special place. These bursts of realization can be intense, even overwhelming.

You may be filled with rage and anger when the shock and denial begin to wear off. The anger may be directed at fate or God, or at physicians or other caregivers whom you feel might have done something more to prevent the loss. You may even feel bitterness toward the person who has gone for the unfairness of his or her leaving you. This anger is natural and unavoidable, as is feeling helpless to do anything about the situation, especially helplessness to bring the person back. Even though you know it is "irrational" to have these feelings, your heart knows otherwise, feeling empty, alone, and abandoned.

You may find you are impatient with others, even when they try to make you feel better. You may find fault with them, feel put-upon, or hold them somehow responsible. You may refuse to be consoled; you don't want to be comforted—you only want back what you've lost.

Fear and anxiety is another common reaction to loss. You may feel that you've lost control over life. Or you may have the sudden sense that the world is not a just or predictable place. Such feelings can lead to a sense of paralysis, vulnerability, even momentary panic or terror.

Sometimes the reaction to loss is physical. You may feel waves of bodily distress—tightness in your throat, choking, shortness of breath, muscle tension, stomachache, and the like—without any physical source for it. People often lose their appetite and have difficulty sleeping.

Common psychological reactions include becoming preoccupied with thoughts of the persons or things lost. They may show up repeatedly in dreams, or you may think you have seen them, but on closer inspection find you are mistaken. Sometimes people who are grieving take on certain mannerisms or symptoms of the person who is gone.

Guilt, too, is common, especially if the loss was a death that was a "relief" after a long and draining illness. Feelings of guilt will be greater if at times you had found yourself wishing the person would die or be gone from your life, or if you felt you could have done more. Guilt feelings also stem from remorse over things you wish you hadn't done, such as argue. You may be haunted by all the times you were mean, angry, critical, or unloving.

As the reality of the loss seeps in, feelings of depression occur. For a while this can manifest as anger, anxiety, confusion, and guilt, followed by apathy, restlessness, despair, or the inability or active refusal to pick up the pieces and go on.

The depression associated with grief and mourning is normally different from a major or biological depression (see p. 462). Though it may share many of the same symptoms, such as guilt, listlessness, and preoccupation, in grief such symptoms come and go. And depression born of grief typically does not include the feelings of worthlessness that typify a depressive disorder.

A vital part of adjusting to loss is sadness, which may leave you for a time with the sense that everything is tasteless, pallid, or pointless. This quiet period of withdrawal from your usual interests helps you to slow down, reflect on your loss, and acknowledge what has happened, both emotionally and intellectually.

Whether with deep sadness or wistful melancholy, it is natural to review how your life has been, and at times, be flooded with memories. Memories may flow from the start or emerge after months have passed. These reminiscences may come with such intense sadness that it is hard to concentrate on anything else.

Slowly, in fits and starts, you will come to accept the loss and direct your energies to what is possible in the future.

Normal grief, with its phases of screening out the pain and of being immersed in sometimes overwhelming feelings, usually is most intense for three to six months after a major loss. But it can go on for a year, and in some cases—such as the death of a child—linger in a subdued form for many years.

Some people show their feelings freely, with frequent outbursts of weeping and anguish; others are quiet. Both are normal responses. What is most helpful and comforting at such moments is simply to have someone you trust sit with you. You should be permitted to have your feelings and express them as you wish, no matter how intense. This is almost always better than sedating yourself with medication, unless you are in danger of losing control and may hurt yourself or others.

The course of normal grief is highly individual, too. Feelings occur in no set order, no well-defined "stages," no "right" way. Some people, for example, may never mourn openly. Others may be filled with grief from time to time months or even years later. While all these feelings are normal, if you feel especially distressed at any time, therapy can help.

Signs to Look For

The hallmark of problems in bereavement is that they represent *extremes of the normal process* of grief. These include:

- panic; being overwhelmed by fear and grief
- frenzy; extreme efforts to put the loss out of mind, such as abusing drugs or alcohol, sexual excess, or burying oneself in work
- recurring nightmares about the loss
- overwhelming despair, guilt, rage, or fear that interferes with functioning
- emotional numbness that does not lift

□ Milly and Sam had been married for forty-five years when he died of a heart attack at sixty-six. Milly, two years his junior, temporarily collapsed. She was in tears constantly and wouldn't leave their apartment. She told her daughter she no longer had any reason to live.

After a year, Milly was still filled with sadness. She had difficulty resuming gardening, her favorite activity, and since she found it hard to socialize with friends without her beloved Sam, she would often stay in her apartment all day with the shades drawn.

What Therapists Recommend

Approach. Supportive therapy is the main approach recommended. About half of therapists also suggest a psychodynamic approach, in which the emotional meaning of the lost relationship is clarified.

Medication. The general guideline is that it is better to let people express their grief than to sedate them so they don't feel it, unless depression or anxiety become temporarily overwhelming.

Setting. The therapist's office.

Format. Individual therapy is the most common, but some therapists also recommend group therapy or a peer support group of others who have faced or are facing a similar loss. Hospitals and clinics often offer such groups. A few therapists suggest family therapy, especially when the loss has affected the entire family, or when the family can give support to a member who is particularly hard hit by the loss—a widowed parent, for instance.

Frequency. Most therapists believe once a week is sufficient, though a particularly intense reaction may require extra meetings.

Duration. One to six months should normally be sufficient, though more complicated and prolonged grieving can take much longer to resolve. Long-term support may also be needed.

What You Should Know About Therapy

When grieving isn't resolved in a normal way, or when a particular reaction or phase is unduly intense and prolonged, therapy is probably called for. Short-term supportive therapy may be able to get you through a particular emotional block. Any therapy should help you review the meaning of your loss—how important the person you lost was to you, what losing him or her means, what life without him or her will be like. It should also help you confront any unfinished "emotional business"— resentments, ambivalence, anger, or words of love and forgiveness that were never spoken.

If the loss is still too overwhelming—you are flooded with thoughts and feelings about it—therapy should focus on getting these feelings under control first. If you are too out of touch with your loss, then therapy should have the opposite focus, helping you get in touch again.

Before an anticipated death. If you or someone close to you is suffering from a terminal illness, therapy can help you avoid extremes. One of these is denying that death is inevitable or imminent, which may keep you and the other from sharing your feelings of how special you are to each other. The result is often regret on the part of the survivor, and a feeling of isolation on the part of the one dying. A therapist, counselor, or hospice worker can help you or your family find a way to talk about what is happening.

Acute grief. When a death is unexpected, the result of violence, or that of a child, reactions can be particularly intense. If a person becomes psychotic, out of control with rage, or self-destructive, an emotional emergency exists.

If so, the person should not be left alone but rather kept in the company of trusted friends or family who are continuously available, until the crisis passes or until professional help is obtained. If the person is in immediate danger of harming himself or others, then the crisis is best handled in a psychiatric emergency room. If the person cannot be managed or will not take your advice, call the police and an ambulance and have him taken to the nearest emergency room.

CHAPTER SIXTEEN

■

EMOTIONAL AND BEHAVIORAL PROBLEMS OF CHILDHOOD AND ADOLESCENCE

Raising a child is both rewarding and frustrating; at times all parents overreact or simply don't know what to do. But the days are over when "bad parenting" was blamed for all the child's problems. The more current thinking is that many children's problems have multiple causes, one of which may be the styles of parenting. And usually if those styles are creating a problem, they can be changed through therapy.

Parents often feel ashamed and exposed—even angry and guilty—when they bring their child to a therapist. They usually fear the child will tell the therapist about their failings as parents or that these will be all too apparent in the child. Parents may also be glad their child is getting help, but feel that *they* are the ones who really need help or need help, too.

Child therapists are very aware of parents' feelings and usually welcome the opportunity to discuss them with you. They will also give you credit for recognizing your child's difficulties and seeking out help for them.

Choosing a Therapist for Your Child

The guidelines described in Part I for finding a therapist for adults apply to children, too. You should take the time to look around before settling on a therapist, whether therapy involves the entire family or just you and your child. If your child is to have individual sessions with the therapist, the rapport between child and therapist is particularly important in your selection.

Realize that the therapist who does the initial evaluation may very often recommend another therapist to treat your child, particularly at a child-guidance clinic. But you do not have to stay with the first therapist who is recommended if you think he or she is not right for your child, or for you.

Your child should feel comfortable with the therapist within the first few sessions. If you feel there could be a better match between your child and the therapist, try two or three other therapists for a few sessions before making a final choice. If the child, especially an adolescent, is feeling forced into therapy, he or she may reject all of the clinicians, and then the parent and the therapist should make the choice.

In child therapy, parents are almost always involved in treatment, especially in behavioral and family approaches, but usually in psychodynamic approaches as well. The younger the child, the more important the parents' involvement. Therapists will rely on you for information and feedback and may enlist your help with assignments between sessions. They may put you in charge of implementing the overall treatment plan. Or they may want you to join with your child in learning new ways of interacting together. They may also suggest resolving certain conflicts between you and your spouse, which is frequently an effective way of resolving a child's difficulties.

Even if your child's therapy will be mainly individual—as in play therapy with the psychodynamic approach—you will have meetings with the therapist, too. In every case, you should feel you have a good working relationship with him or her.

All children's problems have to be evaluated relative to what's normal for their age. Acting like a three-year-old at three is fine; at twelve it is a problem. Emotional stress often makes children regress, and most symptoms in children were normal behaviors at an earlier age. The most common example is the older sibling who starts acting like a baby when a new brother or sister is born, but a divorce, a death in the family, or moving can cause regressive reactions as well. But children's problems have many other causes, and sometimes multiple causes. A child who is anxious or depressed, for example, may be overly identifying with someone else in the family, such as a parent or grandparent. Or a child may act up as a way of taking the spotlight off an alcoholic parent. Still another frequent cause of children's problems is the inadvertent rewarding of a problem behavior. A child who gets to come into her parents' bed whenever she is scared at night, for example, may increasingly have nighttime anxiety attacks.

What Children Think About Therapy

Some children may think that they're "crazy" or "retarded" if they are taken to see a therapist. If your child expresses these concerns, explain that going to see a therapist does not mean he or she is "crazy," that many other children have found it helpful to see a therapist, and that he or she will be happier. The risk of a child's feeling stigmatized has to be balanced against the opportunity for lasting resolution of painful problems and a lifetime of psychological growth. You also want to assure the child that you will be there and are committed to doing whatever it takes to help.

You may want to keep your child's therapy a "family matter," not something you talk about with just anyone. This will minimize the likelihood that your child will run up against other children's teasing for "seeing a shrink." Confidentiality is even more important to children relative to their peers than it is to an adult.

ADJUSTMENT PROBLEMS AT SCHOOL

School is the first main arena where a child is challenged to adjust outside the family. Many emotional landmarks occur there: our first leave-taking from the family; getting acclimated to new people and settings; learning to compete with others and assert ourselves; having our performance evaluated; and making new friends.

The most common sign of trouble for a child at school is, of course, a dip in academic performance and generally not performing up to his or her ability. Doing poorly in school leads to a chain reaction of feelings in the child: fear, shame, anger, self-blame, and helplessness. At some point along the way, behavioral problems often start—the next most common sign the child is experiencing difficulties.

In older children and adolescents, other common signs of trouble include undue anxiety at having to take tests, write papers, or speak up in class; intense fear of failure or of not performing well; boredom; a lack of direction and sense of purpose; procrastination or failing to get work done; and trouble getting along with classmates or teachers.

A child's difficulties in school may not always mean the difficulty is *with* school. A drop in school performance is often the first behavioral sign that something is wrong at home. Changes in the family, such as a move, a new baby, a sibling leaving home, a parent losing a job, a death in the family, or a divorce, almost always affect a child's academic performance and his or her behavior at school. Most of the problems at school will resolve as the child and the family adjust to the change at home. But if your child continues to seem unduly upset at school, continues to misbehave, or does not return to his or her former performance level, the school will normally see this as a sign the child needs help, and so should you.

Difficulty handling important issues and stages in individual development can also be reflected in academic and behavioral problems at school.

Signs to Look For

The hallmark of school problems is that your child has difficulty functioning in school up to his or her natural abilities. Some typical forms this can take in younger kids include acting out, withdrawal, somatic complaints, tardiness, or absenteeism. In older students, difficulties may be reflected in anxiety about tests, perfectionism, procrastination, or boredom with schoolwork.

What Therapists Recommend

Approach. Psychodynamic therapy is highly recommended. This approach encourages children to talk about what may be producing their reaction to school and affecting performance. Also recommended: behavior therapy, in which the focus is on changing problem behaviors, and for older students, cognitive therapy, which helps identify and change self-defeating, distorted ways of thinking about the demands of school.

Medication. Medication has no role unless the problem has grown to include depression or overwhelming anxiety. And even then there are nondrug alternatives.

Setting. Office visits are the norm.

Format. Individual therapy is the usual recommendation. For children whose school problems are a reaction to difficulties at home, family therapy is appropriate.

Frequency. Once a week is usual. If a child is going through a crisis, though, such as panic at flunking a test, he or she may need meetings more than once a week until some calm is restored.

Duration. Most therapists estimate one to six months should be long enough.

What You Should Know About Therapy

School problems: is therapy the answer? Don't assume your child needs therapy. Start by asking for a consultation with his or her primary teacher, then with the school guidance counselor or psychologist. Consult with them to get an objective view of what the sources of the problem might be: what is happening in the class-room, or your child's social life (e.g., being the target of a bully), as opposed to, e.g., adjusting to separation or divorce at home.

If the main problem is that your child is performing below his or her intellectual ability, then tutoring should be the first response. If that is not sufficient, then therapy should be considered.

If you wonder whether your child is, indeed, performing below his or her ability, you can ask your school to do testing. Often a child who is doing poorly has a learning disability, which calls for special classes or tutoring with a specialist. In such cases, therapy makes sense only as a supplement to special education, to deal with any problems in self-esteem a student may have as a result of having done poorly in school. Learning disabilities sometimes do not become obvious until the higher grades of grammar school or even junior high.

If the problem is in your child's social life at school—for instance, feeling an outcast, bullied, or discriminated against—then you might consult with your child's teacher or the school principal to find a solution there. And if the trouble is how a particular teacher is treating your child, then a meeting with the teacher is called for.

If the problem is due to circumstances at home or school, try to change the situation before you try to change your child. For instance, if your child is inattentive at school because he or she is upset by your fights with your spouse, then marital counseling may help your child as much as it does you. If the problem at school is traceable to some other difficulty in the family, or between you and your child, then family therapy is the best course to pursue.

CONDUCT PROBLEMS

Every normal child goes through periods of being "bad," such as refusing to do as told, bullying, stealing, lying, or getting in trouble at school. Ordinarily these conduct problems pass with time—in a few days, weeks, or months.

But some children's problems don't go away, though they may take different forms as time goes on. These children are usually difficult to manage—or barely manage-able—both at home and at school. They get in trouble not just with parents and teachers, but with potential friends and classmates as well. They get a reputation for being unruly, mean, and even dangerous; other children often shun them. Their schoolwork suffers, too. They are frequently sent to the principal's office and pay little attention to lessons.

Children who are bullies or otherwise aggressive seem to misinterpret certain social cues from other children: they tend to see hostility or a threat where none was intended. When they subsequently pick a fight, they are thus "defending themselves," albeit against an imagined slight or threat.

Conduct problems often go hand in hand with hyperactivity (see p. 374). Being so restless and impulsive makes it all the easier for children to get into trouble. Hyperactivity may also be another reason children with conduct disorders often do so poorly in school. One theory holds that the conduct disorder is the expression of the frustration and anger hyperactive children feel at being unable to keep up with their peers in learning.

The great majority of children with conduct disorders come from homes where abuse is common. In these families there is often alcoholism, violence, or pervasive chaos. In this light, these children's behavior can be seen as a learned response to a dysfunctional family system, a means of coping with a highly stressful and unpredictable environment.

Conduct problems are also more common in families where parents' discipline is both harsh and erratic—a pattern that can itself provoke behavior problems. But more is at play in causing conduct problems than just these factors because the problem is also found in families when none of these is present.

These children—particularly highly aggressive boys—are at high risk of becoming troubled adults. Such boys are three times more likely to become involved with the law by the time they reach their twenties as are less aggressive boys. Apart from the risk of committing crimes, these children are at greater risk for alcoholism or drug addiction, other psychiatric problems, or simply a lifetime of lost jobs and broken relationships.

Conduct problems are relatively common: estimates range from 2 to 8 percent of children. Young boys are much more likely than young girls to have such problems, though by early adolescence it does show up in girls, too.

But remember, an otherwise "good" child or teenager who gets into trouble— even serious trouble—once or twice does not have the kind of pervasive conduct problem that demands therapy.

Signs to Look For

The hallmark of conduct problems is a *longstanding pattern of getting into many kinds of trouble.* Look for several of the following:
In children:

- impulsivity
- acting out
- low self-esteem
- becoming easily overwhelmed

- low tolerance for frustration
- gives up easily
- usually very angry

In adolescents:

- stealing, whether "borrowing" without giving back, shoplifting, breaking into houses, or robbery, such as purse-snatching, stealing bikes or cars, taking money from smaller children
- running away from home repeatedly
- lying to parents, teachers, other children
- setting fires
- cutting school or (if employed) cutting work regularly
- vandalism
- cruelty to animals or to people
- rape
- picking fights; using a weapon in fights

□ As a preschooler, Frankie was the terror of his play group, snatching toys from other kids, getting into fights in which he kicked and bit ferociously, cruelly taunting and threatening younger kids. At five he attacked a neighbor's cat with a hatchet. At six he stole another child's bike, then when he was caught, claimed the child had "loaned" it to him.

In grammar school Frankie was known as a bully, forcing smaller kids to pay tributes of candy and money or face a beating. In class he was a cutup, defiant to his teachers, and never paid attention. He often cut school to hang out at a video game shop in the local mall.

In junior high Frankie was the first in his grade to smoke, and by eighth grade he was selling marijuana. Because Frankie picked so many fights, he was finally expelled in ninth grade when he broke another boy's arm with a baseball bat. But his first arrest, at fourteen, was for breaking and entering a neighbor's house.

Defiance

Not quite so bad, but still troubling and frustrating for parents and teachers, are children whose problem takes the form of defiance without the more serious conduct problems described above. Defiant children will not do what they're told, pick arguments with parents and teachers, tease other children, lose their temper easily, and are often angry. They are annoying, rebellious, and resentful.

But they are also in control of their meanness: when an adult they do not know is present, they tend to keep their defiance under wraps and can seem perfectly obedient—until that adult turns his back or leaves. And if told they are "defiant," such children will retort that they are justified, that other people deserve it.

What Therapists Recommend

Approach. A behavioral approach is the therapy of choice. This usually means a regimen of clear rewards and punishments according to an explicit contract or set of rules stating what is expected and what is not allowed. Also recommended is a family systems approach, in which the family is the focus of treatment. Sometimes the two are combined, so that the family becomes the main reinforcer of the rules.

Medication. There is none for conduct problems themselves. But it may help if, as is often the case, hyperactivity accompanies conduct problems.

Setting. Conduct problems can be treated with the child living at home and making office visits. But treatment might begin in a children's residential treatment program if a child cannot be handled at home or has been in constant trouble with the law. An alternative is hospitalization, again for children too out of control to be kept at home. This makes sense only if the hospital has a special unit geared to such children, and only in extreme cases.

Format. Family therapy is the most highly recommended format, with individual therapy following. Typically this means combining both approaches. Also highly recommended is group therapy, presumably with others of the same age with similar problems.

Frequency. Once a week, though twice or more a week may be needed when a child is at the beginning of treatment and close monitoring is called for.

Duration. Open-ended.

What You Should Know About Therapy

If your child has conduct problems, expect to play a key role in therapy. The therapist should work with you to help you find ways to better manage your child, and to encourage him or her to be more sociable.

Frequently parents of such children have become desperate when it comes to discipline, resorting to threats, criticism, or violence—none of which work well. This often creates a spiral of anger, with you becoming more and more frustrated each month and your child increasingly defiant. It ends with you becoming fed up, blowing up, or giving up.

A first step might be helping you to see the situation as a problem to be solved rather than something to get angry about. And you may be encouraged to praise your child when he or she behaves appropriately—not just lash out at misconduct—and to spend more time with your child doing something you both enjoy.

In a behavioral approach, you may be asked to become more methodical about exactly how and how often your child misbehaves so as to pinpoint the problems you want to correct: is it stealing, not obeying requests to help out, lying? Then you may be coached in making clear requests, spelling out exactly what you want done. And most important, you will have a clear idea of how to handle disobedience in a way that will not lead to a frustrating spiral of anger.

Your child may also see a therapist on his or her own. These sessions may also extend to group experiences, in a setting that fosters cooperation.

Hospitalization. If your child is dangerous and unmanageable, if he or she has hurt other children, say, or set fires frequently, then therapy may have to begin in a hospital or juvenile home. You may also be told that hospitalization for a short time would be helpful for observation to rule out neurological problems and make a thorough diagnostic assessment. While this is a standard approach in extreme cases, you may want to weigh the advantages (presumably, a more effective treatment plan) against the disadvantages (including the stigma of being hospitalized and the disruption in your child's life, such as stopping school) if you have a choice.

ANXIETY PROBLEMS

Fears are natural for a child, who is so small and vulnerable in such a large and sometimes dangerous world. Indeed, most children pass through periods of intense fearfulness, with specific fears typifying each age. But these fearful episodes usually end in a few weeks.

A child's fears may indicate a problem, though, if they are far out of proportion, persist for long periods, are too "childish" for the child's age level, or interfere with the child's day-to-day functioning.

Extreme anxiety is one of the most common problems that bring children to therapy, second only to getting in trouble repeatedly or being unable to control anger. But only when fears become so pronounced or relentless that they interfere with your child's ability to lead a normal life should you consider therapy.

For the anxious child, worry is a constant. While most every child will have worries that preoccupy him or her from time to time, the anxious child is worried more days than not and worries about all kinds of things rather than having just one or two concerns. Just exactly what causes the worries can change from week to week, but the worry is constant.

Certain kinds of worries frequently show up in children who are anxious. One is not bearing to be separated from their parents—fright at being left at school, for instance, or at going to camp. If that seems to describe your child, see page 369. Another is being exceedingly shy and shrinking from meetings with strangers or even playmates (see p. 371). And then there are children who are just overly anxious in general.

But remember, one or two episodes of intense anxiety does not mean a child needs therapy. If your child's fears and worries are short-lived, are assuaged when you reassure him or her, or do not interfere in any major way with the demands of family, friendships, and school, then there is no need for the help of a therapist.

Signs to Look For

Excessive fears are the main sign of anxiety problems, of course, but not the only ones. What sets an anxiety problem apart from the ordinary worries of childhood is its intensity and persistence, as well as a variety of accompanying signs of distress:

- *Excessive, unrealistic worries.* Typically these worries are about the main features of a child's life: school, friends, family, sports, being liked. The worries are widespread, not just focused on one or two issues, and although the specifics may change, they persist for months on end.
- *Physical tensions.* This tension may show up as twitching or trembling, a general restlessness, or even getting tired easily. Sometimes it takes the form of sore, achy, or tense muscles.
- *"Motor racing."* The child's body shows signs of the "fight or flight" reaction: clammy hands; racing heartbeat or palpitations; shortness of breath or a sense of being smothered; dizziness or light-headedness; stomach troubles such as nausea or diarrhea; hot flashes or chills; trouble swallowing. Of these signs, the most common is stomachache.
- *On edge.* The child seems overly vigilant, as though dreading something that is about to happen. He or she may become startled or irritated easily or have trouble sleeping. Worrisome thoughts may make concentrating on schoolwork or on what is being said difficult or cause the child seemingly to "go blank."

For these signs to indicate a need for therapy, you should notice a number of them. Since most children go through periods of anxiety from time to time as they grow, it is considered a problem only if the child has more days than not over some months when he or she is anxious.

Anxiety attacks. Sometimes children with these problems will have episodes of anxiety where the physical symptoms become extremely intense. These attacks are similar to the *panic attacks* that occur in adults (see p. 490). In addition to the "fight or flight" signs mentioned above, the child may feel a sense of panic or terror, cry or seem frightened, describe bizarre and intense physical changes (e.g., "My heart is stopping" or "I can't breathe"), and be terrified of being deathly ill—a common reaction during panic attacks. Such attacks can last anywhere from a few minutes to an hour or more and can be triggered by seemingly trivial incidents or come from "out of the blue."

Separation Anxiety

The term *separation anxiety* means becoming intensely upset at being parted from one's home, mother, father, or anyone who usually takes care of one. This anxiety is normal in infants starting at around nine months and can last for months or even years in many forms. At that time in children's psychological growth separation anxiety is considered a healthy sign: it means they have a strong bond to their parents and are beginning to be able to distinguish other people from them.

Although children gradually become more comfortable with separation as they grow, the fear of being separated from parents often waxes and wanes through much of childhood, particularly in response to new situations such as a new baby-sitter, going to preschool for the first time, or starting back to school after vacation. The normal anxieties of separation can be worsened during stressful times, such as when you or your child is sick, when a younger sibling is born, or during a move to a new home or school.

Some children seem to be born prone to becoming upset at separations. A child with a lifelong pattern of holding back may not necessarily need therapy. But if your child is developing problems at school, with playmates, or in leading a normal life, then you should consider it.

Signs to Look For

The main signs of separation anxiety include:

- Unrealistic worry about parents, such as the persistent fear that something harmful will happen to them or that they will leave and not come back.
- Fears about calamities that might separate the child and parents, such as being kidnapped, lost, or hurt in an accident.
- Refusal to go to school, wanting to stay home instead.
- Reluctance to go to sleep alone or fear of sleeping away from home.
- Avoiding being alone, clinging to parents or following them around.
- Nightmares about being separated from parents.
- Physical complaints, such as headaches, stomachaches, sore throats, especially on days when a separation from parents is about to occur.
- Anticipatory distress, such as temper tantrums or crying, when the child is about to leave parents.

The child may have one or another of these behaviors from time to time without there being a serious problem. But if several of the signs occur simultaneously and last for more than two weeks with great intensity, then your child would probably benefit from therapy.

School Refusal

One of the most common forms of separation anxiety in children six to ten is refusing to go to school. But this can also be a sign of other kinds of anxiety problems, perhaps a *simple phobia* about something connected with school such as riding on the bus, or a *social phobia* such as fearing disapproval from other kids. Often school refusal begins after the child has been staying home with his parents for a long time, during an illness or an extended vacation. It can also be triggered by a stress, such as the death of a relative or pet, changing schools, or moving to a new neighborhood.

Typically a child who dreads school will complain of some illness, perhaps a sore throat, just as it is time to leave for school in the morning. Once the child is allowed to stay home, the illness magically subsides, only to reappear the next day.

Paradoxically, once some children who refuse to go to school are in the schoolroom, their fears and resistance fade. These children are calmer in school because their fear centers around leaving home rather than being in school. The fears may resurge, though, during changes in routine, such as a new lunch period.

Other children resist school because they have a difficult time there, particularly with other children. They yearn for the safety of home and are genuinely frightened about life at school. They may have a hard time adjusting to rules set by strangers, being compared with other children, or failing at a particular task. Or they may dread having to recite or answer questions in class, or undress for gym. For such children, the sudden refusal to go to school is often in response to a minor crisis: a new teacher, an encounter with a bully, or general teasing by other children.

Sometimes the threats the child imagines have some basis in fact. If so, it makes more sense for you to try to deal directly with the problem, for instance, by talking to the school principal about a bully. Often, though, the child is reacting to relatively minor situations as if they were major crises—which they temporarily are for the child.

Still other children dread school because they are frightened that something bad will happen to a parent while they are away. This danger—which the child feels as urgent and real—can be completely imaginary or have some small basis in fact, such as a parent's illness. Such fears are a key sign of separation anxiety.

If your child refuses to go to school, you have a problem you cannot afford to ignore. Keep in mind, though, that school refusal connected with separation anxiety is not the same as truancy, in which children lie both to their parents and teachers about skipping school. Truancy is a sign of a conduct problem (see p. 363).

□ Robbie hated school. At least that's what he told his mother whenever she tried to get him ready for the school bus. The problem had started a month or so after he began second grade. Robbie came down with the flu and was home for a week with his mother. When his doctor said he was well and should go back to school, Robbie refused.

He cried and cried. Surprised by the intensity of his feelings, his mother gave in and let him stay home, hoping that he would feel better about it the next day. But for days afterward, the same small melodrama unfolded: Robbie's mother would start to pack his lunch for school, and he would start crying. Then, once his mother would let him stay home, Robbie's tantrum would subside.

Extreme Shyness

Shy or "avoidant" children, as the new diagnostic term calls them, are more often girls than boys. Such children shrink from the presence of strangers, even when they have reached three or four, ages when most children have resolved the normal stranger anxiety of the toddler stage.

Children between the ages of five and seven are most likely to express their extreme shyness by refusing to go to school. But such children have often given signs of their shyness earlier in life. Typically they become silent, blush, and cling when other children or adults are around. They hang back from playing with other children, avoiding playground games and other social situations, such as birthday parties, that are part of a child's life.

The first major crisis for very shy children is often having to go to preschool or kindergarten. More typically, shyness becomes most problematic in late childhood and early adolescence. At whatever point shyness becomes so incapacitating that it prevents a child from leading a normal life, therapy is called for.

But remember, it is perfectly normal for a child to be shy from time to time. And some children, by nature of their temperament, tend to be shy more often than children who are naturally outgoing. Shyness may require therapy only when it *seriously* interferes with your child's day-to-day activities.

Children's Fears: What's Normal?

Some fears are normal at some ages, but may signify difficulties in older children. For instance, three-year-olds are often afraid of being separated from their parents, but ten-year-olds shouldn't be. Here are the typical fears of children arranged by age:

Birth to six months: Loss of physical support, unexpected noises.

Seven to twelve months: Strangers, heights, sudden, unexpected, or looming objects.

One year: Separation from a parent, injury, strangers.

Two years: Loud noises (vacuum cleaner, alarms, trucks, thunder, etc.), animals, dark rooms, separation from parents, large, noisy machines, people coming and going, strange children.

Three years: Masks, the dark, animals, separation from parents.

Four years: Separation from parents, the dark, noises at night.

Five years: Animals, "bad" people, the dark, separation from parents, being hurt.

Six years: Supernatural beings (ghosts, witches, "boogeyman," Darth Vader), being hurt, thunder and lightning, the dark, sleeping or staying alone, being separated from parents.

Seven to eight years: Supernatural beings, the dark, frightening news (e.g., kidnapping of a child), staying alone, being hurt.

Nine to twelve years: School exams, doing poorly in school, being hurt, physical appearance, thunder and lightning, the dark, death.

Teen years: Social success, sexuality.

What Therapists Recommend

Approach. The two most highly recommended approaches are behavioral therapy and family therapy. While each of these approaches can be used on its own, they are often combined, so that the family cooperates in helping a child follow a program of behavior therapy. Another highly recommended approach is psychodynamic, in which therapy would focus on the emotional meanings and conflicts that underlie the anxiety.

Medication. Not usual for young children, though adolescents may receive medication if the symptoms are extremely disruptive of their lives.

Setting. Virtually all therapists say treatment for children's anxiety should be via office visits. However, in a behavioral approach, therapy may include asking the child to experience directly the situations that elicit anxiety, such as going to school despite fears.

Format. Most therapists agree that therapy should include both individual sessions for the child and sessions for the parents or whole family.

Frequency. Most therapists say therapy should be once a week, but more often if necessary when symptoms are most disruptive.

Duration. Usually one to six months, sometimes longer.

What You Should Know About Therapy

The three main options in therapy for children with anxiety problems are behavior therapy, psychodynamic therapy, and family therapy. A fourth, psychiatric medication, is not strongly recommended for anxiety in children.

Behavior therapy assumes the anxieties have been learned and aims to replace these learned reactions with others that are incompatible or to "extinguish" the habits altogether. For younger children, therapy may engage both parents and teachers as "cotherapists," helping with a regimen that uses real-life situations to counter the learned anxieties. Older children are themselves actively involved in implementing their treatment.

In one behavioral approach, called exposure, the child is confronted with the situation that is so scary, but in a controlled manner so that he or she will experience going through it unharmed. This is often done in graduated doses. For instance, a child terrified of dogs may first be shown pictures of dogs. He or she would then be put near a small, friendly dog, then be encouraged to pet it, then to play with it. The treatment would continue with larger and "scarier" dogs.

Another behavioral approach rewards a child for staying in a situation he or she fears. A shy child might be given points, which can be exchanged for prizes, each time he or she overcomes timidity. These approaches may seem simple, but they work. A behavior therapist will help you design a program tailored to your child's needs and help you implement it.

A *psychodynamic therapy* assumes that children's anxieties are caused by internal emotional conflicts, such as a young boy's feelings of rivalry with his father or fear of the loss of a parent.

Psychodynamic approaches are indirect. The therapist will play games with your child or have him or her draw or tell a story. The therapist engages your child to develop rapport and trust, then uses their interactions to tease out underlying fears of which the child may be only dimly aware and provide indirect and direct reassurances. The goal is to help the child experience a sense of control and mastery, which will carry over to calm the anxieties.

In *family therapy*, the child's anxiety is understood as a reflection of problems within the family unit. The family therapist meets with the whole family, and sometimes with individual members separately, to see how the child fits in the pattern of family interactions, as well as how the family operates as a whole.

The therapist will, for instance, want to explore not just what is going on with the child, but also how the entire system the child is a part of functions, including family members, neighbors, and friends. The therapist may prescribe tasks, such as your comforting your child. The interaction will be studied, along with others, to see what may be producing the anxiety. And the therapist will look, too, for sources of strength in the family that could help the child, such as a particularly strong rapport with another sibling.

Psychiatric medication is not recommended for young children, though it is more often used in adolescents. The considerations in using medications are the same as for adults with anxiety disorders (see p. 498). Low doses of imipramine, an antidepressant, are sometimes used to lower anxiety in children. But there is a general reluctance to use antianxiety medications with youngsters, in part because their safety and effectiveness have not been adequately determined for children.

ATTENTION DEFICIT HYPERACTIVITY DISORDER (ADHD)

Healthy children, by their nature, are highly active, easily distracted, and impulsive. But some children are so energetic and unfocused that it not only exasperates their parents but seriously interferes with their ability to keep up in school and get along with other children. When children seem far more active, disruptive, and distractible than other children of their age, the problem may be an *attention-deficit hyperactivity disorder* (ADHD) or what is commonly called hyperactivity.

Deciding what is normal exuberance and what is hyperactivity is not easy. A professional evaluation by a child specialist—and sometimes a second opinion—is called for before a child is treated for hyperactivity.

Parents and teachers may differ in their tolerance for a child's disruptive behavior. What drives one adult to the limit of patience may bother another very little. That's why parents may be puzzled when the first-grade teacher says their child is hyperactive, while the preschool teacher never mentioned a serious problem.

Hyperactivity can show up in preschool and is almost always identified as a problem by the early grades, since with maturation children normally learn to pay attention and calm down in class. The hyperactive child has considerable difficulty mastering these basic skills for productive school performance. He begins to stand out as a discipline problem, the class "bad boy," and other children may begin to see him as "a baby."

Often it is the teacher or school psychologist who will tell parents that their child may be hyperactive. That does not mean they are right. Sometimes perfectly normal, though exuberant, young boys are called hyperactive by teachers who are having a hard time keeping them in line. The term is overused and the condition easily misdiagnosed. A teacher or other nonclinician who says a child is "hyperactive" is not making a diagnosis but speaking descriptively. Just because your child *seems* "hyperactive" to them, it does not mean he actually is.

But if you, too, think it might be the case, or you have been hearing similar comments about your child from other people—and he or she seems to exhibit some of the signs listed below—*do* have the possibility checked by bringing your child to a child psychologist or other child therapist who is *experienced with ADHD* for a diagnostic workup.

Sometimes hyperactivity leads to social and psychological problems. The child may be continually getting into trouble at home for not finishing things, not listening, or leaving messes, while at school his inability to sit still draws his teacher's displeasure and other children's scorn—all of which can make a child feel bad about herself.

A full evaluation by a child clinician should establish not only if a child is clinically hyperactive but also if any other problems are involved. The evaluation typically includes:

• Checklists that you fill out listing specific ways your child behaves.
• Observation of your child at school or at least an interview with his or her teacher about how he or she behaves. Sometimes the teacher will be asked to fill out a checklist, too.
• An interview in the therapist's office with you and your child. Don't be surprised if your child is on "good behavior" in the office. Parents often say, "He's never this good!" The therapist should not be surprised.
• The usual medical and family history, and sometimes a consultation with your child's pediatrician.
• Consultation with a child psychiatrist or neurologist.

Signs to Look For

A child may be hyperactive if, compared to other children his age, he is far more restless, has a much harder time concentrating, and acts more impulsively. One of the most telling signs is trouble getting along with other kids. A child with ADHD may not show all of these signs. Some children, for instance, have extreme difficulty paying attention and controlling impulses, but are not too active physically. These children may still suffer from an attention-deficit disorder without hyperactivity and can benefit from treatment as well.

A child with only a few of the following signs probably does not need treatment. But if by age seven a child has been showing a half dozen or more of them for more than six months, he or she should be evaluated. The major warning signs of ADHD include:

• Incessant fidgeting; can't sit still or play quietly on his own.
• Is easily distracted; e.g., constantly changes from game to game and toy to toy while playing.

- Rarely finishes what he starts; unable to stick with a given task for more than a few minutes or so, even something he especially enjoys.
- Doesn't listen; interrupts constantly when people are talking to him; has trouble following instructions.
- Gets into trouble with something even immediately after being told not to do it. No matter how much he is disciplined for getting into trouble, nothing seems to help.
- Takes risks and repeatedly gets into dangerous situations; needs to be watched constantly; e.g., as a toddler, runs into the street or climbs in dangerous places.
- Is impatient; can't stand to wait his turn when playing games with other children or disrupts other children's games.
- Speaks out in class without raising his hand, despite frequent reminders.
- Is disorganized; loses what he needs to do his schoolwork, such as pencils or books.
- Talks nonstop; a "chatterbox."
- Has difficulty forming and maintaining relationships.
- Has low self-esteem and is unable to respect others.
- Can't control or soothe himself at times of stress.

Hyperactive children often seem different as early as age three, and sometimes in infancy, when they tend to cry a lot, be irritable, and sleep restlessly. As toddlers, they are noticeably overactive, hard to control, and inattentive compared to other children their age.

□ Joey was always moving, like a little monkey. At ten months his mother found him out of his crib. His sisters, at the same age, could never have climbed out of it alone. As a toddler, he was a terror: he broke things all the time—plates, furniture, toys—and would never share with his two sisters. He couldn't focus on any activity for more than a minute. He'd dump all one hundred crayons out on the floor, scribble for a minute, then run off to something else, crushing the crayons into the carpet.

His parents tried to adapt to Joey's style. His mother bought games that didn't have lots of small parts that could get strewn all over the house. They put locks on his sisters' rooms so he wouldn't ruin their things. But it was hard: one night, when Joey was six, he drew with crayon on a newly painted wall. His mother got so angry she locked him in his room for the night.

By the time Joey started school, his parents were worn down and worried. To be sure, Joey could be sweet, and he seemed intelligent. But the teacher said he never seemed to listen and wouldn't sit still for a second. Most of the kids didn't like to play with him—he would never wait his turn in games and sometimes hit them.

A problem that is easily mistaken for ADHD is a *learning disability*. The frustrations of being unable to read or otherwise grasp lessons that other children take with ease can make the learning-disabled child act up in a way that looks—particularly to his teacher—like hyperactivity. Psychological testing can help distinguish ADHD from a learning disability. On the other hand, children with ADHD often do have specific learning disabilities as well.

What Therapists Recommend

Approach. The best approach, most therapists agree, is behavior therapy. Also suggested is combining a behavioral approach with a supportive or a family approach that gets the whole family involved.

Medication. Most therapists in the survey recommend it, but the use of medication is still controversial. The purpose of medicine is not to sedate children but rather to help them concentrate. Children should have a careful evaluation before medication is tried. Medication should be prescribed and closely monitored for any side effects. The prescribing doctor, the child's pediatrician, and the individual therapist should coordinate closely.

Setting. Therapy in office visits is the norm. However, therapy may also take place in a treatment program, where available, usually run by school districts as a special class.

Format. Individual therapy is recommended, often in conjunction with family involvement.

Frequency. Usually once a week.

Duration. Open-ended.

What You Should Know About Therapy

The three most common treatments for ADHD are behavior therapy, family therapy, and medication. Sometimes a therapist will employ just one approach, but these are most effective in combination.

Medication. The most commonly prescribed medications are stimulants (see p. 638), although these don't work for all children or for all symptoms. These medications produce a paradoxical effect that helps focus the children's attention and composes them. Common side effects include anorexia, trouble sleeping, and headaches. Also used, if stimulants do not help after two to five weeks: tricyclic antidepressants (see p. 610) and clonidine (see p. 639), but these drugs are riskier and less effective.

Many parents do not like the idea of their children taking a psychiatric medication, especially one taken daily. The greatest opposition has been to the stimulant Ritalin, which some think has been prescribed too freely. On the other hand, some parents are ardent supporters of medication because they have observed marked improvements in their children.

Therapy. In either case, *medication alone does not suffice.* Even if children do become calmer, the medication may not help them improve their school performance or repair their self-image. Therapy should focus on self-esteem, mastery, learning to process cognitive information, attentional focusing, and forming relationships.

Psychotherapy addresses not only the symptoms of hyperactivity, but also the unhappiness it causes. A child who gets into trouble all the time, can't make friends, and does poorly at school will inevitably start to feel bad about himself and probably angry at the world for "blaming him all the time." Therapy can help children understand what is going on, that they are not "bad," and help them deal more adaptively with the situations that are so troubling.

The most common alternative or adjunct to medication is behavior therapy. Behavior therapy assumes that systematic management of how the child's parents and teachers react to him can help him get his behavior under control. Part of the problem for a hyperactive child can be a cycle in which his poorly controlled actions lead to his being punished, which in turn makes him feel angry, defeated, and rebellious. That leads to his getting into more trouble, and so the cycle repeats.

Parents can begin to break that cycle by using rewards to encourage the child's good behavior, instead of relying on punishment to control bad behavior. Parents are often asked to track their children's performance of some desired action, such as finishing homework, then reward them after they have reached a certain point. It may take many weeks of experimenting to find the right combination of target behavior and rewards to start seeing a real change.

Many therapists will want to work closely with the child's school as well. The child may be seated in a quieter part of the room or in a study carrel, where distractions are minimal; be given tutoring or special time with the teacher; or be more closely monitored during free times, such as recess and lunch. The teacher may make special allowances for the child, such as letting him use a calculator or allowing him more time for classwork and exams. It often helps if a teacher shows the child how to be more organized in studying, gives clear and simple instructions, and provides books of tailor-made assignments. Ideally, the teacher will work as part of a team with the therapist.

Family therapy is another important adjunct to other treatments since a hyperactive child affects everyone in the family in some way. The hyperactive child, for example, is often the family scapegoat, bearing the brunt of blame for dissatisfactions that actually have other sources.

Diet and hyperactivity. Some contend that sugar, as well as other food additives, worsen the symptoms of hyperactivity. Others argue that no strong scientific evidence shows a connection.

Several controlled laboratory studies have found that sugar does not seem to increase physical activity or aggression in children, hyperactive or not. But studies in which mothers kept careful records of what their children ate at home and their activity level found that sugar snacks made hyperactive children more restless and aggressive.

One possibility is that the culprit is not sugar per se, but carbohydrates, including sugar, which replenish a child's supply of available energy and so allow him or her to be more active—or hyperactive.

While the debate continues, there does seem to be a percentage of hyperactive children who are sensitive to sugar in their diets. It certainly makes sense to restrict your child's diet of sweets to see if it will make a difference.

DEPRESSION IN CHILDREN

For many years, psychotherapists debated whether a child could be depressed at all; most thought that clinical depression occurred only in adults. Now, though, some authorities claim to be able to recognize depression in children as young as two. The new awareness of childhood depression has made therapists recognize that depression is often part of other childhood problems. For instance:

- Neglected and abused children are often depressed.
- Children can be depressed not just after the death of a parent or sibling, but also after other "losses," such as moving away from friends or changing schools.
- Children with a physical disability, such as severe asthma, can be depressed, especially if it interferes with their playing with other children or keeping up in school or makes them feel bad about themselves.
- Children with unrecognized learning problems can become depressed because of the frustration of trying to keep up with their schoolmates.

In such cases, once the full diagnosis is made, the primary problem would be the focus of therapy, and the child's depression would be regarded as a secondary symptom.

Any problem that interferes with a child's schooling, family life, or friendships is likely to make him or her feel miserable. That unhappiness takes many forms.

☐ Joan, an artist, was left alone to raise her three children after Ron, her husband, left her to live with another woman in a distant city. Though Joan was able to talk to her children sensitively about their feelings, her own anxiety and depression was palpable. Each of the children started having emotional problems.

Pete, eleven, was the oldest. His reaction to his father's disappearance was anger. He got into lots of fights at school and was demanding at home, trying to take charge. He stole from his mother and from his friends, then denied stealing even when caught red-handed. He teased and baited his younger brother and sister mercilessly.

Sally, seven, was a quiet, dreamy child. Always obedient at home, Sally was close to her mother, comforting her when she had weeping spells. Somewhat shy, Sally became even more withdrawn after her father left. Although she had done well in first grade, she began to slip far behind despite extra help and even lost some of her ability to read and do math.

Teddy was just four and looked continually forlorn. He became stubborn at nursery school and clung to his mother desperately when she left him at the door. He demanded constant attention from his teachers and made no friends. His favorite spot at school was the teacher's lap.

All Joan's children are depressed, though each shows it very differently. None of these children would tell you he or she was sad, but Pete's angry defiance, Sally's withdrawal, and Teddy's clinging are all common ways children express their depression. A child may not even realize that it is unusual to feel so depressed.

Signs to Look For

Depression shows itself in children in both obvious and subtle ways and is indicated by a pattern of several of these symptoms. For some children, some of these signs are part of their normal personality or are part of a phase of development. They are taken as signs of depression only when they are seen by the child or his or her parents as a cause for worry, and they are a marked change from the way the child usually is.

The signs of depression in children include:

- *Unhappy mood.* The child seems or says that he or she is sad or lonely, feels hopeless, or is generally pessimistic about everything. There can be dramatic mood swings, with the child seeming content one moment and quite unhappy the next. Sometimes, though, the child is just sullen.
- *Negativity or oversensitivity.* The unhappiness can also show up as being "difficult": the child is irritable, easily annoyed, and hard to please. The hypersensitive child, who cries so easily, may also be depressed.
- *Self-criticism.* The child puts himself down, saying he's dumb or ugly, for instance. If complimented, he belittles the remark, but if criticized or if he fails at something, he is preoccupied with it. He may be convinced he is being persecuted—that other kids "hate him" or are out to get him.

- *Death wishes.* Thoughts of suicide are one of the most serious symptoms of depression. At its mildest, the child says, "I wish I were dead." If a child has looked into ways to kill himself, this is a sign that *immediate* intervention is called for.
- *Belligerence.* The child is quarrelsome and hard to get along with; is continually disrespectful of parents, teachers, and other authorities; and is generally hostile and agitated. Sometimes his anger will flare suddenly; he will be quick to pick a fight with other youngsters.
- *Sleep problems.* The child cannot fall asleep at bedtime or awakens in the middle of the night and cannot get back to sleep. Or the child will sleep far longer than usual, having trouble waking up or getting out of bed in the morning.
- *Drop in school performance.* The child no longer makes his or her usual effort at schoolwork and is indifferent to dropping grades. Teachers complain that he or she is daydreaming, can't concentrate, or can't seem to remember anything. The child doesn't do assignments in school or finish homework. Even extracurricular activities are no longer of interest.
- *Dislike of school.* Where before school was enjoyable, the child now doesn't want to go, claiming to "hate" school.
- *Social withdrawal.* The child loses interest in playing with friends or in doing things with groups of children. He or she becomes unfriendly to former chums and is much less outgoing.
- *Physical complaints.* Complains of headaches, stomach pain, muscle aches, or other physical problems.
- *Fatigue and apathy.* Energy level drops noticeably. The child loses enthusiasm for favorite pursuits, becomes lethargic.
- *Appetite change.* The child may lose his or her usual appetite or start eating unusually large amounts. Obvious signs are a large, sudden weight loss or gain. In children under six, this can show up as the failure to make expected weight gains.

□ Toby is a sixth-grader whose temper tantrums, dropping grades, and threats of quitting brought him to the attention of the school psychologist. When his mother brought Toby for his appointment, Toby refused to talk. He sat glaring at his mother while she told his story.

Toby's father had deserted the family the year before. A few months later, Toby's problems began. He would do no homework and so was failing all his courses. He had often been suspended for fighting. At home, he picked fights with his younger sister and refused to do his chores.

Once outgoing, Toby now refuses to have anything to do with his friends, whom he calls "stupid and boring." He spends the day in his room playing with toy soldiers, reading comics, and eating candy and potato chips. He's gained twenty pounds in five months. He often wakes up in the middle of the night with "scary dreams" about his father and has trouble getting back to sleep. When his mother punishes him, Toby says he's going to run away. "He doesn't seem like my son anymore," his mother says.

This classic picture of a depressed child does not include every sign of depression, the most notably absent being sadness. Any depressed child will typically display just a handful, not all the signs of depression.

A child may display some of these signs for up to several weeks without there being any lasting and serious underlying problem. This is especially true when a child is grieving, whether over the loss of a loved one, after a move, or because of some other sad event. Normal grieving in children, as in adults, does not indicate a need for psychotherapy.

Common Variations

When adults become depressed, they fall prey to a pessimistic mode of thinking and can't seem to see hope in anything. With children, the cognitive symptoms of depression often show up as trouble in school. The child is so preoccupied with whatever has caused the depression that he or she has trouble marshaling the concentration to grasp what the teacher is saying. A drop in a child's scores on achievement tests is a common clue to depression. Because it shows up as difficulty in learning, teachers are often among the first to notice.

Subtle signs. Sometimes parents are not as able or willing as a child's teacher to notice the signs of depression, particularly when they are less obvious. In part this may be because parents do not have many other children of similar age with whom to compare their child as a teacher does; in part it may be a reluctance to admit there is a problem. Remember, the parent who gets help for his or her child when needed is doing the best thing, even when it means facing up to a problem in the family.

Another reason parents may not notice a child's depression is that the signs may be "silent." A child who is obsessed by burdensome guilt, worries, and sadness, bad feelings about himself, or even thoughts of suicide, may say nothing at all to his parents or anyone else. This is more true the older a child is. When the only signs on the surface may be a sullen mood, withdrawal, or apathy, it may be especially hard for a parent to judge just how serious the problem is. A psychotherapist who interviews the child can best gauge this.

Depression commonly shows up in children, especially young children, as physical complaints. This is not because they're "faking" a tummy ache, but because physical pain is a more concrete way to express their deepest feelings. The physical problem is a way of saying "something hurts me" or "I feel bad."

Depressed children, unlike depressed adults, frequently become aggressive. The child who suddenly becomes hard to handle, picks fights with other children or siblings, or displays an uncharacteristic defiance may well be depressed. He is not a real troublemaker, but is showing the world that he is in pain.

Age and depression. Children show depression differently depending on their age. Very young children typically show depression by apathy. Usually children will not have periods of prolonged sadness until they reach five or six. Between five and eight, depressed children tend to withdraw or be very angry. Though they feel sad, they often cannot talk about it. Instead they give clues through their moping and apathy or irritability.

As children grow, the potential causes of depression change, too. As children become far more attuned to other people and what others think of them, they may blame themselves for things that have little to do with them, such as parents' arguing or separating. Their self-blame may lead them to depression. Or, for instance, a girl with a learning disability may be emotionally unaffected by the problem at age five, but at nine she may become depressed by it, see herself as a failure, feel ashamed of disappointing her parents and teachers, and feel she isn't measuring up to her friends.

A depressed teenager is likely to feel hopelessness along with many other symptoms. In the depressed teenager's mind, a small setback takes on huge proportions: a single social rebuff means a life as an outcast; a bad grade means academic disgrace. These same thinking patterns are found in adults with depression. The full gamut of adult symptoms can appear in the depressed teen. But for adolescents who have not lived long enough to see life problems resolve themselves, setbacks can seem intractable problems. That is one reason that, say, a failing grade can lead to suicidal thoughts. Indeed, it can be helpful to point out to a teenager that such problems can resolve and may even seem trivial with the passage of time.

There is an especially high risk of depression for girls in the year or two after puberty.

What Therapists Recommend

Approach. No one treatment approach is clearly preferred for childhood depression. Substantial numbers of clinicians would use each of the major therapies. The most frequently recommended, though, was a psychodynamic approach that would help children understand what's troubling them. But not far behind were family therapy and a supportive approach that helps children develop better ways of coping with and managing their day-to-day problems. Many therapists would use some combination of these three approaches. Also recommended is cognitive therapy, an approach that is fast becoming a preferred therapy for depression in adults.

Medication. Therapists seem evenly divided on the question of whether a depressed child should receive antidepressant medication along with psychotherapy. Almost half recommend that a child receive such medication if the symptoms warrant, but half recommend psychotherapy without medication.

Setting. Office visits are the norm. But if the depression is extremely severe, or the child seems suicidal, then brief hospitalization in a child unit or some other form of brief residential treatment may be needed until the crisis passes.

Format. Individual sessions are recommended for the child, along with family meetings involving parents or the entire family. If a child has been withdrawn for very long, group therapy can help rebuild social skills and confidence.

Frequency. Once-a-week therapy is the norm, unless a crisis demands meetings more often.

Duration. Open-ended. The length of time a child may need therapy for depression can vary greatly.

What You Should Know About Therapy

Why treat depression in children? Won't it go away with time? Sometimes, but not always. And if it does fade, it may recur later when the child is under stress. The longer a child is depressed, and the older he or she becomes, the more deeply entrenched and harder to change the depression is likely to become. That means it makes sense to treat depression even in the very young child.

Before a child is treated for depression, the psychotherapist will want to evaluate the child's recent life, to better understand any stresses and traumas that might be causing it. The evaluation typically includes interviews with the parents, sometimes with the whole family. Teachers' impressions are important, too: most children spend as much time at school as with their parents.

One of the difficulties in therapy of any kind with depressed children is that they tend to withdraw into silence, which demands the therapist be more active and directive.

If the depression seems due to a specific loss or trauma, such as the death of a parent, the treatment will usually be shorter, under six months. If there is no clear cause for the depression, and it is long-standing, the treatment can go on for a year or more. Your therapist should be able to estimate how long treatment will last after a session or two of consultation.

If therapy alone doesn't work, antidepressant medication can be tried along with therapy. Some scientific reports suggest that the antidepressants commonly used with adults are effective with some children, but there is no strong, conclusive evidence. One particular drug, imipramine, a tricyclic antidepressant, has been reported by some researchers to help with depression in children. But imipramine is not technically approved by the FDA for use with children under twelve except for treating enuresis (see p. 614, on medications). Even so, it is commonly used by many child psychiatrists in treating depressed children.

Note: A child should not take any psychiatric medication without a full medical evaluation first. *Never give a child medications prescribed for someone else.* There is a special danger for children from tricyclic antidepressants (see p. 610), which are commonly prescribed for adults with depression. In children, tricyclics can cause severe heart problems.

OBSESSIVE-COMPULSIVE BEHAVIOR

Many children will develop their own rituals, such as always carrying a particular piece of cloth, being sure to count the squares on the sidewalk as they walk by, or carefully jumping over the cracks on the sidewalk instead of walking on them.

Such rituals are normal. But when a child comes to rely so much on private rituals that they get in the way of normal daily life, then psychotherapy is called for. These disruptive rituals may take the form of *obsessions,* constantly repeated thoughts that the child cannot seem to get out of his head, such as the idea that everything is covered with germs and he will become ill if he touches things, or the incessant fear that his parents will get sick and die. Such obsessions often go hand in hand with *compulsions,* actions that the child feels compelled to repeat over and over, such as washing his hands or taking a shower many times a day, or compulsively counting things.

The children who suffer from these problems are typically of normal intelligence, and although they may see the illogic of their compulsions, they are at a loss to explain both their actions and the repetitive thoughts that underlie them.

Children do not necessarily realize that their compulsions are a problem unless their parents or others tell them so. But just telling a compulsive child to stop is not enough to end the problem. When a child tries to resist a compulsion, the result is a buildup of tension; yielding to the compulsion relieves the tension. The more the compulsion is indulged, the less likely a child is to try to fight it.

While older children may recognize that their compulsions are illogical or in excess, young children may firmly believe that their compulsions are a reasonable remedy for whatever they are trying to prevent.

There is something soothing about rituals; they help us control our anxieties. Religions everywhere offer them to handle the large uncertainties that surround birth and death. There is reassurance in the cadence of a christening, or the solemnity of a funeral. Common superstitions are garden-variety rituals: not walking under ladders, avoiding black cats.

Likewise to control anxieties, people often develop private rituals: wearing a "good luck" piece of clothing or jewelry, for instance. The reliance on such private rituals begins early in life. It is common among children and is perfectly normal— within limits. For very young children, bedtime and feeding rituals offer a sense of security, and they can be reassuring to older children, too, particularly in times of stress.

Signs to Look For

It is quite normal for a child to entertain some ideas that seem obsessive or some habits that are compulsive: touching all the pickets on a fence or all the lampposts passed on the way to school, for instance. Some obsessive thoughts are part of the "magical" thinking typical of young children. The most common of these magical beliefs is that some dreaded event will be prevented if the child repeats some action that, somehow, will influence the course of events: "If I fold all the clothes in my drawer, then my parents won't fight."

Such thoughts and habits are benign if they remain occasional flights of fancy. But should they become intense compulsions, then your child will experience them as unwelcome, unpleasant, and even disturbing. *When they interfere with your child's life, then they require treatment.*

□ At seven, Josh's whole life was ruled by rituals. He could only sit down to eat if he had opened and closed the kitchen door four times, then touched each corner of the table four times. He had to chew his food twenty times before swallowing. He would only take a toy from his toy chest after he had tapped the lid three times, and he would have to put the toy back and start over if it touched the chest while he was taking it out. If he dropped a toy while playing with it, he would immediately put it back in the toy chest, passing it in and out three times before finally leaving it inside. Josh was quiet and passive at school and had no friends.

Josh is typical of children whose compulsions are so severe they require treatment. While many children briefly adopt one or another of the kinds of compulsive habits that are seen in obsessive-compulsive disorder, they rarely reach these extremes.

The main signs of a serious problem include:

• *intrusive, repeated thoughts.* These obsessions can take the form of ideas, impulses, or images that seem disturbing to the child—for example, the persistent impulse to do something the child knows is "bad," or the incessant fear that something bad is going to happen. The child tries to counter these thoughts with some other thought or action.

- *repetitive, stereotyped actions.* These compulsions are in response to the child's obsessions and are meant to neutralize them—for instance, to prevent something bad from happening, the child will perform a specific action. The actions, however, are not logically connected to the danger—the connection is magical.
- *distress or detriment to the child's life.* Typically the obsessions or compulsions are time-consuming, lasting up to an hour a day or more, and interfere with the child's having a normal family, school, or social life.

□ Ellen, nine, would panic whenever her parents would go out and leave her at home. She was certain that they would fall victim to some calamity: an auto accident, or that the building they were going to—whether a movie or a PTA meeting at school—would catch fire. Or, if they had to drive over a bridge, Ellen was petrified by the thought that it would collapse.

Thinking it might somehow magically save them, Ellen would frantically draw a picture of the horrible fate she imagined for them. The pictures were graphic in their depiction of the blood and gore of the calamity that, in Ellen's vivid thoughts, befell her parents. To "make sure it won't happen," she would tear her drawings into hundreds of tiny pieces. This, she explained, would ensure that her parents could return home safely

What Therapists Recommend

Approach. The treatment of choice is fast becoming behavior therapy, often in combination with cognitive therapy, in which treatment would focus on directly changing the symptoms or thoughts that underlie them. Also recommended by some therapists is a psychodynamic approach, in which part of the treatment would focus on exploring the symbolic meaning and origin of the obsessions or compulsions.

Family therapy is almost always included, especially with younger children.

Medication. For teenagers, Anafranil (clomipramine) is often helpful in reducing the intensity of symptoms, helping the child regain calm and some sense of control over the problem, making psychotherapy more effective.

Setting. Clinicians are virtually unanimous in recommending that obsessive-compulsive disorder be treated in office visits. With behavior therapy, that typically includes interventions at home as well. If the disorder is extremely disabling, treatment may involve briefly hospitalizing the child.

Format. The consensus is that obsessive-compulsive disorder should be treated in individual sessions, combined with family sessions or consultation with parents as needed.

Frequency. Once a week, or more often in behavior therapy.

Duration. Open-ended.

What You Should Know About Therapy

The three major approaches to treating obsessive-compulsive disorder in children are behavioral and psychodynamic therapy, and medication. Of the therapies, behavioral approaches seem most effective.

Therapists with a psychodynamic orientation will focus on identifying the anxieties that lie behind your child's symptoms. The theory is that if a given obsession or compulsion disappears while the fear remains, another obsession or compulsion will take its place. This approach can often help with children who are able to confront underlying anxieties with the help of a therapist.

But the growing consensus is that a behavioral approach, which focuses on limiting the symptoms, is generally more suitable. A behavior therapist will spend little or no time trying to discover the symbolic meaning of symptoms.

In the behavioral approach, for example, your child might be directed to resist compulsions for steadily increasing periods of time—a simple approach that, if your child is motivated enough, can be quite effective in learning to resist them entirely.

Behavior therapists will first find out the specific details of compulsive ritual: when and how they are performed, how often, exactly what they involve. Then they will restrict the time the child is permitted to engage in them. The usual method is response prevention combined with exposure, which means the child is exposed to the feared objects (such as "contaminated" items), but prevented from enacting the compulsion. This requires repeated sessions several times a week, with parents asked to continue the regimen between sessions.

The medication that has come into use for obsessive-compulsive disorder is clomipramine (trade name Anafranil). For many people, it seems to weaken the power of obsessive thoughts and of the urge to perform compulsive rituals. Ordinarily used as an antidepressant, Anafranil has some side effects, such as dry mouth, constipation, and drowsiness (see p. 612).

If a psychodynamic or behavioral approach is not enough in itself to overcome your child's obsessions or compulsions, then Anafranil will probably be recommended in addition.

POSTTRAUMATIC STRESS

Unfortunately, far too many adults believe that the best way to handle a child's trauma is to ignore it. The belief is that if you don't talk about it, the problem will go away. However, just as with adults, children need help recovering from trauma and can suffer serious consequences if it is not dealt with. And if children receive therapy soon after the trauma, they can often recover more fully and completely than adults.

Children experience some of the same traumas as adults, such as hurricanes, floods, auto accidents, and the like. Children can also be traumatized by witnessing acts of violence. A large proportion of murders, for instance, are witnessed by a child of the victim. The same is true for rapes and assaults. Children who are the victims of sexual, physical, and emotional abuse all show degrees of posttraumatic stress.

Sexual abuse of children, which is being reported at an alarmingly growing rate, can be exceptionally traumatizing, particularly when the abuser is a loved one, such as a parent, relative, or friend of the family, which is most often the case. Often the child who is being sexually abused will turn to a parent or relative to report the abuse and be disbelieved, ridiculed, or angrily dismissed. Because it is a betrayal of trust by the very people the child is dependent on and needs to trust, this sexual abuse is the most insidious and traumatizing form. Disbelief of the child's story only continues the abuse in another form and compounds the injury.

Posttraumatic stress in children differs somewhat from the reaction in adults, depending on the age of the child, though by adolescence, children start to react much as do grown-ups. Instead of burying the trauma, as many adults do, and because they typically feel they can't mention it to anyone—or they have been threatened into silence—young children act it out over and over in their games or artwork. This is especially true in children who have been severely traumatized and have gone undiagnosed or untreated.

These repetitive games are usually grim and obsessive. A young girl who had been kidnapped in a van, for instance, played "Traveling Barbie," in which her doll would go somewhere in a van but not come back. Second-grade boys who had survived an attack on their recess by a man who killed five children with a submachine gun made that one of their favorite games: someone with an automatic rifle shoots a group of children at play.

These repetitive games tend to continue and change unless the traumatic experiences are somehow resolved.

Signs to Look For

The main signs of posttraumatic stress in children include:

- Nightmares of the trauma or of events like it, such as being chased; and night terrors, terrifying dreams so vivid the child acts as though they were real.
- Sleep problems, such as inability to go to sleep or fear of sleeping alone.
- Fear of "ghosts" or "monsters" or other imaginary terrors.
- Startling easily, such as becoming frightened by a sudden sound.

- Apathy and indifference to games, schoolwork, or playing; listlessness.
- Being on guard against some imagined danger, or hypervigilance.
- Defiance of authority, including parents and teachers; a good child suddenly turning "bad."
- Physical complaints, including stomachaches and headaches.
- Repetitive games that reenact the trauma.
- Fears of anything even remotely related to the trauma.

Therapy for Children with Posttraumatic Stress

Therapy aims to help the child overcome the trauma: to remember what happened, speak about it, understand it, and tolerate the feelings the trauma evokes.

If a child is reluctant at first to talk about what happened, the therapist may ask the child to make a drawing or play. Usually something in the drawing or play is a hidden reference to the trauma or a link the child may make in telling a story about the drawing.

When children are able to talk about traumas, it can create an emotional distance from the events that frees them up. During treatment children are gradually encouraged to express their feelings and to try to master them. Alternatively, it may not be necessary to talk about the trauma directly. Young children, especially, can often "work through" their feelings in play alone, with the help of a therapist. *Play therapy*—drawing, game playing, use of dolls and figures—can be a prelude to talk or be healing in itself.

Such therapy can be a great relief for children. Finding someone who wants to know what they've been through, and who can listen without backing away, lets the child feel less vulnerable about what happened, easing fears. Because a child's friends and family typically cannot listen to his or her stories without becoming upset themselves, a professional is better able to play this role.

However, if a child's trauma is from abuse or neglect at home, no amount of therapy will help while the child remains there. In such cases, the child may have to be placed elsewhere, such as in foster care, and family therapy is almost always indicated. The family will have to undergo treatment, too, if the child is to be safely returned to the home.

BED-WETTING AND POOR BOWEL CONTROL

Most every toddler will have an episode or two of bed-wetting or poor bowel control after being toilet trained. Only if it becomes a problem to the child—for instance, by preventing him from sleeping at a friend's house or making him feel ashamed— or if it occurs at least twice a month in a six-year-old, or even once a month in an older child, should you consider therapy for your child.

Children may also wet themselves while they're awake. Most bed-wetting occurs during the first third of the night; sometimes the child will dream of bed-wetting. Loss of bowel control typically occurs during the day. The problem can occur after a child has had a year or even longer of good bladder or bowel control, or it may persist from the beginning of toilet training.

Bed-wetting is a fairly common problem in children. About 7 to 15 percent of boys and 3 percent of girls have the problem at age five. By age ten bed-wetting is still a problem in 3 percent of boys and 2 percent of girls. And even at eighteen, almost 1 percent of boys have problems with wetting the bed at night, although it is virtually nonexistent in girls at that age. Poor bowel control, by contrast, is much rarer: only about 1 percent of five-year-olds have the problem.

Children who bed-wet typically feel embarrassed and ashamed. They are reluctant to go to a slumber party or may refuse to consider summer camp. If children feel ridiculed by their parents, siblings, and friends, this can undermine their self-esteem even more.

Getting angry at your child will not help solve the problem and will add to the emotional burden. Try not to make your child feel judged and do let him or her know that you realize the bed-wetting is not intentional.

Many children "outgrow" the problem, but if it does not seem to be clearing up on its own, therapy can help. Explain to your child that seeing a therapist may help and that you will support him or her in these efforts.

Signs to Look For

- Repeatedly being unable to control urination; wetting bedclothes or bedding during sleep, or clothes during the day.
- Doing so at least twice a month at age five or six, or once a month or more after age six.

Poor bowel control. Children sometimes develop poor bowel control because they are anxious about using a toilet, experience painful defecation, or because refusing to move their bowels has become an expression of emotional opposition or defiance. Often their incontinence occurs after a period of constipation or voluntary retention, which builds up pressure in their bowels that they can no longer control.

What Therapists Recommend

Approach. The most highly recommended approaches are behavioral therapy and family therapy. Often these are combined, with the family in charge of the behavior modification regimen.

Medication. Yes, but it is usually only partially effective and is definitely not the treatment to try first.

Setting. Office visits, unless the problems are so severe that the behavior cannot be managed at home. In that case, a brief hospitalization may be necessary.

Format. A combination of individual sessions with a child therapist and sessions where parents come, too.

Frequency. Normally, once a week.

Duration. Treatment should typically take somewhere between one to six months.

What You Should Know About Therapy

In some cases bladder or bowel control problems begin after a child has had good control for a year or so. But if there never was good control, the problem is more likely to be physical and require medical treatment. *In either case, treatment should begin with a medical workup.*

Possible physical causes include an obstruction in the urinary tract, delayed development of the urinary tract, infection, or diabetes. Once your pediatrician has given your child a physical exam and determined that there is no underlying medical cause, then therapy is an option.

A therapist will need a clear picture of the circumstances that surround the bed-wetting. You will probably be asked to keep track for several weeks of such details as the frequency of your child's bed-wetting and any significant changes in his or her feelings, your feelings, or your interactions that may accompany or precede the incidents.

Common-sense steps you can take on your own to increase the chances of a dry night include restricting your child's fluid intake before bed, keeping him away from caffeine drinks such as colas, and making sure he takes a trip to the toilet at bedtime. If there is a real problem, though, these preventive measures seem to make little difference.

Therapy typically begins by seeking to discover if something is upsetting the child that might, for example, make him reluctant to use the bathroom. Or there may be a subtle reinforcement for incontinence, such as mother's getting into bed with the child in the middle of the night. If such fears or reinforcers are discovered, therapy will focus on changing them. Another standard method is to have the child take charge of changing and washing his sheets or clothes when they are soiled.

Another effective treatment—but usually tried later—is an alarm that awakens your child when he or she starts to wet the bed. These "bed alarms," available through pharmacists, have a bell that rings when urine completes a circuit between two small electrodes clipped on the bedclothes. The better models go off when they detect just a drop or two of urine.

The alarm suddenly wakes the child, making him or her spontaneously contract the bladder sphincter. Then the child can get up and go to the bathroom. The theory is that the child becomes more aware of nighttime bladder pressure. The devices don't work immediately and need to be used for two or three weeks after several consecutive dry nights. But among children who use them, about two-thirds are cured.

Another behavioral approach has your child keep track of wet and dry nights or days. Each dry night or day earns the child a reward. Obviously, wet ones do not get a punishment. This technique can be used with others, such as the bed alarm.

A method called retention control training, in which a child is taught to delay urinating a few minutes each day, is sometimes used. However, it is time-consuming and frustrating for parent and child alike, and the bell alarm seems simpler and more effective for most children.

A psychodynamic therapy may help with other emotional problems, such as low self-esteem, that can arise as a result of prolonged bed-wetting. But psychodynamic psychotherapy is not, in itself, the most effective way to stop this problem.

Medication. If behavioral methods do not help, and if your child is upset by the problem, you may want to consider medication. Imipramine, an antidepressant (see p. 610), has been found effective in some children. But the medication usually does not make a child completely "dry"; it simply lowers the frequency of bed-wetting.

Note: A few urologists recommend surgical treatments that enlarge the bladder. But there is slim evidence, if any, that these are effective, and they can traumatize a child. Behavioral treatments should definitely be tried first and the surgical approaches be avoided unless there is another compelling medical reason.

EATING DISORDERS

The two main eating disorders are anorexia and bulimia. In *anorexia* people so dread gaining weight that they effectively starve themselves. In *bulimia* people gorge themselves, often in secret, and then purge themselves, usually by making themselves throw up what they have just eaten. The underlying problem in both is a morbid fear of getting fat. And along with that fear is another problem: poor self-esteem.

The two eating problems can go together. As many as half of anorexic people also sometimes go through the eating binges and purges of bulimia. Many bulimics have been anorexic before, while others may lose a drastic amount of weight and become anorexic.

Most people with these problems are women in their teenage or early adult years. As many as one in ten to one in twenty women in those age groups may have these problems to some degree, and the problems seem to be getting more common and beginning earlier. There are reports of the problems in girls as young as seven and eight.

Anorexia and bulimia are usually found among middle- or upper-class women. One theory is that they learn to emphasize thinness as a criterion of female attractiveness. Anorexics carry the famous saying of the Duchess of Windsor that one can never be too rich or too thin to a pathological extreme. People in certain groups in which thinness is at a premium are also at risk: dancers and fashion models, for example.

Eating problems are dangerous. They are among the few emotional disturbances that can lead to death, usually through starvation. Other complications include depression and often a difficult family situation, such as overprotective or rigid parents. Parents of people with eating disorders are sometimes themselves preoccupied with physical appearance, dieting, making a good social impression, and a perfectionistic standard of attractiveness—all of which can contribute to eating problems.

Anorexia

People with anorexia starve themselves, thinking that they are too fat when in fact they are dangerously thin. They react to gaining a pound or two with the same intensity that most people feel if they gain ten or twenty.

The weight loss goes far beyond ordinary dieting: it's at least 25 percent of body weight, and often more. Because anorexics typically are not obese to start, their weight loss is all the more dramatic. In adolescent anorexics, the loss of weight is so extreme that it can interfere with normal growth.

The extreme weight loss is due to a severe cutback in the number of calories eaten, especially from carbohydrates and other "fattening" foods. Anorexics also purge—by vomiting or taking laxatives—and often fast, skipping meals entirely. Some engage in vigorous aerobic exercise to work off what little they've eaten. Often an anorexic will try to avoid eating with anyone else, including her family.

Many anorexics also go through eating binges, like bulimics. These are typically at night and in secret, and trigger a sense of guilt and anxiety, which is relieved by inducing vomiting.

Once the cycle of extreme weight loss begins, it feeds on itself through the effects of what soon becomes starvation, or close to it. The symptoms include intense preoccupation with eating (or not eating), combining unusual foods in meals, and substituting caffeine beverages and chewing gum for meals. Anorexics often enjoy cooking for other people, collecting recipes, and otherwise thinking about food—but not eating it.

One of the early signs of extreme weight loss is the halting of menstrual periods. Among the many metabolic changes that semistarvation brings in anorexia is a sense of calm that belies the seriousness of what is happening physically. This state reinforces an apathy toward eating and may lift the depression present in many cases. Other metabolic changes can create medically dangerous conditions. As the starvation becomes more extreme, it actually leads to loss of appetite.

Oddly, anorexics very often were "model children" before developing the problem. Once the problem emerges, eating often becomes a battlefield between parents and child. As the parents become more frantic, the anorexic becomes more stubborn. The underlying issue for the anorexic is one of control ("they're trying to run my life"), while for her parents, it is rejection ("if she won't eat my food, it's me she doesn't like").

Several psychological problems often accompany anorexia, though none is part of the problem per se. Among these are depression, anxiety, phobia or panic attacks, obsessions, irritability, stealing (often of candy and laxatives). Sexual problems are common, too, particularly a loss of interest in sex, or with teenagers, a delay in sexual development.

Many anorexics are fragile socially and feel an overwhelming sense of ineffectiveness. This puts them at a loss when they leave their family or are confronted by other demands, such as in a new job or at college. Many cling to home and family, even long after most people their age have left home.

Most people treated for anorexia will gain weight in the short term, and over the next several years they will return to a normal life. But a small number—around 5 percent—are in grave physical danger and may die from starvation or metabolic difficulties.

Anorexia: Signs to Look For

The hallmark of anorexia is "dieting" to the point of extreme weight loss. The signs include:

- Refusing to eat enough to keep one's weight from dropping 15 percent or more below the standard level for one's height and age.
- Dread of becoming fat or gaining weight, despite already being skin-and-bones.
- Unrealistic body perception, so that what is thin seems "fat." Small weight gains are perceived as the first step toward obesity, and the person feels that some part of the body (thighs, waist) is "much too fat" when it is not.
- Missing three or more periods because of thinness.

Several medical signs of being severely underweight are having low blood pressure, a slowed heart rate, or growing baby-fine hair. A physician can detect other metabolic markers of semistarvation.

□ Somehow Miriam got the idea that she was way too fat. Wherever it came from, that conviction was firm by the time she was fourteen. When she looked at her own body, which to other's eyes was already reedy and thin, Miriam saw only chubbiness. An avid dieter, Miriam began to take her diets to extremes. Some days she'd eat only a bowl of rice and nibble at an orange. Other days she'd eat nothing and drink only fruit juice. Along with her diet, she began a strict program of vigorous aerobics.

The result was that Miriam's already thin frame lost 20 pounds, down to 90 from 110. Given her 5'8" height, the weight loss made her look positively skeletal. But whenever anyone (usually her mother or father) said she was much too thin, she'd point to her thighs or stomach and say, "No I'm not—I've still got a lot more weight to lose."

Despite her own reluctance to eat, Miriam was always in the kitchen at home. She'd gladly help her mother cook, and collected recipes for desserts, her specialty. But when the family sat down to eat, a battle ensued: though Miriam had cooked, she'd take just a teaspoonful, saying that was all she wanted. And her parents, distraught, would spend the entire meal trying to get her to eat more.

Bulimia

Bulimia is closely related to anorexia, and the two problems sometimes occur in the same person. In bulimia, people go on uncontrollable eating binges, then "purge," using laxatives, vomiting, or going on a fast or strict diet to lose weight. But unlike anorexics, bulimics may be of normal weight; they do not usually diet or purge so extremely that they take on the skeletal look of an anorexic, though that sometimes happens. More typically bulimics go through extreme changes in weight, sometimes up to ten pounds in a day.

Of course, most people who put themselves on diets are tempted to "pig out" from time to time, and many do. But the bulimic does so to an extreme, both in terms of how much she eats and how often she does it (sometimes ten or more times in a weekend). And few dieters who slip and overeat try to remedy the lapse by purging afterward. Though they may feel remorse, the slip may even stiffen their resolve to follow the diet.

The bulimic's binges are secretive, done late at night or behind locked doors. Sometimes they are done with a friend who shares the same pattern. Bulimic practices, such as vomiting after an eating binge, are frequently passed from one friend to another. In some settings—such as college campuses—they are common among many women who do not carry it to extremes and so are not (or not yet) bulimic.

Binges are typically triggered by feeling down, a sense of guilt, worrying, or just a vague discomfort. The binge appeals as a way to comfort oneself.

During the binge, which can last anywhere from a few minutes to an hour or two, a bulimic typically feels "out of control." Bulimics say they feel almost as though in a trance: they don't feel hungry and eat way beyond the point of being and feeling full.

The foods bulimics like are usually sweet and fattening—cakes and pastries, ice cream, cookies. For most, these are foods they don't ordinarily permit themselves. The amounts consumed during a binge are, for most people, unimaginable: several cakes, quarts of ice cream, or boxes of cookies.

The next step is purging, usually self-induced vomiting, which banishes the discomfort of stomach distension. Purges can also take less rapid forms, such as heavy laxatives or diuretics, extreme exercise, or fasting.

Paradoxically, vomiting may itself encourage binges. Knowing that she can undo the effect of a binge may make the bulimic feel less need to control the urge to binge. Vomiting, by emptying the stomach, also leads to an increase in appetite. And the acids in vomit may deaden taste receptors in the mouth, which normally help people stop eating when they've had enough.

While the binge temporarily soothes the troubled feelings that brought it on, as time passes, the bulimic begins to regret it. She feels disgust or shame over it and may simply get depressed. Most see their binges as a compulsion they are unable to control.

Unlike anorexics, most bulimics are sexually interested and active. Their preoccupation with how their body looks and being sexually attractive may be one root of the problem. As many as half of bulimics have been objectively overweight and may have turned to purging at first as a way to lose weight.

Rapid weight loss and gain can create metabolic imbalances. Signs of these include swollen hands, feet, and ankles; weakness and dizziness; bloating and stomach pain; puffy cheeks and a painful swelling of salivary glands; and damaged teeth.

Bulimia usually begins during the teenage years or in the twenties. Like anorexics, the vast majority of bulimics—more than 95 percent—are women.

Bulimia: Signs to Look For

- *Binge eating.* Huge amounts of rich foods are gobbled, usually in secret, at least twice a week.
- *Loss of control over eating.* The person feels unable to keep from consuming huge amounts during the binge.
- *Purging.* To ease discomfort and the fear of weight gain, the binge is followed by induced vomiting, an extreme diet or fast, intense exercise, or the use of laxatives or diuretics.

☐ Susan had been a dieter since grammar school. By high school, she'd tried dozens of different diet plans, often encouraged by her mother, who was also an avid dieter. But her freshman year in college, her roommate told her about a new way to keep her weight under control: making herself vomit. The first week she tried it, she lost five pounds.

Knowing she could vomit freed Susan from something she'd always hated: constantly feeling half-starved. Now she felt she could eat as much as she wanted, and not have to pay a price. But as Susan began to use vomiting regularly, her eating began to get out of control. If something made her feel upset, she'd soothe herself by going on a binge: she would buy and eat an entire cheesecake, a tin of shortbread cookies, and a quart of chocolate ice cream, lock her door, and gobble it down in an hour's orgy of nonstop eating.

Though she always felt bad about it after, the binges seemed irresistible. Most nights she'd wait until her friends had gone to bed, then binge, vomit, and fall asleep.

What Therapists Recommend for Anorexia

Approach. About equally recommended are psychodynamic therapy, focusing on the patterns that have brought the eating problem about; behavior therapy, typically a systematic program for correcting eating habits; or a systems approach in family therapy, aimed at changing unhelpful patterns of interacting in the family.

Medication. Only if needed for depression or anxiety.

Setting. Therapy often begins with hospital treatment, then continues in office visits. Hospitalization is almost always necessary when an anorexic is dangerously underweight or medically unstable. If there is no immediate medical risk, therapy can be started on an outpatient basis.

Format. One-to-one therapy, often along with family treatment. Group therapy or a self-help group with other anorexics is also useful.

Frequency. Twice or more a week, especially for anorexics who are in physical danger. Once there is no emergency, once a week is usually sufficient.

Duration. Open-ended. It could take a year or two. In general, the less extreme the problem, the shorter the time needed.

What You Should Know About Therapy for Anorexia

Treatment for anorexia should begin with a medical examination to determine if there is serious physical danger or damage from malnutrition. At the outset, the person should be checked by several specialists, an internist and a nutritionist at a minimum, in addition to a psychotherapist.

The first goal of therapy is simple—to keep the person alive. This means getting her to put on weight. Other goals are equally concrete: get her to eat a diet that is nutritionally adequate and to overcome quirky eating habits. If the family is overly involved in an unhealthy way, then addressing family relationships is also a priority. And if the patient is too dependent or insecure, then boosting her self-confidence and independence will also be important goals.

Denial. At the outset, people with anorexia usually do not see themselves as needing therapy. Since part of their problem is a skewed perception of their body, they tend to minimize the seriousness of their weight loss, if they admit it at all. For some, being so thin is a kind of solace, a reassurance of being adequate.

All that makes it hard to convince someone with anorexia that she has a problem, let alone that she should get help. Anorexics rarely seek help on their own and often refuse it, at least at first. If you are trying to convince an anorexic to go into therapy, it may help to emphasize that this will help with secondary problems, such as feelings of depression or insomnia, rather than to emphasize that it will help her gain weight.

Hospitalization. If the weight loss has not been too drastic, therapy can take place in office visits while the person lives at home. But often cases of anorexia have progressed to the point of physical harm from malnutrition. If there is serious danger, a physician or psychiatrist is obligated to hospitalize, involuntarily if necessary.

Hospital treatment generally includes a behavioral program designed to gradually increase body weight by encouraging better eating habits. It may be too much to try to get the person back to a normal body weight, but every effort will be made to get her weight high enough to protect her from medical danger.

Gaining weight will undoubtedly make the anorexic anxious. Psychotherapy at this point will aim, in part, at supporting her efforts to gain weight and calming her fears of getting fat. After she leaves the hospital, therapy will continue, as will monitoring of her weight to be sure she is maintaining her gains.

What to expect in therapy. Treatment usually begins with a contract in which the anorexic agrees to make weight gain a goal. The agreement will specify the target weight and a series of steps to help her meet that target. It will help immensely if family members can help the patient work out the contract and support her in following it. She will also need to be monitored medically to ensure that she is not at physical risk.

What counts most is gaining weight, getting a nutritional balance, and being able to live more adaptively. At first, behavioral approaches, such as the weight-gaining contract, are the most important. Also important is correcting distorted thinking about what is "fat" and what is "thin." Later, however, gaining insight into what caused the problem may help keep the anorexic from falling back into the old habits.

Group therapy can be extremely helpful. In a group, people with anorexia find others who understand what they are going through. Some groups are psychodynamic, focusing on inner experiences and personal relationships. Others are cognitive-behavioral, trying to help group members correct the distorted ways of thinking that have led them to starve themselves, and to help them restore better eating habits.

Family therapy can be useful if the patient lives at home or is very close to her family. One technique sometimes used is having a therapy session over lunch, to change the kinds of interactions and power struggles that focus on how the recovering anorexic eats.

Self-help or support groups for anorexics can be an important adjunct to therapy, and most therapists will recommend joining one. See Appendix I, "Eating Disorders," for the listing of the National Association of Anorexia Nervosa and Associated Disorders, which can direct you to their local chapter.

Medication. No medication specifically helps with anorexia. Indeed, because weight loss makes the body extrasensitive to medications of all kinds, they should be used with great care. Antidepressants, to help when depression is part of the problem, are the most commonly prescribed medications.

What You Should Know About Therapy for Bulimia

Unlike most anorexics, people with bulimia usually feel they do have a problem and often welcome help. But too often bulimics wait for years before getting it.

If you have the problem, you should understand that change will be gradual, not sudden. Be patient with therapy at first. The most effective treatments for bulimia tackle it on a broad range of fronts: in addition to psychotherapy, you should get a good physical and consult a nutritionist.

Therapy can be individual or in a group, or a combination of both. Group therapy with others who share the problem is particularly effective for bulimia. Self-help groups and support groups also usually help.

Of the three approaches most common in treating bulimia, cognitive-behavioral therapy should probably be tried first. This approach focuses on helping you control your eating habits by using a gradual series of goals, and on correcting distorted thinking by tracking your moods and thoughts as they trigger the urge to binge.

Also effective is psychodynamic therapy, particularly if it focuses on your relationships and what your eating habits mean in terms of these. Family therapy is sometimes useful, particularly if you are still living at home. Therapy with your family can help you straighten out tensions that may lie behind some of your eating habits. And having your family know what you are trying to do can lead to essential support in overcoming bulimia.

Medication. Certain antidepressants seem to help in some cases. The two most commonly tried are tricyclics (see p. 610) and MAO inhibitors (p. 616). But if you have bulimia, you may be hypersensitive to medications or their side effects. And the MAO variety require you to keep certain dietary restrictions (no cheese, for instance), which may be difficult for you to comply with.

For medication to work, it usually has to be taken over a long period, since relapse rates are high when medication is stopped. This poses a problem for young women who plan to become pregnant.

Hospitalization. Hospitalization should not be necessary for bulimia, unless it is combined with anorexia or your purging has led to severe medical complications.

AUTISM

The most severe of all children's psychological problems is autism, or "pervasive developmental disorder," as it is now officially called. The reason for the new name is that there are a variety of such problems, the best known of which is autism. All the developmental disorders share the same feature: a devastating failure of normal psychological growth.

Autism and the other developmental disorders show up early in life—typically by age two or three. For instance, instead of cooing and smiling back when his or her mother or father smiles and talks, the infant may be indifferent, uninterested in any contact.

Most parents realize their child may have a serious developmental problem when the child is around age two or so, when the lack of normal sociability or speech begins to be noticeable. Other parents—particularly those of an only child—may not realize there is a problem until the child is three, four, or even five, when their child begins a play group or kindergarten, and the differences from other children become obvious.

These problems are quite rare, found in only one or two children in every thousand, with boys affected three or four times more often than girls. While these disorders seem to be due to a brain abnormality, no strong evidence suggests exactly what that abnormality might be or just what causes it. Autism has also been thought to be associated with a wide range of medical problems, from the mother's having had measles during pregnancy to lack of oxygen during childbirth. None of these is clearly related to autism, however.

Some evidence suggests that the tendency toward autism and related problems is inherited—siblings of a child who is autistic are more likely than other children to have a similar problem. But the tendency is slight: most siblings of autistic children are normal.

In earlier decades, some psychotherapists proposed that autism was due to the way parents interacted with their infants, or to some personality problem in one or the other parent. But careful studies have shown these theories to be unfounded. Worse, they needlessly stirred guilt in parents who already had the stress of life with a child who is difficult to care for.

If you suspect that your child may have a serious developmental problem, you should have an evaluation done by a child psychiatrist or psychologist familiar with treating infants and toddlers. Autism is difficult to treat, and the earlier in life treatment begins, the better the outlook.

There is no general prognosis for therapy with developmental disorders because the range of difficulties they present for a child vary tremendously. No therapy can "cure" autism or other developmental disorders, but some interventions can make a large difference in the kind of life your child will lead. For fewer and fewer children, the best outcome will be living in a supervised facility; for increasing numbers it will be joining other children at school. Some will even go on to college and lead a normal life.

Signs to Look For

The child who has a pervasive developmental disorder will seem different from children of the same age, even to the casual observer, displaying any of a range of deficits in abilities. As the child grows older, these deficits become increasingly marked. Generally, the younger the child when the deficits begin to show up, the more severe the problems are likely to become.

No single pattern or problem is displayed by every child with a developmental disorder, but areas of difficulty include social interaction, communication, and bizarre behavior or activities.

Social Interaction

The child shows no interest in other people or responds strangely. This may mean not liking to cuddle, look you in the eye, or smile back at you. Toddlers and young children may show no interest in playing with other children. The main signs of problems in social interaction include:

- Absence of interest in other people, ranging from treating others as though they were inanimate objects (in the most troubled children) to an indifference to the emotional needs of others, such as the right to privacy (in less troubled children).
- Lack of the need to be comforted when upset, hurt, or ill. The child does not turn to anyone to be soothed or may soothe himself in a fixed, bizarre way, such as by rocking back and forth intently.
- Fails to learn by imitating, such as by saying a word such as *doggy* back to a grown-up or by waving hello or good-bye. Sometimes this takes the form of imitating a word or movement completely out of context, in a mechanical style.
- Lack of social playfulness. The child prefers to play alone or doesn't respond when others try to play with him or her.
- Makes no friends, either because the child does not seem at all interested in having friends or because he or she is awkward and out of touch with the conventions of playing.

Communication

One of the first signs of trouble most parents of children with severe developmental problems notice is that the child fails to learn language or develops odd habits of speech. Unlike deaf children they seem altogether indifferent to communicating with their parents, family, or anyone else. If they do speak, they often display bizarre speech mannerisms. Typical signs of communication difficulties include:

- lack of speech or other means of communicating, such as facial expressions or gestures. As an infant, the child does not babble; when older, he or she ignores others' attempts at conversation.
- odd gestures or expressions, such as a fixed stare or deadpan look or strange gesticulations.
- absence of fantasy play, such as the story enactment common to young children; indifference to fantasy children's stories.

- strange-sounding speaking voice, such as being abnormally high-pitched, lacking intonation, or speaking in a monotone or some other habitual way that is jarring to the listener.
- odd use of words, such as repeating the same phrases (such as a television jingle), irrelevancies, strange grammatical constructions.
- inability to sustain conversation, either because the child does not respond to the cues, such as questions put to them, or digresses into long, irrelevant monologues.

Bizarre Activities

Some of the most readily recognized signs of autism are the bizarre, repetitive movements and strictly stereotyped daily routines preferred by such children. These favored activities reflect a sharply restricted range of activities in comparison to other children of the same age. Typical signs include:

- Distress over small changes, so that the child becomes intensely upset at a slight change in routine or in the placement of some object.
- Obsessive interest in one narrow subject, with a lack of interest in most everything else: a preoccupation with collecting paper clips or license plate numbers or memorizing phone books, for instance.
- Repetitive, odd movements, such as hand-flicking, walking on tiptoe, or standing and rocking back and forth.
- Extreme attachments to objects, such as a certain pencil or string of rubber bands, or a fascination with a certain object, such as auto headlights.

Perhaps the most disturbing sign of autism is self-mutilation, often in the form of biting, hitting, or scratching oneself, or head-banging.

□ Joey's way of talking was what first made his parents realize something was different about him. He was late to speak, but when he was three, he began to repeat words back to people exactly as they were said to him, with a precise imitation of the intonation and lilt of the speaker's voice. Indeed, the next few years showed that Joey was a remarkable mimic: he could repeat a line of dialogue from a movie, TV show, or ad on the radio almost exactly as he had heard it.

But even though he was a remarkable mimic, Joey never really talked with anyone. He would either repeat back what had just been said to him or recall a line of dialogue he had overheard long ago to get his needs across. For instance, when he was hungry, Joey would say, "Do you want to eat?" in just the way his mother asked the question.

Joey's mother remembered him as a difficult baby prone to tantrums. He never engaged in any of the usual games babies enjoy, such as peekaboo, and when she picked him up to cuddle him, his body would go stiff with resistance instead of softening with warmth.

An only child, Joey kept to himself, ignoring the neighborhood children. He was fascinated with things, particularly watches and clocks. He always carried a worn travel alarm that his father had thrown away. He also had a remarkable memory for license plate numbers. He would sometimes sit and scribble license plate numbers on pieces of paper with earnest intensity, then show them to his parents as though they were urgent messages.

Music also fascinated Joey. When he listened to his favorite songs, he would dance around on tiptoes, flapping his hands—a gesture he made whenever he was excited. Sometimes he would rock to and fro for hours at a time, ignoring everything around him.

Familiar routine was crucial. If he didn't get exactly the same cereal for breakfast or have precisely the right place setting at a meal, Joey would scream and bang his thighs until the problem was fixed. His thighs were continually black-and-blue from his tantrums.

Complications and Variations

Not every child who displays such signs is autistic. Children who have been subjected to extreme physical abuse or emotional neglect may have some of the difficulties with speech and the bizarre mannerisms common in autism. But if such a child is adopted or taken into a caring and responsive foster home, the symptoms typically improve or disappear altogether.

Mental retardation. A common complication in developmental disorders is an extreme slowness in learning that lowers the child's mental age. *Not all children with developmental disorders also have mental retardation; some actually have superior intelligence.* But the greater the mental handicap, the more severe a child's overall impairment is likely to be.

The large majority of the mentally retarded—about 85 percent—fall in the "mild" range, with an IQ between fifty and seventy. Such people are educable, though they learn slowly and with effort. By their late teens the mildly retarded can learn up to about the sixth-grade level, and by adulthood can live independently, needing help or supervision only under unusual stress.

The more seriously retarded have an IQ of thirty-five to fifty. They can learn up to about the second-grade level and by adulthood can often work in a semiskilled job and live in a supervised home in the community. Even those with more severe retardation can learn enough that they are able, eventually, to work in a supervised setting and live in a group residence or with their families.

Though they often occur together, mental retardation and autism are *two distinctly different disorders.* For instance, mentally retarded children, unlike those with autism, are typically warm and sociable. To the degree an autistic child is retarded, it adds to the difficulties in treatment.

Seizures. About one in four children with autism also develop epileptic seizures at some point in childhood. This is most likely to occur in children with severe mental retardation. The seizures themselves require neurological examination and treatment with medication apart from any other therapy the child receives.

What Therapists Recommend

Approach. Behavior therapy is the most recommended approach, along with a family approach. This almost always means combining the two, so that family members apply behavior reinforcement techniques with the child at home.

Medication. Sometimes prescribed for other symptoms such as hyperactivity. But no medication has an effect on autism itself.

Setting. Survey results are mixed on this point, with about equal numbers of therapists saying that treatment should be in a completely supervised setting, at least at first; in a hospital; or in a special residence. The emerging consensus, though, is that, whenever possible, treatment should be carried out in "integrated" settings— a normal school classroom or at home.

Format. Because autistic children require an intensive treatment regimen, all formats are highly recommended. In practice, this usually means combining individual and family therapy. Teachers may also be involved as cotherapists. These formats are sometimes supplemented with group therapy.

Frequency. Autistic children require a continuously structured and monitored milieu throughout the day at school, at the treatment program, or at home.

Duration. Treatment has to be open-ended. Typically that means that therapy of one kind or another continues throughout childhood and sometimes beyond, as the child's development dictates.

What You Should Know About Therapy

If you suspect your child may have a developmental disorder, the first step is a thorough physical examination, including hearing and speech tests, a neurological examination, and tests for metabolic abnormalities. Cognitive and psychological tests are especially important. *Each case of developmental disorder is unique in its pattern of deficits and symptoms.* Ideally, a treatment plan is tailored to fit your child's pattern.

Autism is typically treated with a *total program* of behavior training designed to encourage ordinary behavior and discourage bizarre habits. It requires an all-out effort. If your child is to continue to live at home, all members of the family will almost certainly be called on to join in this effort, as will those in charge of your child's day care program or any classroom teachers. For therapy to work best, all those who have daily contact with your child must act consistently and in concert.

You should be frank with your child's therapist about those habits of your child that are particularly bothersome for you, such as poor toilet habits, temper tantrums, self-destructive behavior, sleep problems, odd food preferences, and the like. These— along with habits, such as running into busy streets, that represent a direct physical danger—will be top-priority targets for change. You and the therapist will also want to focus on things your child does that make it hard for other people in the community to accept him or her.

Another top priority is changing habits that might keep your child out of the best available educational program. These might include poor toilet training, odd eating habits, or the inability to wait in line or respond to a teacher. These basic social skills can be essential for a child to be accepted by teachers and fellow students and are more crucial at first than are academic skills. More and more, however, schools are accepting autistic students regardless of disability.

Living arrangements and education. The wide spectrum of recommendations for the setting for treatment reflects the great differences among children with developmental disorders. The guideline is that your child should live in the *least restrictive setting possible.* Supervised residential settings are a second choice to living at home, if at all possible.

In the past, the only two residential choices for an autistic child were home or large impersonal institutions. Now, however, the wider range of options includes "respite care," a residence where an autistic child can go for anywhere from a few hours to a month, to give his or her family time out to restore themselves. For older autistic people, programs exist to help them live in the community, in supervised apartments, or in group homes.

Autistic children who are kept in the community generally adjust better than do those of equal ability who are treated in a residential setting with other autistic children. One reason is that those who spend their days with other autistic children do not have the benefit of exposure to models of ordinary behavior.

Beyond these considerations, the law requires that autistic children, like all other handicapped children, be educated in the same kind of setting as other children, to the extent possible. Your child's general behavior will determine how well he or she will fit into a regular school, or what kind of special program may be required.

If your child is too disturbed or self-destructive to live at home, then you should choose a residential facility that has a well-established treatment program for autism.

Medication. Medication is used in autism for controlling specific problems, as part of a more general treatment approach. Medications are not sufficient in themselves and may not always be helpful or necessary. The best evidence suggests that the only symptom for which medications are of much use in autism is hyperactivity. The goal of medication treatment is to make it easier to use other therapies with a child, and to allow him or her to learn more readily.

As a rule of thumb, medications should be used only if other treatments have failed to control the problem, and even then only in conjunction with other therapies. Although a majority of therapists surveyed recommended the use of medications for autism, strong doubts exist about using them at all with children, particularly if a nonrisk therapy such as behavior modification will work as well or better. Medications can have damaging side effects, such as tardive dyskinesia (see p. 624), which would only complicate the child's difficulties.

Generally medications should be used with caution in treating autism. A medication will be started at very low doses and gradually increased over a period of weeks to find the optimal balance between benefits (if any) and side effects. There are typically no standard dosages; each child reacts to medications very differently.

A given medication will usually be tried for a month. Its continued use is justified only if there is some significant improvement. And even then the medication should be discontinued every six months or so to see if it is still necessary.

Perhaps the strongest reservation comes simply from the fact that autism is not a single, well-identified syndrome, but seems to be a group of problems with similar symptoms but varied biological bases. More often than not, in any individual case the underlying biological cause is a mystery. Thus no single medication is clearly *the* choice for treating autism, unlike such disorders as manic depression. Instead, each case may require several trials to see which medication, if any, will help.

Aversive techniques. A small number of behavior modification programs use "aversive conditioning" for children who may mutilate or otherwise harm themselves. A dangerous or undesirable behavior is paired with some adverse consequence so that the child will learn to associate the behavior with the consequence and thus avoid it. "Aversives" range from electrical shocks to sniffs of ammonia, to being tied down in a restrictive device. Aversives, understandably, are controversial.

Those who support their use argue that they are necessary to prevent even worse harm. Those who oppose them argue that more humane and effective ways exist to keep children from harming themselves, and that the aversives may sometimes just make things worse. Most who treat autistic children oppose the use of aversives, favoring approaches that positively reinforce desirable behavior.

A SPECIAL CASE: CHILD ABUSE

Abuse takes many forms, from physical or sexual abuse to emotional or physical neglect. In terms of emotional impact, all these kinds of maltreatment send very similar messages to children, the most harmful of which is that their world is not safe, and that they themselves are not worthy of nurturance and affection. The effects of abuse in childhood can be lifelong; the earlier the problems are treated, the better the outlook for an untroubled later life.

The psychological damage done will be worse:

- the more severe the abuse
- the longer it lasts
- the closer the relationship between the child and the abuser
- the more harmful the child perceives the abuse as having been
- the colder the emotional environment of the child's family

Current studies report that 1 to 1.5 percent of children are abused in a given year. This figure is widely disputed, however, since the vast majority of abuse continues to go unreported. Other studies reveal that by the time children have reached adulthood, up to a third of men and women will have experienced at least one incident of serious abuse.

Adults who were abused as children are at higher risk for a range of problems, including alcohol and drug abuse, violent crimes, depression, and other psychiatric disorders. Virtually all patients with multiple personality, and a high proportion of those convicted of brutal murders, were extremely severely abused as children. Those who were sexually abused have a greater likelihood of sexual complications, ranging from prostitution to the inability to trust in intimate relationships.

About a third of those who were abused as children will go on to become child abusers themselves and/or find themselves in abusive relationships. Apart from helping children handle their own emotional difficulties, early treatment can keep the cycle of abuse from repeating in the next generation.

On the other hand, the majority of abused children do *not* go on to abuse their own children; many become capable and caring parents. In almost every such case, a supportive adult helped the child see that he or she was not to blame for the abuse, that the abuser was wrong, and that the child was deserving of better care. Helping abused children come to these realizations is among the most important goals of therapy.

One of the difficulties in treating abused children, and in particular those who have been physically abused, is that they, as well as their parents, may not consider what is going on as "abuse." Many abusive parents have distorted views of what is "normal" or "justified" punishment. This is particularly true for those who were themselves abused in childhood, many of whom may never have accepted the fact that the punishments they received were, indeed, abusive. Some studies have found that as many as three-fourths of adults who were, by objective standards, abused as children do not think of themselves as having been abused.

Such parents are particularly likely to carry on the cycle of abuse since they think of themselves as being "good parents" in carrying out their harsh discipline. Others who engage in physical abuse often do so because they have an unrealistic understanding of what can be expected of children at different ages. Such parents may overreact, for instance, by punishing a one-year-old for making a mess with his or her food, though that is perfectly normal at that age.

Only in the early 1960s was what was then called "the battered-child syndrome" recognized as a problem by physicians. Before then, parents were largely able to punish their children as they wished, with minimal monitoring by authorities. While there is now widespread concern by authorities and psychotherapists alike about child abuse, no official diagnostic category for abused children exists.

The child being abused is not the only problem. Treatment needs to begin with the abuser, who also should be brought into therapy, if only to protect the child. It also may include another spouse who, if not the abuser per se, abets the abuse by passively allowing it to continue. Other siblings who witness or know about the abuse may also be troubled, even if they are not themselves abused, and thus require treatment.

Signs to Look For in Physical Abuse

Often children who are being physically abused will not complain of the abuse to others for fear of being subjected to more abuse. Typically other adults in the child's life—relatives, neighbors, teachers—are the first to notice unusual behavior in the child and come to suspect abuse. Since the abusing parent or parents frequently do not think of themselves as abusive, they will typically deny it if confronted.

Signs that children are being physically abused include:

- Unusual injuries, such as multiple fractures or bones that when x-rayed reveal a history of many such fractures; the injuries seem more severe than fits the explanations given for them.
- Negative self-esteem, a sense of worthlessness.
- Self-destructive acts, such as taking wild physical risks that can result in injury.
- Suicidal gestures, in which the child makes a serious attempt at suicide, threatens to do so, or talks about it as a "solution."
- Poor school performance, often due to cognitive difficulties that make it hard to learn or keep up with peers.

- Loss of interest in school or in activities, such as sports, that the child formerly enjoyed.
- Distractability, as though preoccupied.
- Poor peer relations; social withdrawal or mistrust, so that the child seems a "loner."
- Aggressiveness toward other children and toward adults; quick to anger and pick fights.
- Defiant toward teachers and other adults.
- Hyperobedience; the child overly strives to be cooperative and is compulsively "good," e.g., giving detailed answers to questions.
- Anxious and mistrustful of adults and other children; fretful and whiny; clinging and dependent—especially in younger children.

No child who has been abused will exhibit all these symptoms, but several will show up in any given abused child. Some of these patterns are behavioral opposites: being anxious and withdrawn versus being aggressive and defiant, for instance. In general, the more severe the abuse, the more marked the signs in the child will be.

□ Harold thought his son, Jack, was obstinate and "wild." The only thing that would keep him in line, Harold felt, was "a strong hand."

When Jack, just nine, forgot to put his bike away for two days in a row, Harold locked him in a closet for an hour. When Jack broke a glass in the kitchen, his father whipped him with an electric cord—a frequent punishment—leaving welts that turned into scars. Several times, infuriated when Jack came home too late from playing, Harold threw him against the wall. And once while the family was driving in the car when Jack was just three and was "being too noisy," his father dangled him outside the car window.

Whenever Harold's wife objected that he was being too hard on Jack, Harold's reply was, "Spare the rod and spoil the child," and at times he would hit her for "interfering." Besides, Harold's parents had been just as "firm" with him; he was simply being a "good parent."

□ At eight, Ellen stood out from the other children in her third-grade class. She was the only girl who picked fights with other children; she talked back to her teacher, refusing to sit still or stop talking. The other children shunned and teased her, often about the shabby way she dressed. Although her family was not poor, she always came to school in dirty or torn clothes.

During lessons, Ellen would stare into space vacantly or bother other children. As her teacher put it, "she just didn't have any interest in the work, no matter what the subject—not even music or art." And when the teacher tried to give her special tutoring, Ellen would give up, saying, "I'm just too dumb."

The school nurse was the first to notice the scars on Ellen's legs. Her father would hit her with a metal yardstick when she was bad, Ellen said. And then the nurse saw in Ellen's record that she had missed school several times for injuries—a broken leg, and twice for broken fingers. Ellen explained these injuries by calling herself "a klutz."

Sexual Abuse

Sexual abuse includes adults or adolescents fondling a child or telling the child to fondle them; an adult's being overly suggestive or seductive (for example, while undressing or bathing the child); exposing a child to an exhibitionist or pornography or photographing a child for pornography; or engaging in sexual foreplay, fellatio, or having intercourse with a child.

As with all forms of abuse, the closer the sexual abuser is to the child—a parent, sibling, or stepparent, for instance—the more damaging it is likely to be for the child. If the sexual abuse is an isolated instance perpetrated by a stranger, children may suffer fewer lasting consequences, particularly if their families are supportive—especially by not blaming the child.

While most attention has focused on girls who are abused by men, about two in five victims of sexual abuse are boys. And while the vast majority of perpetrators of sexual abuse are adult men, adolescents and even children sometimes abuse other children. Women, though rarely perpetrators, may abet men, such as boyfriends, in sexual abuse of their own children.

Sexual abuse breeds a great deal of *guilt* in the child, a problem that is rarely found in other forms of abuse. Some of the guilt may be over having had physical pleasure during the abuse, while for others the guilt may come from keeping the secret or having been sexually intimate with a parent's spouse, lover, or relative. Children often keep sexual abuse secret for years because they have been threatened by the perpetrator, are ashamed, or they fear that revealing the secret will destroy the family or that they will not be believed and will be ridiculed or rejected.

Signs to Look for in Sexual Abuse

- *Social isolation* is common in sexually abused youngsters. The sexual exploitation and the shame it evokes leave them feeling different from their peers. Girls may keep their distance from other girls for fear of sharing their awful secret and may stay away from boys for fear of being taken advantage of sexually.
- *Mistrust* in sexually abused children typically revolves around sexual issues. Such children may be reluctant later to become involved in romantic relationships or may end relationships as they are becoming more emotionally intimate. Abuse can also lead to a dislike for sex or difficulty in becoming aroused as an adult.
- *Precociousness,* especially in sexual matters, is common in children who are sexually abused. Their precociousness is sometimes social as well, a response to being forced into an adult role. This "pseudomaturity" is often seen with daughters in incestuous relationships with their fathers.
- *Sexual aggressiveness* is frequent in younger children who have been molested. While playing they will sometimes engage in sexual acts they experienced during the abuse.

□ Rachel was only eight when her father first brought her to his bed. Her mother, who was alcoholic, was unaware of this sexual intimacy. Rachel's parents often fought, and Rachel's father physically abused her mother. Her father treated Rachel as his "substitute wife," which both appalled and flattered her.

Rachel grew up fast; people who met her were impressed by her maturity. By twelve, she was shopping and cooking for the family, tasks her mother no longer seemed up to. At school, though, she was aloof, a way of ensuring that she would keep what she thought of as her terrible secret.

At thirteen Rachel became pregnant and then miscarried in an emergency room. There the incestuous relationship was discovered. She became extremely anxious and was plagued by guilt. In the months following, Rachel became deeply depressed and threatened suicide.

Neglect

While abuse involves outright cruelty or mistreatment, neglect is the consistent failure to nurture a child— failing to provide food, clothing, shelter, and other basic necessities. This form of maltreatment is more likely in homes where parents, often a single parent, are overwhelmed and unprepared for parenthood, have little money or education, and live under chaotic circumstances. Caretakers who are negligent were typically neglected and abused as well.

In emotional neglect, the child's feelings and psychological needs are ignored. Emotional neglect takes two very different forms: *indifference* or *constant negativity*—criticism, belittling, and harsh berating.

The effects of neglect, particularly if it occurs when the child is very young, can be psychologically devastating. At its worst, it can result in a "failure to thrive" syndrome in which the child becomes apathetic and listless, gains little height or weight, and without medical attention may even die.

An early experience of such pervasive insensitivity leaves children with a sense that their needs will not be met. Emotionally neglected children come to feel that people—indeed, the world itself—cannot be trusted, and that they are not worthy of proper care.

Adult Victims of Childhood Abuse

Since abuse in childhood leaves such deep psychic scars, adults who were victims can frequently benefit from psychotherapy. A range of psychological problems emerge in adulthood as a result of abuse early in life. The emotional legacy of abuse is at its worst in those people who came to believe in childhood that their parents were justified in abusing them because they were worthless or bad. Apart from the general debilitating effects of low self-esteem, these people may be vulnerable to depression or self-damaging behavior. Another legacy of abuse, the sense that people cannot be trusted, makes intimate relationships highly difficult.

Victims of sexual abuse are prone to specific problems in close relationships ranging from an abiding sense of guilt to a lack of sexual desire or enjoyment. Some—particularly male victims of sexual abuse—have gender-identity difficulties. Others are promiscuous or become prostitutes.

Lastly, adults who were sexually abused as children may develop symptoms of either a chronic or delayed posttraumatic stress disorder (see p. 505). PTSD can have an acute and devastating onset in adulthood after years during which memories of the abuse were dissociated or repressed.

What Therapists Recommend

Approach. The two most highly recommended therapeutic approaches for children of abuse are a combination of family therapy (when possible and not contraindicated) and a supportive individual relationship with a therapist. Since abuse is always a family problem, therapy with the entire family can ideally help both the child victim and the family members who are perpetrating the abuse. And a supportive approach to individual therapy can nurture the child's ability to cope with what has happened, begin to correct faulty perceptions of what happened and why, and also identify who is responsible. A goal of treatment is to begin to repair children's trust in relationships and alter their image of themselves as guilty and "bad."

Also frequently suggested was a psychodynamic approach, which would focus on the emotional meaning of the abuse to the child, and the internal confusions it has spawned. Also, group therapy with other abused children can be useful as well as reassuring.

Medication. Normally none, unless the child comes for treatment in the throes of an acute posttraumatic stress reaction, or PTSD symptoms erupt during the course of treatment.

Setting. Office visits. Unless children's reactions are so severe that they require hospitalization, or they are still at risk and need to be removed from the home, much of the work with abused children is often done in and by child social-service agencies. In most cases when the perpetrator is living in the home, the adult should be the one to leave the house and not the child. This eliminates the danger that other children will be abused and places the responsibility on the abuser and not the child.

Format. A combination of individual sessions for the child with family sessions with or without the child, depending on the therapist's assessment.

Frequency. Normally, once a week, unless the child is in crisis.

Duration. Open-ended.

What You Should Know About Therapy

Therapy for abuse or neglect is almost always complicated by the legal and other issues they raise: whether a parent or someone else will be prosecuted, the need to protect the child from further harm. The immediate goal is always to *stop the abuse*. In cases of sexual abuse, particularly, it is often difficult to determine if abuse actually occurred. It is usually the child's word against the adult's, and more often than not, the adult denies the allegations and is believed. Sometimes false accusations are made by spouses, most often during a divorce. Beyond these issues, because children may be removed from their families for protection by the courts, abuse is again often denied.

Abuse is usually not treated voluntarily. Therapy often comes about through a social service agency or legal action. Unfortunately, legal action can be as negative for the child as therapy can be positive.

The first step in therapy is to assess what immediate danger the child may be in. In most states, if child abuse comes to a therapist's attention, he or she is *obligated under law to report* it to the local or state office for the protection of children or to the department of social service, which in turn is obligated to evaluate the child's safety within a specified period of time. At this point, legal proceedings may be started. If the abuse or neglect took place at home, the child may be removed from the home until the time that the parents or caregivers can show that they are able to provide adequate protection.

If a child is removed from the home, it may be to the care of a relative; if no relative is willing or able, to a foster home or residential setting. The former is far preferable since it is less traumatic for the child and the parent alike. If the child is sent to a foster family, many agencies will not allow contact between the parents and the foster family.

CHAPTER SEVENTEEN

PSYCHIATRIC DISORDERS

ALCOHOLISM

Without doubt, alcoholism, along with drug abuse, is the number one mental health problem in America today. Close to 9 percent of Americans abuse alcohol or drugs—or increasingly, both—to the point that it interferes with their ability to work, raise a family, or otherwise lead a fulfilling life. Over the course of a lifetime, 16 percent of Americans, or about one in every six, will have such a problem. One in three American families will have a member with the problem.

Alcoholism has always been with us. In the past, drinking to excess was not considered a problem, but part of normal life. But the last decade or so has seen a new mood of sobriety, some of it fueled by increasing evidence of the disastrous effects of hard drinking on physical health, some by anger at the senseless deaths caused by drunken drivers.

The trouble is not alcohol consumed in moderation, but when it is turned to more and more for solace. The alcoholic's plight is that the more he or she turns to drink as a refuge from pain, anxiety, or turmoil, the worse things get.

Alcoholism is one of the most difficult of problems to treat, not because effective treatments don't exist, but because most people who are alcoholics don't think they have a problem. In our society alcohol is still the recreational drug of choice. Its use is sanctioned, even largely encouraged socially, despite the new mood of sobriety. Ads make its use glamorous; business lunches and meetings scheduled over drinks make it part of doing business.

Besides, there is no single moment when a person becomes an alcoholic. The pattern is noticeable over weeks, months, or years, but can be elusive from day to day. Symptoms, and the problem itself, may fluctuate, making it hard to distinguish with certainty whether your drinking habits are a lasting problem, just a temporary binge that will pass with no persisting effects, or part of the norm in a society where there is still so much heavy drinking.

The good news about alcoholism is that some people seem to be able to help themselves quit. About a quarter of those with drinking problems—and perhaps more—give it up on their own. A common pattern, for instance, is the young man who drinks to excess in his teens and twenties, then lets up by his early thirties as marriage, family, and work make their demands.

Many people hold that an alcoholic will straighten up when he or she "hits bottom." That has been true for some, who were shocked out of their drinking habit by a serious illness, blackouts, or an arrest for driving while intoxicated.

But don't count on it. Such crises are all too common in the troubled life of an alcoholic, and most often they do not lead to a turnaround. Instead, they can lead to even more drinking.

Those who have given up a heavy drinking habit on their own are lucky. For most, the journey out of alcoholism is one that demands hard work, help, and patience.

Bad habit, addiction, or illness? That alcohol can be abused is an idea as old as the legal codes of ancient China and Egypt. But that its abuse is an illness is a new concept, one that is widely accepted now among many psychotherapists, especially in psychiatry. Still, some psychotherapists prefer to think of alcoholism as simply a bad habit, while others see it as a psychological addiction rather than an illness. Just how a psychotherapist views alcoholism is important because it will shape his or her treatment philosophy.

The most visible alcoholics are the stereotypic grizzled denizens of the streets who ask passersby for a quarter toward the next bottle of cheap wine. But that image is misleading. The typical alcoholic is a married man in his thirties who holds a good job, has a home and family—and does not realize he is alcoholic.

Of course, the alcoholic may also be his wife, who joins him for cocktails or a beer every night after work, keeps drinking through the evening—and starts the next morning with an "eye-opener." Women tend to be less noticeable in their alcoholism, though the toll is just as great. Although alcoholism is five times more common among men than women, that seems to be changing. Among younger men and women, the rates are more similar, although men still have a higher incidence.

On average, the highest rate of alcohol consumption is for men and women between twenty-one and thirty-four. That is also the age range at which problem drinking is highest, despite the stereotype of the elderly wino.

Younger alcoholics do not have the same severity of physical symptoms as older alcoholics. Also, emotional and behavioral signs of alcoholism vary widely among younger people, but tend to be more similar in older alcoholics.

Many younger people who drink so much that, by objective standards, they are dependent on alcohol manage to taper off their drinking by the time they reach their mid-thirties. But those who start drinking heavily in early life and continue drinking suffer the worst physical damage and are often the most difficult to change.

Causes. There is no "alcoholic personality," a specific character type that is prone to excessive drinking. But *excessive drinking does leave its mark on personality.* Common effects of alcoholism include anxiety, depression, hypochondria, hostility, and an antisocial attitude. Any given person with a drinking problem may not develop them, but many may develop more than one.

Some people are at risk for alcoholism mainly because of the lifestyle of their profession. Among these are bartenders, longshoremen, musicians. Authors and reporters (as judged by the rate of death from cirrhosis of the liver) also have high rates of alcoholism.

Contrary to common belief, emotional problems in one's past do not have a strong link to later alcoholism. Having had an unhappy childhood, growing up in a family with heavy tension, having had parents who did a poor job—even being abused as a child—do not lead to alcoholism so much as emotional problems in general. Many people began drinking as a form of "self-medication" for depression or other unpleasant feelings.

Although alcoholism tends to run in families, not all alcoholics are children of alcoholics, nor do all children of alcoholics become alcoholics themselves. But having an alcoholic parent or history of alcoholism in the family does heighten the odds of problems with drinking, especially for men. Some studies have found that 20 to 25 percent of sons of alcoholics become alcoholic, and between 5 and 10 percent of the daughters. On the whole, children of alcoholics are four or five times more likely to follow their parents' lead. While some children of alcoholics react against it and end up as total abstainers, those who do develop a drinking problem tend to do so earlier in life and have a worse dependency and harder time giving up drinking.

Properties of alcohol. Alcohol has so many toxic properties that were someone to try to introduce it as a new product in America today, it would probably be banned by the Food and Drug Administration. The social acceptability of alcohol blurs the fact that these toxic properties call for special caution in its use.

Alcohol is the main contributor to the three leading causes of death in men under forty: suicide, homicide, and accidents. It is involved in one in four hospital admissions for disease. Its use makes a person susceptible to heart disease, stomach problems, some kinds of cancer, and most notably, cirrhosis of the liver.

For women, the risks of drinking extend to the fetus, should they become pregnant. An alcoholic mother has about a one in three chance of having a child born with "fetal alcohol syndrome." Symptoms include facial abnormalities, hyperactivity, attention deficit disorder (see p. 374), mental retardation, stunted growth, and heart defects. Even if a child does not have fetal alcohol syndrome, a mother's drinking can still cause deficiencies in her child's IQ.

One of the most pernicious health problems among chronic drinkers is malnutrition: people who drink a lot often lose their appetite. The reason seems to be that wine, beer, and hard liquor have so many calories that they may give you the sensation of having eaten your fill, leading you to neglect the foods you actually need. Alcohol can also interfere with the body's absorption of nutrients. People who drink excessively are prone to vitamin-deficiency diseases such as pellagra and beriberi.

Interaction with other drugs. Without question the most dangerous substance alcohol can be combined with over a long period of time is also the most common—tobacco. These two substances in combination account for more deaths than any others.

Drinking while you take certain psychiatric drugs can be dangerous, even fatal. For instance, if you are taking sedatives or tranquilizers (see p. 628), alcohol will interfere with the body's properly metabolizing them. The result can be an accumulation to toxic levels. Beyond that, alcohol and sedatives both depress the central nervous system. Taken together, they can sedate you to the point it becomes dangerous to drive or operate machinery; at higher doses, the combination can be lethal.

What happens when you drink. When you drink, alcohol is absorbed into your bloodstream. The quicker it is absorbed, the quicker you become drunk. If you have food in your stomach, it slows the absorption. If you have a mixed drink (water or carbonated beverages combined with your alcohol), it speeds up the absorption so you get intoxicated more quickly.

There is a natural limit to how much alcohol the body can metabolize in a given time before a series of changes begin to occur in the brain and central nervous system. On average, the body can absorb about three-quarters of an ounce of 80-proof alcohol an hour—roughly the equivalent of one bottle of beer or a glass of wine. If you drink more than this, you'll start feeling drunk. That is why a drink you might nurse for half an hour without getting tipsy will make you drunk if you down it in a few minutes.

Some people say they drink to feel good, while others say they drink not to feel bad. Both are true. Alcohol is *both a stimulant and a depressant* to the central nervous system. At first, it stimulates the brain, giving you the pleasant "buzz" that makes you feel good.

But as the body absorbs more alcohol, it starts to act as a depressant on the central nervous system, switching your mood from euphoria to depression. This "downer" effect can lead you to reach for another drink in a futile attempt to recapture the high you felt only moments before. Now you're drinking not to feel bad.

This two-pronged mood switch is one of the most insidious effects of alcohol, leading people to drink more and more, and as time goes on, to become dependent on alcohol for an ever more elusive high.

In technical terms, the impact of alcohol on your brain and body can be gauged in terms of its level in your blood. For women and for lighter-weight people it takes less alcohol to have the same effect. But for a 160-pound man, at roughly two to three drinks—a level of 0.05 percent—you feel loose: your thoughts flow easily, and your judgment and restraint are freed from inhibition. You may feel woozy, as though you can't quite think straight. With five or more drinks in an hour, you reach a concentration of 0.10 percent; your movements start to get clumsy. You've approached the blood alcohol level most states consider "legal intoxication," 0.10 to 0.15 percent.

Beyond that, effects get increasingly severe. At about 0.20 percent a marked depression of the entire area of the brain that controls your movements occurs. You may stagger if you try to walk and weave all over the road if you try to drive. At 0.30 percent, you are certain to be confused, and perhaps even stuporous. If you reach the 0.40 to 0.50 percent level, you may go into a coma. If you keep consuming alcohol beyond this point, you could die: the brain centers that control breathing and heart rate become depressed and cease to function.

Are you alcoholic? (**Or is someone close to you?**) That may be one of the hardest questions of all to answer about yourself. Of all psychological problems, alcoholism is among the most invisible to its victims. It is all too easy to ignore the signs that you are in trouble.

For one, the problems may be at their worst while you are drunk, when you are least able to take stock of what is going on. If, for instance, your family is distressed while you are drunk, it will be far less visible to you while you are sober—and able to notice—because they will not be feeling it as acutely.

Besides, when so many people around you drink—perhaps just as much or more than you do—it's hard to tell if your drinking is out of line. But ask yourself some key questions about your drinking habits:

- Do you often drink to soothe some emotional pain, such as after an argument or some disappointment?
- Do you find yourself drinking while you are alone, during the day, or at times other than meals?
- Does the feeling of being under pressure make you want to have a drink?

- Do you keep telling yourself you should cut down on your drinking, but never quite seem able to?
- Do you find yourself wanting more drinks than are offered in a social situation, feel uncomfortable if no drinks are offered, or want to keep drinking when your friends have stopped?
- Does your drinking make you feel guilty so that you try to keep your family or friends from knowing just how much you are really drinking? Do you ever lie to hide how much you've actually been drinking?
- Do you often find yourself sorry afterward about something you've said or done while drinking? Do you have to apologize afterward?
- Do you find yourself trying to justify how much you drink to your family or friends?
- Do you forget details or conversations that occurred during drinking?
- Do you have trouble falling asleep or staying asleep?

Other key questions to ask your family or friends are:

- Does your drinking create an atmosphere of tension or ever ruin family times together, such as dinner or holidays?
- Does your drinking make your family or friends feel worried about you? Do you act in a way that makes them embarrassed when you drink?
- Do members of your family fear you might hurt them while you are drunk? Have you ever done so?
- Do friends or people in your family worry about how much you drink or talk about it amongst themselves?

Answers of yes to several of these questions are signals you may be alcoholic. If you suspect you might have a problem, try this test: tell yourself that you will only have one drink a day, say, for two months. No more, no matter what. If you fail, you may be on the road to alcoholism or have already arrived.

Some alcoholics are able to abstain from drinking for a time if they know that they will eventually be able to drink. Another effective test is to choose a conservative number of drinks (say two) you will have in a given time and write it down. See if you can stick to that number. Usually an alcoholic will not be able to control his or her drinking once they have started. If you are not able to stay within your drink quota and find yourself making excuses for exceeding the limit, then you are drinking alcoholically. Or you can take what's called the "CAGE test":

- Have you ever felt the need to CUT DOWN on your drinking?
- Have you ever felt ANNOYED by people who criticize your drinking?
- Have you ever felt GUILTY about drinking?
- Do you sometimes have an EYE-OPENER in the morning?

Denial and collusion. It is all too easy to tell yourself that the troubles in your life are due to problems besides alcohol, and that you drink to ease the pain those troubles cause. The truth, however, is almost always that those troubles—such as a divorce or a lost job—are a *result* of your drinking. You might say, "I'm drinking because my girlfriend left me." But there's a good chance that she left you because of your drinking.

The ease with which alcoholism is denied is abetted by the tendency of those close to a person with a drinking problem to look the other way and try to accommodate them. A spouse may be reluctant to broach the problem for fear of the anger it may arouse in a partner who is prone to physical abuse when drunk. Sometimes people in a relationship with an alcoholic find a certain emotional satisfaction in caring for the needs of their partner. Because such a person unwittingly permits an alcoholic to continue his or her dependence on alcohol, such a person is sometimes called a *codependent.*

Beyond that, other people in an alcoholic's life—coworkers or friends, for instance—may be aware of clear evidence that someone has a problem with drinking. But they tell themselves "it's none of my business," they "don't want to intrude," or simply don't want to take the responsibility for speaking up. The result is that the alcoholic continues oblivious to the problem, or that anyone else notices. An alcoholic's denial is so steadfast and severe that often people give up trying to penetrate it.

Patterns. There are many different patterns to alcohol abuse, some very complicated. Many of the violent acts, accidents, health problems, sleep disorders, missed work days, and arrests that stem from alcohol abuse occur with people whose drinking habits do not technically qualify them as chronic alcoholics. And yet their lives are plagued by drinking problems.

A common pattern is *episodic* drinking, which makes it harder to recognize that there is a problem at all. People with this pattern do not drink too much every day. Instead, they may drink only on weekends or even be abstinent for months at a time—only to go on a binge that can last days or weeks.

Some people assume that severe alcoholics continue to drink to avoid the symptoms of withdrawal, but this is rarely the case. Rather, one of the most frequent reasons people are unable to stay off alcohol is because they react to negative emotional states by wanting a drink and so relapse.

Signs to Look For

There is no surefire test for alcoholism, no single symptom that is invariably present. All the signs can come and go, and the problem can take different forms in different people.

Like any substance addiction, alcoholism can exist on two levels: "dependence" and "abuse."

Alcohol Dependence

Dependence on alcohol can be *either psychological or physical*. If you are psychologically dependent on alcohol, you turn to it time and again, or fairly continuously, as the main means to soothe yourself. The main signs of alcohol dependence, though only some will pertain to any given person, include:

- Giving in to the temptation to have more than you intend or continuing to drink for a longer period. In either case, you often drink until you "feel high," despite telling yourself you want to stay sober.
- Being unable to quit drinking, despite repeated attempts to cut down or stop.
- Spending a lot of your day drinking or drunk, or recovering from being drunk. The time spent actually drinking may be a matter of hours, or it might continue through most or all of the day. You spend a lot of time worrying about when and how you'll get your next drink.
- Being drunk or hung over when you should be working, at school or studying, or taking care of duties at home.
- Being drunk where you or someone else is put at risk—for example, while driving or taking care of children.
- Ignoring problems created by drinking. Even though your drinking causes psychological or medical problems or interferes with your social or family life, you keep drinking, despite the fact that it makes things worse.
- Increasing tolerance makes you need to drink more and more in order to get the same effect. Where you once drank three glasses of vodka, now you find yourself drinking half a bottle. Tolerance for alcohol does not escalate continually as happens with other drugs. Heavy drinkers typically reach their upper limit quickly and keep that amount as their "usual."

With heavy, constant drinkers, the following frequently develop:

- Withdrawal symptoms if you try to stop drinking. If you've been drinking heavily and cut down or stop, a few hours later you will get "shakes" or tremors in your hands, tongue, or eyelids. You might also feel headachy or nauseous, weak, keyed up, moody, or angry. Sometimes people going through withdrawal have hallucinations or seizures. Usually they have trouble sleeping.
- Drinking to avoid withdrawal. Some people undergo severe withdrawal symptoms when they try to stop drinking, an experience so awful that it spurs them on to drink more than ever, starting in the morning and continuing throughout the day.

□ Herb was a highly talented man who somehow always seemed to engage in self-defeating behavior. At law school, he began to drink steadily. Although under the influence much of the time, he somehow managed to graduate and get his degree.

His first job, with a prestigious law firm, ended after a year and a half, when he was let go. While everyone at the firm saw Herb as brilliant, he had a steady record of failing to finish briefs on time or doing them sloppily. No one at the firm knew that Herb drank every night after work or that he would sometimes come in the next morning after having been out drinking until dawn.

Herb's marriage ended soon after he was let go from the firm. While his wife had supported him through law school by working as a nurse, she complained bitterly that he was never home, leaving her to care for their two young children by herself. Herb always claimed he was "working late at the office."

Alcohol Abuse

Some people abuse alcohol but are not dependent on it. For instance, if you usually don't drink, but every few weekends go on a drunken binge that makes you miss work for a day or two, or you drink even when a physician has told you it worsens some medical condition, then you are abusing alcohol. People who as college students went on weekend drinking binges may never develop dependence on alcohol, but they may retain the habit of bingeing, a form of abuse.

That you can abuse alcohol without becoming dependent on it is small consolation. Abuse is still a form of alcoholism and can be just as disruptive and self-destructive as dependence. It is just as much a problem that needs treatment. Its main signs are:

- Disregard for the consequences of drinking, despite the realization that it is intefering with your psychological or physical health or your social or work life.
- Repeated use despite obvious hazards, such as drinking while you are driving or smoking in bed.

Apart from the formal signs, if you are an alcoholic—or know someone who might be—some of the more obvious habits or traits you may notice include:

- Being unable to cut down or stop despite repeated efforts to control your drinking.
- Binges during which you are drunk for most of the time for a few days at a time; drinking an entire fifth of liquor (or a bottle of wine or case of beer) on a single occasion.
- Having amnesia after you have been drinking.

But remember, it is not the absolute amount of alcohol you drink that determines whether you are an alcoholic, but whether your drinking habit is destructive in your life.

Apart from the signs of alcoholism listed above, some of the ways this destructiveness might show up include:

- becoming aggressive or violent while drunk
- legal troubles that stem from your drinking
- getting in arguments with your friends or family while you drink, or because of it
- troubles in your closest relationships because of your drinking
- being unable to work, study, or attend to family duties
- changing jobs often because of problems due to your drinking
- not knowing how long you will drink or how much once you start
- having difficulty falling asleep or staying asleep

□ Janet, the thirty-four-year-old mother of two teenage daughters, was urged to see a psychotherapist when she confessed to her minister the problems caused by her drinking. Every two weeks or so, when her husband was away on business trips, Janet would binge on Scotch that she kept hidden in the house. Her husband never knew she drank; when he was around, she kept her drinking under control. But on the morning he would leave, she would reach for the bottle and be drunk by the time her daughters came home from school.

Whenever she went on one of these drunken binges, she would become angry with her daughters, berating them for even slight infractions of house rules—coming home a few minutes late from a date, not doing the dishes quickly enough, leaving their clothes in the bathroom. What troubled Janet the most was that lately she had gotten so out of control that she hit them. Although her daughters would not tell their father about their mother's drinking, it had gotten to the point that they would not speak to her at all.

What Therapists Recommend

Approach. A behavioral approach was the most frequent recommendation for psychotherapy, with supportive close behind. This typically means a combination of the two. Also recommended: family therapy, especially when the family can help a person spot and deal with signals of relapse.

Medication. More appropriate for dependence than abuse. The main treatment medication is Antabuse, which makes people feel sick if they drink alcohol. However, few people who could really benefit from it are willing to take it for very long, if at all. Minor tranquilizers such as Librium, less often Valium, are frequently used during detox. Antipsychotic medication may be needed if withdrawal produces the hallucinations, delusions, and psychotic perceptual distortions that accompany DT's.

Setting. For those who *abuse* alcohol, the trend is increasingly toward outpatient treatment. Inpatient treatment, say in a hospital or residential rehabilitation facility, would be resorted to only after outpatient had failed. But for alcohol *dependence,* especially long-term dependence, treatment should often begin in a psychiatric hospital or special alcohol treatment center because of the medical risks associated with withdrawal.

If detoxification is needed (see p. 429), then you need an inpatient facility with a medically supervised detox unit. If you don't need detox, but feel you do need help going through the first days of withdrawal, then a residential setting, such as an alcohol rehab halfway house, will do.

If neither of these are problems but you need a program that will give you daily supports you don't have on your own, then a day program is called for. And if you don't need detox and do have enough people in your life who can give you daily support, then an outpatient treatment facility geared exclusively toward establishing and maintaining sobriety is an excellent choice.

Format. The most common recommendations for both abuse and dependence were for group treatment in combination with individual sessions. Typically, this means attending a twelve-step group such as Alcoholics Anonymous, or another recovery group, in addition to individual support. Family involvement was also highly recommended.

Frequency. In an outpatient setting, treatment for alcoholism needs to be intensive, especially at first. Individual sessions twice a week or more are recommended, even daily if necessary during the initial phase of recovery. Most therapists and outpatient clinics will recommend—or insist on—daily AA meetings to start with, or at least a few meetings a week, at which you should be given a sponsor to work with.

Duration. Open-ended. For many, this means an ongoing involvement in AA to support and continue sobriety.

What You Should Know About Therapy

The Role of Psychotherapy in Recovery

Many counselors who are themselves recovering alcoholics oppose traditional psychotherapy. Many of them have had unsuccessful therapies at a time before there were effective psychotherapies for alcoholism. Individual psychotherapy alone is not the treatment of choice for alcoholism; it is typically combined with group treatment, and often with involvement by spouses, parents, or children. The most effective treatments in general use self-help groups such as Alcoholics Anonymous or Al-Anon. Those who do not have a religious orientation may be more comfortable in programs such as Rational Recovery, which are not predicated on a belief in a higher power. Many alcoholics trying to stop are helped by going to outpatient treatment facilities that specialize in treating alcoholics, though this is not necessary.

All the treatments for alcoholism that have been effective follow certain principles. One is that *alcoholism itself is the problem that must be treated,* not some other "underlying" psychological problem. Anxiety, depression, or chronic irresponsibility may bring an alcoholic into therapy, but these are most often the result of drinking, not its cause.

Indeed, until the drinking is under control, therapy for any other issues is impossible—an illusion. Trying to focus on other problems while the drinking continues, or while sobriety is still shaky, such as an insight-oriented approach to get at "the source" of the drinking, runs the additional risk of creating more anxiety and making relapse all the more likely.

Cognitive-behavioral therapy. Once drinking is under control, other therapeutic approaches can be taken to support sobriety. The most highly recommended approach, cognitive-behavioral therapy, assumes that it is relatively easy to stop drinking; the hard part is keeping yourself from relapsing into your old drinking pattern again. Cognitive-behavioral treatment focuses in part on helping a recovering alcoholic cope with moments that are likely to trigger a "slip," as AA terms it. The goal is to prevent these slips from becoming a relapse.

Most recovering alcoholics do slip. How often varies. The cognitive-behavioral approach assumes that a slip can be turned into an opportunity to learn what triggers your drinking, and to prepare yourself to abstain next time the same situation occurs. Whereas this time you had a drink at a party when your host pressed some wine on you, you can rehearse how you would turn down the wine next time.

The cognitive-behavioral approach also stresses developing positive alternatives to drinking as part of a more balanced lifestyle—e.g., finding friends who enjoy pursuits such as hiking, rather than hanging out in bars.

Treatment formats. Individual psychotherapy is helpful for alcoholism when it focuses on stopping the drinking, but not when it tries to explore the causes of your drinking problem. Individual therapy works best when it is part of a combined treatment approach. Most treatment programs for alcoholism revolve around peer support groups. You can get more from other people who are going through the same problem with drinking—or who have already gone through it and know something about recovery—than you can from just about anyone else. You can also use recovery groups to rebuild social skills and relationships that you've lost or damaged through your drinking. Support groups provide a sense of "family": you become part of the group, helping others while you help yourself.

If you have family nearby or are married, they can be especially helpful in treatment. They will be there with you when temptation is greatest. And they know better than anyone else what the destructive effects of drinking are for you. If they have fallen into a codependent role with you, they will also need help in changing their behavior, and you will need help seeing that these changes don't mean they are rejecting you or love you less.

Your family may have an agreement with you that they will boycott you if you drink, but spend time with you if you do not. They can also take steps to minimize moments in your life that have been cues to drink. They can encourage you to leave a cocktail party after the first hour or talk you through moments when you get the urge to drink. And they can help by laying off: not nagging you about your drinking, but helping to arrange life so you are less tempted. This may mean keeping alcohol out of the house and family arguments to a minimum, being more accommodating around the house, socializing more with nondrinkers.

Getting Help for the Resistant Alcoholic

The majority of people with a drinking problem are unable to see or admit that they have it. If someone you care about is like that, you may want to try to get him or her into treatment despite the denial.

The difficulty in caring about such people is that you cannot, in good conscience, just wait for them to hit rock bottom. Even then, there is no assurance that they will seek help on their own. And yet treatment will only help someone who wants to be helped. You need to find a way to motivate them.

One way is a *managed confrontation*. This means getting together as many of the key people in their life as possible—close family and friends, people from work, neighbors, minister or rabbi—in short, anyone and everyone who cares about them. The confrontation should be rehearsed. It is helpful—perhaps essential—to have the advice of someone experienced in orchestrating such confrontations, such as a staff member from an alcoholism treatment center. Some therapists and recovery personnel now specialize in helping families arrange these interventions.

The confrontation should be at a time when the person being approached has not been drinking. In the meeting, one by one each person should describe an instance where the drinking caused real concern and express the hope that the person will get help. The atmosphere should be one of warmth and concern, not blame and accusation.

Alcholics typically respond by denying that there is a problem or by being evasive, saying that they are getting better on their own (when they are actually just between episodes). They may try to put off getting help until some vague time in the future, saying that some other difficulty in their life—a divorce or a death in the family—is the real problem, and that once they deal with that, the drinking will stop by itself.

Everyone needs to be firm in rejecting such excuses. Instead, come prepared with a specific way for the person to start treatment: a treatment center to go to, a group to join, a psychotherapist to see. And let the person know that you will all continue to support him or her through the inevitable difficulties that will come on the road to sobriety.

A caution: interventions are high risk and can sometimes backfire. An alternative approach is "motivational interviewing," in which a seasoned counselor talks to the people with a drinking problem about their life situation and helps them see the need for change. If your family member's or friend's health is seriously at risk, however, or the drinking is breaking up a marriage or family, you should not be worried about an intervention's backfiring. You should be concerned only about getting him or her help, whatever the cost.

Do You Need an Alcohol Treatment Center?

Follow the principle of "stepped care." This means you start with trying to quit on your own. If that is not successful, then try a self-help group or self-help group plus psychotherapy. If that does not work, then you may need an inpatient treatment center, especially if you have tried and repeatedly failed to give up drinking in outpatient or in day-treatment programs.

This is particularly true if no one is available in your life to support your attempt to stop drinking. If you have to go through it on your own, or if your spouse or family have not been able to help you stay dry in your previous attempts, then an inpatient program is advisable. This may even need to be followed by a stay in a structured residential setting such as an alcohol rehabilitation halfway residence to continue intensive outpatient treatment until the danger of relapse is lessened.

There are alcohol treatment centers in most cities. Most are based on a two-week program of inpatient treatment. Most health insurance covers inpatient care but not partial care, so you may need to go to a hospital-based program even if you'd do fine as an outpatient. On the other hand, if you'd have trouble getting time off from your job to go to a hospital or inpatient facility, then outpatient care is a good alternative.

Detoxification. Only a small portion of people with alcoholic dependence need to go through inpatient detox. If you have a physical addiction so strong that you experience withdrawal symptoms when you stop drinking for a day or so, then detoxification is the first step in treatment. Make the decision in consultation with your doctor or therapist. For someone who drinks heavily, the signs of withdrawal begin within the first several hours of stopping. They include:

- nausea or vomiting
- sweating, heart palpitations, increase in blood pressure
- anxiety, depression, or irritability

- feelings of extreme fatigue or weakness
- intense nightmares or insomnia
- "the shakes": tremors of hands, tongue, or eyelids
- "DT's" or delirium tremens, hallucinations, disorientation

If you've never had any of these symptoms—especially DT's or seizures—and you're in good physical condition, then detoxing at home is a viable option. In home detox you try to dry out in your own home, with help from friends or family, ideally under the supervision of a doctor or therapist. Your spouse or some other family member must be able to stay with you throughout the first few days. You need to be supervised to be sure you resist taking a drink, and a psychiatrist or doctor should be available for daily contact.

The psychiatrist may prescribe some minor tranquilizers, such as Valium or Librium (see p. 628), to help you handle such symptoms of withdrawal as anxiety. But you should be able to stop taking medication within three to five days after you've given up drinking.

If you do begin to experience severe withdrawal symptoms, especially DT's, whoever is with you should take you to the nearest hospital emergency room for evaluation. If you have experienced severe withdrawal symptoms or DT's in the past, or you have a medical condition such as diabetes that may complicate withdrawal, you should begin treatment in a hospital or other medically supervised detox unit.

Help for the Alcoholic's Family

Alcoholism is always a family problem. Being the child, spouse, sibling, or other relative of an alcoholic can be devastating. Children or spouses may blame themselves for the drinking. They may feel responsible for "saving" the alcoholic and feel guilty when they cannot. Often husbands who drink become abusive or violent toward their wives and/or children while drunk. Children of alcoholics may express the problem through failure in school or misbehaving.

For all these reasons, most programs will involve the family in treatment. Some sessions may be with the family alone without the alcoholic, and the family may meet with other families who have an alcoholic member and are going through the same struggle.

An alcoholic parent can leave a lifelong emotional legacy that can cripple relationships in the child's adult life—and that may require therapy. A nationwide network of self-help groups for children of alcoholics now exists. The two best known and most widespread of these are Al-Anon and Adult Children of Alcoholics (ACOA) (see Appendix I).

Medication

Many therapists recommend that dependence on alcohol be treated with psychiatric medication, and some suggest the same for alcohol abuse. But no medication has any claim to being a cure for alcoholism per se. Little convincing evidence exists that medication is very useful in the treatment of alcoholism apart from detox, and sometimes, prevention. If an alcoholic is clearly suffering from a major depression, for instance, antidepressant medication may be called for. During withdrawal, symptoms such as anxiety, restlessness, agitation, and sleeplessness may be eased by a tranquilizer such as Librium or Valium (see p. 628). For people with DT's, antipsychotic medications may be used temporarily to control hallucinations and perceptual disturbances.

In the weeks after withdrawal, tranquilizers are sometimes prescribed for anxiety and antidepressants for depression, though most doctors and psychiatrists will be reluctant to risk substituting one drug for another when the goal is abstinence. Lithium is also sometimes used to block the euphoria alcohol brings and so cut the desire to drink.

The only medication specifically helpful in treating alcoholism is Antabuse (disulfiram). It works by interfering with the way your body normally absorbs alcohol, causing an alcohol by-product to accumulate to the point that you become nauseous. This reaction can be quite severe. You might have heart palpitations, sweats, flushing, or trouble breathing; become so nauseous you vomit; feel dizzy or have blurred vision. Your blood pressure may drop significantly. In rare cases, people have died.

For those reasons it is essential that you let your family and friends know you are taking Antabuse, especially in case you accidently ingest alcohol. You could have a reaction from an over-the-counter medication with alcohol, such as cough medicine, or eat food containing alcohol. You should also tell any physician who is treating you that you take Antabuse since it can also cause a reaction with other medications.

Antabuse is a deterrent to drinking, not a treatment. It does little to change your desire to drink, although it definitely helps you resist it. If you take Antabuse every morning, you'll know that taking a drink will make you feel sick.

If you take Antabuse, it's best to take the pills at the same time every day, such as with your breakfast. Even better is having someone there, such as a spouse, who can help you remember. Taking Antabuse in the presence of someone in your family is a statement that you are fighting an active battle against drinking.

A standard dose is 250 milligrams a day. Taking more than that is no more help, and taking a lot more can be dangerous should you drink. It takes three to five days for Antabuse to be secreted. That means that it will continue to work over an entire weekend if you took it last on a Friday.

Antabuse is most useful for recovering alcoholics who have been treated in a treatment center and are in the midst of the transition back to their normal routine.

Alcoholics Anonymous (AA)

By far the best-known self-help group for alcoholism, AA is a fellowship of recovering alcoholics. AA is highly recommended in addition to any psychotherapy or other treatment you might seek. It is the most popular, respected, and effective form of social support for people recovering from alcoholism. Far more people find treatment for their drinking problem through AA than in psychotherapy or treatment centers.

Almost every town in America has at least one AA group; cities have several. Many places of employment have AA meetings on the premises for their employees. *To find an AA group, simply look in the phone book under Alcoholics Anonymous.*

AA groups meet at least weekly and often daily, noontimes as well as evenings, Saturdays and Sundays as well. Membership is anonymous; you give only your first name. Since there are usually several groups in an area, and each group has its own meeting times, you should have no difficulty finding one that fits your schedule. If you are having trouble "fitting it in," that's probably just another excuse.

AA groups are run on a drop-in basis—there are no attendance requirements. Nevertheless abstinence and sobriety are best supported by regular attendance. During the initial recovery phase following detox or a decision to stop, after a relapse, or during a crisis, many go to AA meetings as often as once a day. On average most AA members go three or four times a week in the beginning.

AA doesn't care *why* you drink, just that you *do* and don't want to. The philosophy is "one day at a time," putting long-term goals aside for a more practical attack on the present and its problems. This also gives you a manageable unit to focus on— getting through the day without a drink. When you get to the end of a dry day, you can feel the sense of accomplishment.

While the groups vary in composition and focus, you can expect a warm, family feeling—you'll be among people who understand you and accept you. Once you join a group, you can and should ask a specific person you feel attuned with to be your "sponsor." He or she will also be a recovering alcoholic, but further along the road than you. Your sponsor will understand the pressures you face and help you in moments of crisis by being available by phone or in person.

The AA philosophy hinges on the well-founded assumption of "once an alcoholic, always an alcoholic." That is, though you may stop drinking, your vulnerability to abusing alcohol will always remain. There is no permanent "cure." AA therefore doesn't talk about being "recovered" but about "recovering." No matter how long your sobriety, you are always "recovering" from alcoholism.

AA groups are based on the "Twelve Steps." Briefly, this program begins by first admitting your powerlessness over alcohol and your need to seek help from some higher power (you can interpret *higher power* in any way that is compatible with your beliefs). You then take a "moral inventory" in which you acknowledge whatever wrongs you have done people through your drinking, ask forgiveness, make amends where possible, and commit to helping other alcoholics in their recovery. Some alternative groups modeled on AA replace belief in a "higher power" with that of depending on a higher power within oneself.

In years past there was often mistrust between AA and psychotherapists. Today that is largely gone. Most psychotherapists who work with alcoholics recommend that their clients join AA as part of treatment. For many alcoholics, being in AA is itself enough. While they may go into therapy for other problems, they do not need it to stay sober.

A more likely source of possible mistrust or misunderstanding involves the use of psychiatric medication. In the past, AA was decidedly against the use of psychiatric medication because of the concern over substituting one form of chemical dependency for another. Today there is a growing recognition that alcoholism often accompanies other major psychiatric disorders that require pharmacological treatment—manic depression, for instance. Negative feelings toward the use of *any* psychiatric medication for emotional problems still linger in some AA groups. If you are on medication for another disorder and encounter this attitude, try another group. You should be able to find one that you feel comfortable in.

Al-Anon is for spouses and family members of alcoholics. Its goal is to help them with the problems of "codependency," such as feeling responsible for their spouses' drinking, or not being able to recognize that there was a problem in the first place. Alateen does the same with teenage children of alcoholics.

Adult Children of Alcoholics (ACOA) was formed in recognition of the special problems—such as low self-esteem—that often develop in people who grew up with an alcoholic parent. This is an increasingly popular and effective resource. Therapists refer clients who are "adult children" to it as they refer alcoholic clients to AA.

Your Outlook Can Help

Certain factors that bode well for those going into treatment for alcoholism include being married, doing well at a stable job, and being better off financially. These factors may not be crucial in themselves but rather indicate that one's personal resources and ability to turn to others for emotional support are at a level conducive to staying on the wagon. Also, the more the meaningful people in your life—your spouse, children, relatives, and friends—are invested in your giving up drinking, the better the outlook.

Certain attitudes on your part will be particularly helpful:

- Accepting that to drink again carries the risk of falling back into alcoholism.
- Seeing and accepting the damage that drinking brought into your life.
- Forgiving yourself for that damage, while resolving not to repeat it.
- Being honest with friends and family about your decision to stop drinking, and being able to refuse a drink openly.

• Keeping your treatment appointments and doing any assignments connected with the program.
• Being patient with yourself.

SUBSTANCE ABUSE

Any substance that can change your mood or state of mind—suspend reality, induce euphoria, stimulate or sedate—can be addictive. Any such "psychoactive" substances can be abused to the point of *addiction,* psychological or physical dependence.

To be sure, many people experiment with drugs without ever developing an addiction, just as most people who drink never become alcoholics. Some antidrug campaigns exaggerate the dangers of mild drug use in a sometimes overzealous attempt to scare young people away from drugs. Simply using a drug from time to time for "recreational" use does not constitute an addiction, though it may be illegal.

Over the last decade or so the pattern of addiction has changed. The hallucinogens, such as LSD, have declined in popularity, as have marijuana and hypnosedatives such as Valium. On the other hand, use of more addictive drugs like the opiates— such as heroin—cocaine, amphetamines, and certain drugs like PCP have soared.

What Is Addiction?

A person is considered addicted to a drug is he or she (1) is *psychologically dependent* and so repeatedly needs it to maintain a preferred state of mind; or (2) is *physically dependent,* so that being without the drug produces uncomfortable symptoms of withdrawal; and (3) the person's physical or psychological state deteriorates as a result.

In recent years, however, it has become clear that people can abuse drugs to a destructive degree without ever becoming dependent on them. Some drug abusers go for a period of days, weeks, or months between binges when they abuse drugs to an extent that endangers their physical health or destroys their ability to work, go to school, or function in social relationships.

The most commonly abused substances are both legal: alcohol, which is both a stimulant and a depressant, and nicotine in tobacco, which is a mild stimulant. Other commonly abused depressants are barbiturates, methaqualone (Quaalude), and tranquilizers. Stimulants that become addictive include cocaine, amphetamine, and caffeine. Opiates such as heroin, hallucinogens such as LSD, and other drugs such as marijuana, PCP, and even solvents round out the list.

By current estimates, in any given six-month period 2 percent of Americans are addicted or abuse drugs, although this figure may be low. Over their lifetime, close to 6 percent of Americans will abuse drugs at one point. If tobacco is counted as a drug, one in three Americans will have abused drugs at some point. Each year 350,000 Americans will die from smoking, up to 150,000 from the effects of alcohol, and under 10,000 from all the other drugs.

The opportunities for addiction are ample, even without using illicit drugs. For instance, of the close to one and a half billion prescriptions written each year in the U.S., about a fifth are for drugs, such as tranquilizers and sedatives, that can be addicting.

The vast majority of drug problems occur during the late teens and twenties. By middle age drug abuse drops markedly, with the notable exception of alcoholism, which becomes more of a problem.

The specific state induced by a given drug depends on its chemistry:

- The *opiates,* such as codeine, opium, morphine, and heroin, induce a drowsy euphoria; they also diminish appetite and sex drive. If you become a chronic user, opiates can blunt your sensitivity to pain and discomfort, leading you to neglect your health. Injections carry further risks: infected veins, blocked arteries, hepatitis, and AIDS.
- *Stimulants,* such as amphetamine and cocaine, make you feel alert, talkative, and euphoric. They can also make you irritable, aggressive, agitated, and paranoid. Beyond that, they can lead to temporary impotence, exhaustion, malnutrition, hallucinations, tremor and dry mouth, weight loss, heart disease, and even convulsions. Chronic cocaine use can put a hole in your septum, the cartilage that divides your nostrils. Even minor stimulants have serious side effects: tobacco increases your risk of lung cancer, heart disease, and emphysema.
- *Depressants or "downers"* include barbiturates, methaqualone (Quaalude or "ludes"), and tranquilizers such as Xanax, Librium, or Valium. They offer a dreamy drowsiness that can leave you confused and unable to pay attention. They can also lead to heart conditions, delirium, and seizures.
- Other abused drugs include *cannabis, PCP,* and *solvents.* Their highs are marked by euphoria and fluent ideas, peaceful feelings, and a sense of unreality. Among the adverse symptoms: anxiety and panic, and for solvents, kidney and liver damage.

So why, then, do people beome dependent on any of these drugs? Many do not. A large but unknown number of people have experimented with these drugs and not become dependent, or they have stopped on their own when the side effects became worrisome or unwelcome.

But some who start to take drugs for their recreational uses or as solace from unhappiness find they cannot stop. Some of these do not realize they have a problem; they do not see (or choose not to notice) the detrimental effects of drug use on their families, their friendships, their work or school. For others, the hold of the drug is so strong that even though they know full well the damage it does them, they cannot stop.

Denial and drugs. People addicted to drugs rarely want to face the fact of their addiction, nor do they want to be treated. They want their drug. To get it they will often lie, cheat, steal, and deceive those who love and trust them the most. The drug addict operates under a double onus: his habit is something he wants to deny or keep secret, and in the U.S. at least, it is illegal. That pressures drug addicts to be not just secretive about their habit, but devious.

Often a double denial is at work: the person hides his addiction from others and denies to himself that it is a problem that requires help. If such a person goes to a physician for such problems as infections or liver disease that are caused by drug use, he or she may either conceal the role of drugs or acknowledge it without also seeing it as a problem or without having any intention of trying to kick the habit.

Note: No matter which drug you or someone you are concerned about use, the use of a given drug and its treatment have much in common with other drugs. The introductory part of this chapter applies to all drug abuse, while the later sections focus on what is unique to a given drug.

Signs to Look For

Because subterfuge and denial come so naturally to people who are addicted, the signs of drug abuse are not always as obvious as in other disorders—such as depression, say, where the person is quite willing to admit the emotional pain he or she feels and wants help.

Still, the signs of addiction are clear if the person is willing to face up to the facts. If you know someone well, many signs that he or she is addicted to a drug should be clear to you, too.

Three or more of the following symptoms indicate *dependence:*

- Loss of control over the drug use; e.g., taking ever-increasing amounts or spending more and more time taking the drugs, or taking more than you originally intended.
- Being unable to cut down.
- Large amounts of time spent getting, taking, or recovering from the drug. At the extreme, virtually the whole day revolves around drug use.
- Being intoxicated while fulfilling responsibilities at home, school, or work.
- Giving up other activities because of drug use.
- Continued drug use despite awareness of its toll on your social, psychological, or work life.

- Drug tolerance, which requires that more and more of the drug be used in order to get the same effect.
- Withdrawal symptoms if drug use is stopped.
- Taking the drug to avoid withdrawal.

Drug *abuse* follows two main patterns: the person continues to use the drug even though he or she realizes it is affecting his or her work, relationships, family life, or health; or the person continues to use the drug even when it is hazardous, despite the risks.

People who abuse drugs may not be dependent on them, but the abuse puts them at serious risk nevertheless. For instance, some may drive while high on drugs; others may continue to share needles despite the risk of contracting AIDS; and some may continue occasional use even though it exacerbates a disease such as diabetes.

What counts is not how much of a drug the person uses, but whether using it has painful consequences to himself or others. Often the cost is social: getting violent and hurting people while high, or having repeated arguments with family or friends about using drugs. As the drug becomes an increasing focal point of the addicted person's life, he or she becomes less reliable, from failing to take proper care of children to not showing up at work.

People addicted to a drug tend to share certain traits regardless of the particular drug they use, including:

- A low tolerance for frustration; being quick to anger.
- A self-centered, demanding attitude.
- Lack of advance planning for even the basics, such as how to pay the rent.
- Fixation on fulfilling whatever need or desire presents itself.
- Preoccupation with what other people can do for them.
- Continual pushing of the limits, testing to see how far they can go and what they can get away with.

Multiple-drug use. Your problem may not be just with one drug, but with several. The more drugs you use, the more complicated the effects will be and the more difficult stopping becomes. Abusing more than one drug—a pattern that has become increasingly common—means, for instance, that the person is prone to more severe withdrawal when he or she stops.

If someone is brought to an emergency room intoxicated on several substances, the mix of symptoms can confound those trying to treat him. Someone being "dried out" for heroin use, for example, may suddenly start having convulsions from barbiturate withdrawal.

☐ Jimmy, nineteen, hung around with a "wild" crowd. No one worked; they lived off their families and committed petty crimes to raise money. Jimmy's speciality was car stereos. All his money went for drugs and "good times."

At fourteen Jimmy had started drinking beer, wine, whiskey—anything he could get his hands on. At fifteen he added marijuana and hashish. The next year he began using "speed" and "ludes" (amphetamine and Quaalude). And by seventeen he had added cocaine to the mix. He had no particular favorite among drugs; he'd use whatever was at hand.

One night, though, Jimmy's friends brought him to the emergency room, terrified he would die. Jimmy was shouting angrily but making little sense. His breath came in irregular gasps, his heart was racing, his pupils were completely dilated, and he was shouting at someone no one else could see. None of his friends could—or would—say exactly what drugs he was on. Three days later, Jimmy went into convulsions; luckily he was still in the hospital. When he could talk again, he admitted to having taken barbiturates in addition to "lots of cocaine, lots of beer, and lots of joints."

What You Should Know About Treatment

Resistance and Denial

Most everyone who goes into treatment for drug use confronts some degree of denial that they have a problem. But to succeed, you have to face the extent to which your drug use is a problem. Often people secretly hope that they can use the treatment to get enough self-control that they can still use the drug, but without its use having devastating effects in their lives. That is a fantasy. To help you overcome denial, many programs will require you to make a detailed list of the problems that drug use has caused in your life, or in the lives of those close to you. This list will be used again and again to counter your attempts to downplay the effects of your drug use.

Expect, too, to encounter resistance to the changes in your life that getting off drugs demands. You'll have to stop seeing the people with whom you've been taking drugs, and to stop hanging out where you habitually got or used drugs in the past.

Getting someone else with a drug abuse problem to face the fact of his or her problem can be even more difficult. One effective means is to have someone else who has successfully overcome an addiction to the same drug have a straight, no-punches-pulled talk with him or her. Below, we'll discuss a newer method of arranging an intervention that uses the entire family.

Even after one accepts the need for help, the power of the drug continues. Unlike most people who come for help, those who do so for drug abuse are typically still under the control of the drug: they want help, but they still long for the high, can't forget it, and often still crave it.

Inpatient vs. Outpatient Treatment

The first decision is whether you need "detox," a period of medically supervised withdrawal from the drug, or whether you can safely stop taking the drug on your own. That decision depends on whether you show any signs of withdrawal or dependence, and if the drug you are abusing produces serious withdrawal symptoms. The decision also depends on whether you have been abusing several different kinds of drugs, have a drug-related medical problem, or are suicidal or prone to violence. If any of these conditions apply, inpatient detox is called for. This will normally take place in a hospital or detox center, where withdrawal symptoms can be carefully monitored and where access to the drug can be controlled when the urge to use again is strong.

(*Note:* Withdrawal from sedatives cause the most dangerous reactions. These include barbiturates such as phenobarbital and Seconal; Quaalude; benzodiaze-pines—tranquilizers such as Valium and Librium; and alcohol. If unsupervised by medical personnel, withdrawal reactions from these substances can be fatal.)

On the other hand, inpatient or residential detox is unneeded if:

- The drug you have been abusing doesn't produce dependence or withdrawal symptoms.
- Withdrawal from this particular drug is discomforting, but not potentially serious. Withdrawal symptoms do not need constant medical supervision.
- You have been abstinent for periods before without having had any withdrawal symptoms.
- You have no serious complicating conditions, such as a medical or emotional problem apart from the drug abuse itself.
- You've been able to discontinue or cut down on your own in the past.
- Family or friends are willing to stand by and help you stay away from the drug.
- You prefer staying at home while being treated instead of going to a drug treatment facility.

Once detox is completed, most people can be discharged and continue treatment on an outpatient basis. Some may need follow-up residential treatment to support recovery, either in a short-term rehabilitation center or a halfway house specializing in substance abuse rehabilitation. This is more likely if the drug use has been heavy, especially if it has reached the point of compulsion. If you freebase cocaine, smoke crack, or inject opiates, you may fall into this category. Continued residential rehab may also be necessary if you have been dealing drugs to support your habit.

Short-term residential treatment may also be indicated if you have few social supports—no family or close friends who can see you through stopping and give you emotional support in staying off the drug—or if you have repeatedly tried to give up on your own without success.

Once outpatient treatment begins, whether immediately or after detox and inpatient rehab, therapy focuses on the same issue: maintaining abstinence.

Abstinence

Your goal has to be to get off the drug and *stay off*. That demands you immediately stop using it when you begin treatment. It also means getting rid of any drug paraphernalia and supplies and stopping all contact with other users or dealers. Going into therapy without stopping your drug use is pointless, especially if you are drug dependent.

Staying off is as important as stopping. Many addicts stop their drug only to start again weeks or months later. Each time you stop and start again makes it that much more difficult to stop for good.

Trying to continue drugs just for "recreational" use is not a viable alternative, especially if your habit has been serious enough to fit the description of dependency on page 434. Trying to give up one drug while continuing to take others is only fooling yourself. A new drug, including alcohol, can also trigger a craving for the drug you're trying to stop. A single beer can lower your resistance to the temptation of drugs.

Your long-term goal is to change your life so that it is satisfying without drugs. That may mean, for instance, changing your favored ways of socializing, avoiding friends whom you used to take drugs with, and finding new friends who don't use and won't tempt you to use. One strong argument for a peer self-help group such as Narcotics Anonymous is that there you will be with people like yourself who are fighting a drug use habit.

The first phase of treatment—the first six months or more—will focus on abstinence from all drugs. During this phase the most effective treatment usually includes participating in a recovery group with others who have had the same problems with drugs as yourself. They can help you face the day-to-day challenge of resisting the temptation to turn to the drug when you are feeling tense, anxious, depressed, hopeless, or inadequate—whatever feelings trigger your desire for the drug most intensely. You will be encouraged to join a self-help group such as Narcotics Anonymous, Cocaine Anonymous, even Alcoholics Anonymous, which has also proven helpful to people with substance abuse problems. Daily or near-daily meetings with people like yourself who are recovering from drug use will help you stay straight with yourself. The people in these groups are sensitized to the lies and self-deceptions that accompany drug use.

Individual psychotherapy can be a helpful adjunct to the group approach, particularly if it focuses on practical problem-solving—for instance, how to handle those moments when you are most tempted to use drugs. Exploratory therapies that seek to find why you became addicted, or that encourage intense expression of your feelings, are *not* helpful at this point. These approaches run the risk of precipitating a relapse. You may need more frequent sessions with your counselor or therapist in the beginning—perhaps several times a week. The counselor, or another staff member if you are being seen in a clinic, may need to be available by phone after hours. These sessions should be for support and encouragement, straight talk about supporting abstinence, dealing with recurrent cravings and urges to use, handling whatever situations or feelings are giving you the most trouble from day to day, and rebuilding your life without drugs.

Another help will be getting your family to groups or meetings where they will learn about the nature of drug abuse and addiction and what you are likely to go through during recovery. The better informed they are, the better they can support your recovery. This will also help them get support for themselves, which they probably need by this point.

Urine Testing

To help you stay straight, your therapist, doctor, or rehab program may require regular urine testing as a part of treatment. While you may be skilled at fooling people about drugs you're taking, a urine test will not lie.

The point of urine tests is not to catch you in a lie. Instead it is to help you in your battle for self-control, to help in the struggle to resist the impulse to take the drug. Knowing that a single lapse will show up in a urine test can strengthen your resolve and commitment. It can make the difference in a moment of indecision.

Urine tests are part of most drug treatment programs. The specific consequences of a positive test will vary from program to program, but they are usually clearly stated at the beginning of treatment. For instance, you might sign a contract agreeing to disclose your slip to someone important to you if your urine test comes back positive.

Resisting the Craving for Drugs

As you go through treatment, your main challenge will be resisting the urge for drugs. The urge will likely recur time and again, often unexpectedly. Typically the urges are triggered by people and places that are associated with past drug use. But the urge can also come from an emotional state—anxiety, depression, anger, frustration, boredom—that you habitually turned to drugs to avoid.

Try not to see these cravings as signs of failure, or signs that treatment isn't working. They are a normal, even predictable, part of treatment. The urges do not build and build until you inevitably have to give in to them. They typically peak in an hour or two and then pass. Learning to resist these urges is a key to treatment. You will learn some techniques in therapy, such as for relaxation, that can detach you from the urges, enabling you to watch them come and go without feeling compelled to give in.

Preventing Relapse

An occasional slip is not the end—if you use it to learn. If and when you do slip, this is almost certain to trigger a cascade of bad feelings about yourself. You can be left feeling like a failure for giving in to temptation, and that you're helpless to stop the drug from taking over your life again. Many treatment programs emphasize using a slip as an opportunity to understand the inner forces and social settings that trigger your craving. Once you see that, you then rethink how to handle these same moments more effectively, without giving in to the drug.

One of the best ways to deal with slips is to head them off while they are still just cravings. When you first recognize a craving, for instance, take action to make it harder to get drugs or seek out friends or family who are not users. In treatment you'll learn to devise alternative plans for those moments of temptation. Each time you let the craving pass without acting on it, you weaken its hold on you.

If you start to have more frequent lapses, then there should be major consequences for your treatment program. Individual therapy may be suspended, or you may be given a more intensive treatment contract that has stronger consequences for lapses. Or you may be required to check into a drug treatment facility for a time.

Once you've managed to remain abstinent for several months, the focus of treatment typically shifts to making changes that will keep you from relapsing. Being in a group of others recovering from drugs is a major help at this point, as is psychotherapy, whether by yourself, with your partner, or with your family. At this point programs often cut back on the frequency of therapy and groups, perhaps to a twice-weekly recovery group and therapy once a week. Whatever the program or your therapist recommends, however, do whatever it takes to support your sobriety. For many, this might mean daily NA or AA groups.

During this stage of treatment you'll deal with such issues as fond memories of the high you used to get from drugs, and the temptation to turn to them again when you feel tense, depressed, or otherwise upset. This recall of the drug is distorted: it ignores the unpleasant and destructive side of drug abuse, and its very high costs. You'll need to remind yourself often why you stopped in the first place.

You'll also need to be watchful of slipping back into the habits that supported your drug-taking. These include contacting friends you used drugs with, visiting the places where you used to get or take drugs, or letting stress build up without doing anything to relieve it, so that the thought of the drug seems more and more desirable.

Recovery: An Ongoing Process

People who have been addicted to drugs are always at some risk of a flare-up that may start a spiral into abuse and addiction again. The final goal of therapy for drug use is to consolidate the gains you've made so you are immune to temptation, but realistic: not overly confident or denying once again that you had a problem.

Ongoing membership in a recovery group will be invaluable at this point, both because of the demand for honesty and the support you'll feel. But as time passes, the issues that will loom largest for you are likely to be feelings of low self-esteem or having to catch up for time lost to drugs in your social, emotional, or work life. Once your focus shifts to these issues, you may find that psychotherapy is especially helpful. At this point, you may benefit from a therapy that is not just supportive or behavioral, but exploratory.

SPECIFIC DRUGS: WHAT TO LOOK FOR AND SPECIAL TREATMENT CONSIDERATIONS

Sedatives

Barbiturates

Barbiturates are medications prescribed as sedatives. Those that reach the black market are usually diverted from legitimate sources. Prescriptions of barbiturates are as tightly regulated as those for morphine. People dependent on barbiturates often get around this by obtaining prescriptions from a number of different physicians simultaneously.

The high of barbiturates is a drowsy sense of euphoria, warm and pleasant. The signs that someone is on a barbiturate high are similar to what you would see in someone who is drunk: sluggishness and slurred speech, poor coordination and a "drunken" gait, a spaced-out state with poor memory and attention, open expression of sexual impulses, quickness to anger. Sometimes the person will be suicidal or seem paranoid.

Barbiturates are often used along with certain other drugs to boost their effects. Used with alcohol, they enhance the sense of intoxication; they can also be used to relieve withdrawal symptoms. For heroin users, barbiturates are a way to intensify weak heroin. Using barbiturates with amphetamines adds a soothing sense that guards against feelings of paranoia or agitation. People who inject barbiturates— the most intense use—often do so as a cheap alternative to heroin.

Barbiturates are extremely dangerous. You can die from taking too much. When taken along with alcohol, barbiturates are particularly lethal.

The barbiturates most commonly abused are:

- phenobarbital, which lasts twelve to twenty-four hours
- Amytal (amobarbital), which lasts six to twelve hours
- Nembutal (pentobarbital), also known as yellow jackets and nembies
- Seconal (secobarbital), or "reds," "red devils," or "downers," which are short-acting, lasting three to six hours

While occasional use does not lead to an increased tolerance or withdrawal re-action when you stop, regular use for a month or two generally does. This means that you need steadily greater doses to get the same effect, and that withdrawal symptoms will occur when you stop.

A mild withdrawal reaction from barbiturates includes anxiety and irritability, sweating and weakness, nausea or vomiting, shaking and tremors, and a racing heart. More severe withdrawal symptoms can include convulsions as intense as grand mal seizures. At its most severe, the withdrawal reaction can lead to a lethal car-diovascular collapse.

Of all the addictive drugs, barbiturates have the most severe withdrawal reactions. If you go through withdrawal as part of treatment, it is essential that you do so in a hospital or treatment center with a medically supervised detox unit.

Quaalude (Methaqualone)

Although chemically different from barbiturates, Quaalude is another sedative with similar effects. The drug is no longer legally manufactured in the U.S., although it is made in illicit labs as well as smuggled into the country.

Called ludes, mandrakes, or soapers on the street, Quaalude is used mostly by teenagers and younger adults. One appeal is the belief that the drug intensifies sex.

A particularly dangerous use of Quaalude is taking it with alcohol. Like all sedatives, Quaalude can be fatal when taken with alcohol. The signs of a Quaalude overdose include restlessness and agitation, delirium, muscle spasms, and convul-sions.

Note: A Quaalude overdose requires emergency medical care, including having the person's stomach pumped.

Tranquilizers (Benzodiazepines)

While tranquilizers were the most commonly prescribed medication in the early sixties, they are used less frequently these days. But because they are still prescribed, those who are addicted to them can often get them from a physician. The high of tranquilizers is a drowsy, easygoing sense of euphoria.

Among the most common of the some two dozen brands of tranquilizers are Valium, Dalmane, Serax, and Librium. Tranquilizers are often taken by cocaine addicts who want to ease their crash after a cocaine high. Among heroin addicts the appeal of tranquilizers is their enhancement of the euphoria when used along with heroin.

Withdrawal symptoms from regular use usually begin two or three days after stopping the drug. Symptoms of withdrawal include anxiety and an uneasy feeling, hypersensitivity to intense sounds and sights, nausea and vomiting, muscle twitches, and at high doses (100 mg/day or more), convulsions. The body rids itself of tranquilizers very slowly, so symptoms can last several weeks.

Preferred Treatments for Sedative Dependence

Approach. A behavioral approach to stopping sedative abuse in combination with a supportive therapy are the two most frequently suggested approaches.

Medication. Yes, to handle the symptoms of withdrawal.

Setting. All therapists agree that treatment for sedative addiction should begin in a hospital or other inpatient treatment facility. At later stages in treatment, a residential or day-treatment setting may be called for. And as treatment continues after the person has left those settings, many therapists advise continued outpatient treatment.

Format. The most highly recommended format is individual therapy in conjunction with group treatment. About half of therapists also recommend the family be involved in the treatment where possible.

Frequency. Most therapists say that therapy should be frequent—twice or more a week during the recovery period. Recovery group meetings should be daily to begin with.

Duration. Inpatient detox, and rehab if necessary, may take from several days to two to three weeks. Continued outpatient treatment needs to be open-ended.

Stimulants

Cocaine

Cocaine produces an intense euphoria, a sense of well-being and self-assuredness. Since the 1970s cocaine has been steadily gaining in popularity, and by the late 1980s was second only to marijuana in numbers of people using it in the U.S.

The cocaine high, which usually lasts a half hour to an hour, is followed by a crash into depression and anxiety. To cushion against the crash, most cocaine users habitually take other drugs with the cocaine, such as marijuana or tranquilizers.

Occasional users most commonly take cocaine by snorting it. This method is the least addicting, since it does not offer the intensity produced by the other two methods, injection or the smoking of crack, crack being a pellet form of pure cocaine. Injecting or smoking cocaine delivers a far more potent high than does snorting; those who prefer these methods are far more likely to become addicted.

Cocaine produces an extremely intense craving in those who become addicted. Addicts are obsessed by the thought of cocaine. Since the cost of the habit is high, addicts frequently turn to crime or to dealing the drug to supply their own habit.

One frequent pattern of cocaine abuse is a binge, lasting a day or two, followed by a crash of a day or so. The binge is typically marked by lack of sleep and food; the crash is a period of exhaustion, depression, excessive sleep, overeating, and sometimes muscle pain and chills.

During the crash, cocaine addicts often turn to alcohol, sedatives, or narcotics to ease their misery. The craving then leads to another binge. This cycle of bingeing and crashing often goes on until the person's body (or family and friends) reach a crisis point.

Signs of cocaine addiction. One of the central signs that someone is addicted to cocaine is that he or she is preoccupied by the drug, obsessed with getting it. Other signs include:

- the jitters
- hypersensitivity to bright lights or loud noises
- irritability and agitation
- trouble concentrating
- being unable to sleep (or during the crash, sleeping for extremely long periods)
- losing weight
- loss of interest in sex
- compulsive absorption in meaningless acts such as sorting, scribbling, pacing, or taking objects apart and putting them back together
- paranoid thoughts, such as that he or she is the object of a conspiracy by some group

Other indications are suddenly frequenting after-hours clubs, which is a common place for cocaine to be sold; suddenly falling into debt; becoming self-absorbed and undependable in meeting work or family obligations. Another telltale sign: frequently disappearing during social events (to take cocaine).

Specific health risks are also associated with long-term abuse. If someone snorts cocaine, his nose will eventually become chronically runny and clogged, inflamed and swollen, and may develop an ulcer. Heavy snorting will result in a perforation of the septum, the tissue separating the nostrils. Those who smoke crack can damage their lungs, sharply reducing their lung capacity. And those who inject cocaine open themselves to the dangers of all drug users who share needles: hepatitis and other diseases, especially AIDS.

If users take too much cocaine or have been taking it for a long time, they may have a reaction that includes intense anxiety and paranoia, dangerously elevated blood pressure, and a racing heart. They may also become hyperactive and agitated, extremely vigilant and hyperaware of what is happening around them, and experience mental confusion that makes their speech rambling. Along with these symptoms they may get violent—cocaine is one drug that readily gets its users into trouble with the law for their violence.

The physical toll of cocaine, especially when smoked or injected, can include seizures, stroke, or death from respiratory arrest or heart failure. An overdose can be fatal. The risk of death is even higher among those who combine cocaine injection with heroin, a combination known as a speedball.

The psychological toll of cocaine abuse is, at the extreme, psychosis: the person may become lost in a paranoid delusion, go on a sexual binge, or have hallucinations, such as that bugs are crawling under the skin. Often the delusions are jealous ones, where the person becomes convinced that a partner is cheating on him or her. One particular danger: sometimes these delusions lead to murderous impulses that are acted on.

What Therapists Recommend

Approach. A cognitive-behavioral approach to stopping cocaine use is by far the most highly recommended therapy. This approach is typically employed in combination with supportive therapy. The focus is on learning to master the urges and situations that compelled you to use cocaine.

Medication. No medication yet exists for the treatment of cocaine dependence, though antidepressants may reduce cravings. Medication may be prescribed for symptoms such as severe depression or anxiety as an adjunct to treatment during recovery.

Setting. Therapists are divided; some think a hospital or other inpatient treatment center is required for treatment of cocaine abuse; others see it as best treated in office visits or other outpatient settings. In general, the principle of least-restrictive setting applies. If you and your therapist think you can succeed in stopping cocaine use while living at home with help, you should try this first.

Format. Group therapy in combination with individual therapy is the most highly recommended approach. But family therapy is also highly recommended—in practice that means involving the family in your treatment plan if at all possible.

Frequency. Daily sessions with a group and/or individual therapist are usually necessary in the withdrawal phase and during the immediate postwithdrawal period. Frequent meetings will continue to be necessary until some sobriety has been achieved.

Duration. Open-ended.

What You Should Know About Therapy

Withdrawal. If you have been using cocaine heavily for several days, stopping will produce an intense withdrawal reaction that will peak about two to four days after you stop. The typical symptoms of cocaine withdrawal include fatigue, apathy, and depression; insomnia or sleeping for long periods; and a general malaise. Some feelings such as irritability, depression, and a general malaise may last for weeks.

Perhaps most important is that withdrawal brings a severe craving for the drug. At times you will find yourself obsessed with the thought of getting more cocaine. Since your goal is to stay off the drug, that means staying away from people and situations that have been sources for you.

Since cocaine withdrawal does not usually involve dangerous physical symptoms, medical supervision is usually unneeded if cocaine is the only drug of abuse. But if you have been using other drugs along with cocaine—sedatives and alcohol are the most common ones—then you *do* need to be medically supervised while going through withdrawal, since stopping these drugs can trigger life-threatening physical reactions.

People with severe cocaine habits sometimes undergo overwhelming anxiety or a manic high, or even a psychosis, during withdrawal. If so, emergency psychiatric care is essential.

An inpatient facility, such as a treatment center that specializes in treating cocaine and other substance addictions, is called for if you have been unsuccessful in attempts to quit on your own. This is especially true if checking into a facility is the only way you can keep yourself away from people and places that have been sources of the drug.

Along with cocaine, you have to give up other drugs you might have been using, such as alcohol or sedatives. Because you've taken them as part of the cocaine use cycle, they are likely to trigger your craving for cocaine, while lowering your ability to resist. The only way to go straight is across the board.

Psychotherapy. Psychotherapy alone is not enough in treating cocaine; it has to be part of a larger treatment program. The best approaches are cognitive-behavioral and supportive. Behavioral programs are set up to reinforce success in staying off the drug and to discourage habits that might lead you back to it.

A supportive approach involves help and encouragement in staying away from sources of cocaine and in dealing with the practical day-to-day problems you now face off the drug.

More introspective therapies that seek to help you understand what in your past might have made you vulnerable to cocaine addiction are not a helpful approach, especially at the start of treatment when your main struggle is to get through each day without cocaine.

Group therapy is extremely helpful. Groups especially for cocaine abusers exist in such organizations as Cocaine Anonymous, Alcoholics Anonymous, and Narcotics Anonymous. These groups are modeled on the successful twelve-step approach of AA.

Amphetamines

There are several kinds of amphetamine, or "speed," which are also major stimulants and also widely abused. Most brands of amphetamines that are available as a legal pharmaceutical substance are also commonly abused. The best known include Dexedrine ("dexie"), Methedrine ("meth"), Ritalin, and Benzedrine ("bennies").

The amphetamine high is typified by a euphoric sense of well-being and energy, a sharpening of speaking and related abilities, a loss of appetite, and an insensitivity to pain. Prolonged use often leads to agitation, paranoia, and malnutrition.

While amphetamine was once prescribed for weight loss, that is no longer the case. People quickly develop a tolerance to amphetamine so that higher and higher doses are necessary to produce the same effect. Within just three days, for example, a "speed freak" can jump from taking fifteen milligrams of amphetamine to two thousand milligrams a day in order to get the same high.

Amphetamine shares many characteristics with cocaine. Like cocaine, amphetamine produces a state of chronic suspiciousness and paranoia in longtime users, and an overdose of either can be fatal. As with cocaine, withdrawal from amphetamine after lengthy use or a binge brings a crash. Regular users find the craving for the drug dominates their lives.

The typical pattern is a cycle of heavy use for several days to a week, followed by a crash, which ends with resumed use. The viciousness of this cycle stems in part from the mounting psychological effects of the drug. People who suffer feelings of inadequacy or depression may at first feel drawn to amphetamine because its high buoys their spirits and self-confidence. But when they crash, the depression is even deeper, so they are compelled to turn again to amphetamine for relief.

Signs to Look For

During the amphetamine high, a person typically shows many or most of the following:

- restlessness and talkativeness
- sleeplessness
- irritability and hostility; proneness to violence

- confusion and anxiety
- "the shakes": tremors, twitches, jitteriness

Physically, amphetamine intoxication brings several health risks. These include a sharp rise in blood pressure, hemorrhages and strokes, convulsions, and coma. Cardiovascular shock from amphetamine can be fatal.

During the crash, chronic amphetamine users typically show:

- anxiety and fearfulness
- discomfort and dissatisfaction
- lethargy and fatigue
- nightmares
- insatiable hunger

They may also complain of such symptoms as stomach and muscle cramps, headaches, or nausea. Other long-term effects include "amphetamine psychosis," which resembles a paranoid psychosis. The psychosis is usually triggered when a heavy user takes even larger amounts than he is used to. The person is seized by the delusion that some person or group is persecuting him, believes that trivial events have great personal meaning, or has terrifying hallucinations. While the psychosis usually passes within a few days or weeks, the suspiciousness can persist for months afterward.

What You Should Know About Therapy

Amphetamine addiction presents special complications during withdrawal, which usually peaks in two to four days after use of the drug stops. During withdrawal, amphetamine users typically become deeply depressed and often feel suicidal.

This means that withdrawal should be done in a supervised medical setting, such as a psychiatric hospital or drug treatment center. During the peak of withdrawal, the person may have to be under continuous supervision, and even under physical restraint.

If the person has been paranoid, as few people as possible should be involved in his care, and his surroundings should be simplified. Anything he considers a threat should be removed. Antipsychotic drugs are typically prescribed if the person becomes psychotic during withdrawal, or tranquilizers if he becomes extremely agitated. A subsequent depression may be treated with antidepressants.

Opiates

Opiates are chemicals derived from the juice of the opium poppy. The best known of the opiates are morphine, heroin, and codeine. Synthetic versions include Dilaudid,

Demerol, and Darvon. Of these, the most common addiction is to heroin. The majority of heroin addicts use other drugs as well, most often downers such as alcohol and sedatives.

Because heroin is injected, sharing needles is a major hazard: one of the highest rates of spread for AIDS and hepatitis is among heroin addicts. But the death rate among heroin addicts is high apart from these diseases. Addicts also die from overdoses, infections from dirty needles, a generally lowered resistance to disease, and murder.

Statistically, if a heroin addict survives to his or her mid-thirties, there is a good chance of a decline in use, and by forty of stopping altogether—though whether for psychological or biological reasons is unknown. Treatment can help the abuser stop using heroin at any age.

The high from opiates includes numbness to pain (its main medical application), a drowsy tranquility and pleasant mood, a sense of warmth, heaviness, and relaxation, and a cloudy, dreamy state of mind. Along with these psychological changes come dry mouth and itchy skin, flushing, and a slowing of metabolism.

Heroin is about twice as powerful as morphine. If heroin is injected, there is an immediate high, a rush that is described as akin to orgasm. The rush is followed by drowsiness, or "nodding off." First-time users, however, often do not experience these pleasant states. Instead they feel nausea.

Of course, in cases of terminal illness such as cancer, medically prescribed opiates can make the intense pain at the end more bearable.

Once people start using opiates, a rapid tolerance develops, pushing the user to seek more each time in order to get the desired effect. The high risk of death from overdose makes heroin tolerance particularly dangerous. While someone who has a strong tolerance can take hundreds of milligrams of morphine, only sixty milligrams could kill someone who has not built up tolerance.

Signs to Look For

The most common addiction to opiates involves shooting morphine or heroin. When someone "shoots up," the fleeting rush is followed by a longer-lasting period of floating drowsiness. These longer-lasting signs of addiction include:

- slurred speech and slowed movements
- trouble paying attention or remembering
- self-absorption and apathy to surroundings
- difficulty in relating to others or completing tasks
- feeling ill at ease between times of drug-taking

The telltale sign of addiction: needle tracks on the arms, legs, ankles, or groin. The signs of overdose include:

- slowed breathing
- coma
- low body temperature
- pupils dilated to a pinpoint

Note: An overdose is a medical emergency. Take the person to the nearest hospital emergency room at once.

The risk of sudden death from heroin extends beyond overdose. Two kinds of psychiatric drugs, MAOI antidepressants (see p. 616) and antipsychotic medications (see p. 621), enhance the chemical action of opiates. Taking heroin while you are on either type of medication significantly heightens the risk of death from respiratory failure.

Withdrawal. Withdrawal begins four to eight hours after taking the last dose and can last up to ten days. Signs of withdrawal include:

- craving: pleading, scheming, threatening, begging to get the drug
- anxiety and restlessness
- misery: loss of appetite, nausea, aches, spasms, twitches, cramps

The physical misery of heroin withdrawal is intense. The person may have severe diarrhea and vomiting, be unable to sleep, develop a rapid pulse and high blood pressure, and suffer dehydration. Some end up in the fetal position, aching from severe stomach cramps.

Heroin withdrawal has lent two phrases to the language. One symptom of withdrawal is goose bumps; *cold turkey* derives from their resemblance to the skin of a turkey. And the phrase *kicking the habit* may derive from the muscle spasms and twitches of addicts going through withdrawal.

In treatment, withdrawal can be initiated by the injection of a substance that blocks the chemical activity of opiates. Ordinarily, the full panoply of withdrawal symptoms occurs only when the drug is stopped in someone who is heavily addicted.

What You Should Know About Therapy

There is disagreement among those who treat opiate abuse and dependence. Some favor a "soft" approach, which uses methadone, a heroin substitute, as part of treatment. Others advocate a "tough" approach—a total elimination of all drugs rather than substituting one drug to combat another, since methadone itself is addicting.

Methadone is a synthetic version of heroin that can be taken by mouth as a substitute. It is mildly addicting, but much less so than heroin. Taking methadone produces a pleasant, euphoric feeling and wards off the symptoms of withdrawal, which addicts understandably dread. Most important, it blocks the effects of heroin.

Other chemicals, such as naltrexone, also block the effects of heroin, but do not produce a euphoria. These have proven less successful in treatment because addicts are reluctant to use them instead of their drug.

The strategy in methadone maintenance therapy is to gradually lower the daily dose until withdrawal is complete. Although there is still a withdrawal reaction, it is less severe than with heroin.

Methadone does have certain advantages. For one, it is legal and can be dispensed by prescription. That prevents the desperate daily search for heroin, as well as the criminal behavior that often pays for the daily dose. People on methadone can hold a job and otherwise resume a normal life.

Another advantage of methadone is that it keeps people from using needles. Many of the health hazards associated with opiate addiction are due to dirty needles, which transmit the AIDS virus, hepatitis, and systemic infection.

Perhaps the strongest argument for methadone is that after several years on methadone maintenance, the majority of those who stay in the programs are able to live a productive life.

Many people on methadone never withdraw; maintenance can go on for years. One argument against methadone is that it is a substitute addiction; the person remains dependent on methadone. The use of methadone has also led to an illicit market in the drug, with some addicts getting high taking methadone instead of heroin. Finally, heroin can still be abused along with methadone.

The alternative to methadone is "going cold turkey," that is, stopping entirely. Because the withdrawal is so severe, it should be done in a treatment facility where there is medical supervision.

Programs that do not use methadone are usually based on intense group therapy with other recovering addicts in a clinic or program specializing in recovery from substance abuse, less often in a residential setting such as a halfway house run as a "therapeutic community." The therapeutic community is a residence of people who all share the same drug problem. The rules demand total abstinence; joining requires high motivation.

The therapeutic community aims to change completely the drug addict's lifestyle. In addition to taking him off the drug and out of the friendships and locations that have been the basis for his drug use, it attempts to develop personal qualities that will serve as armor in the fight to resist drugs: honesty, responsibility, useful social skills, and avoidance of criminal behavior.

Staff are typically former addicts themselves. The group sessions, which are daily, are confrontational. Any lies, self-deceptions, or other shams are baldly confronted by the others, who are all too familiar with the ways addicts alibi and cheat to maintain their dependency. The community members become the person's key peer group; contact with old friends who are addicts is forbidden.

While these programs are demanding and difficult, and the dropout rate is high, those who stay with them are highly successful in getting off and staying off drugs.

Group therapy is the main emphasis in most outpatient treatment programs for opiate addiction. For ex-addicts who are "graduates" of a therapeutic community, groups such as Narcotics Anonymous, where other members are going through the same process of recovery, are recommended. You're more likely to listen to what people have to tell you if they've been where you are.

If you live with or are in close contact with your family, then family involvement in treatment can be helpful. If you are close to your family, then your addiction is of concern to everyone in your family and has affected them in some way. Meeting together, family members can consider ways they may have been abetting your habit and can find ways of being with you that will help you get free of drugs. Once you are off drugs, your family can be of immense help in supporting your resolve to stay clean.

Individual therapy is not the first choice for treating opiate addiction. If you are in individual therapy, the focus should be on abstinence—getting off and staying off drugs—nothing else. It should also be combined with regular participation in an ongoing peer recovery group, such as Narcotics Anonymous, or a substance abuse recovery program. The focus should be twofold: to support abstinence, and to help with the day-to-day struggles to get your life back together. Once sobriety is solidly established—six months to a year—therapy can be added to begin to address some of the longer-standing problems that preceded, and may have precipitated, your drug use.

The occasional relapse will not undermine therapy, but a pattern of continued relapse or a return to using will. For this reason, many therapists will want an understanding beforehand that if relapses persist or you resume regular use, therapy will be suspended until you stop.

Hallucinogens

The hallucinogens are a family of drugs so named because hallucinations are among their effects. They have a long role in human history as part of religious rituals for spiritual exploration. Their history as drugs of abuse is, historically speaking, very recent.

Hallucinogens are not physically addicting. People can become psychologically dependent on them, but that happens less than with other drugs of abuse, since each experience is highly unpredictable. There is no assurance, for instance, of the kind of euphoric feeling that opiates induce.

While hallucinogens are not addicting in the sense that opiates or stimulants are, they can lead to the need for therapy for several reasons. One is the effects of "bad trips," nightmarish experiences that can worsen preexisting emotional problems. Another is when they are habitually used, most often along with other drugs of abuse, to an extent that seriously interferes with the user's ability to function in life.

The hallucinogens include the peyote cactus and its synthetic form, mescaline; psilocybin, which is an analog of a substance found in a mushroom; and the most commonly used, LSD.

The effects of LSD are a prototype for all hallucinogens, though each has its own unique effects. LSD, which acts within an hour of taking it, profoundly alters consciousness. This can include:

- Altered perceptions: sights, especially colors, become brilliant and intense, and other sensations, such as touch, taste, and smell, are heightened. Kinesthesias can occur across the senses so that sights are heard and sounds are seen.
- Changes in the sense of one's body, and in the sense of time and space. The body may seem to melt and merge into the world or become separated from the self.
- Hallucinations, particularly visual.
- Intensely felt and highly changeable emotions.
- Introspection and religious or philosophical insights; mystical states.
- States of ecstasy or terror.

Flashbacks. A flashback is a sudden, unexpected reexperiencing of the drug experience. It might include, for instance, visual distortions or other hallucinations, a sense of unreality, or being swept away by an intense emotion. Flashbacks usually last a few seconds or minutes, but sometimes longer. Like the drug experience itself, they can be pleasant or troubling, blissful or terrifying. Flashbacks are most disturbing when they occur repeatedly and lead to disorientation. Most people who experience flashbacks mainly need to be reassured that the flashback does not mean they are "going crazy."

Bad trips. The adverse experiences of a "bad trip" can vary, but are always unwanted and disorganizing. They generally end when the drug's physiological effects do, within eight to fourteen hours. The specific experience can include any of those listed above, along with a sense of overwhelming fear or terror. The person forgets that the unpleasant experiences are drug-induced and will pass as the effects of the drug wear off. This can lead the user to believe he or she is "going crazy" and will never regain sanity. The worst effect of a bad trip is the triggering of a psychotic state, which is marked by intense anxiety and fearfulness, agitation, paranoid delusions, and ongoing hallucinations.

"Set and setting" are critical influences on one's experience with hallucinogens. "Set" refers to a person's expectations, while the "setting" is the circumstances under which the drug is taken. People who use hallucinogens in carefully controlled environments, and in a secure setting with someone they trust monitoring their experience, are far less likely to have a bad trip than is someone who injects a hallucinogen among strangers at a party or casually mixes a hallucinogen with other drugs while out on the town.

What You Should Know About Therapy

The best treatment for a bad trip is to reassure the person that they are in someone's care who will protect them, and to remind them their experience will pass. If the frightening experiences do not subside within the eight or so hours that the drug is most active, or the person remains highly agitated despite reassurances, medical attention is advisable. Tranquilizers can be used to help calm him or her down. If a person who is going through a bad trip is brought to a hospital emergency room, someone they know and trust should stay with them and explain to the attending physician exactly what drug they have taken.

Since hallucinogens can magnify internal conflicts, such as buried feelings of anger or fear, there is no specific form adverse reactions take. But when these disturbing feelings do not fade with time, therapy is called for. However, if you are seeking therapy for conditions connected with hallucinogen use, you should find a therapist who has some familiarity with the drugs' psychopharmacology, and who has experience working with other people who have used them.

Marijuana

Marijuana is a drug prepared from the hemp plant. Its strength varies widely, depending on the part of the plant it comes from, as well as on the particular type of plant. Marijuana is usually smoked, but it can also be eaten. THC, its active ingredient, can also be taken in capsules.

Mainly because of refinements in growing, the marijuana sold today is often up to thirty times stronger than that sold a decade or two ago. It is not as benign as many people who have not used it in many years remember it to be.

Marijuana is the most commonly used illegal drug today. Some estimates put the number of adults who have tried it at least once at 60 percent. Perhaps 10 million Americans use it regularly. In some social circles, it is as common a recreational drug as alcohol.

Just as with social drinking, the occasional use of marijuana is not considered a psychological problem or reason for psychotherapy. But when a person shows signs of abuse or dependence, therapy is indicated. Marijuana use is serious enough to treat, for instance, when people regularly depend on it to avoid unpleasant moods; when its use hampers their performance at work, school, or in family life; or when they habitually use it in situations where its effects are dangerous, such as while driving or using power tools.

Tolerance to marijuana can develop after frequent use of high doses. There is also a withdrawal reaction after stopping frequent use at high doses, including possible sleep problems, nausea and vomiting, sweats and shakes.

The biggest difficulty for those trying to stop smoking marijuana is the craving to smoke again. As a psychological dependence, marijuana can be one of the hardest drug habits to break.

The most worrisome use is by those who take it along with other drugs in a mix that can be highly unpredictable. This is a particular concern when it is used to ease the crash from cocaine or amphetamines. This combined use is typically harder for the person to control and more complicated to treat.

The active ingredient in marijuana, a chemical called THC, has been found to help cancer patients taking chemotherapy ease side effects such as nausea. This medical application is the only use for which marijuana is legal.

Signs to Look For

The most common effects of the marijuana high include:

- euphoria
- flood of ideas
- mild visual hallucinations
- sensitivity to stimuli, such as touch or sound
- altered sense of one's body or the passage of time
- discontinuity in thought; a spaced-out disconnected style of talking in irrelevant trains of thought
- serenity and lethargy
- uninhibited thoughts, which are more often expressed in fantasy than action

As with hallucinogens such as LSD, the specific effects are highly influenced by set—the person's expectations—and setting, the situation in which marijuana is smoked. Adverse reactions (a bad trip) are more likely in those who smoke because of social pressure when they don't really want to; in those who believe smoking marijuana can produce bad side effects; and in people who are already unstable. A bad trip is most likely in someone who has smoked little or no marijuana before, does so in a situation where he or she feels uncomfortable, and takes an extremely strong dose.

At very high levels, marijuana can produce some of the same effects as hallucinogens: hallucinations, a sense of unreality, hypersensitivity to stimuli. While some marijuana users may take such a shift in perception in stride, others may become anxious or panicked.

In general, the signs of a bad trip with marijuana use are:

- anxiety and agitation
- confusion and bewilderment

- disorientation
- clinging to illusions
- hallucinations

In extreme cases, the person may develop a delusion, usually that he or she is being persecuted in some way. With the delusions come strong fear and anxiety, intense mood swings, and a sense of unreality. The episode usually lasts a day or so.

Repeated marijuana use can worsen existing emotional problems. People who are depressed, for instance, may become even more depressed when they smoke. People who are vulnerable to psychosis may have a psychotic episode.

The most common adverse reaction to marijuana is a state of anxiety. Smoking can trigger an episode of intense anxiety that can escalate to panic. The anxiety often centers around paranoid thoughts of some sort, such as that some group like the Mafia or the CIA is plotting against you. Other beliefs that can become the focus of the anxiety and panic include something's being direly wrong with your body—a shift in the perception of the body is interpreted as meaning you are ill or dying. Another common cause for the panic is the fear that the psychological changes induced by marijuana mean you are "going crazy."

For those marijuana users who have also used hallucinogenic drugs, smoking marijuana may induce a flashback in which they spontaneously reexperience hallucinogenic states. These episodes are usually transient.

What Therapists Recommend

Setting. The large majority of therapists recommend treating marijuana abuse on an outpatient basis.

Format. Individual therapy is the most strongly recommended, but in conjunction with recovery groups. Many therapists also recommend family therapy as well.

Approach. As with other drug abuse problems, a cognitive-behavioral approach is the most widely recommended. Supportive therapy is also highly recommended, as is family involvement in treatment.

Medication. Unless there is some other, accompanying psychiatric disorder, no medication is recommended in the treatment of marijuana abuse, nor is there any medication specifically intended for that purpose.

Frequency. Individual sessions and group meetings usually need to be frequent during the withdrawal phase, daily if necessary. Individual therapy can then taper off to once a week to support recovery. Group meetings may still need to be more frequent until abstinence is solidly established.

Duration. Open-ended.

What You Should Know About Therapy

Hospital or residential treatment is rarely necessary in treating marijuana abuse, except when other drugs are also involved that require medically supervised withdrawal. Apart from this, the same principles of drug abuse treatment apply to marijuana.

The goal of treatment is abstinence. The most important support and the backbone of treatment is meeting several times a week or more in groups with others who are also trying to give up marijuana or other drugs. These can be groups in a structured outpatient substance-abuse rehabilitation program, at a clinic, agency, or HMO, or through one of the well-known self-help organizations such as Narcotics Anonymous (NA) or Al-Ateen. Alcoholics Anonymous has organized groups for marijuana users in many parts of the country.

As with opiate addiction, individual therapy is not the first choice of treatment. If you are in individual therapy, the focus should be abstinence and little else. Therapy should also be combined with regular attendance in peer recovery groups. Once sobriety has been firmly established, therapy can begin to address some of the underlying problems that may have precipitated your drug use.

If you are helping someone who has smoked marijuana and has become intensely anxious, agitated, paranoid, or panicky, remember that simple reassurance that the feelings will pass is the best approach. During a bad trip, people need to be in the company of someone they trust, and in a place that is familiar and safe to them.

Bringing someone in this state to a new place, or a new person—even a physician—can itself be upsetting. If help is needed to get the person calm again, it is best to have someone whom he or she knows stay with them while they are being treated. Psychiatric emergency rooms are used to dealing with people having bad trips. If you accompany someone there, be sure to tell the physician on call about any drugs the person may have taken in addition to marijuana.

PCP

The drug PCP is also known as angel dust or crystal. It is usually taken by snuffing, in a pill, or smoked by sprinkling it on a marijuana cigarette. Made by street chemists, PCP has about thirty chemical variations. The closest chemical cousin is the drug Ketamine, which is used medically as a short-acting anesthetic and is also used illegally.

PCP is considered one of the most dangerous street drugs. It is often used by mixing it with several other drugs, making its effects wildly unpredictable. A PCP trip usually starts within minutes of ingestion, reaches its peak in about a half hour, and lasts three to five hours. Its effects can last for several days, however, and it can take one or two days to recover from the high.

Signs to Look For

The PCP high includes any of the following, especially during its peak:

- indifference to what is happening nearby; absorption in fantasy and sensation
- euphoria; a peaceful, "floaty" feeling
- altered sense of one's body
- delusions; hallucinations
- confusion and disorganized feelings
- an intense "clingy" feeling of needing other people
- mood swings: friendly and talkative at one moment, hostile the next
- lessened sensitivity to physical pain, putting people at risk for hurting themselves unintentionally
- muscular stiffness, grimaces, head-rolling
- a chanting, rhythmic speech

Sometimes the high is followed by depression. During this phase the person may become impulsive or violent: irritability and hostility may give way to paranoid accusations and belligerence. This can be quite dangerous: PCP users in this state can assault others or become suicidal.

Apart from depression and violence, the signs of a PCP bad trip depend on whether the person has taken a low dose or a high one. At a low dose, the bad trip takes the form of anxiety and fearfulness, confusion and agitation. The person may seem "blank," not responding to what is said to him, staring blankly.

At a high dose, these signs grow more intense. The high-dose PCP user can become delirious, paranoid, or enter a psychotic state in which he acts out of control. The signs of PCP psychosis include:

- stripping and masturbating or urinating in public
- uncontrollable crying or laughing
- odd, repetitive movements
- muscle jerks or twitches; muscle contractions

The physical dangers of PCP include vomiting and nausea, seizures, fainting and coma, and death from respiratory arrest.

What You Should Know About Therapy

While friends and family of PCP users sometimes try to handle the symptoms of a bad trip on their own without getting professional help, that is extremely unwise. The symptoms can worsen steadily over several hours or days to the point that they become a psychiatric emergency.

At the peak of a bad trip, it is useless to try to talk the person down. At that point hospitalization is necessary. This is especially true because of the danger of physical complications that can be fatal.

The usual treatment is an antipsychotic medication that makes the person less disturbed, or a tranquilizer to handle the person's agitation. If the person is in a coma from PCP, he or she may need to be restrained, since many people become violent as they come out of the coma.

Withdrawal from PCP often includes an intense craving for the drug. For that reason, along with the need for medical supervision, treatment of PCP abuse is best begun in a residential treatment facility, where access to the drug can be controlled. Once the person has gotten off the drug, treatment is as for other drug addictions, with recovery groups the main modality.

DEPRESSION

Everyone feels sad or hopeless from time to time, yet even during a down mood, most people still feel some control over their emotions, that the sad feelings will eventually pass. But people with a serious depression may feel that a terrible heaviness and hopelessness has descended that they are powerless to prevent, and that it will go on and on. The intensity of despair that people can feel in serious depression goes far beyond the lows of normal life. It destroys the person's ability to continue in life's usual roles and can lead to utter confusion, mental paralysis, or the brink of suicide.

Just because you may feel blue, therefore, does not mean you are suffering from a serious depression. Your feelings may be a normal, even healthy, reaction to some loss—be it of a job, marriage, or loved one. While the unhappiness of daily life or adjustment to a loss comes and goes, the unhappiness of depression stays on. With normal unhappiness, for instance, going to a movie may cheer you up, at least for a while. With depression even your favorite comedy will leave you unmoved.

If you are seriously depressed, your family and friends may not realize how upset you really are. To them, you may seem to be no sadder than they become now and then. But if you are depressed, you know that your feelings are far more distressing than anything people ordinarily go through. Your friends and relatives may try to reassure you or cajole you into feeling better, but nothing they say will make much difference.

Depression has no one pattern. The clinical terms *depression* or *mood disorder* refer to an overall category for extremes of mood. These extreme moods can take several forms. For those with *major depression,* it is a plunge into deepest gloom. For those in the grip of a *manic episode,* it takes the form of a "high" of expansive elation that, on its surface, would seem to have no relationship to depression. For those with *manic depression,* it entails swings in mood that plunge them from the heights of mania to the depths of depression and back again. And for those with *dysthymia,* a mild depression lingers for months or years at a time.

In one form or another, depression is the second most common emotional problem after anxiety. About 5 percent of Americans have a serious depression during any given month. And about 8 percent of Americans will become seriously depressed sometime in their lives. About twice as many women experience a major depression as do men.

The likelihood of depression has been increasing in recent decades, particularly among women. Baby boomers have a higher rate of depression than do those generations born before the war. And in recent years, depression has begun earlier and earlier, to the point that it is now being recognized for the first time in children.

Major Depression

The hallmark of major depression is the loss of all joy in life. Even good news or a happy event fails to lift one's mood, even briefly. And in that gloom, people are obsessed by the worst thoughts about themselves and their lives. Because depression tinges everything so negatively, people should postpone any major life decisions until after they have recovered.

Depression is always accompanied by characteristic physical symptoms as well, such as insomnia, weight gain or loss, change in appetite. Even the simplest chores may, all of a sudden, be more than the depressed person can manage.

The course of depression also varies. For some there may be just a single, brief episode. For others, depression may be recurrent with two or more episodes occurring over months or years.

The average age of onset for major depression is around forty. For those people with a history of depression in their family, the onset is likely to be earlier. For those with no family history, it's more likely to begin in the forties or fifties.

Major depression can first appear gradually, over several days or weeks. Occasionally, it can erupt in a single day. While some episodes seem to come out of the blue, with no particular relationship to the course of a person's life, others are clearly triggered by some event.

The most common length of an untreated episode of major depression is between six months and a year. When treated, though, most episodes of major depression lift within a few weeks to three months. Generally the earlier in the episode you get treatment, the sooner the depression wanes.

The large majority of people with a major depression recover completely. Only about 15 percent of depressive episodes last more than twelve months. When they do, the residual problems tend to be minor, such as irritability or trouble sleeping.

If you have an episode of major depression, the likelihood of its repeating lessens as time goes on. The greatest risk of recurrence is within a half year after recovery.

About half who suffer a major depression will have another episode, and about half of those will go on to have a third episode.

But if you have had several episodes of depression, you may also be prone to manic episodes as well as time goes on (see p. 478). Those episodes may not occur until years after your bouts with depression.

The outlook for recovery from depression is very favorable, but the course of recovery fluctuates. Don't be discouraged by a period when your mood worsens after you have begun treatment—it's common and does not mean a dim outlook for recovery.

Signs to Look For

There are four main categories of symptoms in major depression. *Mood* is the most obvious; closely connected are *depressing thoughts:* guilt, self-blame, worthlessness, or hopelessness. Other symptoms are purely *physical,* showing up in such things as loss of appetite. The final variety of symptoms are *marked changes in behavior,* such as a sudden loss of pleasure in favorite activities.

Mood

- *Sadness.* Most everyone who is depressed feels an intense, perpetual sadness, a feeling of despondence, hopelessness, and gloom about everything.
- *Loss of pleasure and interest.* Some people with major depression feel a profound loss of interest in life rather than overwhelming sadness. They feel hopelessly indifferent to things that used to give them pleasure. Nothing seems to matter anymore.

    Moods of sadness or loss of interest—or both—typically prevail. If you find yourself shifting quickly from these moods to others such as anxiety or anger, you may not be suffering from a major depression.
- *Boredom.* A sense of ennui, no sense of humor.
- *Anxiety.* A sense of apprehension, anguish, tension, or feelings of panic. In some "anxious depressions" it can be difficult to tell which mood is paramount,

anxiety or depression, and whether you are suffering from a mood disorder or an anxiety disorder. It is important to distinguish them since the treatments are different.

- *Turmoil.* Brooding, worrying, and irritability.

Thoughts

- Persistent *thoughts of being worthless or of guilt.* An obsession with all one's faults and failures, including some imaginary ones, and remorse about wrongs one has committed.
- A *negative view* of the world, yourself, and life. Nothing seems good or worthwhile.
- *Hopelessness and helplessness.* The sense that the depression will go on forever, that there is no way to change it, and that the future is entirely bleak.
- *Inability to concentrate or remember.* Even minor demands, such as reading a newspaper article, watching a TV show, or remembering a phone number are difficult.
- *Confusion and indecision.* The sense that your thoughts are jumbled, or that they have slowed down; difficulty making even minor decisions, sometimes to the point of mental paralysis.
- *Hallucinations and delusions* (in psychotic depression). Seeing or hearing things that are not there or believing that imagined events have actually occurred.
- *Thoughts of death and suicide.* Actively thinking about killing yourself or passively just wanting to die.

Physical Symptoms and Complaints

- *Changes in appetite and weight.* Either eating voraciously and gaining weight or losing appetite and losing weight.
- *Disturbances in sleep.* Difficulty falling asleep or staying asleep; waking in the middle of the night and brooding; frightening dreams; or waking up too early. Sometimes sleeping too much but still feeling fatigued; or sleeping too little despite feeling extremely fatigued.
- *Sluggishness.* Everything is slowed down—walking, eating, thinking, reacting. It may take twenty seconds to answer a simple question.
- *Agitation.* Fidgeting, pacing, wringing hands.
- *Lethargy.* A loss of vitality and stamina, making it hard to get going. Feelings of mopiness, being washed-out, constant fatigue.
- *Loss of sexual appetite.* Both an absence of desire and lack of enjoyment in sex.
- *Bodily complaints.* These include back and neck aches, muscle cramps, headache,

blurred vision, and the like. Gastrointestinal disturbances, including nausea, heartburn, indigestion, and abdominal pain, are particularly common.

Behavior

- *Loss of interest in usual roles,* such as spouse, parent, student, or employee.
- *Loss of interest in normal activities,* even those that you usually enjoy.
- *Clinging and demanding* in relationships; pleading for special attention. Sometimes takes the form of compulsive sex.
- *Escape,* such as withdrawing into solitude, staying in bed all day, or sleeping excessively.
- *Excess,* such as eating too much, taking drugs, or drinking heavily in an attempt to escape the misery.
- *Restlessness.* Constant fidgeting, nail-biting, chain-smoking, spending sprees, taking reckless risks, and the like.
- *Suicidal gestures.* Attempts on one's life that are survived, such as taking pills and then letting someone know, or taking them at a time when someone is sure to discover it.

While no one will have all these symptoms, people with major depression always have one of the first two (sadness or apathy) and four or five of the others. Even in the same person, the symptoms can vary as time goes on. But if a half dozen of these symptoms persist for two weeks or longer, then you are likely experiencing a major depression.

As these symptoms lift during recovery, they tend to disappear in a rough sequence. Very often trouble with sleep is among the first problems to improve, followed by a return of appetite and an increase in physical energy. After the physical symptoms have begun to clear up, mood begins to brighten, and depressing thoughts and attitudes such as hopelessness, self-criticism, and pessimism begin to fade. Note that the depressed mood itself is usually the last symptom to go.

☐ Jan, thirty-six, was a free-lance writer and the mother of two small children. Everyone knew her as a high-energy woman who enjoyed what seemed to be a golden period of her life. She was content with her marriage, loved caring for her children, and had found steady and lucrative outlets for her writing. She had a reputation as a superb juggler, somehow finding time for writing, car pools, gourmet cooking, and managing a busy household.

But the bubble burst for Jan a few months after her husband got a promotion that required him to be out of town half the week. Her children suddenly started to be obstinate, she found that her household chores doubled, and she felt lonely and abandoned.

Now she felt anxious and blue all day, so lethargic and overwhelmed by the easiest task that she gave up even trying. Her mind felt sluggish and confused; she could no longer concentrate enough to make the small decisions of household life, let alone write.

Her mother started spending the day at the house to help, something Jan would never have allowed before. Jan was haunted by thoughts like "I'm a complete failure at everything" and "I'm a terrible mother and wife." She spent hours sitting up in bed, brooding and tearful.

The pleasures she had taken in cooking, caring for her children, and writing vanished. The very thought of food made her nauseous. Already thin, she lost seven pounds in a week. She felt no reason to go on living: nothing in life gave her joy.

Masquerades: Depression or Physical Illness?

Very often people who are depressed do not realize they need psychotherapy; they think their problem is purely medical. Though they know something is wrong, they frequently focus on their physical symptoms rather than their depressed mood or thoughts. This is more likely to happen with the elderly, or with people who are not comfortable focusing on and talking about their feelings. While more and more physicians are aware that depression can masquerade as physical complaints, many fail to recognize it.

Still, the physical changes brought on by depression, such as insomnia and loss of appetite, can aggravate already-existing illnesses such as diabetes, hypertension, and lung disease. These problems are real, not "just in your head."

Nevertheless, the physical symptoms of depression can lead you on an endless round of medical tests and specialists. Though the changes—such as fatigue, sleeping troubles, or sexual disinterest—are very real for you, these complaints will not show up as abnormalities in diagnostic tests. What's more, they can lead to your being referred for inappropriate treatments, such as behavior therapy at a sleep clinic or sex therapy, while the real problem—your depression—goes undiagnosed.

On the other hand, many medical conditions can mimic aspects of depression, among them senility, Parkinson's disease, severe infections, AIDS, strokes, adrenal or other endocrine imbalances, mononucleosis, some cancers, and vitamin deficiencies.

Also, some medicines have side effects similar to symptoms of depression: anti-inflammatory drugs or analgesics, antifungal medicines and antibiotics, antihypertensives (such as beta blockers), steroids and hormone supplements, and drugs taken for other psychiatric or neurologic conditions.

Start with a complete physical. If you are taking any medications, be sure to mention them to your physician during your physical. This is particularly true for elderly people, who often have serious medical conditions for which they are taking multiple medications.

Variations and Complications

Suicide

The risk of suicide is, of course, the most serious of all complications of depression. About two-thirds of people who commit suicide do so while suffering from depression. Many of the rest are alcoholic. Still, suicide is rare. Though thoughts of suicide are common in people who are depressed, very few attempt it, and even fewer succeed.

Thinking about suicide is not the same as intending to try it. The danger begins when a person makes the transition from simply thinking about suicide to actually planning an attempt.

The more explicit a person is in talking about how to take his or her life, the greater the danger. Contrary to myth, those who talk about suicide are *more* likely to try, not less. Danger is particularly high in people who have made previous attempts, who have thought through how to take their lives, and who have the means (a gun or pills, say) at hand.

Paradoxically, *one of the riskiest periods in the course of depression is after some of the symptoms have begun to improve.* This is because in many people the physical symptoms, such as sluggishness, clear up first while the dark depressive mood and hopelessness lags. This partial recovery can give people the energy to carry through on their suicidal impulses.

One subtle warning sign of suicide can be a sudden calmness in someone who has been distraught. That outward calm may signal that the decision to attempt suicide has been made. The calm reflects the sense of relief and resignation. Sometimes the suicidal urge comes after a setback, which activates feelings of hopelessness and despondency.

If you are depressed and worried you might act on suicidal thoughts, *tell someone immediately,* especially your therapist if you have one, or a family member or friend.

How to handle a suicidal person. Preventing suicide is crucial. If you think someone is suicidal, don't put off helping. Drop everything and attend to the situation. If the threat seems serious, seek professional help. If the person is in psychotherapy, ask for an appointment for the person with the therapist that day, or for a daily phone call. If the person does not have a therapist and the threat is more urgent, many cities have suicide hot lines where a counselor is always available.

Decide what to do in consultation with a psychotherapist who is experienced in dealing with suicidal patients—many therapists are not. If in consultation with the therapist you agree that the depressed person can stay at home, you should get advice from the therapist on how to act as part of a "treatment team": warning signs to watch for, topics to avoid or to discuss, and the like.

For instance, it often helps to draw the person into activity, no matter how mundane. As simple a thing as asking him or her to do some useful chores can counter the sense of inertia and passivity.

Hospitalization is another alternative. Hospitals that have psychiatric emergency services are prepared any time of day or night to accept as patients people who are suicidal. The main advantage of a hospital is that the staff is trained to monitor closely people in danger of killing themselves.

But hospitalization may not be necessary if you and your family or friends are able to be with the person throughout the day and night. The important thing is that the suicidal person not be left alone.

Don't try to go to heroic lengths to keep a friend or family member out of the hospital. Realize that there are limits to how well you can handle this situation and that the stakes are high. Be ready to admit when you just cannot—and should not—take responsibility for what can get out of control.

Psychotic Depression

Along with all the usual signs of major depression, here the person becomes psychotic as well, losing contact with reality. The loss of contact can take the form of delusions, hallucinations, or a deep stupor, with the person just sitting mute and unresponsive.

Delusions or hallucinations in psychotic depression have a depressive content that distinguishes them from other psychoses. Typical themes are feelings of utter inadequacy, guilt over some terrible deed, deserved punishment for some misdeed, being the carrier of a disease, or the loss of all meaning and consequence.

In psychotic depression, the risk of suicide is especially high.

Melancholia

Historically, the term *melancholia* was used to describe all types of depression. Today it is used to describe a particular form of depression that sometimes occurs in people who have recovered from an episode of major depression. Melancholia seems to come out of the blue for no particular reason.

People with melancholia do not suffer the most severe symptoms of depression, but a general gloom sets in. They lose interest in life's pleasures: activities they once enjoyed no longer make them feel good. Or they awake a few hours earlier than usual and feel especially gloomy during the morning hours.

Like people with more severe depression, those with melancholia can sometimes lose weight suddenly, feel lethargic, or become quite agitated.

Pseudodementia

In this form of depression, the most noticeable complaint is of mental difficulties, notably trouble remembering things, confusion, and disorientation. When pseudodementia occurs in the elderly, it is often misdiagnosed as senility or "dementia." Careful evaluation, though, will reveal many symptoms of depression.

Some of the signs that distinguish this kind of depression from true dementia:

- In pseudodementia the person complains of a poor memory; in dementia the poor memory is obvious to all except the person who has it.
- In true dementia, a person can't remember a half dozen items seen a few minutes before; a depressed person will remember them, though after fretting about it.
- In dementia, a person will try to answer questions; the person with depression resists, answering with silence or "I don't know."
- Someone with dementia likes company; a depressed person wants solitude.

Seasonal Depression

Some people are prone to "winter blues." They get depressed as the days grow shorter in fall and winter and start to feel better in spring as the days get longer. This variety of depression is apparently a symptom of out-of-kilter biological rhythms. The treatment of choice, oddly enough, is exposure to bright fluorescent light for two to six hours a day. Another treatment option is going to bed earlier than usual, or sleeping less. Seasonal depression also improves within a few days if the person travels to another climate where the days are longer.

Substance Abuse and Depression

One of the frequent complications of depression is alcohol abuse. One theory why men are diagnosed with depression less often than women may be that more men "treat" themselves for depression by turning to drink or drugs, including cocaine, amphetamines, or sedatives.

When people try to "self-medicate" their depression with alcohol or drugs, they inevitably worsen the condition. Alcohol or drugs may offer some short-term relief, but the feelings of anxiety and depression will return that much stronger, increasing the need to get "high" and precipitating a vicious cycle.

This is particularly true of alcohol, the only drug that has a biphasic action on the central nervous system; it acts first as a stimulant, then as a depressant.

What Therapists Recommend

Approach. The most frequently recommended approach for severe depression is supportive, in which treatment focuses on helping the person handle immediate problems and regain the ability to function day to day. A psychodynamic approach is also highly recommended, in which the emotional issues accompanying the depression are explored. Cognitive therapy, also highly recommended, focuses on the negative thoughts that trigger the depressed person's feelings of gloom and hopelessness. Some current research suggests that cognitive therapy may be the more effective approach.

These approaches are typically used in combination, with a supportive phase at the beginning. During the most acute phase of depression, medication and a supportive treatment are warranted until such major symptoms as extreme apathy lift enough so that the therapy can shift to a more active psychodynamic or cognitive approach.

Medication. The vast majority of therapists recommend antidepressant medication in combination with psychotherapy. This combined approach is supported by current research.

Setting. Major depression can usually be treated in a therapist's office, though a particularly severe episode may require a short hospitalization if the person is suicidal, psychotic, or temporarily unable to function.

Format. Most psychotherapy for depression is individual. But individual treatment can be supplemented by group therapy, or by family sessions.

Frequency. During the acute phase of a severe depression, most therapists recommend that therapy sessions be twice a week or even more frequent, though if the person is not suicidal or otherwise severely incapacitated, treatment can be on a once-a-week basis. Typically, more frequent sessions are needed at the beginning of therapy, during those weeks or months when the depression is at its worst. They can then be tapered off to once a week or less as the person begins to feel better.

Duration. Most therapists recommend leaving treatment for severe depression open-ended since it is impossible to know how long an episode will last. Therapy can also continue when the depression lifts, particularly to prevent relapse.

What You Should Know About Therapy

Remember, even though you may feel hopeless, depression is one of the most treatable of all emotional problems. At worst, a depression will pass in its own natural course.

At best, combined treatment with psychotherapy and medication will lift depression much sooner and make its recurrence less likely or less frequent.

But the treatment of depression can be frustrating in the short run. Antidepressant medications take several weeks to a month or more before having a substantial effect; psychotherapy usually takes longer. You may need to try several medications before finding one that's effective.

It is especially important that you feel a warm rapport with your psychotherapist. You want to be able to talk openly and feel free to phone your therapist in a crisis when you really need support. But you do *not* want a therapist who promises you too much too soon: you want hope that is realistic, not wishful thinking.

Major depression is hard on the entire family. They often need support, too, and a place to express their frustration and fears. Many therapists will want to contact your family with your permission so as to better understand what you are going through. The therapist can also educate your family about depression, offer encouragement, and help them support you.

Approaches. *Supportive therapy,* the most highly recommended approach, offers common-sense advice on day-to-day problems, encouragement during the difficult periods, such as waiting for a medication to take effect, and help reestablishing work habits and personal ties that have been disrupted by the depression. Psychodynamic and behavioral approaches should also offer this kind of support during the acute phase.

Psychodynamic therapies for depression seek to find the emotional issues in past or present conflicts that may be related to the depression. While this approach has been adapted from psychoanalysis, full psychoanalysis is not recommended for the treatment of severe depression.

One of the psychodynamic approaches is *brief dynamic therapy*. This typically lasts fewer than thirty sessions. The therapist is more confrontational than in traditional psychoanalysis, exploring issues associated with the depression. *Interpersonal therapy,* another psychodynamic approach, concentrates on improving your close relationships, using the therapy sessions as a microcosm of the feelings those relationships evoke. Interpersonal therapy was developed specifically for the treatment of depression and has been found highly effective.

The technique most strongly recommended on the basis of research findings is *cognitive therapy*. For depression at its most severe—when, for example, a listless person spends all day in bed—cognitive therapy begins with therapists working out a schedule of activities for the day. They begin with small challenges, such as taking a shower, going for a walk, calling a friend. As the person becomes more able, the activities become more challenging, such as going to a movie. All are meant to attack the depressed person's sense that life has no pleasure or meaning, and that he or she is helpless to do anything.

As the depression begins to lift, the cognitive therapist typically moves on to tackle the self-defeating and discouraging thoughts that underlie the depression. The depressed person is asked, for instance, to keep a record of situations and the thoughts they trigger. For example, a fight with a child might evoke such thoughts as "I'm a terrible parent" or "I'm no good at anything; nothing ever works out for me." The therapist helps the person see the distortions in such thinking and to learn to challenge such thoughts as they happen—e.g., "It's normal for parents and children to fight sometimes. I'm basically a good parent."

When marital problems loom large in the depression, *couples therapy* can be useful. The aim will be to improve communication between the partners, alleviating strife.

Medication. Medication is a standard recommendation for treatment of major depression. Medication and psychotherapy work together, but to different ends. Medication acts most powerfully to alleviate the more biological symptoms such as sleeplessness, agitation, fatigue, and the depressed mood. Psychotherapy, on the other hand, addresses the patterns of thinking that lead to a sense of hopelessness and helplessness.

No single antidepressant medication works for everyone. Finding a medication that alleviates symptoms without undesirable side effects may take several trials.

The final decision is yours. If a medication you are trying makes you feel strange or has some worrisome side effect, talk to the prescribing physician or psychiatrist about trying something else.

The main medications used in treating major depression are:

- *Tricyclic antidepressants (TCAs; sometimes called heterocyclic).* Typically tried first, these have been found effective in up to two-thirds of cases (see p. 610 for details on TCAs). They usually take two to six weeks to be effective.
- *Monoamine oxidase inhibitors (MAOIs).* These are generally the next medication tried for those who do not respond to tricyclics (see p. 616 for details). MAOIs are the first choice if anxiety is a prominent symptom.
- *Serotonin-specific medications.* The most common of these, fluoxetine or Prozac, is sometimes used because it has fewer side effects than other antidepressants. Introduced as a third drug to try, after TCAs and MAOIs, Prozac is increasingly being tried first for this reason (see p. 619).
- *Benzodiazepines,* mainly alprazolam (Xanax). This is often used with people who have a combination of depression and anxiety, since it can sometimes alleviate both (see p. 630).
- *Bupropion.* An antidepressant unrelated chemically to any of the others, this has few of their side effects (see p. 621).

Hospitalization

Most people can safely be treated for severe depression with a combination of medication and psychotherapy while staying at home. Yet for a few, being in a hospital during their darkest hours can be lifesaving. Typically hospitalization lasts less than a month.

The signs that hospitalization should be considered include:

- threats of suicide or homicide
- extreme apathy, so that the person cannot, e.g., feed himself or herself
- severe agitation or psychosis
- a dangerous concurrent medical condition, such as severe diabetes, which the person is no longer caring for properly

On the other hand, factors diminishing the need for hospitalization include psychotherapy several times a week and close friends and family available to tend to the person's daily needs, monitor his or her condition, and be supportive.

Electroconvulsive Therapy (or ECT)

In this treatment, also known as "electroshock therapy," an electric current is passed through the brain, resulting in something like a controlled seizure. ECT got a well-deserved bad reputation in its earlier years, largely because it was often used, if unwittingly for disorders for which it was not effective. In the worst cases it was used simply as a threat to enforce order in some mental institutions. When administered carelessly, ECT occasionally resulted in broken bones and other adverse effects.

Today ECT is far safer, and in some cases, is the treatment of choice. When properly administered, and with recent technical improvements, ECT can be remarkably effective in lifting the severest episodes of depression. Even so, it is recommended mainly for the most dire instances: when someone is so depressed they risk starvation, suicide, or are in a stupor. It is also tried when the usual drug treatments fail.

In the early days, ECT was sometimes given for twenty, thirty, or even more sessions. The modern treatment is usually six to eight treatments, or less often, ten to twelve every other day or three times a week. The standard procedure is to give ECT in a hospital, with an anesthesiologist attending, but it can be administered to outpatients. ECT is often started during a hospitalization and completed with sessions after discharge.

During ECT a controlled pulse of electric current passes through the head. Typically this is administered on one side of the head only, instead of bilaterally as before. This helps to minimize the side effects. One effect of the current is a muscle convulsion throughout the body, but no longer the kind of grand-mal-like convulsion you have probably seen in the movies and associated with ECT. The convulsion is controlled through an anesthetic, sometimes with muscle relaxants. People who undergo ECT are always surprised they feel no pain. They don't since the brain has no nerve endings that sense pain.

The immediate side effects are some confusion and memory loss, a mild headache, and often some muscle pain. These tend to pass within a day or slightly longer, and to be most pronounced after the first one or two sessions. The modern method prevents the fractures that, in the past, were the occasional result of wild convulsions and unfortunately are still part of the popular stereotype. There is no evidence that ECT results in any long-term memory loss or causes any brain damage.

Most people respond with some brightening of mood within six to eight sessions—usually after about two to three weeks.

What the Family Can Do

Sometimes troubles in the family can aggravate depression. You will need to bend a bit to ease family burdens for your loved one. Do not, for example, pressure someone going through a depression to make any major decisions. At the same time, you can only do so much to relieve the misery of someone suffering from depression.

For women who tend to take primary responsibility for problems in the family or in a marriage, other problems can worsen depression. In such cases, family or marital counseling, along with individual treatment, can help. Likewise, depressed teenagers or young adults can often benefit from family therapy in addition to individual psychotherapy.

Dysthymia: Chronic Mild Depression

The most common form of depression is dysthymia. It's main sign is a more or less chronic dysphoria or mildly depressed mood. This mood persists most of the day, more days than not. But unlike major depression, the dour mood is not overwhelming. Instead, it can be such a steady feature of life that it almost seems to be a part of a person's temperamental makeup. But mild depression can be treated successfully, even if it has been a problem for years.

If you suffer from this kind of depression, you may laugh and joke from time to time and enjoy yourself on occasion. At times you even feel cheery or at least normal. But your typical outlook is gloomy. You often feel irritable, frustrated, or find yourself complaining. Minor disturbances that others seem to take in stride upset you.

You are not alone; in any given month, 3.3 percent of Americans suffer from mild depression. It is found in about 5 percent of women, but in just about half as many men. About one in ten people who come for psychotherapy have mild depression.

Signs to Look For

The main symptoms of mild depression are constantly feeling down in the dumps and unable to take any pleasure in life. Besides these, most symptoms of major depression can also occur. But while people with major depression are so debilitated they cannot work or socialize, those with mild depression continue to do so, though not at their peak.

☐ Sarah said she'd been depressed ever since she could remember. As a teenager she spent hours in her room, brooding. She first saw a therapist for a year when she was seventeen. She complained then that she was inferior to other people and that she just couldn't focus on her schoolwork. To her parents she complained bitterly about her lack of boyfriends and her unpopularity.

Sarah came into therapy at twenty-nine, two years after her marriage. Her complaints were much the same: she berated herself for what she saw as her inferiority; she was distracted at work; she was continually unhappy about her home and her marriage.

Her marital problems had prompted her to come into therapy. At first she had been happy with her husband, whom she had met at work. But soon she found herself critical of his sloppiness, the way he dressed, his inability to earn enough. They fought often. Sarah found herself uninterested in sex, a major point of contention. In fact, she found that nothing seemed to bring her much pleasure. As she put it, "I can't remember a time that I was really happy."

The main signs of mild depression are at least two of the following:

- feeling depressed or irritable for days or months on end
- overeating or loss of appetite
- fatigue, chronic low energy
- being self-critical or having low self-esteem
- trouble concentrating that interferes with doing one's best work
- difficulty making decisions that other people don't hesitate about
- feeling hopeless or helpless, not up to life's demands, or that it's always such a struggle

Other occasional signs include:

- lack of sexual desire
- chronic complaints and brooding, getting upset over things others take in stride
- preoccupation with health, worrying that something is seriously wrong at the slightest sign of a problem

Variations and Complications

The symptoms of mild depression entail many of the same complications as with major depression. One is suicide, discussed on page 467.

Sometimes the complaints in mild depression may be mainly physical, such as loss of appetite, lack of energy, and vague but persistent medical problems. These can lead you on an endless round of diagnostic tests that never show any physical problem, or to treatments for maladies that don't exist though the symptoms are real. The mild depression, meanwhile, goes undiagnosed and untreated.

Some of the symptoms of mild depression, such as the tendency to complain and bicker, combined with a general lack of pleasure that can lead to a disinterest in sex, can cause difficulties in marriage or other close relationships.

People with mild depression sometimes turn to alcohol or drugs for relief, which can lead to abuse or addiction. Drugs or alcohol will themselves speed up this process, because after the temporary relief, they tend to increase the feelings of depression.

Since mild depression is chronic, it is possible for a major depression to coexist with it. This condition has been called double depression. The major depression may never quite seem to clear up because the milder form lingers on after the most severe symptoms pass.

Atypical depression. In this variation of mild depression people have regular episodes of feeling unhappy and demoralized, during which they are hypersensitive to life's minor ups and downs. A flattering comment can induce a near ecstasy, while a criticism or rejection can evoke deep despair. People with this pattern tend to feel anxious and tired much of the time and complain of numerous physical maladies, none with a clear medical basis. They are also prone to eating binges, sleeping too much or too little, and phobias.

What Therapists Recommend

Approach. The most frequently recommended therapy for mild depression is psychodynamic, in which the focus is the underlying emotional issues. Also highly recommended are supportive treatment, emphasizing the ability to function fully in life, and cognitive therapy, which concentrates on correcting the self-defeating thoughts that prime depressed feelings.

Medication. Only as needed to control symptoms, and not in every case. Just half the number of therapists who think medications are needed to treat major depression see the need for it in minor depression.

Setting and format. Therapists almost unanimously recommend treating mild depression in office visits on an individual basis. Some recommend complementary family, couples, or group therapy.

Frequency. Once a week, with sessions more often if the depression intensifies to major proportions.

Duration. Because mild depression is so long-lasting, most therapists see it as needing longer-term treatment with therapy open-ended.

What You Should Know About Therapy

Changing mild depression, which may by now seem to you just part of your nature, is possible, but will require persistence on your part.

On the basis of studies comparing the effectiveness of therapies for depression, *cognitive therapy* is the treatment of choice and is often superior to medication in alleviating symptoms of mild depression. Cognitive therapy is typically limited to twenty or so sessions, but because mild depression is so persistent, may take longer.

Psychodynamic therapy—the approach most often recommended by therapists in the national survey—also has the support of research studies. One variety of psychodynamic therapy that research has shown to be especially effective for depression is *interpersonal therapy*. In this approach, your relationship with your therapist becomes a gauge for other key relationships in your life. Many psychodynamic therapists who may not think of themselves as practicing this specific approach do, in effect, the same thing.

Supportive therapy for mild depression is used in tandem with other approaches. If problems in your marriage or with your parents or other family members (if you still live with them) play a major role in your unhappiness, *couples* or *family therapy* may be helpful if your partner or family members will join you.

Note: Begin with a physical examination from a physician. Some of the symptoms of mild depression can also be caused by purely medical or neurological problems, so get a physical to eliminate these possibilities before seeking psychotherapy.

Medication. Fewer than half of psychotherapists recommend medication for mild depression. Still, drug treatments should be tried if, after several months, psychotherapy alone has not brought about any discernible improvement, or if you have other members of your family who have been seriously depressed and were helped by medication. A third instance is if your symptoms are severe and long-standing and approach the paralyzing effect of major depression.

Tricyclic depressants (see p. 610) are usually tried first, or increasingly, Prozac (see p. 619). MAO inhibitors (p. 616) may be the medication of choice if your main symptoms are biological—e.g., sleeping or eating too much, feeling worse as the day goes on, or diffuse physical complaints. If these don't help, then lithium is often tried (p. 633). But no strong evidence indicates that medication will do much to help with mild depression in many or most cases. Unlike in major depression, some studies have found psychotherapy alone as effective or more effective than medication.

MANIC DEPRESSION

Most of us feel a mild elation when things go well for us, and occasionally we feel euphoric, confident, productive, and expansive. But mania begins when such feelings intensify, becoming reckless, destructive, and out of control. When a person swings from episodes of such unbounded elation to episodes of inconsolable misery, it is popularly known as manic depression, which mental health professionals now call *bipolar disorder*.

The mild form of manic depression is called *cyclothymia*—moderate swings of moods from elation to mild depression. Next in severity is *hypomania,* in which a person feels euphoric, and creative, though a bit impulsive, and can sometimes irritate others by being overbearing. Because of its desirable qualities, people do not usually think of themselves as having a problem when they are hypomanic. The next most severe form is *manic-depressive disorder,* described below, and the most severe is *rapid-cycling bipolar disorder,* described on page 482.

The hallmark of bipolar disorder is a mercurial mood of euphoria and expansiveness that can suddenly turn to irritation and anger. Most people with bipolar disorder also go through bouts of depression, though about one in ten have manic episodes without depression. But even if the person experiences only mania, the diagnosis is the same and so is the treatment. Occasionally a person can have both manic and depressive symptoms at the same time.

While manic, the person will be extraordinarily cheerful, friendly, and outgoing, talking a blue streak and rattling off great idea after great idea. Sometimes people who are manic become extremely persuasive, like a good salesman, snaring those around them in wild schemes. They are likely to start numerous ambitious projects and then just as abruptly abandon them.

People going through a manic episode seem to have tapped some reservoir of energy that lets them stay up to all hours, talk endlessly with boundless enthusiasm, and make jokes and puns they find amusing, even if no one else does. They seem audacious, talking to total strangers as though they were old friends, calling people in the middle of the night, and embarking on whatever adventure their whim dictates.

But their elation has a dark underside. In their enthusiasm, they can be overbearing and abrasive. Their cheerfulness can change to rage in a moment, leaving them belligerent and paranoid. When the manic episode is at its height, the person may seem completely bewildered, making no sense at all.

During the periods of depression, the symptoms are like those of major depression: gloom, lethargy, sleep problems, self-doubt, hopelessness, physical complaints, and the like.

There is no predictable rhythm for the recurrence of manic episodes or for their alternation with periods of depression. Some people with bipolar disorder have several episodes of depression before another manic episode, while others go from high to low and back over a period of months or years. In rapid-cycling bipolar disorders, the alternation between mania and depression can occur several times in a year.

About one person in two hundred suffers from a manic episode in a given half year. Over the course of a lifetime, about one person in one hundred and twenty is likely to experience one. The disorder is most common in people between eighteen and forty-four; it rarely occurs in the elderly.

As with major depression, strong evidence suggests that the susceptibility to bipolar disorder is inherited. Some studies show that if one parent has bipolar disorder, the chances of its affecting one of his or her children are about one in four; if both parents have the disorder, the odds are greater than 50 percent.

Bipolar disorder often begins not with a manic episode but with a serious depression during the later teen years or more commonly in early adulthood. In these instances, the first manic episode may not occur until years later. During the intervening period, it will not be clear that the first episode of depression was the beginning of a bipolar disorder.

Less often, the problem begins with a sudden manic episode. Mania can erupt within hours on a single day, though often it takes weeks to unfold. The depressed phase typically comes and goes more slowly, over a period of weeks or months.

Bad judgment. While in the depressive phase, people with bipolar disorder may become convinced they are "a terrible person" or "completely incompetent" and so try to divorce a loving spouse, quit a perfectly good job, or make some other drastic—and damaging—decision. During the manic phase, their decision-making ability is just as prone to error, but for opposite reasons: a sense of grandiosity may lead them to initiate a divorce or quit a job because they are "too good."

Note: If you or someone close to you is going through either phase of a bipolar disorder, *try to delay any major life decisions until the crisis has passed.* What may feel like an intolerable situation during the most intense episodes will seem very different afterward.

Signs to Look For

The most obvious sign of bipolar disorder is the "high" of mania. The manic person's mood of elation is so strong that it is sometimes contagious. For people who do not know him or her well, nothing may seem strange. But if you are familiar with the person going through a manic episode, the change will be clear to you.

The main signs of a manic episode disorder are:

- Extreme elation, an expansive mood that lasts for days or weeks at a time.
- Irritability and belligerence if thwarted or frustrated; elation can suddenly turn to hostility and anger.
- Grandiosity, an unrealistically inflated self-image.
- Poor judgment, such as buying sprees, sexual binges, foolish investments, which come from acting on whim.
- Incessant activity and excitement in pursuit of an ever-changing set of goals.
- Pressured speech: talking a blue streak, often with utter disregard for what others say. During the peak of excitement, speech may become incoherent.
- Fluidity of thought and free association, jumping from one topic to the next in an unrestrained flow of ideas, puns, wordplay, and a stream of jokes.
- Lack of need for sleep; staying up for days at a time, or getting by on only a few hours sleep, especially as the manic episode intensifies.
- Distractibility, so that attention is readily drawn by trivial things or irrelevancies, or disregard for details, such as forgetting to hang up the phone.
- Intrusiveness and thoughtlessness; acting headstrong and demanding, pushing family and friends to their limits; a Dr. Jekyll–Mr. Hyde personality that can be ingratiating and charming one minute, obnoxious and alienating the next.

A manic episode can be considered under way if a person displays several of these symptoms for at least a week, to the point that they disrupt that person's life or intrude on others who are close to them.

People who are manic can be quite charismatic and manipulative. They are skillful in shifting blame to other people, at exploiting people's weaknesses, and adept at playing one person off against another. Since all this is in the service of their grandiose and impulsive schemes, they are apt to leave a wake of havoc in the lives they touch while manic.

□ Jenny, at thirty-four, was the head of marketing for a small cosmetics firm. She had always been outgoing and gregarious, but she suddenly became much more so. One summer week Jenny changed: she began to stay up through the night, barely sleeping. She started making plans to leave the company she worked for and start her own, but she couldn't seem to decide just what kind of company it would be. One moment it was fashion accessories, the next a dating service, the next a travel agency.

Jenny would call friends and people she hadn't been in touch with for years at any time of the day or night. With endless enthusiasm, she would tell them of her latest plans, often changing those plans in the middle of a conversation just on the basis of a casual remark. She was confident that her talents were extraordinary and that she would make millions no matter what business she went into.

Although she had always been reticent about dating men she did not know well, she now frequented bars and made advances to men she had just met. Although she was normally careful in budgeting her money, she went on impulsive spending sprees, running up all her credit cards to their limit.

After weeks of not coming to work, Jenny was fired. With that, her mood changed from ebullient to hostile. She began to tell people that she was being persecuted by "the Mob," and that they had convinced her boss to fire her. She made threatening calls to people at work and somehow interpreted even casual remarks as confirming her theory that she was the target of a huge conspiracy.

Although the manic state is the most evident sign of bipolar disorder, it is not the most frequent. The depression can last six to nine months, while the manic episodes typically last a matter of weeks.

Even though their symptoms partially overlap, *it is important to distinguish bipolar depression from major depression* because the treatment for the two conditions differs markedly. The diagnosis should be made by a trained clinician. Sometimes the differences between the disorders are subtle, particularly when manic episodes do not play a prominent role.

Variations and Complications

Bipolar disorder with psychosis. When a manic episode reaches its frenzied peak, the person may become psychotic, suffering from full-blown delusions. One common delusion is of being persecuted by some person or group, such as the Mafia or CIA. Most manic delusions fit with the overall mood of elation and grandiosity: being very wealthy, famous, or having some special power or ability. Another sign of this frenzy is that people become so disorganized in their thinking that their speech makes little or no sense, though they do not seem aware that this is so.

Bipolar disorder mistaken for major depression. Sometimes people will suffer from severe depressions that come and go. In between they experience a mild manic state or "hypomania," literally, a "lesser mania." These hypomanic periods, which usually occur within a half year of a major depression, are so pleasant by comparison that people welcome them and do not think to report them as a problem. While hypomanic they feel particularly alert, effective, and on top of things.

But if the hypomania is not brought to the attention of the psychotherapist treating the depression, then the result may be a misdiagnosis. In such cases, clinicians may prescribe the wrong medication, which will not be as effective in treating the problem and might even make it worse in the long run.

The greatest danger is that a tricyclic antidepressant (see p. 610) will be prescribed. These can trigger a manic episode in someone who has never had one before. For that reason, you should be sure to tell your therapist and especially whoever is prescribing your medication if you have a history of mild mood swings or periods of mild elation and "highs."

If the depressive phase of bipolar disorder occurs first, it is also likely to be diagnosed as a major depression. Not until the first appearance of a manic episode—which can be years later—will it be clear that the problem is bipolar disorder, not major depression.

Rapid cycling. In this form of bipolar disorder the episodes of major depression and mania follow each other in rapid succession, four episodes or more a year. The resulting roller coaster from paralyzing depression to the reckless abandon of mania can make a shambles of a person's life. In some instances, this pattern seems to be brought about by taking the wrong antidepressant (see p. 633 on medication for bipolar disorder).

Suicide. Although it is not obvious, a person undergoing a manic episode is at risk for suicide. Even while manic, a person can suddenly flip into a mood of deep despair. And the energy of the manic phase can help a person carry through on a plan for suicide that they might be less able to act on while depressed and lethargic (see the discussion of suicide in major depression, p. 467).

If there is a danger of suicide, it may be necessary to commit the person to a hospital against his or her will—always a painful decision to make and carry out (see p. 268). The dilemma with people who are manic is that they usually do not see themselves as having a problem or needing help. They may resist the idea of entering a hospital, or even seeing a psychotherapist.

Alcohol and drug abuse. As with major depression, people with bipolar disorder often turn to drugs or alcohol to make themselves feel better during the depressive phase. This ultimately backfires since both drugs and alcohol tend to increase anxiety and depression.

During a manic episode, on the other hand, people may turn to drink or take drugs to stay "up." The danger of excess is extreme because mania leads such people to feel invulnerable, immune to any danger and oblivious to their physical limits.

The danger from alcohol is perhaps greatest. Because alcohol initially acts as a stimulant on the central nervous system, it can seem to sustain or intensify the "high" (as, of course, do other stimulants such as amphetamine). But in its next phase, alcohol depresses the central nervous system, which can worsen feelings of depression.

Instead of stopping, however, people tend to develop tolerance and typically increase their use, trying to get the same effect. A vicious cycle can set in, leading to an additional problem of alcohol or substance abuse, even dependence, super-imposed on the bipolar disorder.

What Therapists Recommend

Note: Recommendations for treating the manic and the depressive phases of bipolar disorder differ somewhat. Where they differ, recommendations for each are given.

Approach. The most frequently recommended approach by far for the acute phase of both bipolar depression and mania is supportive therapy. More active approaches are usually impossible until some of the acute symptoms subside. For bipolar depression, once the acute phase has passed, psychodynamic therapy was highly recommended as was cognitive therapy.

Medication. Almost all therapists recommend medication for treating both bipolar depression and mania. The usual medication is lithium (see p. 484).

Setting. Bipolar disorder can be treated in the office or clinic when the symptoms are not exteme. But hospitalization may be necessary during the acute phase of either mania or depression if the symptoms threaten the safety of the person or those around him or her (see p. 486 for a discussion of hospitalization).

Format. Most psychotherapists recommend individual therapy for both bipolar depression and mania, which can be supplemented by group therapy or by family or couples therapy when the person is not too depressed or too manic to participate.

Frequency. Therapists recommend once a week for bipolar depression, though twice a week or more may be necessary during an acute phase and hospitalization may still be necessary.

But during a manic episode, for as long as hospitalization can be avoided, or after the more severe symptoms have begun to subside, the strong consensus is that contact with the therapist should be frequent: a large majority of therapists endorse sessions twice a week or more. As with depression, these would be cut back as the intensity of the manic episode subsides.

Duration. For bipolar depression, therapy should be open-ended according to almost three-quarters of therapists. But for manic episodes, supportive therapy can often be shorter, since most manic episodes run their coarse within a few weeks or one to two months.

What You Should Know About Therapy

If you or someone you know has the major signs of a manic episode or the mood swings of a bipolar disorder, *the first step should be a thorough physical examination.* As with major depression, a wide range of medical disorders can cause symptoms of bipolar disorder, among them neurological, endocrine, and kidney diseases, as well as infection and vitamin deficiencies.

Many medicines can also produce mania or depression as side effects, or because of interactions with other drugs. This makes a physical especially important with older people, who may be taking several medications.

Manic episodes tend to recur, especially without treatment. A manic episode can last anywhere from a few weeks to two or three months if left to run its course. If manic episodes repeat, they tend to become more severe, last longer, and become more frequent—a strong argument for getting treatment the first time one occurs.

If you are under treatment for a manic episode, you may go through a bout of mild depression before you feel back to normal. That seems to be part of a natural progression. If it happens, realize that it is probably a sign that you are getting better, and that time is the best prescription.

Remember that treatment may be frustrating in the short term: it can take weeks for medication or psychotherapy to start working.

If someone you know needs treatment for bipolar disorder, you may have to make special efforts to get him or her into therapy. People who are depressed may be too despairing to seek help, thinking that nothing or no one can help them. And those who are manic may not believe anything is wrong.

Medication. Lithium, a natural salt like sodium, is the treatment of choice. While lithium does not work for everyone, it is effective in about four out of five cases to calm a manic episode. It is less effective during the depressive phase, but is often used along with an antidepressant.

If used during a manic episode, lithium will usually calm things down within ten to fourteen days, though sometimes it takes even longer. If it does not seem to work at first, the trial period can last as long as a month or longer.

Be patient if you are trying lithium. To be effective, lithium needs to reach a certain concentration in the bloodstream. Finding the dose that will protect you against recurrent episodes with a minimum of side effects may take several months (see p. 634 for details on lithium's side effects). You may have relapses in the meantime.

If a person is out of control—becoming combative or destructive, say—during a manic episode, antipsychotic medications are usually prescribed. Sometimes these have to be given intramuscularly, by injection, against the person's will if his or her own or someone else's safety is at stake. Antipsychotics take effect quite rapidly, reducing the intensity of the manic agitation within thirty minutes, and calming excitement and psychotic thinking within a few days. But in the long run antipsychotics do not have nearly as broad gauge an effect on mania as does lithium.

Before you start on lithium, a psychiatrist will ask you to have a medical workup, including urine and blood samples. Periodic blood samples will also be necessary while you take lithium to be sure that the dosage stays in the optimum range.

For most people with bipolar disorder, taking a maintenance dose of lithium lessens the severity and frequency of both the manic and depressive episodes. For people who do not respond well to lithium, other medications are sometimes given in combination or as a substitute. Tegretol, an anticonvulsant, is a common one (see p. 637). Some antidepressants have the paradoxical effect of causing a switch from the depressed phase to a manic one, and these need careful monitoring.

Therapeutic approach. Lithium and other medications are typically used in tandem with psychotherapy once the person is stable and calm enough to engage with a therapist. Studies have shown that the two together are the most effective treatment in most cases, though lithium is more effective than therapy in preventing relapses. During a manic episode, therapy should concentrate on offering support in helping you to handle your excitement and its effects on your life. During a period of intense depression, therapy should also be supportive in the main.

One of the important contributions of a supportive therapy if you are taking lithium is encouraging you to take the medication regularly. Your euphoric feelings may make you feel you don't need it. Once it starts to work, you may begin to miss the high of the manic state and want to stop.

For some people, manic episodes can be triggered by interpersonal conflict. In such cases, a therapy that helps people handle their relationships better can make such relapses less likely.

Psychodynamic therapies are largely impossible with someone during a manic episode since insight—the focus of these approaches—is virtually absent. Such approaches may also be unhelpful during a depressive phase, since uncovering conflicts while you are severely depressed may worsen feelings of helplessness and self-reproach.

What family or friends can do. If someone in your family or a close friend is being treated for a manic episode, you can help by seeing that his or her home life does not worsen the condition. In general, this means keeping things as quiet and calm as possible: not too much talk, too many people, or too many changes.

Arrange to call the person's psychotherapist at any time for advice if things seem to be getting out of control. Be sure the person takes any prescribed medication. Watch for signs that someone in the depressed phase may feel suicidal and so try to overdose with the medication. Suicide can be a risk during a manic episode as well, particularly during the recovery phase with the loss of the high. Usually people in an acute manic episode are given only a few days worth of pills at a time to avoid this danger.

Beware of getting caught up in the manic excitement—for instance, being drawn into some grandiose scheme. During a depressive episode, try not to get drawn into the mood of hopeless pessimism.

Hospitalization. Because of the frenzied energy and hostility that can be part of the peak of a manic episode, it can easily present an emergency to family, friends, and coworkers. If the person is out of control and seems to be a danger to himself or to others, hospitalization may be called for until the mania subsides. Signs that hospitalization may be needed include:

- threats of suicide or of harm to someone else
- indifference or carelessness so extreme the person is not adequately caring for himself
- extreme disorientation or psychosis
- disregard of care needed for a dangerous medical condition, such as diabetes
- loss of self-control, unrestrained excess, and impulsivity that is self-destructive

If someone in your family is going through a manic episode and you feel overwhelmed and threatened, you should not hesitate to consider hospitalization at once. Notify his therapist if he is in therapy. If not, bring him to the emergency room of the local hospital. If he refuses to go, ask the emergency room for advice. If he is out of control and dangerous to himself or anyone else, call the police. Don't wait.

The average hospital stay for someone with bipolar disorder is two to six weeks, depending on how intense the episode is, how soon the person gets treatment, and how well they comply with it—especially with medication. Hospitalizations for mania typically last longer than for bipolar depression.

Between acute episodes, bipolar disorder can be treated while living at home. This is especially true if the person is being seen regularly by a therapist; if there are no signs of severely impaired judgment, agitation, or psychotic delusions; and if a strong network of family and friends can help.

Cyclothymia: Mood Swings

Mood swings, or cyclothymia ("cycling mood"), is a more muted version of bipolar disorder. The moods are not so severe but still present definite problems, particularly during the depressed phase. Instead of feeling wildly euphoric, as happens during mania, you may feel a sense of elation, energy, and well-being on the upswing, and a mood of gloom, fatigue, and irritability on the downswing.

Most people with mood swings tend to feel depressed more often than elated, although they will also have periods of euphoric productivity from time to time.

While the extreme swings in mood in manic depression take weeks or months, those in this milder version are typically short—from a few days to a week, sometimes even shifting in a matter of hours. Between these irregular highs and lows, your mood is likely to be normal for weeks or months at a time.

Mood swings often begin to be noticeable for the first time in late adolescence or your twenties. Once they begin, they tend to become chronic. They are more common by far in people who have relatives with manic depression or who also are prone to mood swings. A small number of people who are prone to mood swings go on to develop the more severe symptoms of manic depression.

Even in this milder version, the roller coaster of up-and-down moods can be disruptive, leading to breakups in intimate relationships, and to unevenness in school performance or at work. It can feed a chronic dissatisfaction that leads to a wanderlust or frequent changes of residence. More seriously, it can also lead to abuse of drugs and alcohol, either to self-medicate a depressed mood or to keep an elated mood going.

In relationships, for instance, you may feel extremely romantic, even hypersexual, during the up phase, then lose all interest in intimate contact and sex and feel irritated with your partner while you are feeling down—an unpredictability that will be as hard on your partner as it is on you.

While some people do actually become more productive during their upswings, many or most may find themselves becoming disorganized and ineffective—for instance, starting dozens of projects but finishing none.

In short, because mood swings are so unpredictable and powerful, you may feel your emotions are out of control.

Signs to Look For

While the ups and downs of mood swings are far less severe than in manic depression, the symptoms are almost identical—just less intense. The main signs during the *depressive phase* include:

- a depressed mood or
- loss of interest in activities you usually find pleasant, plus some of the following:
- insomnia or sleeping too much
- listlessness and fatigue
- loss of productivity at work or school or of effectiveness at home
- distinterest in sex
- tearfulness for no apparent reason
- loss of sociability; not feeling like talking, for instance
- pessimism about life and the future, brooding over things that have happend

The main signs during the *manic phase* include:

- feeling euphoric or
- feeling irritable, as well as some of the following:
- less need for sleep than usual
- increased energy and restlessness
- heightened self-esteem; a sense that you can tackle anything; overoptimism and exaggeration of your achievements
- heightened productivity, often by working long and unusual hours
- unusually creative thinking; "good ideas" flow readily
- sociability; outgoing and uninhibited in seeking out people; talkative
- heightened sexuality, with disregard for consequences of liaisons
- impulsive decisions; sprees and binges without taking responsibility for the outcomes—for example, making foolish investments or buying things you can't afford
- extreme joviality, even when no one else is laughing; jokes and puns punctuate conversation

▫ For Derek, songwriting came easily—at least when he was feeling "wired," as he put it. His first song was recorded when he was only twenty-two. In the ten years since, he had sold dozens more. The songs would come to him effortlessly when he was in one of his "good" periods. For days at a time since his late teens he'd be confident and happy, talking a mile a minute and going with just a few hours' sleep a night. His friends knew him then as charming and hilarious.

But just as often Derek would have a "bad" spell when his inspiration would leave him completely: he couldn't write a note. He would take to bed for days, sleeping up to fourteen hours at a stretch, lacking energy, confidence, and interest in anything but watching TV. He'd feel like a "vegetable," withdrawn and irritable.

These ups and downs had led to a school record that mixed A's and B's and F's. Derek had tried six different colleges before giving up without a degree. Although his ambition was to start a band, each time Derek had tried it would disintegrate during a "down" time.

What You Should Know About Therapy

If you suffer from mood swings, you are most likely to consider seeking treatment during a period of depression. During the upswing, you may feel on top of the world, energetic, and highly productive and so see no need for treatment.

Just as the symptoms of mood swings are muted versions of those in manic depression, the treatments are similar, too. The usual medication is lithium (see p. 484), which often calms the disruptive ups and downs. But it can take two to six weeks for lithium to work, and several months to find the right maintenance dose.

A caution about medication. If you come for treatment during a down phase and are misdiagnosed as depressed, you may be given an antidepressant that has a boomerang effect: it may induce a hypomanic, "up" reaction. This is a sign that you are, indeed, prone to mood swings.

While psychotherapy alone may not help you control your mood swings, a supportive approach can help you ease or repair the disruptions they bring to your personal, social, or work life. Cognitive therapy can help you manage the problems that occur during your depressed periods. Family, couples, or group therapies can help you maintain the support and understanding of the people in your life whom your mood swings affect most strongly.

ANXIETY DISORDERS: PANIC ATTACKS, AGORAPHOBIA, PHOBIAS, AND GENERALIZED ANXIETY DISORDER

Anxieties are normal. People worry from time to time about how their children are doing in school or whether they will be able to pay all their bills. But when people's anxieties are continual, or are so strong that they keep them from living a normal life, then they are considered to have an "anxiety disorder," serious enough to treat.

Anxiety disorders are the single most common emotional problem bringing people to therapists. In a given month, 7 percent of Americans suffer from an anxiety disorder. Over a lifetime, close to 15 percent of Americans will have the problem. Anxiety disorders are about twice as common in women as in men: the rate is about one in ten for women, about one in twenty for men.

People with anxiety problems feel fearful and worried in situations where most other people do not. For those who suffer from phobias—an intense fear of a specific situation—the fear is far stronger than average. For instance, while almost everyone feels nervous before giving a speech, those with a phobia of public speaking find their fears so paralyzing that they may refuse to even try, even if refusing prevents them from advancing in their career.

The main anxiety disorders are:

- Panic attack, a frightening and intense combination of anxiety symptoms occurring in a sudden rush that can lead a person to fear he or she is about to die.
- Agoraphobia, a fear of becoming panicked in a public place, such as a busy store. The fear can be so intense that a person refuses to leave home.
- Phobias, fears of specific situations that can be so strong that a person becomes

anxious even thinking about them. These are by far the most frequent anxiety disorder.

- Generalized anxiety, being filled with free-floating anxiety that is not just about some specific thing, but a changing range of worries that leave a person continually preoccupied by minor matters that don't warrant so much concern.

If you are prone to one of these anxiety disorders, your anxieties go far beyond ordinary fear. As you have probably found, these fears can't be talked, threatened, or ridiculed away: they are real, not imaginary. But they can be faced and overcome with help.

Panic Attack

Panic attack is one of the most terrifying of psychological problems. Victims of panic attack may be convinced that they are having a heart attack. A sizable proportion of people who come to hospital emergency rooms for heart attack are actually found to be suffering a panic attack.

Since some symptoms of panic attack *do* resemble a heart attack—for instance, chest pain and heart palpitations—the fear of dying is not unreasonable. Because many of the symptoms of panic attacks mimic medical problems—or at least seem to—the person who suffers them may spend months or years fruitlessly seeking a medical diagnosis for what is actually a psychological problem.

The most common age for a first panic attack is in the twenties, though they can begin during the teen years or during later decades of life. They are equally common in men and women, though when they become linked with agoraphobia (as is frequent), they are about twice as common in women as men.

Signs to Look For

The first sign of a panic attack for many people is a *building feeling of doom or dread.* As the feelings build, the person may become acutely aware of physical sensations that become increasingly intense.

Other signs of panic attack include any combination of the following:

- A sense of smothering, choking, or difficulty breathing; this can include hyperventilation, where your breath is rapid, but you don't feel you are getting enough oxygen.
- Feeling dizzy, shaky, or trembling, as though you are losing control of your steadiness.
- Sweating, hot flashes, or chills that make you feel your body's temperature is rapidly changing.
- Nausea or feeling sick to your stomach.

- A sense of depersonalization, feeling strange or unreal to yourself, or that what you experience is happening to someone else.
- Tingling or numbness throughout your body.
- Chest pain or pressure in your chest.
- Fear that you are dying, about to go crazy, or somehow lose control.

Panic attacks can occur several times a week, although over a year there may be long periods between attacks. Although they sometimes last for an hour or more, panic attacks generally last just a few minutes.

The attacks are unpredictable. If you are prone to them, you may be constantly apprehensive that an attack might begin at any minute. As the attacks become more frequent, you may have a better idea of when they might begin. Certain circumstances—such as being under deadline pressure—may be more likely to bring them on and lead you to avoid them.

□ Margie's panic attacks first started when she was nineteen. She had gone off to college at a large state university, her first venture away from the small town where she grew up. She had gone to school all her life with people she knew well. Now she was surrounded by strangers.

The first attack came one day out of the blue when a professor called on her in class and she was unprepared. She had nothing to say and found herself shaking, ashen white, her heart pounding, feeling that she would faint.

From then on school was a nightmare. Two or three times a week at the most unpredictable times she would suddenly find herself suffering an attack, sometimes again during class. Fearing these classroom attacks, Margie finally dropped out of school.

Agoraphobia

Agoraphobia, in its most general sense, is the fear that you will be trapped in a place you cannot easily leave while you are having an incapacitating or embarrassing experience. These include losing control of your bladder, fainting, or since most people with agoraphobia are susceptible to panic attacks, having a panic attack in public.

That anxiety typically leads to one of three debilitating fears: fear of being alone, of leaving home, or of being caught someplace where it is hard to leave—buses, planes, elevators, restaurants, theaters, crowded stores—or where it would be awkward to leave abruptly, such as a doctor's office or a dinner party. If the problem escalates, the person with agoraphobia can become a virtual prisoner in his or her own house, especially when it combines with panic attacks.

□ Elinor first felt the fear one night when she was riding a train from her office to her home in a suburb. The day had been sweltering and the train was packed so tightly she couldn't get a seat.

Standing hemmed in on all sides, she suddenly felt herself gasp for breath and thought she might suffocate. With that, her legs started trembling, her face broke out in sweat, and she felt herself flush with redness. Terrified she might be dying, Elinor ran from the train at the next stop and took a cab the rest of the way home.

After that, she was never again comfortable riding the train, though if a trusted friend rode with her, she would feel all right. She had several repetitions of the first episode, and each time she bolted from the train at its next stop. Finally she refused to ride the train at all. Instead, she managed to find a job within walking distance of her home.

But one day, while walking to work, Elinor again had that panicky sense that she could not breathe. Trembling and scared, she somehow managed to get home. Too frightened to try to walk to work again, she quit her job.

Signs to Look For

The most obvious sign of agoraphobia is that a person has somehow limited life's normal activities to avoid being out in public for fear of having a panic attack or losing physical control. While the fear is most often of panic attack, it could also be of some other embarrassing problem, such as vomiting, losing bladder control, or fainting.

Usually, though not always, the person has had such an experience before and dreads it happening again. Sometimes the person merely fears that such an episode might occur and is mortified at the prospect of being humiliated by it.

Agoraphobia can range from mild, in which the person goes on with his or her normal activities but endures certain situations with distress, to severe, in which the person's extreme need to avoid public places leads to virtual confinement at home.

What Therapists Recommend for Panic Attack and Agoraphobia

Approach. The most highly recommended approach is behavioral, often combined with cognitive therapy. Though research clearly favors a behavioral approach, psychodynamic approaches are almost as highly recommended by practicing therapists.

Medication. Clinicians are divided, particularly for agoraphobia, which was the index disorder for the question. More therapists favor medication for panic attacks, particularly to control the attacks in conjunction with other therapies that would aim to reduce the patient's vulnerability to them.

Setting. Treatment is normally in the therapist's office or clinic. That may be difficult for an agoraphobic who is housebound, but making the trip is one of the important steps toward recovery.

Format. While almost all clinicians recommend individual treatment, many also suggest supplementing it with sessions in groups made up of people with similar problems.

Frequency. Normally once a week. But two or more sessions a week may be needed during the beginning of treatment when the problem is at its worst. Some more intensive therapy programs also involve more frequent sessions.

Duration. Most clinicians view treatment as relatively open-ended. Virtually none see panic attack or agoraphobia as being treatable in less than a month or needing more than year, unless there are other problems as well.

What You Should Know About Therapy for Panic Attack and Agoraphobia

The cognitive-behavioral approaches, recommended most highly in the survey, have shown strong results with panic attack and agoraphobia. Some outcome studies have reported success rates of 80 percent and above, with follow-up studies showing the improvement persisting at two years or longer. Generally, these therapies expose the person in gradual steps to the situations he or she dreads most and try to change the habitual thoughts that feed those fears.

Cognitive-behavioral therapy for panic attacks typically involves helping a person learn to recognize the physical cues that signal the onset of an attack, and teaching him or her relaxation and breathing techniques to help the feelings of panic recede. This approach also involves learning to recognize the situations or thoughts that can trigger panic attacks, and to counter them with more realistic appraisals—e.g., being out of breath does not mean a heart attack is beginning; it's probably just a symptom of anxiety or physical exertion.

Behavioral approaches can be combined with psychodynamic therapy, in which the therapist would encourage you to explore emotional factors associated with your fears while using behavioral methods to learn to confront them head-on.

When spouses or family members participate in therapy for panic or agoraphobia, their role is typically to help patients with homework where they place themselves in the situations they fear. The active participation of a spouse or other family member can improve the overall effectiveness of therapy. Some studies have shown that when husbands helped their agoraphobic spouses during therapy, the wives had a more powerful recovery two years later than did those who were treated on their own.

Medication often plays a key role in psychotherapy for panic attacks (see Chapter 18), controlling the symptoms while therapy continues. The most commonly prescribed medications are antidepressants; more rarely, benzodiazepines (Xanax is the most common). While these medications will control panic attacks for many who take them, they will not prevent a recurrence if the medication is stopped. For that reason, those who take medication should combine it with psychotherapy.

Phobias

Phobias are the common cold of anxiety disorders. In any given six-month period, about one in twelve Americans suffer from them. Over the course of a lifetime, 13 percent of Americans will have a phobia. Despite their prevalence, simple phobias can have a profound impact on a person's life, as well as on the life of the person's family.

The most frequent phobias are of animals: dogs, insects, snakes, and mice. But other common phobias include flying, elevators and heights, being in a closed space (claustrophobia), driving, thunderstorms, and seeing an injury or blood. The fear is not of the object itself, but of some dire consequence associated with it. Someone afraid of dogs or other animals, for instance, typically fears being bitten; a claustrophobe fears suffocation; the "fear of heights" is actually of falling.

Phobias of animals typically begin in early childhood and are lifelong. But other phobias can develop at any point in life. Often they begin with an upsetting or traumatic experience: a near-crash on a plane flight may trigger a fear of flying; an auto accident may lead to fear of driving.

In many phobics, the anxiety can be as severe as in a panic attack. But while panic attacks happen at unpredictable times, the anxiety in phobias is specific to the thing feared. Even thinking about it can start the anxiety flowing.

If you have a phobia, you have probably found that the nearer you are to the thing you fear, the stronger your fear grows. Likewise, the more threatening the thing you fear seems to you—the bigger the dog, the taller the building—the stronger the anxiety.

Although you may know rationally that "there is nothing to be afraid of," that belief will do little, if anything, to calm your fears. If you are like most phobics, you will go to great lengths to avoid a confrontation with the thing you fear, even though it may mean limiting your comings and goings.

Signs to Look For

The hallmarks of phobia include:

- enduring fear of a specific object or situation
- immediate anxiety that occurs when the person is exposed to that object or situation
- avoidance of the object or situation
- interference with normal social or work life because of the fear

- recognition that the fear is unreasonable, although unable to do anything to control it

□ Darrell's fear of flying began after an experience of severe turbulence on a flight. Darrell flew often on business. He was an account executive and had clients across the country whom he called on regularly.

The flight had been fine until it encountered a severe thunderstorm over the Rockies. The turbulence was so bad at one point that the plane seemed to drop like a stone, plunging several thousand feet before it began a steep climb. During the fall several passengers shrieked; Darrell got sick to his stomach and threw up.

When the plane stopped in Denver, Darrell finished his trip by bus. The very thought of flying terrified him now. If he visualized himself on a plane, he could feel himself shake and tremble. To avoid having to make trips by plane again, Darrell opted to take early retirement at his firm and find a job that required no travel.

Common Variations: Social Phobia

The fear in social phobia is that you will embarrass yourself in front of other people. Perhaps the most common specific fear is of speaking in public but others include eating in public, using public bathrooms, being at parties, meeting strangers, and being interviewed. While some people fear just one of these situations, some are afraid of several or many of them.

As with simple phobia, the fear in social phobia is of what the person *imagines might happen*. The fear is almost always of some form of public humiliation: forgetting everything you were going to say while giving a speech, saying something particularly stupid while being introduced to someone else, being the object of ridicule at a party.

Often the specific fear is that others will notice just how nervous you are: seeing your trembling, stuttering, or sweating, for instance. The anxiety evoked by the social phobia can itself contribute to the behavior—stammering, for instance—that you are trying to avoid or conceal.

To prevent such embarrassing moments, many phobic people avoid those social situations they fear, limiting their lives severely if they dread a great many of them.

Social phobia typically begins in late childhood or during adolescence and is thought to be somewhat more common in men than in women. It is different from simple shyness, in which a person shrinks from contact with strangers, but will endure it if necessary. Social phobia marks an extreme of shyness: the anxiety is so intense that the person typically tries to avoid the situation altogether.

Signs to Look For

The typical signs of social phobia include:

- Intense fear of a specific social situation that could cause embarrassment or humiliation.
- Anxiety while in that situation, or even at its prospect, despite knowing the anxiety is irrational.
- Avoiding the situation, even if it hampers one's personal or work life to do so, or enduring it with extreme distress.

☐ George's fear was speaking in public. The fear had begun in high school, when classmates had on several occasions laughed at his stammering an answer to a teacher's question in class. Through college George had done everything he could to avoid taking courses that required class discussions.

Graduating in accounting, George built a one-man operation into an accounting firm with several branch offices. One year the local chamber of commerce decided to give George an achievement award. Knowing that he would have to get up in public and accept the award, George went through a miserable week beforehand. His palms were sweating constantly, he became irritable and short-tempered at home and with his employees, and he found it almost impossible to sleep. Finally, on the evening of the award dinner, George went to bed, pretending to be ill, and asked his secretary to accept the award for him.

The anxiety caused by social phobia can be every bit as intense as in other phobias. People commonly try to sedate themselves by drinking or taking drugs. While intoxicated they do not feel the anxiety that would ordinarily plague them and so are able to get through what would otherwise be an unbearable time.

Performance anxiety or "stage fright." Perhaps the most common variety of social phobia is the narrowly focused fear of performing, commonly called stage fright. The panic is induced by anything ranging from giving a speech in front of a large crowd to having a job interview. Performance anxiety is surprisingly common even among professional performers. A survey of members of symphony orchestras, for example, found it in one in four.

The main fear in performance anxiety is usually that you will become so anxious that others will notice, embarrassing you; or that your anxiety will make you muff your performance. People with performance anxiety typically get thoughts like "My mind will go blank and I won't know what to say" or "My hands will shake so much everyone will see." This nervousness then creates the kind of tension that can sabotage performance.

What Therapists Recommend for Simple and Social Phobia

Approach. Behavior therapy is by far the most highly recommended treatment approach for phobias, along with cognitive therapy, which is often combined with it. Psychodynamic therapies were also recommended.

Medication. Few therapists see medication as the preferred treatment for phobias, although sometimes it can play a role in combination with therapy.

Setting. Phobias should be treated in office or clinic visits.

Format. Individual therapy. But one-to-one visits can be supplemented with group therapy with others who share similar phobias.

Frequency and duration. Most clinicians recommend treatment be once a week. Most say phobias can be treated in short-term therapy, lasting from one to six months.

What You Should Know About Therapy

The main behavioral therapy technique for handling phobias is for the person to actually confront the feared situation and learn that nothing dire really happens. Typically this involves a sequence of graded steps, beginning with imaginative rehearsal and continuing through successive stages to the real situation itself. Cognitive therapy, used in tandem, aims to quiet the thoughts that feed the phobia.

The most frequently prescribed medications for treating phobias are benzodiazepines (especially alprazolam or Xanax), buspirone, and beta blockers (see Chapter 18 for a fuller discussion). These medications act by suppressing the symptoms, which can recur when the medication is stopped, and are usually used only to control the most severe phobias. But during behavioral therapy for phobias, the blunting of anxiety during treatment can sometimes be counterproductive since people need to feel they have survived the feared situation on their own.

For performance anxiety, the most effective medication is a beta blocker, propranolol. Many professionals with stage fright take it routinely, as needed. Propranolol works mainly by calming the physical symptoms of anxiety, such as hand tremors, that can trigger an escalating cycle of anxiety. But for people whose performance anxiety is mostly based on worries rather than on physical symptoms, propranolol is often of little or no help, since the worrisome thoughts continue unabated.

For such people, an especially effective approach is cognitive-behavioral group therapy with other people who share performance anxiety. In this approach, each person may give a performance with the rest of the group becoming a simulated audience. During the "performance," the therapist can help the person capture the thoughts that escalate anxiety, such as, "Everyone can see how nervous I am," and check them against the actual impressions of the "audience." Typically people discover that most of the thoughts that escalate anxiety are unrealistic. Each person can then practice catching those worrisome thoughts and countering them with a more realistic appraisal, thus short-circuiting the anxiety.

Generalized Anxiety Disorder

If you worry almost all the time or are anxious about a great many things that are actually not realistic causes for worry, then you may suffer from generalized anxiety disorder. Unlike in phobia, the anxiety is free-floating, not attached to a specific situation.

For instance, if you are a parent, you might continually worry about how your children are doing in school, whether they are safe when they are out playing, and if they are going to get sick. In addition, you might worry about your finances, the security of your job or your spouse's, or simply have vague apprehensions about what the future will bring.

Unlike ordinary worries, which come and go after a few days or weeks, the worries in generalized anxiety disorder preoccupy you at least for a half year or longer. The anxiety is marked; anyone looking at you would notice that you are worried. Several habits of thought are typical of people with this condition. One is "castastrophizing": you seize on a minor problem and blow it up out of all proportion. For instance, if you notice a mole, you become frightened you have cancer and will die. If your boss rebukes you or makes a mildly critical remark, you imagine a chain of events in which you will lose your job, be unable to pay your rent or mortgage, and end up homeless.

Another habit is selectively picking out the most upsetting detail in a situation and dwelling on that. For example, a student who gets a C on a report card on which all the other grades are A's and B's might fixate on the low grade and worry she will flunk out of school.

Generalized anxiety most often begins during the twenties or thirties, but it also occurs in children and teenagers. Without psychotherapy, it usually lasts for years.

Signs to Look For

The characteristics of generalized anxiety are:

- Unrealistic worries about a number of aspects of life simultaneously.
- Long-lasting anxieties, so that the worries are bothersome more days than not for half a year or longer.

- Physical tension, such as trembling or shakiness, sore or tense muscles, restlessness or tiredness.
- Physiological signs of anxiety, including a speeding heart rate, clamminess or sweating, trouble breathing, dryness in the mouth, feeling light-headed, a lump in the throat, upset stomach, chills or hot flashes, the need to urinate often.
- Edginess, including being keyed up, easily startled or irritated, trouble keeping focused, and sleeplessness or fatigue.

What Therapists Recommend

Approach. The most recommended approach for treating generalized anxiety is psychodynamic; therapy would focus on the emotional origins and meaning of the anxiety. Many therapists also suggest a supportive approach, in which the therapy would build on those strengths in coping with anxiety that the person already has.

Medication. More than half of psychotherapists think medication can be a useful supplement to therapy. The usual medications are tranquilizers (see p. 628)

Setting. In the office or clinic.

Format. Individual therapy is recommended nearly unanimously.

Frequency. The majority of therapists believe the standard once-a-week schedule is best.

Duration. Most believe the length of treatment must be left open-ended.

What You Should Know About Therapy

Because of the pervasive nature of the worry, many psychotherapists believe general anxiety disorder has a biological basis. For that reason, a large proportion of therapists suggest medication along with psychotherapy. But medication alone will not solve the problem. Without psychotherapy, the worries will come back if the medication is stopped. And for some people medication alone does not stop the worrying.

STRESS DISORDERS

What is stress? There's no denying it: deadlines, illness, family arguments, moving, changing jobs—modern life is stressful. Of course much of the zest in life comes from the challenge of meeting pressures head-on. Too little challenge can be boring, but too much becomes stress.

Exactly what makes for stress varies from person to person. For one person, moving to a new city may be an exhilarating adventure, while for another it is a confusing and frightening ordeal. Stress is not so much in the things that happen to you, but rather in *how you perceive and experience* them. If events seem threatening or overwhelming, they they are stressful, even if someone else might shrug them off.

Stress is really the inner response you have to events that tax your ability to manage. Each of us has an optimal level of challenge in life that we find pleasant. But going beyond that is not: struggling to get kids who are fighting ready for school on a stormy day when you are already late for a crucial business appointment can feel overwhelming. The result is the combination of emotional and physical reactions we call stress.

Beyond normal stressors, there are outright traumatic events: being in an auto accident, being raped, being the victim of a violent crime or even witnessing one. Then there are natural catastrophes: hurricanes, floods, earthquakes, fires, tornadoes. Beyond that, there are man-made disasters: building collapses, riots, wars, airplane crashes. Though these events are rare in any one person's experience, the daily papers make all too clear that they strike thousands of people on any given day. Such traumas touch most of us at least once.

An exceptionally stressful but normal event such as a parent's dying, a spouse's suddenly announcing he or she wants a divorce, or suddenly finding yourself without a job can produce a reaction that is temporarily overwhelming and disabling—a severe but short-lived *adjustment reaction* from which you recover without long-term debilitating effects. The psychological and physiological effects of traumatic events outside the norm—abuse, violence, natural catastrophe—can be devastating even years later and result in a *posttraumatic stress disorder*. Thousands of Vietnam vets, for instance, have suffered from posttraumatic stress years after they went through the original harrowing encounters on the battlefield.

Normal stress response. The body's normal reaction to stress is the "fight or flight" response. Every animal's nervous system is arranged to trigger that response when danger looms. The trouble is that modern life presents us with too many events the body reacts to as potentially "dangerous," so that the stress response is on too often. Or some traumas are so castastrophic that the body keeps acting as though the emergency were continuing long after it has passed.

The stress response mobilizes the body by shunting more blood to the organs and brain, pumping the liver to escalate the energy available to cells, raising blood pressure and heart rate, speeding up breathing, and raising muscle tension levels. Emotionally, you feel fear, anger, or a sense of apprehension. Your mind focuses on the event that triggered the response. Even when you try to think of something else, the thoughts intrude.

Normally, the reaction subsides with time, in minutes. But in some people, particularly those who have gone through a particularly intense and traumatic event, or who are struggling to adjust to some major upsetting changes in life, the reaction lingers on as a stress problem.

The most common sign of stress problems is when some aspect of the upsetting event constantly intrudes on your thoughts. The intrusion can be a recurring nightmare or anxiety-filled dreams, troubling images or thoughts that keep coming back, or a recurring sense of sadness, fear, or anxiety similar to what you felt during the event itself.

Particularly when the original event was shocking, the details—the sounds, sights, smells, feel—can be etched in your memory with great intensity and can return in a fragment or in full vividness time and again. Along with the memory there are common psychological reactions, including the fear it will happen again, shame over having been helpless to prevent a tragedy, rage at whatever caused it.

A stress problem can make you unable to concentrate at work or to sleep well at night. You may find yourself extremely irritable or teary for no obvious reason. You may be jumpy and nervous, fearful of most everything.

The normal course of adjustment after a trauma is for strong memories and feelings to alternate with a tuning out of painful thoughts. It's as though we give ourselves a breather to collect strength for another "dose" of the painful memories. Going through the entire sequence repeatedly seems to help people come to grips with what happened and to finally put an end to its more disruptive effects and make some sort of peace.

People go through these phases of adjustment at their own highly individual pace. If a close friend is killed in an accident, for example, one person may need to talk about it over and over in the following days, while another will not be able to mention it for weeks or months before dealing with the pain. Someone who seemed to be "over" the effects of a trauma, on the other hand, may begin having a reaction months or years later.

The lasting effects of a stress problem can take many forms, not all of which may seem to be connected with the original trauma or even signal a poor adjustment. For instance, in coming to grips with trauma, people normally try to put thoughts and memories of the troublesome event out of mind for a time. At its extreme this can mean resorting to drugs, alcohol, or "psychic numbing," the cutting off of all emotion altogether. People normally have occasional intruding thoughts about the event that interfere with concentration, but at the extreme, this can become a flood of overwhelming images and memories.

If you do not "work through" the upset well, the lasting result can be a chronic state of anxiety or depression, a sense of being "frozen" and unable to initiate things, or vague physical complaints.

ADJUSTMENT DISORDERS

Adjustment disorders are serous stress problems that occur within three months or so in response to some specific event or change in your life, rather than as a reaction to a severe trauma. A move or loss of a job could trigger an adjustment disorder. A catastrophic experience, on the other hand, such as being raped or injured in an auto accident, would more likely lead to a more severe and long-lasting posttraumatic stress disorder (see next section).

While the events that precipitate adjustment disorders are quite normal, the reaction itself can be severe—depression, temporary inability to function at home or at work, even a suicide attempt.

The hallmark of adjustment disorders is that they hit you harder than is normal for most other people going through the same change. Many people, for instance, find retirement a relatively smooth and welcome change, while some find it deeply upsetting. An adjustment disorder is more than a single outburst. It involves a sweeping *pattern* of difficulties, such as depression and anxiety, along with, say, a sudden irritability with your spouse or uncharacteristic lethargy and apathy.

It is not always immediately obvious that the reaction was triggered by the stressful event, since the reaction may not emerge until several weeks later. The trigger can be a single event, such as a divorce, or a series of upsets one after the other: the death of a loved one just after losing your job or coming down with a serious illness. Some triggering events are recurrent, such as a seasonal downswing in your business. Others are relentless: caring for a helpless relative or your own chronic illness.

The decisive factor is the *emotional meaning* of these events. Some that seem mild may produce devastating reactions, while others that seem dramatic may leave you unfazed. Most people will experience at least one adjustment reaction at some point in their life, though no one knows exactly how common they are.

Sings to Look For

The signs of adjustment disorder include difficulty at work, school, or in relationships that begins suddenly, and reactions to an event, such as anxiety or depression, out of proportion to what most people would experience.

□ Karen, twenty-two, graduated from college and moved to a large city to look for work. Unfortunately, though she answered many newspaper ads and sent in numerous résumés, no one offered her a job. Interview after interview ended without success.

Within a month of moving to the city, she had given up looking for work. In despair, she would stay in bed in her apartment all day. She would cry, feeling she was a failure in life, and thought the future so hopeless that she began to consider suicide. Whenever her mother called, Karen would pick a fight. Finally she wouldn't even answer the phone.

The specifics of an adjustment disorder vary widely. Physical symptoms such as stomachaches and headaches are most common in children. Adolescents frequently "turn bad" suddenly: cutting school, drinking or using drugs, being defiant at home and school, lying or vandalizing.

In adults adjustment disorders include depression and anxiety, financial recklessness, careless driving, picking fights, drinking to excess, shirking responsibilities, and suicide attempts.

What Therapists Recommend

Approach. Most therapists recommend a supportive approach through the period of intense reaction, combined with a more psychodynamic approach to help you understand the intensity of your reaction as it subsides. The primary focus, however, should be on helping you manage your reaction and its effects.

Medication. Certain symptoms that often accompany adjustment disorders, such as anxiety, depression, and insomnia, do respond to medication. If these symptoms are severe, a therapist will probably recommend a medication evaluation from a psychiatrist. If the reaction is severe enough to warrant hospitalization, the symptoms are usually severe enough to warrant medication, though this shouldn't be automatic. Medication alone is not enough to help with adjustment reactions.

Setting. Many adjustment disorders can be treated in the office or clinic. However, severe reactions that involve depression, intense anxiety, inability to function, psychosis, or suicidality may require a brief hospitalization until these symptoms subside.

Format. Individual therapy is the usual recommendation, though if your spouse or family is somehow involved, it may help to include them in couples or family therapy. Group therapy with others who have gone through the same stressful event—a divorce, a business failure, the death of a spouse—can often be just as effective.

Frequency. Once a week is the usual recommendation, though more frequent sessions may be necessary in the days or weeks immediately following the onset of the reaction.

Duration. The length depends both on the intensity of your reaction and the orientation of the therapist. Many people find a month or two of supportive therapy is enough.

Others may need six months or more, though if you find you haven't substantially recovered by then, the problem may be more than just an adjustment reaction.

What You Should Know About Therapy

Even though adjustment disorders are so distressing, for many people going through a troubled time and pulling through means emerging with greater assurance and maturity. Most people return to their earlier level of well-being within three or four months.

Because adjustment reactions tend to pass with time anyway, therapy may not be necessary at all. However, if your reaction is so intense you are continually disturbed, therapy is probably a good choice. But it should be brief, time-limited, and focused on helping you with the problems triggered by the event.

POSTTRAUMATIC STRESS DISORDER

Unlike the milder adjustment disorders, posttraumatic stress reactions are caused by true traumas: catastrophes that would be incapacitating to most anyone. Not a financial loss in a business, for example, but a fire that destroys the business entirely; not just the death in old age of a husband or wife, but witnessing the rape or murder of a spouse.

The two main causes of posttraumatic stress are *natural disasters,* such as floods and tornadoes, and *human aggression,* such as rape or assault. Generally the reaction to human aggression is more severe than to natural catastrophe. In either case, the event is traumatic because it overwhelms a person's normal sense of reality and ability to cope.

Normal reactions to catastrophe. Catastrophes can destroy your sense that the world is a safe and predictable place: that catastrophic things only happen to other people; that you can control the events in your life. For a time, they leave you feeling vulnerable, uncertain, and unwilling to trust the world. You may live in fear that the catastrophe will happen again or feel frightened by perfectly innocent events: the sound of a siren, for instance, may flood you with panic.

If the disaster was perpetrated by a person—a rape, an assault, abuse—it may leave you feeling suspicious and fearful. You may find yourself panicked by seeing someone or something that reminds you of the perpetrator.

In coping with these kinds of catastrophic events, almost everyone experiences a *characteristic series of psychological reactions.* The first reaction is often an *outcry* of fear, sadness, and rage. This is typically followed by either a state of *denial* and a refusal to face the trauma and its consequences, or a state of *intrusion,* in which unwanted thoughts, memories, or recollections of the traumatic circumstances intrude into consciousness. During the phase of denial, it is typical to feel "numb": a sense of detachment from others and a feeling of unreality about the catastrophe itself. There is a tendency to minimize the effect the event had on you, or even to forget that it happened at all. Or you might feel cut off from your feelings, temporarily unable to laugh or cry or renew your interest in life.

This tuning out of the catastrophe often alternates with an oppposite reaction, where you become all too aware of what happened and unable to get it out of your mind. You may be on edge, startle easily, find yourself unable to concentrate. It may take you hours to get to sleep, or you may wake up in the middle of the night and be preoccupied with unsettling thoughts of the catastrophe. You may have nightmares. You may suddenly start crying over nothing or lash out in anger at people.

Over the course of time, it is typical to alternate between phases of denial and intrusion until the experience is worked through and the reality of what has occurred to them has been dealt with. These reactions are normal and should gradually weaken in intensity and pass within a few months or so.

Posttraumatic stress disorder (PTSD). But sometimes the duration of these symptoms is prolonged, they are exceptionally intense, or their working through is blocked. If they do not abate after six months or so and continue to disrupt your life, then the normal posttraumatic stress response has become a posttraumatic stress *disorder*.

The main feature of PTSD is the recurrent *re-experiencing* of the traumatic event in dreams, nightmares, "flashbacks", unwanted waking thoughts, or in sudden reactions to stimuli associated with it.

The normal psychological reactions to trauma become exaggerated and extreme. The initial outcry of fear, sadness, and rage leads on to panic, emotional and physical exhaustion, even temporary psychotic reactions. The phase of denial can become a state of extreme avoidance and psychic numbing. Memories of the event itself may be dissociated from consciousness: you may not remember it, or forget it happened at all. There may be a kind of psychic and emotional "numbing": a deadening of feeling and responsiveness, an inability to laugh or cry, a lethargy and marked lack of motivation or interest in life. This is often abetted by losing oneself in daydreams, drinking, drugs, sex, or some kind of compulsive activity which will distract you and help you forget.

When the traumatic event does intrude on consciousness, memories and experiences tend to rush in in an overwhelming flood that can't be checked. Various aspects of the event are not just remembered but vividly relived and reexperienced in flashbacks, nightmares, dreams, waking thoughts, frightening day images, and sudden reactions to associated stimuli. The sound of a siren, for instance, may flood you with panic.

Some consequences of ongoing traumatization are psychological. The randomness or senselessness of the events tends to shatter basic assumptions and beliefs: that life is meaningful; that the world is a safe place; that others can be trusted; that you can trust yourself; that you can keep yourself safe; that tragedy always happens to someone else and you are immune. The unusual degree of helplessness you experienced tends to erode your sense of yourself as an effective and worthwhile person. Everyday difficulties may get "catastrophized".

Some posttraumatic stress problems are biological: becoming hypersensitive, in a chronic state of stress arousal, so that anything a little more intense than usual—a loud noise, for example, or a strange sound in the middle of the night—triggers anxiety or dread.

Or paradoxically, you may become compelled to seek out things that will excite and thrill you, to re-create the heightened state of arousal you experienced during the traumatic event. You may even become "addicted" to trauma, craving the overwhelming intensity you first experienced then. You may want to lose yourself in sex or anything else that induces the same level of intensity.

Other lasting effects can include a drastic deterioration in your relationships, with you feeling estranged even from those closest to you. If someone has died, you may feel an intense guilt for having survived. You may find that nothing seems to interest you anymore, or that past pursuits you enjoyed now leave you listless. Or you may find yourself simply full of rage, deeply depressed, or utterly passive.

One theory holds that, in order to fit a trauma into their view of themselves and the world, people have to review it over and over again. The review can become almost obsessive, since the trauma fits so poorly with anything people have ever experienced.

Posttraumatic stress can go unrecognized for several reasons. Denial can last for years. Its signs can be subtle. It is easy, too, to think that what happened to you so long ago "doesn't matter" anymore. Or you may be ashamed or embarrassed to admit that something from your past can still be bothering you so much.

Most posttraumatic stress reactions are acute: they occur immediately or shortly after the traumatic event. But posttraumatic stress reactions can also be delayed: the symptoms of PTSD may not be experienced for many months or even years after the events.

A posttraumatic stress disorder can also take a "disguised" form as chronic low-grade depression, chronic anxiety, substance and alcohol abuse, chronic physical complaints without apparent cause, and antisocial behavior.

Posttraumatic stress can occur at any age, though children generally react differently from adults (see p. 511).

Signs to Look For

The hallmark of a posttraumatic stress reaction is that the problems show up or persist long after the original event. An *acute* form surfaces within the first half year of the trauma, then passes, generally within a half year. The *delayed* form does not surface until a half year or more has elapsed, sometimes many years, and lasts for at least six months and usually longer, even years.

The trigger for symptoms is sometimes an event that is strongly reminiscent of the original trauma. The intensity of the problem can wax and wane over the years, intensifying when life becomes more stressful. The most intense symptoms are typically seen in people who were exposed to human violence or atrocity. Perhaps the most telling signs of posttraumatic stress are *repetitive nightmares* that relive the trauma and *flashbacks*. These two symptoms are red flags for a diagnosis of posttraumatic stress.

The main signs include:

- Being easily startled and hypervigilant.
- Trouble concentrating, especially because of intrusive thoughts of the trauma.
- Disturbing dreams or nightmares that review the trauma; recurring anxiety dreams.
- Flashbacks, the sudden vivid sense of reliving the trauma. Flashbacks are usually intense visual images.
- Disturbing preoccupations with the trauma; thoughts, feelings, and images that come unbidden into mind.
- A feeling of confusion or disorganization when thinking about something related to the trauma.
- Distress at reminders of the trauma.
- Being overcome with the same emotions, such as sadness or rage, that the event originally triggered.
- Nervousness, such as heart palpitations, nausea, shaking, diarrhea, the sweats—especially in response to something reminiscent of the trauma, such as its anniversary.
- Being in a daze: not noticing important things or not appreciating what things mean.
- Sleeping too much or too little.
- Forgetfulness: not being able to remember aspects of the trauma, or other important things that have happened since.
- Avoiding reminders of the trauma and obliviousness to things that might be reminiscent of the traumatic event.
- Getting lost in daydreams or fantasies to deny the reality of what happened.
- Feeling estranged or distant from people who used to be close.
- Emotional numbness, such as being unable to express tender feelings to loved ones.
- Physical symptoms such as bowel trouble, fatigue, headaches, muscle pain.
- Withdrawal from usual activities, such as favorite pastimes.
- Indecisiveness and confusion.

□ Vivian and her college roommate had been out at a "midnight movie." On their way back to their apartment they noticed a man following them. As they began to walk faster, he overtook them and seized Vivian's roommate. Vivian ran off, desperately seeking help. Her roommate was found the next morning, dead. Her throat had been slashed and she had been raped.

Vivian was upset at first, but not overly so. She helped the police in their investigation and helped her roommate's parents arrange a memorial service. But a year later, on the anniversary of the murder, Vivian had a nightmare in which a man was chasing her down a dark street. She awoke screaming.

The nightmare returned once or twice a week for months. Vivian started to obsess about the details of the night her roommate died. She could not keep her mind focused enough to study: the memory of that night kept flooding her thoughts. When her professors called on her in class, she couldn't answer: she had been thinking about the rape and murder. Vivian started to forget her notebooks and textbooks, leaving them behind wherever she had last been using them.

Whenever she heard a siren, she would start shaking. She became afraid to go out at night alone. She felt intensely guilty and kept reviewing each small detail of that ill-fated night to see what she might have done to have saved her friend.

Flashbacks. Flashbacks are one of the hallmarks of posttraumatic stress, but some psychotherapists may mistake them for a psychosis, for schizophrenia, or for something like an LSD flashback. If you know that the images represent something that actually happened to you, be sure to tell the therapist.

Disguised forms. Posttraumatic stress can show up in several disguised forms in which the problems are more muted. These include:

- chronic mild depression or anxiety
- alcoholism or drug abuse
- physical complaints such as headaches, stomach problems, or backaches
- problems focusing attention or with memory
- getting into trouble and defying authority
- disturbing dreams

What Therapists Recommend

Approach. Therapists recommend a *sequence* of approaches in testing PTSD. A supportive approach is recommended first, which focuses on containing and managing the acute posttraumatic stress reaction. Once symptoms have subsided and some safety and stability have been achieved, a psychodynamic approach can be taken to gradually work through the memories, feelings, and impact of the trauma. Some therapists also recommend a cognitive approach to the threat the trauma poses to ordinary ways of making sense of experience.

Medication. Only for cases with specific symptoms that respond to medication, such as anxiety, agitation, or depression.

Setting. Office visits, usually. A small minority of therapists, perhaps with Vietnam vets and special Veterans Hospital programs in mind, suggest day treatment programs or a psychiatric hospital, but these are only appropriate if the symptoms are extremely debilitating or the person feels suicidal.

Format. Individual treatment is the standard, often supplemented by groups designed for those with posttraumatic stress. Such groups have been successful in helping Vietnam vets and victims of violence, abuse, and incest. Another important supplement is family therapy: a supportive family can be instrumental in recovery.

Frequency. Usually once a week, but twice a week or more during acute or intrusive phases. The more severe the symptoms, the more often therapy may be needed. On the other hand, if a person is not ready to confront the full impact of the trauma, intensive therapy that takes place too frequently can trigger overwhelming anxiety.

Duration. Most therapists recommend leaving it open-ended. Others think it should resolve within a half year to a year. That may be optimistic in cases of prolonged or delayed PTSD. If the trauma has altered one's personality in some enduring way, therapy will take longer.

What You Should Know About Therapy

In general, the problems of posttraumatic stress clear up most quickly when the symptoms appear within a half year of the original trauma. Other positive signs are having functioned well in life, and the absence of other emotional problems or physical illness. Feeling support from the important people in your life is extremely helpful.

If your reaction has occurred *within the first half year* or so of the trauma, a particularly effective approach is often cognitive therapy in combination with supportive therapy. The cognitive approach aims to help you understand the thoughts and feelings you are having, and to distinguish between those that are realistic and those that only feed your turmoil. The supportive aspect of therapy helps you find ways to feel more secure and deal with daily challenges. In these instances, therapy can be fairly brief, often only a month or two.

If your reaction is *long-standing* or *delayed* more than a half year, then a supportive approach together with psychodynamic therapy is called for. This approach will allow you to build a strong relationship with a therapist and help you deal with residual problems such as feeling overwhelmed by memories or rage.

One effective approach is to use cognitive and psychodynamic therapies sequentially. In this combination, cognitive therapy is used first and as a preparation for the relationship-building of a psychodynamic approach.

It is generally *not* useful to engage in a therapy that encourages the direct reliving of what happened or the intense expression of your emotion. These are likely to be the very problems that you are in therapy to recover from.

If you are blocked emotionally, however, your therapist may work with you to recover the feelings tied to the trauma. But this should be done a little at a time, in doses you can handle. This will give you a sense of control over the trauma. You should discuss this strategy with your therapist at the outset. Be sure you both agree on how to handle probing the memory of the trauma and the feelings it brings up in you.

Steps. At first, therapy may focus on making clear to you what the links are between your present problems and the original trauma. You may be asked to track your symptoms by keeping a notebook of such things as anxiety attacks and nightmares. You and your therapist may also work on helping you find specific ways to handle these symptoms.

As some of your symptoms start to wane, you and your therapist may start to probe your memories of the trauma and feelings about it. This is typically done gradually, uncovering a piece and then stepping back to digest it. This process can take months, or even years, if your reaction is a complicated one.

As your overall symptoms begin to wane, you and your therapist can turn to any enduring impact the trauma has had on your personality. For instance, if you never became committed to an intimate relationship as a result of the trauma, you would explore that problem.

Self-help groups. These can be of immense help if you can find one that deals with the type of trauma you suffered. There are many, ranging from victims of rape and assault to groups for combat vets. Such groups are usually established anywhere there has been a major catastrophe, such as an earthquake or a hurricane.

Others who have gone through the same tragedy and are at different stages of recovery can give you both hope and practical advice. They can ease the sense of stigma or isolation you may feel from other people who just don't really understand what you endured.

Journal-writing—like a diary, but focused on your thoughts, memories, and feelings of the trauma—can be therapeutic in itself or as an addition to therapy.

Family therapy. If the trauma involved your family or your problems currently involve them, getting your family into therapy with you can be of great help. This should go on, though, in addition to individual treatment, not as the exclusive approach.

Your family's understanding of what you are going through and their active support can make your recovery much more bearable.

Hypnotherapy. Hypnosis is increasingly used in treating long-lasting trauma as part of both supportive and psychodynamic therapy. However, you should first have established a relationship of trust with your therapist. Hypnosis can then be used to help you develop a "safe place," a state of mind you can return to at will to reassure yourself when your feelings become overwhelming. Once this is established, hypnosis can then help to uncover memories or feelings about the trauma that have long been blocked. But if doing so makes you too agitated, you should go back to using it only to create a safe refuge or postpone it until later.

Medication. While medications may be useful and even necessary during an acute phase for some specific poststress symptoms such as depression or agitation, they do not treat the main problem of the trauma's impact. Only therapy will do that.

Note: If you are experiencing acute problems, such as flashbacks that temporarily flood your consciousness and overwhelm your ability to concentrate, you may be cautioned not to drive or operate dangerous machinery until the symptoms calm.

Finding a therapist: experience counts. The events that cause posttraumatic stress can be disturbing for the therapist as well as for you. If you have lived through brutal wartime scenes or were the victim of political torture or a vicious assault, it may be hard for some therapists to dwell on the details. If after several sessions your therapist seems to be avoiding talking about what happened to you, you might consider asking for a referral to a therapist who is more experienced in dealing with posttraumatic stress.

On the other hand, don't be too eager to change therapists. You may enter therapy with a burden of mistrust that is a residue from your trauma. It may take you several weeks or even months to feel that you can trust your therapist, but relearning trust is especially important after a trauma.

SEXUAL PROBLEMS

WHAT IS NORMAL SEXUALITY?

Popular ideas about sexuality are often superstitions and half-truths. One of the most prevalent false assumptions is that sex is simple, obvious, and comes as naturally as falling off a log. Nothing could be further from the truth. Quite normal and healthy individuals can occasionally experience problems—temporary impotence or frigidity, for example, or temporary loss of interest in sex.

The range of what has to be considered "normal" sexual behavior is much wider than most people assume. This means you might be concerned that some aspect of your sexuality, a bizarre sexual fantasy for instance, is a problem requiring therapy, when in fact, it may be well within the range of "normal." From a therapeutic point of view, sexual behavior can be considered normal even when it isn't exclusively monogamous or heterosexual, uses other parts of the body than the genitals to produce sexual arousal, or doesn't culminate in mutual orgasm. Clinically, it is not so much the specific act that makes sexual behavior deviant or unhealthy, but whether it is compulsive, obsessive, destructive to either partner, or is accompanied by a lot of anxiety and guilt.

Sexuality Has a Large Psychological Component

Sexuality is an extremely complex area of human behavior that interacts with almost every other aspect of life. It does not have a life of its own, separate from what is going on in the rest of your life. It is closely entwined with the total personality. It also involves much more than just genital pleasure. What you are thinking and feeling is as critical in your sex life as your hormones are.

At the same time, all pleasure is not ultimately sexual. Few therapists today hold that view. Pleasure can come from any number of sources: the experience of competence or aesthetic achievement, for example. On the other hand, you can use sex to satisfy many other impulses that have nothing to do with pleasure: dominance, dependency, power, aggression. Sex can be used to assuage insecurity or to promote self-aggrandizement and status.

Sexual Learning in Childhood

As Freud proposed and subsequent research has confirmed, sexual activity and sexual learning begin in childhood. As early as infancy, children normally play with their genitals because the sensations it stimulates are pleasurable. The important thing is not that children experience sexual sensations and begin to explore their sexuality, but what parents and other caretakers make of this innocent and necessary exploration. How they respond to their child's sexuality and how he or she reads their responses begins to shape sexual attitudes for better or worse. Someone whose parents reacted with disapproval and punishment, for instance, may grow up feeling inhibited and timid about sex.

Although childhood experiences can have a deep and lasting effect on a person's feelings about sex in adulthood, most of the crucial lessons about sex are imparted without much deliberate thought on parents' part. Such seemingly nonsexual interactions as vigorous play and physical contact between a parent and child instill a basic attitude about physical contact and sensuality that will become a factor in how natural and at ease a person is with a sexual partner in adulthood.

Sexuality

Sexuality refers to your own individual patterns of sexual desire, arousal, and orgasm. Crucial in understanding sexuality is the idea of a "sex print," or "lovemap" as it is sometimes called. Your sex print is your characteristic pattern of sexual expression and satisfaction. It dictates your preferences for a particular kind of partner, the sexual activities you enjoy the most, the particular way you become aroused and experience orgasm, even the type of sexual fantasies you tend to have.

Sexual Identity

In addition to characteristic patterns of sexual expression and satisfaction, we also develop a *sexual identity* and a *gender identity*. The two are not the same.

Sexual identity is a sense of being biologically a male or female. Your sex print is an important component. By the age of two or three, nearly every boy or girl has a firm conviction that he or she is a "boy" or a "girl." Nevertheless sexual identity is finally consolidated only after the biological changes of puberty.

Gender identity does not concern one's biological sex, but one's self-image and *subjective experience* of oneself as psychologically male or psychologically female. Normally, biological sex and gender identity coincide. But not always. They are closely related but separate lines of development; and they can develop independently of each other. When they do, gender identity becomes a problem. The psychological sense of gender can lead a woman with female sexual identity (she knows she is biologically a woman) and a masculine gender identity (she feels psychologically she is a man) to feel as though she is "a man trapped in a woman's body." A man with a female gender identity can feel like a woman trapped in a man's body. Men who enjoy dressing as women, and men and women who seek sex-change operations, have gender identities at odds with their biological sex.

Both biological and psychosocial factors shape gender identity. The timing and levels of male and female hormones play a role. So do parental and cultural attitudes—the way parents dress children, for instance, whether they respond to them in gender-typical or atypical ways, or need them to be the gender of a child they lost or wanted. Gender identity *isn't* simply a by-product of sexual development. Developing a psychological sense of maleness or femaleness, masculinity or femininity, is a separate task and achievement.

Homosexuality

Homosexuality in and of itself is *not* a sexual problem. While social conventions used to demand that homosexuality be seen as "deviant," today most therapists at home and abroad consider homosexuality to be within the range of normal sexual preference and orientation. Homosexual men and women, like heterosexual men and women, have no inherent problem in their ability to love, to work, and to play. They are not impaired in any way merely by virtue of being homosexual. No evidence suggests that any of the primary psychiatric syndromes or personality disorders cause, or are caused by, homosexuality in any way. Nor is homosexuality associated with any psychiatric syndrome or condition more than any other.

Nevertheless, special problems can obviously arise for homosexual men and women in our society, given many of the attitudes that still prevail: rejection by their parents after "coming out," for instance, or coping with the death of a friend or partner from AIDS. Because of social attitudes toward homosexuality, gay men and lesbians may experience years of turmoil and confusion over their sexual orientation before understanding it, and perhaps years more before accepting or openly acknowledging it to family and friends. Many continue to struggle with feelings of discomfort and anxiety at best, and with shame, guilt, even thoughts of suicide at worst. They also seek help for the same reasons heterosexual men and women do: a failed relationship, the death of a loved one, professional problems. They are more likely to implicate their sexual orientation in these problems, but being gay or lesbian in our society often *does* affect nearly all the normal problems in everyday living in some way.

There may be a biological component in homosexuality since its prevalence has been more or less constant through history and in cultures around the world. Both biological and psychosocial explanations have been hypothesized, but the fact is that its cause is just as unknown as the cause of heterosexuality. What does seem clear is that homosexual men and women no more "choose" to become homosexual than heterosexual men and women "choose" to become heterosexual.

Lastly, sexual orientation is relative, not absolute. It is not uncommon for heterosexuals to have had sexual experiences with someone of the same sex or to have had homosexual fantasies at some point in their development. This often occurs as part of normal adolescent experimentation with emerging sexuality. It sometimes serves male or female bonding in adolescence or young adulthood. It can even serve to confirm adolescents' sexual identity, prowess, or attractiveness in their own eyes before their same-sex peers. Over half of all adolescents have homosexual fantasies, and occasional homosexual urges during adulthood are also common. Many if not most men and women who are clearly heterosexual in their orientation and activity may still find themselves entertaining homosexual fantasies on occasion. And many homosexual men and women are attracted to and enjoy partners of the opposite sex. By and large a person can be considered homosexual if he or she mainly enjoys homosexual fantasies and prefers sexual partners of the same sex.

The Sexual Response Cycle

Most sexual problems are malfunctions in what research has identified as the "sexual response cycle." This is the normal progression in sexual activity from desire, to arousal and excitement, to orgasm, to quiescence. This does not mean that all sexual behavior *must* progress through every stage in this cycle. It doesn't. Only that there are stages of response, and that when sexual activity progresses, it does so in this sequence. The patterns with which the phases unfold are also more variable in women than they are in men.

The great value in understanding the normal response cycle was that it made sense of the different sexual dysfunctions: each was associated with a particular phase of the cycle.

The cycle begins with *desire*. The psychology and physiology of sexual desire are quite different. You can experience a lack of normal desire although your ability to actually make love remains unimpaired. One of the fastest-growing areas of sex therapy is in treating people who "never seem interested anymore." Lack of desire can also be expressed in an absence of normal sexual fantasy.

Desire leads to *arousal or excitement*. This involves both the sense of sensual pleasure and the physical changes of arousal: erection in men, vaginal swelling and lubrication in women. As excitement mounts and intensifies, it culminates in *orgasm*. Both phases, excitement and orgasm, can be the focus of sexual problems. Dysfunction during the excitement phase may lead to impotence in men, the inability to get an erection, or frigidity in women, the inability to become aroused.

No matter how orgasm is achieved—through intercourse, vaginal or clitoral stimulation, or even masturbation—the *physiology* of sexual climax is the same. This contradicts the old "dual orgasm" theory of vaginal versus clitoral orgasm that has burdened a lot of women, as well as men, with feelings of anxiety, inadequacy, and guilt.

Following orgasm, a short "refractory" period occurs in men, though not in women, during which men will not be able to reexperience orgasm—another age-old source of confusion and shame.

But sexual response entails far more than just biology. Emotions, fantasies, underlying conflicts—all come into play and can interfere. The moments of lovemaking bring to bear years of sexual and emotional history. How you react may have as much, or more, to do with what has happened to you before as what is going on in the moment. Sex doesn't just happen "automatically"—another misunderstanding that creates a lot of self-blame and distress.

Masturbation

Many patterns of sexual response are reinforced during masturbation, an almost universal practice. Among American men, virtually 100 percent masturbate at some point; among women the figure is close to three-quarters. While masturbation is most common during adolescence, it is also relatively frequent among married men and women. The myth that masturbation causes mental illness or interferes with sexual potency is without foundation. Masturbation is a concern only when it becomes a compulsive activity or comes to replace normal sexual relations with a partner or spouse.

Love and Intimacy

Finally, sexuality is part and parcel of the human capacity to love. In its most mature form, sexual desire goes hand in hand with mutual love. Intimacy develops when you feel comfortable giving and receiving love. An impairment in either your capacity for love or for full sexuality will affect the other.

SEXUAL PROBLEMS

Some estimates put the prevalence of sexual problems at 50 percent, meaning that half of all Americans experience a sexual problem at some point in their life. The problems are often mild and respond well to brief therapy.

The causes of sexual problems range from nonspecific stress to a wide variety of specific psychological issues: performance anxiety, lack of self-worth, guilt or shame, self-consciousness. Ongoing emotional struggles in relationships are also often involved: fear of abandonment, lack of trust, jealousy. Sexual problems can also stem from a moralistic upbringing or may be the result of another psychiatric disorder that affects sexual desire and capability, such as depression. Too often people let sexual problems persist for years before doing anything about them.

Disruptions in the normal sexual response cycle are most likely to occur during a first sexual encounter or in young adulthood—suddenly finding oneself impotent or frigid, for instance. A sudden inability to function as he or she expects to can be particularly confusing and distressing to a young man or woman just coming to maturity. Other problems, especially loss of sexual desire, tend to be more common during middle age.

What Therapists Recommend

Approach. Sex therapy has evolved as a distinct speciality in the last decade or two, specifically for the treatment of sexual dysfunctions and more recently for disturbances in sexual desire. The standard procedure in sex therapy is to combine approaches: a psychodynamic and/or systemic approach to explore the factors in the couple or in one of the partners that have led to the problem; and a behavioral approach for treating the specific sexual dysfunction itself. This will typically include "homework" assignments between sessions that gradually increase the individual's or couple's sexual mastery and pleasure.

Medication. Only for secondary problems such as depression or anxiety, rather than for the sexual problem itself.

Setting. Treatment for sexual problems is usually offered in an office or clinic.

Format. Either individual treatment or couples therapy, or some combination of the two, depending on where the problem resides. Even if the problem is an individual one, a sex therapist may suggest involving spouses or partners in therapy if they are willing. Group sessions with other individuals or couples having a similar problem are sometimes useful, though you may feel excessively self-conscious at first.

Frequency. Once a week is standard.

Duration. One to six months is usually sufficient. Certain problems can take longer, particularly if a partner or the couple have related psychological issues that need to be addressed as well.

What You Should Know About Therapy

The good news is that problems in sexual functioning by and large respond well to therapy. Some problems have an extremely high rate of success, in the 80 to 90 percent range. These include premature ejaculation in men and failure to have an orgasm in women. Generally, the more "mechanical" the problem, the easier to solve; the more it depends on emotional factors or a troubled relationship, the more work it requires.

Many sexual problems can have an organic cause. Lack of sexual desire, for instance, can be a symptom of endocrine pathology, kidney disease, epilepsy, or a chronic immune infection, among other things. *A full physical examination is the first step in therapy for sexual problems.*

A diagnostic evaluation for other emotional problems is also a first step. Loss of interest in sex or other sexual difficulties can result from a large number of psychological problems: from depression, anxiety, and panic disorder to alcoholism and drug abuse.

The obvious choice of a therapist for sexual problems is a certified sex therapist. While other kinds of therapists may be willing to treat sexual problems, a sex therapist is likely to be most effective. Marital therapists are also often a good choice, especially when the problem is symptomatic of tensions between the partners.

When you go for treatment of a sexual problem, you can anticipate certain kinds of questions. Some will deal with your sexual behavior itself: are you anxious while making love? What images float through your mind during lovemaking? Do you reach orgasm? These questions will help your therapist gain a detailed picture of exactly where the problem may lie.

Sometimes deeper issues are at play, stemming from your past, so your therapist may also probe into early sexual experiences, your family history, and the like. If you are with a partner, your interaction as a couple will also be considered. Often improving sexual problems depends on improvements in your relationship. The most crucial question may be whether you actually like each other.

In general, the following rules of thumb can guide you to the right kind of therapist, whatever the specifics of the sexual problem:

- Sexual problems stemming from serious psychological difficulties, such as personality problems (see p. 568) or deep-seated conflicts about sex, respond best to long-term individual psychotherapy that is mainly exploratory.
- Sexual problems that stem from tensions between a couple are symptoms of destructive interactions between partners and respond best to couple therapy. Until there is some improvement in the relationship, sex therapy should be postponed.
- Moderate sexual problems in a basically sound relationship usually respond well to brief sex therapy.

What to Expect in Sex Therapy

The setting for sex therapy is almost always the therapist's office, or a clinic that specializes in treatment of sexual problems. If you are in an ongoing relationship, expect that both you and your partner will be seen in therapy. The assumption is that whenever there is a sexual problem, both partners are involved in some way. Even if the trouble seems to be just with you—premature ejaculation, for instance, or inability to have an orgasm—your partner may be contributing to the problem in some way and certainly can help you with the solution.

Another reason for both of you to see the therapist is that sexual problems frequently signal emotional troubles in your relationship. If so, then the relationship itself needs to be dealt with in therapy, with an emphasis on the sexual problems. Of course, in order for this to work, both of you must be willing to enter therapy.

Along with therapy for the couple, each partner, or sometimes just one, may see a therapist individually. This is particularly useful when one of the partners has some conflict about sexuality that not only creates problems in the relationship but may make it difficult to participate in sex therapy at first.

Group therapy is sometimes also used, either in conjunction with couples or individual therapy, or as the main therapeutic approach. The advantage of groups is that they allow you to deal with problems that may make you feel ashamed or anxious with others who share your problems and feelings. Open discussion—say among men who share the problem of premature ejaculation—can help you correct any misconceptions you may have, as well as make you more comfortable about the problem itself. Groups can work well, too, when they are composed of couples who have sexual problems. But they won't work if you or your partner are opposed to participating or are excessively shy or inhibited in groups.

The sex of the therapist you see may be important to you, especially at first. It is sometimes hard to confide a sexual problem to a therapist of the opposite sex. While these concerns may guide your choice of therapist at the outset, if you have only mild reservations, they are likely to fade as therapy progresses.

The usual focus in sex therapy is on the more immediate causes of the sexual problem: the anxiety you feel as you start to make love, say, rather than on the antisexual attitudes that were instilled in you during childhood.

The most common approach to sex therapy combines behavioral techniques with an exploration of what has caused the problem. Typically you will be given specific assignments to carry out in the privacy of your home, for instance, "sensate focus." In this, you and your partner take turns giving each other a slow, sensual massage, designed to induce sexual arousal but going no further.

Such exercises, tailored to your specific problem, will be your homework between sessions. At sessions you will report on your progress with these assignments and new ones will be prescribed. The goal is to guide you and your partner through a gradual series of naturally reinforcing steps. Since sexual problems often result from conflicts in the relationship, therapy may shift back and forth from focusing on the sexual problem to working on the relationship.

SPECIFIC SEXUAL DYSFUNCTIONS AND THEIR TREATMENT

Lack of Sexual Desire

People vary greatly in their desire and need for sex. Some, though not many, are happy with intercourse once a month; others prefer making love once a day. Generally men complain that their wives do not want enough sex and women that their husbands want too much. For instance, in one survey of couples married an average of nine years, more than 12 percent of men said they preferred intercourse more than once a day, and 3 percent of women said the same. On the other hand, 10 percent of women and about 4 percent of men said that once a week was enough. Most men and women preferred sex three or four times a week.

But the reality was different from the desire. Only 2 percent of men and 1 percent of women said they actually made love more than once a day, while 12 percent of both men and women said that the actual frequency of lovemaking in their marriage was once every two weeks to a month.

You or your partner may have a problem with a lack of sexual desire if there has been a sharp drop in desire for more than just a few weeks or months. Many people go through periods when their desire wanes, only to pick up again. One survey of couples found that a third did not make love for up to two months at a time. Typical causes of such temporary waning are personal losses, such as the death of a loved one, or an increase in pressures at work. But a sudden, lasting drop may signal ongoing marital conflict.

Another problem with lack of sexual desire is if a large discrepancy exists in how frequently partners want sex. Remember, most couples disagree on this, typically with the man wanting sex more often than the woman. It is too easy, though, to blame the partner who wants less as being "undersexed," or to accuse the other of being "oversexed." The real difficulty is in the *imbalance*, not in the degree of desire of the other partner.

True low sexual desire may include both a lack of sexual fantasies and a lack of desire for sex itself. Or, a person may have sexual fantasies but is "turned off" by actual lovemaking. But if you find yourself simply turned off when you are with someone you find unattractive, or in a situation that is unsexy for you such as lack of privacy, that is not a difficulty with desire.

Usually, though, the person with low sexual desire still finds his or her partner desirable. The condition is puzzling: how can you feel love and affection for someone for whom you also feel no sexual desire? Yet this is exactly the situation.

The loss of sexual desire is sometimes *limited:* you feel the lack only with your sexual partner, while you still have interest in others, in sexual fantasies, or in masturbation. This pattern typically signals an underlying conflict in the relationship.

Sometimes the loss of desire is *pervasive:* you not only lose interest in your partner but in everyone else, in fantasies, and in masturbation. In this case the problem is with some factor in you, not in the relationship.

Even if you have low sexual desire, you may be able to force yourself to go through the motions, though you don't enjoy lovemaking. Or you may still enjoy kissing and cuddling, but find they don't lead to erotic arousal. Some people, though, develop a strong aversion to all physical contact, sexual or not.

A loss of interest in sex is likely to trigger strong counterreactions in your spouse. The most common are feelings of rejection and abandonment, which lead to hurt and anger. Those reactions may in turn intensify your lack of interest. Even if you are not particularly disturbed by your waning interest in sex, you may want to consider therapy because your spouse is upset by it.

The causes of waning sexual desire may be purely biological. Medical conditions that lower levels of testosterone will markedly lower sexual desire, especially in men. Many medications, such as some antidepressants, antipsychotic medications, and those for heart disease, can also lower sexual desire. So can a major illness or surgery, or a chronic depression.

More commonly, though, the problem in sexual desire is a symptom of marital conflict. Difficulties with emotional intimacy easily spread to trouble with sex.

Signs to Look For

The signs of low sexual desire include:

- lack of sexual fantasies, whether about one's partner or others
- loss of desire for sexual contact of any kind
- aversion to genital contact with a sexual partner

□ Rachel and Steve have been married for seventeen years. While their sex life was rather predictable for most of that time, for the last two years it has been almost nonexistent. Rachel, as she puts it, "just never feels interested." When Steve persists, she sometimes goes through the motions to please him, but never feels any arousal herself. Sometimes she gets angry when he pursues her.

The trouble started soon after Steve got a new job. When he left his job as a partner in a bookstore to become a representative for a textbook publisher, Steve had to go on the road half the year and they had to move to a different state.

Steve's absence upset Rachel. She felt isolated and abandoned. She had a house that was much nicer but no one to enjoy it with. When Steve would return from one of his trips, the first thing he would want to do was make love. Rachel would go along with it, but with little enthusiasm, and finally she lost interest altogether.

What Therapists Recommend

Approach. The most highly recommended approach is psychodynamic; next is behavioral. Many sex therapists combine these two. The psychodynamic phase is typically at the beginning, focusing on personal issues in the relationship. Once these are identified and begin to clear up, a more directive, behavioral approach focusing on the sexual problem itself is usually undertaken.

Medication. Only in those rare cases where a lack of testosterone or another problem, such as depression, is at fault. Even there be cautious: some antidepressants can lower desire.

Setting. Office visits.

Format. Therapy should be individual usually supplemented by couples therapy if there is a partner or spouse.

Frequency. Normally once a week.

Duration. Anywhere from a month to a year or more. The issues behind a loss of sexual desire normally take longer to resolve than a problem in sexual functioning.

What You Should Know About Therapy

If your therapist gives you "homework" assignments between sessions, be careful to observe how you fulfill them. A failure to follow the recommendations can be as useful in what it reveals as a success, particularly in bringing to light hidden emotional conflicts. Otherwise, the general discussion on sex therapy applies here (see p. 518).

Several medications can lower sexual desire. These include steroids, estrogen, and progesterone, some medications for hypertension, for depression, and for schizophrenia, as well as sedatives. Excessive drinking can, too, as well as many drugs of abuse. If any of these apply to you, tell your therapist.

Sexual Arousal Problems: Impotence and Frigidity

Since desire and arousal are two different aspects of sexuality, you can have a problem with one but not the other. You may want to have sex, but find yourself unable to become aroused. In men this takes the form of impotence, inability to get or sustain an erection. In women, it means being unable to experience the physical signs of sexual excitement.

Impotence. The most common complaint among men in sex therapy is impotence. Of the three patterns of impotence, the rarest is never having been able to get an erection hard enough for intercourse. The second, more common, is having been successful in getting an erection in the past, but not now. The third, also common, is being able to function sexually with some partners or in certain situations but not others, such as a man who can get an erection with a woman he is having an affair with but not with his wife.

Even though a man may be unable to get an erection, it is still possible for him to become excited enough to ejaculate. But shame about the inability to get an erection often leads such men to avoid sex altogether. Nevertheless, impotence in itself *does not mean* you are lacking in desire.

Some men are impotent with partners, but have no trouble masturbating. Others complain they can get an erection but lose it, say, when they undress, are about to enter their partner, or while they are inside the vagina. Others lose their erection when they start to feel pressured about performing well, or with certain types of women. The notion that many men become impotent because of overly aggressive "liberated women" is a myth, however. Most partners of men with impotence are, if anything, too passive.

Most men have had an occasional bout of impotence. The condition is a problem *only if it persists*. Impotence becomes more frequent with age. The fear of impotence increases as well. While impotence is common in men over eighty, it is not universal.

Impotence can be due to organic causes or can be purely psychological. Sometimes it is both. Injury to or loss of the testicles does not necessarily lead to impotence.

The diseases that can cause impotence include mumps, arteriosclerosis, kidney failure, cirrhosis of the liver, malnutrition, many endocrine and neurological disorders, pelvic fracture, and any severe systemic disease.

Abuse of alcohol or drugs is also a common cause of impotence. Heroin, methadone, morphine, cocaine, amphetamines, and barbiturate use can all do the trick, as can some medications for hypertension.

Many psychiatric drugs can also interfere with the ability to get an erection, though not always. These include tricyclic antidepressants such as imipramine (Tofranil) and clomipramine (Anafranil), and MAO inhibitors such as Parnate, Actomal, and Nardil. The mood stabilizer lithium can also have this effect, as can major tranquilizers—fluphenazine (Prolixin), thioridazine (Mellaril), haloperidol (Haldol)—as well as minor tranquilizers such as chlordiazepoxide (Librium).

If you get erections at night, while dreaming, or when you have to urinate, then your impotence is most likely not organically caused.

Signs to Look For

The signs of impotence are straighforward:

- inability to get an erection, either persistently or often
- inability to maintain an erection to or through intercourse
- lack of sexual pleasure during sexual activity

Arousal Problems in Women. You may feel the desire for sex and want to make love, yet find that once you begin you have little or no response. Sometimes this difficulty is also connected with the inability to have an orgasm, though not always.

Because you do not experience the vaginal swelling and lubrication that normally accompanies sexual arousal, intercourse itself can be painful for you as well. This can cause additional problems, such as vaginal irritation and loss of sexual desire altogether.

Sometimes the problem is a waning of arousal once lovemaking begins. These difficulties are more common than are often thought: one survey found that a third of married women reported some difficulty in becoming aroused or maintaining sexual arousal during lovemaking.

Women with this problem tend to feel more sexual excitement just after their menstrual period or during ovulation. If this is true for you, you should let your partner know so that you can time your lovemaking accordingly before you seek therapy.

While no one knows for sure, an imbalance in sex hormones may be one of the causes of inhibited arousal. Women are far less likely to have the problem because of a medication they are taking. The most common causes are psychological, particularly conflicts in the relationship. The same factors that can lead to lack of desire also can impair arousal (see discussion of lack of desire, p. 519).

However, if your partner fails to offer stimulation that is intense enough or is too quick, then the problem may be your mutual pacing and rhythm: your partner needs to give you more time and attention during sex.

Signs to Look For

The signs of inhibited sexual arousal in women are simple:

- Inability to become physically aroused during lovemaking; lack of vaginal swelling or lubrication that may be persistent or recurring, partial or complete.
- Absence of pleasure and excitement during sexual activity.

Therapy for Arousal Problems

The treatment of choice is sex therapy that combines exploring issues in your relationship with behavioral therapy. Expect therapy to involve your partner or spouse. The treatment will involve specific "homework" to be done in the privacy of your bedroom, which you will discuss during sessions with your therapist.

Typically, the homework will include sessions in which you "pleasure" each other, but do not proceed to intercourse. The pleasuring will proceed in gradual steps, at a pace you are comfortable with. It may start with a simple massage, for instance, and increase in sensuality, but involve switching from sexual to nonsexual contact until you feel ready to proceed.

Orgasm Problems in Women

The term *frigid* has commonly been used in the past to describe women who are unable to have an orgasm. That term has been replaced by the more technically correct and less judgmental *inhibited orgasm*. Women with this problem are by no means "cold": they may be interested in sex, loving and caring, and enjoy sexual pleasure. They may even be highly aroused, with all the physical signs of sexual excitement. But it takes them "forever" to have an orgasm, if it happens at all.

Some women can have an orgasm with no direct contact, simply through fantasies or kissing, and most women can climax during intercourse. For many women, direct clitoral stimulation is essential for orgasm; this is a normal pattern.

But other women cannot achieve orgasm with a partner, though they can by masturbating alone. And about one in twelve women have never had an orgasm through any means. Women in these last two categories can benefit from sex therapy.

Of course, some women find sex perfectly enjoyable even if they do not have a climax. Such women should not be pressured into therapy unless they are unhappy with the situation. Some men are more upset by their partner's lack of an orgasm than are the partners themselves.

The causes are usually psychological. Among them are hostility toward or rejection of your sexual partner, fear of pregnancy, fear of losing control, and guilt.

Signs to Look For

Signs of orgasm problems in women are straightforward:

- Delay or absence of orgasm during sexual activity that is otherwise intense and long enough to produce climax.

Therapy for Orgasm Problems in Women

Here therapy is often individual. If you have never had an orgasm, your therapist may give you "homework" that involves guilt-free self-stimulation in gradual steps, culminating in orgasm. The homework may include Kegel exercises to strengthen the muscles involved in orgasm, the use of visualization and fantasy, or the use of a vibrator.

After you are able to achieve orgasm on your own, your partner or spouse will gradually be introduced at a pace that is comfortable for you. You will also be encouraged to experiment with a variety of ways to become sexually stimulated.

Orgasm Problems in Men

Retarded ejaculation. Like women who cannot have an orgasm, some men are unable to ejaculate, even though they have no difficulty with erection. The range of severity differs, from those men who experience the problem only in certain situations (e.g., during oral sex) or with certain women, to those who never have orgasm at all, or once used to but no longer do. Men are typically more disturbed by the problem than are women who do not have orgasm.

The problem is sometimes the result of surgery—of a prostate condition, for example. Some medications and neurological disorders can also cause the problem. *Check with a physician first* before seeking sex therapy.

Psychological causes include a rigid or puritanical upbringing that has instilled a deep sense of guilt about sexual pleasure. Conflicts in your relationship, ambivalence about it, or disinterest in your partner can also lead to the problem.

Premature ejaculation. The problem here is ejaculating too soon, usually before or immediately after entering the vagina. Typically men with this problem enjoy sex, have a high sex drive, are attracted to their partner, and find it easy to get an erection. The problem may occur with all partners, no matter what the situation, or only with some partners or in certain situations. The difficulty seems to be in learning voluntary control over the reflexes that control ejaculation.

The problem may not be crucial if, for instance, a couple paces lovemaking so that the man brings his partner to orgasm in other ways. But many women feel angry and rejected, thinking that the problem means the man dislikes her or is trying to deprive her of pleasure. This is likely to make the man feel more guilty, more pressured—and more likely to ejaculate prematurely. A troubled, tense relationship will intensify the problem.

Premature ejaculation is more common among well-educated men and is the chief complaint in about a third of men who enter sex therapy. Anxiety may be one cause. Another is having developed sexual habits under conditions where speed was essential: with prostitutes who wanted the man to "hurry up" or when discovery was a fear. Guilt over sex can be another factor.

Creams that dull sensation do not help nor does trying to distract yourself. Inattention is itself part of the problem: premature ejaculation is ususaly due in part to a failure to notice your own erotic feelings well enough to pace yourself. By the time you notice what is going on, ejaculation is virtually inevitable.

Signs to Look For

- Ejaculation just before or immediately after entering the vagina, which recurs persistently and is troubling.

Therapy for Orgasm Problems in Men

Sex therapy for premature ejaculation is usually brief. One remedy is to become more aware of the erotic feelings that accompany sexual arousal and lead up to ejaculation. Greater awareness of these sensations allows you to pace yourself better and leads to greater voluntary control of the reflexes controlling ejaculation. Treatment often involves homework with your partner or spouse. In one common approach, your partner stimulates you manually to the point of ejaculation, then stops. The treatment proceeds in gradual steps until you learn to gain control.

Sexual Phobia

Some people have an aversion to sexual contact: a phobia of sex. While it is not strictly speaking a sexual dysfunction, when couples have sexual complaints, the problem may actually be a sexual phobia in one of them. This condition tends to respond well to sex therapy.

The problem usually takes the form of a persistent fear of sexual experience and an active avoidance of it. While the person with the problem knows the fear is unreasonable, he or she feels helpless to do anything about it.

You may avoid all sexual contact or just certain aspects of it, such as genital contact. Sexual phobia can make it difficult or impossible to pursue romantic interests, to get married or stay married, and can severely restrict social life. Some people handle the problem by remaining virgins.

If people with this phobia do engage in sex, they typically feel panic, intense rage, or revulsion while making love. They want to "get it over with" and see sex as an ordeal to survive rather than as something to enjoy. Partners of people with a sex phobia frequently feel hurt and become angry themselves.

Signs to Look For

- Aversion to sexual contact and seeking to avoid it if possible

Therapy for Sexual Phobia

A sexual phobia is best handled in individual therapy using the same behavioral approach that is effective with other phobias (see p. 494). However, if the phobia has roots in other psychological conflicts, you may need psychodynamic therapy in addition, or before you are ready for behavioral methods.

Typically behavioral therapy for a simple phobia can be carried out relatively quickly, in a few months. Therapy will take longer, though, if other psychological or relationship problems are involved.

Unusual Sexual Preferences (Paraphilias)

There is nothing abnormal in occasional sexual fantasies that are unusual or bizarre—sadistic or masochistic fantasies, for instance, or fantasies of voyeurism or exhibitionism. Many normal people entertain such fantasies or imagery from time to time, but they aren't prerequisites for arousal, nor do they become special obsessions. Some unusual behavior can also be a normal part of sexuality when both partners are willing and neither is hurt or abused by it. An unusual or bizarre sexual fantasy or activity only becomes abnormal when it is fixed, repetitive, and compulsive; it is a prerequisite for sexual excitement or orgasm; it is the predominant or preferred mode of sexual pleasure; or it causes harm.

These types of fantasies and activities were once called perversions, a term since abandoned because of its connotations. They are now known as paraphilias: unusual sexual preferences. Each is characterized by a specific sexual fantasy or activity. Each has an imperative quality. Suppressing it feels difficult if not impossible. The fantasy or impulse typically becomes increasingly insistent, creating a pressure that builds until people have to engage in the fantasy or action to get relief from the tension. If they don't give in, they experience severe anxiety, depression, or a feeling of profound emptiness.

The actual content of the fantasy or activity can be either pleasurable or distressing—what matters is that it facilitates sexual pleasure. The fantasy or activity typically terminates in orgasm, either through a direct sexual encounter following the fantasy or activity, or through masturbation.

People with paraphilic sexual preferences often see their behavior as essentially normal, although they know their preferences are unusual. Nevertheless, their fantasies and practices are sources of humiliation and guilt. They also tend to be prone to depression, often in the form of a feeling of ongoing emptiness. Alcohol and substance abuse are unfortunately common, perhaps as attempts to self-medicate these feelings.

Paraphilic fantasies and practices also tend to spill over into the rest of life, creating serious psychological and legal problems. This is especially true for those whose fantasies involve sex with children, sex with a nonconsenting partner—someone they take by force or sadistically mistreat—exhibiting themselves, or making obscene phone calls. If acted out, these can lead to seriously harming someone, criminal behavior, and imprisonment. Fears of discovery and legal retribution tend to be constant preoccupations. Even apart from such dire consequences, these kinds of fantasies and practices tend to exact an interpersonal toll. They interfere with the development of emotional intimacy, for example. If the person does establish an intimate relationship, it is often difficult to sustain unless the partner joins in acting out the preferred mode of sexual gratification.

Paraphilic fantasies often first begin during the teen years, sometimes even in childhood. Many can be traced back to key events that became sexually charged. These fantasies are far more common in men than in women. Their actual prevalence is unknown since most people are understandably secretive about them and most people with them do not come into therapy for them.

Signs to Look For

The more common fantasies and preferences include:

- *Fetishes*. In a fetish the sexual charge comes from an object, often an object of clothing such as boots, high heels, or furs. The fetish is usually something closely associated with the body. Fetishes typically date back to childhood and are incorporated into masturbation or sexual activity with a partner—for example, demanding that a partner wear heels and panty hose with garters.
- *Exhibitionism*. The urge to exhibit one's genitals to a stranger typically involves a man exposing himself to a woman. The sexual excitement is in anticipation of the exposure and usually culminates in masturbation during or after. Much of the excitement comes from watching the expression on the woman's face.

Obscene phone calls are a variation of exhibitionism. The sexual excitement occurs during the call, with the caller masturbating during or after.

- *Voyeurism.* The voyeur's preference is for watching someone who is naked, dressing, or engaging in sex. The voyeur masturbates while watching or with the fantasy in mind.
- *Masochism and sadism.* These involve becoming aroused from inflicting real or simulated pain on oneself or someone else. This often takes the form of allowing oneself to be sexually dominated or sexually dominating another. Unlike most other paraphilias, these occur in both men and women, heterosexual and homosexual. Masochistic fantasies, often enacted with a sexual partner, include being bound, whipped, or spanked, even urinated on. Sadistic fantasies complement these. Often both masochistic and sadistic fantasies occur together. These are the most prevalent of the paraphilias. Mild versions of these fantasies, when acted out between consenting partners as part of lovemaking, are not considered a sexual problem.
- *Transvestism (cross-dressing).* Transvestites are typically men who find sexual arousal in dressing in women's clothing. The degree can vary from wearing a single article of women's clothing such as panties under regular masculine dress to full cross-dressing, in which the transvestite may appear convincingly female.
- *Pedophilia.* The sexual preference for young children is often found in men who were sexually abused in childhood, though the preference may not emerge until midlife. One of the most destructive of paraphilic preferences when acted on, pedophilia frequently leads to child molesting, child sexual abuse, and child rape.

Other unusual tastes include: *rubbing,* excitement at rubbing against the body of a fully clothed woman in a crowded place such as a subway; *getting enemas,* often self-administered; and *being urinated on* (golden showers).

Often people with one specialized fantasy will be excited by several others. A person who enjoys masochistic activity, for instance, may also enjoy fantasies about dressing as a woman. Sometimes the fantasies change over the years, a fetish giving way to masochism or sadism as the favored preference.

Therapy for Unusual Sexual Preferences

Few people with unusual sexual preferences come into therapy for that reason. Why give up something that is a source of pleasure? But if the preference leads to problems for yourself or others—marital dissatisfaction, trouble with the law, or harm to others—then you need help. Therapy is appropriate, too, when the preference has become an obsession or compulsion, replacing all other sexual contact.

The goals of therapy are to make the unusual sexual preference less appealing, while increasing sexual arousal from more usual tastes. Often when the unusual sexual preference has become an all-consuming passion, the person's social skills have withered. In that case, bolstering assertiveness—such as how to meet women and make a date—is another goal of therapy.

The sexual preference is harder to treat the earlier it began, the more often you have acted it out, and the less shame or guilt you feel about it. Success is more likely the more you have also engaged in regular intercourse, and the more you want to change. Your motivation is crucial, since changing sexual preferences requires a steady effort on your part in such things as monitoring your sexual fantasies.

Success in therapy may not mean that the fantasy disappears entirely, but that it no longer has the power to compel you to act it out or to masturbate to gain relief.

Unless your sexual preference has gotten you into trouble with the law—most common with pedophilia—therapy can be done in an office or clinic.

Two approaches are the most appropriate. One is psychodynamic, which will give you the chance to understand the events that led to your sexual preference. Understanding is not enough, however. The most important issue is either changing the pattern of preference, or if the preference can't be modified, at least controlling the impulse to act on it. This means learning to be sensitive to the daily encounters that stimulate the fantasy and controlling your reactions to them. Other, less unusual sexual preferences can then sometimes be developed. Psychodynamic or couples therapy, if you are married or in a long-term relationship, can also help with the way the central fantasy has inevitably interfered with intimacy in marriage or relationships. If he or she has not already been alienated, a partner or spouse can often be an aid in establishing and maintaining control of the impulse and behavior associated with the fantasy.

The other main approach is behavioral. This typically includes the use of "aversion" techniques that will lead to your associating your sexual preference with unpleasant things, and so diminish your appetite for it. Other self-control techniques will be taught as well, again based on increasing awareness of internal and external stimuli that cue the impulse or the behavior. At the same time, techniques that increase the appeal of more normal sexual tastes will be used.

No medication can change a sexual preference. But some medications—antiandrogens—do block the activity of sex hormones. These medications are used when your sexual drive is out of control and has gotten you into trouble. They reduce the level of desire, but they do not change the preference.

OBSESSIVE-COMPULSIVE DISORDER

Obsessions and compulsions are symptoms of the same disorder. Obsessions are thoughts that completely preoccupy a person, while compulsions are actions that people feel they must perform.

Often obsessions take the form of a single, circumscribed worry, such as believing that no matter how often you wash your hands, they are still dirty. Compulsions are frequently ordinary acts repeated over and over, such as checking appliances to see that they are off.

Many people have a few minor habits that are obsessive or compulsive. Some people like to count things, such as telephone poles they pass. Others like to check their door several times to be sure it is locked. And children normally develop compulsive habits for a time as they grow up.

A bit of obsessiveness—being well-organized and neat, for example—is not a problem. A compulsive attention to detail can even be an advantage in life.

But when obsessions or compulsions start interfering with living your life spontaneously, then they become a problem that needs treatment. So it is all right to be very neat, but if you spend all your time straightening up your house and never get around to other important things, your neatness has become a compulsion.

Many people who suffer from obsessions or compulsions manage to keep them secret from those around them. They may wait until they are alone to indulge the compulsion or never mention that they are utterly preoccupied by some thought that won't leave them alone.

At their most serious, obsessions and compulsions can be so overwhelming that they completely dominate a person's life. In these extreme cases, they almost always occur together.

Some obsessive-compulsive people will take hours to leave their house because they feel compelled to check and recheck all the windows to make sure they are closed. Others feel compelled to perform private rituals, such as driving over and over the same route to be sure they have not struck a pedestrian, or repeating some phrase over and over before they can act.

Although people with such obsessions and compulsions often know very well that their thoughts are strange or undesirable, they feel powerless to stop them. People with compulsions say that although they often do not want to perform the act, if they don't, a sense of anxiety builds until it is unbearable.

For many years clinicians believed that such obsessions and compulsions were rare, afflicting only about one in two thousand people. But a national door-to-door study of more than eighteen thousand men and women discovered that as many as one in forty Americans will suffer at some point in their life from them.

Signs to Look For

Typically people suffering the obsessions or compulsions recognize them as their own thoughts, rather than thinking someone else is imposing them on them—a sign of psychosis. And often—at least at first—they know that their symptoms are strange, though later, they may come to identify with the thoughts so much that these will seem normal.

A person may suffer from either obsessions or compulsions or both. The main signs include:

- *Obsessions,* preoccupying and unwanted thoughts that recur again and again. Sometimes the thoughts seem senseless to the person, but they are compelling nevertheless, such as the thought that one might harm a loved one.
- *Distress* over the obsessing thoughts, so that the person having them typically tries to suppress them or resorts to some other thought or deed that, at least for a time, will put the thought to rest. Thus someone obsessed by germs may feel a transitory respite while washing.
- *Compulsions,* acts that the person repeats in responding to an obsession. The acts are ritualistic, following fixed rules or formed in a rigid, stereotyped manner. The compulsion is meant to ward off some dread event or mounting anxiety, but is an excessive response to it or not logically related.

The most common obsessions are:

- A preoccupation with dirt, germs, bodily wastes such as urine, or impurities in the environment.
- The intense foreboding that something terrible might happen, such as a fire, or the death or illness or a loved one or oneself.
- A need for order, exactness, or symmetry.
- Having to scrupulously follow some arbitrary set of rules.
- Fixation on certain numbers as lucky or unlucky.
- A battle against "forbidden" sexual thoughts or dangerous impulses.

The most frequent compulsions are:

- Excessive cleanliness, such as repetitive handwashing, showers, or baths, toothbrushing or flossing, or general grooming.
- Repetitive rituals, such as having to go in and out of a door a set number of times before finally passing through, or getting up and down from a chair many times.
- Repeatedly checking to see that things are safe, such as that doors are locked, appliances are off, or the car brakes work.

- Overly zealous cleaning or other rituals done to sanitize "contamination."
- Touching things as one passes them or counting things.
- Constantly ordering or arranging things.
- Private rituals meant to protect oneself or others from harm.
- Hoarding or collecting objects of little or no value.

□ Cary was always given to worries, even as a young child. Years later, she could remember having an overwhelming fear that something awful would happen to her parents or brother if she didn't keep her room in order.

As she grew, the worries intensified each time someone close to her died. At twelve her grandmother died, and her compulsive attention to her room increased so that everything had to be not just clean, but perfectly symmetrical. When she was twenty-five, her brother died in an auto accident, and soon after she lost a baby during pregnancy.

After that she was driven by the thought that the only way the people she loved would be safe from harm was if she kept her house scrupulously clean. She would vacuum the rug because someone had walked on it; clean the whole bathroom each time it was used. The labels of all the foods in her pantry had to face out, and each container had to be a certain distance apart.

Her compulsions ruined her family life. She couldn't have guests over because she spent all the time cleaning up after them. Her children were not allowed to play with a toy unless they washed it afterward and put it back in a specified spot. If these rules weren't followed, Cary would feel pressure building in her "as if I were going to explode." Performing her cleansing ritual was the only way of relieving the pressure.

What Therapists Recommend

Approach. Therapists most often recommend psychodynamic psychotherapy, in which part of the treatment would focus on the symbolic meaning and origin of the obsessions or compulsions. Also highly recommended are behavior therapy and cognitive therapy, in which treatment focuses on directly changing the symptoms or thoughts that underlie them.

Medication. In the survey, a minority of therapists recommended medications. However, research findings, more recent than the survey, suggest that new drugs, clomipramine and fluoxetine, can help in many cases.

Setting. Obsessive-compulsive disorder can be treated in the office or clinic. On rare occasions, when the disorder is extremely debilitating, treatment may involve a brief hospitalization.

Format. The consensus is that obsessive-compulsive disorder should be treated individually. Group sessions with others who suffer the same problem are often useful. At some point, treatment may involve the whole family, with life at home arranged to be more supportive of the person's efforts to recover.

Frequency. Once a week is normally sufficient.

Duration. Usually open-ended.

What You Should Know About Therapy

Even though many therapists continue to recommend a psychodynamic approach for obsessive-compulsive disorder, a behavioral approach is becoming the preferred treatment. Sometimes called "exposure and response prevention," it consists of graded exposure to the thing that is most feared with techniques for suppressing the urge to perform compulsive rituals.

If you have obsessions or compulsions, you may be reluctant to try this approach. It demands that you face directly the things you fear the most or resist your compulsions. But you can learn to resist your compulsions, even if only for a few minutes at a time, until gradually you can resist them entirely. Studies have shown close to an 80 percent rate of improvement among those willing to try these methods.

The drugs clomipramine or fluoxetine (see p. 618), which work by affecting levels of serotonin, a brain chemical, can halt obsessions or compulsions in many people. But once you start, you may have to take it indefinitely.

Try behavior therapy first. If that does not work, then consult a psychiatrist or psychopharmacologist about trying clomipramine or fluoxetine. It can also be used in tandem with behavior therapy.

In addition, supportive or psychodynamic therapy may help you deal with more general feelings of anxiety, depression, or other problems due to the disruptive effect of your obsessions and compulsions.

SOMATOFORM DISORDERS: PHYSICAL COMPLAINTS WITHOUT A MEDICAL CAUSE

A range of physical complaints—fatigue, back and neck aches, stomach problems, headaches, chronic pain, and the like—often occur with no underlying medical condition to explain them. For some people these complaints are continual, present more often than absent, or come and go according to some mysterious rhythm of their own.

The dilemma for people with these problems is that they are told, "It's all in your head"—but it isn't. *The physical distress is real,* not faked or imagined, even though medical test after medical test finds no biological basis for the symptom. Although these problems present themselves as physical discomfort, they may be signs of psychological pressures in your life.

However, you should consider psychotherapy only after thorough medical testing finds no known physical cause for your complaints. Psychotherapy might help either by making it easier to live with the complaints—chronic pain, for instance—or by actually easing them, by lessening some underlying emotional cause.

People who suffer from these kinds of complaints tend to be exceptionally sensitive to what goes on inside their body. Sensations that do not bother other people can be extremely distressing to them.

If you have had a history of going from doctor to doctor in a fruitless search for a diagnosis and cure, you may be told by one of these physicians to see a psychotherapist. Don't be dismayed or offended. Because of the close connection between mind and body, a category of physical complaints exists called *somatoform disorders*, which seem to express emotional distress as physical symptoms. In these conditions, it is believed, the body becomes a language for expressing that something is seriously wrong. This does not mean that the complaints aren't real. They are a genuine way of both experiencing and expressing distress.

These discomforts differ, too, from what are called psychosomatic conditions. With psychosomatic problems, a clear medical problem, such as hypertension or a tension headache, is triggered or made worse by emotional stress. But in the problems we're talking about here, no identifiable underlying medical condition accounts for the discomfort.

If you have a somatoform disorder, you may have a history of physical complaints with no known medical basis as far back as your teenage years or twenties. You may have consulted many different kinds of specialists and may even have undergone surgery for problems that turned out not to have required it. You may see yourself as "sickly" or as particularly prone to getting sick.

Signs to Look For

The hallmark is having a long list of physical complaints, most of which have lasted for years, with no known medical cause, such as:

- Stomach problems, including nausea, queasiness, and vomiting; stomach pain; diarrhea and gas; getting sick from various foods.
- Pain in the back or neck; in the joints; during urination; in the arms or legs.
- Heart and lung complaints, such as being short of breath, racing heart, being dizzy, or chest pain.
- Sexual difficulties, such as a burning or other bothersome sensation in the genitals or rectum; painful intercourse; being unable to get an erection; or lack of interest in sex.
- Menstrual troubles: irregular periods, bleeding too much, or painful periods.

- Nervous symptoms, such as forgetfulness; trouble swallowing or laryngitis; trouble hearing or seeing; fainting spells; seizures; trouble walking or weak muscles; trouble urinating.

Variations. Sometimes the problem takes the form of chronic pain that cannot be accounted for medically, or pain that seems far out of proportion to an underlying medical condition.

Another variation is preoccupation with being ill. The person is convinced that certain sensations or other physical signs mean that he or she has a serious disease, even though careful medical evaluation finds no evidence for any illness.

Still another form is preoccupation with an imaginary physical defect in appearance.

□ Arlene's troubles started when she was still in high school. She often missed days of school for stomach pains and nausea. When her period came the pain would be so intense that she had to take to bed. At the same time she developed allergies to such a wide range of foods that she could eat only grains and hard boiled eggs. If she ate other foods, she said, she'd get sick to her stomach. But her doctors could not seem to find anything wrong with her.

In college, she began to be bothered by vague pains in her legs and joints. Though Arlene thought she had arthritis, her doctor could find no sign of it. For a time she became so fatigued that she was convinced she had mononucleosis but tests did not confirm it. Some mornings she'd wake up with her back and neck so stiff that she could not get out of bed. Sometimes she would get up only to have a dizzy spell. Although she liked boys, Arlene never had sexual relations: "Sex never interested me," she said. At twenty-five, Arlene had an operation for what had been diagnosed as a "slipped disc." The surgeon was puzzled to find there was no medical problem.

What Therapists Recommend

Approach. Most therapists recommended a psychodynamic approach, to address the stresses that might be exacerbating the physical complaints. However the majority also recommended combining this with a supportive approach to day-to-day struggles and the confusion of not being able to find a medical basis for genuine physical complaints. Cognitive therapy was also recommended, also in conjunction with a supportive approach.

Medication. Medication was recommended by some therapists for the symptoms of depression or anxiety that often accompany this condition.

Setting. Office or clinic.

Format. The great majority of therapists recommended individual therapy. But group therapy and family therapy were also recommended.

Frequency. Most therapists recommend once a week.

Duration. Most therapists recommend leaving therapy open-ended. But a quarter believe therapy should take between six months and a year, and a significant percentage believe short-term therapy—under six months—can be sufficient.

What You Should Know About Therapy

You would probably not be considering therapy unless you had already consulted a number of physicians and had had numerous tests—most inconclusive or negative. If for some reason you haven't, the first step in treating physical complaints of any kind is, of course, a thorough medical examination. If this shows nothing, then the next step should be a psychiatric evaluation. See a psychiatrist rather than a nonmedical therapist since the chief and often only complaint is physical symptoms that look as if they should have a medical basis.

If neither a medical nor a psychiatric evaluation reveals any underlying disorder, then the best approach to treatment is a combination of ongoing medical supervision and psychotherapy. Therapy doesn't have to be with a psychiatrist, but may be with a nonmedical therapist who is experienced in working with this condition.

The physician's role in ongoing treatment is to protect you from needless lab tests, medical treatments, or surgery. They can also help you avoid becoming addicted to narcotic painkillers and other medications that offer little help for these conditions. They should evaluate any new symptoms to make sure you get timely and adequate medical care if an underlying medical condition comes to light.

You should not have to be "sick" in order to see your physician. You should schedule regular brief visits whether or not your symptoms have changed. These visits should include physical examinations as needed, especially whenever a new symptom develops. A physician you see regularly is in the best position to judge how to proceed in each case. The visits with your physician can be brief, but not so brief that they don't have a chance to talk with you about other ongoing issues and concerns in your life; and you should take this opportunity to talk with them, however briefly.

A word of warning: many physicians have a hard time treating people with this problem. For one, as practicing professionals they want to help someone get better. They may get annoyed by your complaints or frustrated when your symptoms fail to respond. They may prescribe medication just to satisfy your feeling that you need "something."

It is important that you find a physician who understands and accepts that your complaints and symptoms are real, even if medical tests don't confirm a physical cause, rather than treating them—even sympathetically—as if they are "only in your head." You will need to trust what your physician tells you so that you can stop endlessly searching for medical solutions that do not exist.

In addition to ongoing medical supervision, some medical centers have behavioral medicine programs designed to help people reduce the distress and stress of chronic pain or other disabling physical conditions. If you can find one—and your physician may be able to guide you to one—it can be very helpful.

The overall goal of both medical care and psychotherapy is not to "cure" the physical complaints, but to help you handle them better and to diminish their effects on your life. You may never feel completely better, but you can go a long way toward keeping your physical problems from completely controlling your life.

One focus of therapy should be to help you understand better the difference between physical sensations and your emotional reaction to them. For instance, part of pain is the emotional reaction to sensation; when you are anxious, the same sensations will seem more "painful" than when you are calm. Focusing on physical problems also amplifies their seriousness. Learning how to differentiate between sensation and your emotional reaction to it will reduce the distress of the symptoms.

It usually is not helpful to enter therapy that focuses on making you more introspective or emotionally expressive than you already are. An exploratory approach was recommended by most therapists in our national survey, but this should be undertaken gradually and cautiously. Usually morbid introspection about your physical state is enough of a problem already. Nor is a therapy that dwells on factors from your distant past likely to be of immediate help to you. Your focus should be on the here and now, on the problems your physical complaints cause you.

You may find supportive group therapy helpful along with individual treatment. In a group you may be able to talk to people who will listen to you, appreciate your distress, and be supportive of your troubles.

Preoccupation with being ill. If you are not plagued by a long list of physical complaints but primarily by the *fear* that you are ill, you will want to learn to better distinguish between your actual sensations and your emotional reactions to them. You are very likely overreacting. A cognitive approach that helps you control your emotional overreaction would be beneficial. You may also benefit from working at identifying and expressing your emotional reactions to problems in your life more directly.

Chronic pain. Pain control programs are better than most kinds of psychotherapy for chronic pain. Such programs are typically run in groups, though there is sometimes a parallel option for individual sessions of therapy. The best pain control programs combine a range of approaches. They will teach you about the physiology of pain, as well as train you in specific techniques to help you control your pain better. These include biofeedback, hypnosis, or meditation, all of which can be effective in pain management. One effective technique is the practice of mindfulness, a mental training that allows you to break the experience of pain down into pure sensation—throbbing, pressure, heat—without the accompanying emotional reactions of fear, resistance, judgment, despair, and blame. This makes the pain far more bearable.

A pain control program should also include physical therapy and exercise, tailored to your needs and abilities. Simple yoga techniques adapted to this purpose have proven quite effective. In addition, cognitive techniques can help you control the tendency to overreact emotionally to pain sensation, and stress control methods will minimize turmoil that can worsen pain. Many of these programs are short-term—once a week for three or four months—with regular follow-up as needed.

Painkillers—analgesic medications—are appropriate for the treatment of acute pain, but are not ideal for managing chronic pain. The strongest painkillers are narcotics, and dependency is a major risk. They should be used cautiously under close medical supervision. Antidepressant medication is occasionally effective for chronic pain since it shares many of the features of major depression. For most people, however, antidepressants don't affect the pain, even when depressive symptoms improve.

Pain control programs aim to help you manage the pain without resorting to powerful painkillers. Many such programs will help detox people from narcotic analgesics if their use has become an addiction.

Preoccupation with a physical "deformity." This problem most often brings people to a plastic surgeon for a solution. But psychotherapy can be an alternative. The goal is a more realistic and accepting image of yourself—a goal you may still want to pursue in therapy even if you have already gotten plastic surgery.

Medication. Significantly, only a minority of psychotherapists recommend using medication in the treatment of physical complaints for which no medical cause has been found. Chronic pain is the occasional exception. Medication seldom brings relief since there is no demonstrable biochemical or neurological problem. It also frequently leads to abuse. You may nevertheless be in the habit of getting prescriptions from physicians and expect the same from psychotherapy. Indeed, you may feel comforted when you get a prescription. But unless you have pronounced psychiatric symptoms as well, such as acute anxiety or depression, a psychiatrist will probably be reluctant to prescribe. If you do have acute psychiatric symptoms, you should be evaluated for those.

Impulse Control Problems

While everyone is impulsive on occasion, some people's inability to control impulses gets them into chronic difficulties. Impulse problems include running up deep debts through shopping or gambling, shoplifting, having bouts of explosive anger, or even setting fires.

One common feature of all these problems is the feeling of an inner pressure building and building, finally becoming so intense that the act—gambling, stealing—is virtually irresistible. All sense of self-control or of reining in crumbles. It feels as though the only relief will be repeating the act, whatever its consequences.

If you have an impulse problem, even though you may feel a great sense of confusion or guilt afterward, while you are in the midst of it, there seems to be no alternative. You may think of yourself as "spineless" or "weak" when you are facing the consequences of what you have done. Or you may see yourself as unable to resist temptation. But those very feelings make you more vulnerable.

Problem Gambling

Millions of people gamble without its becoming a problem. For most people who play lotteries, go to casinos, have private poker games, or bet at horse races, no compulsion is at work. But others are unable to resist the impulse to bet, even when the debts they accrue threaten to destroy their family, ruin a business, or bring bankruptcy.

Problem gamblers find an excitement in gambling that they find nowhere else in life. Many describe the thrill of gambling as a "high" or a "rush," akin to that of using a drug.

As many as one in fifty Americans may have a problem with gambling. The problem is actually not just with gambling. Many compulsive gamblers find they have to lie to borrow money or to hide how extreme their involvement with gambling has become. For some, a final step is fraud or embezzlement, always with the idea of repaying the money—but rarely with the possibility of doing so.

More common in men, problem gambling typically starts in late adolescence, waxing or waning as the years go on. Often a person gets hooked by some early, big win. But once the habit becomes rooted, even the most cautious gambler starts becoming careless. As the habit grows, life begins to revolve around gambling.

Over a number of years, chronic gambling almost inevitably leads to disaster. It disrupts every part of life: jobs are lost, marriages break up, friends become estranged. Huge debts can lead to a frenzy of desperation.

Signs to Look For

The hallmark of the problem gambler is a preoccupation with gambling or with getting the money to gamble. Other signs include:

- Betting more than intended over and over.
- Betting more and more to get the same level of excitement.
- Tension relieved by gambling; a sense of discomfort and restlessness if you're not able to gamble.
- "Chasing" losses by returning with more money again and again to recoup the money you've already lost.
- Futile efforts to stop; time after time the resolve to quit ends in a return to gambling.
- Gambling instead of meeting other obligations, whether family, social, or work; willingness to put other aspects of life at risk in order to gamble.
- Gambling despite unpayable debts, or in the face of legal or other problems caused by the gambling.

Sometimes gambling is the root problem that lies behind other emotional problems, such as depression, drug abuse, alcoholism, or suicide attempts.

What You Should Know About Therapy

Getting help for someone who has a destructive gambling habit can be difficult. Such people rarely seek therapy on their own, though they may agree to it under family pressure. Sometimes when a chronic gambler is sentenced for illegalities stemming from gambling debts, a judge makes therapy a condition of probation.

Some treatment facilities have inpatient units that specialize in treating gamblers. The advantage of starting therapy in such a setting is that it removes the gambler from temptation. He can escape the pull of gambling until the therapy is under way and he thus has more support in resisting. But this restrictive setting is by no means necessary for everyone, nor might it be affordable.

The most effective treatment format is group therapy; the most successful group program is Gamblers Anonymous (see the listing in Appendix I). Those who go through inpatient programs are typically introduced to a Gamblers Anonymous group before they leave and continue with it once they are discharged.

You should attend the Gamblers Anonymous group as often as you need: daily if necessary. Gamblers Anonymous works on the Alcoholics Anonymous (AA) model. If there is no Gamblers Anonymous group in your area, an AA group can serve the same purpose if you attend regularly. Individual psychotherapy is more effective if it is coupled with attendance in such a group.

The best approach to therapy is a combination of behavioral techniques, focused on stopping gambling, and supportive therapy to help you deal with the chaos gambling has brought to your life. The first goal of therapy is getting your impulse to gamble under control. Psychodynamic approaches, such as seeking the roots of your gambling in childhood or emotional conflicts, are distractions at first and will not help you control your gambling at the outset. Once you have gotten some control and have not gambled for at least three months, a psychodynamic approach may be fruitful.

If you enter therapy, watch for several attitudes that can slow its progress. One is to see lack of money as the problem, rather than your compulsion to risk it. Or you may expect an instantaneous cure, think that life without gambling is unbearable, or believe that repaying your debts is impossible. With self-discipline, you can both keep from gambling and get your finances in order.

You might benefit from vocational counseling if you have lost a string of jobs due to gambling. And if it has been your only real pleasure, you might also gain from recreational therapy, aimed at broadening your range of ways to enjoy yourself.

Your therapist should be slightly skeptical toward your assurances; after all, you are likely to have a history of broken promises. What will count is what you do. The success of your therapy should be judged on how long you are free of gambling, on your progress toward paying debts, and on your developing interests other than gambling. Your ability to offer psychological insights on why you gamble is no gauge of success.

Expect therapy to be long-term. You may have an occasional relapse, but that does not mean that therapy is a failure *if* you use the slip as an opportunity to learn how to resist temptation.

Compulsive Stealing (Kleptomania)

People with kleptomania have a secret compulsion to steal, even though more often than not, they can easily afford the stolen goods. The goal is not to gain what's stolen; the payoff is the act of stealing itself.

The kleptomaniac feels the impulse to steal build and build until the tension becomes irresistible. The actual theft brings a feeling of pleasure or release from the tension. Even so, most people feel guilty and nervous afterward.

Shoplifting and kleptomania are not identical. Most people who shoplift are not suffering from a compulsion to do so. Only about one in twelve shoplifters are thought to have kleptomania, but those with kleptomania may be slightly more likely to get caught. Often those who steal for pleasure do so with less regard for the consequences than do those who are simply thieves. Also, the person with a compulsion to steal does not restrict it to shoplifting: he or she will steal things from friends or people at work, too.

The problem often begins in childhood or adolescence, although most children who steal, and most do at some time or other, do not become kleptomaniacs.

Sometimes kleptomania is a symptom of another problem altogether, such as a neurological disorder, depression, or an eating disorder. People prone to compulsive stealing often do so when they are under stress—in reaction to a loss, for example. The problem typically waxes and wanes and often burns out with age.

Signs to Look For

- a buildup of tension before stealing until the impulse to steal is irresistible
- stealing things one does not want or need
- feelings of tension release or pleasing excitement while stealing

What You Should Know About Therapy

The outlook for kleptomaniacs in therapy is good, but few seek therapy on their own. Often they end up in therapy after being caught.

Therapy for kleptomania can be individual or group or family. The latter two may be best, especially when the stealing is in reaction to dissatisfaction with relationships.

At the outset of therapy, the focus should be on getting the stealing under control and on finding alternative pleasures. A cognitive-behavioral approach is most effective. Once the stealing is under control, a psychodynamic approach might be fruitful.

If you are in therapy for the impulse to steal, expect your therapist to put less stock in what you say you're going to do and more on what you actually do. The mark of success will be in controlling the impulse to steal.

Kleptomania can relapse, even after you have gotten the habit largely under control. However, a slip does not mean failure if you use the experience to understand what triggered the impulse and to rehearse how to resist it.

Fire-Setting

Children are often fascinated with fires, particularly between the ages of five and eight. But most just toy around with matches and don't intentionally set destructive blazes. Most fire-setters trace their thrill at setting fires back to childhood, but instead of waning with age, their fascination continues into adolescence and adulthood.

In the fire-setter, the urge to set a fire builds and builds until it seems irresistible. Even while planning the fire, fire-setters feel a pleasant thrill. After setting it, they invariably stay to "enjoy" it. Some actually sound the alarm and join in trying to control it. Others join the bystanders, savoring their secret involvement. And some are so excited by the thrill of the flames that they become sexually aroused.

Most arson, however, is not by people who have this psychological problem, but rather for profit or revenge. Psychologically motivated fire-setters typically have a complete and utter fascination with fire: they show up at fires whether they set them or not, may set off false alarms, and love fire trucks and other fire-fighting equipment.

Signs to Look For

- setting fires for the pleasure of it rather than for money or some other motive
- buildup of tension is relieved by fire-setting or watching a fire
- attraction to fire and anything associated with it, such as fire trucks and equipment

What You Should Know About Therapy

Anyone who sets fires for pleasure, whether a child or adult, should receive therapy. By adulthood, however, most fire-setters are not interested in stopping; they get into therapy because they were caught. Unfortunately, therapy that is forced on a person is nowhere near as effective as therapy freely chosen. A better outcome is more likely if the fire-setter sees therapy as a way to control an impulse that brings suffering.

Since people who have set fires usually need to be incarcerated, therapy for fire-setters typically begins in a prison or psychiatric hospital and is court ordered. As therapy progresses, parole or supervised release is possible.

Behavioral therapies are more useful than psychodynamic, with concrete goals such as controlling the impulse, improving social skills, finding friends, and discovering other means of gratification.

BRIEF PSYCHOTIC REACTIONS

Episodes of brief psychosis are just that—brief. Before the episode, the person is well adjusted. But he or she then abruptly becomes psychotic for a few days or weeks, sometimes a bit longer. During the episode, the person will be out of touch with reality, saying or doing bizarre things completely out of keeping with his or her personality before the episode.

These brief psychotic episodes are a reaction to some specific stress, often overwhelming. For instance, a brief psychosis might be triggered by the unexpected death of a spouse or by suddenly finding yourself in a strange culture or country. But it might also be in reaction to something as seemingly innocuous as starting freshman year in college, facing a crucial exam, or joining the army. Whatever the event that triggers the psychosis, it will have been an emotionally trying one for the person, even if many other people weather such events without difficulty.

The outlook for this kind of brief psychosis is very good. Most people who go through them recover fully and never experience another.

Such brief psychotic breaks are thought to occur most frequently when people are in their late-teenage or young-adult years. But they can occur at virtually any point in life.

Psychosis seems to come out of nowhere, without warning, peaking abruptly within a matter of days or even hours after the triggering event. When the psychosis passes, some people may feel depressed for a time afterward.

If someone you know becomes psychotic, however, you can't assume at the outset that it is just a brief reactive episode, even if it seems to have been triggered by a clearly stressful event. That event could be merely coincidental, or it could have triggered another psychiatric problem that resembles brief psychosis, such as a manic episode (see p. 479).

Always consider whether the psychosis might have been caused by alcohol, drugs, exposure to toxic chemicals, or a physical illness with neurological effects, such as epilepsy or fever-induced delirium. All of these can produce conditions resembling brief psychosis, but need to be treated differently. Since someone who is psychotic may be unable or unwilling to tell you if they have been using drugs, drinking, or the like, you should try to find out from anyone who might have been with them before the onset.

If possible, the person should be taken to a physician for a thorough examination to eliminate these possibilities or for proper medical care if they are present.

Signs to Look For

During the psychosis, the person may act in bizarre ways. He or she may dress strangely, adopt weird postures or movements, act or speak in peculiar ways. The key symptoms include:

- Impaired sense of reality, such as incoherence or strange ways of thinking, delusions, hallucinations, or extremely disorganized behavior.
- Tumultuous emotions, including rapid-fire shifts from one emotion to another—rage to sadness to elation, for example—or profound confusion and a sense of perplexity.
- Onset triggered by one stressful event or several events that taken together are stressful.
- Sudden onset and end, so that the whole episode lasts no longer than a month or is as brief as a few hours.
- Absence of any other cause. Because the symptoms are so similar to those caused by drugs, illness, and the like, these must be eliminated as causes.

☐ George had always been shy, a loner through high school. Still, when he graduated and went away to a large state university, he seemed confident. But his family heard from him less and less as his freshman year went on. While he never told anyone, his grades rapidly deteriorated: going into his exams just before the Christmas break, he had D's in most courses. After he finished his last exam, he was supposed to take a bus home for the holidays, but he wasn't on it when his parents came to meet him.

The next they heard was three days later when the police in a distant town called to say George was in their custody. He had been found walking shirtless and barefoot through the snow, saying he was a "traffic cop from the sixteenth dimension," and that he was "sent to find the archangel of Hizbollah." He seemed extremely agitated and confused, his eyes darting wildly around as though he were seeing phantoms. George could not answer the simplest question without intense emotion. He would swing from crying one moment to angry attacks on the police officers the next.

After being brought to the local emergency ward and admitted to the psychiatric unit, George was started on antipsychotic medication. He was coherent within several days and a week later was home with no trace of psychotic behavior.

The outlook is generally better for people like George who have functioned reasonably well in life before the psychotic episode, who become psychotic in response to a specific severe stress, and in whom the onset of symptoms is quite abrupt. Among other signs of a good prognosis: the symptoms included intense emotions; the person seemed perplexed by the psychosis; and the most florid symptoms were short-lived.

What Therapists Recommend

Approach: The most highly recommended therapeutic approach is supportive, where the therapist helps the patient reconstitute and return to normal functioning, the main task during a brief psychotic episode. Family therapy and psychodynamic approaches were the next most frequently suggested approaches, as supplements to a primarily supportive approach.

Medication. Yes, particularly in calming the more disruptive symptoms of the psychotic episode.

Setting: A reactive psychosis normally requires brief hospitalization. Once the most disorienting symptoms subside, therapy can continue in an outpatient setting.

Format. Individual therapy. Family therapy may also help, particularly if the person is young and still living at home or is in close touch with his or her family, as is often the case. Group therapy is often a supplement to individual therapy, especially during hospitalization.

Frequency. Therapists strongly recommend two or more times a week, so that contact is strong during the most intense part of the crisis.

Duration. Some therapists say the episode would generally require treatment for a month or less, primarily during the period of peak intensity. Others say that treatment should last one to six months, continuing after the crisis to help people resume their normal life. And a small percentage believe that treatment should continue for at least six months or longer. Therapy probably needs to be left open-ended, varying from case to case.

What You Should Know About Therapy

The *immediate* decision to make is *whether hospitalization is necessary* until the symptoms subside. Hospitalization is absolutely called for if the person is suicidal or homicidal, especially if he or she is hearing voices telling them to harm themselves or others. It should also be considered if they are so confused they cannot take care of themselves or can't be managed by those they usually live with.

Sometimes a brief psychotic episode can be handled outside a hospital if family or friends are willing to take turns providing constant monitoring and support, and if the person already has an ongoing relationship with a psychotherapist, or with an outpatient clinic where he or she is known.

Medication. Antipsychotic medications (see p. 621) are normally prescribed for brief psychosis, though not invariably. Medication is more likely if people are experiencing hallucinations or delusions or their behavior is disorganized or out of control. Low doses are likely unless the person is extremely agitated, anxious, or confused. Medication is typically stopped as quickly as possible. Sometimes sleep medication is prescribed if the person has been unable to sleep.

Length of therapy. Therapy should normally be limited to the time of the crisis and continue for a month of two after, unless the psychosis has created other severe problems in its wake. Continuing therapy briefly is especially helpful if the person feels the temporary depression that often occurs afterward. Or if he or she feels shaky about handling daily life for a time, or to help him or her or the immediate family understand what has happened.

Frequency of therapy. Some people do better with frequent brief meetings with a therapist or group during the most intense part of the psychosis, with sessions decreasing to once or twice a week afterward. Other people cannot tolerate frequent close contacts while they are psychotic. They do better with short, supportive contacts at first that gradually become extended meetings as their feelings of confusion and vulnerability wane.

DELUSIONAL PARANOIA

In paranoia, a person holds tenaciously to a fixed belief that no evidence to the contrary can dislodge. In all other areas of life, however, the paranoid person seems perfectly rational.

While *paranoia* is the earliest term used for the problem and is still the most widespread, the new technical name is *delusional disorder*. The modern understanding of the disorder is that paranoia, suspiciousness, per se may not always be the most prominent or sole feature. Rather, the common element in the different varieties of delusional disorder is a body of *tenaciously held, irrational beliefs.*

Common delusions are, for instance, the conviction that someone you love is passionately in love with you when he or she is not, or that something is physically wrong despite all medical assurances to the contrary. Extreme jealousy is another variation, as is a fixed belief in some elevated, special status or mission you believe you have.

In each case, the delusions are fabrications based on slim shreds of evidence. For instance, a man whose delusion is that his wife is being unfaithful may seize on runs in her stockings as "proof." The delusion that the CIA is spying on you may be "confirmed" by each bit of static or each unusual click on the phone line.

If suffering from a strictly delusional disorder, people rarely seek help on their own. Since they believe so firmly in their delusions, they see nothing to treat. They are not disturbed by their beliefs, though they may have some consternation about the disturbance those beliefs produce in other people. Usually it is the family or friends of a delusional person who finally get him or her into treatment.

The delusions are generally systematic and logically consistent, once one accepts the basic premise. Because the delusions are typically isolated in one sector of life, those who hold them may get along well at work or in other areas that the delusions do not touch. The delusions are also plausible, involving situations that might actually occur in life, rather than the bizarre ones encountered, say, in schizophrenia.

Delusions of being persecuted by a particular group are more common in men and often come to light when they finally lead to some act of violence or other lawbreaking. Romantic delusions tend to be more common in women.

When the delusions begin suddenly, they are often in response to a loss or a major life change, such as childbirth or marriage. Sometimes they seem to be an attempt to make sense of confusing experiences, such as a strange accident. Emigrating to a foreign country is a common trigger.

Often, though, the onset is slow and gradual, gaining momentum as the delusions become rigidified. This can occur, for instance, in elderly people who lose those close to them, become increasingly isolated, and begin to lose their hearing.

At the start of the delusions, the person may realize how strange they seem to others and so conceal them. The delusions may lead them to move or make some other life change in order to feel safe, at least for a time. Sometimes the delusions turn family or friends into imagined enemies. Outbursts of delusional thinking can also alienate them. The resulting social isolation may increase the strength of the delusions.

People typically end up being brought to treatment when their delusions reach the point that they cause ruptures in their personal relationships or their work life or lead them to harass others who play a role in their delusional beliefs.

Signs to Look For

The hallmark of delusional disorders is that the person's unfounded beliefs are internally logical and are tenaciously held to, despite all evidence to the contrary. The person's concern with the delusions may disappear for a long period of time, only to recur later.

Even when the delusions are in full bloom, the person holding them typically has no problem in other realms of life. Such people seem quite normal when talking about other topics.

Since delusions are common symptoms of neurological diseases such as drug toxicity or brain tumor, possible physical causes should be eliminated by a physical examination.

The main signs of delusional paranoia include:

- Delusions that are plausible, such as being followed, deceived by one's spouse, or having some disease.
- Delusions that are durable. The delusions should have lasted at least a month—those that begin suddenly and are short-lived typically are symptoms of other problems, such as a physical disease.
- No hallucinations.
- Other behavior is rational and appropriate apart from the delusions.

Common Variations

Several distinct types of delusions, each built around a dominant theme, are:

Persecution. The most common type of delusions, these often revolve around a group—the FBI, communists, foreigners—that is plotting against the person. The person may fear being poisoned or drugged, cheated, spied on, followed, or the like. Delusions of persecution make a person touchy; minor slights, for instance, may be blown up into major attacks. Such delusions can frequently get the person who holds them into legal tangles, either as a litigant in trying to "right" some imagined wrong, or as the result of a violent reaction toward someone who is imagined to be a persecutor.

☐ Archie was an assistant manager for a bank branch office. One day, however, his boss loudly upbraided Archie for a mistake in the daily accounts. The upbraiding was public, visible both to bank tellers and customers. Archie objected that he was not at fault, and should not be criticized. When the branch manager continued to criticize him, Archie stalked out. Thereafter, he began to talk about how his manager was "out to get" him, and would seize on small events or irrelevant statements he overheard as evidence that the manager was organizing everyone at the branch against him.

Archie lodged a complaint against his manager with the vice-president in charge of their division, demanding an apology for the original rebuke. When that got no response, he complained to the bank's president, then to the chairman of the board. Then Archie brought a lawsuit against the manager and the bank, at which point he was fired.

Jealousy. The theme of jealous delusions is usually that a spouse or lover is being unfaithful. Though the suspicions are unfounded, the person seizes on trivial details—e.g., spots on a sheet or marks on clothing—as "proof" of the infidelity. Such people usually confront their partners with their suspicions and will sometimes impose restrictions, such as not letting the partner out alone, to prevent further "infidelities." The jealous partner may even attack the other partner or the partner's supposed lover.

☐ Huang, thirty-six, was a secretary who had come to America from her native Vietnam. Bright and capable, she worked for the vice-president of a large bank. One day he asked her to type a letter to a women's health clinic that had asked him to join its board of directors.

Huang refused to type the letter because the clinic performed abortions, "like the ones my husband's mistresses have." She explained that she had first discovered the affairs one day when she answered the phone and a woman asked for someone with a different name and hung up. Her husband claimed he knew nothing about it.

Since then, she had found more and more evidence of his affairs: her husband read novels in which people had extramarital affairs, he was sometimes late coming home from work, and he worked as a waiter in a restaurant where "loose women" went. Huang said her husband changed into street clothes from his waiter's uniform before coming home to conceal lipstick stains and other telltale signs of his affair.

Other than this single lapse, Huang was impeccable in her job.

Romantic. Romantic delusions are typically directed at someone of higher status and a stranger, such as a celebrity, who is fancied to be irresistibly attracted to the person who holds the beliefs. Particularly with women, the delusion focuses on an idealized, nonsexual union. While the romantic delusions are often kept secret, when they are acted on, the result may be harassment—phone calls and letters to the fancied lover, or even stalking the person. The delusions may lead to trouble if, for example, the supposed lover is in danger and must be protected from some evil plot.

Grandiose. These delusions revolve around a greatly exaggerated sense of power, knowledge, and the like. This inflated self-view often takes the form of being convinced one has some insight or talent of immense importance. People who believe this about themselves may try to contact such agencies as the FBI or government officials, even the president. Some have delusions that they are special prophets or have privileged religious insights. Sometimes a person joins a social movement with a "special mission," though such people typically remain on the fringe because of their fixed, idiosyncratic beliefs.

What Therapists Recommend

Approach. The most fruitful psychotherapy approach for paranoid delusions is a supportive one. The focus would be on helping the patient strengthen those areas of functioning in life that are strongest, instead of challenging the person's delusions or seeking insights into what brought them about. In addition to the supportive approach, some psychotherapists suggest cognitive therapy, focusing on correcting distorted beliefs.

Medication. Almost all clinicians feel that during the acute stages of paranoid disorder, patients should receive medication. Antipsychotic medications are most likely.

Setting. Because of the special difficulties in treating those with paranoid delusions, most clinicians recommend that they be treated as inpatients. Treatment might be possible in outpatient settings if the person were somehow convinced that he or she should seek treatment and so come voluntarily.

Format. Therapists agree that this problem is best treated individually. Establishing a trusting relationship with a therapist is crucial to treatment. But individual therapy can also be supplemented by sessions with the whole family or group therapy.

Frequency. The need for intensive treatment is clear: most therapists recommend sessions be twice a week or more.

Duration. Most therapists believe treatment should be open-ended.

What You Should Know About Therapy

Because people with delusions do not see themselves as having a problem needing treatment, it usually falls to relatives or friends to get them into therapy. For those who have persecutory delusions, however, this can be especially difficult, since the very attempt to provide help may be construed as a conspiracy against them.

Since delusions can accompany many physical illnesses or brain trauma, careful physical and neurological examinations should be done. Only if these show no physical basis for the delusions should it be assumed that psychotherapy is needed. This is especially true for older people, where delusions may mark the onset of senility or may be due to side effects of medication. Delusions are also a common side effect of the extreme abuse of certain drugs, especially alcohol, amphetamines, cocaine, cannabis, and hallucinogens.

Medical and Neurological Conditions That Can Cause Delusions

- Neurological diseases such as Parkinson's or Huntington's chorea
- Vitamin deficiencies, such as B_{12} or niacin
- Alzheimer's disease and other forms of dementia
- Drug-induced intoxication, especially from alcohol, cocaine, amphetamines, or hallucinogens
- Side effects of medicines, including those used for illnesses such as hypertension
- Endocrine disorders, including those of the adrenal and thyroid glands
- Epilepsy, strokes, brain tumors
- Diseases that affect the nervous system, such as encephalitis, uremia, and hypoglycemia

---

Since other psychiatric problems, such as schizophrenia, can also lead to delusions, a psychiatric examination should be done. The examiner will usually carefully draw the person out about the delusions, but not confront him with their absurdity. Instead, the examiner will listen carefully and sympathetically. This is done to build rapport and to avoid an angry confrontation, which might end treatment or obstruct gathering necessary information. If asked what they think about the delusional beliefs, however, the examiners will probably say that they do not agree with them or understand them, and that they seem to be causing the patient suffering.

If you accompany the patient, you may be interviewed, too, probably in the presence of the person you've brought to avoid arousing suspicions. Like the examiner, your tone should be one of respectful disagreement regarding the delusions, making the point that they seem to be causing difficulties, and that your concern is for the best care.

Because people with delusions rarely seek help voluntarily, their first feelings toward the psychotherapist are often angry. The therapist will need to spend a great deal of time at the beginning simply forming a bond of trust and rapport. People whose delusions make them suspicious are prone to breaking off therapy prematurely, especially if they have begun it unwillingly.

Caution: some delusions can lead to violence. Be particularly attentive to any plans for suicide or violence toward someone else. If the person has a history of violence or has specific plans, hospitalization will almost always be necessary. It also may be needed if the person's delusions lead to severe impairment in their life, or to an unbearable burden for his or her family.

Delusions often pass after a few months of treatment. Once gone, they rarely return. The more recently the delusions began before treatment, the better the outlook.

Medication. If a person with delusions is brought to a psychiatric emergency room in an agitated state, he will probably be given an injection of antipsychotic medication for short-term relief. But for long-term treatment, the evidence is mixed that medications are helpful.

In any case, someone with paranoid delusions generally sees no need for medication and is likely to refuse it even when it is prescribed. What's more, medication itself can easily become incorporated into the delusion, particularly in those with persecutory beliefs. Any potential side effects, as well as the way medicines work, should be well explained so that the person with delusions will not later suspect that he or she has been lied to.

Individual psychotherapy: what to expect. Developing a trusting relationship with the therapist is crucial. At first, the therapist is likely to focus on helping with anxiety or irritability rather than the delusions themselves. That can only begin in later phases after trust has been built. The psychotherapist will not try to prove the illogic of the delusions, but rather deal with the symbolic meanings and feelings that lie behind them.

The goal of therapy may be improvement in the person's relationships rather than total disappearance of the delusions. This is especially true in behavioral therapy, where the focus is easing the hypersensitivity to criticism that can lead to social isolation.

Therapy may involve family members to mend the ruptures in relationships that delusions often lead to. This is especially important when the delusions have caused the person to suspect, accuse, or attack family members. The more accepting the person's family can be, the easier it will be for the person to regain his footing.

One danger is that the family and the therapist will be seen as conspiring together behind the person's back. For that reason, family members must respect the confidentiality of the relationship between the person in treatment and the therapist.

SCHIZOPHRENIA

Schizophrenia can be the most disabling and long-lasting of mental disorders. But while in the past schizophrenia often meant a long sojourn in a psychiatric hospital, today the outlook is different. With proper medication and help, most people can live in the community and lead productive lives. While the disorder was once thought to be lifelong, recent studies have shown that schizophrenic symptoms can diminish over the years and in some instances remit entirely.

The causes of schizophrenia are unclear. At one time it was blamed on the way families communicated, or on flawed relations between mother and child. But such explanations—which created an immense amount of guilt among the families of those afflicted—are now seen as unfounded and unhelpful. There is no known difference between the early family life of schizophrenics and that of others. To be sure, there are difficulties in such families, but the strain of having a family member afflicted with schizophrenia seems enough to explain them.

Though families don't cause schizophrenia, it does tend to run in families. The most likely explanation is a genetic susceptibility that makes a person vulnerable to reacting to the stresses of life with the symptoms of schizophrenia. Exactly how this happens and what level and type of stress might be the critical threshold are still unknown. How the vulnerability may be genetically transmitted has also not been identified. The best bet is that schizophrenia is a complex illness with multiple causes. One reason the causes are so difficult to identify is that what is called schizophrenia may actually refer to a group of similar disorders with overlapping symptoms, rather than to a single entity. Alternatively, the pattern of symptoms identified with schizophrenia may be what is called a "final common pathway" for a group of conditions that are related but different in origin.

The incidence of schizophrenia tends to be the same across cultures, countries, and historical periods. The best estimate from pooled studies is that close to one out of every one hundred people is afflicted over a given six-month period. Over the course of a lifetime, somewhere between 0.5 to 1.5 percent of people will develop symptoms.

Stress sometimes triggers the first episode of schizophrenia, though not always. But once the symptoms develop, stress almost always makes them worse.

In most instances, the symptoms of schizophrenia first appear during mid- to late adolescence or early adulthood. For some, the onset is abrupt and dramatic—an acute psychotic episode that occurs with little warning. This is characterized by the so-called *"positive" or "active" symptoms* of schizophrenia, which are bizarre and dramatic.

The most prominent are delusions—though all too real and terrifying—of being persecuted, punished, or controlled; or of being or encountering God or the devil;

or of being caught up in a cosmic conflict of good and evil. Most though not all also experience hallucinations, usually voices that may whisper or shout, be intelligible or incoherent, comment on the person's behavior—usually harshly, witheringly—or demand they do or say something morally offensive ("command hallucinations"). It may be the voice of someone they know—a dead parent or grandparent, for example—or of a stranger. The voices may go on and on or be just one or two words or phrases repeated over and over. Visual hallucinations are usually bizarre, frightening, or threatening: mutilated bodies, snakes crawling out of skulls. Olfactory hallucinations are more rare, usually disgusting smells coming from one's own body. Tactile hallucinations are also uncommon: bugs crawling under one's skin, or one's skin stretching or contracting in grotesque ways. Speech often becomes rambling and incoherent—to the listener, though not to the individual. To the listener, the connections between thoughts are illogical or missing; thoughts seem to go off on weird tangents. An individual sentence may make sense, but the whole sounds like nonsense. The person may have little or nothing to say; they may be uncommunicative, even mute and unmoving. Or they may have too much to say and seem flooded by ideas without being able to filter out the important from the unimportant. Emotions and moods may swing wildly and uncontrollably from one moment to the next.

When the acute episode passes, the psychotic symptoms may abate for the most part, but a precipitous drop in the person's ability to handle the day-to-day demands of life often follows.

For most, however, the onset is more gradual. An acute episode occurs only after a period of growing withdrawal from family, friends, and former interests, a gradual loss of touch and increasing turn inward to a world of ideas, fantasies, and preoccupations that seem more and more real and compelling. This is usually accompanied by some of the so-called "negative" symptoms of schizophrenia, which can emerge almost imperceptibly long before the first acute psychotic episode occurs. They also tend to characterize the periods between psychotic episodes. If recovery is not complete, they can last for years in the nonpsychotic long-term course of the disorder.

These symptoms are referred to as *"negative"* or *"deficit"* *symptoms* since they mark an absence of some ability. They include withdrawal from family, friends, social contacts—or keeping these to a minimum; a marked drop in ability to handle the normal demands of life; difficulty feeling motivated; low energy; poor hygiene and self-care; a disconcerting flatness in expressing emotion, or a blunting of feelings altogether; emotional responses that aren't appropriate to the situation—grinning or laughing in describing something unbearably sad; difficulties paying attention; wandering trains of thought that are difficult to follow; a narrowing of focus to certain fixed, idiosyncratic ideas that dominate and color the perception of everything else; feelings of inner emptiness or unreality, as if no one were home inside, or of the world's being unreal and disconnected.

Whether the onset is abrupt or gradual, the years following the first acute episode are difficult for most people. The active symptoms tend to be in the forefront. These can be not only overwhelming and disruptive in themselves, but they also tend to follow a roller-coaster pattern at first, periods of relative calm alternating with acute psychotic episodes that may require rehospitalization.

Schizophrenia is often referred to popularly as "split" personality. When the term was first introduced, however, it meant a "shattered" personality. What makes the disorder so shattering is not just the nature of the symptoms themselves, but the larger pattern. Whereas individuals with other severe psychiatric disorders may have one or two of the symptoms of schizophrenia, the person with the disorder itself is afflicted by all of them. It also tends to strike just when people are trying to establish themselves in the world and form an adult identity. Schizophrenia interferes with all of the important developmental tasks of this stage: leaving home, doing well at school, getting started in a career, forming relationships, getting married, and starting a family.

Schizophrenia is likely to last longer the earlier in life it begins, the more gradually it emerges, the more diffficulties the person has had previously with social, sexual, and work adjustment, and the more unusual and idiosyncratic the person's behavior before the onset.

On the other hand, the later in life it begins, the more sudden and acute the onset of symptoms, the better the person was functioning before it began, and the more supportive his or her family, the less severe it is likely to be and the greater the eventual likelihood of a good recovery.

As devastating as it can be, schizophrenia is *treatable*. Individuals and families should not give up hope. With proper treatment it can be controlled in almost all cases. In some cases, there can be a nearly complete recovery from symptoms, especially from the more active, bizarre, and disruptive symptoms. Even without treatment, the active symptoms tend to subside on their own. In studies of people whose schizophrenia had occurred decades earlier, two-thirds had shown significant improvement or had virtually no signs at all of the disorder. If symptoms remain, they tend to be of the negative type.

With the help of medication, appropriate psychotherapy, and some help in managing day-to-day affairs, even if recovery is not complete, most people with schizophrenia hold a job, live independently, and enjoy a circle of friends. Many marry and raise families as well.

Signs to Look For

No single symptom is the hallmark of schizophrenia. Symptoms can come and go unpredictably, and not all of them occur in everyone. Each of these symptoms is found in at least one other mental disorder as well, also in certain medical conditions, leading schizophrenia to often be overdiagnosed.

A reliable diagnosis requires that a combination of these symptoms persist for at least half a year. If they occur in their most intense form for a few weeks and months and then clear up, schizophrenia can't be the diagnosis. Even if some of the symptoms are "schizophreniform" in nature—"schizophrenialike"—the episode still has to be seen as brief psychosis (see p. 544), not as schizophrenia.

As schizophrenia develops, there is a *deterioration* in a person's ability to function. This can occur in a week or so or be extended over several years. Signs of the deterioration include:

- *Change in personality,* so that he or she no longer seems to be the same person to friends and family.
- *Neglect of grooming and hygiene.*
- *Inability to function* in life's roles, such as student, worker, parent, or spouse.
- *Withdrawal* from friends and family, and social life in general.
- *Loss of initiative and energy,* and an indifference to pursuits that used to bring pleasure.

As schizophrenia develops, the signs generally intensify at some point into an acute phase, during which these symptoms are at their most bizarre and obvious, "active" or "positive." This phase is often triggered by a specific incident, but other signs will typically have been building toward the crisis.

Signs during the *acute phase* include:

- *Confused speech:* the person does not make sense when he or she talks. This can take the form of completely incoherent sentences that are one long stream of consciousness or just incoherent words.
- *Delusions:* bizarre beliefs out of touch with reality—such as that he or she is being spied on or poisoned, that someone is "putting thoughts in my mind," that he or she can directly transmit thoughts to others, that the person has some special secret or divine mission, or role, that some apocalyptic event is at hand, that they are a witness to or participant in some titanic struggle between God and the devil or the forces of good and evil, or that things having nothing to do with them refer to them or carry some special message for them.
- *Hallucinations,* usually hearing voices that offer a running commentary on their actions, criticize or torture them, or command them to do certain things they find repugnant or morally offensive—including hurting or killing themselves. Hallucinations in schizophrenia can appear in any of the five senses, but hearing voices is the most common.
- *Disturbed thinking,* a loose stream of consciousness that shifts rapidly from one topic to some other unrelated topic without seeming to notice that the connection makes no logical sense.
- *Perplexity and confusion* because the person may not be able to discern whether

what he or she perceives is real or not. The perplexity is fed in part by mixed-up thoughts, in part by hallucinations and delusions.

- *Blunted emotions,* little or no emotional response to situations that evoke strong feelings in others.
- *Odd emotions,* in which the person's emotional reaction is incongruous or disconcerting—laughing when they should be crying, for instance. What they express and the way they express it don't match.
- *Heightened drive* and vitality, with abnormal levels of enthusiasm and excitement, but which is unfocused and confused.
- *Distress* at all this: anguish, desperation, even despair.

Any of these signs can continue on for months or years after the acute phase subsides. Psychotic disturbances in thinking tend to be controlled by medication, but some of the other symptoms may continue in a muted form for years. Long-entrenched delusional beliefs may also persist in a less active form.

Oddly, after the acute symptoms fade, some people become depressed. The depression seems to be over the passing of the sense of heightened reality and intensity in life that accompanied the acute symptoms: they feel abandoned to life's mundane problems and feel poorly equipped to deal with them.

The periods between acute episodes, and the long-term course of schizophrenia, are characterized by so-called "negative" or "deficit" symptoms. These include:

- *Social isolation,* in which the person continues to withdraw from social contacts or retreats into a circumscribed daily round, shying away from making new acquaintances or from contacts in general.
- *Impaired functioning* in school, at work, or at home.
- *Peculiar habits,* such as hoarding food, picking through garbage cans, collecting odd items, or talking to oneself.
- *Lack of emotionality or odd emotional reactions.*
- *Strange ways of talking,* such as vagueness, constant digressions, or overly elaborate ways of putting things; a poverty of speech, such as making minimal responses to queries.
- *Odd beliefs,* such as that others can read one's mind or control one's thoughts.
- *Unusual perceptions,* such as "sensing" that someone is present who actually is not, or strange feelings in the body.
- *Apathy* and loss of initiative.

These symptoms do *not* mean people with schizophrenia are utterly out of touch with reality. Even during the most acute phase, they will know that people eat and sleep, that cars run on streets, how to buy something, and other basics of living. They also have some insight—often excellent insight—into what is happening. This means they appear and think and act normal much of the time, except when acute symptoms erupt.

Daniel: The Acute Phase

Daniel had been an outstanding student all his life. But while he was working days and into the nights on his research project for his doctorate in microbiology, something began to change. His roommates noticed that Daniel, formerly meticulously clean, began to leave messes in the apartment: pans with burnt food in the bottom, piles of dirty towels in the bathroom, a huge pile of unwashed laundry in his bedroom. He seemed to be neglecting himself, too; he had not washed in weeks.

At about the same time, Daniel began to mention a strange "whooshing" sound that he heard deep in his ears, and he seemed to think that his roommates could hear his thoughts. His lab partners noticed he had abandoned his microbiology research and had begun to build a contraption that he said was meant to "contact the archangels."

When his adviser told him that he would have to take down the device, Daniel began to yell that the adviser was with the "Mafia and the Vatican" and had been spying on him and planting thoughts in his head. As he went on and on, Daniel's speech became incoherent. He ran out of the building, screaming that "terrible evil" was to be visited on the college, rambling on about archangels and voices telling him what to do.

Daniel: The Long-term Symptoms

Daniels' first episode with schizophrenia led to hospitalization for several months. Upon discharge, instead of returning to the university, he went back to his parents' home. There he spent most of his time alone in his room, reading religious books for hours on end and making profuse notes. He refused to see any of his old friends. He would come out of his room for meals, but sat eating in silence.

Over the months, Daniel's room became packed with piles of dirty clothes, books and magazines, and bits and pieces of junk that he salvaged from neighbors' garbage cans during early-morning forays. When his parents got him to talk, Daniel would tell them that he was engaged in an important secret research project "for the Defense Department and the KGB," but when pressed to explain, he would only mumble vaguely that it had to do with gamma rays and auras. He showed no interest in trying to resume his studies at the university or in getting a job. "There's too much whooshing in my head for that," he explained.

Variations and Complications

Schizophrenia can take several forms, although most people with the disorder have prominent symptoms typical of one of the types mixed with symptoms from other types. These symptoms can come and go, and any of the various symptoms can predominate at a given time.

The disorganized type. The main symptom of this type of schizophrenia is incoherence. The person may not make sense at all when speaking, jumping loosely from one idea or association to another, or the words spoken are a complete jumble. The person's behavior is typically disorganized and bizarre as well.

Along with the disorganization, the emotional reactions are often inappropriate—strange laughter, for instance, or few, if any, emotional responses at all. This type of schizophrenia usually has a long and gradual onset beginning early in life and unfortunately tends to be fairly chronic.

The catatonic type. The most obvious symptom is catatonia, a rigidity of the body, such as holding a particular position for a long time, a "waxiness" in movement, or assuming bizarre postures. People who are catatonic can stay rigid despite all attempts to make them move. On the other hand, they are also prone to agitated excitement, during which they may make rapid, odd movements, and then sink once again into a stupor. Catatonia is relatively rare, though it was once one of the more common types of schizophrenia.

The paranoid type. Delusions of being persecuted are the main symptom in this form. Sometimes the delusions are compounded by hallucinatory voices that the person thinks belong to persecutors. The delusions are not always of being persecuted, however. The person may believe he or she is entitled to some elevated status or role or has some special, secret, or spiritual mission.

Paranoid schizophrenics are also typically anxious, suspicious, hostile, and quick to argue or take offense. They may become violent if they feel they have been provoked.

What Therapists Recommend

Approach. The large majority of psychotherapists recommend supportive therapy for both acute and long-term treatment. During the acute phase, no other approach is strongly recommended. During long-term treatment, family and behavioral approaches are suggested most often.

Medication. Almost all therapists see the need for medication concurrent with therapy, particularly during the acute phase.

Setting. The vast majority of therapists agree that acute episodes of schizophrenia are best handled in a hospital. But once the intense disruption of the acute phase passes, long-term schizophrenia is best treated outside the hospital in a community setting, usually in office visits, at day treatment centers, or in special residences providing help in managing day-to-day affairs.

Format. Individual psychotherapy is highly recommended for both the acute and long-term phases. In addition, group therapy and/or family therapy are also recommended by many clinicians during both phases.

Frequency. During the acute phase, supportive treatment needs to be intensive: sessions twice a week or more, usually daily during a hospitalization, though inpatient therapy may be provided by a member of the hospital staff. But during long-term treatment, as symptoms fade, supportive sessions may be tapered off to every other week, once a month, and eventually check-ins once every other month or less. Long-term developmental psychodynamic therapy usually takes place weekly, or bimonthly if weekly contact is too intense.

Duration. Treatment for the acute phase should be open-ended, though this phase often ends within six months. As the more intense symptoms calm down and treatment becomes long-term, some people may need therapy for months, others for years.

Certain kinds of frequently recommended behavioral therapy are time limited: social skills training or assertiveness training, for instance. Developmental psychodynamic therapy is long-term work that has to be left open-ended.

What You Should Know About Therapy

While there is no sure "cure" for schizophrenia, some people do recover completely from its major symptoms. And in those whose symptoms continue even with treatment, schizophrenia can be managed with the proper care. It is no longer the hopeless illness it was once thought to be.

In the treatment of schizophrenia, psychotherapy is typically part of a combination of needed interventions. Medication is almost always considered essential, especially during the acute phase, and usually in a lessened dose if the symptoms continue and become long-term. In general, psychotherapy and medication—in combination with a structured and, if necessary, supervised daily milieu—have been shown to be more effective treatments than either alone. A strong and stable relationship with a therapist helps greatly.

The immediate goal of treatment is to help the person manage his or her symptoms. But beyond that, the goal is to improve the quality of his or her life by preventing relapses, and by helping the person to work, to live as independently as possible, to enjoy friends, and to reduce the stress on his or her loved ones.

One of the key elements in helping a person with long-term schizophrenia is managing the stresses of living. Under severe stress, the symptoms may return; if life is relatively calm, problems can be minimized. Most people with schizophrenia can live a normal life in the community. Many marry, raise a family, and work. But as is the case with people who have chronic illnesses like diabetes and heart disease, they may require intensive treatment or hospitalization from time to time.

Medication. Nearly two dozen major medications are used for the treatment of schizophrenic symptoms, all referred to as "antipsychotics." They all have basically the same effects on brain biochemistry, but they differ somewhat in potency and side effects—a major concern in the treatment of schizophrenia.

If your therapist is not a psychiatrist and you are not already under medical care, your therapist will probably refer you to a psychiatrist for medication. Since the medications for schizophrenia are potent, expect the psychiatrist to prescribe only a certain amount and to want to meet with you regularly to monitor your reactions.

People with schizophrenia often forget to take their medication, take it at the wrong times, or decide to stop because they don't like the side effects. Stopping is your right, but you should know that ceasing medication arbitrarily is one of the major causes of relapse.

If you have worries or complaints about the medication you are taking, discuss them frankly with your psychiatrist. Do this rather than simply deciding on your own to stop. No antipsychotic medication is better than the others in every case. You may have to try a medication for four to six weeks before you will know what its effects will be. Often side effects that show up in the first week or so will stop after a week or two.

If you don't find your symptoms improving by about six weeks, talk to your doctor about trying a different medication. For more information on antipsychotic drugs see page 621.

Antipsychotics are most effective in calming the active symptoms of schizophrenia: reducing agitation, controlling hallucinations and delusions or diminishing their vividness, and making thought and speech more coherent and organized. But with the possible exception of clozapine, they have less effect on the negative symptoms of apathy, loss of initiative, social withdrawal, and emotional aloofness.

For that reason, they are prescribed in stronger doses during the acute phase when the active symptoms are most bothersome. The dosage is then reduced markedly during long-term care when their main function is to prevent a recurrence of the more intense symptoms. Some studies have found that 50 percent of those who do not take antipsychotics relapse within two years, while only 20 percent of those taking the medication do so.

A common error in prescribing antipsychotics is to give too large a dose. Recent thinking and research holds that smaller doses than have been standard in the past can have the same effects. But some psychiatrists and physicians still continue to prescribe in the larger doses they have been accustomed to (see pp. 622 for dosage guidelines on antipsychotics). On the other hand, when medication does not seem to help, it is sometimes because a large enough dose has not been tried.

One of the most serious potential side effects is *tardive dyskinesia* (see p. 624).

Psychotherapy. Psychotherapy alone usually has limited success. But different kinds of therapy may be appropriate at different phases, each with their own goals.

During the acute phase, the focus should be on controlling the more severe psychotic symptoms. During this phase people typically feel lost, confused, and overwhelmed, their attention scattered. Therapy sessions at this point are often kept relatively brief in order to avoid further overload, emphasizing support and a consistent, reliable point of contact that is not caught up in the confusion, the terror, or the flood.

Once the more disruptive symptoms are under control, continuing long-term therapy has to be primarily supportive to start. Most people with schizophrenia will have to learn to live with some residual symptoms. This means, for example, that they may continue to hear voices or to hold odd beliefs, though usually with medication these are not as compelling. But it helps if they come to realize that the voices are not actually real or that others will view their beliefs as odd and they should be discreet about them. A supportive approach can be very helpful with these kinds of issues.

Once the acute phase passes and symptoms are stabilized, other kinds of therapy are possible. One is *developmental psychodynamic therapy.* This does *not* aim at uncovering underlying conflicts, but rather to help the person build or rebuild basic social and psychological capacities whose growth has been impaired by the severe disturbance. Such capacities include a coherent and consistent sense of self; a more realistic body image; a capacity to experience, tolerate, and express emotion; more reliable boundaries between inside and outside, self and others. This approach, not yet widely known or practiced, even by many psychodynamically oriented therapists, represents a major advance in treatment, not just for schizophrenia but for all forms of severe disturbance with developmental arrests. If you seek help from a psychodynamically oriented therapist, make sure he or she is experienced with schizophrenia and will be taking this "developmental" approach, *not* an insight-oriented approach.

Group therapy for schizophrenia is also a relatively new approach and has the advantage of being less intimate and emotionally demanding than one-to-one therapy for someone trying to rebuild the capacity to handle emotion and intimacy. Each person in the group can learn from the problems of the others and can practice needed interpersonal skills in a supportive atmosphere.

For those who have been socially isolated for a long time, the skills of daily life have usually atrophied. They often need to relearn such simple things as listening to what someone is telling them in a conversation, how to hold a conversation, or how to stand up for themselves, let alone advocate for their rights. Skills training and assertiveness training are two *behavioral approaches* that can be helpful during recovery.

In skills training, people rehearse a difficult life situation they are likely to confront, such as interviewing for a job or looking for an apartment. They watch a therapist and others act it out, then rehearse the situation themselves. Assertiveness training is a related approach that focuses specifically on developing self-assertiveness skills.

Another type of behavioral approach used for those with debilitating symptoms living in a longer-term psychiatric hospital—rare these days—or a group home, is a "token economy." Tokens are given on a mutually contracted basis for controlling disruptive symptoms or for developing a particular social skill. The token is redeemable for something extra the person wants.

Caution. People with schizophrenia should avoid therapies that provoke intense emotions, such as gestalt therapy or primal scream, or therapies that are confrontational, or demand self-disclosure. Experiencing or expressing intense feelings can be confusing and overwhelming, and can induce a relapse into acute psychosis.

What the Family Can Do

The family is no longer seen as part of the problem, but as part of the solution: they can do much to ease the life of the afflicted family member and help prevent relapses. At the same time, the family itself often needs guidance and support.

What had previously been seen as "disturbed" communication in the family is now understood to be the result of the stress of living with someone afflicted with schizophrenia. Every family has difficulty coping with the symptoms of schizophrenia in a loved one who may be hallucinating, delusional, in a state of confusion, terror, or extreme agitation, and acting strangely.

Today, most psychiatric hospitals and clinics have programs to educate families about how to create a home environment that will facilitate recovery, and programs to provide direct support to the family itself.

The main thing families can do to help is to keep family tension as low as possible. Some general principles:

- Be tolerant. Try not to criticize in a way that seems to judge your family member. Avoid comments like, "You don't care what anyone thinks about you." On the other hand, constructive criticism in the form of an explanation or advice can be helpful: "People want to be friendly. If you were more friendly to them, you'd probably find them being more friendly to you."
- Be understanding of the symptoms of schizophrenia. Talk to your family member's therapist, case manager, or social worker and have the symptoms explained. Don't demand that the schizophrenic "act normal" or be critical when he or she does not. Usually they cannot.
- Avoid holding the schizophrenic to unrealistic expectations for the future, such as returning to college or a high-pressure job. The pressure will only create stress and increase the risk of relapse. Wait and see what level of adjustment to

life residual symptoms will allow, and try to help your family member find a niche that fits.

- Try not to be too emotional yourself about the problem. If you get upset whenever your family member shows any symptom, it is likely to make things worse.
- Don't try to talk the family member out of delusions or ideas that you find strange. It won't help. But you don't want to reinforce these beliefs either by passively accepting them. When they come up, you can make it clear in an understanding way that you don't share them.
- Don't think in terms of finding a "cure." Focus your efforts on the practical ways you can help your family member deal with living.
- Be straightforward about what you are thinking and feeling about the situation. Hold down anger, criticism, and blame, but don't walk on eggshells. Don't try to turn yourself inside out to be accommodating. That will only add to your family member's burden of guilt and responsibility.
- See that the family member takes his or her medication as prescribed.
- Don't let the family member be irresponsible or do whatever he or she pleases. Make clear what the rules are and be firm—not hostile or aggressive—in sticking to them.
- If the family member's behavior creates a specific problem time and again, meet with his or her therapist or case manager to try to find a creative solution.
- Consider family therapy for yourself. The family therapist can advise you whether it might be useful to include the afflicted family member.
- Contact other families who have experience with schizophrenia. It will help you to know what they have gone through and how they have handled situations similar to yours.

The main organization of families is the National Alliance for the Mentally Ill. They can provide useful information and both practical and moral support for families. They have local chapters in most parts of the country. To find one near you, contact:

National Alliance for the Mentally Ill
2101 Wilson Blvd., Suite 302
Arlington, VA 22201
(703) 524-7600

Hospitalization

Before the advent of antipsychotic medication, schizophrenia was almost always treated in a psychiatric hospital. Many people with the disorder spent much of the rest of their life there. No longer. Now, people with schizophrenia typically require hospitalization only during the acute phase.

If the person is threatening others, is suicidal, or is unable to care for himself, hospitalization may need to be involuntary (see p. 268).

The hospital can offer a thorough evaluation, a reliable diagnosis, safe and adequate trials of medication, and stabilization of symptoms. Hospitalization usually need not be for more than several weeks to a month or two. The goal should be to return the person to the community with the most severe symptoms under control, an ongoing relationship with a therapist or case manager established, and a comprehensive plan for continued treatment and supervised living after discharge.

The discharge plan is crucial to the continued success of treatment. If the person has no one to see that medication is taken and appointments kept, for instance, the chances of stopping medication and missing sessions with consequent rapid deterioration are high.

Many people with long-term schizophrenia do have relapses of acute symptoms from time to time and need to be readmitted. It helps to understand that this is simply part of the recovery process. Another acute episode does not necessarily mean a step backward or that treatment isn't working.

Living Arrangements

Many people with long-term schizophrenia live with their family or in supervised apartments or group residences if they are unable to live on their own.

These arrangements work best if people are visited regularly by assigned case managers or social workers who help them keep appointments, find paid or volunteer work or join a day treatment program, get and take medication, and generally assist with the demands of daily living.

The general rule of thumb: find the housing arrangement that allows the most independence, but has enough support to make it workable.

Homelessness

This is a real danger for someone with long-term symptoms of schizophrenia. As many as a third of the people who become homeless in America's major cities may suffer from schizophrenia. Many of them have been treated in hospitals—some several times—only to be released to a faulty network of supports that eventually leaves them without income, housing, medicine, or any other care.

One key to preventing this is "case management," in which someone helps an ex-patient with the problems of daily life. People who are disabled by mental illness, for instance, are entitled to government benefits that will meet basic living expenses. But getting those payments demands a round of bureaucratic appointments that is sometimes too much for someone who is already confused and apathetic.

If no one sees to it that the person keeps appointments for therapy and medication, or takes medication once it is prescribed, the symptoms of schizophrenia may emerge again in full force. Too often, the sad result is that the person may end up on the street, confused and psychotic. If the person's symptoms become florid, the police may bring him or her to a psychiatric emergency room, only to begin the same round through the hospital and out again. If the symptoms are less obvious—apathy and social withdrawal, say—the person may end up living in a doorway or on a park bench, noticed by no one.

Other Treatments: Caution

In the past, before the introduction of antipsychotics and appropriate forms of therapy, other medical treatments were standard for schizophrenia. One of these was electroshock therapy, but this has little effectiveness. Some studies have shown it may be useful during acute episodes of depression and emptiness that occur in some forms of schizophrenia, or during the postpsychotic depression that can occur after an acute episode when the risk of suicide is high. But apart from these specific instances it is not recommended unless medications fail to have an effect on the most intense symptoms, or the person continues to be severely suicidal.

Psychosurgery, an operation in which part of the brain is severed from the rest, was also originally an accepted treatment for schizophrenia. However, there is little evidence for its therapeutic value and no reason for its use in treating schizophrenia today.

Suicide

The highest risk of suicide in schizophrenia is in the first half year, especially in the first three or four months after discharge from the hospital for treatment of an acute episode. This can be a particularly dangerous period when the person is more aware of the illness and is most likely to feel hopeless about the future, become depressed, give up on treatment, and think of suicide as the only way out.

The danger signs that a person is at risk for suicide include:

- If he or she becomes depressed after the psychotic symptoms abate.
- If the person becomes discouraged about treatment, thinks "nothing will help," and becomes hopeless.
- If the medication produces feelings of depression and futility as side effects.
- If he or she stops taking medication against his or her therapist's or psychiatrist's advice.

Family and friends should be alert to these risks and notify whoever is in charge of treatment if there is reason for concern.

A SPECIAL CASE: PERSONALITY DISORDERS

The idea that certain temperaments or dispositions make people prone to a specific set of problems is one of the oldest in mental health, dating back to ancient Greece and India. The idea is summed up in the saying "character is destiny." The word *personality* refers to ingrained habits of acting, feeling, and thinking that a person brings to every situation, whether a new job or a marriage.

Which traits are most prominent often depends on the situation. It pays to be compulsive when you are doing your taxes, for instance. And under the right circumstances, most of us can be self-absorbed or suspicious. Only when these personality traits become exaggerated and pervasive do problems begin.

About a dozen patterns of personality are currently recognized as problems that can be helped by psychotherapy. These problems, referred to as *"personality disorders"* in the *DSM-III-R,* often exist along with, and complicate the treatment of, other problems such as depression or anxiety. But they can also cause a great deal of suffering in themselves, and their presence alone frequently calls for help.

Estimates of the prevalence of personality disorder are high, ranging from about 5 to 15 percent of people. In people treated for emotional problems, the incidence is thought to be far higher: a third to a half, by some estimates.

Among the personality disorders that psychologists have identified for many years are the obsessive, who is fixated on details in a situation, but oblivious to the emotional nuances; the narcissist, who tends to be arrogant and self-absorbed; and the paranoid, who is prone to suspiciousness. Others have been recognized only in the last few decades: the "borderline" personality, for example, marked by chaotic ups and downs, impulsivity, and a bent toward self-destructiveness.

Often people have traits of more than one personality disorder. Personality disorders also tend to be associated with other kinds of disorders, such as drug abuse, alcoholism, or depression.

Personality disorders start to become obvious in the teen years or early adulthood, often when people leave home to find their own identity. These problems—which may result in repeated difficulty in holding a job or in forming intimate relationships—tend to characterize most of the person's adult life, though the most pronounced problems often subside by middle age.

The person who has a trait—be it suspiciousness, self-absorption, or compulsiveness—may not see it as a problem. Instead of seeing the pattern of job or relationship disasters as the result of a problem, he or she may simply blame it on everyone else involved. But even when people do feel that they have a problem, they typically feel helpless to change it on their own.

For good reason. Personality disorders are among the most difficult to treat. For one, the traits are deeply ingrained, a part of the person's identity. The traits feel natural and "right" to the person, rather than the source of troubling symptoms.

That can be the source of much resistance to treatment: when the therapist points out the troubles the traits are causing, the person may take it personally, as a criticism or rejection.

The Nature of Personality Disorders

In a sense, the essence of a personality disorder is a *deficit:* some task of emotional development has not yet been accomplished or has gone awry and needs some reparative experience. One of the key tasks of psychological growth is becoming comfortable with the full range of emotions and their expression. In many personality problems, the difficulties involve such feelings as anger, disgust, shame, or fear. In certain personality problems, the difficulty is not being able to distinguish between such feelings—in other words, not really knowing exactly what it is you feel.

In some people the trouble is being unable to tolerate strong feelings or being unable to express them freely. They are afraid that if they become angry or sad, these emotions will overwhelm them.

Sometimes the result is a sense of boredom and emptiness, which results from avoiding any and all feelings of any significance. For people who have never really mastered their emotions, their feelings may fluctuate between quiet periods of boredom and emptiness and emotional storms and outbursts, a fluctuation that can be quite bewildering to close friends and family.

Once they get agitated, they have trouble calming down on their own. They need someone else to help them feel soothed. Even then, the emotional storm may take a while to calm.

Strong emotions seem to have a life of their own to those with personality disorders, who feel at a loss to control them. Strong emotions always seem to be caused by someone else. The feeling is sometimes expressed directly: "Why did you make me feel that way?" "If you hadn't done/said . . ."

Personality disorders leave people chronically unhappy, with a sense of being empty and alone, even when they are with others. They feel they can't really connect with others and often feel isolated, rejected, or abandoned emotionally even in the company of others. That makes them particularly sensitive to losses, large and small. A slight rejection can leave them abjectly saddened, as though someone close had died.

In some people with personality disorders, their own body—like their emotions—does not quite seem to belong to them. At the extreme, this can lead to treating their body as though it were a foreign object, without sensing that they are hurting themselves. They may cut or burn themselves and not seem to feel it nor feel that it was they who did it to themselves. Such self-inflicted pain can also be a way of releasing pent-up tensions.

Sex often has a special importance to people with personality disorders as a way to make up for the lack of feeling emotionally close. For some, sex can be compulsive, and is all too often unsatisfying; others may fear the contact and intimacy that sex brings. Typically, sex is a vehicle to get their own needs met instead of a chance for mutual sharing and giving.

In their relationships, people with personality disorders tend to have trouble seeing both the good and the bad in someone else; they tend to think in all-or-none categories. "You're my friend or my enemy; you either love me unconditionally or you don't love me at all." They also see themselves in the same stark terms: admirable, lovable, and special; or worthless, shameful, and at fault. And so they either love or hate themselves and other people, depending on their mood. This extreme vacillation leaves others perplexed; one minute the person will be friendly and warm, the next enraged and hurt.

Understandably, such people have great problems with their relationships. They enter relationships either with extreme caution or with great impulsivity. Personality disorders lead people to be intensely ambivalent about intimacy. They can feel utterly depressed when they are alone, but can't manage emotional intimacy without blowing up every small disagreement into a crisis that threatens the relationship itself.

Many of these difficulties stem from a basic lack of an ongoing sense of oneself and of others. Such people find it hard to keep in mind what people they are close to are like. They often can't seem to remember things you've said to them; when they are angry with you, they won't be able to remember anything kind you've ever done for them.

People with personality disorders often feel inadequate. They may feel ineffective in their work, or believe that no one will ever find them lovable.

In the most severe personality disorders, people do not feel any "cohesion": they have the sense that they are not the same person from situation to situation, mood to mood, or day to day. Many of the experiences they go through seem impersonal, as though they had little or nothing to do with them.

People with moderate personality disorders have a sense of continuity, but also a sense of helplessness and passivity. Events in life, such as problems in a relationship, seem to happen *to* them, instead of being in their control.

Those with less severe personality disorders still suffer from low self-esteem. No matter how well they have done in life by objective standards, they still do not feel they are admired for themselves or that they are "good" people.

In most people with personality disorders, those close to them are their main source of good feelings about themselves. They constantly need reassurance and demonstrations of love and caring. Without it, they can't feel good about themselves and slide into depression or anxiety.

In their work life, such people often don't have trouble getting a job, but they frequently have chronic problems keeping one. A job that at first engenders enthusiasm soon pales. They get little satisfaction from work, tend to become increasingly frustrated by something about the job, or get into conflicts with supervisors or coworkers. They tend to have a lot of complaints and feel unappreciated or exploited by employers. They may be absent more frequently or late to work. They are prone to quitting impulsively or being let go. They have trouble finding a lasting work interest and so tend to move from one job or one line of work to another. They tend to perform far below the level their innate talents and intelligence would allow.

Signs to Look For

Personality disorders are hard to recognize for several reasons. One is that people will not necessarily display the troublesome pattern in every situation. Someone who is unbearably arrogant or sadistic in his intimate relationships may be perfectly civil and kind to his business associates. And while others may be fully aware of the problem, the person himself may not be. Thus people often cannot see themselves in the descriptions of their problem, though people close to them find it easy.

Some general signs that a pattern of traits has intensified into a personality disorder include:

- When a trait becomes inflexible, so that the person reacts in a set way no matter what the circumstances, and no matter how damaging. For the person who is inflexible, it may seem that other people are unreasonable and demanding, while for those who deal with the person, it will seem that he or she is stubborn, out of touch, or unresponsive.
- When the trait causes the person emotional distress, often experienced by that person as caused by someone else. Someone who is paranoid may complain, for instance, that his current boss hates him—but over the years he will feel that way about a string of bosses.
- When the trait leads to impaired social relationships or failures at work. These are the most common problems, marked by a strong pattern of similar relationship breakups, or by the same kind of difficulty arising at work over and over.
- When the trait leads to problems that are not just occasional, or a passing reaction to stress, but are an enduring pattern in the person's life. For example, being unable to sustain a lasting intimate relationship because each time what starts as a passionate affair ends in bitterness and recrimination.

What You Should Know About Therapy

Persuading people with a personality disorder to get help can be hard. But if things aren't working well in their life—if they've become frustrated or dejected by a series of lost relationships or failures at work, or otherwise are in despair over how things are going—then the suggestion that therapy might help is easier for them to accept.

They do not need to know that you think they have a personality disorder. The therapist should recognize that fact.

Not all therapists are eager to treat people with personality disorders. Some therapists see treating these problems as extremely difficult, if not futile, and fear that they will have little to show for a great deal of effort. People with personality disorders can be highly demanding as clients and feel that no matter how hard the therapist tries, it is not enough. Beyond that, some therapists are reluctant because of the risk that during treatment the person will become self-destructive or even suicidal.

But things have begun to change as more therapists see personality disorders—even the most severe—as treatable. Since the early 1970s, psychotherapy has made major advances in treating these problems. Many therapists now make working with personality disorders a speciality.

The usual approach is to try to use the relationship between therapist and client to help remedy the developmental deficits that underlie the problems. Since the developmental tasks that need to be mastered mainly have to do with relationships, the relationship with the therapist can be the arena where the repairs occur, through corrective emotional experiences and the opportunity to learn relationship skills that have, at best, been poorly mastered.

But the very difficulties with relationships that so often bring those with personality disorders into therapy come into play with the therapist, making it hard to form a working alliance. If you believe you may have a personality problem, you can go into therapy with any one of several goals. One might be support for an emotional crisis in your life. Once the crisis passes, you can consider with your therapist whether you want to continue in therapy to work on underlying problems or just stay in treatment for long-term support.

Or you may go into therapy to address the personality traits—the underlying patterns of behavior—that continually cause you trouble. This is usually long-term work, several years or more.

What to Look For in Therapy and Your Therapist

Since people with personality disorders can express their most troubling feelings in ways that are self-destructive, including suicide attempts, alcohol and drug abuse, and high-risk behavior, a climate of safety in therapy is a paramount concern. It can best be created if you and your therapist have some mutual understandings at the outset. You both should discuss the following conditions:

- A *stable framework* for therapy, including explicit appointment times, a policy on missed or canceled appointments, payment expectations, and the like. Your reactions to any departures from these should be discussed between you.
- An *active therapist* who will engage with you, not hide behind a "therapeutic"

attitude of silence. You want your therapist to be someone who interacts with you and feels like a "real" person, and who will maintain the framework of therapy agreed on at the start.

- *A flexible therapist* who will bend a bit to give you the kind of support you may need in a crisis: schedule extra appointments in an emergency or let you call between appointments in agreed-upon situations.

- *A strong therapist* who can withstand the strong and stormy feelings you often have that may have driven people away from you in the past. You want your therapist to be consistent and caring—even in the face of your rage or rejection. You also want a therapist able to set limits on anything you do that threatens your safety, the therapist's, or the therapy itself.

- *A therapist who focuses on the here and now,* instead of on your past. Especially in the beginning of therapy, delving into your past can be a distraction from the more urgent problems you face right now. Later in therapy, you may spend more time on the roots of your problems.

- *An understanding therapist* who is familiar with personality problems and has enough patience to commit to treating you over the long haul. Change may be slow; your therapist should not demand to see changes in you too quickly.

You Can Expect Certain Difficulties in Therapy

In therapy for personality disorders certain difficulties can arise because the therapy relationship recreates the emotional reality of your formative relationships. The same responses you learned early in life with your primary caretakers are likely to be reenacted with your therapist.

That may lead you, for instance, to test your therapist, to challenge his or her competence, regard for you, or ability to set limits. Or you may express feelings in behavior that you find too upsetting to put into words. Thus, instead of talking about how distressed you get by some of the topics touched on in therapy, you may forget your next appointment. Or be unable to express feelings of hurt and rejection and hurt yourself instead.

You may be afraid that therapy will open you up to feelings that are too intense or too shameful to handle. Or you may be anxious that you'll become too intimate with your therapist or too dependent.

You will tend to overly idealize your therapist and expect unreasonable things of him or her. Such excessive hopes can lead to disappointment when the therapist does something that is only human—doesn't understand what you are saying on occasion or how you are feeling.

You may also expect to be treated as someone "special" and try to get your therapist to make exceptions for you. You may resent being held to the standard expectations of a client, such as keeping to scheduled appointments, showing up on time, or ending on time.

Formats

Many therapists who treat people with personality disorders recommend a combination of individual sessions and group therapy. The group will be mainly of other people who are dealing with problems similar to your own. A group, like your individual therapy, can be short- or long-term depending on your goals.

Hospitalization

Because many, though not all, personality disorders can occasionally lead to episodes of depression, anxiety, self-destructiveness or suicidality, even transient psychosis, and because they are often compounded by problems with alcohol and drug abuse, brief hospitalization may sometimes be a necessary part of treatment. When hospitalization is necessary, it should be kept as brief as possible—only until the crisis is over or the person is out of danger. Usually this should require no more than several days to a week or two at most. An extended hospitalization tends to create additional problems by encouraging dependency and regression. These days it is almost never recommended as the main setting for treatment.

If you should be hospitalized during a crisis, psychotherapy with your regular therapist should continue if possible. You can meet in the hospital if your therapist is willing and able. You can also maintain contact by phone, perhaps at your regularly scheduled appointment hour.

Your therapist should work closely with the hospital team. He or she will know you far better than they. If the hospital staff resists your continuing to work with your own therapist while you are there, you should not accept that decision without consulting with your therapist. You will be working with your therapist long after you leave the hospital, and it is important to maintain that contact.

Your therapist will need your permission to talk with hospital staff because of laws protecting your confidentiality. Since it is in your best interest to have coordinated care, you should normally give that permission. This does not mean that your therapist will need to share all the personal things you have discussed in therapy, only what is necessary to coordinate treatment. If you are uncomfortable about what might be said, discuss it with your therapist.

Medication

There is no medication for personality disorders per se, but they are sometimes accompanied by symptoms that medication can address: depression, anxiety, or transient psychosis.

You may welcome medication as a way to soothe feelings of unhappiness or anxiety, but the most significant changes will come from your relationship with your therapist. On the other hand, you may resist medication, perhaps seeing it as an attempt to control you or as a violation of your physical integrity. You should weigh your resistance against the possibility that the right medication at the right time could relieve some of your distress.

If you have a history of substance abuse or have abused prescription medications in the past, expect your therapist or psychiatrist to be hesitant about prescribing medication, especially any medication that can be lethal on overdose. Also expect him or her to prescribe it in small doses and to monitor your drug use closely.

Expense

Of all the difficulties people bring to therapists, personality disorders often require the longest treatment—typically several years or more. That means finances are a special concern. You should consider how you will cover the cost of treatment before you enter and should talk to your therapist in the first few sessions about what the likely cost will be and how you might be able to afford it. Be frank about your limits. If you both know what to expect about costs at the beginning, painful misunderstandings are less likely later on.

PERSONALITY DISORDERS: CHARACTERISTICS AND TREATMENT

Note: Personality disorders are not mutually exclusive. Often people have features of several rather than just the traits of one type.

The Entitled Person (Narcissistic Personality Disorder)

When people feel a deep sense of unworthiness or shame, they sometimes protect themselves by taking on compensating attitudes that will shore up their sagging self-esteem. Among these attitudes is a sense of being special, of being entitled to more attention, praise, and admiration than are other people. Along with the sense of entitlement goes a self-absorption rather like that portrayed in the myth of Narcissus, who fell in love with his own reflection.

The pivotal problem for the entitled person is a self-defeating and often self-destructive vanity that conceals feelings of shame and inferiority. On the surface, many people with this trait seem to be doing very well: they seem confident, cheerful, and unflappable. But because deep down they harbor feelings of inadequacy, they exaggerate their accomplishments and need a continual admiration or adulation from others in order to reassure themselves.

Entitled people do not experience genuine mastery, the sense of being able to act effectively on their own behalf, particularly when it comes to getting other people to respond to their needs. Nor do they feel valued by other people, feeling instead that they are not really heard, seen, or understood by others. Thus they feel they must do something special to be valued.

When the facade of self-confidence wanes, such people most often complain of a mild dissatisfaction and depression, of frustration and envy, of an anxiety about being fraudulent. This often happens in their life when career and creativity peak or even begin to crumble, or when parts of this personality pattern undermine success. This dynamic is often at play, for instance, in cases of the politician whose sexual affairs are exposed, or of the successful entrepreneur whose business goes bankrupt because he is so overextended.

Other blows are simply part of aging. Those who have prided themselves on their beauty, strength, and energy confront the hard reality of the toll of time. The resulting depression, shame, or rage is what often brings entitled people to therapy.

Origins. The roots of those traits, according to the most widely accepted theories, lie in certain childhood experiences. One is the feeling that your parents did not let you be yourself, but instead held you to fixed expectations. Either they were aloof and unempathetic or were overly involved. In either case, parents were so caught up in their own needs that they paid insufficient attention to yours.

In essence, children tested this way come to feel that in order to be loved or accepted, they must meet the parents' expectations and set aside their own needs. They must, for instance, prove themselves by accomplishments in school, sports, or other activities to obtain their parents' love. Such children depend on others' opinions in order to feel good about themselves—the entitled person's basic predicament in life.

Such people rely on a lifelong strategy of fantasies of great success, perfection, wealth, power, fame, or good looks. Such daydreams of accomplishment serve to bolster a fragile self-esteem: if others don't give you enough admiration, you can imagine it. People with this trait also gravitate toward careers where applause is explicit: entertainment, politics, modeling, and the like. In other lines of work, they seek the spotlight as public figures.

Relationships. Because of their deep need for adulation, entitled people combine an outer appearance of extroversion and self-confidence with a self-protective emotional distance. They are charming, but not really interested in other people's needs; they lack empathy and seek an admirer. If that admiration wanes, they feel betrayed. But when hurt, the entitled person adopts a veneer of self-sufficiency, saying, "I don't really need anyone—I'm all right on my own."

That stance does not last, though, because of the need for others to validate the entitled person's fragile self-esteem. The theme most often repeated in their relationships is one of great expectations at the beginning and disillusionment at the end.

An entitled person may hope to inflate his or her own stature by a close association with a powerful person: someone with money, fame, beauty, status. But to do this, they give up their own needs, becoming submissive.

Such relationships evolve quickly and with great passion and can be quite stable. Their disadvantage is that the entitled person actually loses self-esteem over the course of the relationship. For one, the fantasy that the other person will somehow share power and meet their deepest needs is invariably disappointed. But once in such a relationship, it is often hard to leave, since that would also be a blow to self-esteem. This dynamic is sometimes at work, for instance, in marriages where the wife is physically or emotionally abused.

Another common pattern is called the "as if" relationship. In this the entitled person keeps people at a distance emotionally, while being seductive and charming to lure them on. But when the fantasized satisfactions fail to materialize, they quickly drop the relationship, moving on to someone else whose power, position, etc., holds out the hope of inflating their self-esteem.

Signs to Look For

- Inability to stand criticism without feeling ashamed and humiliated or enraged.
- Exploitive relationships; being interested in others only so far as they can be useful.
- Self-importance; boasting and exaggerating achievements and abilities; unfounded confidence.
- "Specialness" and entitlement; a feeling of being beyond the rules that apply to others, and having unique problems only other "special" people can understand; expecting to be treated better than others.
- Need for the spotlight and constant admiration, compliments, and attention.
- Little empathy for others' feelings.
- Envy and intense competitive concern about how rivals are doing.

□ Emil, at thirty-four, had been working on his dissertation as a graduate student at a large university for ten years. He had a reputation around his department as a perennial student and a procrastinator. He scraped by as a research assistant on whatever project was funded that year.

Emil, however, as he was quick to tell anyone he met, saw himself as the brightest student the department had ever had. His thesis, he was sure, would revolutionize the field. That was why, he explained, he was taking so long to do it: his dissertation would attract so much attention that he had to make it a magnum opus. Meanwhile, he sometimes confided, he felt deep envy for his peers who had "gotten by" on "trivial" dissertations, gotten their Ph.D.'s, and gone on with their careers in the field.

Emil felt the faculty in the department owed him endless extensions on his dissertation as well as the top research assistant job available in any given year. Since he was going to make the department even more prestigious, he felt, he should be exempt from the usual rules governing graduate-student jobs. He regarded himself as virtually a faculty member, though he had actually never gotten more than halfway through writing his dissertation.

In private moments, though, Emil felt a deep insecurity about his ability to write a passable dissertation. He was frightened that when he did finally hand in his dissertation, he would fail, a thought that filled him with deep shame. He lived for the moments when he could impress some naive undergraduate with his brilliance and dreaded the thought of actually finishing his thesis.

Healthy Versus Unhealthy Narcissism

All successful people have a bit of narcissism. A healthy adjustment and a successful life are based to some degree on having a positive image of oneself. But a definite line exists between healthy narcissism at the core of solid self-esteem and the traits of the entitled person that lead to serious problems in careers and in relationships.

Some of the rules of thumb that distinguish healthy from unhealthy narcissism:

- Healthy self-esteem appreciates praise, but can live without it; the entitled person has an insatiable need for it in order to feel good about himself.
- Healthy self-esteem may be hurt by criticism, but the hurt fades; the entitled person is crushed or enraged by criticism and will brood about it.
- After a failure, healthy self-esteem feels unhappy, but not worthless. For the entitled person a failure triggers feelings of worthlessness and shame.
- Healthy self-esteem realistically acknowledges genuine talent, capability, or specialness to a degree, but the entitled person feels superior to everyone and expects to be recognized for it.
- A setback will throw healthy self-esteem off for a time, but the person will take it in stride. But life's hurts and rejections elicit rage or depression in the entitled person.
- Rejection, disapproval, or an attack will not destroy healthy self-esteem, while for the entitled person such rebukes evoke deep depression or sharp rage.
- Healthy self-esteem expects no special treatment and feels no hurt if it is not given, but the entitled person expects it and feels hurt if it is not forthcoming.
- While the healthy narcissist is sensitive to the feelings of others, the entitled person is exploitive and insensitive.

What Therapists Recommend

Approach. Most therapists recommend a psychodynamic therapy where the focus is on understanding the emotional patterns that underlie the entitled person's traits and on seeking to remedy deficits in emotional growth.

Medication. Medication is prescribed only in a crisis, usually precipitated by a radical collapse of self-esteem, when the person may become severely anxious, depressed, or suicidal.

Setting. Office visits.

Format. Individual therapy is the preferred format, although sometimes group therapy is a beneficial adjunct.

Frequency. Most therapists recommend once a week; some recommend twice or more a week.

Duration. Open-ended. Therapy may take several years or more to address the underlying patterns.

What You Should Know About Therapy

It may be a life crisis that finally brings you to therapy—the loss of a job, a lover or spouse, or some other setback or humiliation. If you find yourself devastated and depressed, it is a good time to start therapy. You will be more open to a candid self-appraisal, instead of trying to impress your therapist.

The treatment of choice for the entitled person is long-term, individual, psychodynamic therapy. For people who are functioning fairly well in life and can afford it, psychoanalysis, with four to five sessions a week, is a good choice. But if you are having repeated problems with self-destructiveness, such as drug abuse or suicidal feelings, or are prone to strong emotional outbursts such as rage, you might do better in a less intense psychodynamic therapy that meets once or twice a week. The more upsetting your problems, the more supportive you will want your therapist to be.

Your aim in therapy is to gain a more realistic sense of yourself, so you neither need to make yourself "special" nor to feel terrible if you fail at something.

Group therapy can sometimes be useful. At some point in the therapy, you are likely to want a special relationship with the group leader or feel envy for those whom you see as closer to the leader. You may also find yourself avoiding confrontations with other group members. Both situations point to your need to feel special and the sense of unworthiness it makes up for.

Hospitalization and medication are usually appropriate only if you become extremely depressed, which can happen following some setback or loss.

What to expect in therapy. A lifelong tendency to deny your own vulnerability may make you reluctant to enter therapy at all. Because therapy demands that you look at your shortcomings as well as your strengths, it may make you uneasy and feel threatening at first. You should be wary of a tendency to hold back information or feelings that might embarrass you or make you seem weak in the eyes of your therapist. Such feelings are natural, but will get in the way of your exploration of the patterns in your life you are there to change.

At first you may find yourself sensitive to what seem to be criticisms by your therapist. But it is part of therapy to probe the truth, and your therapist is inevitably going to reflect aspects of your habits that are not always as positive as you might like to think.

Quick results or magic turnabouts are unlikely; the changes you are seeking are in deep-seated patterns that will take a while to shift. You will also want your therapist to see you as "special." Don't be hurt if he or she does not feed this need of yours: that is part of the therapy.

You may, too, find yourself wanting to believe that your therapist is "special." But whenever he or she falls short of your ideal, you may become disappointed or even contemptuous. Again, these swings are part of the course of therapy.

Points when you feel vulnerable, with the parts of yourself that you feel ashamed of brought to light, will be critical in therapy. At these times you are particularly likely to have a reaction against your therapist or therapy itself. But if you can learn to tolerate the shame and self-criticism and still experience your therapist's concern and regard for you, an important Rubicon will have been crossed.

The Volatile Person (Borderline Personality Disorder)

Volatile people stand out because of their striking instability. Their moods are always on a roller coaster from deep depression and boredom to frustrated anger to keen excitement. Their relationships are always in turmoil. Their behavior is as unpredictable as their mood. At one time such people were considered to be on the "border" between neurosis and psychosis. While that notion was first applied to the entire range of personality disorders, it gave rise to a name that stuck as a designation for one of them: "borderline personality disorder."

The volatile person is not always in the throes of some emotional storm. Indeed, they often look much better than they actually are, especially to people who are meeting them for the first time or are just beginning to get involved with them. But as you get to know such a person, you will find yourself pulled into a series of emotional crises.

Their single strongest characteristic is a morbid aversion to being alone. They are likely to feel alone *even in the presence of another*. This dread springs from a deep sense of emptiness and boredom that leads such people to depend on someone else— or a never-ending string of others—to make them feel engaged and alive.

This search for companionship has a desperate quality: no matter how unsatisfactory the companionship, any is better than none. That means trying to make strangers into friends, or plunging into sexual activity with someone with whom no other real relationship exists.

Paradoxically, tempestuous people fear intimacy and closeness as intensely as they crave companionship. The result is tumultuous, unstable relationships that often begin impulsively and with intense passion. At the start of a relationship they are full of hope that this is the person who will finally make him or her feel better: understood, respected, cared for, truly loved. During this "courtship" phase, charm and seduction take over. But once their ceaseless demands and clinging begin to provoke a reaction from the other person that can be interpreted as a rejection, the emotional storm is unleashed.

The "rejection" may be slight—a mild cooling of intensity, a small criticism, a minor disappointment. But for the tempestuous person it represents an immense abandonment, which triggers a complete turnabout. Where once the other person was all good, now he or she suddenly becomes a villain, the object of indignation, rage, and scorn.

Most of the time stormy people feel depressed, lonely, and bored. The quality of the depression is that of someone who feels empty and abandoned, unable to replenish himself without help from someone else. On top of this basic foundation of depression other feelings come and go with great intensity and rapidity: elated one moment, disappointed and angry the next, irritable and anxious the next. A small frustration can rapidly escalate into a catastrophe or rage. While these mood shifts are sometimes triggered by some event, they also come and go for no particular reason.

The intense emotional swings of the volatile person can lead to impulsive, self-destructive acts: drug or alcohol abuse, sexual promiscuity, shoplifting or other minor crimes, accidents or fights. Most troubling are suicide attempts and self-mutilation. The suicide attempts are typically a desperate cry for help and attention. Self-mutilation—cutting oneself or burning oneself with cigarettes, for example—paradoxically seems to be a way to feel alive. These outbursts of impulsivity are typically triggered by something that makes volatile people feel rejected or abandoned.

Because of the turbulent life they lead, such people rarely perform up to their capabilities. Their school history is likely to be marked by missed classes and truancy; their work life suffers whenever they are consumed by some overwhelming emotional crisis, which can be often.

In addition, such people often feel a sense of unreality—that they are mere masks or shells instead of people. They may have a blurred sense of boundaries with other people and continual confusion about their personal loyalties or goals in life.

Particularly in moments of crisis, volatile people's fragile sense of self can collapse into a feeling of being overwhelmed, cut off from everyone, and a frantic desperation that no one will respond to them. This desperation makes them cling to someone else as a source of stability.

In its most intense form, this can become a short-lived psychotic episode—but one not related to schizophrenia or other kinds of psychoses. The psychosis is often triggered by alcohol or drug abuse, or intense stress, and is typically fleeting and well-defined.

While a borderline personality disorder is diagnosed about three times more often in women than in men, that ratio is disputed. Men and women with the problem may express it differently so that it is more obvious in women. A subtle bias in some clinicians may make them more likely to make the diagnosis in women, with men being given other diagnoses—or none at all.

Many people with this personality disorder—particularly women—have an extremely troubled early history, including neglect, physical or sexual abuse, incest, or traumatic separations. The volatile personality usually emerges as a problem in late adolescence or early adulthood. During this time of life, and extending into the thirties, people with this trait have extreme difficulty finding their way into lasting relationships, a stable career path, or a job.

The thirties can be an extremely stressful decade for women with this disorder who feel pressured by the hope of having a child. As their chances for finding a stable relationship seem less likely and the chances for a child fade, such women may throw themselves into impulsive sexual liaisons or have an unplanned pregnancy.

But for many, the tempestuous quality of their personality often cools during their late thirties and early forties. This means they can settle more easily into a career path or find their way into a marriage that lasts. Yet even at this point they may turn for comfort to alcohol or drugs or end up tolerating abuse for stability in a relationship.

Signs to Look For

- Rocky relationships that shift from an idealization of the other person to an explosion of resentment.
- Impulsiveness and self-destructiveness, such as sexual or spending binges, minor crimes such as shoplifting, driving recklessly, drug or alcohol abuse. Can also take the form of suicide attempts or self-mutilation.
- Intense mood swings from emptiness, boredom, and depression to anger and irritability, to nervousness and anxiety.
- Outbursts of anger that are frequent and inappropriate; a hair-trigger temper and frequent fights or arguments.
- Confusion about one's identity and course in life, self-worth, sexual preferences, friends, and values.
- Feelings of emptiness and lethargy, chronic boredom, and the need for people or events to lift one's mood.

- Clinging and neediness; the inability to feel content while alone, and desperate need to avoid loss or abandonment.
- All-or-nothing thinking: people tend to be seen as all good or all bad.

□ Jesse never knew a stable living situation. Her mother, who never married, had a string of boyfriends but never held a steady job. Jesse and her mother would move every few months, when the rent on their current apartment was due.

Jesse's first suicide attempt was at twenty-one, when her roommate said she was moving out to live with her boyfriend. Jesse slashed her wrists that night, but did so in a way that her roommate was sure to find her. Jesse said she couldn't bear the thought of living there without her roommate; the roommate, guilt-stricken, agreed to delay her move until Jesse could find someone else to take her place.

The episode was a familiar theme in Jesse's life. Since leaving home at seventeen, she'd lived with a succession of roommates and boyfriends. At first, she'd find the other person "wonderful," and would try to engineer their lives so they spent as much time as possible together. In periods when she was alone, Jesse felt "like an empty shell"; she dreaded solitary moments. If she had to be alone, she'd either go on a drinking binge or pick up a man at a bar and bring him home for the night.

Jesse would put immense efforts into trying to keep the boyfriend or roommate from seeing other people. Her suicide attempt was a gesture that, out of desperation, she was to repeat several times, all in an attempt to provoke such guilt and concern that the other person would not leave her.

At some point the other person would make a move that Jesse would interpret as a major slight: it might be simply not coming home for dinner on time, or not wanting to do something together. If Jesse couldn't get the other person to change plans to suit her, she'd fly into a rage. From that time on Jesse would "hate" the other person, who suddenly stood revealed to her as a "bastard" or "bitch."

What Therapists Recommend

Approach. Two approaches are particularly favored: *psychodynamic,* especially with a developmental focus; and *supportive.* These are often combined, so that, for instance, the therapist focuses on helping the person through any day-to-day problems in living, but also seeks to correct some of the key emotional experiences that went awry earlier in life by building a strong, dependable relationship.

Medication. Only for specific symptoms, such as pronounced depression or anxiety. But the focus of treatment is the relationship with the therapist, not medication.

Setting. The vast majority of therapists recommend an office or clinic setting. Hospitalization is appropriate only during a crisis, such as a suicide attempt.

Format. Likewise, therapists are almost unanimous in recommending individual therapy, sometimes complemented by group or family therapy.

Frequency. Once a week, but extra sessions or contacts may be necessary during periods of crisis, or at a certain stage of therapy. You may need your therapist to be available for a scheduled phone call between sessions, for instance, or in an emergency. Since these extra sessions or contacts can become something you crave or become dependent on, it is better to build an explicit agreement into the therapy contract at the start as to how and when and under what circumstances these will be available. If not, they will need to be explicitly spelled out and agreed to if and when they become necessary later on.

Duration. Definitely long-term and open-ended. Therapy typically takes several years or more. But short-term therapy of a few weeks or months can be useful to handle specific crises or problems. Modifying the underlying patterns, though, requires much more time.

What You Should Know About Therapy

The main work of therapy for the volatile person is the effort to establish a stable, long-term relationship with the therapist. By doing this the reactions and patterns that have distorted and destroyed past relationships can be understood and changed and more satisfying behaviors learned.

Many psychodynamic approaches will work equally well. But traditional psychoanalysis is not recommended. Therapy will become a testing ground for your fluctuating fears, needs, and moods, and the therapist needs to be highly responsive, emphasizing the here-and-now.

Perhaps more important than the specific approach of your therapist are his or her personal qualities. Your therapist should give you a feeling of stability: that he or she is consistent and reliable. You need a therapist who is firm with you, who helps you set limits that will protect you from your impulsiveness and self-destructiveness. In short, you want someone who will not be pulled onto your emotional roller coaster.

If you are a tempestuous person, you will find the therapy session becoming a microcosm of all your patterns in relationships. But the therapy relationship also differs from any other in your life. Your therapist is there to help you see the effects of your actions, to still accept you after you have exploded in anger, and support you through times of despair.

During the first year or two in therapy you may continually test the boundaries between you and your therapist. You may feel a need to pull your therapist into your life—to try to get him or her to intervene actively in the large and small crises of life by having contact outside the therapy sessions. Don't expect your therapist to go along with these desires.

The first phase of therapy may also find you trying to provoke your therapist by putting yourself at risk. You may go on a self-destructive binge—eating, sex, drugs, drinking—or make a suicide attempt. The best response from your therapist in the long run is to set firm limits on what you do. Your therapist may require an agreement, for example, that self-destructive acts such as suicide attempts or drug binges will result in your being hospitalized.

If you and your therapist stay together through such stormy episodes, your tests may gradually give way to feelings of dependency on the therapist. You will gain much from being able to tolerate the discomfort these feelings bring up in you. You may also find yourself more freely able to express your feelings of disappointment and anger toward your therapist as they well up.

With time, you will find yourself becoming more aware of the unpleasant feelings that have driven much of your troubling behavior—feelings such as emptiness or depression. You will learn how to get your emotional needs met by someone else—an essential skill that you can take to all the other relationships in your life.

Difficulties. Volatile people have a harder time than most establishing a good working relationship with the therapist. Your feelings toward the therapist can shift dramatically from session to session, or sometimes over the course of a single session. Therapy itself can be quickly pegged as either the best thing that has ever happened to you or the worst. As therapy continues, you should come to see the therapist and therapy itself more realistically, in complex, changing terms, like the rest of life.

Limits. Expect your therapist to set some ground rules for therapy, including limits on your contact outside the session and, if you have been self-destructive in the past, perhaps on your behavior. You may be told, for instance, that if you go on a drug-taking or drinking binge, or make a suicide threat, you'll need to go to a hospital until you regain control.

You may react to these limits with a sense of outrage or anger, feeling that you are being punished. But the limits are an important part of therapy, a way to help you control both self-destructive impulses and unreasonable demands on your therapist. You will need to be reminded, too, that other people are not the cause of all your difficulties, nor are they to be expected to rescue you: you will gradually need to take more responsibility for your problems.

Hospitalization. A small minority of psychotherapists feel that therapy for this personality disorder requires hospitalization. The argument for a hospital is that it is a safe place where the caregiving is consistent and limitations and expectations are clear. But most therapists think therapy should be done in office visits, with the person learning to deal with life situations as they occur. Beyond that, they argue that being in a hospital can encourage a regressive dependency. However, brief hospitalizations during crises are generally agreed to be helpful—but only when the person's safety or stability is at risk.

Hospitalization for such crises should be kept as brief as possible, however, ideally not more than a few days to two or three weeks. Going to a hospital is often difficult: you may feel constricted and suffocated when you enter, and angry that it is unjustified. On having to leave, though, the symbolic abandonment can trigger another self-destructive episode.

Some hospital programs specialize in treating people with borderline personality, especially adolescents and young adults. But hospital-based treatment has come under criticism as unnecessary and too expensive (much of the criticism has come from insurance companies and health plans, which are reluctant to pay the high rates that hospitalization entails).

Complements to individual psychotherapy. In addition to one-to-one therapy, group therapy can also be helpful. But it should not start until after you have formed a strong working relationship with your therapist. Being in a group offers you the chance to practice interacting with and confronting people in a more balanced way.

If it is especially hard for you to manage day-to-day life, you may also benefit from a day hospital or day treatment program, or from living for a while in an independent but supervised setting such as a halfway house.

If you are young and still in close contact with your family or living at home, family therapy may also be beneficial. This is especially true if a stormy relationship with your parents is a major problem.

Medication. Psychiatric medications can be useful to help with specific symptoms that often accompany this personality disorder: depression, anxiety, anger, and sometimes, psychotic episodes. But medication will not change the underlying patterns that bring on your problems—therapy does.

The Perfectionist (Obsessive-Compulsive Personality Disorder)

The perfectionist becomes obsessed with a given thought or preoccupation; their diligence is driven and compulsive. The technical name for this personality disorder is "obsessive-compulsive." However, an obsessive-compulsive personality is quite different from an obsessive-compulsive disorder (see p. 531), in which a person becomes haunted by *obsessions*—thoughts that are often groundless that persist and intrude on other thoughts—or in which a person is bound by *compulsions* to endless repetitions of ritualistic acts. By contrast, perfectionists suffer no delusional ideas, and while they can be dogged, their efforts are aimed at real tasks. However, people with this character trait are strongly predisposed to developing a full obsessive-compulsive disorder.

To be sure, perfectionists can do quite well at work, even excel, and can be highly productive, but they can also be inflexible. Perfectionists see one way to do things: the "right" way, i.e., their way. They can be dictatorial and frustratingly stubborn, refusing even to consider alternatives. That attitude, of course, creates great friction at work, in a family, or in a couple.

The perfectionist is often a workaholic, a trait that is rewarded at work with praise and promotions. But the person who habitually works evenings and Saturdays, then brings home work on Sundays, has little, if any, room left for sociability, meaningful relationships, or a family life.

Perhaps the most troubling trait of perfectionists for people in relationships with them is how overcontrolled they are in their ability to feel or express emotions. They have great difficulty expressing warmth or tenderness, rarely if ever cry, and usually find it hard to laugh. They may manage a dutiful "I love you" from time to time, but rarely express that emotion spontaneously. They find little enjoyment in life.

Perfectionists are dogged in their pursuit of duty, but paradoxically, if they have to grapple with a problem on their own, they freeze. They are far more comfortable being told what to do and executing it.

On the other hand, once a decision is made, they are ferociously thorough in sticking to it and applying the rules. Indeed, they are often moralistic and judgmental, interested in the letter of the law, not its spirit.

Their concentration on detail is intense and relentless, and they make excellent accountants, computer programmers, and mechanics. But in a situation where intuition, tenderness, making a big decision, or adapting to changing circumstances is called for, the perfectionist is often at a loss.

Signs to Look For

- Unreasonably high standards that undermine actually getting a task accomplished.
- Fixation on details, rules, and organization, while losing touch with the major goal of the effort.
- Dogmatic and overbearing in insisting that things be done exactly their way.
- Workaholism, placing more value on getting work done than on personal relationships, leisure, and other obligations.
- Difficulty making decisions: putting them off and relying on others to decide.
- Rigidly moralistic.
- Unemotional; little sense of humor.
- Tightfisted and reluctant to lend a hand except for personal return.
- Hoarding things long after they have served their use.

□ Edward is the successful editor of a magazine for lawyers. He rose to the top out of sheer dogged dedication: he habitually works fifteen hours a day, coming in at six A.M. and going home at nine P.M. However, his wife is threatening divorce.

She complains that she never sees him during the week, that he spends most of Saturday at the office, and half of Sunday in his office at home. They haven't taken a vacation in ten years. She complains of his lack of expressiveness and affection. Though they see each other mainly in bed, he never seems to be in the mood to make love. Instead he spends his time reading over articles for the magazine, until he falls asleep.

At work, Edward has trouble deciding which article to use, how it should be edited, and what to title it. He is most comfortable making grammatical corrections and looking for spelling errors, work he should delegate to a copy editor but refuses to. His staff is up in arms because he keeps putting off decisions they need him to make.

What You Should Know About Therapy

The most appropriate therapy for perfectionism is individual and long-term. But psychodynamic therapies that dwell on the causes of a problem can be slow-going.

Perfectionists tend to swamp their therapists with details. Instead of connecting thoughts with feelings, which should be one of the major goals of their therapy, perfectionists may use their insights as rationalizations to explain away their behavior.

What you need in therapy is to focus on how you are feeling at this moment, how you treated a situation yesterday, what you can do differently tomorrow. You need to measure your progress in concrete changes in your actions, not in insights.

Group therapy, too, can be beneficial. Since much of what you are seeking to change about yourself has to do with your relationships, the group can offer a social microcosm where you can have your behavior reflected back to you with candor, and you can try out new ways of relating.

There is no medication for the character traits that constitute this disorder. Medication will be prescribed only if an actual obsessive-compulsive disorder emerges, or if accompanying symptoms of anxiety or depression become severe.

The Dramatic Person (Histrionic Personality Disorder)

People with histrionic personality disorder are highly dramatic and demanding of attention. Life is an ongoing drama; minor crises become major catastrophes. They not only overreact, but they tend to exaggerate their own reaction. This used to be identified as a "hysteric" personality style. Because of its negative and sexist connotations, that term has now been dropped.

The stereotype of the dramatic personality is the superficial and demanding actress who is happy only when she is center stage and everyone else is caught up in her drama. She can be utterly charming and seductive, but when thwarted, she becomes enraged. If her boyfriend so much as looks at another woman, she stalks out; if she gets a bad review, she threatens suicide.

Histrionic people tend to jump to conclusions based on first impressions rather than gathering facts to make an informed decision. They are often gullible and easily become dependent on someone else for guidance in daily life. They find it hard to concentrate for very long and are prone to physical complaints that have no basis in a medical disorder.

In relationships, the main complaints about them are their stormy emotions, flightiness, and shallowness. They often put much effort into making themselves sexually attractive, though they may be dismayed if someone takes them up on what seems like an invitation to intimacy.

Histrionic personality disorder is most often diagnosed in women, and in effeminate men. But this may be due in part to a gender and cultural bias that does not recognize the pattern as easily in men.

Signs to Look For

- Seeking reassurance, praise, or approval as though playing to an audience.
- Sexually seductive in appearance and bearing, often inappropriately so.
- Preoccupation with appearance and attractiveness.
- Exaggerated emotional expressiveness, overly dramatic in conversation.
- Self-centered attention-seeking, unhappy if not the focus of attention.
- Shallow emotions that change capriciously.
- Demanding instant gratification of desires and whims; low tolerance for frustration.
- Impressionable and suggestible, with little grasp of details.

□ Eleanor was the life of the party and always had been. In adolescence she was flirtatious, sexually precocious, and dressed and wore makeup beyond her years.

She has never had any close friendships with women, whom she sees as rivals. Women are afraid she will go after their boyfriends. She dresses in an attractive, even seductive manner and is extremely outgoing with men. But once a man gets serious about her, she is likely to be catching someone else's eye.

Eleanor works in a beauty shop but may soon be fired, as she has been many times before. Her coworkers complain she is self-centered, thoughtless, and demanding. She often shows up late or not at all. She hopes to set up her own shop one day, but just can't seem to focus on the business arrangements. When she talks about her problems, Eleanor comes to tears easily, but stops just as quickly; moods never seem to last very long with her.

What You Should Know About Therapy

As with most personality problems, the approach of choice is individual, psychodynamic therapy, usually once a week. The goals of therapy include getting some control over the excessive emotional reactions, and to understand how the habitual "center stage" approach to people undermines relationships and work life. Other goals include developing self-assurance in order to be less demanding of attention;

approaching things less haphazardly; and expressing emotions in a more appropriate manner.

Group therapy can also be quite beneficial. The group offers the chance to learn directly how you come across, and to try new ways of being with other people.

No medication will help in the treatment of this personality disorder. However, medication might be prescribed for specific accompanying symptoms such as anxiety or depression.

The Dependent Person (Dependent Personality Disorder)

Every healthy individual has an emotional need for other people. We all want to be taken care of when we're ill, or even when we're just feeling down. A common occasional fantasy is of someone coming to our rescue or taking on the burdens of life for us. But those who are overly dependent have that wish all the time. Such people dread being on their own; it makes them feel helpless or scared.

Such people often manage to find someone else to take care of them: a relative, parents, a spouse. If that person should abandon the arrangement, they are vulnerable to depression. Apart from that, dependent people are particularly susceptible to anxiety, to drug or alcohol abuse, and to a general sense of being out of sorts and unhappy.

Many dependent people are fine, even highly productive, while they are being supervised closely or when they feel taken care of emotionally. Left on their own, they fall apart.

Dependent people need at least one key, sustaining relationship, a person on whom they count on for direction, security, and stability. To the partner in the relationship, the dependent person is a loyal and devoted companion, eager to please, but also often demanding of attention and overindulgence. Dependent people feel such an intense need for a partner, they are easily manipulated and dominated or even physically abused in their intimate relationships.

The problem that brings most dependent people to treatment is an intense disturbance, such as anxiety, depression, or drug or alcohol abuse. But the trigger for this problem is usually the loss of someone they depended on.

Signs to Look For

- Being unable to make decisions without guidance from someone else, including everyday decisions and major life decisions.
- Fear of rejection leads to agreeing with others even when they are wrong.
- Lack of initiative and inability to do things alone.

- Intense need to please, offering to do unpleasant things in order to be liked.
- Fear of being alone; going to extremes in order to be with someone else; often becoming obsessed with the fear of being left.
- Dreading the end of a dependent relationship; feeling devastated, helpless, or depressed when such a relationship ends.
- Craving approval; deeply hurt if criticized.

☐ At age forty-eight Ralph still lived at home with his parents. His domineering father lorded it over Ralph and his mother. While Ralph had spent two years away at college, he had transferred to a local college in his third year so he could continue to live at home.

From college Ralph went straight to work as a salesman in his father's furniture store, giving up his aspirations for a career in architecture. Over the years he has had several job offers from others in the furniture industry, but he preferred to stay in the family business.

Although he has occasionally dated and once had a girlfriend he thought of marrying, his father found the girl unworthy and vetoed the plan. Ralph's social life revolves around a bowling team the store sponsors, which includes several friends he has known since boyhood.

When Ralph's father had a heart attack and was hospitalized for several months, Ralph became intensely anxious and depressed. He was unable to go into the store to work, feeling that he didn't "know what to do."

What You Should Know About Therapy

The goal of therapy is to increase your sense of autonomy and assertiveness, and your ability to function well on your own. That means, for instance, being able to make large and small decisions without needing constant reassurance, or being able to be content by yourself without experiencing anxiety and depression.

No specific therapy approach is recommended—a behavior therapy may be as effective as a psychodynamic one, so long as it includes your finally taking the risk to change the patterns in your relationships. When you begin to assert your own feelings, you may feel torn between your therapist's encouragement to be assertive and your fear of losing a relationship, but this is a crisis you may have to face. Even so, your therapist should respect your feelings of attachment and help you find the pace for change that is workable for you.

Since the therapy relationship is a microcosm of others in your life, you are sure to form a dependency of sorts on your therapist. But it should gradually become a healthy dependency, one in which you work with your therapist to free yourself to some degree from a crippling reliance on others. The final "crisis" in therapy may be the moment you end your relationship with your therapist—an experience that in itself can be therapeutic for you.

The Withdrawn Person (Avoidant Personality Disorder)

While everyone may feel shy from time to time, for the withdrawn person the fear of being rejected is a private agony. The dread of being criticized or judged by others is so strong, such people lead a life of social withdrawal, even though they crave affection and acceptance. Because they tend to avoid unnecessary social contacts, the technical term for people with this trait is "avoidant personality disorder."

The withdrawn person is distinct from the person who has a *social phobia* (see p. 495). The phobic person fears specific social situations such as speaking in public; the withdrawn person is anxious about them *all*. Understandably, however, social phobias are common in the withdrawn person.

For instance, in order to feel safe in a relationship, the avoidant person needs especially strong assurances that he or she will be accepted uncritically. It takes a long time—often years—for such people to develop enough trust to be comfortable with someone. Their friendships tend to be with their own relatives and a handful of people whom they have known for a long time.

Part of the difficulty is a low sense of self-worth, popularly known as an "inferiority complex." If you have this trait, you are often self-effacing, feel a lack of self-confidence when you are talking with someone, and are continually afraid of being criticized. You are most likely timid about speaking up in groups or making a request of anyone, and hypersensitive to slights.

Your need for friends and relationships, coupled with your fear of rejection, may lead you to be overly compliant, always seeking to please others. At work, you are likely to seek jobs for which you are overqualified but that demand little contact with people and consequently can be done with little or no risk of criticism.

Signs to Look For

- Hypersensitivity to criticism; being hurt easily.
- Lack of friends other than relatives and reluctance to enter new relationships unless certain of being accepted.
- Avoiding social contacts and shunning activities that bring contact with other people.
- Reticence and timidity in social situations; fear of seeming foolish or being judged.
- Fear of embarrassment or of showing signs of nervousness such as blushing.

☐ Maxine had worked in a library for fifteen years at a small college in the town where she had grown up. She had started in the job, cataloguing new acquisitions, after graduating from high school. She worked behind the scenes with two librarians.

Because of her experience, Maxine was offered a promotion to oversee both her own department and the library checkout desk. While the job was far better than the one she had, the very thought of having to deal with subordinates and people checking out books made Maxine tremble with anxiety.

All her life Maxine had been shy. In high school she was known as a wallflower. She would sometimes feign illness and stay home from school if she knew she had to speak in front of a class. She refused to go to college, making up a series of excuses to cover her dread of having to meet a sea of new faces. Her only friends were two women she had known since kindergarten. She had dated just twice.

She ended up declining the job offer.

What You Should Know About Therapy

For the avoidant person, a relationship with a therapist can be frightening at first—like any other relationship. The most effective approach is support for your specific day-to-day challenges, and gentle guidance in becoming more outgoing. The goal of therapy is to help you overcome the obstacles to the social life you desire.

You want a therapist who will understand your special sensitivity to criticism and respect your need for extra reassurance. Do your best to make these needs known, and give the therapist a session or two to recognize them. If you feel from the start that a therapist is not sensitive enough or is too confrontational, then try someone else.

Be patient with your anxieties about trusting someone you do not yet know. Expect that trust will develop gradually, and that you will have many moments of doubt, fear, and the wish to stop.

As you develop trust and feel ready, you should begin to move out into the world in small, safe ways. Your feeling of readiness is crucial; you and your therapist should discuss it to determine whether your reaching out is proceeding at a pace you can tolerate and learn from.

Assertiveness training, in which you learn to express your wishes openly, without being too passive or too demanding, may be especially useful. Another technique is behavior modification, in which you purposely put yourself in the situations you have been avoiding, one step at a time, to gradually conquer your fears. Group therapy can be helpful, but only if your sensitivity to slights and rejections is respected. If so, the group can be an excellent place to practice social skills to help you gain confidence with other people.

The Passive-Aggressive Person (Passive-Aggressive Personality Disorder)

Certain people have a way of frustrating and angering others by agreeing to do something but never actually getting around to it, or doing so only with great reluctance and after much prodding. The other person—parent, spouse, teacher, boss, coworker—experiences their passivity as aggressive. Most people express aggressive feeling by *doing* something; these individuals express aggressive feelings by *not doing* something. Their apparent passivity allows them to conceal and disown their aggression—even from themselves.

By refusing to take responsibility for what they are supposed to do, such people in effect become dependent on the angry urgings and complaints of others for motivation. Other people, in exasperation, often end up doing their chores for them and feeling resentful.

Indeed, passive-aggressive individuals often derive a degree of sadistic pleasure from the irritation they cause others. Unlike the obsessive person, who simply cannot make up his mind, this individual actually tries to provoke others by his continuous vacillation.

The pattern can wax and wane throughout life and tends to collect several associated difficulties, including irritability, anxiety, depression, alcoholism, and substance abuse. For obvious reasons, such people usually have a lifelong history of troubled relationships at home, at school, and at work.

Signs to Look For

The key trait is a stubborn unwillingness to comply with obligations. The signs include:

- Procrastination: not meeting deadlines, putting everything off until the last possible moment, or seeking an extension by pleading some complaint.
- Sulkiness when asked to do something that is part of his or her responsibilities. Resenting being asked and arguing about it.
- Deliberate dawdling or sabotaging of a task that he or she resents doing.
- Unjustified protests of unfairness regarding a reasonable request.
- Convenient "forgetting" of deadlines, requests, and the like.
- Overestimating how well he or she has done on a task.
- Resenting advice on how he or she could improve.
- Sabotaging a group effort.
- Scornful of those who try to help or who are in a position of authority over them.

□ Harold, a lawyer, was in danger of losing his position at the large law firm where he had worked for five years. He was chronically late to work and appointments, even with important clients; was sometimes days or weeks late on legal briefs; balked on taking advice on the cases he handled; and would not turn in his records for client billing for months at a time.

Harold had been willful since childhood. When he played with other children, he would insist that they play the games he chose or he would have a tantrum. In school he did outstanding work for teachers he liked, but would not turn in a single assignment if he resented the teacher. Often his intelligence allowed him to do things his own way. But when he couldn't, he wouldn't.

Harold was married for a year, but it ended in divorce. His wife became completely exasperated with his "forgetting" to do chores he had promised he would take care of. He said she was a "bitch" who was "always trying to control me and tell me what to do." Harold seemed to find a certain satisfaction in describing how his forgetting to do things made his wife frustrated and angry.

What You Should Know About Therapy

The most fruitful therapy for passive-aggressive people is a supportive, individual approach. They are likely, of course, to resist therapy when others whom they continually thwart suggest it to them: it is simply another opportunity to passively battle. However, they do become genuinely distressed by the resentments and difficulties they breed for themselves, and therapy can be presented as a solution.

If you are passive aggressive, you may find yourself doing subtle battle with your therapist, even though you actually want help. You may postpone paying your bills, come late, find fault with what the therapist says, or quit therapy before it is done.

Expect your therapist to keep pointing out the consequences of your passive aggressiveness. A pragmatic approach, where your therapist helps you deal with situations as they arise in your day-to-day life, will be more immediately helpful than trying to explore the origins of your stubbornness.

Some people with this pattern become so depressed by their personal relationships that they become suicidal. In such cases, treatment may include antidepressants or hospitalization, but no medication is beneficial for passive-aggressive traits themselves.

The Emotionally Detached Person (Schizoid Personality Disorder)

The detached person has a lifelong pattern of social withdrawal and isolation. In part this isolation is preferred: such people tend to be shy. But it is also the result of their lack of emotionality: other people experience them as detached and aloof. But their aloofness is due to their shyness.

Throughout their life, such people have few friends and seem indifferent or insensitive to what others feel. They tend to develop solitary interests and are most comfortable in work that puts them in contact with few people.

They strike others as not just quiet and reserved, but unconcerned about sociability. As they go through life, they show little longing for emotional closeness to others and seem content being on their own. Criticism or praise, or feelings in general, are of little concern to them.

Detached people sometimes seem "spacey" or "in a fog" to other people. They seldom marry or even date; their dispassion extends to sex. But they can put impressive energy into abstract activities, such as science or mathematics. And despite their emotional detachment, they can make genuine contributions in the fields they choose to pursue.

Though it's not apparent, behind their detachment they typically lead very active fantasy lives. They may spend a lot of time daydreaming, which sometimes makes it hard for them to concentrate on the task they are engaged in. Their mind tends to wander off into reveries of accomplishments, intimacy, sex, power, prestige, and position—everything they don't have in the real world. This world of fantasy is a place of refuge they can escape to, much more vivid and compelling than the life they are actually living. And yet they know these are only fantasies that will never be realized, no matter how soothing or consoling for a time—ultimately only making their isolation and detachment more painfully apparent.

The detached personality style usually begins in early childhood as extreme shyness. By adulthood, such people usually find a comfortable niche in life and are not especially disturbed by the traits that make them so socially withdrawn. For instance, they are often at peace with their social isolation, rather than feeling extremely lonely. Because this trait is not disturbing, they rarely seek therapy on their own.

Signs to Look For

The key indicator is an indifference to other people and to emotions. The main signs include:

- Socially distant, neither seeking close friendships or intimate relationships, nor minding being on the social fringe.
- Preference for solitary pursuits, including being comfortable in activities with long periods of isolation or few social contacts.
- Emotional flatness; coolness and aloofness; unresponsive to emotions in conversation; never seeming to feel extremes such as anger or excitement.
- Lack of interest in sex or in romantic relationships.
- Few, if any, close friends apart from immediate family.
- Unswayed by criticism or praise from others, and unresponsive to their feelings.

☐ As a child, Lloyd kept to himself. Through school he made few friends and preferred to spend his spare time alone reading rather than out playing. He did well in school, although he was reticent about speaking up in class.

When he was a young man, Lloyd's family pressured him to get married or at least to date. But his few attempts at dating never led to a second date, and he gave up trying.

Lloyd, now in his fifties, has settled into a routine he rarely varies. Weekdays he works nine to five in the catalogue department of a university library. While he is cordial to his coworkers, he keeps his distance. After work he walks to a diner where he sits alone and has one or two favorite meals: meat loaf or a hamburger. He then goes home to his small apartment and watches television until he falls asleep. On Sundays he calls his sister, who lives in the next state, and has a conversation that is more or less the same every week.

While on the outside Lloyd seems to be untroubled, he sometimes feels miserable being so isolated and wishes he could make better contact with people.

What Therapists Recommend

Approach. The favored approach is supportive therapy, typically combined with a psychodynamic approach.

Medication. There is no medication that helps the main traits of the detached personality, though some medications may help with anxiety in certain cases.

Setting. Therapy normally takes place in the office or clinic.

Format. Individual therapy is the usual format.

Frequency. Once-a-week sessions are the norm, though frequency—and length of sessions—depends in part on how much contact is tolerable.

Duration. Open-ended; often several years or more if the underlying pattern of detachment and emotional withdrawal is to be addressed.

What You Should Know About Therapy

Those with a strong trait of detachment rarely seek therapy on their own. If they come to therapy they are usually there because someone else has strongly urged them to go. If you are one of these people and have been told by your therapist that you have this kind of personality pattern, your relationship with your therapist may be the beginning of building more ties with other people, which should be one of the main goals of therapy for you.

While individual therapy is the best format, at some point when you feel ready for it, you may want to join a therapy group or other group activity that will give you the chance to interact with more people.

Expect your therapy to be long-term—if you want to work on these personality traits—and to focus in the beginning on supporting you in your day-to-day challenges. Expect, too, that it will take quite some time before you begin to feel real trust in your therapist. And don't worry about long silences during your sessions—

they're natural for someone trying to overcome a trait of detachment. But you want a therapist who is comfortable with such silences, too.

It will not be helpful, though, to be in therapy with someone who pushes you to "get in touch with your feelings" before you feel ready. If you feel uneasy about your interactions with your therapist, you should discuss those feelings with him or her as frankly as you can.

If you join a therapy or other group, you may find yourself reluctant to join in at first—maybe for quite a while—watching and listening rather than saying much. Ideally, the other group members should be comfortable with your long silences and not push you into being more actively involved than you feel ready for.

No medication will directly change a trait of detachment. Mild tranquilizers may help you if you feel anxious at times, but only for brief periods. No other medications are appropriate.

The Overly Suspicious Person (Paranoid Personality Disorder)

People who are intensely suspicious of just about everyone have a "paranoid personality disorder." They see the world in terms of real or possible conspiracies against them.

While other people who have suspicions will abandon them when contradictory evidence presents itself, not so the overly suspicious person. Their belief that the world is hostile, filled with devious people and enemies, is beyond question. This leaves them chronically vigilant for signs of hostility or unfairness. They are quick to take offense and easily angered. Criticism or even a slight contradiction raises their hackles. However, they are quick to find fault in others and are often critical and judgmental.

Typically, people with such a paranoid bent will seize on some slim evidence of an injustice, blow it out of all proportion, and distort the facts to prove their point. They are often litigious and may be involved in several lawsuits at one time.

Despite their paranoia, such people are often bright and manage to fit in, though they typically have a reputation for being difficult. Such people are not psychotic and so do not go to the extremes seen in delusional disorder (see p. 548). They are, however, likely to have chronic difficulties with certain kinds of people: those in authority, such as a supervisor at work, and those who try to become emotionally close, such as a lover or spouse. Such people easily become the target of the suspicious person's resentment and mistrust, and a long history of broken relationships and lost—or quit—jobs is often the result.

A person with an overly suspicious personality will almost always resist the idea that he or she is, indeed, overly suspicious or might need psychotherapy or any other kind of help.

Signs to Look For

- Expecting to be exploited, tricked, or cheated.
- Vigilance for signs of threat or exploitation, or taking unnecessary precautions to guard against them.
- Suspecting friends, family, or associates of disloyalty or betrayal; jealousy.
- Seeing hidden meanings in events that make them seem threatening or insulting; taking things out of their context to support suspicions.
- Holding grudges and finding it hard to forgive people once they have given offense; never really making peace with an "enemy."
- Quick to anger; counterattacking at the slightest provocation, even imagined ones.
- Secretive and guarded; will not confide in anyone.
- Cold and aloof; little sense of humor, especially about himself or herself; emotionally unresponsive, especially to tenderness.

□ Gerald was a lawyer, a profession that suited him well. Though an effective courtroom opponent, Gerald ran into problems from the start of his career. He quit the first firm he worked for in a rage, sure that the partners who ran the firm were conspiring to cheat him out of a promotion and a raise he deserved. He then went into partnership with another lawyer, but before the first year was out, Gerald accused his partner of cheating.

Gerald ended up working alone. But his enemies list grew over the years. Certain judges, he was sure, were against him. Other lawyers were conspiring against him; he could tell because they would become quiet when he entered a room. His own accountant, he was sure, lied to him about how much he owed in taxes.

Taking his suspicions seriously, Gerald began to sue people he suspected of injustices. Gradually his own lawsuits took over his practice: he was suing so many people that he spent only a third of his time working on other cases.

What You Should Know About Therapy

Individual psychotherapy is the best format, but there are obvious difficulties. One is getting the suspicious person to admit that anything is wrong; another is getting him or her to trust a therapist.

Typically trust develops slowly, over several months or more. It helps if the therapist is straightforward and open. For example, if the therapist makes a mistake such as being late for an appointment, he or she should acknowledge it, apologize, and get on with the session. The best kind of therapist here is gentle, respectful, and professional.

Group therapy is generally not advisable. Therapy groups can be too confrontational or demand too much emotional involvement for the suspicious person to feel at ease.

Once you and the therapist have established a rapport, you can begin to explore together the specific problems that the suspiciousness is causing. The more concrete that exploration, the better. One goal of therapy is to allow you to see things from another perspective, to get a corrective view that will help you realize that there are other ways of seeing things.

Medications are useful only to control episodes of extreme agitation or anxiety.

The Eccentric Personality (Schizotypal Personality Disorder)

Some people seem "odd," "spacey," or "strange," but are not schizophrenic. They get along all right, though they are prone to eccentric habits, beliefs, or involvements. They may claim to have contact with the supernatural—be clairvoyant or have other magical powers. They tend to join fringe, cultish groups. Such people hold strong beliefs that resemble the delusions seen in schizophrenia, but they are otherwise completely rational and have none of the cognitive deficits or other problems of schizophrenia.

These people often keep to themselves, living alone or having few friends. One common belief among such people is that they or other people are not "real," but are, for instance, aliens from another planet. Understandably, they have trouble making emotional connections.

Their behavior may sometimes appear schizophrenic, but is not. They do not have hallucinations, and while they may subscribe to odd beliefs, they are able to make their way in the world without falling victim to confusion or agitation. On the other hand, many people with schizophrenia who are between acute episodes resemble this personality disorder.

Some do finally develop schizophrenia, but they are a minority. However, the pattern is especially common among relatives of schizophrenics, and there may be a common genetic basis.

Signs to Look For

- Unusual beliefs and bizarre fantasies, such as having the ability to read minds or tell the future, or of being "an agent from outer space," for example.
- Odd perceptions, such as "sensing forces" of people or things that are not present.
- Strange appearance or oddities of behavior, such as muttering to oneself or being chronically sloppy and somewhat disheveled in dressing.
- Strange ways of speaking, such as vagueness or speaking in long, abstract digressions.
- Inappropriate emotions; being unable to match another person's mood (e.g., being silly when the other person is sad), being aloof, being "off" in responses.

- Social discomfort and anxiety about being with others; often keeping to oneself.
- Reading meanings into things, especially seeing a reference to oneself that is not there.

☐ Sally was strange from childhood. By junior high she had a reputation for oddities and social awkwardness. Once she went up to a boy she liked, poked her finger in his chest, and said, "Bzz, bzz, I'm a buzz saw," then ran off. When she was called on in class, her responses were no less unpredictable.

By her college years, Sally was regarded as "spacey." She claimed she could see people's auras, that she could read their thoughts, and that she had a special mission to establish contact with visitors from another galaxy. She would spend long hours alone, lost in fantasy. She tried to work as a waitress, but would confuse the orders or simply forget them, staring off into space, lost in thought. By the time she was twenty-five, Sally was on welfare, living in a dingy apartment filled with books on the occult.

What You Should Know About Therapy

People with schizotypal personality disorder do not change much in therapy, though they may learn to get along better. Such people can become anxious if they are pushed too hard to change, or to express strong feelings. Psychodynamic therapy is not recommended. A supportive, social-skills-oriented therapy is most appropriate. The best therapist is one who will not seem to criticize or ridicule eccentric beliefs, but who can help you address day-to-day problems and can foster better contacts with others.

Hospitalization is normally neither necessary nor helpful. It can make such people even more socially withdrawn. However, sheltered workshops or day treatment programs can help draw them out.

Medications are typically not appropriate, either. The side effects of antipsychotic medications (see p. 622) outweigh their advantages, although such medications in low doses can sometimes diminish disturbing symptoms such as anxiety, minor delusions, or a feeling of being "unreal." But the medications will not help the core problem or improve social relations and should only be used as an aid to supportive psychotherapy.

The Antisocial Person (Antisocial Personality Disorder)

The antisocial person is often charming and extremely adept socially, but at bottom lacks any genuine concern for the feelings or rights of other people. The hallmark is an underdeveloped conscience; his life centers around satisfying his own desires, acting on impulse, and being guided by whim. Often the antisocial person has a long history of major or minor brushes with the law.

In the past, other terms have been used: *sociopath* and *psychopath*. The term *antisocial* captures the key feature, a willingness to break standards or laws to get what one wants, but it is slightly misleading. Such people are not necessarily rebels or at odds with established rules; if they can get what they want without bending the rules, then they will play by them.

What causes an antisocial personality to develop is uncertain. Such people are found in a variety of cultures, in families rich and poor, with no specific style of childrearing. One theory holds that the antisocial person suffers from an anomaly in brain function that makes them relatively fearless and unable to empathize with other people's feelings—a combination that makes it easy to be ruthless.

In boys, antisocial behavior shows up in childhood in such things as lies, stealing, and skipping school. In the relatively few women who become antisocial, the pattern doesn't emerge until adolescence, when it typically shows up in drinking and drugs, promiscuity, and truancy.

Though many youngsters and adolescents go through periods of getting in trouble, for the antisocial person getting in trouble is a steady trait throughout life. An antisocial boy who steals bikes in childhood will steal cars as a teenager and rob stores in adulthood. An antisocial person is irresponsible and uncaring about others in everything he does, and throughout life. The peak years for antisocial activities are the twenties through the forties. After that, many antisocial people settle down, though many continue as alcoholics or drug abusers.

Although they are reckless and impulsive, antisocial people are perfectly rational. Whether by intimidation, persuasion, or deception, they are expert at manipulation. Such people are especially glib and experts at "conning," able to shift effortlessly into whatever pose will work for the person they are with at the moment. They are particularly adept at reading and responding to social cues, which enables them to be charming while opportunistically looking for the main chance.

Antisocial people have a shallow emotional life, devoid of love, loyalty, or caring. They are also devoid of guilt or shame. They have a lifelong history of casual relationships and temporary partners, but no lasting friendships. They may marry for expediency, but will not be a devoted spouse or parent. They are likely to be exploitive, neglecting, or abusive with anyone in an intimate relationship.

The antisocial person is oriented to immediate gratification. His life is a continuing saga of jobs left, lovers deserted, bills unpaid, temptations pursued. The antisocial person takes the easy way, whether it be cheating on exams or petty crime.

While not all criminals have an antisocial personality, the large majority of antisocial people flirt with crime, if they do not pursue it full-time. While they can tell right from wrong, they simply do not care: their interest is in what will work to get them what they want, whether it is forgery, lies, seduction, their fists, or someone else's money.

Because antisocial people are glib and artful in telling others what they want to hear, they may sometimes seem to have insight into their problems or to feel some remorse. But this is a pose and does not change their ways.

Signs to Look For

- Childhood troublemaking, such as petty theft, cutting school, acting up in school, fights, running away from home, setting fires, vandalism.
- Trouble with authorities, usually from childhood: a history of arrests, suspension or expulsion from school, fired from work for breaking rules.
- Promiscuity: history of one-night stands and a chain of short-lived romantic involvements.
- Cruelty: a bully or cruel to animals in childhood, forced sex or assaultiveness in adolescence and adulthood.
- Financial irresponsibility: bad checks, loans unpaid, failure to support children.
- Failure to hold jobs: out of work for long periods, quitting jobs impulsively, absent with no good reason.
- Lawbreaking such as harassment, theft, property destruction.
- Assaultiveness, such as picking fights, beating one's children and/or spouse.
- Impulsiveness and general lack of planning, sometimes indicated by wandering aimlessly from place to place or job to job or relationship to relationship.
- Recklessness, such as driving dangerously or while drunk, thoughtlessness about taking care of others' property.
- Lying and con games.
- Irresponsibility as a parent.
- Remorselessness over the consequences to others of what one does; a sense of being justified in hurting others.

□ Gerald first got in trouble at eight, when he was caught stealing a bicycle at the local pool. Being arrested did not discourage him; at nine he was caught again, this time for a series of thefts from teachers' desks at school. He reacted to being suspended by seizing the opportunity to sneak into the rooms of schoolmates and stealing toys. When Gerald was twelve he forced the girl next door to have sex. At thirteen he stole his first car. The next year saw Gerald's first robbery.

When confronted with what he had done, Gerald always denied it, then, when the evidence was overwhelming, said, "They had it coming." Although he often feigned remorse when he thought it would win him sympathy, Gerald never really seemed to feel it. Despite his criminal history, Gerald was charming, able to talk his way out of almost anything. He never lacked companions or girlfriends, though he was constantly moving on to new people as those close to him started to catch on to his lies.

By his late teens, Gerald had established himself as a cocaine dealer, and was seen around town in flashy clothes and a Mercedes. He carried a gun, and would often pick fights in bars. If someone dared to start fighting, Gerald would pull his gun. When he was finally arrested and sentenced to his first stint in prison, Gerald seemed to change. He joined the prison choir, said he had "found the Lord," and became a model prisoner.

But when he was paroled, he fled the state, took a false identity, and started dealing drugs all over again.

What Therapists Recommend

Approach. Behavior therapy, usually with a straightforward agreement or contract on what the specific target behaviors for change are.

Medication. There is no medication that is effective for the main traits of the antisocial person.

Setting. Outpatient, if the person will cooperate.

Format. Individual therapy, usually in combination with a group.

Frequency. Once a week is the norm.

Duration. Open-ended: the patterns of the antisocial person do not change easily or quickly, if at all.

What You Should Know About Therapy

Antisocial people almost never enter therapy on their own, and no psychotherapy has been found particularly effective with the antisocial person. For one, such people do not agree that they have a problem that needs therapy. They feel perfectly comfortable with their traits, disturbing as these are to others. They are more likely to see therapy as a joke or an opportunity to gain some advange or escape blame, and to see the therapist as someone to con, seduce, or otherwise use.

Likewise, if such people are in an "insight" therapy, where causes for their irresponsibility are sought in childhood, those insights may become justifications for them for what they do rather than leading to any change in their ways. If, as sometimes happens to them in correctional institutions, they are coerced into treatment, they may pretend to be helped, until they are once again in a position to take advantage of someone.

From time to time, though, antisocial people may see the destructive course they follow and want to change. But as with most other things, they tend to approach therapy in search of instant results. They find it hard to put sustained effort into it.

But antisocial people are not free from suffering. They do feel sadness and anxiety on occasion, though they typically try to escape it by seeking solace in thrills of one kind or another. In therapy they may come to experience the pain they feel without escaping into instant gratification, and to realize the consequences of their impulsiveness and irresponsibility. But the most reasonable goals for therapy are a limited increase in self-awareness and self-control. Therapeutic failures with antisocial people are legion.

Antisocial people sometimes respond with positive change when they are part of a community that sets limits on them and holds them responsible for what they do by directly confronting irresponsibility. But even then they may have problems maintaining the improvement after they leave and live once again on their own.

CHAPTER EIGHTEEN

◼

IF YOU NEED MEDICATION

By Eliot Gelwan, M.D.

If your therapist suggests taking medicine, you should be aware of several general issues. In addition, you should know the specifics of the medication you will be using: its benefits, its drawbacks, what to expect, and what to watch out for.

Medication is most often useful in conjunction with psychotherapy, in "combined treatment," i.e., the shared treatment of a patient between two clinicians, one responsible for the psychotherapy and the other—a physician, a psychiatrist, or psychopharmacologist—for medicating the patient. In such cases you work with your therapist, but go to a "medicating doctor," who oversees your psychiatric drugs and reports back to your therapist. Of course, if you are in therapy with a psychiatrist, there is no need for a medicating doctor.

The decision to try medication is often made after therapy has begun. The medicating doctor's role is that of a consultant to the ongoing psychotherapy. This may occur relatively early in therapy if a therapist suspects a strong biological component to the patient's distress or if the patient's symptoms are too disruptive to therapy. Another reason to try medication is for diagnostic clarification; for instance, some forms of depression respond to certain medications.

Often, however, the issue of medication will arise further along in psychotherapy.

Sometimes this is because the growing closeness and trust in the therapy relationship has allowed painful feelings to emerge, amplifying the patient's distress. A difficult or stormy therapy relationship can also prompt a therapist to consider medication. And sometimes only well into the unfolding of the therapy, as the therapist has gotten to know a patient better, does the suspicion arise of a biologically treatable disorder.

If you think that medication might help you, and your therapist has not suggested it, bring it up. If your therapist agrees, too, but does not prescribe medications, you can request a "medication consultation" with a psychiatrist or psychopharmacologist.

Finding the right medication, or the right dose, always involves trial and error. Even a diagnosis made by rigorous psychiatric criteria does not automatically imply you will benefit from medication. Patients classified under the same diagnosis may react very differently if medicated the same. Thus there is not a one-to-one correlation between a given diagnosis and a specific medication. Diagnosis does not imply a certain treatment.

If not by diagnosis, then on what basis are medication decisions made? The alternative is to target symptoms—the specific problems you have, such as insomnia or lethargy. The effectiveness of medications is much more closely related to symptoms than to diagnoses.

If medication does help you, its effects on therapy can be somewhat unpredictable. A positive response can help if, relieved of your distress, you are more comfortable to pursue the issues behind your emotional problems. But you may also find that, with the calming of your symptoms, the motivation to do the work of therapy is diminished.

An ineffective medication, serious side effects, or a referral to a medication doctor with whom you do not get along can all disrupt your alliance with your therapist. How your therapist handles your taking medication can make a crucial difference. If your therapist is positive and encouraging, you are more likely to feel good about the medication and so more likely to take it as prescribed.

Legal precedents are changing to suggest that if you have a serious condition where a medication has been shown to be effective, your therapist is duty bound to encourage you to take it.

The Medication Referral

Therapists who themselves cannot or choose not to prescribe psychiatric drugs often have an ongoing relationship with a psychiatrist or a psychiatric group or clinic to provide medication for their patients. The therapist's referral to the doctor providing medication should include a thorough description of both the symptoms for which treatment is being sought and the pertinent details about the therapy to date. An established, familiar relationship between your therapist and the medicating physician is a great help.

You and your therapist should discuss some key issues about medications before you go for your first appointment with the medicating physician. For instance, will you make the appointment or will your therapist make it for you? Or will the physician contact you after getting the referral from your therapist?

You should be aware that no medication may be prescribed for you at the first appointment, or indeed, at all. That decision is up to the physician, who can make that judgment only after seeing you. And your therapist should make clear to you the trial-and-error nature of medication trials—it takes some experimentation to find the right medication. And it is no instant cure. It often takes time—weeks or sometimes months—before a medication becomes effective once you begin taking it.

Your ongoing appointments with the medicating physician will be on a different rhythm from your therapy appointments. Typically these appointments are short—fifteen or thirty minutes is common—and the meetings can be every two or four weeks rather than weekly. And your medicating physician will ask pointed questions, focusing on your symptoms and other feelings. The point is to monitor how you are doing on the medication.

The medicating physician is usually a psychiatrist. In rare cases, especially in areas with few or no psychiatrists, the medication backup for a psychotherapist may be an internist or general practitioner. Straightforward symptoms may be manageable in this fashion, but your therapist and you should not hesitate to seek a more specialized consultation if you do not respond readily to the internist's treatment. Even if this means traveling to consult with a psychiatrist in a distant city, it is worth it.

Often, the nonpsychiatric physician will have less time, as well as less expertise, to offer. Because psychiatry as a discipline straddles the fence between the biomedical and psychological approaches to emotional disorders, psychiatrists have had training and experience in both medication treatment and the "talking cure." They are far better suited by training and experience to prescribe psychiatric medications than are other physicians.

But the balance that a given psychiatrist has struck between these two elements can vary. A "general psychiatrist" as a rule is well equipped to evaluate for and prescribe medication treatment. Some psychiatrists, however, especially those who practice psychoanalysis, may emphasize psychotherapeutic approaches to the exclusion of the medical. They are generally not as competent or as inclined to prescribe for their own patients and typically will not make themselves available as a medication consultant despite their M.D. degree. They may themselves refer their patients to another more medically inclined psychiatrist.

At the opposite extreme are some psychiatrists who emphasize a biological understanding and medication treatment strongly or exclusively. Referred to as "psychopharmacologists," their practice often revolves around the provision of medical backup to nonmedical therapists and consultation to their less expert psychiatric colleagues about medication issues.

The initial evaluation for medication will often take from one to several sessions, each an hour or longer. Over and above the referral information offered by your therapist, the interview with you is the most important source of information for the medication decision.

The medicating psychiatrist must have an overall picture of your distress, your symptoms, and your general life situation. The degree of detail the psychiatrist wants may surprise you, but is necessary. Where it is dispensed with, patients often have the opposite complaint, namely that the psychiatrist "does not see me as a whole person. I'm just a collection of symptoms."

The territory covered in the initial evaluation will include a thorough examination of your current difficulties and any prior episodes of psychiatric distress, their attempted treatments and their outcomes. Your life history, including childhood and upbringing, education and work record, living situations past and present, and current social circumstances, will all have a bearing. Because of the genetic factors in both psychiatric illness and treatment response, any history of nervous or emotional troubles in blood relatives will be especially pertinent. There is no set order in which this information must be obtained, and the psychiatrist will probably balance free-form conversation with more structured specific questioning.

One key function of this initial workup is to exclude the possibility that your symptoms are being caused by a covert medical illness. Psychiatric symptoms should never be treated until such medical conditions are ruled out. For one, a medical condition could interact adversely with medication. More importantly, a potentially reversible medical condition could be missed, with possibly dire consequences.

An extensive history of your past medical conditions will be taken, including any past or present use of illicit drugs (your answers are completely confidential and will not jeopardize you). Often, records of recent medical evaluations will be obtained and the patient's medical doctor(s) may be consulted. Blood tests may be ordered if they have not been done recently or if some pertinent ones had been omitted from recent testing. Other laboratory tests might include cerebral CT or CAT (computerized [axial] tomography) or MRI (magnetic resonance imaging) scans to visualize the brain; EEG (electroencephalograph, brain-wave recording); or particularly in an older patient whose cardiac health must be considered in prescribing safely, an EKG (electrocardiogram). The psychiatrist will do some testing of such cognitive factors as concentration, memory, and the ability to do simple calculations. These may occasionally include some paper-and-pencil tasks or rating scales, and on occasion, a referral to a psychologist for further testing.

Important: You should always inform any physicians prescribing for you of what other medications you are already taking. Many medications do not mix. Their interactions can make you sick or even be fatal.

COMMONLY PRESCRIBED PSYCHIATRIC MEDICATIONS

ANTIDEPRESSANTS

Broadly speaking, three classes of antidepressant medications are in use—the *tricyclics,* the *monoamine oxidase* (MAO) *inhibitors,* and the newer, so-called *second-generation agents* by and large developed in the 1980s. While their actions and uses overlap considerably, these different categories of antidepressants work by distinct mechanisms, have different side-effect profiles, and are more effective with different symptoms.

Tricyclics

The tricyclics first came into broad use in psychiatry in the early 1950s with the introduction of imipramine (Tofranil and others), still one of the most-used medications in this group. Other tricyclics include amitriptyline (Elavil, Endep), desipramine (Norpramin, Pertofrane), nortriptyline (Pamelor, Aventyl), trimipramine (Surmontil), protriptyline (Vivactil), and doxepin (Adapin, Sinequan). Clomipramine (Anafranil) is a somewhat specialized tricyclic agent only recently introduced into the United States and approved specifically for the treatment of obsessive-compulsive disorder, in contrast to the other members of this class, which have a broader range of accepted uses.

Uses

Although the tricyclics were accepted first and foremost for the treatment of depression and are called antidepressants, they are useful with a wide range of disorders. These include, in addition to major depression and "atypical" depression, panic disorder, social phobia, bulimia, attention-deficit disorder with hyperactivity, bedwetting, and obsessive-compulsive disorder.

Depression accompanying other major disorders such as manic-depressive disorder and schizophrenia is also treated with tricyclics, with certain caveats discussed below. These medications may also be useful for milder depression, including pathological mourning, for agoraphobia without panic attacks, and for some of the symptoms (such as intrusive nightmares) in posttraumatic stress disorder.

What It's Like

Some people suppose taking an antidepressant produces some kind of "high." This is not the case. Usually people taking antidepressants are not particularly aware of any subjective effects of being on a medication except that their depression, panic disorder, or other main symptom becomes less intense or their ability to function in the face of their problem is enhanced—including the ability to use therapy. The exception is when a person experiences side effects.

Often, the benefits take several weeks to become apparent, and then only in retrospect, when you realize that gradually your depression is lifting. But in some cases the relief, especially from depressive symptoms, may be more dramatic; this more dramatic relief can bring a sense of mild elation.

You do not "escape," ignore, or become numb to your problems or sadnesses through taking an antidepressant. Being aware of this in advance can help you make a realistic appraisal with your therapist of what to expect from an antidepressant medication. To know that the medication will not end your need to explore the issues underlying your depression will be a relief to some and may well be disappointing to others!

Antidepressants are not addictive. Taking more than the prescribed dose of a tricyclic is not an attractive but rather a disagreeable experience. In addition, patients do not describe craving or yearning for the experience of being on the medication after it is stopped.

How you stop the medication is important. Do not end it all at once or on your own. It is possible to have a rebound of depressive symptoms, especially if the medication is stopped prematurely. Furthermore, there is a withdrawal syndrome, with malaise, nausea, and headaches, if the medication is stopped too abruptly.

When a tricyclic works in the treatment of depression, some of the discernible effects, in addition to lifting the sadness, include sounder or more restful sleep, decreased dreaming (particularly a decrease in troubling dreams), increased energy and ability to concentrate, and a normalizing of your appetite.

How Tricyclics Work

Tricyclics increase concentration of two brain chemicals (or neurotransmitters), norepinephrine and serotonin. Underactivity of these brain chemicals, known as monoamines, has been implicated in depression and other disorders. After these brain chemicals have been released and been active for a time, they are taken up again into the brain cells that secreted them. Tricyclics delay this re-uptake so that the monoamines remain active longer after secretion. This seems to compensate for the underactivity that brought about many of the symptoms of depression.

Some tricyclic side effects are due to the fact that these medications have similar effects on other neurotransmitters apart from the monoamines, notably histamine and acetylcholine.

Side Effects and Risks

While people differ in the degree of side effects they suffer with tricyclics, these medications can produce quite similar and troubling side effects. With many tricyclics, the most troublesome effect with ongoing use is sedation. They are often administered at bedtime so that this effect is bearable, but it may persist into the following day.

Tricyclics also can cause:

- dryness of the mouth or eyes (of concern particularly if you have dental problems such as bad gums or wear contact lenses)
- a peculiar taste in the mouth
- dilation of the pupils, with a resulting sensitivity to bright light
- disturbances in the rapid adjustment in focus necessary when your gaze shifts (from near to far or vice versa), which can cause momentarily blurry vision
- constipation or trouble urinating

These side effects can occasionally be quite serious or worsen underlying problems. They can lead to conditions requiring immediate medical attention such as acute glaucoma, severe bowel problems, or acute urinary retention. If you experience any such effects, you should inform your medication doctor immediately.

Weight gain is a common complaint. You should take this into account and try to offset it by controlling your intake. It seems that the weight gain is not just due to the restoration of appetite, which had been lost in depression.

In men, another side effect may be difficulty getting an erection, or more rarely, difficulty achieving ejaculation.

Short-term side effects include:

- being restless or anxious
- feeling trembly or feverish
- increased perspiration or night sweats
- difficulty falling asleep or restless and disturbed sleep
- clouded thinking or trouble concentrating

These side effects may be so uncomfortable that you feel like discontinuing the drug during the first few days or weeks of treatment. But by the point when the medication begins to help—usually several weeks into treatment—these reactions usually disappear or become more tolerable.

Other common side effects are cardiovascular problems, such as dizziness upon arising or otherwise rapidly changing posture, or a more rapid heartbeat. Tricyclics can have deleterious effects on an unhealthy heart, e.g., causing EKG (electrocardiogram) changes or arrhythmias (disturbances in cardiac rhythm or conduction).

Much rarer is a worsening or precipitating of angina. Even rarer is heart failure or heart attack.

If you have a history of heart disease, these cardiac effects may eliminate the tricyclics from consideration, although with close ongoing monitoring they may still be safe. A thorough evaluation of their safety if you have a history of heart disease should include consultation with a cardiologist. And in all patients from middle adulthood on, an EKG should be done prior to treatment, as well as whenever dosages are increased substantially.

The cardiac effects make the tricyclics dangerous in overdose. If taken all at one time, a one- to two-week supply can cause serious, potentially lethal, cardiac complications. Tricyclic antidepressants are now the leading cause of death by drug overdose in the United States.

The tricyclics can occasionally cause seizures in patients with a history of head injury, especially those who have already suffered some seizures in the past. If you have such a history, collaboration on your care between your psychiatrist and a neurologist is warranted.

As with all medications to which you have not previously been exposed, an allergic reaction is possible. If you prove allergic to a tricyclic, you must avoid it and other tricyclics that may affect you similarly.

If you have manic-depressive disorder, but it has not yet been diagnosed, it may announce itself when you take a tricyclic by your swinging from a depressed to a manic state. Some people question whether the antidepressants can actually cause mania in someone who would not otherwise have had a manic reaction.

The elderly are particularly susceptible to the side effects noted above and often require lower dosages for comfort and safety. Fortunately, such lower doses can also be therapeutic for them.

The tricyclics may be used in pregnancy, as the *Physicians' Desk Reference* puts it, "only if the clinical condition clearly justifies potential risk to the fetus." A woman taking these medications should not nurse an infant, as the medication may be excreted in the breast milk.

Adverse Interactions with Other Medication

Your primary-care doctor, any specialists, surgeons, and dentists involved in your care should be aware that you are taking a tricyclic. Likewise, your prescribing psychiatrist should know all the other medications you take.

The effects of anticholinergic and sympathomimetic medications (employed in anesthesia, treatment of gastrointestinal disturbances and certain ophthalmological conditions, and allergy and cold remedies) may make the side effects of the tricyclics more severe.

Certain blood-pressure medications may interact with your antidepressant as well, or their effectiveness may be reduced by the presence of the tricyclic. Cimetidine

(Tagamet), ranitidine (Zantac), and other similar medications used for peptic ulcers may raise the tricyclic levels in your body and thus increase the frequency and severity of adverse reactions. If you are receiving thyroid supplements for hypothyroidism, tricyclics may make you more sensitive to their adverse effects, especially on the heart and circulatory system, and they should be more closely monitored.

The tricyclics amplify the brain depressant effects of alcohol and other sedatives (e.g., tranquilizers and sleeping medications), so these should be avoided or used cautiously if you are receiving a tricyclic.

You may also find yourself becoming more fidgety and nervous from caffeine while taking tricyclics. Except for the cold remedies noted above, no difficulty is presented by combining the tricyclics with any over-the-counter remedies, vitamin and other food supplements, or foods.

Medical Preliminaries

Because of all these risks, do not start taking tricyclics until you have gone through a thorough medical screening. It should include blood tests to be sure that a medical illness is not being mistaken for depression. It is crucial as well to determine whether you have the type of heart disease that would make the use of a tricyclic dangerous. This can be detected with an EKG, which should be given to anyone over forty or with a history of heart disease. If you have doubts about the safety of these drugs for you, insist on a cardiology consultation.

Other medical conditions that can make the use of the tricyclics dangerous, such as narrow-angle glaucoma, should be ruled out in your physical, or if there are doubts, in consultation with a specialist.

Choosing the Right Tricyclic

None of the antidepressants has been proven more effective or to act more rapidly than another, despite marketing claims. Choice of one is therefore based largely on their side effects and your symptoms.

There are two broad chemical classes of tricyclics. The *tertiary amines* (amitriptyline, imipramine, trimipramine, and doxepin), which have proportionally more effect in boosting serotonin than norepinephrine, produce more side effects such as drowsiness, dry mouth, and dizziness. Amitriptyline and doxepin are especially sedating. *Secondary amines* (nortriptyline, desipramine, and protriptyline) tend more toward enhancement of norepinephrine levels and hence toward irritability, overstimulation, and disturbed sleep.

The tertiary amines are thus more useful where depression is accompanied by sleep disturbance, agitation, and restlessness; whereas the secondary amines may be better if you are fatigued, withdrawn, or apathetic. Your psychiatrist's initial evaluation, therefore, must go into extensive detail about your depressive symptoms, to tailor the medication to your condition. Overall, desipramine and nortriptyline are perhaps the safest and are often the first tricyclics tried.

How people react to tricyclics may be hereditary. All other things being equal, you should start on the same medication to which a biological relative with the same problem has responded favorably. You may wish to inquire about medication within your family. Of course, where you yourself have previously responded favorably to a particular medication, it should generally be the drug of choice.

Starting on Tricyclics

Your prescribing doctor will draw up a treatment plan for you. Typically, the medication will be started at a low dose to make sure you can tolerate it and to acclimatize your body to its effects. If you are in good health, the dose will be increased every two to four days if tolerated until it is in the therapeutic range. As with any medication, if your physician's instructions are unclear, you should ask for clarification.

For the elderly or infirm, the interval between dosage increases is longer, generally between seven and ten days. Your doctor should do a thorough review with you of what side effects to anticipate. For example, not knowing of the risks of dizziness could mean becoming faint on arising rapidly, falling, and injuring yourself.

During this period of acclimatizing to the medicine, your psychiatrist should be available by phone or frequent follow-up appointment to check on your progress, answer questions about the effects you may be feeling, and reassure you. You should feel free to contact your doctor if you are troubled by anything you are experiencing.

Generally, the medication is taken all at once at bedtime so that side effects will peak overnight and so that sedation will be less inconvenient. But the dose can be divided into two or more portions taken at different times of the day if the side effects of an undivided dose are intolerable for you.

The tricyclics must be taken regularly and consistently to be beneficial. They cannot be used on an "as needed" basis only on the days when you are feeling worst. You must also take them regularly during the two- to four-week lag time until they take effect.

If the medication proves ineffective at levels that should work, you and your doctor may decide to switch to a different medication or try the current medication in combination with other medicines such as lithium carbonate or a second antidepressant. A blood test to gauge the serum level of the medication may also be useful at this point.

Length of Treatment

Patients with major depression can typically be taken off their antidepressant medication after six to eight months of responding well to it. But if you stop the medication too soon, it can often lead to a relapse. However, a patient who initially does well after discontinuing an antidepressant may have a recurrence months or years later. Evidence suggests that up to 50 percent of patients who have had a major depressive episode will have subsequent episodes.

Much less evidence bears on the proper length of tricyclic therapy for other conditions, such as panic disorder. Often, patients with panic disorder require open-ended treatment to avoid relapse, and medication-responsive chronic depression may also relapse if medication is not maintained. Attempts to discontinue tricyclics should take place in a measured way under the supervision of your medication doctor, with the understanding that you may need to resume the medication.

Monoamine Oxidase Inhibitors

Monoamine oxidase inhibitors (MAOIs), like the tricyclics, compensate chemically for depression, but these act by inhibiting the enzyme monoamine oxidase. This enzyme breaks down the monoamines after they have been secreted into the synapse. Inhibiting that process makes more of these brain chemicals available.

Three MAOI medications are in use, primarily as antidepressants: phenelzine (Nardil), tranylcypromine (Parnate), and isocarboxazid (Marplan). While somewhat less widely used than the tricyclics, they have comparable effectiveness in many of the same conditions: major depressive episodes, panic disorder, agoraphobia, social phobia, and attention deficit with hyperactivity. The evidence is less clear for obsessive-compulsive disorder, bulimia, and narcolepsy.

The MAO inhibitors seem to have an advantage over other antidepressants in the treatment of "atypical" depression, a syndrome whose main symptoms are:

- Chronicity; patients may report being "depressed as long as I can remember."
- Mixed emotional features, such as fatigue, anxiety, or panic attacks, and phobias, rather than sadness or melancholy alone.
- The depressed mood may wax and wane over the course of the day with reactivity: i.e., pleasant events cause a significant but transitory lifting of mood.
- Excess rather than deficient sleep and appetite, especially carbohydrate cravings or binge eating.

Whether an MAO inhibitor should be the drug of choice for your depression is somewhat impressionistic and will require thorough evaluation by you and your doctor. Because of their side effects, many physicians do not use MAO inhibitors as the first antidepressant drug with a patient. Some physicians avoid their use altogether.

What Taking MAOIs Feels Like

Like the tricyclics, these medications do not induce euphoria or a high, are not addictive or abusable, and must be tapered off gradually to avoid a withdrawal syndrome. There is a one- to four-week lag time before they start to take effect, although you may begin to feel an improvement on tranylcypromine within ten to fourteen days. Often, the clinical response is most noticeable in retrospect, although a person may feel dramatic relief as soon as the medicine "kicks in."

Risks

By far, the most significant and dangerous drawback of the MAO inhibitors is the so-called cheese reaction. The drugs interact with foods rich in the amino acid tyramine and with other drugs to produce a drastic elevation of blood pressure. This may be signaled by a headache, racing heart or palpitations, visual disturbance or malaise; or it may go undetected but place the patient at risk of fatal hemorrhage or circulatory collapse. Because a headache during treatment may be the first sign of a hypertensive reaction, it is probably wise for a patient with preexisting severe or frequent headaches to avoid the use of an MAO inhibitor for fear of misinterpreting this signal.

Concern over the tyramine reaction has been the major source of reluctance to use these drugs. A strict avoidance of the offending foods and medications is the only way to take an MAO inhibitor safely, and your doctor must be sure of your ability to understand the risks and organize your diet accordingly before prescribing an MAO inhibitor. Some doctors suggest that you go through a "dry run" of the restricted diet for several days without taking the medication. You may be given a potent antihypertensive agent to carry with you and take if you realize you have eaten a substantial amount of a forbidden food. If this occurs, you must seek medical attention from an emergency room to have your blood pressure watched, and if necessary, controlled aggressively until the danger has passed.

You must review the precise list of foods to avoid with your treating physician. It will include aged cheeses (including those in pizza); smoked, pickled, fermented, and otherwise processed meats, fish, and soy products; beef and chicken liver; red wines; beer, ale, and some liqueurs (the tyramine content varies from lot to lot); broad beans; yeasts (not including yeast baked goods); and canned figs. You should make an effort to understand the rationale for the exclusions rather than just memorize a list of dangerous foods, since questions about particular foods not on the list will always arise. The working principle is that you should avoid high-protein food that has undergone protein breakdown through aging, fermentation, pickling, smoking, or bacterial contamination, since this releases tyramine.

Sympathomimetic agents, which are used in cold and allergy remedies, over-the-counter appetite suppressants, and anesthesia, are also dangerous, as are the drugs used in the treatment of Parkinson's disease. Drugs of abuse such as amphetamines and cocaine are hazardous, too. If you cannot convince your physician that you can avoid the use of these drugs—for instance, if you have a history of using them—it should preclude consideration of an MAO inhibitor for you.

The tricyclics also react dangerously with the MAO inhibitors, so a two-week "washout" period must be observed when going from either class of antidepressant to the other, or for that matter, when switching between different MAO inhibitors. Several non-antidepressants such as the antiseizure medication carbamazepine (Tegretol) and the muscle relaxant cyclobenzaprine (Flexeril) are also tricyclics and share the same danger.

There are also some nonpsychiatric medications with MAO-inhibiting activity that should not be combined with the antidepressants. These include the cancer chemotherapy agent procarbazine (Matulane), the antihypertensive pargyline (Eutonyl and Eutron), and the antibiotic furazolidone (Furoxone). The pain medication meperidine (Demerol) has been involved in lethal cross-reactions with MAO inhibitors and should be avoided as well; other narcotic and nonnarcotic pain medications are safe. The antianxiety agent buspirone (BuSpar) may cause hypertensive crisis in combination with the MAO inhibitors and must be avoided.

Important: You must tell any doctor, surgeon, or dentist who may give you anesthetics or medications that you are taking an MAO inhibitor. A Medic Alert or similar bracelet or necklace could be useful, for instance, if you get in an accident and are unconscious or otherwise unable to communicate. It is unwise to begin an MAO inhibitor when you are anticipating elective surgery. Except in an emergency, anesthesiologists should refuse to consider people for surgical anesthesia if they have been exposed to an MAO inhibitor within the prior two weeks. Even local anesthesia can result in enough absorption to have a bad reaction with your MAO inhibitor.

Other Side Effects

Apart from the danger of hypertensive crisis, the MAO inhibitors can cause hypotension—dangerously low blood pressure. Symptoms include feelings of light-headedness, weakness, and the risk of falls. This side effect can often be counteracted by taking the medication with meals. Many foods have at least some scant tyramine content, even in diets designed to minimize them, and this will support your blood pressure sufficiently.

These medications, especially phenelzine, can also cause weight gain, inability to have orgasm, and in males, erectile impotence. Especially early on in treatment, they may be overstimulating, causing headaches (even without blood pressure elevation), increased sweating, anxiety, and jitteriness (as if you had had too much caffeine). This is especially likely with tranylcypromine. For this reason, it's best not to take them at bedtime.

However, MAO inhibitors can be sedating as well, especially phenelzine, and many patients complain of a particularly troublesome mid- to late-afternoon drowsiness. The medications intensify the effects of alcohol and other depressants and you must be careful not to mix them.

As with other antidepressants, the MAO inhibitors can cause a swing from the depressed to the manic state when given to someone with manic-depressive illness. They may have effects on glucose metabolism that make their use in patients with diabetes a cause for close attention.

Newer Antidepressants

A number of "atypical" antidepressants have been added to our inventory in the eighties. The pressure to develop new antidepressants has come in part from a desire to find agents that work more quickly and have fewer side effects. In general, the first goal—greater speed—has not been achieved. But the atypical antidepressants have different, and in some cases more benign, side effects, making them useful additions to the antidepressant catalogue. They are, however, not without their own liabilities.

Trazodone (Desyrel): This nontricyclic agent has effects on both norepinephrine and serotonin, like the tricyclics. It is extremely sedating and so is especially useful when anxiety or insomnia accompanies depression. It is less likely than tricyclics to cause cardiac difficulties, although some arrhythmias have been reported. Its anticholinergic effects are mild, though it can induce dizziness on changing posture. Its otherwise benign side-effect profile makes it especially useful in the elderly. It may also be useful in obsessive-compulsive disorder. A troubling tendency to cause priapism (painful prolonged erection, sometimes requiring surgical correction) has limited its usefulness in men. It may be less effective than tricyclic agents in the treatment of panic disorder. Small doses of trazodone may be added to other less sedating antidepressants to help you sleep.

Amoxapine (Ascendin): Essentially a tricyclic, amoxapine bears a chemical relationship with the antipsychotic loxapine and shares some of its actions. Unfortunately, this includes the tendency to induce some of the most troublesome side effects associated with the antipsychotic class of medications, including the risk of tardive dyskinesia (see "Antipsychotic Agents" below). Furthermore, it can cause seizures in overdose. For these reasons, it has won only narrow acceptance and is often used only where patients have been unresponsive to trials of many other antidepressants.

Maprotiline (Ludiomil): This antidepressant has tricycliclike properties and side effects, but a tendency to cause seizures even in patients who have no previous history of them. It may also cause skin rashes, which clear up when you stop taking the medication.

Fluoxetine (Prozac): This is the first of a new class of antidepressants that are selective re-uptake inhibitors of one of the monoamines, serotonin. Fluoxetine seems to have little effect on other neurotransmitters. It is tolerated well by many patients with little of the anticholinergic, blood-pressure-lowering, or sedative effects of the tri-cyclics. It is as effective as the tricyclics in many patients, and those who are not helped by other antidepressants may be by fluoxetine. It may be especially useful in atypical depressive syndromes. But it often takes longer—typically four to six weeks at a therapeutic dose—to have its effect.

Major side effects of fluoxetine include headaches, skin rash (which clears up when the drug is discontinued), nausea, and jitteriness or raciness, sometimes with an anxious edge and/or insomnia. While some patients quickly become intolerant of fluoxetine and must stop it, many patients experience these side effects only mildly or not at all. Fluoxetine may be more effective than most tricyclics (and comparable to clomipramine, Anafranil) in treating obsessive-compulsive disorder, although this requires higher doses than when it is used for depression.

Fluoxetine also tends to induce mild weight loss; on therapeutic doses, an average 5 to 10 percent reduction in body weight over the first year of treatment has been observed. This is probably from both appetite-reducing and metabolic effects. It is worth noting that investigation has shown that higher dosages do not induce greater weight loss.

Because of its effectiveness, tolerability, and perhaps the weight-reduction effect, fluoxetine is becoming increasingly a first-choice antidepressant drug and has cap-tured an enormous share of the market since its introduction in early 1989; this is despite its high cost compared to other medications. Because of its distinctive mech-anism of action, it may hold promise for at least some depressed patients who have not benefited optimally from agents of other antidepressant classes.

Recently, several doctors' suggestions that fluoxetine can cause suicidal preoc-cupations or violent impulses have aroused a great deal of media attention and medical concern. Patients with depression, regardless of which medication they may be treated with, are at increased risk of suicide due to the nature of their condition. Furthermore, when they are begun on antidepressants, their lack of energy or resolve may respond more rapidly than their hopelessness or despair, leaving them with equal impetus but increased capacity to act on suicidal impulses. Thus, patients undergoing medication treatment for depression must always be assessed carefully and ongoingly for risk.

However, it is possible that some patients receiving fluoxetine in particular may experience the irritability or agitation it can cause as so intolerable that their self-destructive or angry feelings may become more urgent. Nevertheless, it is as safe as other antidepressants when given under the sufficiently careful and close medical follow-up that is warranted for any depressed patient. If you experience destructive or self-destructive urges while taking fluoxetine, these must be brought rapidly to the attention of your caregivers.

The introduction of several other serotonin re-uptake inhibitors is expected in the near future. This class of antidepressants would appear to be the most important psychopharmacological advance in the treatment of affective disorder since the introduction of lithium carbonate in the early seventies.

The effectiveness of fluoxetine in the range of disorders for which the other "antidepressants" have proven useful (eating disorders, panic disorder and other anxiety states, posttraumatic stress disorder, etc.) remains in question at the time of this writing, although extensive research efforts to define its range are under way.

Buproprion (Wellbutrin): This stimulant antidepressant was introduced several years ago but quickly withdrawn after accumulating reports implicated it in causing seizures. It has recently been reintroduced after a finding that the seizure problems were confined to a group of patients with eating disorders, and it is now labeled as contraindicated in such patients. But its potential to induce seizures extends to other classes of patients: those who have had seizures in the past, who have a history of head trauma even without seizures, or who have a history of extensive drug abuse, especially stimulant abuse.

Buproprion is a nontricyclic and works by a novel and as yet not fully apparent mechanism, one unlike other antidepressants. Adverse reactions include headache and nausea. Its distinct mechanism of action makes it useful for patients who were not helped by other antidepressants. Evidence suggests it may be less likely to switch a manic-depressive patient into the manic phase.

ANTIPSYCHOTIC AGENTS

Antipsychotic medications consist of a variety of similarly acting agents from a variety of different chemical classes, including,

- chlorpromazine (Thorazine)
- thioridazine (Mellaril)
- mesoridazine (Serentil)
- trifluoperazine (Stelazine)
- perphenazine (Trilafon)
- fluphenazine decanoate, enanthate, and hydrochloride (Prolixin)
- thiothixene (Navane)
- haloperidol (Haldol)
- loxapine (Loxitane)
- molindone (Moban)

Target Symptoms Helped by Antipsychotics

The antipsychotics are helpful with symptoms of several different psychiatric diagnoses. They are equally useful in schizophrenic, depressive, manic, and drug-induced psychoses. They are indicated wherever there are psychotic symptoms such as paranoia, hallucinations, delusional thinking, confusion, or bizarreness. They are most effective when these symptoms are acute and accompanied by agitation and/or anxiety.

But antipsychotic medications are also used in lower doses to prevent relapse in patients who, although not currently suffering from psychotic symptoms, have in the past. The antipsychotics are of less use with the so-called "negative" psychotic symptoms—social withdrawal, apathy, emotional flatness, poverty of thought and speech—that accompany chronic schizophrenia.

Antipsychotic medications have possible, but more questionable, value in conditions such as posttraumatic stress disorder, severe personality disorders, and anxiety disorders that have been unresponsive to other medications and where anxiety or agitation are sometimes said to reach "prepsychotic" proportions. In these conditions, they are usually used at lower dosages than in the frankly psychotic conditions.

Overprescription

Be particularly cautious if a physician prescribes antipsychotics for you when you do not have the main symptoms for which they are most effective. For instance, if you only have anxiety, these medications are inappropriate. The antipsychotics are not very good as general sedatives or antianxiety medications, and due to the risk of irreversible neurological damage from their use (see discussion of tardive dyskinesia below), they should not be prescribed unless the potential benefits clearly outweigh the risks.

With rare exceptions, they should never be used in patients without clear psychotic symptoms.

How Antipsychotics Feel and Work

You will probably be at least mildly aware of the side effects caused by your medication (see below). You will probably (though not always) feel a calming and sedating effect soon after you begin to use an antipsychotic. Your agitation, restlessness, and anxiety may lessen rapidly, within hours. But relief from some of the other psychotic target symptoms such as paranoia, hallucinations, and delusions may take longer, up to days or weeks.

While they have been referred to as "major tranquilizers," these agents are more accurately called antipsychotics to reflect the fact that they have a specific action on symptoms of psychosis. They are not merely tranquilizers.

The introduction of this class of medications in the early 1950s was a dramatic step in the treatment of patients with psychotic disorders, whose management had previously been with general tranquilizers or sedatives such as the barbiturates.

Indeed, their antipsychotic effects were discovered serendipitously as chlorpromazine underwent clinical trials as a sedative.

While these medications act on many brain centers, their antipsychotic effect appears due to their impact on the dopamine, one of the brain's chemical messengers. Many of the side effects of these medications are due to the fact that they unavoidably block dopamine in areas of the brain not related to stopping psychotic symptoms. Other side effects are due to their blockade of several other brain chemicals in addition to dopamine.

Motor System Side Effects

The major complication of all antipsychotics is their unpleasant effects on the brain's system for motor control of the body. As a result, they have been referred to alternatively as "neuroleptics," literally, "causing neurological changes." These changes in motor control seem linked to their therapeutic effects and may be inevitable. In fact, one way new antipsychotic compounds are identified is if they produce these same neurological changes in laboratory animals.

The problems can begin early in their use, or just after a significant dosage increase, with prolonged and sometimes drastic involuntary muscular contractions of the neck, tongue, face, or back. Young males taking high levels of antipsychotics seem particularly prone to these reactions.

A number of side effects similar to symptoms of Parkinson's disease may arise, usually after a few weeks of antipsychotic treatment and especially in the elderly or those on medications that are particularly potent. These "pseudo-Parkinsonian" effects include hand tremor, an overall increase in muscle tone or rigidity, drooling, and less ease in muscular activity so that the person's gait, actions, and facial expressions seem slow or limited.

These movement effects are reversible if the medicine is stopped or its dosage reduced, and they can often be treated or prevented with the addition of one of several so-called anti-Parkinsonian medications. Akathesia, an uncomfortable and related condition involving restlessness of the legs that causes an incessant need to shift one's position or pace, does not respond as well to the anti-Parkinsonian medications, but can be treated with side-effect medicines of other types such as the beta blockers (discussed below with the antianxiety medications).

Your physician must be knowledgeable enough to recognize these side effects accurately, rather than mistaking them for an increase in psychotic symptoms such as agitation. Such a mistake would lead to your physician erroneously increasing your antipsychotic dosage.

Tardive Dyskinesia

Tardive dyskinesia (TD), a potentially irreversible condition involving involuntary movements of the face, mouth, tongue, and/or extremities, represents perhaps the most distressing complication of antipsychotic medication. TD can arise at any point in your treatment with antipsychotic medications, although it is rare in people who have taken the medications for less than three to six months. The risk of TD may be related to the cumulative level of exposure to the medications. One estimate is that 1 percent of patients taking antipsychotic medications develop TD for every year they are on the medications.

Although there is so far no treatment for the movements of TD once they have developed, its progression can be halted by stopping the antipsychotic medications when the movements have been detected. For that reason, periodic screening by your prescribing physician for the first, often subtle, signs of abnormal involuntary movements is a part of the responsible prescribing of these agents. You should also be given accurate information about the irreducible risk of TD—as well as the other effects of antipsychotic treatment—and discuss them with your physician before you agree to take these medications.

While abnormal movements can often appear while a patient is on antipsychotics, the medications can mask the symptoms and TD may be recognized only when you stop or begin a lower dose. But so-called withdrawal dyskinesias, which are temporary, appear with medication reduction but stop on their own in a few weeks or months. Tardive dyskinesia thus cannot be diagnosed with certainty unless the abnormal movements persist after you have stopped antipsychotic medication or have been on an unchanging, low dose for six to twelve months after their emergence.

The risk of tardive dyskinesia seems to be reduced significantly by keeping antipsychotic dosage as low as possible. One way to do this is to have supportive friends, family, and caregivers who can help with the recognition of signs of an impending relapse of psychotic symptoms. This makes it possible to employ a dosing strategy in which the patient's TD risk is minimized by taking little or no antipsychotic medication except when signs of a return of symptoms become noticeable.

The risk of TD seems greater when an antipsychotic is used to treat a psychotic condition other than schizophrenia, e.g., mania or extreme reactions in posttraumatic stress disorder.

This seemingly gloomy picture of TD has been brightened by data showing that there is not necessarily an inexorable progression of TD with continued use of antipsychotic medication. Many cases may be reversible even though they have been long-lasting.

Other Side Effects

Neuroleptic malignant syndrome (NMS) is an extremely rare but critical, potentially fatal, reaction to antipsychotic medications. Main symptoms include fever, "board-like" or "lead-pipe" muscle rigidity, unstable heart rate and blood pressure, delirium, and other changes in blood chemistry. It appears suddenly, most often in young males, and is a medical emergency that requires management in an intesive care unit. Early recognition of the symptoms and immediate discontinuation of the medication are essential. If you or someone you know shows any of these symptoms while taking neuroleptics, go immediately to an emergency room.

The syndrome can continue for one to two weeks after the medication is stopped. Some patients who recovered and remained psychotic were able to take the original medication again without a recurrence of NMS, but others have had a repeat episode. It is probably wise not to use antipsychotics in a patient who has had an episode of NMS.

Other fairly common side effects of the antipsychotic medicines include: postural hypotension (dizziness on sudden changes in posture, such as standing up), dry mouth, mild to moderate weight gain, and neuroendocrine changes such as the loss of the menstrual cycle in women. More rarely they include: sun sensitivity, skin-pigmentation changes, getting seizures more readily in those prone to them, falling blood-cell counts, and impaired ability to regulate body temperature (which can lead to heatstroke). Jaundice, probably a sign of allergic hypersensitivity to the medications, has also occurred, though rarely.

Antipsychotics may obscure nausea or vomiting that would otherwise be signs of a toxic reaction to another medication or an illness. If you are on antipsychotic medications, always tell any physician or dentist who treats you that you are taking them.

Thioridazine (Mellaril) has a tendency to impede ejaculation in males and causes some change in pigmentation of the retina. A strict daily dosage ceiling of 800 milligrams is recommended for this medication for the latter reason.

While anyone must be watched carefully after taking an overdose of antipsychotics, they are not life threatening. Instead, a patient will experience an uncomfortable and prolonged exaggeration of the range of side effects described above.

Antipsychotics should be avoided by pregnant women; they may cause both short- and long-term complications in infants whose mothers took them during pregnancy. Because antipsychotics are excreted in the breast milk, mothers who must take them should not nurse.

Choosing Among Antipsychotics

All medications in this class are equally effective against psychotic symptoms—and equally likely to cause TD. They do, however, differ in potency, i.e., the number of milligrams needed to achieve equivalent effects. High- and low-potency agents differ in relative prominence of various side effects. Substantial sedation (which may be desirable in some cases) and postural dizziness occur in the low-potency agents (chlorpromazine and thioridazine), while the motor-system effects like Parkinsonism that occur especially in younger male patients are more common with the higher-potency antipsychotics. The lower-potency agents thioridazine and mesoridazine may have less TD risk.

The choice among antipsychotics is thus chiefly a choice between high- and low-potency agents based on the tolerability of various undesirable side effects, and more rarely, the need for certain desirable ones such as sedation. An important factor for your physician in deciding which to prescribe will be any prior history you may have of reactions and responses to antipsychotics. Also important, though to a lesser extent, are reactions of any blood relatives who were treated with antipsychotics.

Most antipsychotics are taken once or more daily as pills. But fluphenazine and haloperidol are also available as injections given once every one to three weeks that slowly deliver the medication into your bloodstream until the next injection. This form is recommended for patients who have trouble remembering to take their medication.

The effects of an antipsychotic can persist for weeks or months after you have taken the last dose. This is because they are effective in minute concentrations and are stored in your body tissues, to be gradually released over time. Thus, you may not have a relapse of your psychotic symptoms for a long while after you have stopped your medication. For this reason, it is often difficult to convince a patient who is having another psychotic episode six weeks or six months after stopping their antipsychotic medication that their relapse is related to the discontinuation, and that they should resume their medication. You should not discontinue your antipsychotic medication except with the agreement and supervision of your medicating physician.

Molindone and fluphenazine probably have less tendency to trigger seizures and so may be the preferable antipsychotics if you have had an epileptic disorder. Molindone may also be less likely to make you put on weight than are other antipsychotics, though the evidence is not entirely convincing. Nevertheless, many psychiatrists choose molindone for the treatment of psychotic patients with weight problems.

Finding the Right Dose or Combination

As you try higher doses or new medications, your physician has to make careful observations of signs of psychosis that warrant dosage increases, and of side effects of the medications that indicate the dose should be reduced or other medications added to counter the side effects, as described below.

Except for treating acute agitation, it is best if you are on a fixed daily dose of an antipsychotic rather than using flexible amounts on an as-needed basis. The medications provide cumulative relief—the longer you take them the more effective they are—rather than immediate relief (so that taking more today will not necessarily help you right away). It is easier for your physician to assess the adequacy of your dose if it is consistent.

If you have certain symptoms, combining other kinds of medications with antipsychotics may be called for. For example, if your symptoms include fluctuating anxiety, you may benefit more from as-needed use of a non-antipsychotic anxiety medication. Other medications that may be used in combination with antipsychotics include lithium, carbamazepine, calcium-channel blockers, or antidepressants.

If Antipsychotics Don't Help

The effective dose of antipsychotic medication varies greatly from patient to patient. If the side effects do not bother you too much, your physician can increase your dosage and experiment with different combinations until your symptoms are relieved.

If you have not responded satisfactorily to antipsychotics, a change to an antipsychotic medication of a different chemical class should be tried. Except in rare instances, combining two different antipsychotics at the same time is generally not warranted (other than combining an oral and an injectable agent).

Interactions with Other Medications

The antipsychotics combine safely with most other medications you may be given. But they will exaggerate the effects of other depressants such as anesthetics, pain medications, alcohol, and sedatives. Because they lower blood pressure to varying degrees, antipsychotics may make a patient more sensitive to the effects of antihypertensive medications. They also may increase blood levels of the anticonvulsant phenytoin (Dilantin), potentially causing toxic reactions unless its dosages are reduced.

As with all other medications, all physicians who play a role in prescribing for you should be fully informed of all the medications that you take.

Neurological complications have occasionally been reported following the combined use of haloperidol and lithium. Patients on this particular combination of drugs must be monitored closely and the medications stopped at the first signs of problems to avoid irreversible damage.

Clozapine (Clozaril)

The 1990 introduction of clozapine, an antipsychotic agent with an unusual mechanism of action, has created a massive stir in the psychiatric world. Clozapine has a different spectrum of activity and side effects from all other antipsychotic agents. Most notably, it seems effective in hitherto medication-resistant psychotic patients.

In particular, clozapine appears to help with the "deficit" symptoms of schizophrenia: apathy, withdrawal, flattening of emotions, slowness of activity, lack of initiative, poverty of speech and thought, and the like, as opposed to other antipsychotic agents, which mainly affect symptoms such as agitation and hallucinations.

It is also claimed that clozapine does not carry a risk of tardive dyskinesia. This recommends it for patients who require ongoing antipsychotic use but have been tempted to discontinue their medication because they have developed tardive dyskinesia.

If continued use confirms the above, clozapine may be the most significant advance in the medication treatment of the psychotic conditions since the introduction of the original antipsychotic medications in the 1950s. Unfortunately, clozapine has a tendency to cause seizures and a rare but dangerous blood disorder called agranulocytosis, in which the body's ability to produce disease-fighting white blood cells is impaired. For this reason, the drug is recommended only for those who have failed to respond satisfactorily to conventional antipsychotic agents and/or have serious tardive dyskinesia. It can only be given under a strict protocol of weekly blood monitoring.

While there had been fatalities from infections due to the loss of white cells in the early years of clozapine treatment in Europe, none have occurred since the monitoring system was introduced.

Clozapine is currently an extremely expensive medication, especially given the monitoring protocols associated with its use. In some states, mental health agencies will not underwrite the cost of clozapine treatment for psychiatric patients who cannot afford it. Ironically, this group makes up a formidable proportion of those who would be ideal candidates for this new medication.

SEDATIVES, HYPNOTICS, AND ANTIANXIETY AGENTS (TRANQUILIZERS)

Anxiety is a perennial and common element of psychiatric disorders, and many medications have been used to ease it through the centuries. The trouble is that all medications that alleviate anxiety are addictive to varying degrees because they induce tolerance. Higher and higher doses are needed to get an effect, and withdrawal symptoms occur when they are stopped. These characteristics mean anxiety medications can be abused like other addictive drugs.

A succession of central-nervous-system depressants has been developed over the years in the quest for a nonaddictive antianxiety agent. The introduction in 1960 of chlordiazepoxide (Librium), and soon thereafter of diazepam (Valium), ushered in the era of the benzodiazepines, now the leading antianxiety and sedative medications and until recently the most widely prescribed class of drugs in Western medicine. This class of medications has virtually replaced earlier classes of sedative-hypnotics used to combat anxiety, which, for that reason, will not be discussed here.

Anxiety relief, tranquilization, and sleep induction are points along the same spectrum of central-nervous-system depression. Further along the same continuum are coma and death, which the benzodiazepines can cause in overdose, especially in combination with other depressants such as alcohol.

The advantage of the benzodiazepines over earlier medications lies in their increased ratio of effectiveness in relieving anxiety to their side effects. For instance, they induce less sedation and dependency and are less lethal in overdose.

Uses and Limitations

The benzodiazepines are useful both for inducing sleep and treating anxiety. When sleeplessness and anxiety occur as part of a severe psychiatric disorder (as is common), the benzodiazepines may be used along with other medications, such as antipsychotics or antidepressants. However, benzodiazepines are rarely useful as the sole agents in treating major mental illnesses.

The limitations of benzodiazepines are related to their effectiveness. The gratification and relief you may feel from taking these medications can be so immediate that you may lose your motivation to manage your anxiety symptoms through therapy or to work on the underlying anxiety-producing situations to seek a more lasting relief without drugs.

Patients tend to like these medications too much, becoming psychologically dependent on them. Combining this psychological dependence with their capacity to produce physical dependency and withdrawal after prolonged use results in a high potential for addiction. Thus, it is important to avoid overuse of these medications, in contrast to most other psychiatric drugs, where dislike of their effects can lead to underuse.

These medications are best used for brief periods, to manage short-term anxiety. Because its effectiveness wears off, usually you do not benefit from using a benzodiazepine continuously for more than five to ten weeks. More drawn-out but sporadic use on an as-needed basis is another acceptable approach.

Thus, benzodiazepines are indicated where short-term treatment is helpful, such as in adjustment disorders when you are anxious, and in acute posttraumatic stress disorder to help cope with sleeplessness, flashbacks, and anxiety. For simple phobias (fears of places or things), these medications may be helpful if you can't avoid what it is you fear. Although other classes of medication may also be used, benzodiazepines may be useful in some cases of social phobia to help you through the feared encounter. In all these anxiety conditions, benzodiazepines offer only symptomatic relief; longer-term relief comes through psychotherapy.

This class of medications has largely proven not useful in the treatment of agoraphobia or obsessive-compulsive disorder, two other conditions classed with the anxiety disorders. Most are not useful with panic disorder, but the high-potency benzodiazepines alprazolam (Xanax) and clonazepam (Klonopin), along with tricyclics and monoamine oxidase inhibitors, do have antipanic effects.

One of the main exceptions to the long-term use of benzodiazepines are people who suffer generalized anxiety. They are prone, probably on a physiological basis, to persistent and markedly elevated levels of anxiety and can be quite disabled. Many with this disorder can benefit from long-term or open-ended treatment with antianxiety agents. One reason is that such people seem not to develop tolerance and thus do not require escalating dosages of the agents over time to achieve a constant effect, as do other benzodiazepine users.

For chronic insomnia, it is not advisable to use benzodiazepines as the sole treatment or for a lengthy period. Tolerance to the sleep-inducing effects of the medications develops within several weeks of continuous nightly use. This can lead to "rebound" worsening of your sleep difficulties when you stop their use. Many cases of chronic sleep difficulty have an underlying cause (medical, psychiatric, or environmental) that must be sought and corrected for lasting relief. Where no underlying disorder can be identified in a vigorous workup by a specialist (usually a psychiatrist) familiar with the sleep disorders, the conservative steps referred to as "sleep hygiene measures" are usually more useful than reliance on medication. These measures include a regular bedtime; relaxation methods; avoidance of excessive caffeine, fluid, or solid food too close to retiring; moderate activity.

Finally, benzodiazepines are widely used in detoxification, the withdrawing of a patient from a dependency on alcohol. The general strategy consists of substituting the antianxiety agent for the alcohol to cover the craving for a drink, then tapering the medication gradually until the acute withdrawal symptoms have ended.

Choosing the Right Antianxiety Medication

The benzodiazepines are all more or less equally effective as antianxiety agents. However, they do differ in potency, i.e., the milligram amount required to produce equivalent effects. They are distinguished primarily by how fast and how long they act. Broadly speaking, rapid-acting agents are useful for immediate relief of situational anxiety, and for difficulty falling asleep.

Intermediate- and long-acting agents, on the other hand, do not provide immediate relief. Instead, they build more gradually to their peak effect, making them useful for people with middle- or late-night insomnia (difficulty staying asleep or early awakening). At a steady dose, they are useful in the treatment of generalized anxiety or for alcohol detoxification.

Side Effects

The most significant complications of benzodiazepine treatment arise from central-nervous-system depression. They include drowsiness, impaired reaction time, and diminished fine-motor coordination. The standard warnings about driving and operating dangerous machinery apply. One manifestation of this CNS depression can be sedation, so that you feel groggy or are "hung over" the morning after use, especially with longer-acting members of this class. These effects are additive with other depressants, in particular with alcohol. This makes it dangerous to drink alcohol if you are taking antianxiety medication.

The relationship between relief from anxiety and performance may be conceived of as an inverted *U;* a little relief from disabling anxiety will improve performance on a wide variety of tasks, but there are diminishing returns from further medication until a point is reached where it impairs your performance.

Memory problems can also be a side effect. Some people report partial amnesia beginning when the drug's activity begins, particularly with the rapidly absorbed higher-potency benzodiazepines such as alprazolam and triazolam. This may be considered akin to an alcohol-induced blackout.

Also like alcohol, the benzodiazepines can be disinhibiting. While it may be therapeutic to lose inhibitions, for example, that make you shy or unable to talk about yourself in psychotherapy, the loss of "useful" inhibitions against impulsive, self-destructive, antisocial, or hostile actions under the influence of benzodiazepines has been reported and must be seriously borne in mind in using them. Patients with various organic brain injuries may be particularly prone to this effect, for instance, becoming combative. If you become more anxious and excitable, have insomnia, or feel increased rage, you should discontinue the medication immediately.

These medications should not be used if you are pregnant or may become so. Children of women using benzodiazepines during the first trimester of pregnancy have an increased incidence of birth defects.

When used in combination with cimetidine (Tagamet), disulfiram (Antabuse), or isoniazid when used with estrogens (e.g., in oral contraceptives and Premarin), the excretion of the benzodiazepine may be impaired, resulting in mounting levels and potential toxicity. Under these circumstances, the dose of the benzodiazepine must be reduced or one of those not metabolized by the liver (oxazepam or lorazepam) should be used instead.

In the elderly or others whose metabolism of these medications is impaired, regular use of longer-acting benzodiazepines can lead to a dangerous rise in their concentrations in the blood. Thus, as with many other medications, shorter-acting agents in lower dosages should be chosen for the elderly.

Two benzodiazepines, oxazepam and lorazepam, are metabolized entirely by the kidneys in contrast to the remaining agents, which are processed through the liver.

Thus, oxazepam and lorazepam are preferable if you have impaired liver function, as for example, in chronic alcohol abuse.

Addiction and Abuse

It has become clear that a withdrawal syndrome occurs if any benzodiazepine, including the long-duration ones, is stopped abruptly after more than several weeks of continuous use. With longer-acting benzodiazepines, the syndrome is more gradual and drawn out (lasting on the order of seven to twelve days, for example, for diazepam [Valium]) but still uncomfortable.

While you may mistake it for the return of your preexisting anxiety, withdrawal from benzodiazepines can also include tremor, nausea, vomiting, loss of appetite, dizziness, perceptual difficulties, flulike body aches, and other bodily symptoms. There is a risk of seizure particularly after the abrupt discontinuation of high-level use. These symptoms, as well as the growing tolerance of the medications with continuous use, are evidence of their addictive properties. This can be accompanied by a psychological addiction as well, with intense cravings and a desperate urgency to get more.

If you have a history of alcoholism or drug abuse, your medication doctor will likely be reluctant to prescribe antianxiety medications for you. Instead he or she may suggest nonmedication techniques for anxiety management, or other nonaddictive and less abusable (and unfortunately, probably less effective) medications. These include sedating antihistamines (primarily used for the treatment of allergies), beta blockers, and buspirone. The latter two are discussed below.

Beta Blockers

These medications are primarily used for the control of high blood pressure, tremors, and prevention of migraine headaches. They include propranolol (Inderal), timolol (Blocadren), nadolol (Corgard), metoprolol (Lopressor), and atenolol (Tenormin). Because they can block the acceleration of heart rate and other bodily changes that accompany acute anxiety, they can sometimes help reduce anxiety. They have proven useful, as well, in blocking stage fright and other forms of performance anxiety. A further psychiatric use has been in controlling rage or impulsive acting out, especially in the mentally retarded. As mentioned earlier, they are also useful for treating akathesia, a side effect of antipsychotic medication.

Side effects of the beta blockers include dizziness and other cardiovascular effects, fatigue, weakness, and impotence. They can cause or exacerbate depression. They can be harmful if you have bronchial asthma, diabetes, or various forms of heart disease.

Buspirone (BuSpar)

This is a recently introduced antianxiety agent that is chemically unrelated to any other class of these medications. The mechanism of action of buspirone is not known, but it does not appear to operate through depressing the central nervous system as other antianxiety medicines do. It is less sedating than other antianxiety agents, does not have addictive effects with alcohol or other nervous system depressants, and does not appear to impair reaction times or coordination. It does not appear to lead to psychological or physiological dependency and so seems to have little likelihood of being addictive.

But how effective buspirone is for reducing anxiety remains to be seen. Patients who have used benzodiazepines extensively have found it comparatively ineffective. It will not block the withdrawal from benzodiazepines, alcohol, or other sedative-hypnotics and should not be substituted abruptly for one of those classes of medication.

A syndrome of restlessness and excitability shortly after beginning to use buspirone has been reported in a small number of patients. Other side effects reported include dizziness, nausea, and light-headedness. The use of buspirone with MAO inhibitors should be avoided.

Recent reports suggest that buspirone may have antidepressant properties either alone or in combination with other antidepressant agents.

LITHIUM AND OTHER ANTIMANIC AGENTS

Since their introduction in the early 1970s, the salts of the common element lithium have assumed the leading role in the treatment of the acute manic phase of manic depression and the prevention of relapse. Between 60 and 80 percent of people with the problem respond well to treatment with lithium. Usually administered in a pill as lithium carbonate (Lithonate, Lithane, Eskalith, Lithobid, and others) or as lithium syrup (Cibalith), lithium has a multiplicity of biological effects throughout the body, and it is not clear what its mechanism of action is.

While remarkably effective, its broad range of effects makes its use complicated and requires vigilance and expertise from your physician—and close collaboration from you.

Lithium is the preferred treatment for manic episodes. But because it will usually not take effect for seven to ten days, antipsychotics are often given in combination with it at the onset. Because acutely manic patients are notably poor at complying with medication regimens, the treatment of an acute manic episode is often begun in the hospital, where medications can be closely supervised.

Between manic episodes, lithium is extremely effective at preventing mood swings to both the manic and depressive extremes. For this reason, you are likely to continue taking lithium after your manic episode passes, at a lower maintenance dose.

More uncertainty exists about the usefulness of lithium in treating the acute depression phase of manic depression or as a sole agent for the prevention of recurrence in depression where there is no manic phase. It is, however, often effective in augmenting a depressed patient's partial response to an antidepressant.

Besides manic depression, lithium salts are used effectively in other conditions in which mood is unstable. These include cyclothymic disorder (milder "mood swings"), some personality disorders, and any conditions marked by angry outbursts. Lithium has been used in combination with the antipsychotics for the treatment of resistant psychosis in some schizophrenic conditions.

How Lithium Feels

Most people who take a maintenance lithium regimen have little or no awareness that anything is different. They feel "normal." If you take it, its effects may be evident to you only in retrospect, by the lessening or absence of manic or depressive extremes of mood. When lithium is used to treat an acute manic episode, some patients report becoming depressed. It is unclear whether this is an effect of the lithium per se or the natural aftermath of clearing up the mania.

Where lithium is used for other conditions marked by emotional instability, especially those with rage or anger, people who benefit remark that it "makes me able to count to ten before acting on my feelings" or "gives me distance on my emotions." Some lithium users have reported a disagreeable flattening of the vibrancy of their emotions, a "graying out" or "loss of the highlights." Occasionally—for instance, in artists—this has been unpleasant enough to lead to a discontinuation of the lithium treatment.

Levels and Toxicity

Toxic lithium levels are not much greater than the effective levels at which you will be maintained, and lithium toxicity can develop insidiously or rapidly. Lithium is rapidly eliminated through the kidneys unless you have preexisting kidney disease or are on diuretics or a salt-free diet (in which case the body will hold on to its lithium as a sodium substitute). In these cases, risk of toxicity is enhanced, and lithium should be avoided or used in much lower dosages. With normal kidney function, about half of the lithium in the body will be eliminated within twenty-four hours if no additional lithium is taken.

This means your lithium level can drop quickly below the therapeutic level with just one or several missed doses. In this case, you will no longer feel lithium's benefits and may experience rapid mood changes, into mania or depression.

Because of the risks both of lithium toxicity and of falling lithium levels, close monitoring of your blood levels is important to make sure you are in the relatively narrow therapeutic range in between. Every patient's dose must be individualized to provide a therapeutic lithium level, as there is no uniform relationship between the amount taken and the resulting blood level.

At the outset of treatment, therefore, dosages are adjusted every three to seven days and the level checked after every dosage adjustment until therapeutic levels are achieved. When that point is reached, blood testing may be done less frequently. If your level was in the correct range the last time it was checked, you stick to your dose, your physical health and fluid balance are unchanging, and your emotional symptoms are under good control, routine blood monitoring can be done every two to three months. If any of these factors change, the lithium level should be checked sooner.

Your stability on lithium will be maximized by having a consistent blood level throughout the day. This is achieved by taking the daily lithium dose divided into three or four portions around the clock or using a time-release preparation that allows twice-a-day or even once-daily dosing. You will pay for such convenience, however. While generic lithium is exceedingly inexpensive, the time-release preparations are much more costly.

Less frequent dosing and the resultant daily fluctuations in lithium level may not detract from its effectiveness. Some patients are taking lithium on a once-a-day, or even less frequent, schedule. Benefits include increased comfort and decreased side effects on the medication. For example, if taken at bedtime, some of the peak side effects will occur while one is asleep. Furthermore, this strategy may protect against the possibility of irreversible kidney damage that may be associated with long-term use of lithium.

The development of lithium toxicity is accompanied by recognizable signs you and those close to you should learn to recognize. You should discontinue taking your lithium and contact your physician immediately if such signs of toxicity as diarrhea, vomiting, tremor, slurred speech, impairment in gait or motor coordination, weakness, or unusual drowsiness occur. Death can occur, usually from coma or cardiac causes, from unrecognized toxicity or intentionally taking massive amounts of lithium.

A toxic interaction with the antipsychotic medication haloperidol can occur even without an excessive lithium level and can lead to irreversible neurological damage. Weakness, fatigue, lethargy, confusion, and fever should cause you to discontinue such combination treatment at once and contact your physician.

Other Side Effects

A number of side effects can occur in treatment with lithium even when your blood levels are in the therapeutic range. These may be evident especially in the first weeks of lithium therapy. Mild effects at the outset can include fatigue and lethargy, impaired concentration and memory, mild weakness, or tremor. These often subside within the first few days of treatment, or if persistent, may be relieved with a reduced dosage or by dividing the daily lithium dose into more frequent, smaller portions.

With ongoing treatment, a number of other complications can arise. Skin changes including acne and worsening of psoriasis have been associated with lithium treatment. These usually respond to dermatologic treatment or dosage reduction. A benign, reversible change in the EKG, usually without consequence to cardiac function, is often noted. A baseline EKG before lithium treatment is necessary for comparison purposes.

A benign decrease in the secretion of thyroid hormone, or more rarely, goiter or hypothyroidism sometimes occurs. This decrease in thyroid activity is reversible by stopping lithium use. Monitoring of the thyroid, along with lithium level, is another important reason for the periodic blood drawing during lithium therapy. Baseline thyroid-function tests must be obtained before initiating lithium therapy.

Lithium has strong effects on the kidneys and the body's fluid balance. Substantial increase in daily urine output is an extremely common effect. As a result of this heightened fluid output, you may be constantly thirsty. Pay attention to your thirst and drink enough to replace the increased daily losses. Dehydration and electrolyte imbalance can be a problem if this is ignored, especially when compounded by heat, perspiration, vomiting, or diarrhea.

There is some controversy over whether lithium has the potential to cause more severe irreversible kidney damage. Baseline renal-function testing with periodic repeat testing while taking lithium is imperative to detect early evidence of impending kidney problems.

Lithium also can irritate the gastrointestinal tract. Depending on the dose and the preparation you are taking, you may experience queasiness, indigestion, or diarrhea. These often occur when the lithium level is at its peak two to four hours after taking your last dose. These inconveniences often respond to adjustments in your regimen or a change in which preparation of lithium you take.

Lithium-induced water retention and weight gain are common and unpleasant effects that you should anticipate. Occasionally, the weight gain is so extreme that patients refuse to use lithium despite its remarkable effectiveness.

Lithium is suspected of causing fetal defects if taken during the first trimester of pregnancy. You should not take it if you are or might become pregnant. Because it is excreted in breast milk, you should avoid nursing while taking lithium.

Nonresponse to Lithium

Around one-third of patients with manic depression are not helped by lithium. While nonresponders cannot be identified in advance, some factors correlated with poor response include: a relative who failed to respond, kidney disease, schizophrenialike features, and rapid cycling (four or more episodes of mania per year). In the latter, cycling can sometimes be slowed down and the patient may become lithium responsive with the addition of thyroid medication. For the treatment of nonresponding acute mania, the lithium level may be cautiously inched upward with close monitoring including EKGs, preferably in a hospital, until side effects limit further increases.

If lithium does not help lift an acute manic episode, electroconvulsive therapy often will.

Where lithium has been ineffective in preventing recurrence of manic depression, the most promising alternative has been the substitution or addition of either of two anticonvulsant medications, carbamazepine or sodium valproate. These medications can also be used where kidney disease interferes with lithium treatment, as they are metabolized by the liver.

Other Antimanic Agents

Carbamazepine (Tegretol) can be as effective as lithium in some people. It may be particularly useful in rapid-cycling manic depression, which often resists lithium treatment.

As with other anticonvulsants and lithium, carbamazepine dosage must be individualized by following blood levels to keep the medication in a narrow therapeutic range between ineffectiveness and toxicity.

Common side effects of carbamazepine treatment include dizziness, gait disturbance, clumsiness, drowsiness, and blurring of vision. These are worst early in treatment and are related in severity to blood levels. Two rare but serious complications are hepatitis and aplastic anemia, in which the bone marrow is compromised in its ability to manufacture new blood cells. These risks are a further reason for stringent blood monitoring throughout therapy. Early changes in liver-function tests or blood counts can also be detected in time to reverse toxic effects and prevent permanent damage. As with lithium, baseline levels must be checked as a preliminary to treatment. Testing must be frequent at the outset—weekly for the first month, then monthly for a while—but with continuing good health and treatment stability, tests four to six times a year are sufficient.

Many of the comments above apply to sodium valproate, also referred to as valproic acid and divalproex and by the brand names Depakene, Depakote, and Valontin. It shows promising effectiveness both alone and in combination with lithium. Side effects include sedation, discoordination or weakness, skin and hair changes, nausea, vomiting, and indigestion. The gastrointestinal effects are more manageable when the medication is taken with food or as the Depakote brand, a coated tablet that reduces stomach irritation. Blood monitoring must be done in valproate treatment both to establish and maintain therapeutic levels and to detect sporadic but potentially severe hepatitis, which has led to liver failure and fatality.

Other very rare serious complications include acute pancreatitis and bleeding disorders.

MISCELLANEOUS AGENTS

Other classes of compounds important in general medicine are possible alternatives to more conventional psychiatric medications. These include the beta blockers, which have restricted applications in the treatment of side effects and of anxiety, the calcium-channel blockers, which may be useful in manic-depressive illness, and stimulants have long been used in psychiatric treatment. Clonidine, a medication primarily used for high blood pressure, has also found psychiatric application.

Stimulants

Amphetamines (Dexedrine and others) were used, until replaced by the tricyclics and the monoamine oxidase inhibitors in the fifties, for depressive disorders. Today, they as well as related substances such as methylphenidate (Ritalin) and pemoline (Cylert) are approved only for the treatment of attention-deficit with hyperactivity disorder (ADHD) in children; they are classified as controlled substances due to their potential for dependency.

Psychiatric interest in the stimulants extends to two further areas: ADHD and related disorders in adults and the withdrawn, apathetic, demoralized state seen in the elderly and medically ill (e.g., stroke and heart-attack victims, AIDS and cancer patients). In the latter conditions, stimulants may be more effective and safer than the antidepressant medications. While frequently prescribed for appetite suppression in the treatment of obesity, this use is probably not warranted, as tolerance to the appetite-suppressing effects of stimulants develops in a matter of a few weeks of continuous use, along with the danger that the user will become addicted.

Pemoline can cause liver toxicity and must be monitored with periodic blood tests. Its advantage is a long persistence in the body, which allows once-daily dosing. In contrast, the effects of methylphenidate last only between two and six hours, requiring frequent redosing and decreased convenience. Amphetamines are intermediate in duration.

Side effects of the stimulants include mood changes such as irritability or anxiety, overstimulation, weight loss, disturbed sleep, headaches, and cardiac stresses. Prolonged use can result in a paranoid psychosis resembling acute schizophrenia. The medications are not safe in pregnancy and can be lethal in overdose.

Clonidine (Catapres)

This medication for high blood pressure has a number of experimental psychiatric uses. These include blocking the discomfort of narcotic withdrawal; acute mania; anxiety disorders; and antipsychotic-induced akathesia. Limiting side effects include sedation and light-headedness from lowered blood pressure. Once started and used for several weeks, the medication must not be discontinued suddenly or a drastic rebound elevation of blood pressure may result.

APPENDIXES

∎

I. SELF-HELP GROUPS LISTED BY PROBLEM

Self-help and support groups, such as Alcoholics Anonymous, can be extremely helpful as a supplement or alternative to therapy. The groups are listed according to the problems they deal with.

ADJUSTMENT-TO-LIFE PROBLEMS

Emotions Anonymous
Emotions Anonymous—Children (ages 5–13)
Emotions Anonymous—Youth (ages 13–19)
P.O. Box 4245
St. Paul, MN 55104
(612) 647-9712

Self-help, nonprofessional organization set up to help people with either short-term or chronic emotional problems. Emotions Anonymous is modeled after Al-Anon and AA and follows a twelve-step program.

Families Anonymous
World Service Office
P.O. Box 528
Van Nuys, CA 91408
(818) 989-7841
1-800-736-9805

Self-help, volunteer organization of parents, friends, and relatives of children with drug and alcohol problems and associated behavioral problems such as running away, delinquency, truancy, low self-esteem, etc. Families Anonymous is modeled after Al-Anon and AA and follows a twelve-step program.

Note: More recently, due to the use of cocaine among adults, Families Anonymous has expanded to include family and friends of adults with drug problems.

Toughlove
P.O. Box 1069
Doylestown, PA 18901
(215) 348-7090

Toughlove is a self-help group program for parents and neighborhood groups who are experiencing out-of-control behavior of teens and young adults.

Toughlove "is a structured curriculum for behavior change" that offers crisis intervention and group meetings to support parents.

ALCOHOLISM

Al-Anon, Alateen, and Adult Children of Alcoholics
Al-Anon Family Group Headquarters, Inc.
P.O. Box 862
Midtown Station
New York, NY 10018
(212) 302-7240
1-800-344-2666

Al-Anon is a fellowship of relatives and friends of alcoholics. Alateen is part of Al-Anon and is designed for younger relatives and friends of alcoholics. It is a self-help, nonprofessional organization that follows the twelve-step tradition to recovery. It offers regular open and closed meetings of Al-Anon and Alateen groups, which share information and give support and makes referrals to groups for Adult Children of Alcoholics.

Alcoholics Anonymous, Inc.
P.O. Box 459
Grand Central Station
New York, NY 10163
(800) 637-6237
Telex: 126822

AA is a voluntary, nonprofessional, twelve-step fellowship organization of men and women who wish to attain and maintain sobriety. AA offers open information meetings to members and nonmembers and closed meetings for alcoholics only. Closed meetings are held regularly and give members an opportunity to share their thoughts and give each other support and help. Meetings groups help members to follow the twelve-step recovery program.

CALIX
7601 Wayzata Blvd.

Minneapolis, MN 55426
(612) 546-0544

Program for Catholic alcoholics who are sober. Works with AA and other treatment programs after the individual is in recovery. CALIX is concentrated in Minnesota, New York, the Midwest, and southern California.

Jewish Alcoholics, Chemically Dependent Persons, and Significant Others, Inc.
197 E. Broadway
New York, NY 10002
(212) 473-4747

JACS seeks to "help recovering Jews and their families to connect with one another, explore their Jewish roots, and discover resources within Judaism to enhance their recovery." JACS currently has approximately twenty-five support groups across the U.S.

Women for Sobriety, Inc.
109 W. Broad Street
P.O. Box 618
Quakertown, PA 18951
(215) 536-8026

Women for Sobriety, Inc. is a self-help program "whose purpose is to help all women recover from problem drinking." Self-help groups for women.

ANXIETY DISORDERS

Anxiety Disorders Association of America
(an expansion of the Phobia Society of America)
6000 Executive Blvd., Suite 200
Rockville, MD 20852
(301) 231-8368

The Anxiety Disorders Association of America (ADAA) is dedicated to promoting the welfare of people with anxiety disorders. It offers a national treatment directory for phobias and related anxiety disorders that educates consumers on how to select a therapist, explains the kinds of disorders and treatments, and contains a comprehensive list of individual practitioners and treatment centers across the country. ADAA will refer a caller to local support groups.

AUTISM

Autism Society of America
 (formerly the National Society for Autistic Children)
1234 Massachusetts Ave., N.W., Suite 1017
Washington, DC 20005
(301) 565-0433

This organization is mostly composed of people with autism and their families. Its focus is to provide information, support, referral, and advocacy services to people with autism and their families. ASA also does legislative lobbying and advocacy on a national level.

 ASA facilitates communication among people with autism, parents of individuals with autism, and family members. ASA will put individuals and families in contact with each other to share experiences, information, and ideas.

BEREAVEMENT

American Association of Suicidology
Box 2459, S. Ash
Denver, CO 80222
(303) 692-0985

"The goal of the American Association of Suicidology (AAS) is to understand and prevent suicide." It is a nonprofit organization that "promotes research, public awareness programs, and education and training for professionals and volunteers. In addition, it serves as a national clearinghouse for information on suicide." AAS maintains a directory of crisis centers and a directory of suicide-survivor support groups.

The Compassionate Friends, Inc.
P.O. Box 3696
900 Jorie Blvd.
Oak Brook, IL 60522
(708) 990-0010

Mutual or self-help organization for parents who have lost a child at any age, due to any cause. Also open to other family members. Local chapters meet monthly and will attempt to match parents with other parents who have had a similar loss. Local groups may have speakers in to talk to parents and family about the grief process.

Pregnancy and Infant Loss Center
1421 E. Wayzata Blvd.
Wayzata, MN 55391
(612) 473-9372

"To provide support, resources, and education on miscarriage, stillbirth, and newborn death." PILC will refer to support groups across the U.S. and other national resources.

SHARE
National SHARE Office
St. Elizabeth's Hospital
211 S. Third St.
Belleville, IL 62222
(618) 234-2120

SHARE is a network of mutual support groups (250 chapters) to help those, parents and others, who have suffered the loss of a child through miscarriage, stillbirth, or early infant death. SHARE arranges a one-to-one contact between parents by phone or mail and makes referrals to other self-help organizations that address the loss of young children.

CHILD ABUSE

National Child Abuse Hotline
Childhelp USA

1345 El Centro Ave.
P.O. Box 630
Hollywood, CA 90028
1-800-422-4453

Focuses on crisis counseling and referrals to professional organizations.

National Domestic Violence Hotline
P.O. Box 7032
Huntington Woods, MI 48070
1-800-333-SAFE
1-800-873-6363 (for the hearing impaired)

To the victims of domestic violence the National Domestic Violence Hotline offers supportive listening, information and referral, and crisis intervention. The hotline will help a caller locate the appropriate resources in her area.

Parents Anonymous
6733 S. Sepulveda Blvd.
Los Angeles, CA 90045
(213) 388-6685
1-800-421-0353

Parents Anonymous is a self-help group for parents who feel "isolated, overwhelmed, or are afraid of their anger toward their children." It "prevents child abuse by providing safe, supportive weekly meetings where parents under stress can discuss their problems with their peers and with trained volunteer professionals."

Parents United International, Inc.
(Daughters and Sons United)
(Adults Molested as Children United)
P.O. Box 952
San Jose, CA 95108

Guided self-help groups provide peer support and sponsorship to victims and their families. Parents United chapters only exist under the guidance of a professional, community-based Child Sexual Abuse Treatment Program. There are three guided self-help components:

1. Parents United (PU)—for the parents.
2. Daughters and Sons United (DSU)—for sexually molested children and their siblings.
3. Adults Molested as Children United (AMACU)—for adults who have not resolved the trauma of being sexually molested as children.

VOICES in Action, Inc.
(Victims of Incest Can Emerge Survivors in Action, Inc.)
P.O. Box 148309
Chicago, IL 60614
(312) 327-1500

The first goal of VOICES is to help incest and child sexual-abuse victims work through the experience of being victims and become survivors. VOICES will make referrals to a therapist, agency, or self-help groups that are recommended by members.

CONDUCT PROBLEMS

Emotions Anonymous
Emotions Anonymous—Children
Emotions Anonymous—Youth
P.O. Box 4245
St. Paul, MN 55104
(612) 647-9712

See listing on page 640.

Families Anonymous
World Service Office
P.O. Box 528
Van Nuys, CA 91408
(818) 989-7841
1-800-736-9805

See listing on page 640.

Toughlove
P.O. Box 1069

Doylestown, PA 18901
(215) 348-7090

See listing on page 640.

DEPRESSION AND MANIC DEPRESSION

Depression After Delivery
P.O. Box 1282
Morrisville, PA 19067
(215) 295-3994

The primary goal of DAD is to "support women who are suffering from postpartum depression and psychosis." DAD is a self-help, mutual aid organization managed by volunteers. "Volunteers staff telephones across the country, helping mothers going through an illness they once experienced themselves."

Depressives Anonymous
329 E. 62 St.
New York, NY 10021
(212) 689-2600

Self-help organization to help people suffering from depression. Offers support group meetings.

Emotions Anonymous
Emotions Anonymous—Children
Emotions Anonymous—Youth
P.O. Box 4245
St. Paul, MN 55104
(612) 647-9712

See listing on page 640.

National Alliance for the Mentally Ill
2101 Wilson Blvd.
Suite 302
Arlington, VA 22201
(703) 524-7600

NAMI is a self-help, advocacy organization for people with *serious* mental illness, their parents, children, spouses, siblings, and friends. NAMI focuses on mutual support groups, public education, public advocacy, research, and lobbying. Local NAMI groups meet to provide mutual support and share information about the mental health system.

National Foundation for Depressive Illness
P.O. Box 2257
New York, NY 10016
(800) 248-4344

A national, nonprofit organization, helps people with depression find professional help in their area. Refers mainly to psychiatrists and also to local support groups.

Recovery, Inc.
802 N. Dearborn St.
Chicago, IL 60610
(312) 337-5661

"A community mental health organization that offers a self-help method of will training at weekly meetings."

DRUG ABUSE

Cocaine Anonymous
3740 Overland Ave.
Suite G
Los Angeles, CA 90034
1-800-347-8998
(213) 559-5833

CA is a self-help, nonprofessional, twelve-step fellowship program for men and women in recovery from cocaine addiction. Services vary from one chapter to another and include regular support group meetings and a "Loner Program"—a one-to-one correspondence for people who are alone for any reason.

800-COCAINE
P.O. Box 100
Summit, NJ 07901

Referrals to local hotlines only.

Families Anonymous
World Service Office
P.O. Box 528
Van Nuys, CA 91408
(818) 989-7841
1-800-736-9805

See listing on page 640.

Narcotics Anonymous
World Service Office
P.O. Box 9999
Van Nuys, CA 91409
(818) 780-3951

Self-help, twelve-step recovery program for men and women who wish to stop using all drugs. Narcotics Anonymous groups exist throughout the U.S., Canada, and in over fifty other countries.

EATING DISORDERS

National Association of Anorexia Nervosa and Associated Disorders
Box 7
Highland Park, IL 60035
(708) 831-3438

ANAD gives counsel and information to anorexics, bulimics, their families, and professionals. ANAD maintains a list of more than two thousand therapists, hospitals, and clinics in the U.S. and Canada to which it makes referrals. ANAD is active in helping to form self-help chapters and refers to these self-help groups.

Overeaters Anonymous
4025 Spencer St.
Suite 203
Torrance, CA 90503
(310) 618-8835

Self-help fellowship of men and women who wish to stop eating compulsively. Offers regular support group meetings.

GAMBLING

Gam-Anon
International Service Office, Inc.
P.O. Box 157
Whitestone, NY 11357
(718) 352-1671

Self-help fellowship for the families of compulsive gamblers. Gam-Anon is a twelve-step organization with regular support group meetings.

Gamblers Anonymous
P.O. Box 17173
Los Angeles, CA 90017
(213) 386-8789
Fax: (213) 386-0030

Self-help, nonprofessional organization that follows the twelve-step program of recovery used by AA. Regular support group meetings for people who wish to stop gambling.

HYPERACTIVITY

Children with Attention Deficit Disorders
1859 N. Pine Island Rd., Suite 185
Plantation, FL 33322
(305) 587-3700

CHADD gives support to parents who have children with attention-deficit disorders. Self-help support groups across the U.S. meet monthly offering parents information, guest speakers, a newsletter, and the support of other parents.

MARITAL PROBLEMS

Batterers Anonymous
1269 N. "E" Street

San Bernardino, CA 92405
(714) 884-6809

Self-help counseling program for men who batter women.

National Domestic Violence Hotline
P.O. Box 7032
Huntington Woods, MI 48070
1-800-333-SAFE
1-800-873-6363 (for the hearing impaired)

To assist victims of domestic violence. The National Domestic Violence Hotline offers supportive listening, information and referral, and crisis intervention.

OBSESSIVE-COMPULSIVE DISORDERS

Obsessive Compulsive Disorder Foundation, Inc.
P.O. Box 9573
New Haven, CT 06535
(203) 772-0565

The OCD Foundation, Inc. is a voluntary organization "dedicated to early intervention in controlling and finding cures for OCD, and for improving the welfare of people with this disorder."

OCD Foundation offers referrals to treatment centers and doctors who treat OCD, assistance to self-help support groups on the community level, and the Find a Friend service, which places people with OCD in contact with other OCD sufferers.

PARENT-CHILD CONFLICT

Families Anonymous
World Service Office
P.O. Box 528
Van Nuys, CA 91408
(818) 989-7841
1-800-736-9805

See listing on page 640.

Parents Anonymous
6733 S. Sepulveda Blvd.
Los Angeles, CA 90045
(213) 388-6685
1-800-421-0353

See listing on page 643.

Toughlove
P.O. Box 1069
Doylestown, PA 18901
(215) 348-7090

See listing on page 640.

PERSONALITY DISORDERS

National Alliance for the Mentally Ill
2101 Wilson Blvd.
Suite 302
Arlington, VA 22201
(703) 524-7600

See listing on page 644.

POSTTRAUMATIC STRESS

Anxiety Disorders Association of America
   (an expansion of the Phobia Society of America)
6000 Executive Blvd., Suite 200
Rockville, MD 20852
(301) 231-8368

See listing on page 641.

SCHIZOPHRENIA

National Alliance for the Mentally Ill
2101 Wilson Blvd.
Suite 302
Arlington, VA 22201
(703) 524-7600

See listing on page 644.

National Association of Psychiatric Survivors
P.O. Box 618
Sioux Falls, SD 57101
(605) 334-4067

This is an organization for people who are or have been in the mental health system. Membership is also open to family and friends of "mental patients." NAPS's focus is on education, political action, and service to its members.

SEXUAL DYSFUNCTION

Impotents Anonymous (IA)
I-Anon (for partners)
Impotence World Service
P.O. Box 5299
Maryville, TN 37802
(615) 983-6064

IA is an international support group network of community self-help chapters for impotent men, while I-Anon is for their partners. At IA meetings presentations are made by the IA group urologist medical adviser, mental health professionals, or a visiting physician.

Sexaholics Anonymous
P.O. Box 300
Simi Valley, CA 93062
(805) 581-3343

Self-help fellowship of men and women who want to stop lusting and become sexually sober. Offers regular support group meetings.

LEGAL HELP

Mental Health Law Project
221 L Street N.W.
Suite 800
Washington, DC 20036
(202) 467-5730

MHLP does test litigation and consultation with attorneys representing mental health patients, and it makes referrals to local lawyers who specialize in mental-health law.

National Association of Protection and Advocacy
   Systems
220 I Street N.W.
Washington, DC 20036
(202) 408-9514

NAPAS is an association of protection and advocacy (P&A) programs that are located in every state. P&A programs provide advocacy services for persons with mental illness and other disabilities.

National Association of Rights Protection and Advocacy
328 E. Hennepin Ave.
Minneapolis, MN 55414
(612) 331-6840

"NARPA is dedicated to increasing the independence of people who have been recipients of mental disability services." Makes referrals to legal advocates across the country.

II. Clearinghouses for Local Self-Help Listed by State

The quickest way to find a self-help group is through local clearinghouses. This list can help you find one in or near your community.

Arizona

The Rainy Day People
P.O. Box 472
Scottsdale, AZ
(602) 840-1029

California

Fresno County Info. Referral Network
2420 Mariposa St.
Fresno, CA 93721
(209) 488-3857

California Self-Help Center
U.C.L.A.
405 Hilgard Ave.
Los Angeles, CA 90024
1-800-222-LINK
(213) 825-1799

Mental Health Association of Contra Costa
  County
604 Ferry St.
Martinez, CA 94553
(510) 603-1212

Sacramento Self-Help Clearinghouse
Mental Health Association of Sacramento
5370 Elvos Ave., Suite B

Sacramento, CA 95819
(916) 368-3100

San Francisco Self-Help Clearinghouse
Mental Health Association
2398 Pine St.
San Francisco, CA 94115
(415) 921-4401

Connecticut

Self-Help Mutual Support Network
Consultation Center
19 Howe St.
New Haven, CT 06511
(203) 789-7645

Florida

Hotline Information Referral
P.O. Box 13087
St. Petersburg, FL 33733
(813) 531-4664

Illinois

Self-Help Center
405 State St.
Champaign, IL 61820
(217) 352-0099

Illinois Self-Help Center
1600 Dodge Ave., Suite S-122
Evanston, IL 60201

In Illinois: 1-800-322-MASH
(708) 328-0470

Indiana

Indianapolis Hotline
(317) 926-HELP

Information and Referral Network
1828 N. Meridian St.
Indianapolis, IN 46202
(317) 921-1305

Iowa

Iowa Self-Help Clearinghouse
33 N. 12th St.
P.O. Box 1151
Fort Dodge, IA 50501
(515) 576-5870

Kansas

Kansas Self-Help Network
Campus Box 34
Wichita State University
Wichita, KS 67208-1595
(316) 689-3170

Massachusetts

Clearinghouse of Mutual Self-Help Groups
Massachusetts Cooperative Extension
113 Skinner Hall
University of Massachusetts
Amherst, MA 01003
(413) 545-2313

Michigan

Center for Self-Help
Riverwood Center
1485 Highway M-139

Benton Harbor, MI 49022
(616) 925-0585

Michigan Self-Help Clearinghouse
Michigan Protection & Advocacy Service
109 W. Michigan Ave.
Suite 900
Lansing, MI 48933
(517) 484-7373
1-800-752-5858 (in Michigan only)

Minnesota

Minnesota Mutual Help Resource Center
Wilder Foundation Community Care Unit
919 LaFond Ave.
St. Paul, MN 55104
(612) 242-4060

Missouri

Kansas City Association for Mental Health
706 W. 42nd St.
Kansas City, MO 64111
(816) 472-5000

Mental Health Association of St. Louis
3617 Shaw Blvd.
St. Louis, MO 63110
(314) 773-1399

Nebraska

Self-Help Information Services
1601 Euclid Ave.
Lincoln, NE 68502
(402) 476-9668

New Hampshire

New Hampshire Self-Help Clearinghouse
Office of Public Education

Division of Mental Health & Developmental Services
105 Pleasant St.
State Office Park South
Concord, NH 03301
(603) 271-5060

New Jersey

New Jersey Self-Help Clearinghouse
St. Clare's Riverside Medical Center
Pocono Rd.
Denville, NJ 07834
1-800-367-6274 (in New Jersey only)
(201) 625-9565

New York

New York State Self-Help Clearinghouse
N.Y. Council on Children & Families
Empire State Plaza Tower 2
Albany, NY 12224
(518) 474-6293

New York City Self-Help Clearinghouse
P.O. Box 022812
Brooklyn, NY 11202

Erie County Self-Help Clearinghouse
Mental Health Association of Erie County
1237 Delaware Ave.
Buffalo, NY 14209
(716) 886-1242

Long Island Self-Help Clearinghouse
New York Institute of Technology
Central Islip Campus
Central Islip, NY 11722
(516) 348-3030

Monroe County Self-Help Clearinghouse
Mental Health Chapter of Rochester/Monroe
One Mount Hope Ave.

Rochester, NY 14620
(716) 423-9490

Onondaga County Self-Help Clearinghouse
The Volunteer Center, Inc.
115 Jefferson St., Suite 300
Syracuse, NY 13202
(315) 474-7011

Westchester Self-Help Clearinghouse
Westchester Community College
75 Grasslands Rd.
Valhalla, NY 10595
(914) 949-6301

North Carolina

Supportworks
  (serving greater Mecklenberg area)
1012 Kings Dr., Suite 923
Charlotte, NC 28283
(704) 331-9500

Ohio

Ohio Self-Help Clearinghouse
Family Service Association
184 Salem Ave.
Dayton, Ohio 45406
(513) 222-9481

Oregon

Northwest Regional Self-Help Clearinghouse
718 W. Burnside Ave.
Portland, OR 97209
(503) 222-5555

Pennsylvania

Self-Help Information & Networking Exchange
Voluntary Action Center of Northeast Pennsylvania

225 N. Washington Ave.
Park Plaza, Lower Level
Scranton, PA 18503
(717) 961-1234

Self-Help Group Network of the Pittsburgh Area
710½ South Ave.
Wilkinsburg, PA 15221
(412) 261-5363

Rhode Island

Support Group Helpline
Rhode Island Department of Health
Cannon Bldg., Davis St.
Providence, RI 09208
(401) 277-2223

South Carolina

The Support Group Network
Lexington Medical Center
2720 Sunset Blvd.
West Columbia, SC 29169
(803) 791-9227

Tennessee

Support Group Clearinghouse
Mental Health Association of Knox County
6712 Kingston Pike, Suite 203
Knoxville, TN 37919
(615) 584-6736

Texas

Dallas Self-Help Clearinghouse
Mental Health Association of Dallas County
2500 Maple Ave.
Dallas, TX 75201-1998
(214) 871-2420

Tarrant County Self-Help Clearinghouse
Tarrant County Mental Health Association

3136 West 4th St.
Fort Worth, TX 76109
(817) 335-5405

Houston Self-Help Clearinghouse
Mental Health Association in Houston
 and Harris County
2211 Norfolk, Suite 810
Houston, TX 77098
(713) 523-8963

Greater San Antonio Self-Help Clearinghouse
Mental Health
1407 N. Main
San Antonio, TX 78212
(512) 222-1571

Vermont

Vermont Self-Help Clearinghouse
P.O. Box 829
Montpelier, VT 05602
(802) 229-5724

Virginia

Greater Virginia Self-Help Coalition
Mental Health Association of Northern Virginia
100 N. Washington St., Suite 232
Falls Church, VA 22046
(703) 642-0800

Washington

Crisis Clinic/Thurston & Mason Counties
P.O. Box 2463
Olympia, WA 98507
(800) 627-2211

Washington, D.C.

Greater Washington Self-Help Coalition
100 N. Washington St., Suite 232

Falls Church, VA 22046
(703) 642-0800

Family Stress Services of D.C.
2001 O Street, N.W.
Suite 6
Washington, DC 20036
(202) 628-FACT

Wisconsin

Health and Human Services Outreach
University of Wisconsin–Madison
414 Lowell Hall
610 Langdon St.
Madison, WI 53706
(608) 263-4432

III. INFORMATION ORGANIZATIONS

CHILD ABUSE

American Association for Protecting Children
The American Humane Association
63 Inverness Dr. East
Englewood, CO 80112
(303) 792-9900

C. Henry Kempe National Center for the Prevention and Treatment of Child Abuse and Neglect
Department of Pediatrics—UCHSC
1205 Oneida St.
Denver, CO 80220
(303) 321-3963

National Child Abuse Hotline
Childhelp USA
1345 El Centro Ave.
P.O. Box 630
Hollywood, CA 90028
1-800-422-4453

National Committee for Prevention of Child Abuse
332 S. Michigan Ave., Suite 1600
Chicago, IL 60604
(312) 663-3520

DOMESTIC VIOLENCE

National Coalition Against Domestic Violence
P.O. Box 34103
Washington, DC 20043
(202) 638-6388

DRUG AND ALCOHOL ABUSE

National Clearinghouse for Alcohol and Drug Information
P.O. Box 2345
Rockville, MD 20852
(301) 468-2600

National Council on Alcoholism and Drug Dependence, Inc.
12 W. 21 St.
New York, NY 10010
(212) 206-6770
1-800-NCA-CALL

National Drug Abuse Information and Treatment Referral Hotline
National Institute on Drug Abuse
12280 Wilkins Ave.

Rockville, MD 20852
1-800-662-HELP
1-800-66-AYUDA (Spanish-speaking callers)

National Drug Information Center of Families in Action
2296 Henderson Mill Rd.
Suite 204
Atlanta, GA 30345
(404) 934-6364

National Federation of Parents for a Drug Free Youth
1423 N. Jefferson
Springfield, MO 65802
(417) 836-3709

PRIDE (National Parents' Resource Institute for Drug Education)
The Hurt Building
Suite 210, 50 Hurt Plaza
Atlanta, GA 30303
(404) 577-4500

EATING DISORDERS

National Anorexic Aid Society
5796 Karl Rd.
Columbus, OH 43229
(614) 846-2833

National Association of Anorexia Nervosa and Associated Disorders
Box 7
Highland Park, IL 60035
(708) 831-3438

GAMBLING

National Council on Compulsive Gambling, Inc.
445 W. 59th St.
New York, NY 10019

(212) 765-3833
1-800-522-4700

HYPERACTIVITY

Association for Children and Adults with Learning Disabilities
4156 Library Rd.
Pittsburgh, PA 15234
(412) 341-1515

MANIC DEPRESSION AND OTHER PSYCHIATRIC DISORDERS

Lithium Information Center
c/o Department of Psychiatry
University of Wisconsin
600 Highland Ave.
Madison, WI 53792
(608) 263-6171

MENTAL HEALTH

National Institute of Mental Health
Public Inquiries Branch
Parklawn Building
Room 15-C-05
5600 Fishers Lane
Rockville, MD 20857
(301) 443-4513

National Mental Health Association
1021 Prince St.
Alexandria, VA 22314
(703) 684-7722

National Mental Health Consumer Self-Help Clearinghouse
311 S. Juniper St., Room 902
Philadelphia, PA 19107
(215) 735-6367

OBSESSIVE-COMPULSIVE DISORDER

Obsessive Compulsive Disorder Foundation, Inc.
P.O. Box 9573
New Haven, CT 06535
(203) 772-0565

TARDIVE DYSKINESIA, TARDIVE DYSTONIA

Tardive Dyskinesia/Tardive Dystonia National Association
4244 University Way N.E.
P.O. Box 45732
Seattle, WA 98145

IV. THERAPIST REFERRAL SOURCES

American Association for Marriage and Family Therapy
1717 K Street N.W.
Suite 407
Washington, DC 20006
(202) 452-0109

Professional organization of marriage and family therapists. Will refer a caller to members.

American Association of Sex Educators, Counselors, and Therapists
11 Dupont Circle N.W., Suite 220
Washington, DC 20036

Professional organization that "certifies the qualifications of sexual health practitioners." AASECT publishes a membership directory, listing its certified members by geographic location. The directory is available, but AASECT will not refer a caller to one of its members.

American Family Therapy Association
2020 Pennsylvania Ave. N.W., Suite 273
Washington, DC 20006
(202) 994-2776

Professional membership organization for therapists. AFTA will refer to members in a caller's area.

American Group Psychotherapy Association
25 E. 21st St., 6th Floor
New York, NY 10010
(212) 477-2677

Membership organization for group therapists. Callers are referred to local affiliates, which will refer to individual members.

American Mental Health Counselors Association (a division of the American Association for Counseling and Development)
5999 Stevenson Ave.
Alexandria, VA 22304
(703) 823-9800

Professional organization for counselors. AMHCA will refer a caller to members certified in the directory of the National Academy of Certified Clinical Mental Health Counselors or to a local community mental health center.

American Nurses Association
2420 Pershing Rd.
Kansas City, MO 64108
1-800-284-2378

ANA publishes a directory of nurses in advanced specialities, including psychology/mental health.

The directory is self-listing so it does not include all of ANA clinical members. ANA does not make referrals to individual nurses over the phone.

American Psychiatric Association
1400 K Street N.W.
Washington, DC 20005
(202) 682-6142

Professional organization for psychiatrists. APA will send out information brochures on fourteen mental health topics and one explaining how to select a therapist. Callers are referred to the local district office where he/she talks to a psychiatrist. The nature of the caller's problem is assessed and he/she is referred to one or more practitioners in the area or a mental health center. An effort is made to match the caller with someone who has experience with the caller's problem.

American Psychological Association
1200 17th St. N.W.
Washington, DC 20036
(202) 336-5500

Professional membership organization for psychologists. APA will refer a caller to the state branch office of APA. At the state level, a caller's name and number is taken. A referral coordinator returns the call and can provide a list of psychologists and mental health centers in the person's area.

Anxiety Disorders Association of America
6000 Executive Blvd., Suite 200
Rockville, MD 20852
(301) 231-8368

Offers a *National Treatment Directory for Phobias and Related Anxiety Disorders* which educates consumers on how to select a therapist, explains the kinds of disorders and treatments, and contains a comprehensive list of individual practitioners and treatment centers across the country.

Association for the Advancement of Behavioral Therapy
15 W. 36th St.
New York, NY 10018
(212) 279-7970

Professional membership organization for behavioral therapists. "AABT responds to requests for referrals by distributing 'Guidelines for Choosing a Behavior Therapist' along with the AABT Membership Directory." Members are listed by area of speciality.

Center for Cognitive Therapy
University of Pennsylvania
133 S. 36th St., Room 602
Philadelphia, PA 19104
(215) 898-4100

CCT maintains a referral list of cognitive therapists and will refer a caller to certified and noncertified cognitive therapists around the country.

National Anorexic Aid Society
5796 Karl Road
Columbus, OH 43229
(614) 846-2833

Maintains an international referral list of professionals and groups.

National Association for the Advancement of Psychoanalysis and the American Board for Accreditation and Certification, Inc.
80 Eighth Ave., Suite 1210
New York, NY 10011
(212) 741-0515

NAAP maintains a registry of accredited institutions and programs and publishes the National Registry of Psychoanalysts. NAAP will make referrals to both accredited institutions and programs and to certified psychoanalysts.

National Association of Anorexia Nervosa and Associated Disorders
Box 7
Highland Park, IL 60035
(708) 831-3438

ANAD maintains a list of more than two thousand therapists, hospitals, and clinics in the U.S. and Canada to which it makes referrals.

National Association of Social Workers
7981 Eastern Ave.
Silver Spring, MD 20910
(202) 408-8600

NASW is the professional organization of social workers. NASW will provide the names of members in its Clinical Registry and will refer a caller to members in the Clinical Registry in his/her area.

National Mental Health Association
1021 Prince St.
Alexandria, VA 22314
(703) 684-7722

Referrals to individual therapists are done at the local level. The national office will refer a caller to its local affiliate chapter.

Obsessive Compulsive Disorder Foundation, Inc.
P.O. Box 9573
New Haven, CT 06535
(203) 772-0565

The OCD Foundation will refer a caller to the nearest treatment center or therapist who treats OCD.

V. National Survey of Psychotherapists

REPORT ON METHODOLOGY

Prepared by Nancy L. Marshall, Ed.D.
Original Sample Design and Analysis Plan Prepared by Joseph Pleck, Ph.D.

Sample Design

The sample was designed to include equal numbers of respondents from three professions: psychiatry, psychology, and social work. In addition, the sample was designed to draw respondents from around the United States. The thirty largest Standard Metropolitan Statistical Areas (as defined for the 1980 census) in the country were used as the sampling frame. These thirty SMSAs were grouped into three blocks, based on the concentration of professionals in these areas. Block 1 included New York City/New Jersey, Los Angeles/Long Beach, Chicago, Philadelphia/New Jersey, Detroit, San Francisco/Oakland, Washington, D.C., Dallas, Houston, Boston, and Long Island. Block 2 included St. Louis, Pittsburgh, Baltimore, Minneapolis/St. Paul, Atlanta, Newark, Anaheim, Cleveland, San Diego, and Miami. Block 3 included Denver/Boulder, Seattle, Tampa/St. Petersburg, Riverside/San Bernadino, Phoenix, Cincinnati, Milwaukee, Kansas City, and San Jose. Goals were set for each block based on the relative proportion of psychiatrists, psychologists, and social workers in the block. Random samples were drawn to meet these goals. In Block 2, we contacted 75% of social workers and psychologists to meet our goals. In Block 3, we contacted 100% of social workers and psychologists to meet our goals. The sample was randomly drawn from three sources: the 1983 Biographical Directory of the American Psychiatric Association, the Division of

Psychotherapy listings of the 1985 edition of the Directory of the American Psychological Association, and the 1985 National Association of Social Workers Registry of Clinical Social Workers.

Each person who was randomly selected was sent a copy of the survey and a letter inviting him or her to participate in the survey. If the survey was not returned within two weeks, a second letter and survey were sent out. We received surveys from 9% of the psychiatrists, 13% of the psychologists, and 15% of the social workers. Psychiatrists in the largest cities were more likely to respond than psychiatrists in Blocks 2 and 3 (12% versus 5%); there were no similar biases for psychologists and social workers. Some of those who did not complete the survey wrote to tell us that they were no longer practicing or had retired; others said the survey was not relevant to their current work, and we were notified that some of the people we had written were deceased. The final distribution of the returned surveys is shown in Table 1.

The sample provides representation from all three professions and from all areas of the country (see Table 2).

Of the 929 surveys received, 4 did not complete the information on treatment approach. All results reported in this book are based on an N of 925.

TABLE 1: Number of Respondents by Block and Profession

	Psychiatrists	Psychologists	Social Workers	Total
Block 1	242	147	195	584
Block 2	34	52	106	192
Block 3	27	42	84	153
Total	303	241	385	929

TABLE 2: Number of Respondents by Area of the Country

	Psychiatrists	Psychologists	Social Workers	Total
Northeast	138	102	137	377
South/Southwest	26	29	38	93
Midwest	55	50	130	235
West	84	60	80	224
Total	303	241	385	929

Sample Characteristics

Slightly over half of the respondents (57%) are men, 44% are women. As might be expected, this ratio varied by profession: 85% of psychiatrists are men, compared to 63% of responding psychologists and 30% of social workers. Two-thirds of the respondents are in clinical practice full-time, and an additional 29% are in clinical practice part-time. Ninety-five percent of the respondents have been in clinical practice for six years or more. Over three-quarters (79%) have been in practice for more than ten years, and 40% have been in practice for more than twenty years. The respondents' average age is fifty-two years.

The respondents practice in a number of clinical settings, as Table 3 indicates. Most are in private practice or in outpatient settings. Almost two-thirds (63%) also supervise, 48% teach, and 64% consult.

TABLE 3: Principal Clinical Setting (N = 835)

	Psychiatrists	Psychologists	Social Workers	Total
Inpatient	43	14	25	82
Day Treatment	5	3	7	15
Residential	2	5	11	18
Outpatient[1]	34	36	115	185
Government Agency[2]	11	4	18	33
Private Practice	174	157	171	502

1. Includes hospital outpatient, community mental health clinic, other outpatient clinic, and private nonprofit agency.
2. Only government agencies not included in other categories.

The respondents were asked to identify their principal clinical orientation. While the three professions are about equally likely to describe their orientation as psychodynamic or eclectic (the two most common orientations overall), there are obvious differences by profession. Psychiatrists are the only ones who use a psychopharmacological orientation, cognitive and behavioral orientations are more likely to be espoused by psychologists and social workers, and social workers are the principal employers of a family or couples orientation.

TABLE 4: Principal Orientation (N = 913)

	Psychiatrists	Psychologists	Social Workers	Total
Psychodynamic	159	117	179	455
Eclectic	82	57	106	245
Behavioral	0	9	14	23
Psychopharmacological	24	0	0	24
Cognitive	2	27	14	43
Family-Couples	6	9	50	65
Other	20	23	15	58

Respondents were asked with which population they usually work. Social workers are less likely than psychiatrists or psychologists to work with individuals, and more likely to work with families or couples. In fact, most professionals (85%) work with either adults or families and couples. However, almost one-third (31%) sometimes work with children, over half (56%) sometimes work with adolescents, and over one-quarter (29%) sometimes work with geriatric clients.

TABLE 5: Principal Population (N = 892)

	Psychiatrists	Psychologists	Social Workers	Total
Adult	235	195	257	687
Family/Couples	6	17	49	72
Children	15	10	34	59
Adolescent	20	14	20	54
Geriatric	8	0	12	20

Fees

Among professionals who see clients or patients privately, the average *treatment* fee per hour was $70 in 1986. Psychiatrists's average fee ($87) was significantly greater than psychologists' average fee ($69), and both were significantly higher than social workers' average treatment fee ($55).

Among professionals who see clients or patients privately, the average *consultation* fee per hour was $84 in 1986. Psychiatrists' average fee ($104) was significantly greater than psychologists' average fee ($80), and both were significantly higher than social workers' average consultation fee ($62).

Almost all of the respondents (91%) report that they sometimes see people for less than their usual fee. Each of the professions is equally likely to use reduced fees.

PART I:
NATIONAL SURVEY OF TREATMENT AND REFERRAL OF MENTAL DISORDERS

1. What is your primary degree: ☐ M.D. ₉₋₁ ☐ Ph.D. ₋₂ ☐ M.S.W. ₋₃ ☐ Other ₋₄ _____

2. Are you: ☐ Male ₁₀₋₁ ☐ Female ₋₂ **3.** Age _____ _{11.12}

3. Are you in clinical practice: ☐ Part-time ₁₃₋₁ ☐ Full-time ₋₂ ☐ Not in practice (Please continue anyway) ₋₃

5. Years in clinical practice: ☐ 1–5 ₁₄₋₁ ☐ 6–10 ₋₂ ☐ 11–15 ₋₃ ☐ 16–20 ₋₄ ☐ more than 20 ₋₅

6. What is your clinical setting:

	Principal Setting (check only one)	Other Settings (check as many as apply)
Hospital In-Patient	☐ 15.16-01	☐ 17-1
Day Treatment Center	☐ -02	☐ 18-1
Residential	☐ -03	☐ 19-1
Hospital Out-Patient	☐ -04	☐ 20-1
Community Mental Health Clinic	☐ -05	☐ 21-1
Other Out-Patient Clinic	☐ -06	☐ 22-1
Govt. Agency (e.g., State, County, City) (other than above)	☐ -07	☐ 23-1

Private Non-Profit Agency (other than above)   □ -08   □ 24-1
Individual or Group Private Practice   □ -09   □ 25-1
Other (please specify) _____   □ -10   □ 26-1

7. **Do you** (check as many as apply):   □ Supervise   □ Teach   □ Consult
                                               27-1   28-1   29-1

8. **What is your clinical orientation:**

	Principal Orientation (check only one)	**Other** (check as many as appl
Behavioral	□ 30.31-01	□ 32-1
Psychodynamic	□ -02	□ 33-1
Psychopharmacological	□ -03	□ 34-1
Cognitive	□ -04	□ 35-1
Family/Couple	□ -05	□ 36-1
Community	□ -06	□ 37-1
Neurological	□ -07	□ 38-1
Neuropsychological	□ -08	□ 39-1
Eclectic	□ -09	□ 40-1
Other _____	□ -10	□ 41-1

9. **With what population do you work:**

	Principal Population (check only one)	**Other** (check as many as appl
Child	□ 42-1	□ 43-1
Adolescent	□ -2	□ 44-1
Adult	□ -3	□ 45-1
Geriatric	□ -4	□ 46-1
Family/Couple	□ -5	□ 47-1

10. **If you see clients/patients privately, what is your** *average:*
    Treatment fee/hour _____   Consultation fee/hour _____   □ Not Applicable
                       48. 49. 50.   51. 52. 53.

11. **Do you sometimes see people for less than your usual fee?**   □ Yes   □ No
                                                                        54-1   -2

Instructions

The following two sections of this questionnaire list a number of mental disorders representative of many major diagnostic categories in DSM III-R which clients/patients frequently present. We want to know what treatment approach you would take with clients/patients presenting these conditions. Because we realize that DSM III-R diagnoses are not necessarily the only basis for making treatment decisions, we invite you to describe other considerations that guide your thinking.

We assume that no clinician is expert in the treatment of all disorders, and so you may not feel comfortable expressing an opinion in every case. *Feel free to leave blank* any items you are uncertain about.

As clinicians of course, we treat individuals, not diagnoses. We know that each set of treatment decisions is based to a large extent on the unique features of each individual case. Still, it is possible to make general decisions about treatment for a given disorder. We are asking you to consider a hypothetical prototypic case.

To make this task easier and more valid:

• Assume the disorder is the primary condition you are treating.

• Assume the client/patient is not otherwise at risk: for example, not suicidal, self-destructive or dangerous to others.

If a multi-modal approach is indicated, please be specific in circling the combination of approaches you would recommend. Remember that you will have a chance to describe other considerations that guide your thinking.

Part II:
Treatment Approach

CHILDHOOD AND ADOLESCENT DISORDERS & PROBLEMS

Column legend:
- **SETTING** (circle one): Out-patient = 1, Day Treatment = 2, Residential = 3, In-patient = 4
- **FORMAT** (circle as many as apply): Individual = 1, Group = 2, Family/Couple = 3
- **APPROACH*** (circle as many as apply, see below): Psychodynamic[1] = 1, Developmental[2] = 2, Behavioral[3] = 3, Cognitive[4] = 4, Systemic[5] = 5, Supportive[6] = 6
- **MEDICATION:** Yes = 1, No = 2
- **FRE-QUENCY** (circle one): Less than 1x/wk = 1, 1x/week = 2, 2x/wk or more = 3
- **DURATION** (circle one): 1 month or less = 1, 1–6 months = 2, 6 months–1 year = 3, Open-Ended = 4

Disorder / Problem	SETTING	FORMAT	APPROACH*	MEDICATION	FREQUENCY	DURATION
Conduct Disorder of Childhood/Adolescence, socialized, aggresssive	1 2 3 4 (55)	1 (56) 2 (57) 3 (58)	1 (59) 2 (60) 3 (61) 4 (62) 5 (63) 6 (64)	1 2 (65)	1 2 3 (66)	1 2 3 4 (67)
Attention Deficit Disorder, with hyperactivity	1 2 3 4 (68)	1 (69) 2 (70) 3 (71)	1 (72) 2 (73) 3 (74) 4 (75) 5 (76) 6 (77)	1 2 (11-7)	1 2 3 (8)	1 2 3 4 (9)
School Phobia	1 2 3 4 (10)	1 (11) 2 (12) 3 (13)	1 (14) 2 (15) 3 (16) 4 (17) 5 (18) 6 (19)	1 2 (20)	1 2 3 (21)	1 2 3 4 (22)
Anorexia Nervosa or Bulimia	1 2 3 4 (23)	1 (24) 2 (25) 3 (26)	1 (27) 2 (28) 3 (29) 4 (30) 5 (31) 6 (32)	1 2 (33)	1 2 3 (34)	1 2 3 4 (35)
Functional Enuresis	1 2 3 4 (36)	1 (37) 2 (38) 3 (39)	1 (40) 2 (41) 3 (42) 4 (43) 5 (44) 6 (45)	1 2 (46)	1 2 3 (47)	1 2 3 4 (48)
Childhood Depression	1 2 3 4 (49)	1 (50) 2 (51) 3 (52)	1 (53) 2 (54) 3 (55) 4 (56) 5 (57) 6 (58)	1 2 (59)	1 2 3 (60)	1 2 3 4 (61)

	Psychodynamic	Developmental	Behavioral	Cognitive	Systemic	Supportive
Child Sexual Abuse	1 2 3 4 (62)	1 2 3 (63)(64)(65)	1 2 3 4 5 6 (66)(67)(68)(69)(70)(71)	1 2 (III-7)	1 2 3 (8)	1 2 3 4 (9)
Pervasive Developmental Disorder of Childhood (e.g., childhood schizophrenia)	1 2 3 4 (10)	1 2 3 (11)(12)(13)	1 2 3 4 5 6 (14)(15)(16)(17)(18)(19)	1 2 (20)	1 2 3 (21)	1 2 3 4 (22)
ADJUSTMENT & PSYCHOSEXUAL DISORDERS & OTHER PROBLEMS						
Marital Problem	1 2 3 4 (23)	1 2 3 (24)(25)(26)	1 2 3 4 5 6 (27)(28)(29)(30)(31)(32)	1 2 (33)	1 2 3 (34)	1 2 3 4 (35)
Parent-Child Problem	1 2 3 4 (36)	1 2 3 (37)(38)(39)	1 2 3 4 5 6 (40)(41)(42)(43)(44)(45)	1 2 (46)	1 2 3 (47)	1 2 3 4 (48)
Phase of Life Problem or Other Life Circumstance Problem	1 2 3 4 (49)	1 2 3 (50)(51)(52)	1 2 3 4 5 6 (53)(54)(55)(56)(57)(58)	1 2 (59)	1 2 3 (60)	1 2 3 4 (61)
Uncomplicated Bereavement	1 2 3 4 (62)	1 2 3 (63)(64)(65)	1 2 3 4 5 6 (66)(67)(68)(69)(70)(71)	1 2 (IV-7)	1 2 3 (8)	1 2 3 4 (9)
Somatization Disorder (multiple physical symptoms without evident physical cause)	1 2 3 4 (10)	1 2 3 (11)(12)(13)	1 2 3 4 5 6 (14)(15)(16)(17)(18)(19)	1 2 (20)	1 2 3 (21)	1 2 3 4 (22)

APPROACH DEFINITIONS The primary method is:

1. Psychodynamic: to increase understanding and resolution of intrapsychic conflicts and problems.
2. Developmental: to remedy structural deficits in ego development.
3. Behavioral: to control or change maladaptive behaviors and increase or learn adaptive behaviors.
4. Cognitive: to correct maladaptive cognitions.
5. Systemic: to restructure patterns of interactions, communications, and roles in family or social systems.
6. Supportive: to help manage problems in daily living by supporting available coping skills.

* If only psychopharmacology is the treatment of choice, skip this column.

Part II:
(continued)

	SETTING circle one				FORMAT circle as many as apply			APPROACH* circle as many as apply (see below)						MEDI-CATION		FRE-QUENCY circle one			DURATION circle one			
	Out-patient	Day Treatment	Residential	In-patient	Individual	Group	Family/Couple	Psychodynamic[1]	Developmental[2]	Behavioral[3]	Cognitive[4]	Systemic[5]	Supportive[6]	Yes	No	Less than 1x/wk	1x/week	2x/wk or more	1 month or less	1–6 months	6 months–1 year	Open-Ended
Adjustment Disorder with Work or Academic Inhibition	1	2	3	4	1	2	3	1	2	3	4	5	6	1	2	1	2	3	1	2	3	4
			(23)		(24)	(25)	(26)	(27)	(28)	(29)	(30)	(31)	(32)	(33)		(34)			(35)			
Adjustment Disorder with Mixed Emotional Features	1	2	3	4	1	2	3	1	2	3	4	5	6	1	2	1	2	3	1	2	3	4
			(36)		(37)	(38)	(39)	(40)	(41)	(42)	(43)	(44)	(45)	(46)		(47)			(48)			
Inhibited Sexual Desire	1	2	3	4	1	2	3	1	2	3	4	5	6	1	2	1	2	3	1	2	3	4
			(49)		(50)	(51)	(52)	(53)	(54)	(55)	(56)	(57)	(58)	(59)		(60)			(61)			
Other Psychosexual Dysfunctions (e.g., premature ejaculation, frigidity)	1	2	3	4	1	2	3	1	2	3	4	5	6	1	2	1	2	3	1	2	3	4
			(62)		(63)	(64)	(65)	(66)	(67)	(68)	(69)	(70)	(71)	(V-7)		(8)			(9)			
SUSTANCE ABUSE DISORDERS																						
Alcohol Abuse	1	2	3	4	1	2	3	1	2	3	4	5	6	1	2	1	2	3	1	2	3	4
			(10)		(11)	(12)	(13)	(14)	(15)	(16)	(17)	(18)	(19)	(20)		(21)			(22)			
Alcohol Dependence (tolerance or withdrawal)	1	2	3	4	1	2	3	1	2	3	4	5	6	1	2	1	2	3	1	2	3	4
			(23)		(24)	(25)	(26)	(27)	(28)	(29)	(30)	(31)	(32)	(33)		(34)			(35)			

Disorder	1 2 3 4	1 2 3	1 2 3 4 5 6	1 2	1 2 3	1 2 3 4
Sedative Dependence (e.g., Valium)	(36)	(37) (38) (39)	(40) (41) (42) (43) (44) (45)	(46)	(47)	(48)
Cocaine Abuse	(49)	(50) (51) (52)	(53) (54) (55) (56) (57) (58)	(59)	(60)	(61)
Cannabis Abuse	(62)	(63) (64) (65)	(66) (67) (68) (69) (70) (71)	(VI-7)	(8)	(9)
ANXIETY & AFFECTIVE DISORDERS						
Simple Phobia	(10)	(11) (12) (13)	(14) (15) (16) (17) (18) (19)	(20)	(21)	(22)
Agoraphobia	(23)	(24) (25) (26)	(27) (28) (29) (30) (31) (32)	(33)	(34)	(35)
Generalized Anxiety Disorder	(36)	(37) (38) (39)	(40) (41) (42) (43) (44) (45)	(46)	(47)	(48)
Obsessive Compulsive Disorder	(49)	(50) (51) (52)	(53) (54) (55) (56) (57) (58)	(59)	(60)	(61)

APPROACH DEFINITIONS The primary method is:

1. Psychodynamic: to increase understanding and resolution of intrapsychic conflicts and problems.
2. Developmental: to remedy structural deficits in ego development.
3. Behavioral: to control or change maladaptive behaviors and increase or learn adaptive behaviors.
4. Cognitive: to correct maladaptive cognitions.
5. Systemic: to restructure patterns of interactions, communications, and roles in family or social systems.
6. Supportive: to help manage problems in daily living by supporting available coping skills.

* If only medication is the treatment of choice, skip this column.

Part II:
(continued)

	SETTING circle one Out-patient / Day Treatment / Residential / In-patient	FORMAT circle as many as apply Individual / Group / Family/Couple	APPROACH* circle as many as apply (see below) Psychodynamic[1] / Developmental[2] / Behavioral[3] / Cognitive[4] / Systemic[5] / Supportive[6]	MEDICATION circle one Yes / No	FREQUENCY circle one Less than 1x/wk / 1x/week / 2x/wk or more	DURATION circle one 1 month or less / 1–6 months / 6 months–1 year / Open-Ended
Post-Traumatic Stress Syndrome, chronic or delayed	1 2 3 4 (62)	1 2 3 (63)(64)(65)	1 2 3 4 5 6 (66)(67)(68)(69)(70)(71)	1 2 (VII-7)	1 2 3 (8)	1 2 3 4 (9)
Dysthymic Disorder (depressive neurosis)	1 2 3 4 (10)	1 2 3 (11)(12)(13)	1 2 3 4 5 6 (14)(15)(16)(17)(18)(19)	1 2 (20)	1 2 3 (21)	1 2 3 4 (22)
Recurrent Major Depression	1 2 3 4 (23)	1 2 3 (24)(25)(26)	1 2 3 4 5 6 (27)(28)(29)(30)(31)(32)	1 2 (33)	1 2 3 (34)	1 2 3 4 (35)
Bipolar Depression	1 2 3 4 (36)	1 2 3 (37)(38)(39)	1 2 3 4 5 6 (40)(41)(42)(43)(44)(45)	1 2 (46)	1 2 3 (47)	1 2 3 4 (48)
PERSONALITY DISORDERS						
Borderline Personality Disorder	1 2 3 4 (49)	1 2 3 (50)(51)(52)	1 2 3 4 5 6 (53)(54)(55)(56)(57)(58)	1 2 (59)	1 2 3 (60)	1 2 3 4 (61)
Narcissistic Personality Disorder	1 2 3 4 (62)	1 2 3 (63)(64)(65)	1 2 3 4 5 6 (66)(67)(68)(69)(70)(71)	1 2 (VIII-7)	1 2 3 (8)	1 2 3 4 (9)

	1 2 3 4	1 2	1 2	1 2 3	1 2 3 4 5 6	1 2	1 2 3	1 2 3 4
Antisocial Personality Disorder	(10)	(11)	(12)	(13)	(14)(15)(16)(17)(18)(19)	(20)	(21)	(22)
Schizoid Personality Disorder	(23)	(24)	(25)	(26)	(27)(28)(29)(30)(31)(32)	(33)	(34)	(35)
PSYCHOTIC DISORDERS								
Brief Reactive Psychosis	(36)	(37)	(38)	(39)	(40)(41)(42)(43)(44)(45)	(46)	(47)	(48)
Acute Paranoid Disorder	(49)	(50)	(51)	(52)	(53)(54)(55)(56)(57)(58)	(59)	(60)	(61)
Manic Episode	(62)	(63)	(64)	(65)	(66)(67)(68)(69)(70)(71)	(IX-7)	(8)	(9)
Schizophrenia, chronic in acute phase	(10)	(11)	(12)	(13)	(14)(15)(16)(17)(18)(19)	(20)	(21)	(22)
Schizophrenia, chronic (longer than 2 years)	(23)	(24)	(25)	(26)	(27)(28)(29)(30)(31)(32)	(33)	(34)	(35)

APPROACH DEFINITIONS The primary method is:

1. Psychodynamic: to increase understanding and resolution of intrapsychic conflicts and problems.
2. Developmental: to remedy structural deficits in ego development.
3. Behavioral: to control or change maladaptive behaviors and increase or learn adaptive behaviors.
4. Cognitive: to correct maladaptive cognitions.
5. Systemic: to restructure patterns of interactions, communications, and roles in family or social systems.
6. Supportive: to help manage problems in daily living by supporting available coping skills.

* If only medication is the treatment of choice, skip this column.

	Marital Problem	Parent/ Child Problem	Phase-of-Life Problem	Uncompli-cated Be-reavement	Adjustment Disorder— Work or School	Mixed Adjustment Disorders
TABLE 1: Problems in Everyday Living						
Setting (totals = 100%)						
Outpatient	99	99	99	99.6	98.4	97.9
Day Treatment	(.4) 0	(.4) 1	(.3) 0	.1	1.0	.8
Residential	(.2) 0	(.1) 0	(.1) 0	.1	.1	.1
Inpatient	1	(.3) 0	1	.1	.4	1.2
N Responding	810	757	775	774	763	748
Format (columns do not total 100%, each entry = % yes)						
Individual	54	64	96	95.2	97.1	98.1
Group	16	12	35	33.6	28.7	28.2
Family/ Couple	96	95	28	24.5	21.5	26.1
N Responding	810	757	775	774	763	748
Approach (columns do not total 100%, each entry = % yes)						
Psycho-dynamic	69	62	71	48.6	74.2	77.1

TABLE 1: Problems in Everyday Living (continued)					
	Marital Problem	*Parent/ Child Problem*	*Phase-of-Life Problem*	*Uncompli-cated Be-reavement*	*Adjustment Disorder— Work or School*	*Mixed Adjustment Disorders*
Behavioral	41	54	28	16.8	47.3	38.2
Cognitive	49	42	51	37.3	53.2	51.2
Systemic	76	80	38	27.6	38.0	40.9
Supportive	48	56	70	83.7	57.2	60.7
N Responding	810	757	775	774	763	748
Medication						
% Yes	4	3	7	9.1	5.1	15.4
N Responding	710	664	682	679	680	669
Frequency						
<1×/wk	6	5	7	10.7	6.1	4.6
= 1×/wk	88	89	85	80.8	81.0	81.2
≥2×/wk	6	6	8	8.5	12.8	14.2
N Responding	786	730	743	741	733	724
Duration (columns total 100%)						
<1 mo.	1	2	5	14.2	3.7	1.2
1 mo.–6 mos.	41	38	49	55.1	44.2	35.7
6 mos.–12 mos.	27	27	20	14.6	23.2	24.4
Open-ended	32	33	26	16.1	28.9	38.6
N Responding	793	738	757	752	736	733

TABLE 2: Problems of Childhood and Adolescence

	Conduct Disorder	Attention Deficit	School Phobia	Eating Disorders	Enuresis	Childhood Depression	Sexual Abuse	Pervasive Developmental Disorders (Autism)
Setting								
Outpatient	67	85	96.3	58	98	89	87	19
Day Treatment	8	11	1.3	3	1	4	3	17
Residential	18	3	1.3	5	1	3	6	31
Inpatient	8	2	1.1	34	1	5	4	34
N Responding	636	571	620	583	526	561	556	494
Format								
Individual	80	83	81.4	95	80	93	92	86
Group	56	19	10.9	58	6	16	41	52
Family/Couple	82	75	81.2	75	77	82	82	81
N Responding	636	571	620	583	526	561	556	494
Approach								
Psychodynamic	51	27	58.8	73	49	69	60	37

Behavioral	71	75	63.0	68	68	30	29	65
Cognitive	40	30	32.2	51	20	45	42	32
Systemic	68	54	62.2	67	53	64	69	63
Supportive	48	54	46.6	55	43	61	73	8
N Responding	636	571	620	583	526	561	556	494
Medication								
% Yes	17	82	14	39	38	47	3	86
N Responding	568	545	544	532	473	507	478	461
Frequency								
<1×/wk	4	13	3.4	2	14	2	2	7
= 1×/wk	54	67	62.8	31	76	56	59	27
≥2×/wk	42	20	33.8	68	11	42	39	66
N Responding	624	543	588	575	505	535	528	475
Duration								
<1 mo.	1	1	5.8	2	5	0	1	0
1 mo.–6 mos.	21	20	45.4	13	50	22	20	3
6 mos.–12 mos.	27	25	20.0	19	17	23	24	7
Open-ended	51	54	28.8	66	28	55	55	90
N Responding	628	557	590	588	501	543	538	490

TABLE 3: Emotional and Behavioral Disorders					
	Generalized Anxiety	Obsessions and Compulsions	Post-traumatic Stress Disorder	Mild Depression	Cocaine Abuse	Cannabis Abuse
Setting (totals = 100%)						
Outpatient	97	97	91	97	38	73
Day Treatment	1	1	5	2	4	4
Residential	(.4) 0	1	1	(.1) 0	13	6
Inpatient	1	1	3	1	46	17
N Responding	765	737	686	759	505	497
Format (columns do not total 100%, each entry = % yes)						
Individual	98	96	97	98	84	83
Group	26	23	52	31	85	74
Family/ Couple	21	21	32	29	59	48
N Responding	765	737	686	759	505	497
Approach (columns do not total 100%, each entry = % yes)						
Psycho-dynamic	80	78	72	84	52	55

TABLE 3: Emotional and Behavioral Disorders (continued)					
	Generalized Anxiety	*Obsessions and Compulsions*	*Post-traumatic Stress Disorder*	*Mild Depression*	*Cocaine Abuse*	*Cannabis Abuse*
Develop-mental	41	44	29	48	34	32
Behavioral	52	57	47	37	78	73
Cognitive	52	51	59	60	57	55
Systemic	36	34	42	44	62	55
Supportive	61	51	78	64	67	62
N Responding	765	737	686	759	505	497
Medication						
% Yes	55	31	40	47	24	12
N Responding	702	665	619	697	459	454
Frequency						
<1×/wk	5	4	3	2	2	4
=1×/wk	69	66	68	68	25	49
≥2×/wk	26	30	30	30	73	46
N Responding	747	722	672	735	486	474
Duration (columns total 100%)						
<1 mo.	1	1	2	(.1) 0	6	4
1 mo.–6 mos.	20	13	26	13	22	28
6 mos.–12 mos.	23	20	28	23	19	18
Open-ended	56	66	44	64	53	50
N Responding	756	732	680	747	497	485

TABLE 3: Emotional and Behavioral Disorders (continued)					
	Simple Phobia	Agoraphobia	Somatoform Disorder	Adjustment Disorder at Work/ Academic Setting	Adjustment Disorder	Inhibited Sexual Desire
Setting (total = 100%)						
Outpatient	99	97	96	98	98	99
Day Treatment	(.3) 0	2	2	1	1	1
Residential	none recorded	(.4) 0	none recorded	(.1) 0	(.1) 0	none recorded
Inpatient	(.3) 0	1	2	(.4) 0	1	(.3) 0
N Responding	736	702	735	763	748	657
Format (columns do not total 100%, each entry = % yes)						
Individual	97	97	96	97	98	90
Group	27	71	23	29	28	13
Family/ Couple	18	27	28	22	26	63
N Responding	736	702	735	763	748	657

	Simple Phobia	Agoraphobia	Somatoform Disorder	Adjustment Disorder at Work/ Academic Setting	Adjustment Disorder	Inhibited Sexual Desire
Approach (columns do not total 100%, each entry = % yes)						
Psycho-dynamic	64	68	79	74	77	80
Develop-mental	29	33	45	35	40	39
Behavioral	76	74	42	47	38	60
Cognitive	49	53	52	53	51	48
Systemic	27	34	42	38	41	51
Supportive	51	58	57	57	61	45
N Responding	736	702	735	763	748	657
Medication						
% Yes	24	51	25	5	15	4
N Responding	659	650	658	680	669	591
Frequency						
<1×/wk	4	4	7	6	5	5
=1×/wk	77	65	71	81	81	80
>2×/wk	19	32	22	13	14	15
N Responding	715	688	717	733	724	628
Duration (Columns) total 100%)						
<1 mo.	4	1	1	4	1	2
1 mo.–6 mos.	42	27	19	44	36	38
6 mos.–12 mos.	22	27	22	23	24	25
Open-ended	32	45	58	29	39	36
N Responding	714	693	733	736	733	638

TABLE 3: Emotional and Behavioral Disorders (continued)

TABLE 3: Emotional and Behavioral Disorders (continued)					
	Antisocial Personality	Schizoid Personality	Reactive Psychosis	Acute Paranoid Disorder	Other Psycho-sexual Disorders	Alcohol Abuse
Setting (totals = 100%)					
Outpatient	69	87	28	15	99	57
Day Treatment	7	6	4	3	(.3) 0	7
Residential	17	2	2	2	none	12
Inpatient	7	5	67	80	1	24
N Responding	602	671	637	605	630	587
Format (columns do not total 100%, each entry = % yes)					
Individual	70	93	98	96	87	84
Group	62	43	37	33	11	90
Family/ Couple	31	27	42	35	65	69
N Responding	602	671	637	605	630	587
Approach (columns do not total 100%, each entry = % yes)					
Psycho-dynamic	52	58	43	38	74	53

TABLE 3: Emotional and Behavioral Disorders (continued)					
	Antisocial Personality	*Schizoid Personality*	*Reactive Psychosis*	*Acute Paranoid Disorder*	*Other Psycho-sexual Disorders*	*Alcohol Abuse*
Develop-mental	52	55	28	28	34	33
Behavioral	68	45	36	37	67	80
Cognitive	52	47	40	48	47	57
Systemic	51	47	43	40	50	64
Supportive	47	68	82	74	46	71
N Responding	602	671	637	605	630	587
Medication						
% Yes	10	23	90	91	5	31
N Responding	550	614	633	604	566	534
Frequency						
$<1\times$/wk	10	10	2	2	6	2
$=1\times$/wk	57	62	16	20	80	38
$\geq2\times$/wk	34	28	82	78	15	60
N Responding	592	660	619	580	602	576
Duration (columns total 100%)						
<1 mo.	2	1	24	16	3	5
1 mo.–6 mos.	7	5	33	30	43	18
6 mos.–12 mos.	16	12	13	12	22	17
Open-ended	75	82	30	42	32	59
N Responding	603	666	634	597	611	590

TABLE 3: Emotional and Behavioral Disorders (continued)						
	Alcohol Dependency	Sedative Dependency	Major Depression	Bipolar Depression	Borderline Depression	Narcissistic Personality
Setting (Totals = 100%)						
Outpatient	25	40	60	64	89	96
Day Treatment	5	3	4	3	5	2
Residential	11	9	2	2	2	1
Inpatient	59	48	34	31	3	2
N Responding	553	535	709	677	727	702
Format (columns do not total 100%, each entry = % yes)						
Individual	84	88	100	100	97	93
Group	88	74	36	32	34	33
Family/ Couple	65	53	40	38	25	21
N Responding	553	535	709	677	727	702
Approach (columns do not total 100%, each entry = % yes)						
Psycho-dynamic	48	52	71	61	67	74
Develop-mental	29	31	43	37	66	67

TABLE 3: Emotional and Behavioral Disorders (continued)					
	Alcohol Dependency	*Sedative Dependency*	*Major Depression*	*Bipolar Depression*	*Borderline Depression*	*Narcissistic Personality*
Behavioral	77	74	40	44	46	36
Cognitive	54	54	59	55	46	44
Systemic	61	56	48	45	47	43
Supportive	69	67	77	76	64	52
N Responding	553	535	709	677	727	702
Medication						
% Yes	55	34	93	95	25	6
N Responding	517	495	719	695	659	641
Frequency						
$<1 \times$/wk	2	2	3	7	5	6
$=1 \times$/wk	23	32	41	49	51	58
$\geq 2 \times$/wk	75	67	56	44	44	36
N Responding	532	510	708	675	718	682
Duration (columns total 100%)						
<1 mo.	17	11	3	3	1	1
1 mo.–6 mos.	20	25	14	12	4	6
6 mos.–12 mos.	14	16	13	11	9	12
Open-ended	49	47	70	74	86	81
N Responding	549	525	725	695	725	691

	Manic Episode	Chronic Schizo-phrenia (Acute Phase)	Chronic Schizo-phrenia
TABLE 3: Emotional and Behavioral Disorders (continued)			
Setting (Totals = 100%)			
Outpatient	17	9	40
Day Treatment	2	4	33
Residential	2	3	14
Inpatient	79	84	13
N Responding	617	626	619
Format (columns do not total 100%, each entry = % yes)			
Individual	96	91	82
Group	31	48	67
Family/Couple	37	47	48
N Responding	617	626	619
Approach (columns do not total 100%, each entry = % yes)			
Psycho-dynamic	32	31	30

TABLE 3: Emotional and Behavioral Disorders (continued)			
	Manic Episode	*Chronic Schizo-phrenia (Acute Phase)*	*Chronic Schizo-phrenia*
Develop-mental	22	27	31
tBehavioral	43	44	52
Cognitive	41	36	42
Systemic	39	46	51
Supportive	75	81	88
N Responding	617	626	619
Medication			
% Yes	96	98	94
N Responding	627	632	634
Frequency			
<1×/wk	2	3	28
=1×/wk	16	18	32
≥2×/wk	82	79	40
N Responding	589	591	623
Duration (columns total 100%)			
<1 mo.	18	14	1
1 mo.–6 mos.	31	24	2
6 mos.–12 mos.	8	7	4
Open-ended	43	55	93
N Responding	610	618	639

ACKNOWLEDGMENTS

▣

In preparing this guide, we benefited greatly from the thoughtful comments and help of many friends and colleagues, and the hundreds of therapists who responded to our survey.

Joseph Pleck, Ph.D., and Nancy Marshall, Ed.D., of the Wellesley College Center for Research on Women lent their considerable research expertise in helping us design and analyze the National Survey of Psychotherapists. Dr. Marshall also supervised the data collection and analysis. Judith Shangold, B.A., our chief research assistant, kept track of the eight thousand questionnaires sent out in the study and collated the returns. Pat Duffy, Psy.D., did the statistics.

Several colleagues at The Cambridge Hospital Department of Psychiatry helped shape the guide in its beginnings: Dan Brown, Ph.D., Fran Givelber, LICSW, Henry Grunebaum, M.D., Dan Jacobs, M.D., and Bob Weber, Ph.D., all offered helpful comments and suggestions about its overall design and structure.

Ann Epstein, M.D., also then of The Cambridge Hospital and Cambridge Child Guidance Center, was of great help in the early stages of writing the sections on therapy for problems of children and adolescents.

A number of colleagues around the country with special expertise in a particular area were kind enough to review the draft of those sections in Part II: Steward Agras, M.D., Stanford University School of Medicine; Anne Marie Albano, Ph.D., SUNY-Albany School of Medicine; David Barlow, Ph.D., SUNY-Albany School of Medicine; Dan Brown, Ph.D., Harvard Medical School; Steven Cooper, Ph.D., Harvard Medical School; Mark Durand, Ph.D., SUNY-Albany School of Medicine; Henry Grunebaum, M.D., The Cambridge Hospital and Harvard Medical School; Alan Marlatt, Ph.D., University of Washington Medical School; Howard Shaffer,

Ph.D., Center for Addiction Studies, The Cambridge Hospital and Harvard Medical School; Ron Siegel, Ph.D., Cambridge Child Guidance Center and Harvard Medical School; Jeffrey Young, Ph.D., Columbia University Medical School and Cognitive Therapy Center of New York.

Henry Grunebaum, M.D., director of the Couples and Family Center of The Cambridge Hospital, suggested a model for organizing the discussion of family therapy approaches in Chapter 2.

George Souza, Ed.D., executive director of the Mental Health Division of Goddard Medical Associates–HMO Blue, reviewed Chapter 7, "Paying for Therapy," and contributed helpful comments on new developments in psychotherapy insurance and managed health care.

A very special acknowledgment goes to our editor, Gail Winston. Therapists and writers are alike in that they tend to say either too much or too little. She made sure we did neither. Her skillful editing and suggestions were invaluable in shaping what we gave her and making this a better book. Therapy is also more art or craft than science and lends itself to different perspectives. Gail managed to keep us on track and pulling in the same direction as we worked with all the complex material in this book and tried to do it justice.

Because this is a practical guide for people looking for help rather than an academic or technical book on therapy, we have taken the liberty of not including references. Obviously we have drawn on many sources, as well as our own personal experience. This is the place, then, to acknowledge the many professionals whose articles, books, lectures, seminars, and consultations we have learned from over the years and who have informed our thinking in preparing this book.

—J.E. and D.G.

No one learns to do therapy without the help of many mentors and supervisors along the way. And no one continues to grow as a therapist without being able to discuss and review his or her work with knowledgeable and able colleagues. I feel I have been singularly fortunate in my mentors, as well as in the professional colleagues with whom it has been my privilege to work. They are the ones who have set the standards against which this book will be judged. I am indebted to all of them, but a few deserve special acknowledgment and thanks:

Seymour Boorstein, M.D., and Sylvia Boorstein, MSW, Ph.D., therapists themselves, who encouraged my first interest in clinical work, were instrumental in helping me get started and have remained a guiding presence and role model for intelligent and compassionate care.

Dan Brown, Ph.D., friend, mentor, colleague, coauthor, teacher extraordinaire, with whom I have grown up in the field, shared interests and ideas for two decades, and learned most of what I know about the psychotherapy of severe disturbance.

Phil Kelleher, M.D., now deceased, on whose unit I interned at McLean Hospital, whose grasp of the inner world of schizophrenia and psychosis was unparalleled, who unfortunately never wrote an article or book, but who was the most original theorist of human development and psychopathology I have known. His Saturday-morning seminars were unforgettable experiences.

Alfred Stanton, M.D., former chief psychiatrist at McLean Hospital and an early supervisor, who thundered at me one day never to use the word *manipulative* about a client's behavior again—I never have—and helped me to see how every client was doing the very best he or she could.

Peter Novotny, M.D., at The Menninger Foundation, for teaching me the basic principles of psychotherapy; and Dan Pershonok, Ph.D., of McLean Hospital, for getting me to take clients seriously and myself less seriously.

Anton Kris, M.D., and Sanford Schreiber, M.D., for showing me how individual psychotherapy actually works and how effective it can be.

Marianne Riche-Ault, ACSW, at The Menninger Foundation; Leonard Hill, LICSW, director of family therapy at the Yale Psychiatric Institute; and Cathy Coleman, LICSW, and Charlotte Temin, Ph.D., both of the Couples and Family Center at The Cambridge Hospital, for teaching me family therapy.

Robert Klein, Ph.D., at the Yale Psychiatric Institute, and Vicki Roemele, ACSW, at The Cambridge Hospital, for their teaching and supervision of group psychotherapy.

My staff and the clients at The Lawrence Schiff Day Treatment Center at The Cambridge Hospital, who tolerated a novice clinical director; together we learned milieu therapy and how to create a therapeutic community.

My colleagues on the Monday Team of The Cambridge Hospital Outpatient Department of Psychiatry; there were few human problems we didn't see, struggle with, and learn from together.

My colleagues in the mental health division of Goddard Medical Associates-HMO Blue, from whom I have learned how good psychotherapeutic care can be when offered in a managed health care setting.

And last but foremost, the many clients I have known and worked with: in clinics, in hospitals, and in my private practice. They have clearly taught me more about therapy over the years than anyone else, not just about the nature of human suffering and what is helpful and healing, but about the resiliency and power of the human spirit.

J.E.

Index

■

ABOUT THE AUTHORS

Jack Engler, Ph.D., is on the clinical faculty at Harvard Medical School and teaches and supervises psychotherapy in the psychology and psychiatry training programs of the Department of Psychiatry at The Cambridge Hospital, Cambridge, Massachusetts.

His clinical practice has included the principal modalities of therapy, as well as the main outpatient and inpatient settings. He works in both the public and private sectors. He is currently coordinator of inpatient mental health services for Goddard-HMO Blue in Brockton, Massachusetts.

Dr. Engler did his graduate work at Munich, Oxford, Magadh University (India), and the University of Chicago, where he received his doctorate. He did his clinical training at The Menninger Foundation, Harvard Medical School at McLean Hospital, and the Yale Psychiatric Institute. He is a former Woodrow Wilson, Danforth, and Fulbright fellow.

Dr. Engler is a licensed psychologist in Massachusetts and a member of the American Psychological Association. He is in private practice in Cambridge.

Daniel Goleman, Ph.D., is a psychologist who covers behavioral science and health for *The New York Times*. Before joining the *Times* in 1984, Dr. Goleman had been a senior editor at *Psychology Today,* where he was on the editorial staff for nine years. He came to *Psychology Today* from the faculty at Harvard University.

Dr. Goleman has written or edited eleven books. His most recent include *The Creative Spirit* (Dutton) and *Vital Lies, Simple Truths: The Psychology of Self-Deception* (Touchstone). In recognition of his efforts to communicate the behavioral sciences to the public, he was elected a Fellow of the American Academy for the Advancement of Science.

Dr. Goleman has received many journalistic awards for his writing. He is a four-time winner of the National Media Award from the American Psychological Association, including a Lifetime Achievement Award in 1988. He has also received awards from the National Association of Mental Health, the National Alliance for the Mentally Ill, and the Robert T. Morse Writers Award from the American Psychiatric Association.

He is a former Alfred P. Sloan Scholar, Ford Fellow, and Fellow of the Social Science Research Council. Dr. Goleman attended Amherst College and Harvard University, where he received his M.A. in clinical psychology and his Ph.D. in personality and development.

Eliot Gelwan, M.D., is a graduate of Yale Medical School and of Harvard College. He is associate director of the Psychopharmacology Clinic of the Department of Psychiatry, The Cambridge Hospital, Cambridge, Massachusetts, and lecturer in psychiatry at Harvard Medical School. He is also in private practice in psychotherapy and psychopharmacology in Cambridge.